Macroeconomic Themes

Macroeconomic Themes

EDITED READINGS IN MACROECONOMICS WITH COMMENTARIES

BY

M. J. C. SURREY

OXFORD UNIVERSITY PRESS

1976

Oxford University Press, Ely House, London W.1

OXFORD LONDON GLASGOW NEW YORK
TORONTO MELBOURNE WELLINGTON CAPE TOWN
IBADAN NAIROBI DAR ES SALAAM LUSAKA ADDIS ABABA
KUALA LUMPUR SINGAPORE JAKARTA HONG KONG TOKYO
DELHI BOMBAY CALCUTTA MADRAS KARACHI

Casebound ISBN 0 19 877059 6
Paperback ISBN 0 19 877060 X

© Oxford University Press 1976

Printed in Great Britain by Thomson Litho Ltd., East Kilbride, Scotland.

Foreword

Contemporary macroeconomics covers a vast range, and at almost every point theoretical and empirical debate continues. In this volume, an attempt has been made to give an impression of the evolution and diversity of views on different topics by including a relatively large number of relatively short extracts from books and articles. In addition, a series of Introductory Notes tries to set out what the various issues are and to summarize the main contentions of the authors of the associated extracts. It is hoped that in this way a useful bridge has been built between the many excellent macroeconomic textbooks now available and the perhaps, to many students, daunting literature of original books and papers.

In selecting and editing extracts of this kind, sometimes amounting to only a fraction of an original contribution, violence is inevitably sometimes done to the range and subtlety of the authors' views. It is hoped that such losses are more than offset by the advantages of the much larger selection of views which such editing allows.

The publication in 1936 of Keynes's *General Theory of Employment, Interest and Money* marked, by common consent, a turning-point in the evolution of economic theory. The development of macroeconomics since then is best seen in the light of Keynes's book. That is not, of course, to say that macroeconomics has subsequently been limited to the refinement of the argument of the *General Theory*. In the early years after its appearance there were, it is true, elements of this; there was also a long debate about the relationship of the Keynesian analysis to the classical, or 'marginalist', orthodoxy of the times. Since then, persistent themes have been (1) the extension of macroeconomic theory into areas not treated explicitly in the *General Theory*: inflation, growth, cycles, and income distribution, for example; (2) the continuation of the 'Keynes and the Classics' debate, and the revival of interest in versions of the quantity theory of money; (3) the attempt to test statistically the various theories; (4) more recently, the debate as to whether post-Keynesian orthodoxy has not over-simplified—or even misrepresented—what the 'Keynesian revolution' really was.

Those, then, are the *Macroeconomic Themes* of this book. The arrangement of the readings is as follows.

Chapter 1 is concerned with the fundamental 'model' of the *General Theory*, with early attempts to set out its crucial features, and with its relationship to the previous orthodoxy. This culminates in the standard 'IS–LM' and 'neoclassical synthesis' models which have recently been under fire as misleading vehicles for understanding the Keynesian revolution.

Chapters 2–4 trace the development of views on consumption, investment, and monetary theory. In these chapters, several themes are interwoven—the refinement of concepts, the confrontation of theory and statistical data, and the revival of interest in neoclassical theory.

Chapters 5–8 deal with problems barely touched on in the *General Theory*—economic growth, business cycles, inflation, and income distribution.

Chapter 9 is concerned with recent reappraisals of macroeconomic theory, notably by the neo-monetarist school on the one hand and by Keynesian monetary theorists on the other.

Finally, Chapters 10 and 11 examine some of the problems involved in macroeconomic policy-making, both theoretical (Chapter 10) and those involved in building statistical models of real economies as a basis for making the analyses and forecasts which underlie policy decisions (Chapter 11).

Oxford,   M.J.C.S.
October 1975.

Contents

1. The Keynesian Revolution

Introductory Note

THIS section begins with extracts from Keynes's *General Theory of Employment, Interest and Money* (1936) and then traces the way in which the 'Keynesian' approach developed and how the novel ideas attributed to Keynes were assimilated into the mainstream of macroeconomic thinking.

It would be very hard to find a representative passage which summarized the orthodoxy which Keynes thought himself to be attacking. Indeed, there has never been a real consensus of opinion on the extent to which there was a single orthodoxy with which the *General Theory* was in direct conflict. Keynes himself set up a 'classical' economist against whom to inveigh, but, as many writers have pointed out, this was a figure of straw corresponding to no single man or school. It therefore seems best to begin with a crude sketch of what Keynes and later exponents of the Keynesian approach took to be the classical approach with which they were in dispute, bearing in mind that there was a great deal more to classical thought than such a sketch implies.[1]

First, we note that the relevant parts of the analysis are 'short-run' in the sense that although net investment is taking place, the effects of the resulting growth in the stock of capital may be ignored. In a given period, 'labour' is applied to the existing stock of capital equipment to produce a homogeneous 'good' which, for the moment, we suppose may be used either as a consumption good or as an investment good. A stock of 'money' exists, whose supply is controlled by 'the authorities', and serves only to avoid the inconveniences of a barter system by financing all the transactions which take place in the economy. There are thus three markets to consider—those in labour, in goods, and in money.

In the labour market, supply is taken to be an increasing function of the real wage. On the demand side, perfectly competitive conditions are assumed and profits are maximized. With the capital stock (and technology) given, real output depends only on the level of employment. Employment and thus output are pushed to the point at which the marginal physical product of labour is brought to equality with the real wage rate. Given diminishing returns, so that the marginal physical product of labour declines as more

---

[1] As Joan Robinson has often pointed out, the economists of the immediate pre-Keynesian era should strictly be termed 'neoclassical', reserving the term 'classical' for nineteenth-century thinkers. But this entails the use of the awkward term 'neo-neoclassical' to describe the approach of modern general equilibrium theorists, and the less correct but conventional terminology will therefore be retained.

labour is applied to the given stock of capital, the demand for labour will depend inversely on the real wage. The intersection of supply and demand schedules thus determines the real wage, the level of employment, and hence the level of real output.

The demand for money depends only on the value of transactions. Provided that institutional arrangements and customs of payment are unchanging, and that the value of transactions increases as the level of money income rises, the demand for money depends only on money income, which is itself the product of real income and the general price level. The supply of money is taken as fixed by the authorities.

The only function of the remainder of the model is to allocate income between consumption and investment and, consequentially, between consumption and saving, for the equality of income and expenditure entails the equality of saving and investment. Equilibrium is attained through movements in the rate of interest. The lower the interest rate, the more investment projects will be profitable to undertake, other things being equal, while the higher the rate, the greater the incentive to save. The intersection of savings and investment schedules thus fixes the distribution of income between consumption and savings/investment, and the equilibrium rate of interest.

This simple 'classical' model has three main features. First, conditions in the labour market alone determine the values of the 'real' variables—employment, output, and the real wage rate. Since the supply of and the demand for labour are equated, there cannot be unemployment, at any rate in equilibrium. Of course, if either the supply or the demand schedule shifts, there will be a new equilibrium real wage and a different level of employment—but there will still be no unemployment in the sense of *involuntary* unemployment. Secondly, the only (analytic) function of money in the model is to determine the price level, for, with the given full-employment level of real output, the price level must adjust so as to procure that level of money income at which the demand for money is equal to the given supply. Finally, the rate of interest is a non-monetary phenomenon, in that it serves only to equilibrate the flows of savings and investment and is unaffected by, for example, a change in the supply of money. Thus the system partitions completely into 'real' and 'monetary' sectors, employment and real output being determined independently of the money supply, whose only role is to fix the price level.

This, then, while a highly schematic and over-simplified model of what the classical economics taught, summarizes the bare essentials of the orthodoxy which the *General Theory* set out to demolish.

The *General Theory* is, by common consent, an exceedingly difficult book, and one in which ambiguities, lack of clarity, confusions, and even inconsistencies, have often been pointed out. At this stage, however, we are more concerned with what economists made of the new ideas than with what

Keynes 'really said'.[2] Reading 1.1 therefore picks out, from several different parts of the book, those passages which seem to incorporate the major ideas in which the 'Keynesian revolution' was taken to consist.

First, the *General Theory* asks what happens when real income increases, rather than taking a full-employment level for granted. The answer given is that consumption will increase, but by less than the absolute amount of the increase in income. The remainder of the increase must, if the situation is to be stable, be accounted for by investment, which in turn depends on the profitability of investment in relation to the level of interest rates. For the economy to be in equilibrium, that is, 'effective demand'—consumption plus investment—must be equal to supply.[3] But since consumption is itself a function of income, it is investment which is the prime mover in determining the level of income. There is, in general, no reason to suppose that investment (and hence effective demand) will be at that level which will procure full employment, and if demand is insufficient there will be unemployment *even if the marginal product of labour exceeds the wage rate* [Reading 1.1, pp. 12–14].

The relation between consumption and income [pp. 15–17] in real terms[4] is positive, but an increment of income will lead to a smaller increment in consumption. The relation between the latter and the former, $\Delta C/\Delta Y = a$, say, is termed the marginal propensity to consume. But since the ultimate increase in income must be identically equal to the consequential increase in consumption plus the initiating increase in investment, we have

$$\Delta C = a\Delta Y$$

and
$$\Delta Y \equiv \Delta C + \Delta I$$

from which
$$\Delta Y = \frac{1}{1-a} \cdot \Delta I,$$

where the factor $1/(1-a)$ by which the change in investment is multiplied is termed the *multiplier*.[5]

---

[2] That there is a great, and important, difference between the two is the theme of some important recent work, to which we return in Chapter 9. The major contribution has been that of Axel Leijonhufvud. See his *On Keynesian Economics and the Economics of Keynes* (New York: O.U.P., 1968).

[3] We take up in Chapter 9 the question of what—if anything—could be meant by 'ineffective demand.'

[4] Keynes refers to measurement in 'wage-units'. Provided that the real wage, w/p, is unchanged, this is equivalent to working in real terms.

[5] This simple algebraic manipulation obscures the important dynamics of the operation of the multiplier. An increase in investment generates factor incomes: a proportion a of these incomes is spent on consumption goods, in turn generating further factor incomes ... and so on. Thus the ultimate increase in income is

$$\Delta Y = \Delta I + a\Delta I + a^2\Delta I + \dots$$
$$= \Delta I(1 + a + a^2 + \dots)$$
$$= 1/(1-a)\Delta I$$

It is this *process*, rather than the 'equilibrium condition' described in the text, which really illustrates the nature of 'the multiplier'.

If income (= output) determines employment, and investment determines income, what determines investment? Here [pp. 17–18] Keynes's break with orthodoxy is least apparent. Any capital asset is expected to produce a stream of returns, against which must be set its cost. There will be some rate of discounting the expected stream of returns which will equate their value to the price of the asset: this is termed the *marginal efficiency* of the asset. The higher investment in any particular type of capital asset, the lower will be the marginal efficiency of further additions—in the short run because increased demand for the investment good will tend to bid up its supply price, and in the longer run because the expected returns will tend to diminish as the stock of the asset increases. For capital goods in the aggregate, therefore, there will be a negative relationship between the level of investment and the marginal efficiency of capital (MEC); investment will naturally be pushed to the point at which the MEC is equal to the rate of interest at which investment funds can be borrowed.[6]

Finally [pp. 18–23], what determines the rate of interest? As in the classical model, one motive for wishing to hold cash balances—and thus to forego the interest which these balances could otherwise have earned—is to finance the current level of transactions. A second motive is precautionary: the fact that future interest rates are uncertain means that it is prudent to keep a reserve of cash as a store of wealth to offset the risk that being forced by an unexpected turn of events to sell a security in order to realize cash may involve a capital loss. Finally, there is the speculative motive. The typical financial asset is taken to be a bond of stated nominal value paying a fixed sum (or 'coupon') per annum. If there exists an organized market in bonds, trading will ensure that the price at which they are exchanged is such as to equate their yield with the going rate of interest. (Thus a £100 bond paying £5 per annum will exchange at £50 if the rate of interest rises to 10 per cent per annum.)

---

[6] The elision from the concept of capital (a stock) to investment (a flow) needs a word of explanation. Other things being equal, a fall in the rate of interest makes some investment projects worth undertaking which would previously have been unprofitable. The desired stock of capital, that is to say, increases. But when the investment has been carried out and the desired capital stock attained, net investment will fall back to zero. In this *dynamic* framework, there are different investment demand schedules at different times for any given MEC schedule. We must therefore understand Keynes to be abstracting from questions involving the lapse of time. The comparison is effectively between what *is* and what *would have been*, had the rate of interest been lower (that is, the analysis is in terms of comparative statics). In this case it is clearly true that were the desired capital stock higher 'now', so would the rate of investment be. Cf. Joan Robinson, *Economic Heresies* (London: Macmillan, 1971), p. 83: 'One thing he [Keynes] could never have said is that a permanently lower level of the rate of interest would cause a permanently higher rate of investment.' See also the Introductory Note to Chapter 3 below.

The use of both comparative static and dynamic modes of analysis (and the corresponding ambiguity about the meaning of the term 'short-run') is one element making for the difficulty of the *General Theory*. Keynes's analysis of liquidity preference, for example, is almost wholly 'dynamic'.

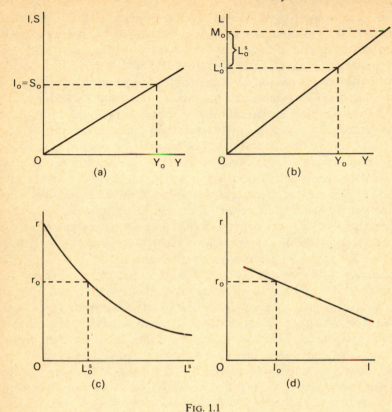

FIG. 1.1

Trading will, of course, only take place if opinions as to the future course of interest rates—and hence of bond prices—differ, for a person will only sell if he expects prices to fall, while the buyer must expect prices to rise. In the aggregate, the lower the rate of interest is in relation to what is generally regarded as its normal level, the fewer people will expect it to fall further (that is, for bond prices to rise further) and the greater will be the tendency to hold cash rather than bonds. Cash balances held for speculative purposes—the 'preference for liquidity'—will thus vary inversely with the divergence of the interest rate from its 'normal' level.

A given supply of money will thus be absorbed in part by transactions and precautionary (or 'active') balances which depend primarily on the level of income; the rate of interest must then be such as to persuade people to hold the remainder as speculative (or 'idle') balances.

The argument may now be brought together [pp. 23–24]. Unlike the 'classical' system, the Keynesian system cannot be partitioned: all markets are interdependent. This may best be seen diagrammatically. Given a certain level of investment (I_0 in Fig. 1.1(a)), income rises to the level (Y_0) at which savings

(S_0) are equal to investment. At that level of income, the transactions (and precautionary) demand for money will be L_0 (Fig. 1.1(b)), leaving L_0^s of the fixed money supply M to be held in idle balances. With an unchanged view about the normal level of the rate of interest, this level of speculative balances will be consistent with an interest rate r_0 (Fig. 1.1(c)), which in turn (Fig. 1.1(d)) must be that rate which calls forth the level of investment, I_0, with which we started. Consider now an increase in the money supply, all other circumstances remaining unchanged. (Assume that the increase comes about through the purchase by the authorities of bonds on the open market, with no change in government expenditure or taxation. The control of the money supply will be considered in more detail in Chapter 4.) In the first instance, with the level of income unchanged, this increase must be absorbed wholly into speculative balances—a result which will be associated with a rise in bond prices and a fall in the interest rate. Investment will be stimulated, and the operation of the multiplier will increase income so as to generate additional savings equal to the increase in investment. It is at once evident that although the increase in the money supply is expansionary in its effects on income and employment, offsetting repercussions are set in train: the higher level of income requires a higher level of active money balances, so that the rise in idle balances is less than the full extent of the increase in the money supply; the fall in the rate of interest is thus less great than might at first have been supposed ... and so on. The system's simultaneity is thus characterized by both positive and negative 'feedbacks'. The operation of the multiplier in magnifying the effect on income of an increase in investment is an example of positive feedback, while the dampening of the initial effect on the interest rate just described is an example of negative feedback.

A number of such experiments can, of course, be performed with this model: one can trace the effects of a change in entrepreneurs' expectations (reflected in a shift in the MEC schedule), for example, or in the community's propensity to save (reflected in a shift in the savings schedule); with a little ingenuity, government expenditure and taxation may be introduced and the effects of fiscal policy explored, or exports and imports brought in and the effects of changes in the trade balance illuminated. All this is the common stuff of large parts of modern macroeconomic textbooks, and to a considerable extent reflects the conventional wisdom of economic policy makers in the years following the appearance of the *General Theory*.[7]

Other economists, however, were asking different questions. How, exactly, did Keynesian economics differ from that of the classics? Were the two reconcilable, in the sense that one was, in some way, a special case of the other? Why did the levels of wages and prices seem so unimportant in the 'new' economics? And so on.

It was to the first of these questions that Hicks addressed himself in 'Mr.

[7] Questions concerning the theory and practice of macroeconomic policy making are taken up in Chapters 10 and 11.

Keynes and the Classics', an article which appeared in the year following the publication of the *General Theory*: a later version of the framework there set out appears as Reading 1.2 below. Hicks begins with the assumption that money wage-rates are constant, so that there is, to all intents and purposes, no need to distinguish between real and money income. The level of investment is determined by the rate of interest and, through the multiplier, this fixes the level of income. To every level of the rate of interest there will thus correspond a certain level of income, and the relationship between them will be negatively sloped: this is the SI (saving–investment) curve of Fig. 1.2 [p. 25]. A second relation between the rate of interest and the level of income emerges from Keynes's account of liquidity preference. With a given supply of money, the demand for active balances will vary directly with income. The remainder must be held as idle balances and, as we have seen, the lower the rate of interest (and hence the higher are bond prices) the less the reward—in terms of interest and possible capital gain—from holding bonds rather than cash. As income increases, therefore, active balances expand while idle balances fall and the rate of interest rises. We should thus expect, on this account, a positive relationship between the level of income and the interest rate. This is Hicks's L Curve. Its shape will be quite complicated, for, in the first place, there is likely to be some low level of the rate of interest (high level of bond prices) at which opinion will be virtually unanimous that interest rates can fall no further. Bond holdings will become virtually zero so that any further increase in the supply of money will be absorbed wholly into idle balances with no effect on the bond market and hence no further reduction in the rate of interest. Thus if income falls, releasing money from active balances, the rate of interest does not fall. This floor to the rate of interest, reflected in a horizontal section of the L curve at low levels of income, is, of course, the 'liquidity trap'. At the other extreme, there will be a certain level of income at which active balances absorb the whole of the money supply and thus no further increase in income can be financed. At this point, the L curve becomes vertical, as it would do in the simple classical model in which there is no relationship between the rate of interest and the level of income.

Superimposition of these two schedules gives at their point of intersection the values of *Y* and *r* associated with the equilibrium state of the economy. Investment is equal to saving and the demand for money is equal to its supply: there is, of course, no reason to suppose that the level of income will be that of full employment. If the equilibrium is one of underemployment, income can be expanded by increasing the money supply, and so shifting the L curve bodily to the right—unless the economy is in the 'liquidity trap', in which case the interest rate will not fall and investment therefore will not rise. Or the SI curve can be shifted to the right by reducing the rate of direct taxation and so raising the marginal propensity to consume and thus the multiplier and the level of income associated with the going interest rate and level of investment—unless income is already at the maximum level permitted by the money supply and reflected in the vertical portion of the L curve.

Hansen [Reading 1.3] emphasizes that Hicks's analysis draws together in an explicit way the elements which, although present in the *General Theory*, were never brought together by Keynes in such a way as to show clearly the *simultaneous* determination of the rate of interest and the level of income. The The IS–LM (Hicks's SI–Ḷ) diagram has become deservedly popular as an expository device which points up very sharply this aspect of the Keynesian system. On the other hand, it can be argued that by directing attention so firmly to the *equilibrium* conditions of the model, it tends to obscure the underlying causal structure—a structure which is perhaps more readily seen from the admittedly more cumbersome four-diagram system presented above.

There are, moreover, important ways in which both modes of presentation over-simplify the workings of the economy. Most notably, the assumption of fixed money wages—which means that the distinction between money and real income is effectively suppressed, and that employment can thus be related directly to the level of money—income obscures significant aspects of the 'Keynes and the classics' divergence. Modigliani's 1944 article, 'Liquidity Preference and the Theory of Interest and Money' [from which an extract appears as Reading 1.4], attempted a more comprehensive confrontation of Keynesian and classical theories in which wages and prices were explicitly introduced and in which, as a consequence, the unique link between the levels of money income and employment was severed. It was noted that Keynes had explicitly accepted the orthodox view that, in the short run, with a fixed amount of capital equipment and with 'competitive' conditions prevailing, diminishing returns implied that the real wage would tend to fall as employment increased.[8] But whereas the classicals had supposed the wage bargain to be struck in (or as if in) real terms, Keynes, according to Modigliani, supposed (a) that wage bargaining took place in money terms, (b) that the existing money wage was 'historically' determined, and (c) that the supply of labour would be infinitely elastic at the going money wage, up to the point of full employment [eqns. (9)–(11), p. 34–35].[9]

Given these assumptions, the 'Keynesian' system splits into a money system and a real system. The money system is precisely that of the IS–LM analysis, with investment, saving, and demand-for-money schedules, together with the fixed money supply, determining the levels of money income and the interest rate [pp. 39–42]. But the price level is not determined, and therefore the levels of *real* income and employment are not either. Given that the forces of

---

[8] Cf. *General Theory*, p. 17: 'In emphasising our point of departure from the classical system, we must not overlook an important point of agreement ... [W]ith a given organisation, equipment and technique real wages and the volume of output (and hence of employment) are uniquely correlated, so that, in general, an increase in employment can only occur to the accompaniment of a decline in the rate of real wages.'

[9] Whether these really were Keynes's assumptions is arguable. See Chapter 9 below.

competition ensure that the real wage will be equal to the marginal physical product of labour, however, output and employment will settle at the point at which the price level—fixed by the ratio of monetarily determined nominal income to the physical quantity of output—is such as to produce, in conjunction with the going money wage, the real wage which satisfies this equality [p. 42]. Again, there is no reason to suppose that the level of employment so determined will be that of full employment. Monetary conditions determine money income and, with a given money wage, to each level of money income there corresponds an equilibrium price level and level of employment, but there are no forces tending to ensure that this will be full employment.

Thus for Modigliani, and for the orthodoxy of the 'neoclassical synthesis' which broadly dominated macroeconomic thinking for the next decade and more, the existence of unemployment equilibrium was to be attributed to the 'Keynesian' assumption of rigid money wages.

To illustrate, suppose the economy to be initially in a state of full employment. Suppose that there is a downward shift in the marginal efficiency of capital schedule (the typical example used by Keynes). The IS curve shifts downwards: in the new equilibrium both money income and the rate of interest will, with a fixed money supply and provided the economy is not in the liquidity trap, be lower. Under a system of freely flexible wages and prices, the fall in money income can take place by means of an all-round reduction in wages and prices, leaving real output, employment, and the real wage unchanged. But with rigid money wages, the new equilibrium will be characterized by lower prices, a higher real wage, and lower employment and output. Only in the liquidity trap will unemployment equilibrium be possible if money wages are flexible downwards, for there no reduction in wages and prices can, by releasing money from active balances, reduce the interest rate to the level required to ensure full employment.

The neoclassical synthesis was thus a synthesis in that it adopted the Keynesian theory of the simultaneous determination of money income and the rate of interest while retaining the older tradition that the tendency to full-employment equilibrium could only be thwarted by 'rigidities' somewhere in the system—rigid money wages, the liquidity trap, or (another 'Keynesian' favourite) the failure of investment to be sufficiently interest-elastic.

Patinkin [Reading 1.5] took this line even further, arguing that, *as a matter of logic*, the existence of involuntary unemployment was inconsistent with equilibrium if all prices (including wages and interest rates) were fully flexible [p. 46]. It follows that unemployment must be a disequilibrium phenomenon. The question then is, why should the disequilibrium be able to persist so long even if prices are flexible? And the answer to this involves more of the spirit of Keynes's original analysis than is usually found in neoclassical writings. Consider [pp. 47–49] a reduction in aggregate demand. In the short run, production may remain unchanged (inventories are accumulated) and, through the reduction in active balances and consequential fall in the interest rate, and through the 'real balance effect', offsetting expansionary effects on demand will be set up. (The real balance effect—a central element in Patinkin's analysis—needs some explanation. The decline in demand will tend to reduce commodity prices and, in the present case where output, employment, and hence real wages remain unchanged, money wages. The price decline increases the value of money balances held, and this is taken to increase commodity demand directly.) However, unless these forces work very quickly, there will be a period of disequilibrium in which the fall in demand will push commodity prices downwards and reduce the desired level of employment. In this disequilibrium, since firms are not on their labour-demand curves, the reduction in employment is not associated with a rise in the real wage; with flexible wages, unemployment will force money wages down and there is, in general, no reason why wages and prices should not fall equally. In such a situation of *disequilibrium*, and in contrast to the *equilibrium* analysis of Modigliani, freely flexible wages are insufficient to prevent persistent unemployment. The Keynesian element in Patinkin's argument is, of course, the re-introduction of effective demand as a primary determinant of employment.

The real balance effect, however, means that this disequilibrium will not last indefinitely, for, as wages and prices fall, there will be an increasingly effective stimulus to demand. And the price decline will also tend to act indirectly through the interest rate. With a sufficiently large deflation of wages and prices, the full employment level of output could be restored, but the scale of the price decline required rules deflation out as a primary tool of full employment policy [p. 51]. It is at this point that control of the money supply is introduced as a way of avoiding the decline in prices otherwise needed to restore full employment. Patinkin here asserts that the 'Keynesian' position rests simply on the interest-inelasticity of investment. In that case, the operation of the real balance effect is indeed the only (non-fiscal) solution to the existence of unemployment, though a solution which may well work so slowly as to be consistent with protracted periods of unemployment.

Finally, the 'liquidity trap' case can be disposed of [pp. 54–58]. Even if there is a floor to the rate of interest, expansion of the money supply will increase money balances so that, again, a real balance effect can operate to restore full employment.

To summarize, Patinkin asserts that, with freely flexible wages and prices, unemployment must be a disequilibrium phenomenon. A decline in effective demand will lead to a disequilibrium in which both prices and wages will tend to fall. There is no inherent tendency for the real wage to decline and hence no reason to suppose that freely flexible wages would prevent the appearance of unemployment. However, the real balance effect can, ultimately, restore full employment if prices fall sufficiently, and, similarly, this rules out the liquidity trap as an explanation of the persistence of unemployment in the face of monetary expansion. A deficiency of effective demand could create unemployment; what it cannot do is create an unemployment *equilibrium*.

In his review of Patinkin's book [Reading 1.6], Hicks attempts to translate the argument into terms of the IS–LM diagram. In contrast to the original presentation, this is now constructed in real (or, strictly, in wage-unit) terms. This charge means that the IS curve terminates at full employment, beyond which an inflation occurs with no increase in real income.[10] The effect of wage and price changes on the LM curve, however, is more serious. Given a money supply fixed in nominal terms, its supply in real terms will vary as wages and prices change. Wage–price deflation increases the money supply in real terms, shifting the LM curve to the right: it is this shift which Hicks recognizes as the real balance effect. Wage–price deflation thus will set up a tendency towards full employment—unless the economy is in the liquidity trap. Since, as we have seen, Patinkin specifically denies that the existence of a liquidity trap opens up the possibility of unemployment equilibrium, Hicks is forced to find an alternative to the 'real balance effect', as incorporated in shifts in the LM curve, in order to account for Patinkin's 'classical' belief in the ultimate impossibility of such an equilibrium. This alternative is a vertical segment of the LM curve 'beyond' (that is, to the left of) the liquidity trap, where, presumably, no bonds at all are held and the links between money and the rate of interest and consequently between money and the levels of investment and income are severed. In such a situation, one must suppose that the bond market ceases to exist. The government is then the sole lender in the economy and can further depress interest rates at will. The disruption of the financial system that is entailed represents, for Hicks, such an extreme case that it can effectively be ignored; the liquidity trap as an explanation of unemployment equilibrium is vindicated even under conditions of wage and price flexibility.

Patinkin's rejoinder [Reading 1.7] is that Hicks has misunderstood the nature of the real balance effect. There will indeed be a shift in the LM curve of the sort described by Hicks, but this is not the direct real balance effect. It is the conventional 'Keynesian' effect of a fall in prices on the transactions demand and hence, via an increase in speculative balances, on the rate of interest. The direct real balance effect, however, is the *direct* effect of the increase in the value of money balances on aggregate demand. Such an effect will manifest itself in a shift in the IS, not the LM, curve. It follows that, even starting from the liquidity trap, the operation of the real balance effect means that a sufficient wage–price deflation (sufficient rightward move of the

---

[10] Hicks describes [p. 61] an analogous 'full unemployment' cut-off point beyond which wages fall with (presumably) no further reduction in real income, but this is unnecessary for the argument. The IS curve remains defined as long as a fall in the interest rate reduces investment, whether or not this is accompanied by a fall in wages.

IS curve) can restore the full employment level of real income.

And there, for some years, the argument effectively rested. What seemed to have been established was that, so far as equilibrium states were concerned, unemployment could only be explained by 'rigidities' of one sort or another — in particular, inflexibility of money wages, the existence of a floor to the rate of interest above that level which would stimulate a full-employment level of investment, or insensitivity of investment to changes in interest rates. If none of these rigidities existed, unemployment could only appear as a disequilibrium phenomenon and there might be no reason to suppose that in such a disequilibrium the 'appropriate' adjustment of the real wage would take place. Even then, balanced wage and price deflation could lead back to full employment equilibrium, first through its effect on the demand for money and on interest rates, and secondly through its direct 'real balance effect' on demand. Even if investment were interest-inelastic, so that the former effect were impotent, the real balance effect could, in principle, assure a return to full employment. Crudely put, the new orthodoxy was that the 'Keynesian' approach was correct in a real world in which rigidities were commonplace, while the 'neoclassical' approach carried the theoretical day in demonstrating that free flexibility of all prices (including wage- and interest-rates) would logically ensure the achievement of equilibrium at full employment.

Meanwhile, many other economists were developing, and adding to, the elements of the macroeconomic system, and it is to the exploration of consumption, investment, and demand-for-money functions that Chapters 2, 3, and 4 are devoted.

1.1 The General Theory of Employment, Interest and Money*

The outline of our theory can be expressed as follows. When employment increases, aggregate real income is increased. The psychology of the community is such that when aggregate real income is increased aggregate consumption is increased, but not by so much as income. Hence employers would make a loss if the whole of the increased employment were to be devoted to satisfying the increased demand for immediate consumption. Thus, to justify any given amount of employment there must be an amount of current investment sufficient to absorb the excess of total output over what the community chooses to consume when employment is at the given level. For unless there is this amount of investment, the receipts of the entrepreneurs will be less than is required to induce them to offer the given amount of employment. It follows, therefore, that, given what we shall call the community's propensity to consume, the equilibrium level of employment, *i.e.* the level at which there is no

* From J. M. Keynes, *The General Theory of Employment, Interest and Money* (London: Macmillan, 1936), chs. 3, 8, 10, 11, 13, 15, and 18; from *Collected Writings of John Maynard Keynes* by permission of the Royal Economic Society and Macmillan, London and Basingstoke, and St. Martin's Press, Inc., N.Y.

inducement to employers as a whole either to expand or to contract employment, will depend on the amount of current investment. The amount of current investment will depend, in turn, on what we shall call the inducement to invest; and the inducement to invest will be found to depend on the relation between the schedule of the marginal efficiency of capital and the complex of rates of interest on loans of various maturities and risks.

Thus, given the propensity to consume and the rate of new investment, there will be only one level of employment consistent with equilibrium; since any other level will lead to inequality between the aggregate supply price of output as a whole and its aggregate demand price. This level cannot be *greater* than full employment, *i.e.* the real wage cannot be less than the marginal disutility of labour. But there is no reason in general for expecting it to be *equal* to full employment. The effective demand associated with full employment is a special case, only realised when the propensity to consume and the inducement to invest stand in a particular relationship to one another. This particular relationship, which corresponds to the assumptions of the classical theory, is in a sense an optimum relationship. But it can only exist when, by accident or design, current investment provides an amount of demand just equal to the excess of the aggregate supply price of the output resulting from full employment over what the community will choose to spend on consumption when it is fully employed.

This theory can be summed up in the following propositions:

(1) In a given situation of technique, resources and costs, income (both money-income and real income) depends on the volume of employment N.

(2) The relationship between the community's income and what it can be expected to spend on consumption, designated by D_1, will depend on the psychological characteristic of the community, which we shall call its *propensity to consume*. That is to say, consumption will depend on the level of aggregate income and, therefore, on the level of employment N, except when there is some change in the propensity to consume.

(3) The amount of labour N which the entrepreneurs decide to employ depends on the sum (D) of *two* quantities, namely D_1, the amount which the community is expected to spend on consumption, and D_2, the amount which it is expected to devote to new investment. D is what we have called above the *effective demand*.

(4) Since $D_1 + D_2 = D = \phi(N)$, where ϕ is the aggregate supply function, and since, as we have seen in (2) above, D_1 is a function of N, which we may write $\chi(N)$, depending on the propensity to consume, it follows that $\phi(N) - \chi(N) = D_2$.

(5) Hence the volume of employment in equilibrium depends on (i) the aggregate supply function, ϕ, (ii) the propensity to consume, χ, and (iii) the volume of investment, D_2. This is the essence of the General Theory of Employment.

(6) For every value of N there is a corresponding marginal productivity of

labour in the wage-goods industries; and it is this which determines the real wage. (5) is, therefore, subject to the condition that N cannot *exceed* the value which reduces the real wage to equality with the marginal disutility of labour. This means that not all changes in D are compatible with our temporary assumption that money-wages are constant. Thus it will be essential to a full statement of our theory to dispense with this assumption.

(7) On the classical theory, according to which $D = \phi(N)$ for *all* values of N, the volume of employment is in neutral equilibrium for all values of N less than its maximum value; so that the forces of competition between entrepreneurs may be expected to push it to this maximum value. Only at this point, on the classical theory, can there be stable equilibrium.

(8) *When employment increases*, D_1, *will increase, but not by so much as* D; since when our income increases our consumption increases also, but not by so much. The key to our practical problem is to be found in this psychological law. For it follows from this that the greater the volume of employment the greater will be the gap between the aggregate supply price (Z) of the corresponding output and the sum (D_1) which the entrepeneurs can expect to get back out of the expenditure of consumers. Hence, if there is no change in the propensity to consume, employment cannot increase, unless at the same time D_2 is increasing so as to fill the increasing gap between Z and D_1. Thus— except on the special assumptions of the classical theory according to which there is some force in operation which, when employment increases, always causes D_2 to increase sufficiently to fill the widening gap between Z and D_1— the economic system may find itself in stable equilibrium with N at a level below full employment, namely at the level given by the intersection of the aggregate demand function with the aggregate supply function.

Thus the volume of employment is not determined by the marginal disutility of labour measured in terms of real wages, except in so far as the supply of labour available at a given real wage sets a *maximum* level to employment. The propensity to consume and the rate of new investment determine between them the volume of employment, and the volume of employment is uniquely related to a given level of real wages—not the other way round. If the propensity to consume and the rate of new investment result in a deficient effective demand, the actual level of employment will fall short of the supply of labour potentially available at the existing real wage, and the equilibrium real wage will be *greater* than the marginal disutility of the equilibrium level of employment.

This analysis supplies us with an explanation of the paradox of poverty in the midst of plenty. For the mere existence of an insufficiency of effective demand may, and often will, bring the increase of employment to a standstill *before* a level of full employment has been reached. The insufficiency of effective demand will inhibit the process of production in spite of the fact that the marginal product of labour still exceeds in value the marginal disutility of employment. [...]

Thus the analysis of the Propensity to Consume, the definition of the Marginal Efficiency of Capital and the theory of the Rate of Interest are the three main gaps in our existing knowledge which it will be necessary to fill. When this has been accomplished, we shall find that the Theory of Prices falls into its proper place as a matter which is subsidiary to our general theory. We shall discover, however, that Money plays an essential part in our theory of the Rate of Interest; and we shall attempt to disentangle the peculiar characteristics of Money which distinguish it from other things.[...]

Granted, then, that the propensity to consume is a fairly stable function so that, as a rule, the amount of aggregate consumption mainly depends on the amount of aggregate income (both measured in terms of wage-units), changes in the propensity itself being treated as a secondary influence, what is the normal shape of this function?

The fundamental psychological law, upon which we are entitled to depend with great confidence both *a priori* from our knowledge of human nature and from the detailed facts of experience, is that men are disposed, as a rule and on the average, to increase their consumption as their income increases, but not by as much as the increase in their income. That is to say, if C_w is the amount of consumption and Y_w is income (both measured in wage-units) ΔC_w has the same sign as ΔY_w but is smaller in amount, *i.e.* dC_w/dY_w is positive and less than unity.

This is especially the case where we have short periods in view, as in the case of the so-called cyclical fluctuations of employment during which habits, as distinct from more permanent psychological propensities, are not given time enough to adapt themselves to changed objective circumstances. For a man's habitual standard of life usually has the first claim on his income, and he is apt to save the difference which discovers itself between his actual income and the expense of his habitual standard; or, if he does adjust his expenditure to changes in his income, he will over short periods do so imperfectly. Thus a rising income will often be accompanied by increased saving, and a falling income by decreased saving, on a greater scale at first than subsequently.

But, apart from short-period *changes* in the level of income, it is also obvious that a higher absolute level of income will tend, as a rule, to widen the gap between income and consumption. For the satisfaction of the immediate primary needs of a man and his family is usually a stronger motive than the motives towards accumulation, which only acquire effective sway when a margin of comfort has been attained. These reasons will lead, as a rule, to a greater *proportion* of income being saved as real income increases. But whether or not a greater proportion is saved, we take it as a fundamental psychological rule of any modern community that, when its real income is increased, it will not increase its consumption by an equal *absolute* amount, so that a greater absolute amount must be saved, unless a large and unusual change is occurring at the same time in other factors. As we shall show subsequently, the stability of the economic system essentially depends on this rule prevailing in practice. This means that, if employment and hence aggregate income increase, *not all* the additional employment will be required to satisfy the needs of additional consumption.

On the other hand, a decline in income due to a decline in the level of employment, if it goes far, may even cause consumption to exceed income not only by some individuals and institutions using up the financial reserves which they have accumulated in better times, but also by the Government, which will be liable, willingly or unwillingly, to run into a budgetary deficit or will provide unemployment relief, for example, out of borrowed money. Thus, when employment falls to a low level, aggregate consumption will decline by a smaller amount than that by which real income has declined, by reason both of the habitual behaviour of individuals and also of the probable policy of governments; which is the explanation why a new position of equilibrium can usually be reached within a modest range of fluctuation. Otherwise a fall in employment and income, once started, might proceed to extreme lengths.

This simple principle leads, it will be seen, to the same conclusion as before, namely, that employment can only increase *pari passu* with an increase in investment; unless, indeed, there is a change in the propensity to consume. For since consumers will spend less than the increase in aggregate supply price when employment is increased, the increased employment will prove unprofitable unless there is an increase in investment to fill the gap.[...]

The fluctuations in real income under consideration in this book are those which result from applying different quantities of employment (*i.e.* of labour-units) to a given capital equipment, so that real income increases and decreases with the number of labour-units employed. If, as we assume in general, there is a decreasing return at the margin as the number of labour-units employed on the given capital equipment is increased, income measured in terms of wage-units will increase more than in proportion to the amount of employment, which, in turn, will increase more than in proportion to the amount of real income measured (if that is possible) in terms of product. Real income measured in terms of product and income measured in terms of wage-units will, however, increase and decrease together (in the short period when capital equipment is virtually unchanged). Since, therefore, real income, in terms of product, may be incapable of precise numerical measurement, it is often convenient to regard income in terms of wage-units (Y_w) as an adequate working index of changes in real income. In certain contexts we must not overlook the fact that, in general, Y_w increases and decreases in a greater proportion than real income; but in other contexts the fact that they always increase and decrease together renders them virtually interchangeable.

Our normal psychological law that, when the real income of the community increases or decreases, its consumption will increase or decrease but not so fast, can, therefore, be translated—not, indeed, with absolute accuracy but subject to qualifications which are obvious and can easily be stated in a formally complete fashion—into the propositions that ΔC_w and ΔY_w have the same sign, but $\Delta Y_w > \Delta C_w$, where C_w is the consumption in terms of wage-units. This is merely a repetition of the proposition already established on [p. 13] above. Let us define, then, dC_w/dY_w as the *marginal propensity to consume*.

This quantity is of considerable importance, because it tells us how the next increment of output will have to be divided between consumption and investment. For $\Delta Y_w = \Delta C_w + \Delta I_w$, where ΔC_w and ΔI_w are the increments of consumption and investment; so that we can write $\Delta Y_w = k\Delta I_w$, where $1 - (1/k)$ is equal to the marginal propensity to consume.

Let us call k the *investment multiplier*. It tells us that, when there is an increment of aggregate investment, income will increase by an amount which is k times the increment of investing. [...]

When a man buys an investment or capital-asset, he purchases the right to the series of prospective returns, which he expects to obtain from selling its output, after deducting the running expenses of obtaining that output, during the life of the asset. This series of annuities $Q_1, Q_2 \ldots Q_n$ it is convenient to call the *prospective yield* of the investment.

Over against the prospective yield of the investment we have the *supply price* of the capital-asset, meaning by this, not the market-price at which an asset of the type in question can actually be purchased in the market, but the price which would just induce a manufacturer newly to produce an additional unit of such assets, *i.e.* what is sometimes called its *replacement cost*. The relation between the prospective yield of a capital-asset and its supply price or replacement cost, *i.e.* the relation between the prospective yield of one more unit of that type of capital and the cost of producing that unit, furnishes us with the *marginal efficiency of capital* of that type. More precisely, I define the marginal efficiency of capital as being equal to that rate of discount which would make the present value of the series of annuities given by the returns expected from the capital-asset during its life just equal to its supply price. This gives us the marginal efficiencies of particular types of capital-assets. The greatest of these marginal efficiencies can then be regarded as the marginal efficiency of capital in general.

The reader should note that the marginal efficiency of capital is here defined in terms of the *expectation* of yield and of the *current* supply price of the capital-asset. It depends on the rate of return expected to be obtainable on money if it were invested in a *newly* produced asset; not on the historical result of what an investment has yielded on its original cost if we look back on its record after its life is over.

If there is an increased investment in any given type of capital during any period of time, the marginal efficiency of that type of capital will diminish as the investment in it is increased, partly because the prospective yield will fall as the supply of that type of capital is increased, and partly because, as a rule, pressure on the facilities for producing that type of capital will cause its supply price to increase; the second of these factors being usually the more important in producing equilibrium in the short run, but the longer the period in view the more does the first factor take its place. Thus for each type of capital we can build up a schedule, showing by how much investment in it will have to increase within the period, in order that its marginal efficiency should fall to any given figure. We can then aggregate these schedules for all the different types of capital, so as to provide a schedule relating the rate of aggregate investment to the corresponding marginal efficiency of capital in general which that rate of investment will establish. We shall call this the investment demand-schedule; or, alternatively, the schedule of the marginal efficiency of capital.

Now it is obvious that the actual rate of current investment will be pushed to the point where there is no longer any class of capital-asset of which the marginal efficiency exceeds the current rate of interest. In other words, the rate of investment will be pushed to the point on the investment demand-schedule where the marginal efficiency of capital in general is equal to the market rate of interest.[1]

We have shown that, whilst there are forces causing the rate of investment to rise or fall so as to keep the marginal efficiency of capital equal to the rate of interest, yet the marginal efficiency of capital is, in itself, a different thing from the ruling rate of interest. The schedule of the marginal efficiency of capital may be said to govern the terms on which loanable funds are demanded for the purpose of new investment; whilst the rate of interest governs the terms on which funds are being currently supplied. To complete our theory, therefore, we need to know what determines the rate of interest.

In Chapter 14 of the *General Theory* and its Appendix we shall consider the answers to this question which have been given hitherto. Broadly speaking, we shall find that they make the rate of interest to depend on the interaction of the schedule of the marginal efficiency of capital with the psychological propensity to save. But the notion that the rate of interest is the balancing factor which brings the demand for saving in the shape of new investment forthcoming at a given rate of interest into equality with the supply of saving which results at that rate of interest from the community's psychological propensity to save, breaks down as soon as we perceive that it is

---

[1] For the sake of simplicity of statement I have slurred the point that we are dealing with complexes of rates of interest and discount corresponding to the different lengths of time which will elapse before the various prospective returns from the asset are realised. But it is not difficult to re-state the argument so as to cover this point.

impossible to deduce the rate of interest merely from a knowledge of these two factors.

What, then, is our own answer to this question?...

It should be obvious that the rate of interest cannot be a return to saving or waiting as such. For if a man hoards his savings in cash, he earns no interest, though he saves just as much as before. On the contrary, the mere definition of the rate of interest tells us in so many words that the rate of interest is the reward for parting with liquidity for a specified period. For the rate of interest is, in itself, nothing more than the inverse proportion between a sum of money and what can be obtained for parting with control over the money in exchange for a debt[2] for a stated period of time.[3]

Thus the rate of interest at any time, being the reward for parting with liquidity, is a measure of the unwillingness of those who possess money to part with their liquid control over it. The rate of interest is not the 'price' which brings into equilibrium the demand for resources to invest with the readiness to abstain from present consumption. It is the 'price' which equilibrates the desire to hold wealth in the form of cash with the available quantity of cash;—which implies that if the rate of interest were lower, *i.e.* if the reward for parting with cash were diminished, the aggregate amount of cash which the public would wish to hold would exceed the available supply, and that if the rate of interest were raised, there would be a surplus of cash which no one would be willing to hold. If this explanation is correct, the quantity of money is the other factor, which, in conjunction with liquidity-preference, determines the actual rate of interest in given circumstances. Liquidity-preference is a potentiality or functional tendency, which fixes the quantity of money which the public will hold when the rate of interest is given; so that if r is the rate of interest, M the quantity of money and L the function of liquidity-preference, we have $M = L(r)$. This is where, and how, the quantity of money enters into the economic scheme.

At this point, however, let us turn back and consider why such a thing as liquidity-preference exists. In this connection we can usefully employ the ancient distinction between the use of money for the transaction of current business and its use as a store of wealth. As regards the first of these two uses, it is obvious that up to a point it is worth while to sacrifice a certain

[2] Without disturbance to this definition, we can draw the line between 'money' and 'debts' at whatever point is most convenient for handling a particular problem. For example, we can treat as *money* any command over general purchasing power which the owner has not parted with for a period in excess of three months, and as *debt* what cannot be recovered for a longer period than this; or we can substitute for 'three months' one month or three days or three hours or any other period; or we can exclude from *money* whatever is not legal tender on the spot. It is often convenient in practice to include in *money* time-deposits with banks and, occasionally, even such instruments as (*e.g.*) treasury bills. As a rule, I shall, as in my *Treatise on Money*, assume that money is co-extensive with bank deposits.

[3] In general discussion, as distinct from specific problems where the period of the debt is expressly specified, it is convenient to mean by the rate of interest the complex of the various rates of interest current for different periods of time, *i.e.* for debts of different maturities.

amount of interest for the convenience of liquidity. But, given that the rate of interest is never negative, why should anyone prefer to hold his wealth in a form which yields little or no interest to holding it in a form which yields interest (assuming, of course, at this stage, that the risk of default is the same in respect of a bank balance as of a bond)? A full explanation is complex. There is, however, a necessary condition failing which the existence of a liquidity-preference for money as a means of holding wealth could not exist.

This necessary condition is the existence of *uncertainty* as to the future of the rate of interest, *i.e.* as to the complex of rates of interest for varying maturities which will rule at future dates. For if the rates of interest ruling at all future times could be foreseen with certainty, all future rates of interest could be inferred from the *present* rates of interest for debts of different maturities, which would be adjusted to the knowledge of the future rates. For example, if $_1d_r$ is the value in the present year 1 of £1 deferred r years and it is known that $_nd_r$ will be the value in the year n of £1 deferred r years from that date, we have

$$_nd_r = \frac{_1d_{n+r}}{_1d_n};$$

whence it follows that the rate at which any debt can be turned into cash n years hence is given by two out of the complex of current rates of interest. If the current rate of interest is positive for debts of every maturity, it must always be more advantageous to purchase a debt than to hold cash as a store of wealth.

If, on the contrary, the future rate of interest is uncertain we cannot safely infer that $_nd_r$ will prove to be equal to $_1d_{n+r}/_1d_n$ when the time comes. Thus if a need for liquid cash may conceivably arise before the expiry of n years, there is a risk of a loss being incurred in purchasing a long-term debt and subsequently turning it into cash, as compared with holding cash. The actuarial profit or mathematical expectation of gain calculated in accordance with the existing probabilities—if it can be so calculated, which is doubtful —must be sufficient to compensate for the risk of disappointment.

There is, moreover, a further ground for liquidity-preference which results from the existence of uncertainty as to the future of the rate of interest, provided that there is an organised market for dealing in debts. For different people will estimate the prospects differently and anyone who differs from the predominant opinion as expressed in market quotations may have a good reason for keeping liquid resources in order to profit, if he is right, from its turning out in due course that the $_1d_r$'s were in a mistaken relationship to one another[4] [...]

The three divisions of liquidity-preference which we have distinguished above may be defined as depending on (i) the transactions-motive, *i.e.* the need

[4] This is the same point as I discussed in my *Treatise on Money* under the designation of the two views and the 'bull-bear' position.

of cash for the current transaction of personal and business exchanges; (ii) the precautionary-motive, *i.e.* the desire for security as to the future cash equivalent of a certain proportion of total resources; and (iii) the speculative-motive, *i.e.* the object of securing profit from knowing better than the market what the future will bring forth....

It may illustrate the argument to point out that, if the liquidity-preferences due to the transactions-motive and the precautionary-motive are assumed to absorb a quantity of cash which is not very sensitive to changes in the rate of interest as such and apart from its reactions on the level of income, so that the total quantity of money, less this quantity, is available for satisfying liquidity-preferences due to the speculative-motive, the rate of interest and the price of bonds have to be fixed at the level at which the desire on the part of certain individuals to hold cash (because at that level they feel 'bearish' of the future of bonds) is exactly equal to the amount of cash available for the speculative-motive. Thus each increase in the quantity of money must raise the price of bonds sufficiently to exceed the expectations of some 'bull' and so influence him to sell his bond for cash and join the 'bear' brigade. If, however, there is a negligible demand for cash from the speculative-motive except for a short transitional interval, an increase in the quantity of money will have to lower the rate of interest almost forthwith, in whatever degree is necessary to raise employment and the wage-unit sufficiently to cause the additional cash to be absorbed by the transactions-motive and the precautionary-motive.

As a rule, we can suppose that the schedule of liquidity-preference relating the quantity of money to the rate of interest is given by a smooth curve which shows the rate of interest falling as the quantity of money is increased....

Nevertheless, circumstances can develop in which even a large increase in the quantity of money may exert a comparatively small influence on the rate of interest. For a large increase in the quantity of money may cause so much uncertainty about the future that liquidity-preferences due to the security-motive may be strengthened; whilst opinion about the future of the rate of interest may be so unanimous that a small change in present rates may cause a mass movement into cash. It is interesting that the stability of the system and its sensitiveness to changes in the quantity of money should be so dependent on the existence of a *variety* of opinion about what is uncertain. Best of all that we should know the future. But if not, then, if we are to control the activity of the economic system by changing the quantity of money, it is important that opinions should differ....

Whilst the amount of cash which an individual decides to hold to satisfy the transactions-motive and the precautionary-motive is not entirely independent of what he is holding to satisfy the speculative-motive, it is a safe first approximation to regard the amounts of these two sets of cash-holdings as being largely independent of one another. Let us, therefore, for the purposes of our further analysis, break up our problem in this way.

Let the amount of cash held to satisfy the transactions- and precautionary-motives be M_1, and the amount held to satisfy the speculative-motive be M_2. Corresponding to these two compartments of cash, we then have two liquidity functions L_1 and L_2. L_1 mainly depends on the level of income, whilst L_2 mainly depends on the relation between the current rate of interest and the state of expectation. Thus

$$M = M_1 + M_2 = L_1(Y) + L_2(r),$$

where L_1 is the liquidity function corresponding to an income Y, which determines M_1, and L_2 is the liquidity function of the rate of interest r, which determines M_2. It follows that there are three matters to investigate: (i) the relation of changes in M to Y and r, (ii) what determines the shape of L_1, (iii) what determines the shape of L_2.

(i) The relation of changes in M to Y and r depends, in the first instance, on the way in which changes in M come about. Suppose that M consists of gold coins and that changes in M can only result from increased returns to the activities of gold-miners who belong to the economic system under examination. In this case changes in M are, in the first instance, directly associated with changes in Y, since the new gold accrues as someone's income. Exactly the same conditions hold if changes in M are due to the Government printing money wherewith to meet its current expenditure;—in this case also the new money accrues as someone's income. The new level of income, however, will not continue sufficiently high for the requirements of M_1 to absorb the whole of the increase in M; and some portion of the money will seek an outlet in buying securities or other assets until r has fallen so as to bring about an increase in the magnitude of M_2 and at the same time to stimulate a rise in Y to such an extent that the new money is absorbed either in M_2 or in the M_1 which corresponds to the rise in Y caused by the fall in r. Thus at one remove this case comes to the same thing as the alternative case, where the new money can only be issued in the first instance by a relaxation of the conditions of credit by the banking system, so as to induce someone to sell the banks a debt or a bond in exchange for the new cash.

It will, therefore, be safe for us to take the latter case as typical. A change in M can be assumed to operate by changing r, and a change in r will lead to a new equilibrium partly by changing M_2 and partly by changing Y and therefore M_1. The division of the increment of cash between M_1 and M_2 in the new position of equilibrium will depend on the responses of investment to a reduction in the rate of interest and of income to an increase in investment. Since Y partly depends on r, it follows that a given change in M has to cause a sufficient change in r for the resultant changes in M_1 and M_2 respectively to add up to the given change in M.

(ii) It is not always made clear whether the income-velocity of money is defined as the ratio of Y to M or as the ratio of Y to M_1. I propose, however, to take it in the latter sense. Thus if V is the income-velocity of money.

$$L_1(Y) = \frac{Y}{V} = M_1.$$

There is, of course, no reason for supposing that V is constant. Its value will depend on the character of banking and industrial organisation, on social habits, on the distribution of income between different classes and on the effective cost of holding idle cash. Nevertheless, if we have a short period of time in view and can safely assume no material change in any of these factors, we can treat V as nearly enough constant.

(iii) Finally there is the question of the relation between M_2 and r. We have seen that *uncertainty* as to the future course of the rate of interest is the sole intelligible explanation of the type of liquidity-preference L_2 which leads to the holding of cash M_2. It follows that a given M_2 will not have a definite quantitative relation to a given rate of interest of r;—what matters is not the *absolute* level of r but the degree of its divergence from what is considered a fairly *safe* level of r, having regard to those calculations of probability which are being relied on. Nevertheless, there are two reasons for expecting that, in any given state of expectation, a fall in r will be associated with an increase in M_2. In the first place, if the general view as to what is a safe level of r is unchanged, every fall in r reduces the market rate relatively to the 'safe' rate and therefore increases the risk of illiquidity; and, in the second place, every fall in r reduces the current earnings from illiquidity, which are available as a sort of insurance premium to offset the risk of loss on capital account....

Let us now attempt to summarise the argument of the previous chapters; taking the factors in the reverse order to that in which we have introduced them.

There will be an inducement to push the rate of new investment to the point which forces the supply-price of each type of capital-asset to a figure which, taken in conjunction with its prospective yield, brings the marginal efficiency of capital in general to approximate equality with the rate of interest. That is to say, the physical conditions of supply in the capital-goods industries, the state of confidence concerning the prospective yield, the psychological attitude to liquidity and the quantity of money (preferably calculated in terms of wage-units) determine, between them, the rate of new investment.

But an increase (or decrease) in the rate of investment will have to carry with it an increase (or decrease) in the rate of consumption; because the behaviour of the public is, in general, of such a character that they are only willing to widen (or narrow) the gap between their income and their consumption if their income is being increased (or diminished). That is to say, changes in the rate of consumption are, in general, *in the same direction* (though smaller in amount) as changes in the rate of income. The relation between the increment of consumption which has to accompany a given increment of saving is given by the marginal propensity to consume. The ratio, thus determined, between an increment of investment and the corresponding increment of aggregate income, both measured in wage-units, is given by the investment multiplier.

Finally, if we assume (as a first approximation) that the employment multiplier is equal to the investment multiplier, we can, by applying the multiplier to the increment (or decrement) in the rate of investment brought about by the factors first described, infer the increment of employment.

An increment (or decrement) of employment is liable, however, to raise (or lower) the schedule of liquidity-preference; there being three ways in which it will tend to increase the demand for money, insamuch as the value of output will rise when employment increases even if the wage-unit and prices (in terms of the wage-unit) are unchanged, but, in addition, the wage-unit itself will tend to rise as employment improves, and the increase in output will be accompanied by a rise of prices (in terms of the wage-unit) owing to increasing cost in the short period.

Thus the position of equilibrium will be influenced by these repercussions; and there are other repercussions also. Moreover, there is not one of the above factors which is not liable to change without much warning, and sometimes substantially. Hence the extreme complexity of the actual course of events. Nevertheless, these seem to be the factors which it is useful and convenient to isolate. If we examine any actual problem along the lines of the above schematism, we shall find it more manageable; and our practical intuition (which can take account of a more detailed complex of facts than can be treated on general principles) will be offered a less intractable material upon which to work.

1.2 Keynes and the Classics*

The ideas which we now want to get out of the Keynes theory emerge very easily if that theory itself is put into a particular form— a form which I myself suggested in an article[1] written a few months after the publication of Keynes's book. I still feel that the diagram which was worked out in that article gives the most convenient summary of the Keynesian theory of Interest and Money which has yet been produced. In itself the diagram is nothing more than an expository device; but since more use can be made of it than has yet been made, it will not be out of place to reintroduce it here.

1. We begin with the provisional assumption that rates of money wages are

* From J. R. Hicks, *A Contribution to the Theory of the Trade Cycle* (Oxford: Clarendon Press, 1950), ch XI

[Professor Hicks wishes it to be made clear that this passage is a summary of what he thought (and still thinks) the central argument of the *General Theory* to be. It did not, and does not, represent his own views. For these, see 'The Two Triads' in his *Critical Essays in Monetary Theory* (Oxford: Clarendon Press, 1967), and his *The Crisis in Keynesian Economics* (Oxford: Basil Blackwell, 1974)—Ed.]

[1] 'Mr. Keynes and the Classics', *Econometrica*, 1937.

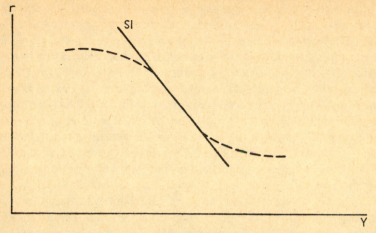

FIG. 1.2

constant. Subject to this assumption, values in Keynesian wage-units are the same as money values. Thus the Marginal Efficiency of Capital schedule shows the money value of investment as a function of the rate of interest. With the accelerator neglected, it is not unreasonable to regard the schedule of the marginal efficiency of capital as independently determined. Other things being equal, the value of investment depends upon the rate of interest, rising when the rate of interest falls. (Just what is meant, or can be meant, by the rate of interest in this connexion is a matter which we shall consider later.)

If, like Keynes, we neglect any direct influence of interest on saving, we can go on to say that with a given value of investment (at constant money wages) the equilibrium value of money income will be determined by the multiplier. Thus, with a given rate of interest, the value of investment is determined from the marginal efficiency of capital schedule; and further, once the value of investment has been determined, the total value of money income is determined by the consumption function. Taking both of these steps together, we can say that with a given marginal efficiency of capital schedule, and a given consumption function, there is a determinate money income corresponding to each rate of interest. If we now construct a diagram with income (Y) on the horizontal axis, and interest (r) on the vertical, the relation between interest and income can be drawn out as a curve, the *SI*-curve of Fig. 1.2. This curve can be defined as showing the level of income which keeps equilibrium saving equal to equilibrium investment at each rate of interest. Since a fall in interest increases investment, and an increase in investment increases income, the *SI*-curve can be relied upon to slope downwards from left to right.

This simple argument gives us the basic generation of the *SI*-curve. But, having got so far, it is obviously possible to relax the assumptions a good deal, without the character of the curve being substantially affected. We can, in the first place, take account of a possible direct effect of the rate of interest on saving. If a fall in the rate of interest affects the volume of saving forthcoming out of a given income, the multiplier itself becomes a function of the rate of interest. But with a given rate of interest there will still be a determinate multiplier, so that income is still a function of interest, as before. If a fall in the rate of interest makes the representative individual save less out of a given income, the multiplier will be increased by a fall in interest, so that the *SI*-curve is made more elastic; if a fall in the rate of interest makes the representative individual save more, the *SI*-curve will become less elastic. We can, I think, be confident that this latter effect will never be large enough to disturb the general rule that the *SI*-curve slopes downwards.[2]

Secondly, we can go some way towards relaxing the assumption of given money wages. Suppose that money wage-rates are fixed in some trades, but are flexible in others. Then a high level of income (in terms of wage-units) is likely to lead to a rise in wages in the flexible trades, so that money income will rise more than it would have done if all wage-rates had been rigid. In the same way a low income in wage-units may be associated with a fall in wages in the flexible trades, so that money income will fall more than it would have done if all wage-rates had been fixed. Thus the assumption of partial wage-flexibility has the effect of making the *SI*-curve more elastic, particularly at its extremities. It is, indeed, not impossible that the lowest conceivable rate of interest might fail to stimulate a rise in employment which was sufficient to call forth an upward movement of wage-rates, so that the elastic stretch on the right would fail to operate. But the characteristic shape of the curve, on the assumption of partial wage-flexibility, is that shown by the dotted line on the diagram.[3]

[2] I may refer to *Value and Capital*, pp. 232–6, for a general argument which seems to show that the tendency of a fall in interest to increase consumption, in the economy as a whole, is more reliable than might appear at first sight.

[3] It is tempting to ask whether the assumption of given money wage-rates could not be relaxed altogether by a further application of this method. As the flexible sector increases in size relatively to the fixed, the elastic stretches of the dotted curve will become more elastic, and the range over which the rate of interest can vary without upsetting the wage-structure will be diminished, so that the elastic stretches will draw together. The curve as a whole will go on flattening out, so that in the limit, when all wages are flexible, it should apparently be replaced by a horizontal straight line.

I think that there is some sense in this construction, and it is useful for some purposes. It is essentially the case of Wicksell's *Interest and Prices*; the height of the horizontal line is Wicksell's 'natural rate of interest'; there is cumulative inflation if the actual rate goes below the natural rate, cumulative deflation if there is a discrepancy in the other direction. Wicksell's theory is the correct theory for a world of completely flexible wages (and prices). The essential difference between Keynes and Wicksell lies in Keynes's assumption of wage-rigidity (at least in a downwards direction).

Where our diagram gets into difficulties is precisely over this last possibility—that wages may be flexible upwards but not downwards. If all wages behave in this way, a sufficient fall in interest will produce a state of full employment, and an indefinite rise in money income; at that point, therefore, the *SI* curve becomes horizontal. Since (*ex hypothesi*) wages do not fall at a low level of employment, there will be ho horizontal stretch on the left; the curve will consist of (1) a

2. Thus the equation of saving and investment can be regarded as giving us one relation between income and interest; a second relation can be derived from the theory of Liquidity Preference. The demand for money, Keynes held, can be divided into two parts: in the first place there is a demand for money to finance current transactions, and in the second place there is a demand for money to act as a liquid reserve. The amount of money required for the first purpose will depend, in the main, upon the volume of transactions in money terms, and this will vary closely with money income (the Y of our diagram). The amount of money required for the second purpose will be a matter of the relative advantage, at the margin, of holding money (considered as a non-income-yielding asset) as against the holding of an asset which does yield interest or profit. The exact nature of this liquidity advantage (on which much might be said) does not greatly signify for our purposes.

Now let us make the provisional assumption that the supply of money is fixed. This fixed supply of money will have to be divided between the above two purposes; the more that is absorbed in one, the less will be available for the other. A rise in money income (Y) will increase the amount of money required for the transactions purpose; if the total supply of money is fixed, this additional demand can only be satisfied if money is drawn away from the other use. If the 'liquidity preference schedule' remains the same, the liquid reserves can only be reduced by giving people an incentive to hold their assets in another form—that is to say, by a rise in the rate of interest. Supposing, on on the other hand, that money is released from the transactions balances (by a fall in Y); then more money will be available for holding in liquid reserves than people will desire to hold at the ruling rate of interest. They will therefore increase their demands for income-yielding assets, which will raise the prices of such assets, and the rise in price is equivalent to a fall in the rate of interest.

It follows, then, that under the assumption of a given quantity of money, and given liquidity preference, the rate of interest is a function of money income (Y). This relation can be expressed as a curve on the same income-interest diagram as we have just been using. Since interest rises as income increases, this liquidity curve L (Fig. 1.3) will slope upwards to the right.

What can be said about the shape of the L-curve? It is an essential part of Keynes's argument that an increase in the supply of money, available to satisfy the demand for liquid balances, cannot reduce the rate of interest

---

relatively inelastic stretch, on which employment is less than full, and (2) a horizontal stretch corresponding to full employment. But if the curve is drawn in this way, a static interpretation of it (such as we shall require) breaks down. Once interest had fallen to the full employment level, wages would rise indefinitely; if interest were subsequently raised, the rise in wages would be checked, and unemployment would appear. But wages would not fall to the old level, so that money income would not contract along the old 'inelastic' curve, but along a new curve to the right of it. The curve, in fact, would not stay put.

Under the assumption which we have made in the text—that some wages are flexible, and flex in both directions, while other wages are absolutely rigid, the curve will stay put, so that we can use it without danger of displacement. These assumptions seem to be to be sufficient for the purposes of our present inquiry.

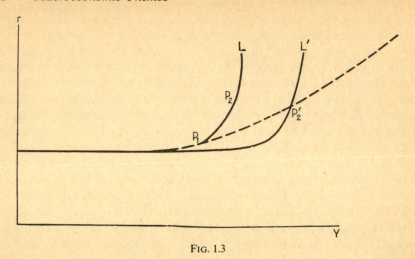

FIG. 1.3

indefinitely; there must be a minimum below which it cannot fall. The exact position of the minimum depends on the method we adopt of choosing a single rate of interest to represent the whole interest-structure. But whatever method is adopted, it is clear that so long as money can be held without cost, it is impossible for any interest rate to become negative, and therefore impossible for *the* interest rate to fall below a certain positive value. Apart from exceptional conditions, in which money is less safe than some non-monetary asset (and such conditions may reasonably be left out of account), the *L*-curve must have a horizontal, or nearly horizontal, stretch at the left of its course. That is the first of the properties which can be laid down.

When we look at the other end of the curve, it seems even clearer that it must tend towards a vertical position. For a point must be reached, as *Y* rises, when all, or nearly all, of the available money has been drawn into transactions balances; beyond that point *Y* cannot rise, however much the rate of interest rises. Thus, on the assumption of a given total supply of money, the *L*-curve must have the shape drawn in the diagram.

If the supply of money increases, the *L*-curve will be moved to the right. The maximum *Y* which can be financed with the available money will clearly be increased, so that there is an undoubted rightward movement of the curve on the vertical stretch. But the increase in the supply of money is unlikely to have much effect on the minimum to which the rate of interest can fall; thus the left end of the curve will be little affected. There will be a shift into some such position as *L'*.

Further, having got so far, we can easily abandon the assumption of a given supply of money. And it is fortunate that we can do so, for the exact meaning of the 'supply of money' in Keynes's theory is one of the things about it which can cause trouble. If, for example, money means bank deposits, then it can be argued that there are bank deposits which do bear interest; and (what is more important) it can be objected that the supply of bank deposits is not fixed, but is to some extent responsive to the same forces of interest and income on which the demand has been made to depend. At the point we have now reached, these complications need cause no difficulty. We can allow for some elasticity in the supply of money—or, more generally still, some elasticity in the monetary system—without changing the essentials of our construction. If the monetary system is elastic, in the sense that a rise in the rate of interest increases the supply of money, a suitable rise in r will allow an expansion, not from P_1 to P_2 on curve L, but from P_1 on curve L to P'_2 on curve L'. By joining P_1 to P'_2 and continuing to the corresponding points on other curves, we can draw an 'L' curve (dotted in the diagram) which shows the relation of income and interest, not with a given 'supply of money' but with a given monetary system—and the curve will be more or less elastic according as the monetary system is more or less elastic. If the supply of money is responsive to changes in Y, we get substantially the same effect. A perfectly elastic monetary system would enable Y to expand without any rise in r—so that the adjusted (dotted) curve would become horizontal; an imperfectly elastic system would be represented by a curve of less elasticity in its upper reaches. We can express the principle of the liquidity minimum by saying that even a monetary system which is in general inelastic behaves elastically when the rate of interest falls to a low level.

3. Having now constructed the savings-investment curve (SI) and the liquidity curve (L) let us superimpose them on the same diagram (Fig. 1.4). Suppose that the curves intersect at a point P. Then at P both the savings-investment and the liquidity relations between income and interest are satisfied. With given marginal efficiency of capital schedule, given consumption function, given liquidity preference schedule, and given monetary system, money income (which we are supposing—in spite of the limited allowance we have made for wage-flexibility—to be correlated with employment) and the rate of interest are simultaneously determined. It is this simultaneous determination at P which effectively sums up the Keynesian system.

Many of the possibilities to which Keynes has, explicitly or implicitly, drawn our attention can now be read off directly from the diagram. If the curves are in the position drawn, intersecting at a level of r which is above the liquidity minimum, and at a level of Y which is apparently well short of full employment, expansion can come about either by an upward movement of the SI-curve (a rise in the marginal efficiency of capital, or in the propensity to consume) or by a rightward movement of the L-curve (fall in liquidity preference, or greater willingness on the part of the monetary authority to create money). If, however, the SI-curve was farther to the left, so that P lay on the horizontal part of the L-curve, monetary action (represented by a rightward movement of the L-curve) would be ineffective; for monetary action

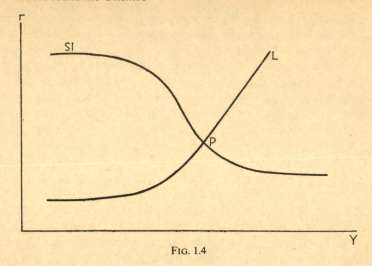

FIG. 1.4

would only affect the upward-sloping part of the *L*-curve, leaving the horizontal part substantially unaffected. And so on; but I may leave the reader to work out the rest of these (mostly familiar) possibilities for himself.

1.3 The Keynesian Theory of Interest*

Keynes attacked the classical theory of interest on the ground that it is indeterminate. According to classical theory the rate is determined by the intersection of the investment demand-schedule and the saving-schedule—schedules disclosing the relation of investment and saving to the rate of interest. No solution, however, is possible because the position of the saving-schedule will vary with the level of real income. As income rises, the schedule will shift to the right. Thus we cannot know what the rate of interest will be unless we already know the income level. And we cannot know the income level without already knowing the rate of interest, since a lower interest rate will mean a larger volume of investment, and so, via the multiplier, a higher level of real income. The classical analysis, therefore offers no solution.

Now exactly the same criticism applies to the Keynesian theory. According to the Keynesian theory the rate of interest is determined by the intersection of the supply-schedule of money (perhaps interest inelastic, if rigorously fixed by the monetary authority) and the demand-schedule for money (the liquidity-preference schedule). This analysis also is indeterminate because the liquidity-preference schedule will shift up or down with changes in the income level. Here we are concerned with the total liquidity-preference schedule including both the 'transactions' demand and the 'asset' demand for money. If we separate the total demand schedule for money into its two component

* Alvin Hansen, 'Classical, Loanable Funds, and Keynesian Interest Theories', *Q. J. Econ.*, 1951.

parts, we could perhaps argue that the 'pure' liquidity-preference schedule is independent of the level of income.[1] But this does not help matters, since we cannot know, given the total money supply, how much money will be available *to hold as an asset* unless we first know the level of income. Thus the Keynesian theory, like the classical, is indeterminate. In the Keynesian case the money supply and demand-schedules cannot give the rate of interest unless we already know the income level; in the classical case the demand and supply schedules for saving offer no solution until the income is known. Keynes's criticism of the classical theory applies equally to his own theory.

Precisely the same is true of the loanable-fund theory. According to the loanable-fund analysis, the rate of interest is determined by the intersection of the demand-schedule for loanable funds with the supply-schedule. Now the supply-schedule of loanable funds is compounded of saving (in the Robertsonian sense) plus net additions to loanable funds from new money and the dishoarding of idle balances. But since the 'savings' portion of the schedule varies with the level of 'disposable' income,[2] it follows that the total supply-schedule of loanable funds also varies with income. Thus this theory is also indeterminate.

In the loanable-fund theory, the relevant supply-schedule is conceived of in terms of loanable funds (i.e. 'voluntary' saving plus new money). In the neo-classical theory of Pigou, however, the relevant supply-schedule is conceived in terms of saving out of current income. 'Saving is defined as the excess of total income received over income received for services in providing for consumption.'[3] Again, in the same vein, 'aggregate money saving' is defined as the 'excess of money income over expenditures on consumption goods.'[4] Here income, consumption, and saving, all apply to the same period. Money savings are that part of current income which is not consumed. Now current income is derived from current expenditures. Whether or not current income is fed in part from the injection of new money or from the activation of idle balances, makes no difference whatever from the standpoint of the Pigouvian or neo-classical definition.[5] Income whether it springs from the spending of funds borrowed from banks or from the spending of 'prior' income; and saving from such income is saving even though bank credit played a role in the process of income creation.[6] Accordingly, in Pigouvian or neo-classical theory, 'saving' is in effect the same thing as 'loanable funds'. In Robertsonian language, however, 'loanable funds' consist of voluntary saving (i.e. saving out

---

[1] In fact since expectations are influenced by the level of income this is not a permissible assumption. The liquidity preference case is therefore even weaker than here indicated.

[2] 'Disposable income' is here used in the Robertsonian sense, i.e. 'yesterday's' income.

[3] See A. C. Pigou, *Employment and Equilibrium*, p. 30.

[4] *Ibid*, p. 31.

[5] 'It is important to be clear about the implications of these definitions when people or governments borrow from banks. Everybody agrees that money so borrowed only becomes income when it is paid out, for services rendered, to factors of production' (*ibid*, p. 30).

[6] *Ibid*, p. 30.

of 'disposable' income) plus borrowed bank funds and activated idle balances. In Pigouvian language, saving out of current income may well exceed 'voluntary' (or Robertsonian) saving in so far as current income is increased by bank loans or the injection of idle balances. Thus the Pigouvian supply-schedule of savings amounts to the same thing as the Robertsonian or Swedish supply-schedule of loanable funds. It is therefore not necessary to distinguish further between them, and hereafter I shall refer only to the neo-classical[7] theory on the one side, and the Keynesian on the other.

The neo-classical formulation and the Keynesian formulation, taken together, do supply us with an adequate theory of the rate of interest. From the neo-classical formulation we get a family of saving-schedules at various income levels. These together with the investment-demand schedule[8] give us the Hicksian '*IS*-curve'. In other words, the neo-classical formulation tells us what the various levels of income will be (given the investment-demand schedule and family saving-schedules) at different rates of interest.

From the Keynesian formulation we get a family of liquidity preference schedules at various income levels. These together with the supply of money fixed by the monetary authority, give us the Hicksian '*L*-curve' (which I prefer to call the '*LM*-curve').[9] The *LM*- curve tells us what the various rates of interest will be (given the quantity of money and the family of liquidity-preference curves) at different levels of income. But the liquidity schedule alone cannot tell us what the rate of interest will be.

The '*IS*-curve' and the '*LM*-curve' are functions relating the two variables: (1) income and (2) the rate of interest. Income and the rate of interest are therefore determined together at the point of intersection of these two curves or schedules. At this point income and the rate of interest stand in a relation to each other such that: (1) investment and saving are in equilibrium (i.e. actual saving equals desired saving) and (2) the demand for money is in equilibrium with the supply of money (i.e. the desired amount of money is equal to the actual supply of money).

Thus a determinate theory of interest is based on: (1) the investment demand function, (2) the saving-function (or conversely the consumption function, (3) the liquidity preference function, and (4) the quantity of money. The Keynesian analysis, looked at as a whole, involved all of these. But Keynes never brought them all together in a comprehensive way to formulate an integrated interest theory. He failed to point out specifically that liquidity

---

[7] The classical theory may be said to coincide with the neo-classical or Pigouvian theory in the special case in which no new money is being created by the banking system and in which idle balances are not being dishoarded.

[8] Perhaps a family of investment-demand schedules, one for each level of income. Everyone will agree that a *change* in the level of income affects the volume of investment, but not everyone will agree that the *level* of income is a determinant of *net* investment.

[9] See my *Monetary Theory and Fiscal Policy*, Chapter 5. The '*LM*' curve represents a situation in which $L = M$ in an equilibrium sense, L meaning the demand for money, and M the supply of money. Similarly the '*IS*' curve indicates a condition in which $I = S$ in an equilibrium sense (i.e. the multiplier process has fully worked itself out).

preference plus the quantity of money can give us not the rate of interest, but only an '*LM*-curve'. It was left for Hicks[10] to supply us with the tools needed for a comprehensive analysis.

1.4 The Labour Market in Keynesian and Classical Models*

[...]   1 THREE ALTERNATIVE MACROSTATIC SYSTEMS

As a first step in the analysis, we must set up a system of equations describing the relation between the variables to be analyzed. In doing this we are at once confronted with a difficult choice between rigor and convenience; the only rigorous procedure is to set up a complete 'Walrasian' system and to determine the equilibrium prices and quantities of each good: but this system is cumbersome and not well suited to an essentially literary exposition such as we intend to develop here. The alternative is to work with a reduced system: we must then be satisfied with the rather vague notions of 'physical output', 'investment', 'price-level', etc. In what follows we have chosen, in principle, the second alternative, but we shall check our conclusions with a more general system whenever necessary.

The equations of our system are:

$$M = L(r, Y), \tag{1}$$
$$I = I(r, Y) \tag{2}$$
$$S = S(r, Y) \tag{3}$$
$$S = I, \tag{4}$$
$$Y \equiv PX, \tag{5}$$
$$X = X(N), \tag{6}$$
$$W = X'(N)P. \tag{7}$$

The symbols have the following meaning: Y, money income; M, quantity of money in system (regarded as given); r, rate of interest; S and I, saving and investment respectively, all measured in money; P, price level; N, aggregate employment; W, money wage rate; X, an index of physical output.[1] We may also define C, consumption measured in money, by the following identity:

$$C \equiv Y - I. \tag{8}$$

Identity (5) can be regarded as defining money income. There are so far 8 unknowns and only 7 equations; we lack the equation relating the wage rate and the supply of labor. This equation takes a substantially different form in the 'Keynesian' system as compared with the 'classical' systems.

[10] *Econometrica*, Volume V, 1937, 147–59. [See also Reading 1.2—Ed.]

*From Franco Modigliani, 'Liquidity Preference and the Theory of Interest and Money', *Econometrica*, 1944; reprinted in American Economic Association, *Readings in Monetary Theory*, Ed. Lutz and Mints (Blakiston, 1951).

[1] This system is partly taken from earlier writings on the subject. See especially O. Lange, 'The Rate of Interest and the Optimum Propensity to Consume,' *Economica*, Vol. 5, N. S. (February 1938), pp. 12–32, and J. R. Hicks, 'Mr. Keynes and the "Classics"; A Suggested Interpretation', *Econometrica*, Vol. 5 (April 1937), pp. 147–59. [See also Reading 1.2—Ed.]

In the classical systems the suppliers of labor (as well as the suppliers of all other commodities) are supposed to behave 'rationally'. In the same way as the supply of any commodity depends on the relative price of the commodity so the supply of labor is taken to depend not on the money wage rate, but on the real wage rate. Under the classical hypothesis, therefore, the last equation of the system takes the form:

$$N = F\left(\frac{W}{P}\right); \text{ or, in the inverse form: } W = F^{-1}(N)P. \tag{9a}$$

The function F is a continuous function, although not necessarily monotonically increasing.

The Keynesian assumptions concerning the supply-of-labor schedule are quite different. In the Keynesian system, within certain limits to be specified presently, the supply of labor is assumed to be perfectly elastic at the historically ruling wage rate, say w_0. The limits mentioned above are given by equation (9a). For every value of W and P the corresponding value of N from (9a) gives the maximum amount of labor obtainable in the market. As long as the demand is less than this, the wage rate remains fixed as w_0. But as soon as all those who wanted to be employed at the ruling real wage rate w_0/P have found employment, wages become flexible upward. The supply of labor will not increase unless the money wage rate rises relative to the price level.

In order to write the last equation of the 'Keynesian' form of our system, we must express this rather complicated hypothesis in functional form. Taking (9a) as a starting point, we may write:

$$W = \alpha w_0 + \beta F^{-1}(N)P, \tag{9}$$

where α and β are functions of N, W, P, characterized by the following properties:

$$\begin{aligned} \alpha = 1, \quad \beta = 0, \text{ for } N \leqslant N_0, \\ \alpha = 0, \quad \beta = 1, \text{ for } N > N_0, \end{aligned} \tag{10}$$

where N_0 is said to be 'full employment'. Equations and inequalities (10) thus state that, unless there is 'full employment' ($N = N_0$), the wage rate is not really a variable of the system but a datum, a result of 'history' or of 'economic policy' or of both. Equation (9) then reduces to $W = w_0$. But after 'full employment' has been reached at wage rate w_0, the supply of labor ceases to be perfectly elastic: W becomes a variable to be determined by the system and (9) becomes a 'genuine' equation. We should add that even in the 'Keynesian' system, it is admitted that the wage rate will begin to be flexible downward before employment has reached the zero level: but in order not to complicate equation (9) still further we can, without serious harm, leave the hypothesis in its most stringent form.

For generality we may also use equation (9) as it now stands, as the 'supply of labor' function of the 'classical' theory. But instead of conditions (10) we have the identities (for all values of N)

$$\alpha \equiv 0, \qquad \beta \equiv 1. \tag{11}$$

Some remarks are also necessary concerning the 'demand for money' equation. According to the 'quantity theory of money', the demand for money does not depend on the rate of interest but varies directly with money income. Under this hypothesis equation (1) reduces to

$$M = kY. \tag{1a}$$

By properly combining the equations and conditions written above we obtain three different systems which we will analyze in turn.

I. A 'Keynesian' system consisting of equations (1) to (7) and (9) and conditions (10).

II. A 'crude classical' system consisting of equations (1a), (2) to (7), and (9), and identities (11).

III. A 'generalized classical' system consisting of the equations listed under II but with (1a) replaced by (1).

2. A RECONSIDERATION OF THE KEYNESIAN THEORY

In reconsidering the Keynesian system we shall essentially follow the lines suggested by J. R. Hicks in his fundamental paper, 'Mr. Keynes and the "Classics".' Our main task will be to clarify and develop his arguments, taking into account later theoretical developments.

Close consideration of the Keynesian system of equations [equations (1) to (7) and (9) to (10)] reveals that the first 4 equations contain only 4 unknowns and form a determined system: the system of monetary equilibrium. We therefore begin by discussing its equations and its solutions.

3. THE TRANSACTION DEMAND FOR MONEY

In a free capitalistic economy, money serves two purposes: (a) it is a medium of exchange, (b) it is a form of holding assets. There are accordingly two sources of demand for money: the transaction demand for money and the demand for money as an asset. This is the fundamental proposition on which the theory of the rate of interest and money rests; it is therefore necessary to analyze closely each source of demand and the factors that determine it.

The transaction demand for money is closely connected with the concept of the income period. We may define the income period as the (typical) time interval elapsing between the dates at which members of the community are paid for services rendered. We shall assume for the moment that this income period is approximately the same for every individual and that it coincides with the expenditure period.[2]

---

[2] This means, for instance, that people are required by custom or contract to pay within the income period for what they have consumed in the period (rent, grocery bill, etc.) or else must rely on 'consumers' credit'.

Each individual begins the income period with a certain income arising out of direct services rendered or out of property and with assets (physical and nonphysical) having a certain market value. In his endeavour to reach the highest level of satisfaction he is confronted with two sets of decisions: (a) he must decide what part of his income he will spend on consumption and what part he will save, (b) he must determine how to dispose of his assets.

The first set of decisions presents no special difficulty of analysis. On the basis of his tastes, his income, and market prices he will make a certain plan of expenditure to be carried out in the course of the income period. The amount of money that is necessary for individuals to carry out their expenditure plans is the *transaction demand for money by consumers*, as of the beginning of the period. The average transaction demand, on the other hand, depends on the rate at which expenditure takes place within the period.[3]

The difference between the individual's money income and the amount he decides to spend in the fashion discussed above is the money value of his savings (dissavings) for the income period. It represents the net increment in the value of his assets.

4. THE DEMAND FOR MONEY AS AN ASSET

Having made his consumption-saving plan, the individual has to make decisions concerning the assets he owns. [...]

There are two properties that all assets, whether physical or not, share in different degrees: liquidity and risk. Following a criterion particularly stressed by Jacob Marschak, we shall define liquidity of an asset in terms of the perfection of the market in which it is traded. An asset is liquid if this market is perfect, i.e. an individual's decision to buy or sell does not affect the price finitely; it is illiquid in the opposite case. It is riskless if the price at which it sells is constant or practically so; it is risky if the price fluctuates widely.

Securities clearly share with money the property of being highly liquid assets. Where there is an organized market, securities will not be significantly inferior to money in this respect. They have, however, two clear drawbacks in comparison with cash:

(a) They are not a medium of exchange. Assets generally accrue in the form of money through savings, and a separate transaction is necessary to transform them into securities. This transaction involves both subjective and objective costs.

(b) They are more risky than money since their market price is not constant. Even the 'safest' type of securities, on which the risk of default can be neglected, fluctuates in price as the rate of interest moves. There are, it is true, some types of loans for which this last risk can be neglected, namely very-short-term loans. Let us assume, for the sake of precision, that the money

---

[3] Thus if expenditure should proceed at an approximately even rate, it would be one-half the initial demand.

market is open only on the first day of the income period; then the shortest type of loans will be those that mature at the end of said period. These types of assets will not be subject to the risk mentioned under (b) since, by assumption, the rate of interest cannot change while they are outstanding.[4]

It is just for this type of assets, however, that the disadvantage mentioned under (a), namely the cost of investment, weighs more heavily: for the yield they promise for the very short duration of the loan can only be small, so that even a moderate cost is sufficient to wipe it out. If, as is likely, the cost of investment does not rise in proportion to the amount invested, then short loans may be an interesting investment for large sums, but not so for small investors. Thus, if this were the only possible form of investment, we should expect that any fall in the rate of interest, not accompanied by a corresponding fall in the cost of investing, would induce a growing number of potential investors to keep their assets in the form of money, rather than securities; that is to say, we should expect a fall in the rate of interest to increase the demand for money as an asset.[...]

In addition, several other reasons can be mentioned that cause a low rate of interest to discourage the holding of securities. In the first place, the risk element involved in holding securities becomes more pronounced when the rate of interest is low, for a smaller fall in the capital value of the asset is sufficient to wipe out the income already earned by holding the asset. Thus, for instance, the smaller the rate of interest, the smaller is the *percentage change* in the rate itself necessary to absorb the yield obtained by holding the asset a given length of time. Again, it has been pointed out by some authors that, as the rate of interest becomes lower, there is some ground to expect that possible movements will be predominantly in the direction of an increase and therefore unfavorable to the holders of securities.

In conclusion then, the lower the rate of interest, the larger will be the number of owners of assets who will prefer to hold these assets in the form of money for the income period; the demand for money to hold (as distinguished from money to spend, previously considered) or demand for money as an asset is a decreasing function of the rate of interest.[...]

On the basis of these considerations we may, in a first approximation, split the total demand for money into two parts: the demand for money to hold, $D_a(r)$, and the demand for money to spend or for transactions, $D_T(Y)$; and write

$$L(r, Y) = D_a(r) + D_T(Y) = M. \qquad (12)$$

This is not really necessary for our argument, but is very useful since it will constantly remind us of the two sources of demand for money and it will permit us to analyze more conveniently the part played by each variable.[...]

---

[4] Even if this assumption were relaxed, the possible fluctuations in the rate of interest would be negligible and the extent to which they would affect the present value of the securities mentioned above could be disregarded.

5. THE MONEY MARKET AND THE SHORT-RUN EQUILIBRIUM OF THE RATE OF INTEREST

There are two ways of looking at this market: (a) in terms of flows (savings and net borrowing) and (b) in terms of stocks. It is from this latter point of view that we shall consider it at this moment.

The supply in this market consists of the stock that is not needed for transactions. On the basis of our first approximation (12), this supply, denoted by S_a, will be

$$S_a = M - D_T(Y),$$

and is determined for any value of the money income and the fixed supply of money.

A position of equilibrium in the money market is reached when a system of interest rates is established at which dealers are willing to hold for the income period all the available supply. Or, from a different angle, the system of interest rates is determined by the price (in terms of forgone income) that dealers are willing to pay to hold assets in the form of money for the coming income period.

This can easily be translated into the usual Marshallian supply and demand apparatus, provided we replace the system of interest rates by a single rate r, as shown in Figure 1.5.

DD is the demand curve for money to hold, sloping downward and to the right (when the price, the rate of interest, rises, the demand falls, as in the case of ordinary commodities). The vertical lines are various supply curves corresponding to different values of Y and the fixed values of M. As the income increases, the supply falls: hence

$$Y_4 > Y_3 > Y_2 > \cdots.$$

Since a fall in supply causes a rise in price, the graph shows clearly that equation (1) gives r as an increasing function of Y.

The characteristics of the D_a function described above are shown in the graph. We noted that, for $r \geqslant r'$ the demand falls to zero; hence the graph of *DD* joins the vertical axis and coincides with it.

On the other hand, when the rate of interest falls to the level r'', the demand for money to hold becomes infinitely elastic. Any increase in the supply of money to hold now fails to affect the rate of interest, for the owners of the extra supply will either desire to hold this in the form of cash; or else they will find some owners of securities, who, being just indifferent as to holding cash or securities, will be willing to sell without any necessity for bidding up the price of securities (lowering the rate of interest). Thus, in Figure 1.5, when the interest rate r'' is reached, the graph of *DD* becomes parallel to the D_a axis; the income corresponding to r'' cannot be more than Y_2; but if income should

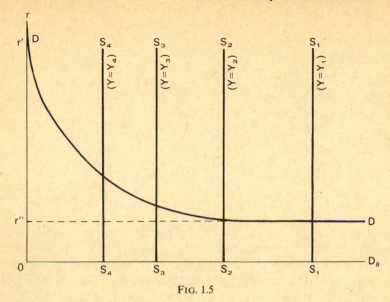

FIG. 1.5

fall below Y_2 it would not change the interest rate.[5] This situation that plays such an important role in Keynes's *General Theory* will be referred to as the 'Keynesian case'. [...]

The equilibrium system of interest rates is determined in each period by the condition that the supply of money to hold, which (given M) depends on the transaction demand for money and hence on income, be equal to the demand for money to hold. We may therefore proceed to draw the graph of equation (1), $M = L(r, Y)$. This is the LL curve of Figure 1.7. Any point on this curve shows the equilibrium value of r corresponding to a value of Y and the fixed value of M: it shows therefore positions of possible equilibrium in the money market. We must prove next that only one point on this curve is consistent with the long-run equilibrium of the system.

6. SAVING, INVESTMENT, AND THE *IS* FUNCTION

The first part of our system yields a second relationship between interest and income. Making use of equations (2) and (3) and the equilibrium condition (4) we obtain: $I(r, Y) = S(r, Y)$. In order to gain some idea of the shape of this curve we may again make use of a graphical method illustrated in Figure 1.6.

Figure 1.6 is the graph of equation (3). Since $\partial S/\partial r$ is usually considered small and of unknown sign we have simplified the drawing by eliminating r. This curve describes the relationship between money income and the proportion of it that people choose not to consume. Its position depends on the

[5] From equation (1) we obtain $dr/dY = -L_Y/L_r$ where the subscripts denote partial derivatives. Hence $dr/dY = 0$ if $|L_r| = \infty$.

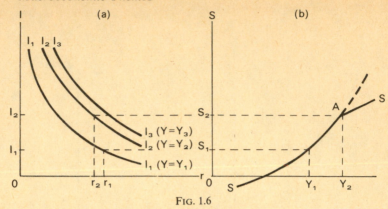

FIG. 1.6

value of the fixed money wage rate w_0: given the wage rate, to any level of money income there corresponds a certain real income and price level and, therefore, a certain level of money saving. In this diagram Y_2 denotes the highest money income that can be reached with the money wage rate w_0 and A is the full employment relationship between saving and income.

The straight line beginning at A gives the relationship between money income and money saving once full employment has been reached and the second part of condition (10) replaces the first.[6] We have then what is usually called inflation: real income cannot change but money income can rise to any level. As all prices rise simultaneously the amount of real income saved is unchanged while its money value rises in the same proportion as the price level and money income.[7] The dotted curved line, on the other hand, gives a potential relation between S and I if it were possible to raise the real income above the full employment level.

Figure 1.6(a) is the graph of equation (2). Each curve in this graph shows the amount of investment that would be undertaken at different levels of the rate of interest and for a fixed value of the income. To larger values of Y correspond investment curves higher and to the right.

Since the vertical scale is the same in both Figure 1.6(a) and Figure 1.6(b), we may use the following method to find the shape of $S(Y) = I(r, Y)$: For any value of Y, say Y_1, the corresponding amount of saving, S_1, can be read from the SS curve. But in equilibrium $S = I$, hence we can draw a line parallel to the Y axis at height S_1 and prolong it until it intersects the investment curve of Figure 1.6(a) corresponding to the income Y_1. We may thus find the the rate of interest r_1 that corresponds to the given income Y_1.

[6] This line is the continuation of the radius vector from the origin to A.

[7] This is strictly correct only if inflation does not provoke any permanent redistribution of income; or if the redistribution does not affect the aggregate propensity to save. Since wages rise with prices we can exclude redistributions from working class to nonworking class. But we cannot exclude redistribution from fixed-income receivers (especially owners of securities) to profits. It is difficult to say whether this will change sensibly the aggregate propensity to save; it is probably a good approximation to assume that the effect will be negligible.

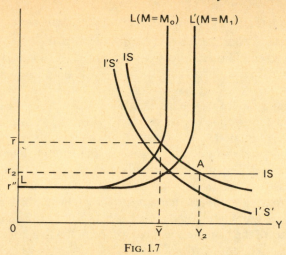

Fig. 1.7

The relationship between r and Y emerging from equations (2) and (3) and the equilibrium condition (4) is shown as the *IS* curve of Figure 1.7. In the normal case it will slope downward and to the right as in this diagram. [...]

The *IS* curve must also have another important property. In Figure 1.7, A denotes the equilibrium relationship between full-employment income (Y_2) and rate of interest (r_2). Money income cannot rise above the full-employment level denoted by Y_2 except through inflation, i.e. if wages and prices rise in the same proportion as income. As the stage of inflationary prices and wage increases is reached, the 'real' value of investment that it pays to undertake at any interest rate is unchanged since yields and costs change in the same proportion.[8] The money value of profitable investments, on the other hand, rises proportionally to prices and money income. As we have seen above, the same will be true of money savings. It follows that inflationary increases in income raise saving and investment in the same proportion and must therefore leave the equilibrium value of the rate of interest unchanged at the full-employment level r_2. It is for this reason that in Figure 1.7, to the right of A, the *IS* curve becomes parallel to the income axis. The dotted curved line beyond A is again the hypothetical relationship between r and Y if it were possible to raise real income above the full-employment level (and if the wage rate should remain unchanged at the level w_0). [...]

[8] Following the example of Mr. Keynes we may define the marginal efficiency of an asset as the discount rate that makes the sum of the expected marginal discounted yields equal to the marginal cost of the asset. The expected yields need not all be equal since they depend on the expected net physical yield as well as on expected future prices; and neither is necessarily constant in time. But the expected physical yield does not depend on prices; and, owing to our 'static assumption' of unit elasticity of expectation, expected prices change in the same proportion as present prices. Therefore the summation of the yields changes in the same proportion as marginal cost and so does the aggregate value of investments having marginal efficiency equal to or larger than r_2. Under unit elasticity of expectation a given change in all present prices does not modify entrepeneurs' production plans.

7. THE DETERMINANTS OF REAL EQUILIBRIUM

It is now time to consider the role of the second part of the system in the determination of equilibrium. Equations (5), (6) and (7) *explain* the forces that determine the real variables of the system: physical output, employment, real wage rate.[9]

The most important of these equations is (7), which states the conditions of equilibrium in the production of goods whether for consumption or for investment.[10] Production will be extended up to the point at which the given and fixed money wage rate w_0 is equal to the marginal net product of labor, or, if we prefer, up to the point at which price equals marginal labor cost.[11] This assumes that the only variable factor is labor and the quantity of equipment is fixed; a condition that is approximately satisfied in the case we are considering. Eliminating equation (5) by substitution into (7) we can reduce this part of the system to two equations in the two unknowns X and N, where X' is used for dX/dN:

$$W_0 = X'(N)\frac{Y}{X}, \qquad X = X(N).$$

Since the money income is determined exclusively by the *monetary* part of the system, the price level depends only on the amount of output. If, at any given price level, the fixed wage is less than the marginal product of labor, the forces of competition lead to an expansion of employment and output which forces prices down. This lowers the marginal product of labor until it becomes equal to the wage rate. If the wage rate exceeded the marginal product of labor, output and employment would contract, which would force prices up. We see clearly from Figure 1.7 that the amount of employment thus determined will, in general, not be 'full employment'; that is, unless the LL curve intersects the IS curve at (Y_2, r_2) or to the right of it.

8. UNDEREMPLOYMENT EQUILIBRIUM AND LIQUIDITY PREFERENCE

This last result deserves closer consideration. It is usually considered as one of the most important achievements of the Keynesian theory that it explains the consistency of economic equilibrium with the presence of involuntary unemployment. It is, however, not sufficiently recognized that, except in a limiting case to be considered later, this result is due entirely to the assumption of 'rigid wages'[12] and not to the Keynesian liquidity preference.

[9] The price level is also necessary to determine the real wage rate, given the money wage rate W.

[10] The equilibrium price of each type of physical asset is found by capitalizing a series of expected marginal yields at the current rate of interest. The expected yields of the marginal unit need not be equal in each period.

[11] This is a sufficient condition under assumption of perfect competition; the modifications necessary in the case of monopolies cannot be considered here.

[12] The expression 'rigid wages' refers to the infinite elasticity of the supply curve of labor when the level of employment is below 'full'.

Systems with rigid wages share the common property that the equilibrium value of the 'real' variables is determined essentially by monetary conditions rather than by 'real' factors (e.g. quantity and efficiency of existing equipment, relative preference for earning and leisure, etc.). The monetary conditions are sufficient to determine money income and, under fixed wages and given technical conditions, to each money income there corresponds a definite equilibrium level of employment. This equilibrium level does not tend to coincide with full employment except by mere chance, since there is no economic mechanism that insures this coincidence. There may be unemployment in the sense that more people would be willing to work at the current real wage rate than are actually employed; but in a free capitalistic economy production is guided by prices and not by desires and since the money wage rate is rigid, this desire fails to be translated into an economic stimulus. [...]

9. LIQUIDITY PREFERENCE UNDER RIGID AND FLEXIBLE WAGES—AN EXAMPLE

In order to see clearly the different implications of the liquidity-preference theory under different hypotheses as to the supply of labor we may briefly consider the effects of a shift in the investment schedule [equation (2)].

Suppose that the system is in equilibrium at money income Y_0: the flow of investments is I_0, and its marginal efficiency, r_0, is the equilibrium rate of interest. Now let us assume that for some reason the rate of investment that seems profitable at any level of the rate of interest falls. In particular the marginal efficiency of the rate of investment I_0 falls to the level $r_1 < r_0$. In order for the system to reach a new position of equilibrium, it is necessary that the rate of interest fall to this level. Except under special circumstances, to be considered later, as the rate of interest falls, the demand for money as an asset rises, and a certain amount of current money savings remains in the *money market* to satisfy the increased demand. If the supply of money is not properly increased, this, in turn, implies a fall in money income.

Under the conditions of our last model (flexible wages) the fall is brought about by an all-around reduction in wages and prices. The price level reaches its new equilibrium position when the supply has been increased sufficiently to satisfy the liquidity demand for money associated with the interest rate r_1.[13] The net effect of the shift is then to depress the interest rate, the money income, and money wages without affecting the real variables of the system, employment, output, real wage rate.[14]

[13] The rate of interest must necessarily fall to the level r_1, for the real income and therefore the amount of real savings will be unchanged, and the marginal efficiency of this amount of real savings is r_1, by hypothesis.

[14] The real wage rate clearly cannot fall. If the real wage rate had fallen, entrepeneurs would try to expand employment while the supply of labor would, if anything, contract. If it had risen, the opposite situation would occur, and neither of these situations is compatible with equilibrium.

But if money wages are rigid downward, the reduction in money income, made necessary by the fall in the rate of interest, becomes a reduction in real income and employment as well. The effect of the shift in the investment schedule is now to start a typical process of contraction so frequently described in Keynesian literature. As producers of investment goods make losses, they have no other choice than to dismiss workers, even though their physical productivity is unchanged. This, in turn, reduces the demand for consumption goods and causes unemployment to spread to this sector. Real income falls along with money income (the price level is likely to fall to a smaller extent). The fall in money income increases the supply of money to hold; the fall in real income decreases saving and raises its marginal efficiency above the level r_1.[15] This double set of reactions leads finally to a new equilibrium, with a smaller money and real income, less employment, higher real wages (since the price level falls) and a rate of interest somewhere below r_0 and above the new 'full employment interest' r_1.[16] In terms of our graphic apparatus, a decreased marginal efficiency of capital (or increased propensity to save), shifts the *IS* curve to the left, as shown by the curve *I'S'*, and lowers interest rate and income, money as well as real income.

10. TWO LIMITING CASES

(a) The Keynesian Case

There is one case in which the Keynesian theory of liquidity preference is sufficient by itself to explain the existence of underemployment equilibrium without starting out with the assumption of rigid wages. We have seen (Section 4) that, since securities are inferior to money as a form of holding assets, there must be some positive level of the rate of interest (previously denoted by r'') at which the demand for money becomes infinitely elastic or practically so. We have the Keynesian case when the 'full-employment equilibrium rate of interest' is less than r''. Whenever this situation materializes, the very mechanism that tends to bring about full-employment equilibrium in a system with 'flexible' wages breaks down, since there is no possible level of the money wage rate and price level that can establish full-employment equilibrium.

From the analytical point of view the situation is characterized by the fact that we must add to our system a new equation, namely $r = r''$. The system is therefore overdetermined since we have 9 equations to determine only 8 unknowns.

The savings and investment equations expressed in real terms are sufficient to determine the value of the real income (since r is already

[15] Except if the *IS* curve is not monotonic decreasing, in which case the process of contraction will be more pronounced.

[16] If there was no full employment in the initial situation, then r_1 is simply the rate of interest that would maintain the old level of employment. This conclusion is also subject to the qualification mentioned in footnote 15.

determined). But this value will in general not be consistent with the value of the real income determined by the last four equations. More workers would be willing to work at the ruling real wage rate than are employed, but efforts at reducing real wages and increasing employment are bound to fail. For any fall in wages and prices increases the supply of money to hold but cannot lower the rate of interest below the level r'' since the demand for money as an asset is infinitely elastic. As Keynes would say, labor as a whole will not be able to fix its own real wage rate.

It appears clearly that, in this case, equilibrium is determined by those very factors that are stressed in the typical Keynesian analysis. In particular, real income and employment is determined by the position and shape of the saving and investment function, and changes in the propensity to invest or to save change real income without affecting the interest rate.

The price level on the other hand is in neutral equilibrium (at least for a certain range of values). It will tend to fall indefinitely as long as workers attempt to lower money wages in an effort to increase employment; and it can only find a resting place if and when money wages become rigid.

In this case the Keynesian analysis clearly departs from the classical lines and it leads to conclusions that could scarcely have been reached by following the traditional line of approach. [...]

(b) The Classical Case

We have the classical case when the equilibrium rate of interest is sufficiently high to make the demand for money to hold zero or negligible. Graphically, the *IS* curve of Figure 1.7 intersects the *LL* curve in the range in which *LL* is perpendicular to the income axis. Under these conditions changes in the rate of interest (except possibly if they are of considerable size) tend to leave the demand for money unchanged or practically so; $L_r = 0$ or negligible and $M = L(Y)$. The properties of a system satisfying this condition have already been sufficiently analyzed in Sections 7 and 8.

11. PRELIMINARY CONCLUSIONS

This brings to an end the first part of our analysis which aimed principally at distinguishing, as far as possible, to what extent the results of the Keynesian analysis are due to a more refined theoretical approach (liquidity preference) and to what extent to the assumption of rigid wages. We may summarize the results of our inquiry in the following propositions:

I. The liquidity-preference theory is not necessary to explain under-employment equilibrium; it is sufficient only in a limiting case: the 'Keynesian case'. In the general case it is neither necessary nor sufficient; it can explain this phenomenon only with the additional assumption of rigid wages.

II. The liquidity-preference theory is neither necessary nor sufficient to explain the dependence of the rate of interest on the quantity of money. This dependence is explained only by the assumption of rigid wages.

III. The result of the liquidity-preference theory is that the quantity of active money depends not only on the total quality of money but also on the rate of interest and therefore also on the form and position of the propensities to save and to invest. Hence in a system with flexible wages the rate of interest and the propensities to save and to invest are part of the mechanism that determines the price level. And in a system with rigid wages they are part of the mechanism that determines the level of employment and real income. [...]

1.5 The Neoclassical Synthesis*

[...]

The norm of reference to be used in defining involuntary unemployment is the supply curve of labor; for this curve shows the amount of employment which the workers of the economy want to obtain in the light of the money wage, price level, and budget restraints with which they are confronted. Hence as long as workers are 'on their supply curve'—that is, as long as they succeed in selling all the labor they want to at the prevailing real wage rate—a state of full employment will be said to exist in the economy. It follows that a state of general equilibrium in the economy as a whole, or even a state of partial equilibrium in the labor market by itself, is *ipso facto* a state of full employment. It also follows that the bench mark of full employment is not an absolute constant, but something which itself varies with every change in the real wage rate or in the subjective or objective determinants of the labor supply curve. [...]

Thus, by definition, the extent of involuntary unemployment is identical with the extent of the excess supply of labor which exists at the prevailing real wage rate. It follows that if the terms are understood in their usual, strict sense, the coexistence of involuntary unemployment and flexible money wages precludes the existence of equilibrium. For 'flexibility' means that the money wage rate tends to fall with excess supply, and 'equilibrium' means that nothing tends to change in the system. Hence, by definition, the foregoing 'coexistence theorem' must be true.

But like any other theorem which is tautologically true, this one too is uninteresting, unimportant, and completely uninformative about the real problems of economic analysis. It tells us nothing about the nature of the forces which generate unemployment. It tells us nothing about the relationship between the height of the real wage rate and the existence of unemployment. It tells us nothing about the proper policies to follow in order to combat unemployment. And—most important of all—it tells us nothing about the central question which divides classical and Keynesian economics: the efficacy of an automatically functioning market system with flexible

* From Don Patinkin, *Money, Interest and Prices* (2nd ed., 1965), chs. XIII and XIV (abridged). Copyright © 1965 by Don Patinkin. Reprinted by permission of Harper & Row, Publishers, Inc., Evanston, Illinois.

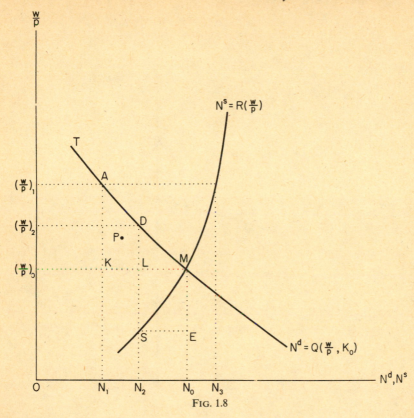

FIG. 1.8

money wages in eliminating involuntary unemployment. It is to this question that we now turn.[1]

1. A THEORY OF INVOLUNTARY UNEMPLOYMENT

Assume that the position of full-employment equilibrium ... is disturbed by a downward shift in the consumption or investment functions. Let this be represented in Figure 1.8 by the movement of the aggregate demand curve from E to E_2. This movement creates a deflationary gap in the commodity market equal to BC. Our task now is to examine the nature of the self-corrective market forces which this initial disturbance sets into operation. For simplicity, we shall deal with a pure outside-money economy; the argument can, however, readily be generalized to an economy with both outside and inside money, as well as interest-bearing government debt. In this case the

---

[1] For textual proof that Keynes's references to 'unemployment equilibrium' were not intended as denials of this innocuous tautology, but were simply based on a usage of 'equilibrium' which differs from the usual one—see Note K:3 [not included here—Ed.].

From this we can see that much of the heated and still continuing debate on whether there can or cannot be a state of 'unemployment equilibrium' is a sterile terminological debate which never would have started had either side bothered to define its terms precisely.

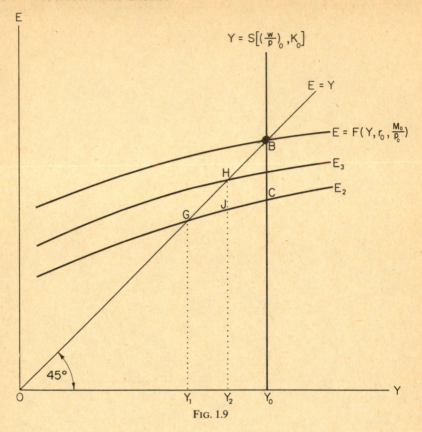

FIG. 1.9

term 'real-balance effect' in what follows should be understood as referring to the analogous real-financial-asset effect.

To the extent that the decreased demand for commodities is accompanied by and finances an increased demand for bonds, an excess demand is created in the latter market, driving the rate of interest down. This, in turn, reacts back on the commodity market and tends to push the aggregate demand curve up again. Here is the familiar classical and neoclassical mechanism by which an increase in savings flows into the loan market, thereby depresses interest, and thus stimulates an offsetting increase in investment. It should be noted that this mechanism will operate even if the obverse side of this increase in savings should consist initially of an increase in the demand for money, without any shift whatsoever in the demand for bonds. In this case, however, the decline in interest must await the impact on the bond market of the positive real-balance effect generated by the downward pressure on prices of the initial deflationary gap. Clearly, in addition to providing this indirect stimulus through the bond market, the real-balance effect also stimulates the commodity market directly.

Thus the downward shift in the commodity demand function automatically creates market forces which tend to offset it. If this demand is sufficiently sensitive to these forces, it will quickly return to a full-employment position at a lower level of wages, prices and interest. Throughout this period of adjustment there will exist a state of excess supply in the commodity market. But due to the assumed shortness of this period, producers will react to their temporary inability to sell by simply permitting their inventories to build up. That is, they will leave their level of production unchanged at Y_0. [...]

Once this assumption is dropped, the whole argument must be drastically modified. In the absence of sufficient interest- and price-elasticity, the adjustment process becomes a long, drawn-out one. It cannot then realistically be assumed that firms will continue producing at an unchanged level, for this would require them to accumulate inventories at ever increasing levels. Hence they must eventually take some step to bring current output—and consequently current input—into line with current sales. And this is the beginning of involuntary unemployment. [...]

In this way the economy is brought to a position described by the point K in Figure 1.8 and its corresponding point G in Figure 1.9. But what must now be emphasized is that this position is *not* one of equilibrium: for at point K there is an excess supply of labor, $N_0 - N_1$, which continues to press down on the money wage rate, and at point G there is an excess supply of commodities, $Y_0 - Y_1$, which continues to press down on the price level. [...]

We can now return to our main discussion and emphasize that it is within the foregoing framework of dynamic disequilibrium—and resulting downward pressures on both the price level and the money wage rate—that we must study the problem of involuntary unemployment. This is the real import of the innocuous tautology of the preceding section: not that involuntary unemployment can be defined away, but that it can have no meaning within the confines of static equilibrium analysis. Conversely, the essence of dynamic analysis is involuntariness: its domain consists only of positions *off* the demand or supply curves. Indeed, it is this very departure from these curves, and the resulting striving of individuals to return to the optimum behavior which they represent, which provides the motive power of the dynamic process itself.

Thus our first task in studying involuntary unemployment is to free ourselves of the mental habit—long ingrained by the methods of static analysis—of seeing only the points *on* demand or supply curve. Once we do this, we find ourselves able to give precise expression to many intuitive, common-sense ideas which have all too frequently been unjustifiably rejected as violating the precepts of rigorous economic analysis. First we see that involuntary unemployment can exist even in a system of perfect competition and wage and price flexibility. In particular, the departure of K from the labor supply curve reflects the existence of involuntary unemployment to the extent $N_0 - N_1$. Second, we see that a deficiency in commodity demand can generate a decrease in labor input without requiring a prior increase in the real wage rate. For since the point K is not on the demand curve for labor either, it is not bound by the standard inverse relation between labor input and the real wage rate which this curve specifies.[2] Both of these implications will be discussed further in the next chapter.

2. A THEORY OF INVOLUNTARY UNEMPLOYMENT (CONTINUED)

As just emphasized, the position represented by point K in Figure 1.8 and point G in Figure 1.9 is not an equilibrium one. In particular, the excess supplies of the two markets described by these diagrams reinforce each other in exerting a downward pressure on both wages and prices. Let us assume for the moment that these decline in the same proportion (so that the real wage rate is not affected) and examine the implications of this movement for the magnitude of involuntary unemployment.

As explained at the beginning of the preceding section, this price decline creates a positive real-balance effect which exerts both a direct and (through its depressing effect on interest in the bond market) indirect upward pressure on the aggregate demand curve for commodities. Assume that as a result of these pressures this curve rises to, say, E_3 in Figure 1.9. If firms continued with their output of Y_1, they would find their inventories being drawn down below the desirable level. Hence, by the reverse of the argument of the preceding section, they will increase their labor input above N_1 and, accordingly, their commodity output above Y_1. Clearly, this process will continue until employment has risen to N_2 and output to Y_2. At these levels there will once again be neither a deficiency nor an excess of actual output—though, as we shall emphasize in a moment, this output is still less than that which firms would like to produce.

This possibility of an automatic decrease in the extent of involuntary unemployment is what is denied by the usual oversimplified statement of the Keynesian position. According to it, any attempt of firms to increase their labor input to N_2 would result in an output Y_2, which could not be sold. Indeed, at such an output there would, in Figure 1.9, be a deflationary gap of HJ which would compel firms to reduce output and, accordingly, input until they had once again returned to Y_1 and N_1, respectively.[3] This argument is clearly based on the tacit assumption that the aggregate commodity demand curve remains unchanged at E_2. In brief, here, as elsewhere, Keynesian economics overlooks the direct influence of the real-balance effect on this demand. Similarly, it overlooks the supply side of the commodity market which, by its excess over the demand, generates this effect.

Leaving this doctrinal issue behind, we now apply the argument of the preceding section to show that the dynamic process cannot stop at the stage

---

[2] It might be noted that this inverse relation characterizes the Keynesian theory of employment no less than the classical. Cf. the *General Theory*, pp. 17–18.

[3] Cf. *General Theory*, pp. 261–62.

represented by the output Y_2 and input N_2. For with the real wage rate unchanged at $(w/p)_0$, there is still at the point L in Figure 1.8 an excess supply of labor exerting a downward pressure on wages. Similarly, there is still at the point H in Figure 1.9 an excess of desired over actual supply of commodities; for since the real wage rate has remained unchanged, so too has the vertical supply curve at Y_0. Hence there remains an excess supply of $Y_0 - Y_2$ (which manifests itself once again in the form of excess productive capacity) exerting a downward pressure on the price level.

Let us continue with our assumption that wages and prices always decline in exactly the same proportion. Then the dynamic process in its entirety can be summarized in the following terms: The initial decrease in commodity demand creates a state of involuntary unemployment. But it also generates a price decline and a consequent real-balance effect which—both directly and indirectly—tends to force this demand up again. As the demand curve rises, it pulls commodity output up after it. And this pulls labor input up concurrently. In particular, as output is pulled diagonally upwards along the 45° radius vector in Figure 1.9, input is pulled correspondingly rightwards along the horizontal dotted line corresponding to the unchanged real wage rate $(w/p)_0$ in Figure 1.8. In this way the extent of involuntary unemployment is continuously diminished. [...]

3. KEYNESIAN AND CLASSICAL THEORIES OF INVOLUNTARY UNEMPLOYMENT

Let us now develop the [preceding] argument ... into an analytical framework for interpreting the debate between Keynesian and classical theories of employment ...

It is ... [the] necessity for a major price decline in the present case which makes this process unacceptable as a primary ingredient of a modern full-employment policy.[4]

Let us, then, temper this process by supplementing it with the traditional discretionary open-market and rediscounting operations of a central bank. The immediate implication of such operations is that a decline in the rate of interest need no longer wait ... for a decline in prices. Instead, open-market purchases replace the real-balance effect as the source of increased demand in the bond market. In this way, by primary reliance on a manipulated lowering of the rate of interest, aggregate demand might be raised to its full-employment level without any prior decline in prices. Indeed, in this Wicksellian world, such a decline would itself be taken as evidence that the rate of interest had not been lowered sufficiently.

It is the belief in the efficacy of this monetary policy which will be identified here with the neoclassical position. Correspondingly, it is the denial of this efficacy which will be identified with the Keynesian one. According to this position, the great degree of uncertainty which surrounds any investment plan makes it unlikely that interest variations of a practical magnitude can

[4] This will be discussed further below.

be depended upon to stimulate such activity significantly.[5] Hence, though working in the proper direction, interest reductions are too weak to justify the reliance placed upon them by monetary policy. For this reason such a policy will not be able to close a deflationary gap with the speed necessary to prevent a protracted price decline.

Thus the success of monetary policy depends ultimately on the stability of the dynamic process initiated by this decline. This brings us back to the analysis of [§2 above]. But now—in order to present the Keynesian position in its entirety—we shall have to introduce into this analysis two hitherto neglected factors.[6]

There is, first of all, the question of distribution effects. As emphasized [above], we cannot assume that the negative indebtedness effects of debtors are simply canceled by the positive effects of creditors. More specifically—and in Keynes' words—'if the fall of wages and prices goes far, the embarrassment of those entrepeneurs who are heavily indebted may soon reach the point of insolvency,—with severely adverse effects on investment'. In brief, a protracted price decline will cause a wave of bankruptcies which will eliminate both the firms' liabilities and the households' assets, and leave only a seriously impaired state of business confidence.

Second, there is the influence of expectations. To the extent that the monetary authorities reduce interest only by slow stages, potential investors may delay carrying out their plans in anticipation of benefiting from still lower rates. Similarly, the decline in prices and wages may create the expectation of still more rapid declines, and thus lead both households and firms to postpone their purchases. Furthermore, the anticipation of a lower future price level has the same effects on the amount of labor demanded as a rise in the current real wage rate. For, in making their plans, firms will compare the wage paid for current input with the lower price that will subsequently be received for its resulting output. Due to these factors, the stimulating real-balance effect of a price decline may be more than offset by its depressing expectation effects.[7]

Thus Keynesian economics is the economics of unemployment *dis*-equilibrium. It argues that as a result of interest-elasticity, on the one hand,

[5] On this insensitivity, see Oscar Lange, *Price Flexibility and Employment* (Bloomington, Ind., 1945), p. 85, and the references to empirical studies there cited. For an excellent theoretical discussion, see G. L. S. Shackle, 'Interest Rates and the Pace of Investment', *Economic Journal*, LVI (1946), 1–17. See also Hicks, *Value and Capital*, pp. 225–26.

[6] The following interpretation of Keynes takes as its point of departure the stimulating discussion of L. R. Klein, *The Keynesian Revolution* (New York, 1947), pp. 80–90, 206–13.

[7] This and the preceding paragraph are largely adapted from Keynes's discussion in the *General Theory* of the effects to be expected from a protracted decline in money wages and prices. See, in particular, *ibid.*, pp. 205–8, 232–34, and 260–69. The quotation in the preceding paragraph is from p. 264.

Note that though in comparing future with present prices it is the *rate* of decline which is relevant in comparing future prices with the present wage rate it is the *level* of these prices that must be considered.

and distribution and expectation effects, on the other, the dynamic process of [§2 above]—even when aided by monetary policy—is unlikely to converge either smoothly or rapidly to the full-employment equilibrium position. Indeed, if these influences are sufficiently strong, they may even render this process unstable. In such a case the return to full employment would have to await the fortunate advent of some exogenous force that would expand aggregate demand sufficiently.[...]

As already indicated, even if monetary policy could definitely restore the economy to full employment, there would still remain the crucial question of the length of time it would need. There would still remain the very real possibility that it would necessitate subjecting the economy to an intolerably long period of dynamic adjustment: a period during which wages, prices, and interest would continue to fall, and—what is most important—a period during which varying numbers of workers would continue to suffer from involuntary unemployment. Though I am not aware that he expressed himself in this way, this is the essence of Keynes' position. This is all that need be established in order to justify his fundamental policy conclusion that the 'self-adjusting quality of the economic system'—even when reinforced by central-bank policy—is not enough.[8]

This interpretation forces upon Keynesian economics the abandonment of the once-revolutionary 'diagonal-cross' diagram with which it swept its way into the textbooks. It compels it to recognize that this diagram takes account neither of the supply side of the commodity market nor of the real-balance effect which its excess over the demand side generates. It therefore compels it to concede that (in terms of Figure 1.9) the intersection of the aggregate demand curve E_2 with the $45°$ diagonal at G does not imply that there exist no automatic market forces to push real income up from the unemployment level Y_1. Indeed, it compels it to accept the classical contention that such forces not only exist, but even succeed eventually in raising income to the full-employment level Y_0.[9]

But this narrowing of the analytical distance between Keynesian and classical economics does not generate a corresponding narrowing of the policy distance. It still leaves Keynes insisting that the inefficiency of the automatic adjusting process is so great as to be remediable only by a program of direct government investment in public works. And it still leaves modern-day adherents of the classical view conceding the inefficacy of monetary policy

---

[8] *General Theory*, pp. 266–67 and 378.

[9] These limitations of the standard Keynesian diagram have already been noted.[...]

One might be tempted to rationalize Keynes' neglect of the real-balance effect—or, more generally, real-financial-asset effect—on the grounds that he was concerned with a pure inside-money economy without government bonds [cf. pp. 297 and 305–307]. I do not, however, believe that textual evidence can be adduced in favor of this conjecture. More important in the present context, there is no reason to restrict the Keynesian argument in this way; for, as we have just seen, its essential point holds for an economy in which outside-money—and hence a real-balance effect—also exist. And, as implied above, a corresponding generalization can be made, *mutatis mutandis*, for an economy which also has government bonds.

by itself, but insisting that it need only be supplemented by an automatic system of contracyclical tax remissions and transfer payments.[10] In brief, our interpretation takes the debate on the degree of government intervention necessary for a practicable full-employment policy out of the realm of those questions that can be decided by a priori considerations of internal consistency and logical validity, and into the realm of those questions that can be decided only by empirical consideration of the actual magnitudes of the relevant economic parameters.

While our interpretation takes off the analytical edge of Keynesian economics in one direction, it sharpens it in another, more vital one. It makes unmistakably clear—what should always have been clear—that the involuntary unemployment of the *General Theory* need *not* have its origin in wage rigidities. Indeed, in this respect we are more Keynesian than Keynes. For by unequivocally placing the center of emphasis on the inadequacy of aggregate demand in the commodity market, and by recognizing the resulting involuntary unemployment to be a phenomenon of economic dynamics, we have freed ourselves from the necessity of static analysis to connect decreases in employment with increases in the real wage rate. We have been able to explain the existence of involuntary unemployment without placing any restrictions on the movement of the real wage rate.[11] Conversely, we have shown that reductions in this rate are neither a necessary nor a sufficient condition for the rapid reestablishment of full-employment equilibrium in the economy.

Correspondingly, our interpretation does not tie the Keynesian theory of unemployment to any special form of the supply function for labor. In particular, it is independent of the all-too-frequent assumption that this theory presupposes a supply curve for labor...[which] remains infinitely elastic at the prevailing—and presumed rigid—money wage rate w_0 until the point N_0. Accordingly, writers who make use of this curve identify the maximum amount of employment that workers are willing to offer at the rate w_0 with the level of 'full-employment', and define involuntary unemployment as the difference between this level and the one actually existing in the economy, say N_1.[12]

4. THE 'LIQUIDITY TRAP'

Noticeable by its omission from the preceeding interpretation of Keynesian economics is the contention that there is a minimum level below which the

---

[10] Thus contrast the *General Theory*, p. 378, with the views of the 'Chicago school' as expressed by H. C. Simons, *Economic Policy for a Free Society* (Chicago, 1948), pp. 40–77, 160–83; L. W. Mints, *Monetary Policy for a Competitive Society* (New York, 1950); Milton Friedman, *Essays in Positive Economics* (Chicago, 1953), pp. 133–56.

[11] As pointed out [in note 2 above], Keynes does accept this restriction; cf. *General Theory*, pp. 17–18.

[12] Cf., e.g., Modigliani, 'Liquidity Preference', *op. cit.*, p. 189. [p. 44 above—Ed.] This also seems to be Keynes' view in the *General Theory*, pp. 8–9, 295, 301–3, and 336. In any event, it is definitely the way Lange interprets him (*Price Flexibility and Employment*, p. 6, footnote 4).

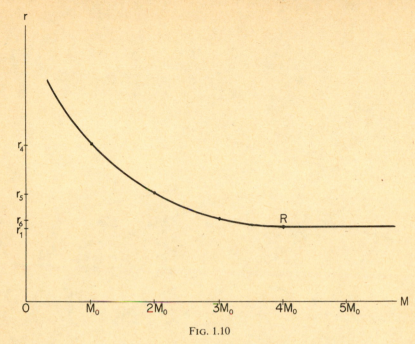

FIG. 1.10

rate of interest cannot fall—the 'liquidity trap'. If this contention were true, then—completely aside from the question of interest-inelasticity which we have emphasized—monetary policy would be confronted with an absolute limitation on its powers to stimulate economic activity. Keynes himself did not seem to attach much importance to this possibility.[13] But later critics—both sympathetic and adverse—have raised it to a key position in the Keynesian argument.[14]

These critics rationalized this limitation by ascribing a special form to their demand curve for money. In particular, they assumed this curve to become an indefinitely extending horizontal line at the minimum level at which 'almost everyone prefers cash to holding a debt which yields so low a rate of interest'.[15] Accordingly, they presented this curve as in Figure 1.10 and argued that it demonstrated the impossibility of driving interest below r_1.

Now ... this cannot be the form of the demand curve for money in the ordinary sense of the term.[16] For when due account is taken of the individuals' planned behaviour in all markets, this curve must retain its negative slope throughout. In particular, the amount of money demanded cannot become

[13] *General Theory*, pp. 203 and 207.
[14] Cf., e.g., J. R. Hicks, 'Mr. Keynes and the "Classics",' *op. cit.*, pp. 469–70 [cf. pp. 24–30 above—Ed.], Modigliani, 'Liquidity Preference', *op. cit.*, pp. 196 and 198–99 [cf. pp. 43–41 above —Ed.], A. H. Hansen, *A Guide to Keynes* (New York, 1953), pp. 132–33.
[15] *General Theory*, p. 207.
[16] The reason for this proviso is explained in footnote 17 below.

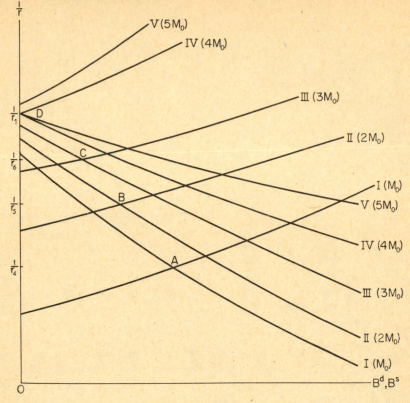

F<small>IG</small>. 1.11

infinite unless the supply of bonds does so; but ... the presence of uncertainty makes it irrational even for a 'bear' to supply such an infinite amount. Nevertheless, as we shall now see, there is a very real limitation on the downward influence that monetary policy—in its usual sense—can exert on the rate of interest. But it is a limitation that flows from the significance of the minimum rate r_1 in the bond market, and not in the money market.

In order to show this let us revert to the analysis of absolute wage and price rigidity under conditions of unemployment ... In this analysis, an increase in the quantity of money permanently shifts the demand curve for bonds rightwards and the supply curve leftwards and thus reduces the equilibrium rate of interest. In terms of Figure 1.11, the successive increases in the quantity of money from M_0 to $2M_0$, $3M_0$, and $4M_0$ shift the demand and supply curves from position *I* to *II*, *III*, and *IV*, respectively, and thus cause the point of equilibrium to move from *A* to *B*, *C*, and *D*, respectively.

Figure 1.11 also reflects the crucial additional assumption that as the demand curve for bonds shifts upwards, its intersection point with the vertical axis approaches the price $1/r_1$ as a limit. That is, no matter how large the value of their initial money holdings, individuals will never agree to hold bonds at a rate of interest below r_1. At such low rates they will always prefer to hold money instead. At the same time, the higher the initial money holdings of firms, the less pressed they are to borrow, and the lower, accordingly, the maximum rate of interest they are willing to pay. It follows that after the monetary expansion has reached a certain point—$4M_0$ in our diagram—the bond market will become inactive: no borrower will be willing to pay the minimum rate of interest on which lenders insist. This situation is represented by the demand and supply curves of position V.

As the reader has undoubtedly realized, the two preceding paragraphs describe a market-experiment identical in general conception with that of Chapter XI:4, though differing in details. In particular, once again we are exogenously changing the quantity of money in the economy and noting the effects of this change on the equilibrium rate of interest. The results of this conceptual experiment can be represented by the curve of Figure 1.10—now cut off at point R and considered to be a market-equilibrium curve, and not a demand curve. That is, this curve is now considered to be the locus of all intersection points of demand and supply curves in Figure 1.11. Its abrupt ending at point R thus reflects the fact that when the quantity of money exceeds $4M_0$, there are no transactions taking place in the bond market described by Figure 1.11, so that the rate of interest is no longer defined. Accordingly, our market-equilibrium curve also reflects the fact that monetary expansion cannot reduce the rate of interest below r_1. Clearly, this limitation flows from the assumed properties of the demand and supply curves for bonds; it therefore holds no matter what the shape of the demand curve for money.[17] [...]

At the same time, it is clear... that even if monetary policy cannot drive interest below r_1, the economy will not remain 'trapped' at a less-than-full-employment level. For this policy also creates a real-balance effect which

[17] Returning now to the proviso mentioned in footnote 16 above, I would like to suggest that Keynesian economists have not been referring to the demand curve in the usual sense of the term, but to a curve generated by changes in the quantity of money, thus see the references to such changes in Hicks, *Trade Cycle*, pp. 141–42 [pp. 24–30 above]; Modigliani; 'Liquidity Preference', *op. cit.*, pp. 198–99 [pp. 36–38 above]; Joan Robinson, 'The Rate of Interest', *Econometrica*, XIX (1951), 101–102; and R. F. Kahn, 'Some Notes on Liquidity Preference', *The Manchester School*, XXII (1954), 247. These writers might, then, have had in mind the market-equilibrium curve of Figure 1.10.

Alternatively, they may have been thinking of a demand curve generated by increasing the individual's *initial endowment* of money and asking him what the rate of interest would have to be in order to be willing to hold this increased quantity. Now, at the minimum rate r_1 there is no real-balance effect in the bond market; nor (according to the usual Keynesian assumption) is there ever such an effect in the commodity market; it follows that at the rate r_1 the real-balance effect expends itself entirely on increasing the demand for money, so that the curve which describes the outcome of this experiment becomes a horizontal line at r_1.

I doubt, however, if this is a proper interpretation of Keynesian thinking, for the notion of a real-balance effect in the demand function for money is quite foreign to it. Note too that this interpretation is inconsistent with any attempt to interpret Keynes in terms of a pure inside-money economy [see note 9 above].

shifts *GG* rightwards until full employment is reached.[18] This, however, does not negate the 'Keynesian Revolution', but only requires us to interpret it as in Section 3 above. Indeed, since this interpretation is free of the special assumptions on which the 'liquidity trap' is based, it actually increases the generality of the Keynesian theory of unemployment.

1.6 Keynes and the Neoclassics*

It is a strange thing that twenty years after the publication of the *General Theory*, doubt should still persist, even among careful thinkers, about the exact nature of the innovations which led Keynes to different *results* from those which had generally been accepted by his predecessors. Some of the innovations of the *General Theory* are innovations of method, which opened the way to new results, or provide better ways of reaching old results; with these I am not here concerned. But there are important cases in which Keynes' predecessors said one thing, and Keynes said exactly the opposite; where Keynes maintains that something is true which earlier economists, who had spoken with authority in their own time, had stated quite definitely to be false. What is the basic reason (or reasons) for this turnabout?

It seems to me that it is the principal contribution of Professor Patinkin's recent book[1] that it does throw some light upon this question. Not quite intentionally, perhaps; for he is not writing to elucidate the 'Keynesian Revolution', but to deny that it is a revolution at all. The theory which Patinkin sets out, though it owes much to Keynes, is not Keynesian; it is a modernised version of the theory which Keynes called 'classical'. It retains (and is shown to retain) complete continuity with the doctrines that were taught by leading economists in the two hundred years before 1936. But it is so carefully and elaborately set out, in such a variety of forms that are shown to be equivalent, that the inessentials fade away, and the crucial points on which the difference remains stand out sharply. When it comes to these crucial points, I should myself take the other line from his; but Patinkin has helped me to understand just why I differ from him. I cannot agree that he has 'integrated monetary and value theory'; but he has performed an extremely useful control experiment.

1. The crucial point, as I now feel quite clear, on which the individuality of

---

[18] It is this rightward shift in *GG* which is overlooked by Hicks in his discussion of the 'liquidity trap' in 'A Rehabilitation of "Classical" Economics?,' *Economic Journal*, LXVII (1957), 286–8 [pp. 63–64 below—Ed.]. For further details, see my 'Keynesian Economics Rehabilitated: A Rejoinder to Professor Hicks', *Economic Journal*, LXIX (1959), 584–85 [pp. 69–70 below —Ed.].

Note that the argument of the text holds even if we accept the Keynesian presentation of the 'liquidity trap'...

* From J. R. Hicks, 'A rehabilitation of "Classical" Economics?', *Econ. J.*, 1957. [See the editorial note to Reading 1.2—Ed.]

[1] D. Patinkin, *Money, Interest and Prices: an Integration of Monetary and Value Theory* (Evanston, Illinois: Row Peterson, 1956). [See pp. 46–58 above.]

the Keynes theory depends, is the implication that there are conditions in which the price-mechanism will not 'work'—more specifically, that there are conditions in which the interest-mechanism will not work. The special form in which this appears in the *General Theory* is the doctrine of the *floor* to the rate of interest—the 'liquidity trap' as Sir Dennis Robertson has called it. But there are other possible ways in which interest may not work, which we shall be considering later. It is very probable that Keynes did not see this clearly at the time when he was writing; he was still in two minds whether he believed in curing unemployment by monetary expansion, or whether he had come to hold that mere monetary stimulus was liable to be ineffective if it was not backed up by more direct methods. On the practical level he was still trying to keep a foot in both camps. But on the theoretical level he was already committed by the logic of his system (it is this which I think is proved by Professor Patinkin's experiment) to the second of these alternatives.

In a world where the interest-mechanism can always operate—where the rate of interest is flexible, and sufficiently flexible, in either direction, for its movements to have a significant effect on (saving or) investment—the Keynes theory is true and the 'classical' theory is true; they lead to the same results. Though the paths of analysis are different, the end-results, achieved when all the same things have been taken into account, are the same. And either analysis can be put into a general-equilibrium form in which it is directly apparent that they come to the same thing.

Thus, for instance, Keynes would argue that an increase in the propensity to save (money wages being fixed) would diminish employment directly; but he would then qualify this statement by an admission that the diminished demand for transactions balances would lower the rate of interest (if interest is flexible), and that this would have a secondary effect increasing investment and hence employment—but to something less than its former level. A properly equipped 'classic' would get to the same result by a different route. He would argue that the increase in saving would *directly* reduce the rate of interest, so that employment would increase in the investment-goods trades as it diminished in the consumption-goods trades; but he could (or should) go on to admit that the increase in saving would carry with it a diminution in the velocity of circulation (some of the saving would be hoarded), so that, with an inelastic monetary system, and the fixed money wages that are being assumed, there would still be a net decline in employment. A general-equilibrium theorist would show the saving operating on interest and employment simultaneously. One can put the systems through their paces in many such ways, and—so long as the interest mechanism functions—one must come in the end to the same result by each method.

Instead of checking over, in the above manner, all the manifold cases which require consideration, it will be more revealing to proceed diagrammatically. And here, instead of making a selection among Patinkin's cornucopia of

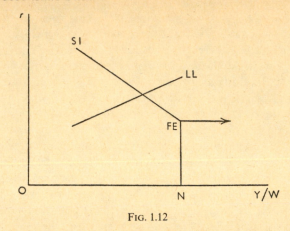

F<small>IG</small>. 1.12

diagrams, I may be allowed to use the apparatus to which I am accustomed myself. So long as money wage-rates are given, it is possible I showed many years ago,[2] to express the essence of the Keynes theory on a single diagram. One measures Income (Keynes' Y) along one axis, and interest (r) along the other; one then draws an *SI* curve (based on the Marginal Efficiency of Capital schedule and the Consumption Function) connecting those levels of Income at which Saving equals Investment, at various rates of interest. Granted that Investment rises as r falls, and Y rises as Investment rises, this must be a downward-sloping curve. We then confront this curve with a *LL* curve showing the rate of interest at which the demand for money will equal a given supply of money, at each given Income (Y). Granted that the demand for money increases with Y, and diminishes with r (as Keynes maintains, and Patinkin does not object), this *LL* curve will be upward sloping. Equilibrium (which can easily be shown to be a stable equilibrium) is established at the point where these two curves intersect.

As this diagram was originally drawn, it laid excessive weight on the assumption of fixed money wages; even for the elucidation of Keynes, it paid insufficient attention to the possibility of Full Employment. For present purposes, it is essential that that gap should be filled. Suppose that (still assuming our given level of money wages) Full Employment is reached at an income *ON*. (Refinements about heterogeneity of labour supply, and such like, need not concern us here.) Further expansion beyond *ON* must be purely monetary in character, so that in money terms the *SI* curve must be horizontal beyond the point *FE*. But it is more satisfactory (Keynes would no doubt agree) to work from this stage onwards in real terms, so that Y is reckoned *in wage-units*. On this convention (adopted in Figure 1.12) the *SI* curve will be unaffected until the Full Employment level is reached, but it will then be

[2] 'Mr. Keynes and the Classics', *Econometrica*, 1937. See also my *Contribution to the Theory of the Trade Cycle*, Ch. XI. [See pp. 24–30 above.]

cut short at the point *FE*. Any attempt to move beyond *FE* will induce a merely inflationary expansion that is *not* represented on the diagram, but of which the arrow that is shown serves as a reminder.

The decision to work in wage-units has no more than this limited effect on the *SI* curve; but its effect on the *LL* curve is more serious. When the price- and wage-level changes the *LL* curve will stay put only if the quantity of money remains unaltered *in terms of wage-units*; but there is in general no reason why it should do so. If the supply of money is fixed in money terms, then (when wages rise) the supply in terms of wage-units contracts, so that the *LL* curve moves to the left.[3] Thus, so long as the supply of money is restrained from expanding (in money terms), wage-inflation must bring its own cure. If, initially, the *LL* curve lies to the right of the *FE* point, the inflation itself will bring it back. (There does, of course, remain the danger that the inflation will have acquired such momentum that the *FE* point is overshot before the leftward movement ceases—but that is not a matter which concerns us here.) Equilibrium will always be reached, if the supply of money is kept under control, at *FE* or on the downward-sloping part of the *SI* curve.

What I want now to emphasise is that the construction so far reached, though it has been expressed in a manner which has a Keynesian tendency, still contains nothing whatever that is inconsistent with 'classical' theory. The only way in which it differs from what was taught by 'classical' economists, from Hume to Marshall and Pigou, is in the assumption that it makes about the behaviour of wages—that they can flex upwards but not downwards; but this is a special assumption that can be incorporated into any theory. Certainly the economists of the past cannot be criticised for not making it, for in their time it would, quite clearly, not have been true. This is not a matter on which there can be any theoretical *contradiction*; it is the kind of change in the exposition of theory which we ought to be making, all the time, in response to changing facts.

If it was desired to apply the above construction to a world in which wages could flex in *both* directions, no major change would have to be made. It would only be necessary to introduce a 'Full Unemployment' point *FU*, beyond which wages would fall, just as they rise beyond the Full Employment point *FE*. Beyond *FU* the curve would be cut off, just as it is cut off at *FE*. If, initially, the *LL* curve lay to the left of *FU*, there would be a fall in prices and wages; but this would *increase* the quantity of money in terms of wage-units, so that the *LL* curve would move to the *right*. Provided that the shape of the *LL* curve is as I have drawn it, equilibrium must be restored on the sloping part of the *SI* curve—at *FU* or at *FE* or somewhere between them.

---

[3] This (substantially) is the 'real-balance effect' of which Patinkin makes so much. I see no reason at all for supposing that it is not (implicitly) included in the Keynes theory. There may, it is true, be a certain 'real balance effect' before wages rise, if prices rise ahead of wages; but that is incorporated in the *LL* curve itself.

2. All the same, it is at this point in the story that more must be said about the *LL* curve. I have drawn the *LL* curve with a gentle rightward slope; this, I think, is the correct form which it would take for an economist who recognised Keynes' *transactions motive*, and also his *precautionary motive*, but not his *speculative motive* (to which we shall come later). And that, I think, is how it would appear to the 'properly equipped classical economist' whom I am using in this paper as an instrument of analysis. In fact, one can find the precautionary motive already in Thornton;[4] there are traces of it in Marshall;[5] after long travail, admirably explored by Patinkin, it emerges in Walras.[6] Any of these writers should have recognised that the demand for money has some elasticity against the rate of interest; and that, in our terminology, should have given his *LL* curve a rightward tilt.

A less perspicacious economist, who recognised the transactions motive only (or some equivalent to it) would draw his *LL* curve simply vertical; if, as is only too probable, he also looked only at full equilibrium, so that his *SI* curve was horizontal, his whole 'diagram' would have reduced to two perpendicular straight lines. The 'dichotomy' is then complete; real and monetary theories have completely fallen apart. This is the case of the crude quantity theorist. But to suggest that such crude quantity theorising was characteristic of the more subtle minds among the older economists is a caricature of the history of economic thought. [...]

3. In Wicksell, the *LL* curve is horizontal, because the banking system is operating in such a way as to maintain a constant rate of interest. If we put this constant market rate against an *SI* curve which has already degenerated into a constant natural rate, we get Wicksell's famous construction. 'If the market rate is below the natural rate...' it all follows. Keynes is using the same kind of construction for the study of temporary equilibrium. But he is maintaining that the *LL* curve becomes horizontal (over certain ranges) not because the banking system is choosing to make it horizontal, but because it is unable to act in any other way. It is not merely that the interest-mechanism may be prevented from operating; there are also circumstances in which it cannot be made to work. We then become *obliged* to analyse what happens in a Keynesian manner.

So long as this possibility is ruled out, we are at liberty to say that saving and investment determine the rate of interest, and that the effects on employment (or on inflation and deflation) depend on the way in which the monetary system reacts to an interest change. Or we are at liberty to regard interest and 'income' as being simultaneously determined, on general-equilibrium lines. But once the Keynes case has to be allowed for, both of these

---

[4] *Paper Credit*, pp. 96–7.

[5] *Official Papers*, p. 268; see Patinkin, p. 418.

[6] Patinkin, pp. 377–412. His detailed examination of Walras is one of the most impressive parts of Patinkin's book.

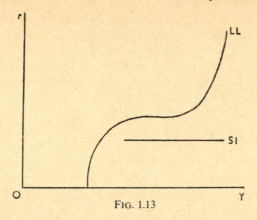

FIG. 1.13

techniques fail us. If the rate of interest is liable to be 'pegged' (not by any action of the monetary authority, but in the nature of the case), then we must treat the effect on income (and employment) as the primary effect, which may or may not be modified by indirect repercussions through the interest rate. It is no longer possible to use the general-equilibrium bridge to show that classical and Keynesian theories come to the same thing.

Since it is the essence of Patinkin's argument that they are the same thing, it is necessary for him to dispose of this critical case. In substance what he argues is the following.

Every economic unit (person or business) requires, on the average, to hold a certain proportion of its turnover (or we may say Income) in *liquid* form; but these liquid reserves do not need to be held in the form of money—they may be held in the form of securities (or bonds) which act as a money substitute. It is the proportion of its total liquid resources which the unit holds in money form which depends on the rate of interest. The lower the rate of interest, the larger the proportion that is held as money. But however low the rate of interest, this proportion cannot rise above 100%. Thus, once the supply of money has increased so far that bonds are no longer held as a money substitute, any further increase in the money supply must be spent upon goods; it must increase investment (or consumption) directly. It must accordingly raise the level of money incomes, on quantity theory lines, by the 'real balance effect'.

Let us look at this in terms of our diagram (Figure 1.13). It is ordinarily admitted that (with a given supply of money) the *LL* curve must be expected to become vertical at its rightward extremity. There is a minimum quantity of money which is needed to satisfy the transaction demand corresponding to a given money income; or (what comes to the same thing) there are units which are unable to use money substitutes as a means of satisfying their demand for liquid resources, however high the rate of interest rises. Thus, if the rate of interest rises very high, bonds will have displaced money in all those uses where they can displace money. It is Patinkin's contention that there is a corresponding vertical stretch at the other end, where money will have displaced bonds in all those uses where it can displace bonds. Thus the *LL* curve is *basically* vertical (the quantity theory is *basically* true); only it has a swerve in the middle, during which the system is switching over from one pattern of demand for money to another.[7]

With a curve of this character, there can be no danger of the *SI* curve falling so low that equilibrium cannot be restored in the end, if wages are flexible; if a (horizontal) *SI* curve lay below the horizontal (or nearly horizontal) part of the *LL* curve, the deflation would still be brought to a stop by an intersection with the vertical stretch to the left. (Or, if we insist that this equilibrium will be indefinitely deferred by the effect of the deflation on past debts, what is theoretically the same point can be made by asserting that equilibrium can always be restored by an increase in the supply of money; a rightward movement of the *LL* curve will always be effective in restoring equilibrium, provided the general shape of the curve is unaffected, as it is reasonable to suppose would be the case.) This, though he sometimes *seems* to rest his argument on different foundations, is the true basis for Patinkin's 'classicism'. If we grant him his vertical stretch on the left, his argument is conclusive; but if we do not grant it, his argument is inconclusive, and we have to go back to Keynes (or something like Keynes) after all.

When it comes to this crucial point, it is a pity that Patinkin does not argue his case more fully; in particular, it is a pity that he does not test it by seeing how it looks when applied to less schematic models, which get a little closer to reality. If he had done so, I believe he would have seen that his 'equilibrium' required not only that the monetary authority should buy up all the 'bonds' which were being used as money substitutes, but that it should go to the point of superseding all the financial intermediaries—banks and other financial institutions—transactions between which regulate the whole *system* of interest rates which exist in reality. What Keynes seems to me to be saying, at bottom, is that a financial system, of the kind that exists in developed 'capitalist' countries, cannot exist if the resultant rate of interest— the rate at which funds pass out of the financial system into real investment— is too low. The most that Patinkin can claim to have established is that the rate of interest might be *forced* still lower if that financial system were abolished, and the supply of funds to business were made directly by government. Whether or not that is the case—how far such a system is itself reconcilable with Patinkin's other assumptions—does not, in my view, affect the main issue. The effective answer to Patinkin is that in the applications we want to make we do not normally desire to proceed to such extremes. The horizontal stretch of the *LL* curve (at the level below which the financial system is unable to allow the rate of interest to go) is relevant to our

[7] The diagram which Patinkin himself uses to embody the above construction is on p. 148 of his book.

discussions. The vertical stretch which may, conceivably, lie beyond it is not relevant.

For the justification of the Keynesian approach to these matters, it is not necessary to consider the limit at which the financial system breaks down. In order to show that we get a better understanding of these problems by considering effects on employment and income first, and then correcting by possible repercussions through interest, all that is necessary is to maintain that there are ranges over which the repercussions through interest will be rather insignificant. To do that no more is necessary than to emphasise the ability of speculative funds to stabilise the rate of interest against considerable disturbances. Which is effectively what Keynes did.

It should, however, be added in conclusion that the Keynes theory would be less important than it is if this were the only limiting case on which it threw light. The interest-mechanism may fail to operate, not only because the rate of interest may itself be insensitive to real changes, but also because (again over certain ranges and in certain circumstances) saving and investment may themselves be insensitive to changes in the interest rate. A Keynesian (non-classical) situation may arise, not only because the *LL* curve may be horizontal over certain stretches, but because the (short-period) *SI* curve may, over certain stretches, be vertical. A vertical *SI* curve, impinging upon a sloping *LL* curve, would show the rate of interest rising when investment increased; but the rise in interest would be a matter of mere financial interest, without real effects. It is because of their desire to cover this case, quite as much as the other, that modern Keynesians are convinced that Keynes, unlike the 'classics', did make the right approach. It is true that when the two theories are properly understood, and fully worked out, they largely overlap; but they do not overlap all the way, and when they fail to do so, the Keynes theory has the wider coverage.

1.7 The Real Balance Effect*

Professor Hicks' recent 'unorthodox' review[1] of my *Money, Interest and Prices* is actually confined to the two chapters (XIII and XIV) of this book which present an interpretation of the Keynesian theory of employment and contrast it with the corresponding classical theory. Professor Hicks' article is essentially an extended criticism of this interpretation. The purpose of the present note is to show, however, that this criticism stems from a failure to understand the main proposition on which my interpretation is based.

Ironically enough, the point at which Professor Hicks goes astray is in the proper extension of his own well-known *IS–LL* diagram of the Keynesian system to a set of assumptions slightly more general than that considered by

* Don Patinkin, 'Keynesian Economics Rehabilitated: A Rejoinder to Professor Hicks', *Econ. J.*, 1959.

[1] 'A Rehabilitation of "Classical" Economics?', *Economic Journal*, Vol. LXVII (1957), 278–89; henceforth referred to as 'Hicks (1957)'. The adjective just quoted is from p. 278. [See Reading 1.6—Ed.]

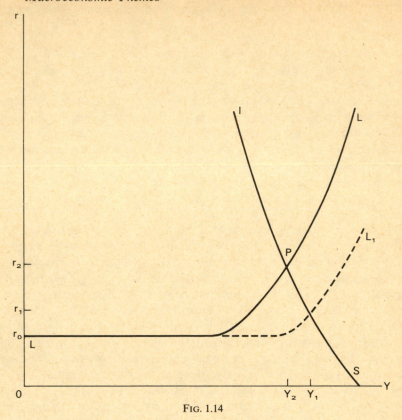

Fig. 1.14

him in his original celebrated article.[2] This diagram is presented in Figure 1.14
—with the difference that Y represents *real*, and not *money*, income. (Since we
shall assume throughout the following analysis that wages and prices move
proportionately, it makes no difference whether we measure real quantities in
terms of price units or wage units.) *IS* represents all combinations of
interest (r) and real national income (Y) for which savings equals investment.
LL represents all combinations of r and Y—as of a given price level and
quantity of money—for which the demand for money is equal to its supply.
The equilibrium position of our economy is given by the intersection of these
curves at P. If prices and wages are absolutely rigid—and if Y_1 represents the
full-employment level of income—the economy will remain permanently at
the level of 'unemployment equilibrium' Y_2.

Let us now drop the assumption of absolute price rigidity and assume

[2] 'Mr. Keynes and the "Classics",' *Econometrica*, Vol. V (1937), as reprinted in *Readings in
Income Distribution* (ed. W. Fellner and B. F. Haley, Philadelphia, Pa., 1946), pp. 461–76;
henceforth referred to as 'Hicks (1937)'. [See Reading 1.2—Ed.]
    I have explained elsewhere (*Money*, p. 229, footnote 21) why the *LL* curve should not be drawn
with a left-hand horizontal segment. Nevertheless, it is drawn here as Hicks draws it in order not
to complicate the present discussion with other issues.

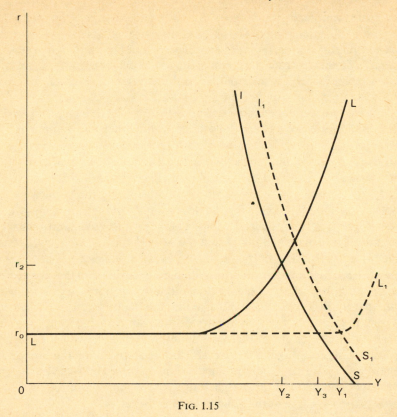

FIG. 1.15

instead that the pressure of unemployment at Y_2 causes wages and prices to fall simultaneously. This causes an increase in the real value of the public's money holdings. Let us first assume—in accordance with the usual Keynesian approach—that this increase affects the system only through its prior effect on the excess demand for money and thereby on the interest rate. Then the fall in the price level has no effect on the *IS* curve in Figure 1.14. On the other hand, it causes a downwards and rightwards shift in the *LL* curve. In Keynesian terminology, at any given level of real income, the real transactions demand is fixed; hence the public will agree to hold the increased real quantity of money only at a rate of interest sufficiently low to increase the speculative demand appropriately.[3]

In Figure 1.14 this process is assumed to bring the economy to its full-employment level: *LL* shifts rightwards to LL_1 so that it intersects *IS* at Y_1. In economic terms the decline in the price level continues until interest has fallen sufficiently (from r_2 to r_1) to stimulate investment and discourage savings to such an extent that they are equal at the full-employment income Y_1.

In Figure 1.15, on the other hand, we have the oft-cited case of the 'liquidity

<hr>

[3] Cf Keynes, *General Theory*, pp. 232, 266–7 and 298.

trap'. (For the moment, the dashed I_1S_1 curve here should be ignored.) Even when the rate of interest has fallen to its minimum level, r_0, the level of demand in the commodity market (as represented by IS) is not high enough to generate full employment. Instead, unemployment to an extent measured by Y_1-Y_3 remains in the system. It follows that in these circumstances no automatic force exists to extract the system from its state of unemployment.

So far we have remained more or less within the analytical framework of Hicks' 1937 article and its later elaboration at the hands of Modigliani.[4] But let us now depart from this framework and assume that an increase in the real quantity of money in the system has a *direct* effect on the level of demand for commodities—in addition to the indirect effect through the interest rate already noted above. In other words, let us investigate the implications for Keynesian economics of the 'Pigou effect'—or, to use terminology which I now find preferable, of the 'real-balance effect in the commodity market'.[5] Then, in addition to the rightward shift it causes in the LL curve, the decrease in the price level generated by the unemployment which exists at the point Y_3 will also cause a rightward shift in the IS surve: for the greater real quantity of money will *increase* the demand for consumption goods—which means that it will *decrease* the level of savings out of any given level of income, and thus require a higher rate of interest in order to bring it (savings) into equality with investment at that income level. Hence even in the 'liquidity trap' case of Figure 1.15 there is no reason for the system to remain stuck at the income level Y_3. Instead, the continued fall in the price and wage levels can—in principle—shift the IS curve rightwards to I_1S_1 in Figure 1.15, so that it intersects the LL curve at the full-employment level Y_1.

This is the argument presented in detail in Chapters XIII–XIV of my book. Unfortunately, Professor Hicks misses its main point. For in his present article—just as in that of 1937—an increase in the real quantity of money is assumed to affect the workings of the economy only through its effect in shifting the LL curve rightwards; there is no recognition of its effect on the IS curve.[6] Needless to say, this omission precludes Professor Hicks from correctly evaluating the argument he is attempting to review. Correspondingly, it leads him to the erroneous conclusion that the validity of the automatic full-employment mechanism depends on the shape of the LL curve —and that if this curve is horizontal in its left-hand segment, then the return to full employment cannot be assured.[7] As has been explained again above—and

[4] F. Modigliani, 'Liquidity Preference and the Theory of Interest and Money', *Econometrica*, Vol. XII (1944), pp. 45–88. [See Reading 1.4—Ed.]

[5] *Money*, p. 21, footnote 11. In a recent article, E. J. Mishan has claimed that these two effects are different ('A Fallacy in the Interpretation of the Cash Balance Effect', *Economica*, Vol. XXV (1958)). It seems to me, however, that Mishan's argument is based on misunderstanding of the nature of the demand function. An attempt to derive such a function from microeconomic analysis (something Mishan does not do) would rapidly make clear that there is only one effect.

[6] Hicks (1957), p. 281, especially footnote 1, where Hicks identifies the real-balance effect of my analysis with the shift in the LL curve! [p. 61, n. 3, above.]

[7] Hicks (1957), pp. 287–8. [p. 64–65 above—Ed.]

as should have been clear from Chapters XIII–XIV of the book that was under review—this just is not so.[8,9]

We now come to a related question: If the real-balance effect can—in principle—restore the economy to a full-employment position, what happens to the Keynesian Revolution? The answer—as I see it—is that the Revolution goes on—though on a somewhat different plane. In particular, the interest of Keynesian economics shifts from 'unemployment equilibrium' (which is the concern of the Hicks 1937 article) to unemployment *dis*equilibrium. And the main message of Keynesian economics becomes that the automatic adjustment process of the market (even with the real-balance effect—and even when supplemented by monetary policy) is too unreliable to serve as a practical basis of a full-employment policy. In other words, though the real-balance effect must be taken account of in our *theoretical* analysis, it is too weak—and, in some cases (due to adverse expectations) too perverse—to fulfil a significant role in our *policy* considerations.

In a way, this shift of interest actually strengthens the Revolution: for it makes it independent of such special assumptions as absolute wage rigidities and the existence of a 'liquidity trap'. Both these assumptions aggravate Keynesian unemployment; but they are not necessary for the validity of Keynes' argument as conceived here. Thus the foregoing interpretation really attributes much more general validity to Keynesian economics than that attributed by the Hicks–Modigliani interpretation.[10]

There is a further point that should be mentioned with reference to the 'liquidity trap'. This has frequently been presented as an economic phenomenon: as due to the shape of the demand curve for money. Actually, though, it is a political phenomenon. Monetary authorities cannot drive the rate of interest below the 'minimum' rate corresponding to the 'trap' because to do so would mean that they would become 'the sole debt-holder—and, by that very fact, the sole lender—in the economy'; an outcome completely at variance with the political motivation of monetary policy in a free economy.[11]

[8] Indeed—though this is unfortunately overlooked by Professor Hicks in his review article (pp. 279–80)—my original argument in these chapters makes use of his *IS–LL* diagram—properly modified. This is explicitly pointed out in *Money*, pp. 227 and 229 (notes 19 and 21, respectively).

[9] It should be emphasised that Hicks' position cannot be salvaged by assuming that the *IS* curve represents the 'savings = investment' condition with the real-balance effect solved out by substitution from the liquidity-preference equation. For the *IS* curve corresponding to such a 'solved-out' equation would not have the uniformly negative slope that is such a crucial element of Professor Hicks' argument. In particular, it can be shown that such an *IS* curve becomes horizontal at the minimum rate of interest. This is consistent—as it must be—with the shift of the *IS* curve to I_1S_1 in Figure 1.15.

[10] This and the preceding paragraph summarise very briefly the discussions in *Money*, pp. 233–40. The main points of this discussion were already presented some years ago in my 'Price Flexibility and Full Employment', *American Economic Review*, Vol. XXXVIII (1948), pp. 562–4.

[11] *Money*, pp. 248–9. Keynes, of course, did not believe that the limitation of the 'liquidity trap' had ever actually been confronted (*General Theory*, p. 207). In this context it might be noted that even during the British 'cheap-money' episode of 1931–39 the monetary authorities never acquired more than 15% of outstanding government securities (see E. Nevin, *The Mechanism of Cheap Money* (Cardiff, 1955), p. 180). A similar statement holds for the Federal Reserve

As indicated, the three preceding paragraphs summarise views elaborated in the book that was under review by Professor Hicks. I repeat them here because I gather from Professor Hicks' article that he would now be ready to subscribe to them.[12] Unfortunately, however, he states this agreement in such a way as to create the impression that he is actually in disagreement![13] This is a pity. For these issues have now been argued for so long that it would be a great help to all concerned (as well as a great saving of time and paper) if it were to be realised that in actual fact substantial agreement has been reached upon them.[14]

---

authorities in the United States (see *Banking and Monetary Statistics* (Washington, D.C.: Board of Governors of the Federal Reserve System, 1943), p. 512, Table 149). In view of this fact—and the general deflationary situation existing in the thirties—it is difficult to believe that the monetary authorities then could not have driven interest down even further by increasing their holdings of government securities. Cf. also Nevin, *op. cit.*, pp. 73–4, 96–8, and F. W. Paish, 'Cheap Money Policy', *Economica*, Vol. XIV (1947), pp. 167–8.

[12] Hicks (1957), pp. 288–9 [pp. 64–65 above—Ed.].

[13] As a case in point, the reader might find it instructive to compare the following two passages —the first of which has just been referred to in the preceding paragraph:

'... if the government is willing to pursue a sufficiently vigorous open-market policy—one that encompasses private as well as government bonds—there is no reason why it should not be able to drive interest down as' low as it wants. But things are not quite so simple. By driving interest down below the 'minimum' rate the government also drives all private individuals out of the bond market. In brief, it succeeds in pushing interest down below the level at which 'almost everyone prefers cash to holding a debt' only by itself becoming the sole debt-holder—and, by that very fact, the sole lender—in the economy. It thus negates the whole meaning of a policy designed to enable government to influence the overall level of activity in the economy with a minimum of direct intervention. Thus there is a limitation on the ability of monetary policy to reduce interest. But it is a limitation which originates in political, and not economic, factors. Furthermore, it is highly unlikely that this limitation has ever yet endangered the efficacy of monetary policy' (*Money*, pp. 248–9).

'When it comes to this crucial point [i.e. the driving of interest below its "minimum" level] it is a pity that Patinkin does not argue his case more fully; in particular, it is a pity that he does not test it by seeing how it looks when applied to less schematic models, which get a little closer to reality. If he had done so, I believe he would have seen that his "equilibrium" required not only that the monetary authority should buy up all the "bonds" which were being used as money substitutes, but that it should go to the point of superseding all the financial intermediaries—banks and other financial institutions—transactions between which regulate the whole system of interest rates which exist in reality.... The most that Patinkin can claim to have established is that the rate of interest might be forced still lower if that financial system were abolished, and the supply of funds to business were made directly by government. Whether or not that is the case—how far such a system is itself reconcilable with Patinkin's other assumptions—does not, in my view, affect the main issue. The effective answer to Patinkin is that in the applications we want to make we do not normally desire to proceed to such extremes' (Hicks (1957), p. 288).

[14] Some other minor errors and misunderstandings in Professor Hicks' article may be briefly indicated here. (1) His implications to the contrary notwithstanding, the dichotomy he refers to on pp. 283 and 284 (between the rate of interest and money national income?) has nothing at all to do with the invalid dichotomy between relative and absolute prices (in a full-employment model *without* a rate of interest!) described in my book (pp. 107–8). (2) Hicks' assertion that the temporary lowering of the rate of interest (after a monetary expansion) was considered by classical economists to be the result of 'forced savings' (p. 283) completely ignores the detailed references to the literature (assembled in Chapter XV: 1 and Note J of my book), which show that this temporary lowering is the direct implication of the loanable-funds theory with which classical economists worked—and has nothing at all to do with 'forced savings'. (3) Furthermore, Hicks also ignores the citations reproduced in Note J, which show that such economists as Mill,

Nicholson, Wicksell and Pigou were quite ready to concede that 'forced savings' could have a *permanent* effect on the interest rate, and not only a temporary one. (4) Finally, Hicks implies that the transactions demand is independent of the rate of interest—and that the validity of the quantity theory depends on the demand for money being independent of the rate of interest (pp. 284 and 287 (line 11)). Both of these statements are incorrect (*Money*, pp. 78, 86–95 and 172–6).

2. Consumption

Introductory Note

The dependence of consumption on income was, as we have seen, a fundamental proposition of the *General Theory*. The precise form of this dependence has, however, been the subject of protracted (and continuing) debate. Keynes's 'fundamental psychological law' implied that the marginal propensity to consume was higher than the average propensity to consume, but less than one. Despite the many qualifications which Keynes mentioned,[1] most 'Keynesian' writers initially adopted some simple version of this relationship. These simple models soon ran into trouble. First, the collection of national accounts data and of family budget data suggested that the consumption/income relationship differed according as it was taken to apply to long-run changes, to short-run changes, or to cross-section differences in family incomes.[2]

Early national income studies suggested that there had been considerable stability in the average propensity to consume over the long run, if cyclical changes were ignored. Kuznets, for example, attempted to iron out cyclical changes by taking averages over overlapping decades between 1869 and 1938, and found that except during the Great Depression the ratio of consumption to income in real terms had only varied between about 0·84 and 0·89.[3] Kuznets commented that 'while the trend in the share of the flow of goods to consumers is upwards and in the share of net capital formation downward, neither is pronounced unless we include the last two decades, which were affected by the 1929–32 depression and its aftermath... [The change] is rather minor, and the underlying estimates are not sufficiently precise to warrant confidence in such small changes.'[4]

Cyclical changes could probably be explained in terms of lags in the adjustment to changes in income, as Keynes had suggested.[5] Far more difficult was the reconciliation of this apparent long-run constancy of the savings ratio

[1] *General Theory*, Chapters 8 and 9.

[2] It should be borne in mind that in this chapter we deal with the consumption function conceived as the relationship between personal consumption and personal disposable income. The relationship between national income and personal disposable income may be quite complex and is obviously important in a complete macroeconomic model: this relationship is discussed, *inter alia*, in Chapter 11.

[3] S. Kuznets, *National Income: a Summary of Findings* (New York: National Bureau of Economic Research, 1946), Table 16, p. 53.

[4] Op. cit., pp. 52–3.

[5] *General Theory*, p. 97; see also T. M. Brown, 'Habit Persistence and Lags in Consumer Behaviour', *Econometrica*, vol. 20, 1952.

with the observation of savings ratios which rose sharply with income in cross-section analysis, and a number of hypotheses were advanced which attempted such a reconciliation.

Secondly, it is noted that the simple consumption theories were no more than rough descriptions of observed behaviour, and lacked a solid theoretical foundation. In particular, it became evident that once the role of saving in increasing *wealth* was recognized, the theory of consumption would have to allow for interrelations between consumption, income, and wealth, rather than simply between consumption and income.

Of the post-war attempts to re-specify the consumption function so as to 'explain' on the one hand both cross-section and time-series behaviour, and on the other hand both short- and long-run changes in the relation between consumption and income, the Permanent Income Hypothesis introduced by Friedman [see Reading 2.1] and the Life-Cycle Hypothesis introduced by Modigliani [see Reading 2.2] have probably had most influence.[6]

Another notable attempt was made by Duesenberry,[7] who accounted for the apparent discrepancy between time-series and cross-section data by suggesting that at any point in time, an individual's propensity to consume depends on his position in the income scale (that is, on his income relative to others) rather than on the absolute level of his income.[8] Thus although the relatively rich will have a higher propensity to save than the relatively poor, over time, as the entire level of incomes rises and provided that the 'shape' of the income distribution does not change, the aggregate marginal propensity to save will remain constant and equal to the average propensity. Finally, cyclical changes in the propensity to save can be explained in terms of inertia (strictly, in Duesenberry's account, by the dependence of consumption on previous peak income, so that consumption remains buoyant in times of cyclically falling incomes).

Friedman's Permanent Income Hypothesis (PIH) [Reading 2.1] makes variations in the observed consumption/income ratio depend on differences between actual income and some concept of 'normal' income—in this case called 'permanent' income. Permanent income reflects the income derived from 'non-human wealth' (capital assets) and from 'human wealth' (earning capacity), while the remainder of actual, or 'measured', income comprises all

[6] The Life-Cycle Hypothesis was first applied to cross-section data by F. Modigliani and R. Brumberg in 'Utility of Analysis and the Consumption Function: An Interpretation of Cross-Section Data', in K. Kurihara (ed.), *Post Keynesian Economics* (London: George Allen and Unwin, 1955). The application to time-series data was carried out by the same authors in a contemporary but unpublished paper, 'Utility Analysis and Aggregate Consumption Functions: An Attempt at Integration', and Reading 2.2 is taken from a later paper by F. Modigliani and A. Ando which recapitulates the argument of this unpublished paper.

[7] J. Duesenberry, *Income, Saving and the Theory of Consumer Behaviour* (Cambridge, Mass.: Harvard University Press, 1949).

[8] The justification for this behaviour is sociological rather than economic-theoretical. Cf. the nation of poverty as a 'relative' concept: W. G. Runciman, *Relative Deprivation and Social Justice* (London: Routledge and Kegan Paul, 1966).

other income elements, attributable essentially to random fluctuations of various kinds. Consumption, analogously, comprises a permanent component which is determined by permanent income, and a random component which is termed 'transitory' consumption. Permanent consumption is taken to be a constant fraction, k, of permanent income, the value of k for each consumer depending on a variety of factors including wealth, rates of interest, tastes and preferences. On the assumption that transitory components of income and consumption are uncorrelated with each other and with permanent components, it is shown (pp. 84–86) that a cross-section of consumers will display a marginal propensity to consume, b, which is less than k (assumed the same for all consumers). This observed marginal propensity to consume is in fact a fraction P_y of k, where P_y is the ratio of the variance of permanent income to that of total income and is necessarily less than one.[9]

The economic explanation of this downward bias in the observed MPC is essentially that higher income groups will include a number of people with positive transitory components of income. On average (assuming that transitory consumption is random) these individuals' consumption will be based on their permanent income, which is lower than their measured income. The top measured income groups will thus be characterized by relatively high measured saving. The average difference in observed consumption for a given difference in measured income, b, will be the fraction of the income difference which is permanent, P_y, multiplied by the proportion of this difference in permanent income which is consumed, k.

The application by Friedman and others of the PIH to time-series statistics of income and consumption depends on the specification of a further hypothesis which explains how permanent income responds to changes over time in actual income. The most obvious hypothesis, suggested by Friedman and almost universally adopted in subsequent empirical work, is to assume that permanent income depends partly on current income and partly on previous periods' incomes. The simplest version of such dependence assumes that the weights attaching to previous periods' incomes decline as we go back in time. This gives a relationship of the form:

$$Y_t^p = \alpha(Y_t + \lambda Y_{t-1} + \lambda^2 Y_{t-2} + \ldots)$$

where Y_t^p is permanent income in period t, Y_t is actual income, and λ is less than one. If we further assume that these weights sum to unity (so that in a long-run equilibrium in which income was constant, $Y_t^p = Y_t$), then α is equal to $(1-\lambda)$.[10] Combining this with the PIH that $C_t = k Y_t^p$ (ignoring random transitory consumption) we have:

$$C_t = k(1-\lambda)(Y_t + \lambda Y_{t-1} + \lambda^2 Y_{t-2} + \ldots).$$

[9] Econometricians will recognize this as formally equivalent to estimation bias due to the problem of 'errors in variables'.
[10] Since the sum of the weights is $\alpha(1 + \lambda + \lambda^2 + \ldots) = \alpha/(1-\lambda)$.

Lagging this relationship by one time-period and multiplying by λ:

$$\lambda C_{t-1} = k(1-\lambda)(\lambda Y_{t-1} + \lambda^2 Y_{t-2} + \ldots).$$

And on subtraction:

$$C_t - \lambda C_{t-1} = k(1-\lambda) Y_t$$

(since all lagged income terms cancel), or:

$$C_t = k(1-\lambda) Y_t + \lambda C_{t-1}.$$

The implication of this form of the PIH for aggregate time-series analysis is thus simply that consumption in any period will depend partly on current income and partly on the previous periods' level of consumption. This results from the assumption that permanent income depends partly on current income and partly on previous periods' incomes (sometimes referred to as the 'adaptive expectations' model of the determination of permanent income). There are important implications for the statistical testing of the PIH using time-series data, for it is clear that it is virtually impossible to distinguish this hypothesis from the much vaguer hypothesis that consumption will depend partly on current income and partly on inertia or habit,[11] represented by lagged consumption, or from the 'generalized Duesenberry hypothesis' that it will depend partly on previous periods' incomes as well as on current income.

A further implication of consumption functions of this type is that the actual propensity to save of an economy will depend partly on the rate of growth of income, for the faster this rate of growth and the more sluggish the response of consumption to changes in income, the lower will the ratio of current consumption to current income become. Thus even if k were equal to one, so that in stationary equilibrium the savings ratio would be zero, a rate of growth of income of 5 per cent per annum and a value of 0.5 for λ would give a savings ratio of 4.5 per cent, while if λ took the (not unrealistic) value of 0.8, the savings ratio would rise to 16 per cent.[12]

---

[11] This suggestion can be found in the *General Theory*, p. 97: 'For a man's habitual standard of life usually has the first claim on his income, and he is apt to save the difference which discovers itself between his actual income and the expense of his habitual standards; or, if he does adjust his expenditure to changes in his income, he will over short periods do so imperfectly.'

[12] These figures are obtained as follows:

$$C_t = (1-\lambda) Y_t + \lambda C_{t-1}, \quad \text{if } k = 1.$$

Thus

$$\frac{C_t}{Y_t} = (1-\lambda) + \frac{\lambda C_{t-1}}{Y_t}$$

$$= (1-\lambda) + \frac{\lambda . C_{t-1}}{Y_{t-1}} . \frac{Y_{t-1}}{Y_t}$$

$$= (1-\lambda) + \frac{\lambda C_{t-1}}{Y_{t-1}} . \frac{1}{1+g},$$

The Life-Cycle Hypothesis (LCH) [Reading 2.2] results from an attempt to derive an aggregate consumption function from the conventional micro-economic analysis of consumer choice. It is supposed that individuals derive utility from their lifetime streams of consumption and from the bequeathing of assets to their heirs. This utility is to be maximized subject to the constraint of the stream of expected earnings, and the function of saving (or dissaving) is then to cope with situations in which current actual income is not equal to the optimum level of current consumption. More formally, if the *proportion* of his total resources which a consumer plans to consume at some future date is determined only by his tastes and not by the size of his resources (and if the receipt and leaving of legacies are neglected), then at any time t the consumption of any individual will be proportional to the present value of his total resources—that is, to his net worth carried over from the previous period *plus* current income *plus* the discounted value of future income receipts. If certain simplifying assumptions are made—that the consumption functions for individuals of the same age are identical, and that the age-structure of the population and the relative distributions of income, net worth, and expected future income are all constant—this relationship may be aggregated over all consumers to give an aggregate consumption function in which consumption depends on net worth, current income, and expected income.

There remains the empirical problem of measuring expected income. From a theoretical point of view, however, what is perhaps the most significant feature of the LCH aggregate consumption function is the substantial reduction in the degree of dependence of consumption on current income. Current income is now only one variable in the consumption function, so that its direct influence is immediately reduced. A rise in current income will, of course, have indirect effects on consumption, both through any induced change in expected future income and (for future periods) through the cumulative effect of higher saving on net worth, but these indirect effects are likely to be relatively weak. So far as cross-section implications are

---

where g is the growth rate of income. In equilibrium,

$$\frac{C_t}{Y_t} = \frac{C_{t-1}}{Y_{t-1}} = 1-s,$$

where s is the savings ratio. Thus:

$$1-s = 1-\lambda+\lambda(1-s)\frac{1}{1+g}.$$

from which

$$s = \frac{\lambda g}{1-\lambda+g}.$$

Further,

$$\frac{\delta s}{\delta g} = \frac{\lambda(1-\lambda)}{(1-\lambda+g)^2} > 0 \quad \text{for} \quad 0 < \lambda < 1,$$

and

$$\frac{\delta s}{\delta \lambda} = \frac{g(1-g)}{(1-\lambda+g)^2} > 0 \quad \text{for} \quad 0 < g < 1,$$

showing that the savings ratio varies positively with the rate of growth of income, and with λ.

concerned, since the upper income groups in any observed income distribution are likely to include a disproportionate number of people whose incomes have temporarily risen, the observed saving propensities of these groups will tend to be above average—and vice versa for low income groups. This explanation of the increase in the savings propensity with rising income in cross-section analysis is very similar to that given by the PIH—in the latter case, temporary increases in income have little or no effect on permanent income and hence on consumption; in the LCH, such increases have only small effects, either directly or via their effects on expected income. As in Duesenberry's theory, the assumption of the LCH that there are no radical shifts in the pattern of income distribution means that this explanation of cross-section data is perfectly consistent with a constant aggregate saving propensity in the long run. And it may be supposed that 'sluggishness' in adjusting notions of expected future income when cyclical changes in actual income occur is again the explanation of cyclical movements in the saving propensity. Finally, this same sluggishness means that in a growing economy there will, just as in the case of the PIH, be a positive relationship between the rate of growth and the savings ratio.

So far as the pure theory of consumption was concerned, the 'new' theories of the consumption function paid little more than lip-service to the dynamic interconnections of saving and the accumulation of wealth. Spiro [Reading 2.3] takes explicit account of this relationship, arguing that saving will take place only when desired wealth exceeds actual wealth. In long-run stationary equilibrium, therefore, net saving will be zero. Positive saving will take place only if there is a secular upward movement in income. Formally (this is a slight simplification of Spiro's argument), suppose that consumption depends both on wealth and on current and lagged income:

$$C_t = \alpha W_t + \beta_0 Y_t + \beta_1 Y_{t-1} + \beta_2 Y_{t-2} + \ldots$$

$$= \alpha W_t + \sum_{i=0}^{\infty} \beta_i Y_{t-i}.$$

Now wealth is accumulated past saving:

$$W_t = \sum_{i=1}^{\infty} S_{t-i}.$$

And, by definition, saving is the difference between income and consumption:

$$S_t = Y_t - C_t.$$

Thus the current level of wealth is equal to the previous period's wealth plus the previous period's saving:

$$W_t = W_{t-1} + Y_{t-1} - C_{t-1}$$

or

$$W_t = W_{t-1} + Y_{t-1} - \alpha W_{t-1} - \sum_{i=0}^{\infty} \beta_i Y_{t-i}.$$

Thus current wealth can be expressed solely in terms of past wealth and incomes. By repeating this substitution for past wealth, current wealth can be expressed solely in terms of past incomes; in general:

$$W_t = \sum_{i=0}^{\infty} \gamma_i Y_{t-i}$$

where the γ_i are unknown weights. Hence the consumption function can be written

$$C_t = \alpha W_t + \sum \beta_i Y_{t-i}$$
$$= \alpha \sum \gamma_i Y_{t-i} + \sum \beta_i Y_{t-i}$$

or $$C_t = \sum \delta_i Y_{t-i} \qquad (1)$$

where, again, the δ_i are unknown weights. The crucial point is that the sum of these weights must be equal to one. If income remains constant and if $\sum \delta_i$ is less than one, saving is taking place and therefore wealth and hence consumption are increasing. But from eqn (1), with constant income consumption must be constant. Hence $\sum \delta_i$ cannot be less than one. By a parallel argument, $\sum \delta_i$ cannot be greater than one. Hence $\sum \delta_i$ must be equal to one.

If it is assumed that the weights decline geometrically, then, given that they sum to one, the consumption function reduces (see above) to

$$C_t = (1-\lambda) Y_t + \lambda C_{t-1}$$

leaving only one parameter, λ, to be estimated.[13] As we have already seen, and as Spiro points out, this leaves the savings ratio dependent on the rate of growth of income. By making consumption depend on wealth and by noting that wealth is accumulated saving, Spiro thus provides a justification for the assumption that in long-run stationary equilibrium, the propensity to consume would be unity, while in a growing economy, the savings ratio will depend (given λ) only on the rate of growth of income.

Clower and Johnson [Reading 2.4] attempt to put the theory of the consumption function on firmer theoretical ground by starting from a micro-dynamic account of household decision-making. At any moment of time, the basic decision is whether to consume or to save, but since saving is an addition to wealth, this is really a decision between consuming and attaining a desired level of wealth. Formally, households maximize a utility function of the form $U = U(C, W)$, where C and W are desired levels of consumption and wealth, subject to the constraint that planned consumption is equal to

[13] This can be done by writing

$$C_t - Y_t = \lambda(C_{t-1} - Y_t)$$

or $$Y_t - C_t = \lambda(Y_t - C_{t-1}),$$

i.e. $$S_t = \lambda(Y_t - Y_{t-1} + S_{t-1})$$
$$= \lambda(\Delta Y_t + S_{t-1}).$$

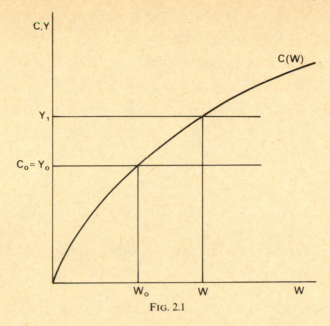

FIG. 2.1

the difference between actual and desired wealth (that is, at a particular instant, lower consumption represents increased wealth). Given indifference curves between desired wealth and desired consumption, consumption is thus an increasing function of actual wealth (for example, for a given desired level of wealth, consumption can be higher the higher is the level of actual wealth). This is illustrated in Fig. 2.2.

The increase in actual wealth is represented by saving, or income minus consumption. In general, income too will be an increasing function of wealth given a positive rate of return on assets. At the point at which the desired level of wealth is reached, saving becomes zero and consumption is equal to income. This equilibrium will be stable if the slope of the consumption-wealth locus (the marginal propensity to consume wealth, MPCW) is greater than the marginal rate of return on wealth.

Suppose, for simplicity, that the rate of return on wealth is zero, so that the stability condition is satisfied for all positive values of the MPCW, and consider an increase in income from Y_0 to Y_1 in Fig. 2.1.

In the initial situation, suppose that equilibrium had been reached so that $C_0 = Y_0$ at the desired level of wealth W_0. If the new level of income Y_1 were sustained, saving would take place until the new equilibrium was reached, with $\hat{C}_1 = Y_1$ at the new desired level of wealth $\hat{W}_1$. In the meanwhile, however, the household will be out of equilibrium as the adjustment is made. Consider the situation after one time-period:[14]

[14] We work in discrete time-periods rather than Clower and Johnson's continuous time to preserve comparability with the other Readings.

1. The increase in wealth is equal to income minus consumption:

$$W_1 - W_0 = Y_1 - C_1.$$

2. In the new equilibrium, if the MPCW is a:

$$\hat{C}_1 = Y_1 = a\hat{W}.$$

3. Meanwhile, consumption is the same function of actual wealth:

$$C_1 = aW_1.$$

4. Thus

$$W_1 - W_0 = a\hat{W} - aW_1$$

$$W_1(1+a) = W_0 + a\hat{W} = W_0 + (1+a)\hat{W} - \hat{W}$$

$$W_1 = \hat{W} - \frac{1}{1+a}(\hat{W} - W_0).$$

5. Since, in the old equilibrium, $C_0 = Y_0 = aW_0$, in the new equilibrium $\hat{C}_1 = Y_1 = a\hat{W}$, and in period one $C_1 = aW_1$, we have:

$$C_1 = a\left\{\hat{W} - \frac{1}{1+a}(\hat{W} - W_0)\right\}$$

$$= a\left\{\frac{Y_1}{a} - \frac{1}{1+a}\left(\frac{Y_1}{a} - \frac{Y_0}{a}\right)\right\}$$

or

$$C_1 = Y_1 - \frac{1}{1+a}(Y_1 - Y_0)$$

which is the 'consumption function' implied.

Consider now the application of this function to a cross-section of households in period 1. The estimated MPC will be

$$b = \frac{\sum c_1 y_1}{\sum y_1^2}$$

(using lower-case letters to denote deviations from means). On substituting the 'consumption function'

$$b = \frac{\sum(y_1 - a'(y_1 - y_0))y_1}{\sum y_1^2}$$

(where $a' = 1/(1+a)$)

$$= \frac{\sum(y_1 - a'y_1 + a'y_0)y_1}{\sum y_1^2}$$

$$= 1 - a' + a'\frac{\sum y_0 y_1}{\sum y_1^2}$$

$$= 1 - \frac{1}{1+a}\left(1 - \frac{s_0}{s_1} \cdot r\right)$$

(where
$$\frac{s_0}{s_1} = \frac{\sqrt{\sum y_0^2}}{\sqrt{\sum y_1^2}},$$

the ratio of the standard deviations of incomes in periods 0 and 1, and

$$r = \frac{\sum y_0 y_1}{\sqrt{\sum y_0^2}\sqrt{\sum y_1^2}}$$

is the correlation between households' incomes in the two periods).

In a stationary state in which aggregate income is not growing, s_0/s_1 will be equal to one, while r will be lower the greater is the variability of individual households' incomes.

Thus we can write

$$b = 1 - \frac{1}{1+a}(1-r)$$

from which it follows that

$$\frac{\delta b}{\delta a} = \frac{1-r}{(1+a)^2} \geqslant 0$$

$$\frac{\delta b}{\delta r} = \frac{1}{1+a} > 0.$$

Thus the observed MPC will be lower (a) the lower is a, the MPCW, (b) the lower is r.

If we assume that there is a correlation between income and wealth, and if the MPCW is lower for higher income groups (the 'negative curvature' hypothesis), the observed MPC out of income will decline with income. Also, the more unstable are household incomes (the lower is r), the lower will be the observed MPC. Both observations are consistent with the evidence from budget studies, and the connection between income instability and low MPC is also consistent with the evidence adduced by Friedman and others that groups such as farmers and the self-employed tend to have low MPCs.

Clower and Johnson thus show that given (a) that consumers maximize utility derived from their flow of consumption and their stock of wealth, (b) that there is a tendency towards stable equilibrium with given income and no saving (that is, no addition to wealth), and (c) that the propensity to consume out of wealth declines with rising wealth,[15] cross-section data and differences between variable income and stable income groups can be explained. The approach has the merit of simplicity: consumers possess indifference maps between consumption and wealth, and there is no recourse to nebulous concepts of 'permanent' or 'normal' income.

On closer examination, however, it is clear that there are no new im-

[15] It should perhaps be pointed out that this last assumption rests on no firmer theoretical foundation than Keynes's 'psychological law', concerning the relation between consumption and income.

plications for the behaviour of consumption in relation to income over time. We have, in any period t, that $C_t = aW_t$.

Now
$$W_t - W_{t-1} = Y_t - C_t$$

or
$$\frac{C_t}{a} - \frac{C_{t-1}}{a} = Y_t - C_t$$

from which
$$C_t = \frac{a}{1+a} Y_t + \frac{1}{1+a} C_{t-1}.$$

This is, of course, the familiar form of the consumption function with consumption depending on current income and lagged consumption; the co-efficients sum to unity, reflecting the fact that in stationary equilibrium a desired level of wealth is achieved and there is no saving.

To summarize: despite its central importance in macroeconomic theory, the theory of aggregate consumption behaviour still lacks a really satis-factory underpinning. At the same time, a number of empirical generaliz-ations seem to have been established. First, consumption depends only rather weakly on current income. Rather, it depends either on wealth or on some notion of normal income, both of which will be only marginally affected by short-run changes in actual income. Secondly, most satisfactory versions of the time-series consumption function relate the current level of consumption to current income and to lagged consumption. When this formulation is adopted, it becomes virtually impossible to distinguish empirically between several apparently competing hypotheses. Thirdly, cross-section data must be explained, at least in part, by the variability of household incomes. Finally, there is a strong presumption that in a long-run stationary equilibrium, savings would be zero; adjustment lags of one sort or another explain cyclical movements in the savings ratio, while the secular growth of real income (and perhaps of population) must be elements in the explanation of the positive aggregate savings ratios which are observed.

2.1 The Permanent Income Hypothesis*
[...]

1. THE INTERPRETATION OF DATA ON THE INCOME AND CONSUMPTION OF CONSUMER UNITS

Let y represent a consumer unit's measured income for some time period, say a year. I propose to treat this income as the sum of two components: a permanent component (y_p), corresponding to the permanent income of the theoretical analysis, and a transitory component (y_t), or
$$y = y_p + y_t.\tag{1}$$

* From M. Friedman, *A Theory of the Consumption Function* (Princeton University Press for National Bureau of Economic Research, 1957), ch. 3.

The permanent component is to be interpreted as reflecting the effect of those factors that the unit regards as determining its capital value or wealth: the nonhuman wealth it owns; the personal attributes of the earners in the unit, such as their training, ability, personality; the attributes of the economic activity of the earners, such as the occupation followed, the location of the economic activity, and so on. It is analogous to the 'expected' value of a probability distribution. The transitory component is to be interpreted as reflecting all 'other' factors, factors that are likely to be treated by the unit affected as 'accidental' or 'chance' occurrences, though they may, from another point of view, be the predictable effect of specifiable forces, for example, cyclical fluctuations in economic activity. In statistical data, the transitory component includes also chance errors of measurement; unfortunately, there is in general no way to separate these from the transitory component as viewed by the consumer unit.

Some of the factors that give rise to transitory components of income are specific to particular consumer units, for example, illness, a bad guess about when to buy or sell, and the like; and, similarly, chance errors of measurement. For any considerable group of consumer units, the resulting transitory components tend to average out, so that if they alone accounted for the discrepancies between permanent and measured income, the mean measured income of the group would equal the mean permanent component, and the mean transitory component would be zero. But not all factors giving rise to transitory components need be of this kind. Some may be largely common to the members of the group, for example, unusually good or bad weather, if the group consists of farmers in the same locality; or a sudden shift in demand for some product, if the group consists of consumer units whose earners are employed in producing this product. If such factors are favorable for any period, the mean transitory component is positive; if they are unfavorable, it is negative. Similarly, a systematic basis in measurement may produce a nonzero mean transitory component in recorded data even though the transitory factors affecting consumer units have a zero effect on the average.

Similarly, let c represent a consumer unit's expenditures for some time period, and let it be regarded as the sum of a permanent component (c_p) and a transitory component (c_t), so that

$$c = c_p + c_t. \tag{2}$$

Again, some of the factors producing transitory components of consumption are specific to particular consumer units, such as unusual sickness, a specially favorable opportunity to purchase, and the like; others affect groups of consumer units in the same way, such as an unusually cold spell, a bountiful harvest, and the like. The effects of the former tend to average out; the effects of the latter produce positive or negative mean transitory components for groups of consumer units; the same is true with chance and systematic errors of measurement.

It is tempting to interpret the permanent components as corresponding to average lifetime values and the transitory components as the difference between such lifetime averages and the measured values in a specific time period. It would, however, be a serious mistake to accept such an interpretation, for two reasons. In the first place, the experience of one unit is itself but a small sample from a more extensive hypothetical universe, so there is no reason to suppose that transitory components average out to zero over the unit's lifetime. In the second place, and more important, it seems neither necessary nor desirable to decide in advance the precise meaning to be attached to 'permanent'. The distinction between permanent and transitory is intended to interpret actual behavior. We are going to treat consumer units *as if* they regarded their income and their consumption as the sum of two such components, and *as if* the relation between the permanent components is the one suggested by our theoretical analysis. The precise line to be drawn between permanent and transitory components is best left to be determined by the data themselves, to be whatever seems to correspond to consumer behavior. [...]

2. A FORMAL STATEMENT OF THE PERMANENT INCOME HYPOTHESIS

In its most general form our hypothesis about the consumption function, which we shall hereafter refer to as the permanent income hypothesis, is given by the three equations:

$$c_p = k(i, w, u)y_p, \tag{3}$$

$$y = y_p + y_t, \tag{1}$$

$$c = c_p + c_t. \tag{2}$$

Equation (3) defines a relation between permanent income and permanent consumption. It specifies that the ratio between them is independent of the size of permanent income but does depend on other variables, in particular: (1) the rate of interest (i) or sets of rates of interest at which the consumer unit can borrow or lend; (2) the relative importance of property and non-property income, symbolized by the ratio of nonhuman wealth to income (w); and (3) the factors symbolized by the portmanteau variable u determining the consumer unit's tastes and preferences for consumption versus additions to wealth. The most significant of the latter factors probably are (a) the number of members of the consumer unit and their characteristics, particularly their ages, and (b) the importance of transitory factors affecting income and consumption, measured, for example, by the 'spread' or standard deviation of the probability distributions of the transitory components relative to the size of the corresponding permanent components. Equations (1) and (2) define the connection between the permanent components and the measured magnitudes.

In this most general form the hypothesis is empty, in the sense that no empirical data could contradict it. Equations (1) and (2) are purely definitional; they add two equations but also two additional unknowns, the transitory components. There are a variety of ways to specialize the hypothesis so that it is capable of being contradicted by observed data. The one I shall use is to specify some of the characteristics of the probability distributions of the transitory components. A particularly simple specification, yet one that seems adequate to explain existing evidence, is to suppose that the transitory components of income and consumption are uncorrelated with one another and with the corresponding permanent components, or

$$\rho_{y_t y_p} = \rho_{c_t c_p} = \rho_{y_t c_t} = 0, \tag{4}$$

where ρ stands for the correlation coefficient between the variables designated by the subscripts.

The assumptions that the first two correlations in (4)—between the permanent and transitory components of income and of consumption—are zero seem very mild and highly plausible. Indeed, by themselves, they have little substantive content and can almost be regarded as simply completing or translating the definitions of transitory and permanent components; the qualitative notion that the transitory component is intended to embody is of an accidental and transient addition to or subtraction from income, which is almost equivalent to saying an addition or subtraction that is not correlated with the rest of income. The merging of errors of measurement with transitory components contributes further to the plausibility that these correlations are zero. [...]

The assumption that the third correlation in (4)—between the transitory components of income and consumption—is zero is a much stronger assumption. It is primarily this assumption that introduces important substantive content into the hypothesis and makes it susceptible of contradiction by a wide range of phenomena capable of being observed. The ultimate test of its acceptability is of course whether such phenomena are in fact observed, and most of what follows is devoted to this question. [...]

A particularly simple special case of the hypothesis arises if, in addition to (4), it is assumed that the mean transitory components of consumption and income are zero, or

$$\mu_{y_t} = \mu_{c_t} = 0, \tag{5}$$

where μ stands for the mean of the variable designated by its subscript. This assumption is eminently reasonable if the probability distribution in question is sufficiently comprehensive. In general, however, we shall want to use conditional probability distributions, for example, the distribution of transitory components in a particular year, or for members of a particular group. In such cases, it will generally be undesirable to assume that (5) holds, just as for the single consumer unit viewed *ex post* it is undesirable to assume that the transitory components themselves are necessarily zero.[...]

3. THE RELATION BETWEEN MEASURED CONSUMPTION AND MEASURED INCOME

Suppose we have observations on consumption and income for a number of consumer units, for all of whom the k of equation (3) can be taken to be numerically the same. Let us proceed, as is usually done in family budget studies, to estimate from these data a relation between consumption and income. For simplicity, let the relation to be estimated be linear, say:

$$c = \alpha + \beta y, \tag{6}$$

where c is to be interpreted as the mean consumption for a given value of y, it being understood that the consumption of individual units deviates from this value by chance. The least squares estimates of α and β (call these a and b), computed from the regression of c on y, are

$$b = \frac{\sum(c-\bar{c})(y-\bar{y})}{\sum(y-\bar{y})^2}, \tag{7}$$

$$a = \bar{c} - b\bar{y}, \tag{8}$$

where $\bar{c}$ and $\bar{y}$ stand for the mean consumption and income respectively of the group of consumer units, and the summation is over the group. In the numerator of the expression for b, replace y and c by the right hand sides of (1) and (2), and $\bar{y}$ and $\bar{c}$ by the corresponding sums of means. This gives

$$\begin{aligned}
\sum(c-\bar{c})(y-\bar{y}) &= \sum(c_p+c_t-\bar{c}_p-\bar{c}_t)(y_p+y_t-\bar{y}_p-\bar{y}_t) \\
&= \sum(c_p-\bar{c}_p)(y_p-\bar{y}_p)+\sum(c_p-\bar{c}_p)(y_t-\bar{y}_t) \\
&\quad +\sum(c_t-\bar{c}_t)(y_p-\bar{y}_p)+\sum(c_t-\bar{c}_t)(y_t-\bar{y}_t).
\end{aligned} \tag{9}$$

From (3)

$$c_p = ky_p.$$

Inserting (3) in (9) yields

$$\begin{aligned}
\sum(c-\bar{c})(y-\bar{y}) &= k\sum(y_p-\bar{y}_p)^2+k\sum(y_p-\bar{y}_p)(y_t-\bar{y}_t) \\
&\quad +\frac{1}{k}\sum(c_t-\bar{c}_t)(c_p-\bar{c}_p)+\sum(c_t-\bar{c}_t)(y_t-\bar{y}_t).
\end{aligned} \tag{10}$$

Given the zero correlations specified in (4), the final three terms will differ from zero only because of sampling fluctuations: they will approach zero as the sample size is increased, or average zero over many similar samples. Since our present concern is not with the problem of statistical estimation but with the interpretation of the results, let us suppose the sample to be sufficiently large so that sampling error can be neglected. In that case

$$b = k \frac{\sum (y_p - \bar{y}_p)^2}{\sum (y - \bar{y})^2} = k \cdot P_y, \tag{11}$$

where P_y is the fraction of the total variance of income in the group contributed by the permanent component of income. More generally, of course, b can be regarded as an estimate of the righthand side of (11).

The algebraic relation in (11) lends itself directly to meaningful interpretation in terms of the permanent income hypothesis. The regression coefficient b measures the difference in consumption associated, on the average, with a one dollar difference between consumer units in measured income. On our hypothesis, the size of this difference in consumption depends on two things; first, how much of the difference in measured income is also a difference in permanent income, since only differences in permanent income are regarded as affecting consumption systematically; second, how much of permanent income is devoted to consumption. P_y measures the first; k, the second; so their product equals b. If P_y is unity, transient factors are either entirely absent or affect the incomes of all members of the group by the same amount; a one dollar difference in measured income means a one dollar difference in permanent income and so produces a difference of k in consumption; b therefore equal to k. If P_y is zero, there are no differences in permanent income; a one dollar difference in measured income means a one dollar difference in the transitory component of income, which is taken to be uncorrelated with consumption; in consequence, this difference in measured income is associated with no systematic difference in consumption; b is therefore zero. As this explanation suggests, P_y, though *defined* by the ratio of the variance of the permanent component of income to the variance of total income, can be *interpreted* as the fraction of any difference in measured income that on the average is contributed by a difference in the permanent component. [...]

Our hypothesis gives a major role to certain features of the income distribution generally neglected in consumption studies. It asserts that some of the most strikingly uniform characteristics of computed regressions between consumption and income are simply a reflection of the inadequacy of measured income as an indicator of long-run income status. In consequence, differences among various groups of consumer units in observed marginal propensities to consume may not reflect differences in underlying preferences for consumption and wealth at all; they may reflect primarily the different strength of random forces, including errors of measurement, in determining measured income. Fortunately, considerable evidence is available on the importance of transitory components of income from studies of changes over time in the relative income status of individuals or consumer units. One of the attractive features of our hypothesis is that it enables us to bring this independent body of evidence to bear on the interpretation of consumer behavior; such evidence can provide some of the additional information required when transitory components of income and consumption cannot be supposed to be zero. [...]

2.2 The Life-Cycle Hypothesis*
[...]

DERIVATION OF THE AGGREGATE CONSUMPTION FUNCTION

The Modigliani and Brumberg model starts from the utility function of the individual consumer: his utility is assumed to be a function of his own aggregate consumption in current and future periods. The individual is then assumed to maximize his utility subject to the resources available to him, his resources being the sum of current and discounted future earnings over his lifetime and his current net worth. As a result of this maximization the current consumption of the individual can be expressed as a function of his resources and the rate of return on capital with parameters depending on age. The individual consumption functions thus obtained are then aggregated to arrive at the aggregate consumption function for the community.

From the above brief description, it is quite apparent that the most crucial assumptions in deriving the aggregate consumption function must be those relating to the characteristics of the individual's utility function, and the age structure of the population. The basic assumptions underlying the shape of the utility function are:

Assumption I: The utility function is homogeneous with respect to consumption at different points in time; or, equivalently, if the individual receives an additional dollar's worth of resources, he will allocate it to consumption at different times in the same proportion in which he had allocated his total resources prior to the addition.

Assumption II: The individual neither expects to receive nor desires to leave any inheritance. (This assumption can be relaxed in either of two ways. First, we may assume that the utility over life depends on planned bequests but assume that it is a homogeneous function of this variable as well as of planned consumption. Alternatively, we may assume that the resources an individual earmarks for bequests are an increasing function of the individual's resources relative to the average level of resources of his age group, and that the relative size distribution of resources within each age group is stable over time. It can be shown that either of these generalized assumptions implies an aggregate consumption function similar in all essential characteristics to the one obtained from the stricter assumption stated here.)

These two assumptions can be shown to imply that, in any given year t, total consumption of a person of age T (or, more generally, of a household headed by such a person) will be proportional to the present value of total

---

* From A. Ando and F. Modigliani, 'The "Life-Cycle" Hypothesis of Saving: Aggregate Implications and Tests', *American Economic Review*, 1963.

resources accruing to him over the rest of his life, or:

$$c_t^T = \Omega_t^T v_t^T. \tag{1}$$

In this equation Ω_t^T is a proportionality factor which will depend on the specific form of the utility function, the rate of return on assets, and the present age of the person, but not on total resources, v_t^T. The symbol c_t^T stands for total consumption (rather than for consumer's expenditure) in the year t. It consists of current outlays for nondurable goods and services (net of changes if any in the stock of nondurables) plus the rental value of the stock of service-yielding consumer durable goods. This rental value in turn can be equated with the loss in value of the stock in the course of the period plus the lost return on the capital tied up. Finally the present value of resources at age T, v_t^T, can be expressed as the sum of net worth carried over from the previous period, a_{t-1}^T, and the present value of nonproperty income the person expects to earn over the remainder of his earning life; i.e.,

$$v_t^T = a_{t-1}^T + y_t^T + \sum_{\tau=T+1}^{N} \frac{y_t^{eT\tau}}{(1+r_t)^{\tau-T}} \tag{2}$$

where y_t^T denotes current nonproperty income; $y_t^{eT\tau}$ is the nonproperty income an individual of age T expects to earn in the τth year of his life; N stands for the earning span and r_t for the rate of return on assets.

In order to proceed further, it is convenient to introduce the notion of 'average annual expected income,' y_t^{eT}, defined as follows:

$$y_t^{eT} = \frac{1}{N-T} \sum_{\tau=T+1}^{N} \frac{y_t^{eT\tau}}{(1+r_t)^{\tau-T}}. \tag{3}$$

Making use of this definition and of (2) we can rewrite equation (1) as:

$$c_t^T = \Omega_t^T y_t^T + \Omega_t^T (N-T) y_t^{eT} + \Omega_t^T a_{t-1}^T. \tag{4}$$

To obtain an expression for aggregate consumption we proceed to aggregate equation (4) in two steps, first within each age group and then over the age groups.

If the value of Ω_t^T is identical for all individuals in a given age group T, then it is a simple matter to aggregate equation (4) over an age group, obtaining:

$$C_t^T = \Omega_t^T Y_t^T + (N-T)\Omega_t^T Y_t^{eT} + \Omega_t^T A_{t-1}^T \tag{5}$$

where C_t^T, Y_t^T, Y_t^{eT}, and A_{t-1}^T are corresponding aggregates for the age group T of c_t^T, y_t^T, y_t^{eT}, and a_{t-1}^T. If Ω_t^T is not identical for all individuals in the age group, however, the meaning of the coefficients in equation (5) must be reinterpreted. It has been shown by Theil that under a certain set of conditions the coefficients of (5) can be considered as weighted averages of the corresponding coefficients of (4).

Next, taking equation (5) as a true representation of the relationship between consumption and total resources for various age groups, we wish to aggregate them over all age groups to get the consumption function for the whole community. Consider the equation:

$$C_t = \alpha'_1 Y_t + \alpha'_2 Y_t^e + \alpha'_3 A_{t-1} \qquad (6)$$

where C_t, Y_t, Y_t^e and A_{t-1} are obtained by summing respectively C_t^T, Y_t^T, Y_t^{eT} and A_{t-1}^T over all age groups T, and represent therefore aggregate consumption, current nonproperty income, 'expected annual nonproperty income', and net worth.

The theorems given by Theil again specify the conditions under which the coefficients in equation (6) are weighted averages of the corresponding coefficients of equation (5). In this case, it is likely that the conditions specified by Theil are not satisfied, because both net worth and its coefficient in equation (5) are positively correlated with age up to the time of retirement. However, a much weaker set of conditions can be specified which are sufficient to insure stability over time of parameters in equation (6). In particular one such set of conditions is the constancy in time of (i) the parameters of equation (5) for every age group, (ii) the age structure of population, and (iii) the relative distribution of income, of expected income, and of net worth over the age groups.

A PRIORI ESTIMATES OF THE COEFFICIENTS OF THE AGGREGATE CONSUMPTION FUNCTION

Modigliani and Brumberg, in order to obtain *a priori* estimates of the order of the magnitude of the coefficients of equation (6) implied by their model, introduced a number of rather drastic simplifying assumptions about the form of the utility function and life pattern of earnings, to wit:

Assumption III: The consumer at any age plans to consume his total resources evenly over the remainder of his life span.

Assumption IV: (a) Every age group within the earning span has the same average income in any given year t. (b) In a given year t, the average income expected by any age group T for any later period τ, within their earning span, is the same. (c) Every household has the same (expected and actual) total life and earning spans, assumed to be 50 and 40 respectively for the purpose of numerical computation.

Assumption V: The rate of return on assets is constant and is expected to remain constant.

Under these assumptions, if aggregate real income follows an exponential growth trend—whether due to population or to productivity growth—the sufficient conditions for the constancy in time of the parameters of (6) are satisfied. The value of these parameters depends then only on the rate of return on assets and on the over-all rate of growth of income, which in turn is the sum of population growth and the rate of increase of productivity.

Table 1 gives some examples of the numerical value of the coefficients under the assumptions described above.

It should be emphasized that assumptions III to V have been introduced only for the sake of numerical estimation of the coefficients and are by no means necessary to insure the approximate constancy in time of the parameters in (6). A change in the assumptions would lead to somewhat different values of the parameters. But both a priori considerations and rough numerical calculations suggest that these values would not be drastically affected, and that it is generally possible to infer the direction in which these

Table 1. *Coefficient of the consumption function* (6) *under stated assumptions.*[a]

Yield on assets (per cent)	0	0	0	3	5	5	5
Annual rate of growth of aggregate income (per cent)	0	3	4	0	0	3	4
$\alpha_1 + \alpha_2$	·61	·64	—	·69	·73	—	—
α_3	·08	·07	·07	·11	·13	·12	·12

[a] Missing values have not been computed because of the complexity of calculation.

values would move when a specific assumption is changed. The recognition of the estate motive would tend to yield lower values for both coefficients, especially that of assets.

On the whole, then, the values shown in Table 1 should be regarded as a rough guide to the order of magnitude of the coefficients consistent with the basic model; i.e., radically different values would cast serious doubts on the adequacy of the life cycle hypothesis.

THE MEASUREMENT OF EXPECTED INCOME

The last point that must be clarified before we proceed to the discussion of the empirical tests is the measurement of expected nonproperty income, Y_t^e, which, at least at present, is not directly observable. A 'naive' hypothesis is to assume that expected nonproperty income is the same as actual current income, except for a possible scale factor. Thus, we have:

$$Y_t^e = \beta' Y_t; \qquad \beta' \simeq 1.$$

Substituting the above expression into (6), we obtain the aggregate consumption function

$$C_t = (\alpha_1' + \beta' \alpha_2') Y_t + \alpha_3' A_{t-1} = \alpha_1 Y_t + \alpha_3 A_{t-1}$$

$$\alpha_1 = \alpha_1' + \beta' \alpha_2' \simeq \alpha_1' + \alpha_2'.$$

We designate this formulation as hypothesis I.

A similar but somewhat more sophisticated formulation is to assume that expected income is an exponentially weighted average of past income, weights adding up to one, or slightly more than one in order to reflect the expected growth. But it is quite difficult to determine the weights from the data we have at our disposal, and Friedman, who favors this formulation, has acknowledged its shortcomings.

The third possible formulation is a slight modification of the first. Under our definitions, Y, and expected income, Y^e, are nonproperty or labor income, excluding, for instance, profits. We may hypothesize that for those currently employed, average expected income, y_t^e, is current income adjusted for a possible scale factor, i.e.,

$$y_t^e = \beta_1 \frac{Y_t}{E_t} \tag{7}$$

where E_t is the number of persons engaged in production. We should expect β_1 to be quite close to unity.

For those individuals who are currently unemployed, we hypothesize that expected income is proportional to the average current income of those who are employed. The proportionality constant in this case represents three factors. First, as before, there may be some influence from expected growth. Second, and probably most important, the incidence of unemployment is likely to be smaller for higher-paid occupations than for lower-paid, less-skilled workers; hence, the average earnings the unemployed can look forward to, if reemployed, are likely to be lower than the average earnings of those currently employed. Third, it seems reasonable to suppose that some of the currently unemployed persons would expect their current unemployment status to continue for some time and, possibly, to recur. We shall therefore assume:

$$y_t^{eu} = \beta_2 \frac{Y_t}{E_t} \tag{8}$$

where y_t^{eu} is the average expected income of unemployed persons; and, for the reasons given above, we expect the constant β_2 to be substantially smaller than β_1. The aggregate expected income is then given by:

$$Y_t^e = E_t y_t^e + (L_t - E_t) y_t^{eu} = E_t \beta_1 \frac{Y_t}{E_t} + (L_t - E_t) \beta_2 \frac{Y_t}{E_t}$$

$$= (\beta_1 - \beta_2) Y_t + \beta_2 \frac{L_t}{E_t} Y_t \tag{9}$$

where L_t denotes the total labor force.

Substituting (9) into (6), we obtain the following variant of hypothesis I,

$$C_t = \alpha_1 Y_t + \alpha_2 \frac{L_t}{E_t} Y_t + \alpha_3 A_{t-1} \tag{10}$$

where
$$\alpha_1 = \alpha_1' + \alpha_2'(\beta_1 - \beta_2)$$
$$\alpha_2 = \alpha_2'\beta_2; \qquad \alpha_3 = \alpha_3'.$$

We designate the formulation embodied in equation (10) above as hypothesis II.

Since β_1 is thought to be close to unity, we have

$$\alpha_1 + \alpha_2 = \alpha_1' + \beta_1\alpha_2' \simeq \alpha_1' + \alpha_2'. \tag{11}$$

The individual values of the observable coefficients α_1 and α_2 are, however, dependent on the nonobservable value of β_2, about which there is little we can say a priori. [...]

RELATION TO THE STANDARD KEYNESIAN CONSUMPTION FUNCTIONS

The standard Keynesian consumption function is usually written in the form:

$$C = \gamma Y^* + \gamma_0 \tag{12}$$

where Y^* denotes personal income net of taxes or disposable income and the γ's are constants. A more sophisticated variant of this hypothesis, which has become quite popular of late, consists in separating income into two parts, disposable labor income Y, and disposable nonlabor or property income, which we shall denote by P. Thus,

$$C = \gamma_1 Y + \gamma_2 P + \gamma_0. \tag{13}$$

This variant, which reduces to (12) when $\gamma_1 = \gamma_2$, is usually advocated on the ground that property income accrues mostly to higher-income and/or entrepreneurial groups who may be expected to have a lower marginal propensity to consume. Accordingly, γ_2 is supposed to be smaller than γ_1 and this supposition appears to be supported by empirical findings.

It is immediately apparent that (13) bears considerable similarity to hypothesis I discussed in this paper, i.e.,

$$C = (\alpha_1 + \alpha_2)Y + \alpha_3 A. \tag{14}$$

The main difference lies in the constant term which appears in (13) but not in (14), and in the fact that the wealth variable A in (14) is replaced in (13) by a closely related variable, income from wealth, P. We can avoid dealing with the first source of discrepancy by working with both hypotheses in first-difference form,

$$\Delta C = \gamma_1 \Delta Y + \gamma_2 \Delta P \tag{13a}$$

$$\Delta C = (\alpha_1 + \alpha_2)\Delta Y + \alpha_3 \Delta A. \tag{14a}$$

Equations (13a) and (14a) are quite useful since they allow a straightforward test of the usefulness of the Modigliani-Brumberg hypothesis as compared with the standard Keynesian one. We have already exhibited in Table 2, row (6),[1] the results obtained by fitting (14a) to the data. In order to complete the test we need to estimate the parameters of (13a). If the standard Keynesian version is correct, the net worth variable in (14) and (14a) is merely a proxy variable for the return from wealth, P, and hence substitution of ΔP for ΔA should improve the fit. On the other hand, if (14) and (14a) are closer to the truth than (13), then the substitution of ΔA by a proxy variable ΔP should reduce the correlation. [...]

The definition of consumption on which we rely, however, is somewhat different from that customarily used in the standard Keynesian formulation in that it includes the current consumption—depreciation—of the stock of consumer durables, while excluding expenditure for the purchase of such goods. The results obtained for hypothesis (13a) are as follows:

$$\Delta C = \cdot93\Delta Y + \cdot07\Delta P \qquad R^2 = \cdot86. \tag{15}$$
$$\quad (\cdot07) \qquad (\cdot29)$$

Comparison of this result with those reported in Table 2, row (6), strongly suggests that net worth is definitely not a mere proxy for current property income. While the coefficient of P is positive and smaller than that of Y as expected, this variable is much less useful than A in explaining the behavior of consumption. In fact, its contribution is not significantly different from zero. [...]

2.3 Wealth and the Consumption Function[*]

The purpose of this paper is to present a new theory that explains the observed relations among consumer expenditure, income, and wealth. The theory, presented in detail below, specifies that savings are the result of a discrepancy between the actual and the desired stock of wealth; when there is no discrepancy, savings equal zero. If income were to remain permanently constant, the desired stock of wealth would ultimately be accumulated and therefore consumption would equal net income. Positive savings will occur only if the secular trend of income is rising.

A GENERALIZED CONSUMPTION FUNCTION

It is convenient to assume temporarily that all decisions and all payments are made at discrete points in time. A generalized consumption function

---

[1] [Not included in this extract. The result in question is:

$$\Delta C = \cdot52\Delta Y + \cdot072\Delta A \quad R^2 = \cdot93$$
$$(\cdot11) \qquad (\cdot018)$$

—Ed.]

* From A. Spiro, 'Wealth and the Consumption Function', *Journal of Political Economy*, 1962. Reprinted by permission of the University of Chicago Press.

may then be written

$$C = f(W_t^*, y_t, y_{t-1}, y_{t-2}, \ldots y_{t-\infty}, e_t^*), \qquad (1)$$

where

C_t = aggregate value of all goods and services consumed during period t,

y_t = total net earnings, received at the beginning of time period t, of all factors of production minus all taxes plus net transfers,

W_t^* = aggregate non-human wealth just prior to the distribution of income,

e_t^* = a measure of the effect of all other forces (than y and W^*) upon consumption of time period t.

The inclusion of past and present levels of income in the consumption function is sufficiently common to require no comment. However, the stock of consumer wealth may also have a considerable effect upon consumption. For example, if wealth were infinite, then a rational society would consume to the point of satiation. Further, non-zero savings must be interpreted as implying a desire to change the stock of wealth. Therefore, it is theoretically plausible that the introduction of wealth into the consumption function will improve the ability of the function to explain the variations of consumption.

THEORETICAL ASSUMPTIONS

To convert the generalized consumption function into an equation for statistical testing, it is necessary to introduce sufficient assumptions to define its form. I make the following three assumptions:

1. When wealth increases, consumption increases.

2. For any given values of y_t, $y_{t-1}, \ldots y_{t-\infty}$, and e_t^* there is some level of wealth at which all income will be consumed and saving will be zero.

Obviously, assumption 1 when combined with assumption 2 implies that if, in some time period, the stock of wealth is decreased below the level associated with zero savings, consumption must decrease and positive savings will occur, and that if the stock of wealth is increased above the level associated with zero savings, the individuals within our economy will dissave.

3. The relationship indicated by equation (1) takes the specific form,

$$C_t = e_t^* + BW_t^* + By_t + \sum_{i=0}^{i=\infty} a_i y_{t-i}, \qquad (2)$$

where B is a fixed coefficient representing the effect on consumption of assets held at the beginning of the time period, and the a_i's are a set of fixed coefficients representing the other influences on consumption of income received in the current and in previous periods. This simply specifies the simplest form of equation (1) that is consistent with the other conditions imposed upon it.

MATHEMATICAL MANIPULATIONS

The above three assumptions are the only assumptions that are required by theoretical analysis. I now perform certain mathematical manipulations and redefinitions that considerably simplify equation (2) and make it easy to obtain statistically testable conclusions from it.

First, it is convenient to divide both sides of equation (2) by an index of the prices of currently produced commodities. This simply specifies the unit of measurement and does not involve any additional assumption or require a change of notation.

Next, we define

$$S_t = y_t - C_t, \tag{3}$$

$$W_t = \sum_{i=-\infty}^{i=t-1} S_i, \tag{4}$$

and

$$e_t^{**} = W_t^* - W_t. \tag{5}$$

e_t^{**} is equal to the capital gains and losses upon the cumulated savings of the individuals within the economy. Substituting equation (5) into equation (2) and setting $e_t^* + Be_t^{**} = e_t$, we obtain

$$C_t = e_t + BW_t + By_t + \sum_{i=0}^{i=\infty} a_i y_{t-i}. \tag{6}$$

Equation (6) is identical to a lagged consumption function of the usual type except that, instead of containing a term that represents exogenous consumption, it contains the terms $e_t + BW_t$.

It is now possible, without introducing additional assumptions, to obtain an expression for W in terms of past levels of y. This is so because $W_t = W_{t-1} + y_{t-1} - C_{t-1}$, where C_{t-1} also contains a term involving W_{t-1}. Further, a similar equation holds for W_{t-1}. As a result, W_t can be expressed in terms of y_{t-1}, y_{t-2}, and W_{t-2}. By continuing this process, W_t can be expressed entirely in terms of earlier values of income and earlier values of e. We can, therefore, eliminate W_t from the consumption function and write it as

$$C_t = E_t + \sum_{i=0}^{i=\infty} b_i y_{t-i}, \tag{7}$$

where

$$E_t = e_t - \sum_{m=0}^{m=\infty} B(1-B)^m e_{t-m-i},$$

$$b_0 = B + a_0,$$

and (for i not equal to zero)

$$b_i = a_i + B(1-B)^i - B \sum_{n=0}^{n=i-1} (1-B)^n a_{i-n-1}.$$

The question now arises as to what can be said concerning the b coefficients of equation (7). We note initially that the b coefficients must sum to a finite limit providing only that

$$0 < B < +2$$

and

$$\sum_{i=0}^{i=\infty} a_i = \text{any finite number.}$$

The first condition must hold since B, the marginal propensity to consume from wealth, cannot exceed unity. Further, the second condition must be accepted if the model is to apply to the real economy, because otherwise consumption would be infinite.

It can now be demonstrated that the finite number, to which the b coefficients must sum, is precisely equal to unity. Consider the case, where, for all time periods, e_t is a constant, so that (from equation (7)) $E_t = \bar{E} = 0$ and y is a constant.

Let the sum of the b coefficients be equal to D. If deflated income has always (that is, from time period $t - \infty$ to time period t) remained constant at $\bar{y}$, then consumption must be equal to $D\bar{y}$. As long as income remains constant at $\bar{y}$, consumption must remain constant at $D\bar{y}$. Can D be less than unity? Proof that this is not possible follows from the fact that, if D is less than unity, $D\bar{y}$ will be less than $\bar{y}$. But if this is the case, then consumers must be saving some positive fraction of their incomes so that W (cumulated deflated savings) must be increasing. However, if W is increasing, consumption must be increasing. But this contradicts the conclusion that consumption is constant; the assumption that D is less than unity leads to a contradiction. The same argument can be used to demonstrate that D cannot be greater than unity. D must therefore be equal to unity, so that the b coefficients of equation (7) sum to unity. These coefficients are the partial marginal propensities to consume from income. Our conclusion, then, is that the sum of the partial marginal propensities to consume from income is equal to unity.

Equation (7), therefore, specifies that, if income and the other influences on consumption represented by e_t were to remain constant indefinitely, savings would fall to zero and consumption would equal income. In other words, consumers would accumulate all of the wealth that they were willing to hold at that level of income. Equation (7) also implies that, if the trend of income were to be continuously upward (so that earlier levels of income were lower than later levels of income), saving would become positive; and that, if the trend of income were to continue downward indefinitely, then saving would become negative. In other words, a rising level of income will ultimately induce consumers to wish to hold more wealth than they initially held, whereas a falling level of income will ultimately induce consumers to draw upon their stock of wealth.

Of course, the other forces represented by e can also cause variations of consumption. Therefore, our hypothesis specifies that the actual time shape of consumption will depend upon the time shape of income and the time shape of e.

The conclusion that our theoretical analysis requires is that the sum of the partial marginal propensities to consume from income is equal to unity. Other models have specified that this sum is less than unity. This is the critical difference between our model and other models.

CONSISTENCY WITH THE THEORY OF CONSUMER BEHAVIOR

Equation (7) has been derived directly from equation (2) without introducing any additional assumptions. Therefore, the foregoing analysis is consistent with any theory of consumer behavior that leads to equation (2).

Consider Duesenberry's well-known theory of consumer behavior: Duesenberry considers the case where a given group of consumers has been permitted to make all adjustments to (what I would term) a given stock of W^* and the set of y's. He then considers the effect of increasing all of these variables by a given factor, k. He argues that, if consumers are permitted to complete all adjustments to the new levels of W^* and the set of y's consumption will increase by the same factor, k. However, this conclusion also follows from equation (2) providing that e^* is set equal to zero. Duesenberry also implies that, if consumers are not in equilibrium, e^* will not be equal to zero. However, my hypothesis is consistent with any time shape of e^*. For example, e^* can be regarded as depending upon the highest level of per capita consumption previously attained. A consumption function of this type is

$$\frac{C_t}{P_t} = \frac{AC_0}{P_0} + \frac{BW_t^*}{P_t} + \frac{a^* y_t}{P_t},$$

(8)

where

P = population,
C_0/P_0 = the highest level of per capita consumption previously attained, and
B, a^*, and A are fixed coefficients.

Multiplying both sides of equation (8) by P_t we obtain:

$$C = \frac{AP_t C_0}{P_0} + BW_t^* + a^* y_t.$$

(9)

But this is simply one form of equation (2) with

$$e_t^* = \frac{AP_tC_0}{P_0}$$

$$a_0 + B = a^*;$$

all the remaining a_1 coefficients (of equation (2)) set equal to zero.

Consider now Friedman's well-known theory of consumer behavior.[1] Friedman imposes the same conditions as do the Duesenberry equilibrium conditions. However, Friedman's theory specifies that these conditions hold regardless of whether or not the consumers are in equilibrium. Further, Friedman indicates that permanent income can be approximated by a weighted average of past and present levels of measured aggregate (or per capita) income. The similarity between equation (2) and Friedman's consumption function can be brought out by noting that equation (2) (with e^* equal to zero) can be written as

$$C_t = \left[\frac{B(W_t^* + y_t)}{\sum\limits_{i=0}^{i=\infty} a_i y_{t-i}} + 1 \right] \sum_{i=0}^{i=\infty} a_i y_{t-i}. \tag{10}$$

Equation (10) is simply a particular form of Friedman's consumption function. In Friedman's terminology this equation specifies that the average propensity to consume from permanent income depends, *ceteris paribus*,[2] only upon the *ratio* between non-human wealth (just after the distribution of income) and permanent income. Friedman also requires this.

In other words, equation (10) (and therefore equation [2]) is simply a particular form of the consumption function implied by Friedman's theoretical mechanism. We can therefore accept without additional justification all of Friedman's theoretical results. However, this cannot be said of his statistical test of time series, since Friedman simply assumed that the average propensity to consume from permanent income remained constant over the period that he investigated statistically (1905–49) even though his theoretical mechanism does not provide any reason for this assumption. This assumption converts equation (10) into an equation of the same form as (7). But in his statistical test Friedman makes use of deflated per capita data, although, as he indicates, he could have as properly used deflated aggregate data. Friedman finds that the sum of the partial marginal propensities to consume from per capita income is less than unity. Friedman's statistical investigation therefore implies an interesting result; if *per capita* income remains constant indefinitely then consumption will be less than income. However, since population was increasing during the period that Friedman

---

[1] [See Reading 2.1 above—Ed.]

[2] In Friedman's view the other things that must remain equal are the interest rate, the tastes of consumers, and the distribution of wealth and permanent income.

investigated, his results are quite consistent with my theory. My analysis applies to aggregate data and implies that, if aggregate income is continuously rising, consumption will be less than income whether aggregate income is rising because per capita income is rising or because population is rising.

In the remainder of this paper, I shall investigate in more detail whether my theory is consistent with the available time series evidence. [...]

WEALTH AND CONSUMPTION

I now turn to consider the secular stability of the savings ratio. In my view this stability is connected with the aspirations of consumers with respect to their stock of wealth. In order to investigate this, consider again equation (6). Consider the case where income has remained perpetually constant so that consumption now equals income—there is no saving and therefore wealth is constant. Using these assumptions and equation (6) we obtain

$$\bar{C} = e_t + B\overline{W} + B\bar{y} + \bar{y}\sum_{i=0}^{i=\infty} a_i, \tag{11}$$

where $\bar{y}$, $\bar{C}$, and $\overline{W}$ are constants.

However, since savings are zero, therefore $\bar{y} = \bar{C}$ so that equation (11) can be written

$$\frac{\overline{W}}{\bar{C}} = \frac{1 - B - \dfrac{e_t}{\bar{C}} - \sum_{i=0}^{i=\infty} a_i}{B}. \tag{12}$$

But one assumption that was introduced in deriving the equation used in statistical testing, was that $e_t = \bar{e} = 0$. Given this assumption it follows, from equation (12), that the equilibrium W/C ratio is independent of the absolute level of consumption (or income) being considered.

In order to test [the] equation it was assumed that the b coefficients of this equation formed a geometric progression. This assumption implies an even more restrictive result: that at *all* times individuals save that fraction of their income which will just maintain a constant W/C ratio. This, obviously, would only be true if deviations from the equilibrium position did not effect the *W/C ratio*. It is, therefore, a matter of some interest to determine whether consumers do seem to be motivated by a desire to maintain a constant wealth/consumption ratio.

The ratios of wealth/yearly consumption, for the non-war years 1905–49, average 6·1. In thirty-eight of the thirty-nine years these ratios lay within 10 per cent of 6·1.

The wealth consumption series was derived by dividing one series (subject to a margin of error) by another series (also subject to a margin of error). The deviations from 6·1 could, therefore, easily be accounted for by errors of measurement. In any event, measured consumption was, in thirty-eight out of thirty-nine years, within roughly 10 per cent of the level that would have maintained the wealth/consumption ratio constant.

If we assume that the length of an income period is one month, our statistical estimate of K implies a ratio of wealth/yearly consumption of between 6·1 and 6·2. There is, therefore, rather good agreement between the estimates computed in the two ways. [...]

CONCLUSIONS

The analysis of this paper has shown that both economic theory and the available evidence are consistent with a model in which (a) the desired wealth/consumption ratio has remained constant so that (b) all saving has in fact arisen from an increase of income that has raised the desired wealth yielding this ratio and hence (c) if income should cease rising, saving would decline to zero.

My analysis therefore requires that a permanent rise of income of $1.00 will (after consumers have completed their wealth adjustment) cause consumption to rise by $1.00. A consumption function of this type has been previously regarded only as a theoretical curiosity, whereas my analysis indicates that it explains the available evidence more satisfactorily than do functions that assume that the (longest run) marginal propensity to consume is less than unity.

2.4 Income, Wealth and the Theory of Consumption*

[...]

THEORETICAL FOUNDATIONS

Household Planning: Basic Concepts

In keeping with familiar procedure, we consider a household whose decision problem at any given moment of time is to choose among alternative combinations of desired consumption (c) and desired wealth (w), subject to a planning constraint that depends on the actual wealth ($\underline{w}$) of the household at the same moment.... We do not inquire into the motives, rational or otherwise, that underlie household attitudes towards spending and saving, nor do we deal explicitly with factors that might influence such attitudes (e.g. expected prices and rates of return, expected income, age, occupation, family composition, previous purchases of durable goods, etc.). On the contrary, we suppose that the household has a short memory and limited foresight, and we ignore all forces affecting choice that conflict with this point of view.... Accordingly, we characterize the household's ranking of alternative wealth-consumption combinations by a preference function of the form

$$u = u(w,c), \tag{1}$$

* From R. Clower and M. Bruce Johnson, 'Income, Wealth and the Theory of Consumption', in *Value, Capital and Growth: papers in Honour of Sir John Hicks*, edited by J. N. Wolfe (Edinburgh University Press, 1968).

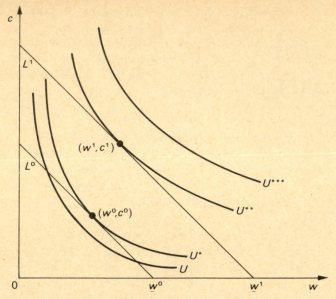

FIG. 2.2. Selection of the optimal plan

in which desired wealth and desired consumption appear as the only explicit variables.

Corresponding to (1), we define the set of currently admissible wealth-consumption plans by the budget equation

$$c + v(w - \underline{w}) = 0, \qquad (2)$$

where v is a given velocity coefficient. The appearance of the parameter v in (2) is dictated by the dimensional difference between the flow variable c and the stock variables w and $\underline{w}$. Since no conceivable experiment will enable us to arrive at independent estimates of v and $\underline{w}$, however, we may gain simplicity without loss of empirical content by setting $v = 1$. On this assumption, the budget equation asserts that the planned (instantaneous) rate of consumption at any given date is numerically equal to the difference between desired and actual wealth at the same date.

Given the choice alternatives defined by (2), we apply the traditional postulate of utility maximization to determine the optimal wealth-consumption combination (w^*, c^*) corresponding to any specified value of actual wealth. This is illustrated in Figure 2.2, where the curves U, U^*, $U^{**}, \dots$, represent the function $u(w, c)$. If w° is the current wealth of the household, the budget line is L° and the optimal wealth-consumption plan, defined by the tangency of L° with the indifference curve U^*, is (w°, c°). Alternatively, if the current wealth of the household is w^1, the budget line is L^1 and the optimal wealth-consumption plan is (w^1, c^1), and so forth.

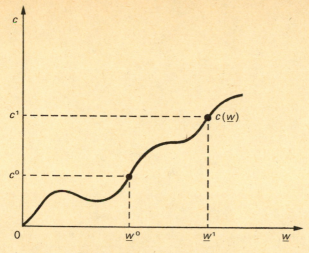

FIG. 2.3. The consumption locus

Supposing that the decision problem has a unique solution corresponding to any given value of current wealth, we obtain planned consumption at any specified date as a single-valued function of actual wealth at the same date:

$$c^t = c(\underline{w}^t). \tag{3}$$

The graph of this function, hereafter referred to as the *consumption locus*, is illustrated in Figure 2.3. Our assumptions impose only one *a priori* restriction on this relation, namely, $c(0) = 0$ (this follows directly from the budget equation (2)). Casual empirical considerations suggest that the slope of the consumption locus, that is, the *marginal propensity to consume wealth* (MPCW), is unlikely to be negative; but no such condition is implicit in our model.

The Intertemporal Adjustment Process

The preceding analysis implies that planned consumption at any date t is a function simply of current wealth. This conclusion is in close accord with views advanced on outwardly different theoretical grounds by Milton Friedman and by Modigliani and Brumberg. Where these writers regard current wealth as an imperfect proxy for 'permanent' or 'expected' income, however, we regard it as a causal variable in its own right. Correspondingly, where they introduce current income to give operational meaning to the otherwise purely metaphysical concepts of 'permanent' and 'expected' income, we shall introduce it as just one factor (the other being current consumption expenditure) that governs variations over time in objective stocks of household wealth.

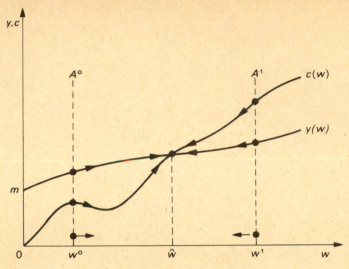

FIG. 2.4. The adjustment process

Specifically, we assume that *the rate of change of current wealth at any date is equal to the difference between measured income* ($\underline{y}$) *and measured consumption* ($\underline{c}$) *at the same date.* Symbolically,

$$d\underline{w}^t/dt = \underline{y}^t - \underline{c}^t. \qquad (4)$$

[...]

We may now characterize intertemporal adjustment processes. The income locus indicates, for each alternative level of current wealth, the maximum rate of current consumption the household can enjoy without drawing on previously accumulated wealth. The consumption locus (reproduced from Figure 2.3 and superimposed on the income locus in Figure 2.4) indicates what the household's actual rate of consumption will be corresponding to any given value of current wealth. The vertical distance between the income locus and the consumption locus measures realized saving; that is, the current rate of change of actual wealth. Thus the income and consumption functions, combined with the asset adjustment hypothesis (4), define a determinate dynamical system in the single variable $\underline{w}^t$ which, starting from any initial value $\underline{w}_0^t$ of wealth at date t_0, generates unique values of measured consumption, income, and wealth for all subsequent dates.

Suppose, for instance, that the value of current wealth at some initial data $t = 0$ is represented by the point w° in Figure 2.4; then current consumption and current wealth will initially tend to increase over time at the rate $y^\circ - c^\circ$. With the passage of time, therefore, the actual values of wealth, income, and consumption all will increase as indicated by the directional arrows originating along the perpendicular A° in Figure 2.4. Alternatively, if the value of current wealth at initial date $t = 1$ is w^1, then consumption will initially exceed income and wealth will tend to decrease over time. The actual values of wealth, income, and consumption will therefore decline with the passage of time as indicated by the directional arrows originating along the perpendicular A^1 in Figure 2.4.

In both of these examples, realized saving will converge to zero with the passage of time. That is to say, current wealth will gradually approach a stationary (and stable) equilibrium value ($\hat{w}$ in Figure 2.4) at which current consumption is equal to current income.[...]

The Consumption Locus

Let us begin by supposing that all households have linear consumption loci, but that the slopes of different loci vary randomly from one household to another. Then cross-section data on wealth and consumption corresponding to a given distribution of service income will yield a random scatter of wealth-consumption points. Alternatively, suppose that the slopes of individual consumption loci tend to cluster about a common value. Then a cross-section scatter will be heavily concentrated within a certain pie-shaped area of the w–c plane. More generally, we should expect any clustering of consumption loci (whether the loci were linear or not) to be revealed by cross-section data. Conversely, if an actual scatter of wealth-consumption points displays a definite pattern, we should infer from this that individual consumption loci tend to conform to a similar pattern.

Unfortunately, consumption research traditionally has been directed not towards relations between wealth and consumption, but rather towards relations between income and consumption. We cannot settle the issue before us, therefore, by running a regression of consumption on wealth. For this to be possible, we should require detailed information about household consumption expenditures at various levels of wealth. Such data are not available in any collection of published statistics. For both the United Kingdom and the United States, however, we do have information about mean consumption and wealth at various levels of income. For the United States alone, moreover, we have some data on the distribution of income and saving within three broad wealth classes. A combination of these materials should tell us something about the existence and probable character of the 'modal' consumption locus even though the scatter it produces fails to satisfy conventional criteria of statistical relevance.

For purposes of comparison, we have plotted the data as separate scatters in Figure 2.5. The similarity between the data for the US and UK is obvious. In both countries, mean wealth and consumption are, by and large, positively correlated with mean income. Moreover, consumption tends to increase less rapidly than wealth as income increases (with double-logarithmic scales, this is indicated by the negative curvature of the scatters for low income levels, by a slope of less than unity in the linear sections of the scatters). There is an evident difference between the US and UK scatters at the lower end of the

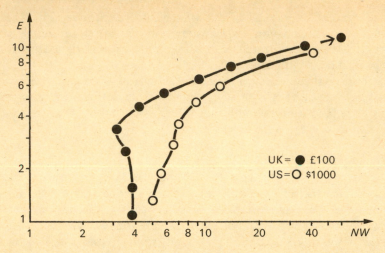

FIG. 2.5. Expenditure and net worth

income scale, where the UK data indicate a negative correlation between wealth and consumption. But it would be a mistake to pay any attention to this phenomenon; for we know that there are many households in both countries with negative or zero net worth (e.g. about 35 per cent of UK households, 15 per cent of US households, and these simply disappear from the wealth distribution when we classify households by income level. That the resulting loss of information is substantial becomes clear when we reflect that the lowest income brackets in both countries will include large numbers of retired people with substantial accumulations of wealth. This alone would explain the truncation of the two scatters and the negatively-sloped section of the UK relation. [...]

The sum and substance of all this may be put more precisely by saying that the modal *w–c* scatter, plotted on double-logarithmic graph paper, is probably linear, and that the corresponding least-squares regression line will most certainly have a slope of less than unity. If this guess is correct, then the implied mathematical relationship between consumption and wealth is given by

$$c = hw^b,$$ (5)

where *h* is a positive constant, and *b* lies between zero and unity.

The graph of the function (2.5) is illustrated in Figure 2.6. In conformity with an old tradition, this relation exhibits negative curvature throughout— suggesting that the marginal urgency of consumption decreases as household wealth increases. In terms of our model, what this means is simply that the MPCW is a strictly decreasing function of household wealth. [...]

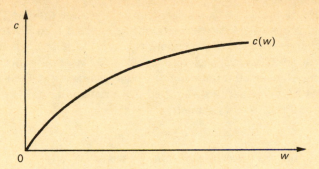

Fɪɢ. 2.6. The 'modal' consumption locus

STATISTICAL IMPLICATIONS

Turning to the task of deriving explicit regression formulae from our model, we begin by assuming that the initial state of the economy at, say, date t_0, is one of stationary equilibrium. Supposing further that $c_i^t = a_i w_i^t$ and $m_i^t = y_i$, we may assert on the basis of the earlier argument that the consumption of a representative household at the end of a unit time interval starting at date t_0 is given by the equation

$$c_i^{t_0+1} = c_i' = a_i w_i^{t_0+1}$$
$$= a_i\{m_i'/a_i - (m_i'/a_i)e^{-a_i}\}$$
$$= y_i' - (y_i' - y_i)e^{-a_i}, \tag{6}$$

where y_i and y_i' denote, respectively, the (average) service income flows of the household at the beginning and end of the interval (i.e. $y_i' - y_i$ represents the change in the average value of the two flows at the beginning of the unit time interval).

Now the least-squares estimates of the slope and intercept coefficients of the regression of consumption on income at date $t_0 + 1$ are defined by the usual formulae as

$$B' = \frac{\Sigma_i(c_i' - \bar{c}')(y_i' - \bar{y}')}{\Sigma_i(y_i' - \bar{y}')^2} \tag{7}$$

$$A' = \bar{c}' - B'\bar{y}', \tag{8}$$

where barred variables, as is customary, stand for group means. Replacing c_i' in (7) by its equivalent from (6), we have

$$B' = \frac{\Sigma_i(y_i' - \bar{y}')^2}{\Sigma_i(y_i' - \bar{y}')^2} - \frac{\Sigma_i(y_i' - \bar{y}')^2 e^{-a_i}}{\Sigma_i(y_i' - \bar{y}')^2} + \frac{\Sigma_i(y_i - \bar{y})(y_i' - \bar{y}')e^{-a_i}}{\Sigma_i(y_i' - \bar{y}')^2}. \tag{9}$$

In general, the weights e^{-a_i} that appear in the last two terms of (9) may be expected to vary considerably from one household to another. Referring back to our initial expression for consumption at date $t_0 + 1$, we note that the response of a household to a change in income will be quicker the greater its marginal propensity to consume wealth (a_i), which is to say that households with large MPCWs will contribute relatively little to the dispersion of the $c-y$ scatter. Neither will such households hold large amounts of wealth. It thus seems plausible to argue that our conclusions about the form of the $c-y$ scatter will not be seriously affected if we replace a_i in (9) by a wealth-weighted average of MPCWs, namely,

$$a = \Sigma_i(w_i a_i/N). \tag{10}$$

Carrying out the indicated substitution, we rewrite (9) as

$$B' = 1 - \left\{1 - \frac{\Sigma_i(y_i - \bar{y})(y_i' - \bar{y}')}{\Sigma_i(y_i' - \bar{y}')^2}\right\}e^{-a}$$
$$= 1 - (1 - s_y r_y)e^{-a}, \tag{11}$$

where r_y represents the coefficient of correlation between the income arrays y and y_i, and s_y represents the ratio of the standard deviation of the array y to the standard deviation of the array y'. Under stationary conditions, however, y and y' differ only in the arrangement of their elements, not in the elements themselves; hence $s_y = 1$ and $\bar{c}_i = \bar{c} = \bar{y} = \bar{y}_i$. Given these restrictions, we obtain the following least-squares estimates of the slope and intercept coefficients of the regression of consumption on income at date $t_0 + 1$:

$$B' = 1 - (1 - r_y)e^{-(a)} \tag{12}$$

$$A' = \bar{y}(1 - r_y)e^{-(a)}. \tag{13}$$

Like any other correlation coefficient, r_y can only assume values between ± 1. If all variations in income flows are strictly random, $r_y = 1$, and the regression line coincides with the 45° line, as indicated earlier. If income permutations are systematic in their effect, r_y will be less than unity; hence B' will be less than unity and its intercept positive. If all households initially have the same service income, $r_y = 0$ and the slope of the regression line will depend simply on the magnitude of the adjustment coefficient $e^{-(a)}$, being smaller the less the value of the exponent (a). [...]

$$\left.\begin{array}{l} \dfrac{\partial B'}{\partial a} = (1 - r_y)ae^{-(a)} \geqslant 0 \\[2em] \dfrac{\partial B'}{\partial r_y} = e^{-(a)} > 0 \\[2em] \dfrac{\partial A'}{\partial a} = -\bar{y}a(1 - r_y)e^{-(a)} \leqslant 0 \\[2em] \dfrac{\partial A'}{\partial r_y} = -\bar{y}e^{-(a)} < 0. \end{array}\right\} \tag{14}$$

In plain words, our theory implies a higher slope and a lower intercept the greater the marginal propensity to consume wealth, and the higher the correlation between income arrays at the beginning and end of the period of observation. For later discussion, it is relevant to emphasize here that the effects of fluctuating income (lower value of r_y) are statistically indistinguishable from the effects of increased wealth (lower values of a). Thus 'entrepreneurial' households may exhibit relatively low income-propensities to consume either because of uncertain incomes or because their holdings of assets tend to be large relative to their consumption. Similarly, 'proletarian' households may exhibit relatively high income-propensities to consume either because their incomes are stable or because their holdings of wealth are slight relative to consumption. Though the implications of our theory are definite, therefore, they are not unambiguous in empirical import. One must be correspondingly cautious in applying them to practical problems. [...]

Other things being equal, therefore, the slope derivatives in (14) may be taken to imply: (i) that cross-section MPCYs will be smaller the higher the average level of household income; (ii) that households with variable incomes will tend to have lower MPCYs than households with steady incomes. A significant portion of Friedman's analysis in the *Theory of the Consumption Function* is directed towards showing that the second of these implications is empirically valid (see particularly his discussion of farm and non-farm families at pp. 58–69, and of occupation characteristics of families at pp. 69–79). His arguments are compelling, considered in the context of his model (which omits explicit mention of adjustment processes); they are merely suggestive in the context of ours. The first proposition accords well with tradition and common sense and has received contemporary support from many writers. Resting as it does on non-linearity assumptions, it is disputed by Friedman—though his own charts of farm and non-farm regressions (p. 59) and of income-change groups (pp. 101 and 105) might be considered to lend firm support to the traditional view. From the standpoint of our model, no judgment is warranted, for in none of the studies that we have examined is proper care taken to ensure that 'other things' are in any degree equal. [...] Our model, like Friedman's, implies an observed regression of measured consumption on measured income for which the ratio of consumption to income declines as measured income increases. Our model, like Friedman's, implies that observed cross-section regressions will shift upward in response to an increase in mean measured income; more generally, that regressions in a growing economy will normally lie farther from the origin of the $y-c$ plane the later the date to which they correspond. Our model, like Friedman's, implies that the mean point of observed regressions will typically lie on or close to a ray of slope $k = a/(g+a)$ through the origin of the $y-c$ plane. Contrary to Friedman's stated belief, his model—like ours—is consistent with Fisher's finding that the marginal propensities to save of certain age and occupational groups are negative. In Friedman's model as in ours, moreover, the slope of the $c - y$ scatter may well be significantly flatter at low than at high levels of measured income, reflecting the influence of life-cycle phenomena. In all of these and in many other *qualitative* respects, there is literally nothing to choose between the two theories of household behavior.

Turning to quantitative comparisons, we begin by observing that our model will yield regression results different from Friedman's only insofar as our estimates of a differ from his estimates of β. This being the case, we confine attention to an issue where the relative magnitudes of a and β are of crucial significance, namely, the close correspondence that Friedman shows to exist between measured income elasticities of consumption and direct estimates of r_y obtained by correlating income arrays for different years. [...]

If we compute the income-elasticity of consumption at the mean point of the $c - y$ regression, the value so obtained is an estimate of the value of $\varepsilon_y = 1 - (1 - s_y r_y)e^{-x}$. The difference between this estimate of the income-elasticity of consumption and the income-correlation coefficient r_y is thus given by

$$\varepsilon_y - r_y = (1 - r_y) - (1 - s_y r_y)e^{-x}.$$

In normal circumstances, however, we should expect s_y to be close to unity, since its value reflects the rate of growth of aggregate income (roughly speaking, $s_y = 1/(g + 1)$). Except in unusual circumstances, therefore, the difference between ε_y and r_y should be approximately equal to $(1 - r_y)(1 - e^{-x})$. Now, this difference clearly will be substantially different from zero unless: (i) income permutations are relatively unimportant (that is, r_y is close to unity); (ii) households adjust very slowly to such income permutations as occur (that is, the adjustment exponent is close to zero). For only in these cases will the slope of the $c - y$ scatter reflect the influence (if any) of income permutations alone—which is what is required if income-elasticities and income-correlation coefficients are to be approximately equal.

As indicated already, the empirical evidence suggests that measured values of elasticities and correlation coefficients are generally very similar. Moreover, both are typically less than unity by a substantial amount. We infer from this that the adjustment exponents β and a must be relatively small (or that our regression formulae are invalid!); for the only alternative is to suppose that s_y is significantly less than unity, and this would require that the rate of growth of aggregate income should typically exceed, say, 10 per cent per annum, which we know to be untrue.

Our estimate of the adjustment exponent a, namely 0·20, is not too large to be consistent with the empirical evidence. Observed differences between elasticities and correlation coefficients are frequently on the order of 0·02–0·04, which is the kind of difference that our model will generate with growth rates of 2 per cent per annum and an adjustment coefficient of $e^{-0.20} = 0.82$.

But Friedman's estimate of the probable value of the adjustment exponent β, namely, $0 \cdot 40–0 \cdot 70$, is much too large to be reconciled with the empirical evidence, for it entails values of the adjustment coefficient $e^{-\beta}$ of only $0 \cdot 50–0 \cdot 67$. This implies differences between income elasticities and correlation coefficients of $0 \cdot 04–0 \cdot 10$ for urban households, and differences of $0 \cdot 15–0 \cdot 25$ for farm households. Our conclusion is that the 'effective horizon' implicit in Friedman's definition of the permanent income concept would have to be considerably longer than the three to five years that he assumes it to be in order to produce anything like the measure of agreement between income-elasticities and income-correlation coefficients that is observed in practice. (The 'effective horizon' implicit in the formula $b = kP_y$, it should be noted, is of infinite length!) Our implicit estimate of the relevant horizon, being based on average rather than marginal consumption-wealth data, may itself be on the small side, and it is nearly 15 years.

The preceding discussion casts doubt on the validity of Friedman's explanation of the temporal relation between consumption and income, for it is largely from his work with time-series regressions of consumption on permanent income that his views about the magnitude of β are drawn. It appears from our analysis that the time-series correlation between permanent income and consumption is spurious: that permanent income is a proxy for a much larger magnitude, namely, household wealth.

This is not the only area where Friedman's theory is open to question; where less idiosyncratic theories—including ours—yield different and rather more plausible results. For example, we should argue that the marginal propensity to save will (other things being equal) tend to decline as we move from lower to higher levels of household income, inferring this result from the negative curvature hypothesis. There is much evidence to support this position, as indicated earlier; but Friedman must oppose it because he assumes that consumption is directly proportional to permanent income.

We should argue that wealth will be distributed much more unequally than income in any advanced society, inferring this from the assumption that the wealth-elasticity of consumption is less than unity and the generalized stability hypothesis (that is, the tendency of consumption to exhaust the whole of income). In the absence of shifts over time in the level of the modal consumption locus, moreover, we should have to argue that the distribution of wealth will tend to become ever more unequal as aggregate real income increases. The validity of the first of these implications is not open to serious argument. As for the second, the evidence suggests no tendency towards greater inequality in the distribution of income or wealth, which suggests that (i) the negative curvature hypothesis is invalid, or (ii) the modal consumption locus is affected in the long run by 'customary' standards of consumption expenditure. We shall consider these alternatives later; here we merely remark that Friedman's model provides no definite link between income and wealth—an absurdity of the first order of magnitude in a theory that purports to say something about saving behavior.

We should argue that receipts of windfall income will, in general, affect consumption in the short run in exactly the same way as an increase in any other kind of income, inferring this from the assumption that current purchasing power consists simply of current wealth, regardless of its original source. There is a large literature on this subject, and all of it seems to support our position. Friedman cannot accept the obvious conclusion because he assumes that changes in measured income affect consumption only insofar as they produce variations in the household's subjective evaluation of its permanent income—and permanent income is so defined that at most a minor fraction of windfall receipts will in fact be counted as 'permanent'.

We do not ourselves have serious doubts about where the truth lies on any of these issues, for we regard the permanent income theory as a statistically ingenious but economically irrelevant and misleading description of household behavior. A detailed defense of our position is hardly possible without vastly better information about household asset holdings than is presently available. Even without such a defense, however, it is clear from the preceding discussion that our model will perform at least as well as Friedman's in relation to every cross-section problem that is considered by him. For where qualitative properties of consumption-income scatters are concerned, the statistical implications of the two theories are observationally indistinguishable. Moreover, our model is at least as simple and plausible as Friedman's in its theoretical foundations, and definetly richer in testable empirical implications. Without further argument, therefore, we may claim that our theory is at least as good as if not marginally superior to, the permanent income theory. [...]

If the generalized stability hypothesis holds, the time path of aggregate consumption should be very similar to the time path of aggregate income in a steadily growing economy. Indeed, if wealth-elasticities of consumption are unity, aggregate consumption should be directly proportional to aggregate income, the constant of proportionality being our old friend $k = a/(g+a)$. [...]

So much by way of speculation. Having indicated in broad outline what time paths we should expect our model to generate, we turn now to historical data for the United States—the only country for which reasonably reliable estimates of household wealth are available over any considerable period of time. Figure 2.7 shows the time profile of consumption-income points for the period 1900–64, together with the time profile of consumption-wealth points over the period 1945–58 and for selected years prior to 1945 (every year for which household wealth data are available.) Since all profiles are plotted on double-log scales, proportionality of variables is implied by a linear relationship of slope $+1$, and proportionality of variables in different relations by parallel profiles.

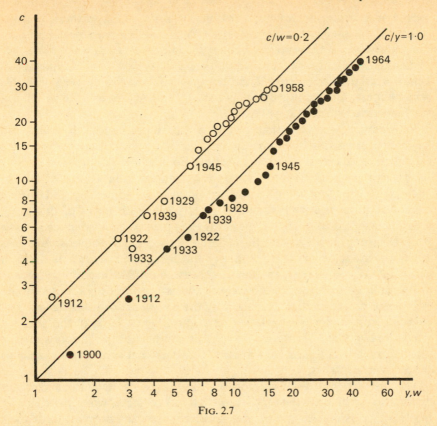

FIG. 2.7

That consumption historically has tended to be approximately 90 per cent of income in the United States is well known; the $c - y$ profile in Figure 2.7 merely confirms this item of textbook information. It is not perhaps so well known, but is equally true, that consumption historically has tended to be approximately 20 per cent of household wealth (both measured in current dollars). This finding constitutes an apparent contradiction of the negative curvature hypothesis. Before commenting on that, however, it is interesting to notice that the consumption-income ratio furnished by the data corresponds closely with the figures suggested by our model. The rate of growth of real per capita income (calculated from a series prepared by Simon Kuznets) was 0·017 in the period from 1900–29, 0·00 (that is, nil) in the period 1929–39, 0·024 in the period 1946–64 and 0·017 for the entire period 1900–64. Given a value for a of 0·20, these growth figures imply a consumption-income ratio of 0·92 for the periods 1900–64 and 1900–29, ratio of 0·00 for the period 1929–39, and a ratio of 0·89 for the post-war period 1946–64. With due allowance for variations in the consumption-wealth ratio (which has in fact fluctuated over time by as much as 25 per cent of its maximum value), these computations seem to lend strong support to the hypothesis that the observed 'constancy' of the saving ratio reflects nothing more profound than the tendency of consumption to equal income at every point in time. We certainly should not expect consumption to display such a regular pattern of behavior relative to income if the majority of households were unstable accumulators. The empirical evidence thus seems to confirm the validity of the generalized stability hypothesis.

Returning now to the time profile of consumption-wealth points, we begin by noting that the apparent constancy of the consumption-wealth ratio is to some extent an optical illusion. For the one period on which we have continuous data (1945–58), the ratio dropped from just under 0·22 in 1948 to just over 0·18 in 1958—a reduction of about 15 per cent in 10 years. Considering the relative magnitudes involved in both terms of this ratio, the decline indicated might well be considered precipitous—so much so as to provide strong support for the negative curvature hypothesis. But this position cannot be defended with any force, for the consumption-wealth ratio in 1900 was precisely the same as the ratio in 1948, namely, 0·22.

It is difficult to reconcile these contradictory positions without running into worse problems than are posed by the contradictions themselves. The evidence from budget-study data is so compelling in favor of the negative curvature hypothesis, however, that one or another reconciliation is almost mandatory. We can think of two rationalizations that seem to us worthy of serious consideration.

The first rationalization is more in the nature of an evasion than an explanation; it involves the supposition that market forces work in such a way that earning assets are valued at a relatively constant proportion of their income yield. The tendency of consumption to exhaust total income at all times would then link consumption with wealth in a similar fashion, producing relative constancy in the proportions between all three magnitudes—income, consumption, and wealth. There is some evidence that a process of this kind is at work. For if one deflates Goldsmith's wealth data with an index of the prices of capital goods, one finds that the ratio of 'real' wealth to 'real' income declines steadily during the period 1900–58. This means that the price level of capital goods historically has increased more rapidly than the price index implicit in the real income (and consumption) series. If we ask, 'Which way did the *true* ratio of consumption to wealth move?', our response must be that we simply do not know. for if we allow for quality changes, the relative rise in market prices of capital goods might be considered to reflect accurately the 'service value' of such goods, leaving us with an approximately constant ratio of real consumption to real wealth; or the relative rise in capital goods prices might be considered to represent an understatement of the service value of wealth held by households, in which case we should argue that the consumption–wealth ratio has after all decreased! One is tempted to conclude from all this that the constancy or non-constancy of the consumption–wealth ratio over periods of more than a decade is not an empirically meaningful problem—and, as we noted earlier, the ratio did decline substantially during the one period for which we have continuous data.

The second rationalization does not require us to question the meaning of the raw statistics on wealth and consumption. It involves the supposition that consumption loci shift over time as per capita wealth rises, marginal consumption-wealth ratios becoming greater as standards of living rise. This conjecture bears an obvious resemblance to Duesenberry's famous 'relative income' hypothesis, and might be defended on similar sociological and psychological grounds. [...]

3. Investment

Introductory Note

The question of the determinants of the level of private fixed investment has undoubtedly led to more controversy than the question of the determinants of private consumption. As we have already noted,[1] Keynes's theory of investment was not particularly novel, but was based on the familiar classical view that a profiit-maximizing entrepreneur would embark on an investment project if and only if the rate at which its expected net future returns had to be discounted to bring their sum into equality with its supply price were greater than the rate of interest—loosely, if the project was 'profitable'.[2] We saw earlier that this approach would provide, at any moment, an array of investment opportunities ranked in order of profitability, but that it was not sufficient to explain the flow of investment over time. This problem was stated explicitly by Lerner[3] in 1944, and is lucidly expressed by Haavelmo in an often-quoted passage:

What we should reject is the naive reasoning that there is a demand schedule for investment which could be derived from a classical scheme of producers' behaviour in maximising profit. The demand for investment cannot simply be derived from the demand for capital. Demand for a finite addition to the stock of capital can lead to any rate of investment, from almost zero to infinity, depending on the additional hypothesis we introduce regarding the speed of reaction of capital users.[4]

Of course, provided we are content with a comparative static analysis, this problem does not arise: in a given state of confidence and expectations and with a given speed of reaction, investment will be higher in a situation characterized by low interest rates than in one characterized by high rates. But in a properly dynamic framework, the objection is clearly valid.

Perhaps the simplest solution is to agree that the fundamental relationship is between the desired stock of capital and the interest rate, and to assume that investment in any period is undertaken so as to make up some constant fraction of the gap between desired and existing capital stock. This would lead to an inverse relationship between the rate of investment and the *rate of*

[1] p. 4 above.

[2] We ignore here the debate as to the relative merits of this 'internal rate of return' approach and the 'present value' approach. According to the latter, if the stream of expected future net returns is discounted at the going rate of interest, the project should be undertaken if the resulting 'present value' is greater than the supply price. Under certain strict conditions the two approaches are equivalent. For a review of this controversy. see J. Hirshleifer 'On the Theory of Optimal Investment Decision', *J. Pol. Econ.* Aug. 1958.

[3] A. P. Lerner, *The Economics of Control* (New York: Macmillan, 1944), Chapter 25.

[4] T. Haavelmo, *A Study in the Theory of Investment* (University of Chicago Press, 1960), p. 216.

change of the interest rate.[5] This solution does not, however, seem to have attracted much attention. On the whole, economists have sought either to provide an alternative rationale for the dependence of the rate of investment on the level of the interest rate, or to seek a fundamental shift of emphasis— in particular by formalizing, via the 'acceleration principle', the role of expectations in determining investment.

The paper by Witte [Reading 3.1] is an exception, attempting to show that the problem can be avoided if we consider the peculiar nature of the capital goods sector. In particular [p. 123], he notes that in this sector *demand* is for a stock of capital goods while *supply* is of a flow of investment goods. So far as the stock of capital is concerned, at a given interest rate there will be a downward-sloping demand schedule relating firms' demand for capital to its supply price. A fall in the rate of interest shifts this demand schedule to the right, raising the market price of the existing stock. This in turn raises the output of the capital goods industry to the point at which the new marginal supply price is equal to the new demand price. Thus a fall in the rate of interest raises the rate of investment (the rate of production of capital goods) —though through the decisions of capital goods suppliers rather than directly through the decisions of those demanding investment goods: 'The essential point is that the rate-of-investment decision, as opposed to the optimum-stock decision, is made by the capital-goods-producing firms, which determine how much they care to produce at the prevailing market price.' [p. 124]

Yet it is not clear that this really solves the problem. Witte's argument depends crucially on the assumption that the potential flow of investment goods is very small in relation to the stock, so that an increase in the demand for capital raises the demand price for a long period. This is an empirical judgement concerning the price elasticity of supply of the capital goods industry which might easily prove to be false. More important, in the long run (however long), we must still conclude that the rate of net investment will return to zero when the desired capital stock is attained.

A different and very much more complex attempt to provide a basis for the dependence of the level of investment on the rate of interest is offered by Eisner and Strotz. [A brief extract from their long, comprehensive, and

[5] Formally, let $K_t^* = a - br_t$, for example, where K_t^* is the desired stock of capital in period t, r_t is the interest rate, and a and b are parameters. Suppose that investment I_t in the period is undertaken so as to close a fraction λ of the gap between desired and existing capital stocks, so that $I_t = \lambda(K_t^* - K_{t-1})$. Since $I_t = K_t - K_{t-1}$ (investment is the change in the stock of capital), we have

$$K_t = \lambda K_t^* + (1-\lambda)K_{t-1}.$$

On taking first differences,

$$K_t - K_{t-1} = I_t = -\lambda b \Delta r_t + (1-\lambda)I_{t-1}.$$

Thus investment varies negatively with the change in the rate of interest; I_{t-1} appears as a reflection of the assumption that investment does not instantaneously respond to a change in the interest rate.

mathematically rather difficult paper appears as Reading 3.2.] Suppose a change takes place—in demand, in the costs of factors of production, or in technology—which increases the desired level of the capital stock. (This is a very general form of the accelerator principle: see pp. 136–145 below.) For each firm, the consequential expansion will involve costs of adjustment which will be higher the more promptly the investment is carried out and the higher the rate of investment. These costs may be both external—the supply-price of capital goods will rise more the greater the short-run rise in demand—and internal—costs of reorganizing the production process. The rate of return net of the costs of expansion will thus be equal to the profit accruing from the given amount of capital less the costs of acquiring the capital *at the chosen rate*, and it is the discounted value of this net return which the firm maximizes.

On certain plausible assumptions about the way in which expansion costs might vary with the rate of investment, Eisner and Strotz provide a rationale for a lagged response of investment to an increase in the desired capital stock. It is argued that the pattern of the lag will be one of geometrically declining weights as we go back in time. This brings us to the central question: how will the speed of response vary when the rate of interest alters? It is shown mathematically [p. 136] that, other things being equal, the investment will be more spread out the higher is the interest rate, 'or, in other words, that a rise in the interest rate delays investment'. Eisner and Strotz do not give an intuitive explanation of this result, but it seems clear that the higher is the interest rate (the rate at which net returns are discounted) the greater will be the weight given to short-run rather than long-run net returns. But these short-run returns will be lower the more rapid is the rate of investment, given the costs of rapid expansion. Thus a high interest rate militates against rapid expansion.

If the firm can be regarded as typical, a similar result will hold for business investment in aggregate. The theory is clearly 'post-Keynesian' in inspiration: an increase in the desired capital stock (upward shift in the marginal efficiency of capital schedule) raises investment, but the rate of investment for a given increment in the desired capital stock varies inversely with the interest rate.

An entirely different approach to the theory of investment concentrates on the determinants of shifts in the MEC schedule, rather than on the causes of movements along it. The majority of these approaches invoke some form of the 'acceleration principle' [see Reading 3.3 by Eckaus]. In its crudest form, the acceleration principle states that, other things being equal, an increase in a firm's rate of output will require a proportionate increase in its stock of capital equipment. This follows directly if it is assumed that the capital/output ratio is some fixed constant, v. In that case, we can write

$$K_t = vY_t$$

and thus
$$I_t = \Delta K_t = v\Delta Y_t,$$

the level of net investment is proportional to the change in output.

This relation is barely plausible as it stands: the assumption of a fixed capital output ratio follows only if there are no changes of technique such as might result from changes in relative factor prices—or if there are fixed technical coefficients in production—and if returns to scale are constant. Furthermore, the time-scale is left vague, and the principle can obviously only work in a limited way for falls in output, since the maximum rate of net disinvestment is limited to the rate of scrapping of capital equipment.

Some of these difficulties can be overcome if the accelerator coefficient v is regarded as a variable rather than a fixed parameter—provided that a coherent account can be given of changes in v. Eckaus lists [p. 139] a number of factors which could influence the value of v at any particular time, but the formal development of the acceleration principle has concentrated particularly on the role of expectations, on the timing of the response to increased demand, and on the influence of the existing degree of capacity utilization.

Let us assume that the entrepreneur has, for any level of output, a desired capital stock, K^*. Then in any period t,

$$K^*_t = v Y_t$$

where, again, v need not be taken as strictly fixed. Now suppose that in any period, net investment is undertaken so as to make up a certain proportion λ of the gap between the desired and existing capital stock:

$$I_t = \lambda(K^*_t - K_{t-1})$$

Again, λ need not be strictly constant: it will tend to be lower the more uncertain the future outlook for demand, the closer to full capacity is the investment-goods industry, the higher (following Eisner and Strotz) is the rate of interest, and so on. Combining these two relationships yields a version of the 'flexible accelerator':

$$I_t = \lambda v Y_t - \lambda K_{t-1}.$$

Net investment will vary positively with output and negatively with the existing stock of capital.[6] We may finally introduce expectations explicitly by acknowledging that the desired capital stock will in practice vary with expected future output, Y^e, at some time or times $t+r$:

$$I_t = \lambda v Y^e_{t+r} - \lambda K_{t-1}.$$

As Eckaus shows, there are a variety of ways in which this flexible accelerator can be developed or extended, and in which it can be made susceptible to empirical testing at an aggregate level.

An entirely different approach—the 'neoclassical' approach—has been

[6] The length of the time-period t need no longer be specified, for changes in its length will be reflected in changes in the size of λ.

proposed by Jorgenson [Reading 3.4]. Jorgenson assumes that the firm maximizes its present value (the difference between the future streams of receipts on the one hand and labour and capital outlays on the other, approximately discounted) subject to the constraints (a) that the rate of change of the input of capital services is equal to the rate of net investment, and (b) that the relationship between levels of output and inputs of labour and capital services is constrained by a production function. Given familiar assumptions, it follows that the marginal physical product of labour is equal to the real wage. So far as capital is concerned, the constraint (a) mentioned above means simply that the increase in the capital stock is equal to gross investment less replacement investment, while (b) requires that the marginal physical product of capital is equal to its 'real user cost'. The user cost of capital, analogous to the wage-rate, has three components. First, there is the opportunity cost of investing money in capital goods rather than in financial assets. If the price of capital goods is q per unit, then this opportunity cost will be qr per unit, where r is the interest rate. Secondly, there is the cost of depreciation. If depreciation is a constant fraction δ of the capital stock, this cost is $q\delta$ per unit of capital. Thirdly, if the price of capital goods is rising, this appreciation of their value will be an offsetting element: user cost will be lower by $\dot{q}$ per unit, where $\dot{q}$ is the rate of change of capital goods prices. Thus the marginal physical product of capital is equated to the real user cost of capital, c/p, where p is the price level:

$$\frac{c}{p} = \frac{qr + q\delta - \dot{q}}{p}.$$

As in any similar microeconomic analysis of the behaviour of the firm, the assumption of a production function relating real output, Y, to inputs of labour and capital, together with the 'perfect competition' assumption that inputs are employed up to the point at which their marginal physical products are equal to their real unit costs, means that the system is complete, given market prices. For example, if the production function is of Cobb-Douglas form:

$$Y = AK^{\alpha}L^{\beta},$$

with

$$\frac{\partial Y}{\partial K} = \alpha \frac{Y}{K} = \frac{c}{p}$$

and

$$\frac{\partial Y}{\partial L} = \beta \frac{Y}{L} = \frac{w}{p},$$

then Y, K and L can be expressed in terms of the three prices p, c, and w.

At first sight, the fact that the demand for capital is thus a function solely of prices (in particular, an inverse function of c, if p and w are held constant) fails to solve the 'Lerner–Haavelmo' problem: a finite addition to the desired capital stock does not lead to a determinate rate of investment. Jorgenson, however, approaches the problem in a different way. Assume that there are no adjustment costs and no uncertainty. Then the firm will always be adjusted to the optimal capital stock, and questions of adjustment to a discrete change in the interest rate do not arise. Instead, the question can be treated as one of comparative dynamics–the comparison of two (optimal) paths of capital accumulation under two different interest rates. The gross demand for investment goods (net and replacement) is given by

$$I = \dot{K} + \delta K,$$

(where $\dot{K}$ is the change in the capital stock and δ is the rate of depreciation of capital) with

$$K = f(p, w, c).$$

Comparing two situations with initial K identical, but with different interest rates, the second equation implies that, with w and p fixed, c must be unchanged in the face of changes in the interest rate. From the expression for c noted above, this in turn implies that interest rate changes must be exactly compensated by changes in the price of investment goods. Jorgenson shows mathematically that from these assumptions it follows that $\partial I/\partial r = \partial K/\partial c \times c < 0$, that is, that investment varies (in two alternative situations) inversely with the rate of interest.

Jorgenson does not give a very clear economic account of this mathematical result. It seems that although capital goods prices change to offset the change in the interest rate, so that the *initial* user cost of capital, c, and hence the *initial* capital stocks in the two situations are identical, the definition of user cost does not imply that *future* values of c will be identical. A rise in the interest rate raises future c's and hence the future optimal path of capital accumulation will be lower than it otherwise would have been.

The basis of this argument can in fact be put very simply. Suppose that all prices except the interest rate are held constant. Then, given the production function, a firm will choose a more capital-intensive technique the lower is the interest rate. In the simplest case, we may assume too that for any *given* interest rate, the optimal capital stock still increases proportionately with output. Combining these two propositions:

$$K = v(r) \cdot Y$$

where v is an inverse function of r.
Differentiating with respect to time,

$$\frac{\partial K}{\partial t} = I = v(r) \frac{\partial Y}{\partial t}.$$

Comparing two situations characterized by identical rates of expansion of output but different interest rates,

$$I_1/I_2 = v(r_1)/v(r_2).$$

Thus if r_1 is less than r_2, $v(r_1)$ will be greater than $v(r_2)$ and investment will be higher.

Put in this crude form, the argument is really rather simple. But it is important to note that the conclusion relates not to the response of investment to a once-for-all change in the rate of interest with output constant, but to the comparative levels of investment in two cases of output growth, the one characterized by a low rate of interest, the other by a high one.[7]

To summarize, the two major propositions of modern investment theory seem to be, first, that one can expect—in very general terms—some sort of systematic relationship between the desired stock of capital and the level of output (and thus between the level of net investment and the rate of change of output), and secondly, that this relationship is likely to vary with the cost of capital, either in absolute terms or—in the neoclassical models—relative to the cost of other inputs.

In addition, a variety of other factors are likely to play a part—notably the availability (as well as the cost) of finance, the degree of capital utilization, the certainty as well as the level of demand expectations, and so on. It is important to note, too, that different kinds of investment may be sensitive in different degrees to these various factors. Long-lived projects whose returns can be predicted with relative certainty—such as construction projects—will, for example, be more sensitive to changes in the cost of finance than short-lived projects of a relatively risky nature—such an investment in machinery— where demand considerations may be expected to predominate. And, of course, by no means all investment can be treated in similar fashion to business fixed investment: investment by the public sector, investment in housing, and investment in stocks (inventories) are the most obvious exceptions.

3.1 Capital, Investment and the Rate of Interest*
[...]
DETERMINATION OF THE PRICES OF CAPITAL GOODS

The aggregate demand curve for a particular type of capital good is derived by summation from the demand curves of all the firms which are actual or potential users of the type of capital good in question. The demand curve in Figure 3.1 relates quantity of the capital good desired to be held to the market price of the capital goods. I am employing a demand curve of the

[7] This argument relates to net investment. A similar argument can be constructed for replacement investment: the higher the capital stock (because of a lower rate of interest), the higher will investment replacement be.

* From J. G. Witte, 'The Microfoundations of the Social Investment Function', *Journal of Political Economy*, Oct. 1963. Reprinted by permission of the University of Chicago Press.

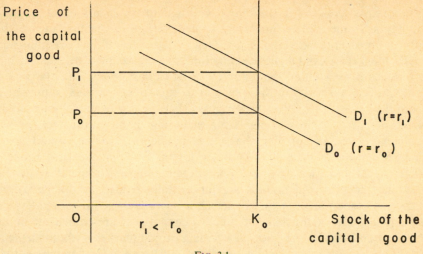

Fig. 3.1

Wicksteed type, in which the reservation schedules of those firms with some initial endowment of the capital good are included in the demand curve. By this procedure the supply schedule of the capital good is inelastic with respect to price; the stock in existence is a given datum at any point in time. The size of the stock will change over time unless the rates of depreciation and production are equal to one another, but at any particular moment of time the stock must be treated as datum. This is particularly important if the annual increment to the stock, resulting from current production less capital consumption, is small relative to the total stock. In this case the influence of demand predominates over that of *flow* supply in the determination of the market price. This can be said without denying the fact that flow supply considerations must dominate the outcome in the long run. In the case of very durable goods, however, a relatively long time must elapse before positive or negative net production produces a significant alteration in the size of the total stock. This is only to say that Marshall's momentary-equilibrium analysis is probably more applicable to houses or office buildings than to special-purpose machinery and certainly more applicable to houses than to merchants' stocks. For clarity we assume that the annual increment to the stock of this type of capital good is so small that we can ignore any influence of the annual flow supply on the market price. Thus variations in demand will necessarily be associated with variations in the market price, for ... price flexibility is necessary to reconcile the freedom of the individual firm to hold all it wishes with the restriction that the entire stock must be held by someone.

In addition to the stock-supply schedule we also have a flow-supply schedule relating the rate of output of capital goods to producers' expectations of market price. This seems to be the ordinary Marshallian supply schedule in which the rate of output is a function of ex ante market price.

With a given capacity in the capital goods industry at any time, the flow-supply schedule will be positively sloped, reflecting the law of variable proportions in the individual firms. There are two conditions of equilibrium in the market for capital goods at any time: the market price must be such as to induce firms to hold the entire stock of capital goods, and the rate of output of capital goods must be such as to equate the marginal supply price with the market price. This presupposes that the law of indifference holds: that is, that two units of the same economic good cannot sell at two different prices. In applying the law of indifference to the capital goods market some allowance must be made for the fact that identical goods of different chronological ages have different remaining economic life spans. We assume that price differentials are functionally related to differentials of expected economic life span. In Haavelmo's words: 'The law of indifference of capital prices states that, for units of capital that are equivalent in any production function, the prices in a perfect capital market, without elements of price expectations or the like, can differ only because of differences in their durability properties.' We conclude that there is a unique rate of output of capital goods, a unique rate of gross investment, associated with each market price of capital goods.

VARIATIONS IN THE RATE OF INTEREST

With the stock of capital goods given let the rate of interest fall. For a given level of firms' sales expectations this fall in the rate of interest raises the present value of the marginal expected profit annuity associated with its capital stock, creating excess firm demand for capital goods at the prevailing price. Thus, in Figure 3.2 the aggregate demand curve shifts to the right and the market price of capital goods must rise so that the market be cleared. The increase in the market price creates a flow disequilibrium, which is followed by a higher rate of output of new capital goods, the rate being that for which the marginal supply price is equal to the new market price. For any conjectural variation in the rate of interest a new rate of output, a new rate of gross investment, can be determined. The essential point is that the rate-of-investment decision, as opposed to the optimum-stock decision, is made by the capital-goods-producing firms, which determine how much they care to produce at the prevailing market price. With the capital stock and the level of sales expectations given, what is determined is a set of rates of gross investment uniquely associated with a corresponding set of interest rates. This set of equilibrium relationships traces out a social investment function that relates aggregate investment to the rate of interest. The point is that this social investment function, or marginal-efficiency-of-capital schedule, is not a demand curve for anything and is not derived by aggregation from similar micro-investment functions. In Patinkin's language, it is a market equilibrium curve rather than a demand curve. Its micro foundations are not suspect, nor is it derived by any expectational *deus ex machina*. Its existence stems from

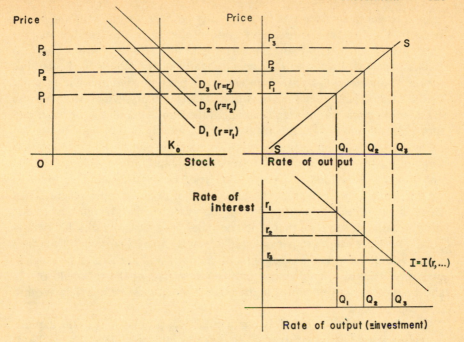

Fig. 3.2

the fact that the aggregate quantity of capital goods cannot be increased very rapidly. Whereas the individual firm can increase its stock of capital significantly within one year's time, when other enterprises are not increasing their demands for capital goods, all enterprises cannot do this simultaneously. The limitation is one of capacity and cost. Thus, the aggregative rate of investment can be regarded as a function of the rate of interest, whereas this would not be possible if there were no constraint on the rate of output of capital goods.

Once again, the rate-of-investment decision is the rate-of-output decision of supplying enterprises and not the rate-of-input decision of capital-using firms.

The interest elasticity of investment is really the interest elasticity of the rate of output of capital goods. Since both a demand and a supply response are subsumed under this relationship... this elasticity is dependent upon two other elasticities. These are (a) the elasticity of demand price with respect to the rate of interest, and (b) the elasticity of the rate of output of capital goods with respect to the market price of capital goods. From my assumption of no feedback from flow supply to stock supply in the relevant time period, I can identify market price with demand price. From this it follows that the elasticity of the rate of interest, *ceteris paribus*, is equal to the multiplicative product of the other two elasticities.

The first elasticity is that of the capitalized marginal profit annuity with respect to the rate of interest. This elasticity governs the extent of the move-ment in demand price consequent upon a change in the relevant market rate of interest. ... This elasticity varies within the limits of almost zero to minus one, with its absolute value a function of the length of the entrep-reneur's time horizon. Its absolute value reaches a maximum value of unity as the entrepreneur's time horizon approaches infinity, which it will if the entrepeneur plans periodic replacement of the capital good into the indefinite future. In all other cases the value of this elasticity is less than unity. An interesting implication of this is that this elasticity should be regarded as a function of the strength of the entrepeneur's expectations and not of the ephemeral expected life of a particular type of capital good. This much is clear as soon as we recognize the possibility of periodic replacement. Thus there is no necessity for the interest elasticity of the demand price for inventories to be less than that of the demand price for more durable capital goods; both are subject to periodic replacement. A short horizon is then seen as the entrepreneur's defense against uncertainty and not as a technological necessity. This is, of course, commonly recognized as the rationale of the short payoff periods on which many businessmen insist before they acquire new capital goods.

The second elasticity is simply the ordinary supply elasticity of the capital-goods industry. The only restriction that can be imposed on its value is that it is less than plus infinity, which must be the case with a given productive capacity in the short run. This elasticity will probably vary inversely with the rate of capacity utilization in the capital-goods industry, being high for a low level of aggregate economic activity and vice versa. From this one should not conclude that the elasticity of the social investment function will tend to be relatively high in periods of recession, however, for the entrepreneur's degree of uncertainty might be relatively high in a period of low aggregative activity. Both elasticities determine the proportionate response of the rate of investment to the rate of interest, and both must be considered in such a judgement.

A necessary condition for there to be a determinate rate of output of new capital goods is that the flow supply curve have less than infinite elasticity. This raises an interesting question concerning the compatibility of this analysis with a model of unemployment equilibrium. If a state of excess capacity prevails throughout the economy during a recession, surely the capital-goods sector must experience some excess capacity. Indeed the durable-goods industries seem to have marked excess capacity in recession years. Does the existence of excess capacity threaten the validity of the assumption of a finitely-elastic flow-supply curve? If so, the consequence is serious, because the analysis developed in this paper would be inapplicable to periods of underemploymnet.

One way out of this problem is to assume, along with Keynes, that marginal costs of the individual firm rise with the rate of output over any relevant range of output. .... Keynes assumed that industrial plant is adapt-able and indivisible. This assumption suffices to generate a supply curve of finite elasticity and a determinate rate of investment, but it is not consistent with many empirical studies of industrial cost behaviour. However, a failure of individual firm marginal costs to rise with the rate of output when there is a great deal of excess capacity does not necessarily rule out the possibility of an industry supply curve of finite elasticity. If each firm's marginal cost curve is flat over ranges of outputs likely to be encountered in a recession, the industry supply curve may still be positively sloped if there is *temporary* exit from the industry. The existence of a flat range of the marginal cost curve implies that average variable cost is approximately equal to marginal cost over some of the range of flatness. Thus it would not be too surprising to observe that some firms would shut down in a recession when price falls to a level that approximates average variable cost. Those firms with relatively pessimistic expectations about the duration of the recession and those with relatively weak financial positions may be the ones expected to shut down. To the extent that temporary exit occurs in recessions, followed by re-entry when demand recovers, the industry supply curve would have a positive slope, and the rate of output would be determinate. Thus there is no necessary inconsistency between the required assumption of finite supply elasticity and conditions of underemployment equilibrium. [...]

3.2 The Rate of Interest and the Rate of Investment*
[...]
THE INTEREQUILIBRIUM APPROACH

Here we begin with the familiar notion of the long-run equilibrium of the firm. We imagine that the rate of profit has been constant and that the size of plant has been chosen so as to make this constant profit level a maximum. The long-run average cost curve is U-shaped and if the firm is in a competitive industry, it is operating at the minimum point of that curve. Complications of language but not of principles are introduced if multiple products are considered. To avoid those complications, we assume that the firm produces a single product, and, to avoid further complications, we suppose that it operates under conditions of complete certainty as to technology, product demand, and factor supply. We next suppose that there has occurred some change—all of a sudden—which defines a new long-run equilibrium position at which the optimal plant size is now greater initially. What sorts of changes might have been responsible for this?

The changes which would produce a new long-run equilibrium position for the firm would be (*a*) changes in demand, (*b*) changes in factor costs or conditions of supply, and (*c*) changes in technology.

* From R. Eisner and R. H. Strotz, 'Determinants of Business Investment', in Commission on Money and Credit, *Impacts of Monetary Policy* (Englewood Cliffs, New Jersey: Prentice-Hall, 1963). © 1963. Reprinted by permission of Prentice-Hall, Inc., Englewood Cliffs, New Jersey.

It is always difficult to state the effects of a change in market conditions upon the equilibrium position of a firm which is in an oligopolistic industry—unless one is willing to assert some definite model of oligopoly behavior. Indeed, even with the competitive or monopoly models, the pure theory of the firm yields very little in the way of definite propositions. About all that can be said short of special restrictive assumptions is that under competition in both product and factor markets, the factor demand curves will not be positively inclined. Nevertheless, we may venture some judgements about what would normally be observed. It seems safe to say that, regardless of the form of industrial organization, an increase in demand facing the firm (or, for the competitive firm, an increase in market price) will as a general rule bring about a rise in the equilibrium level of output for the industry as a whole. The effects on the equilibrium output of the firm are less certain. The appearance of new entrants may absorb much or all of the expansion of industry output and, in certain cases, where the expansion of the industry affects the prices of its factors of production, may even lead to a diminution in the output of existing firms. Nevertheless, *industry* output may be expected to increase in those circumstances. If, by an 'increase in demand' we mean either an equal absolute increase or an equal proportional increase in the amount demanded at each possible price, our generalization seems reasonably safe. We should be less sure of our generalization if the increase in demand is coupled with a more complicated alteration in the form of the demand function. In the case of the imperfectly competitive firm, nothing unique can then be said about the possible shift in the marginal revenue function, and it is possible that the increasing and changing demand may lead to a reduction in the output of the firm and of the industry and to an increase in market price.

To relate plant size to the level of demand, we must next suppose that if the equilibrium level of output increases, this will increase the desired stock of capital. This, too, seems to be a reasonable empirical generalization.

It is these considerations which underlie the acceleration principle in some form: The desired stock of capital is assumed to be positively related to the level of expected demand for output. We may usefully note, however, that if the existing stock of capital, because of underutilization, exceeds the desired stock at the new, higher level of expected demand, no acquisition of new capital would be needed. Thus the acceleration principle may be rendered inoperative by less-than-capacity utilization of capital. In this case, of course, the initial position is not one of equilibrium, as we had assumed.

The effects of changes in factor costs are also ambivalent. If the cost of plant and equipment should decline, one would suppose that capital would be substituted for other factors and that the optimal plant size would increase, so that the sales of both the individual firm and the industry would rise. If, however, there were a change in the price of other factors of production— raw materials prices or the wages of labor—one could not state *a priori* what the effect on the optimal amount of plant and equipment would be. A decline in the cost of other factors may be expected to lead to an expansion of output of the industry as a whole, but this could be achieved either by an expansion of both the amounts of other factors and of plant and equipment employed or by a reduction in the amount of plant and equipment upon the substitution of the other factors which are now relatively cheaper. For the individual firm, there is no certain manner of change in the shape of its long-run average cost curve, and its optimal plant size may become greater or less depending upon the interaction of different factors of production in the production function. In the normal case, however, it seems plausible to assume that a rise in the cost of other factors would lead to a substitution of capital equipment for those factors and that this increase in capital intensity would increase the optimal level of output of the individual firm. The output of the entire industry may, of course, decrease because of the rise in cost.

It is even more difficult to say anything worthwhile at the *a priori* level about the effect of a change in technology. Technological advance may be either labor saving or capital saving and so, even though it may be expected to result in a diminution of cost and expansion of industry output, it is by no means certain that it must lead to an increase in the amount of capital devoted to the industry.

Much of what we have been able to say thus far has dealt with the effect of a change on the demand or cost side on the optimal level of output. Generally, we may suppose that an increase in output entails an increase in the amount of capital equipment, although this inference is not one of logic, but is based upon one's impressions about actual experience. A very simple version of the acceleration principle, of course, might link the level of sales and the level of capital together in a rigid way, so that if the former increases, so would the latter. Investment, being the time rate of change in capital, would then be linked in fixed proportion to the time rate of change in demand. It is clear that the acceleration principle in this form is a rough and ready empirical rule and not a consequence of the pure theory of the firm. We might note explicitly that from its inception the acceleration principle has been based on the 'law of derived demand', and the output changes which were considered relevant were those resulting from changes on the side of demand, not on the side of cost, including technology. [...]

We now wish to provide our own formulation of a dynamical theory explaining the path taken through time by investment when a firm or industry moves from one long-run equilibrium position to another. In the conventional theory of production, which comes to us through Marshall, the analysis, for all its stress on 'time', is essentially one of comparative statics. The adjustment of the firm and the industry from one equilibrium position to another is not formally analyzed precisely because the 'short run' and the 'long run', the 'variable' and the 'fixed' factors of production are conceived as technical characteristics of the production process and are independent of the operating variables of the system. Nothing in the theory describes the speed by which interequilibrium movements occur. We propose to provide here a formal analysis of the course of the interequilibrium movement of a competitive firm resulting from an instantaneous and permanent shift in one of the relevant parameters. The parameter shift may, for example, represent an increase in demand for the product, a change in a cost schedule facing the firm, or an improvement in technology, but in any case we assume that an expansion of plant is indicated. [...]

To be concrete, let us suppose that there is an instantaneous and permanent change in a parameter so that the new long-run equilibrium position for a firm entails a larger plant. We do not expect the new 'long-run' equilibrium to come about instantaneously, or we would not refer to it as 'long-run'. The relative fixity of various factors of production will cause the adjustment to the ultimate, new equilibrium position to take place more or less slowly. In the usual Marshallian analysis, this process is explained by assuming that different productive factors cannot be altered in amount used until a certain length of time has elapsed after an original decision to vary the quantity of each such factor to be employed. The staggering of the lengths of time required to change the quantities of different factors enables one to describe the adjustment process as proceeding by steps and to describe the industry as passing through various states of short- and intermediate-run equilibria before the final adjustment has been made. But the reason for slower rather than more rapid adjustment (in a simple model that excludes uncertainty) is that it costs more (perhaps an infinite amount) to adjust production more rapidly. Indeed, the characterization of productive factors as being more or less fixed in this process ought ultimately to be in terms of the differences in the cost of varying them sooner rather than later, or more rapidly rather than less so. Accordingly, we shall treat a model into which a cost-of-expansion function is specifically introduced in such a way that the adjustment path will be determined not by inflexible technological requirements but by the very principle of profit maximization which determines the equilibrium position itself.

We begin by considering a firm that produces a single product by combining perfectly variable factors of production with another factor of production called its 'physical plant'. By a 'perfectly variable' factor is meant one that can be altered in amount according to a cost schedule which is independent of either the time rate of change in the amount of that factor used or the time interval between a decision to vary the amount of that factor and its actual variation.

The rate of profit earned by the firm may therefore be regarded as a function of the size of plant, since we may assume that the amounts of the perfectly variable factors used with a plant of given size are always optimally adjusted. We therefore write $p = p(s)$, where p is the rate of profit for a stationary plant of given size s, before deducting interest charges on the plant. Since the size of plant may be regarded as changing through time, t, this may be written out more completely as $p(t) = p[s(t)]$. (When the firm is investing, its net current returns will be less than $p(t)$, however, because, by our definition of 'net current returns', we deduct its investment outlay.) Suppose now that the parameter change at time $t = 0$ causes this function to attain a unique maximum for a plant size $\hat{s} > s_0$, s_0 being the size of plant at time $t = 0$. This we suppose to mean that the entrepeneur wishes that the plant were larger, and we imagine him to draw up a plant expansion program, $s(t)$, at time $t = 0$. We next introduce a cost-of-expansion function, $c(t) = c[ds/dt, t]$, where $c(t)$ is a current rate at t. This says that the cost of expansion depends both on the rate of expansion (investment) and on the time that has elapsed between the date at which it was decided to expand, date 0, and the date at which the expansion actually occurs, date t.

If there were no penalty on either the rapidity or promptness of expansion, total investment cost c (a rate), would be proportional to ds/dt, the factor of proportionality representing simply a constant unit cost of the factor called 'plant'. Total investment cost would then be independent of the time path of plant expansion, and expansion would occur all at once at some most propitious time, t. We assume, however, that the cost of investment increases with the rate of expansion. This means that a cost premium must be paid. Perhaps the best way to look at this is in terms of Figures 3.3a and 3.3b where investment cost functions are shown. In Figure 3.3a, the curve $c[ds/dt, t]$ represents the total cost of various levels of investment at any calendar date t. $c_1 = kds/dt$ is a straight line drawn tangent to the function c at the origin, and $c_2[ds/dt, t]$ is simply $c[ds/dt, t] - kds/dt \cdot c_1$ may be defined as the cost component of investment that does not depend upon speed itself. The greater investment, of course, the greater this cost component. But that is because the greater investment (here always regarded as a flow), the greater the amount of additional plant being acquired per unit time. For any increment of plant, Δs (having the dimension of 'bricks', not 'bricks per unit time'), the cost of this capital will be $k\Delta s$ and this cost is in dollars rather than in dollars per unit time. The rapidity or time path of acquiring this additional capital does not affect this cost component. $c_2[ds/dt, t]$ is the cost premium (per unit time) required to elicit a given speed of capital formation. It will be noted that the line $c_1 = kds/dt$ has been chosen tangent to $c = c(ds/dt, t)$ so that the cost component that does not depend upon speed itself (c_1) accounts for as large a share of total expansion cost as possible subject to the condition that c_2 be nonnegative, and therefore so that the component representing the cost premium for speed of expansion (c_2) is minimal. This is the natural meaning of a 'premium': what must be paid for an increment of plant (achieved with a given speed) over and beyond what would have to be paid for that same increment if an eternity were available to acquire it. (c_2 is, of course, not the premium for the acquisition of a given

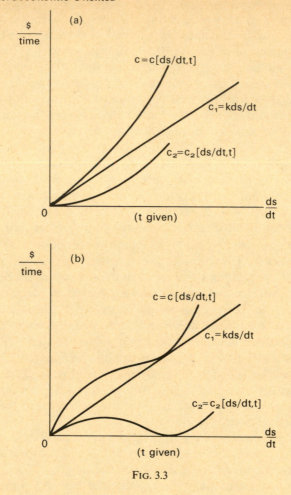

(a)

$$\frac{\$}{\text{time}}$$

$c = c[\mathrm{d}s/\mathrm{d}t, t]$

$c_1 = k\mathrm{d}s/\mathrm{d}t$

$c_2 = c_2[\mathrm{d}s/\mathrm{d}t, t]$

0   (t given) $\dfrac{\mathrm{d}s}{\mathrm{d}t}$

(b)

$$\frac{\$}{\text{time}}$$

$c = c[\mathrm{d}s/\mathrm{d}t, t]$

$c_1 = k\mathrm{d}s/\mathrm{d}t$

$c_2 = c_2[\mathrm{d}s/\mathrm{d}t, t]$

0   (t given) $\dfrac{\mathrm{d}s}{\mathrm{d}t}$

FIG. 3.3

increment of plant in a given length of time; it is the *rate* per unit of time at which a premium is being paid for expansion when expansion is taking place at the rate $\mathrm{d}s/\mathrm{d}t \cdot c$ and c_1 are also *rates* in this same sense.) In Figure 3.3*a*, however, we have assumed that the speed premium increases monotonically with an increase in $\mathrm{d}s/\mathrm{d}t$. In Figure 3.3*b* we do not make this assumption. There we assume that at first it may be more costly to add a given number of bricks slowly than to add them more rapidly, although after a certain point expansion cost is assumed to increase at an increasing rate. In Figure 3.3*b* we have once again chosen the line $c_1 = k\,\mathrm{d}s/\mathrm{d}t$ so that c_2 represents a premium rate in the sense given above.

The rate of return net of investment cost will therefore be

$$p[s(t)] - c[\mathrm{d}s/\mathrm{d}t, t]. \tag{1}$$

We next assume that the firm discounts the net rate of return of all future dates by multiplying (1) by a discounting function which we shall assume is log-linear and represented by $e^{-rt}, r > 0$.

The firm is then assumed to maximize the functional

$$\Phi = \int_{\infty}^{0} e^{-rt}\{p[s(t)] - c[ds/dt, t]\}\, dt = \Phi\{s(t)\}$$

by choosing the proper function $s(t)$.

It should be noted that the form of (2) introduces a special assumption regarding the entrepreneur's preferences among future expected streams of returns. Notably it means that the regularization of returns *per se* is not of consequence to him, or more generally, that there is no intertemporal complementarity in his preference function. Although rather specialized, this is, however, the usual way of thinking about how a future receipts stream is evaluated. If the entrepreneur can borrow or lend at a common rate of interest, the neglect of intertemporal complementarity is evidently justified.

The functional (2) is, of course, to be maximized with respect to the function $s(t)$. To solve this maximization problem we shall assume properties of continuity and of the existence of derivatives that are required for an application of the calculus of variations. [...]

The mathematical conditions for a maximum of (2) are:

$$\frac{\partial^2 c}{\partial(ds/dt)^2} \cdot \frac{d^2 s}{dt^2} = \frac{dp}{ds} + r\frac{\partial c}{\partial(ds/dt)} - \frac{\partial^2 c}{\partial(ds/dt)\partial t}, \tag{3}$$

$$\lim_{t \to \infty} e^{-rt}\frac{\partial c}{\partial(ds/dt)} = 0, \tag{4}$$

$$\frac{\partial^2 c}{\partial(ds/dt)^2} \geq 0 \text{ during expansion.}[...] \tag{5}$$

We focus on two main reasons why a firm may confront greater expansion costs under a program of more rapid expansion: (1) because of a short-run rising supply price in the capital-supplying industry, and (2) because of *internal* increasing costs associated with integrating new equipment in a going concern: reorganizing production lines, training workers, etc.

A firm that is an important buyer of the product of its capital-supplying industry (or that is integrated vertically so as to supply its own capital) will encounter rising expansion costs on both accounts. To get at the contribution of the first reason to the nature of the expansion-cost function requires that we consider the determinants of the supply function of the capital producing industry. But if expansion endures over any substantial length of time there may be a secondary capital expansion in the supplying industry (the accelerator effect) and to understand this requires an understanding of the technology of the supplying industry as well as of the conditions under which it buys its capital from the industries supplying it. The analytical task can therefore be pressed logically to further and further capital-supplying industries. Throughout, the role of monopolistic and bilaterally monopolistic positions must be taken into account. It is to avoid this and to stay within the bounds of partial-equilibrium analysis that we have simply taken the expansion cost function of our 'first-order' firm as given, depending only on ds/dt and t.

A firm that is a competitive buyer in the market for additional plant will not encounter variable expansion costs by reason (1)—rising supply price—if it alone is expanding; but if we are not to fall into a fallacy of composition, we must recognize that during a period of industry-wide expansion an industry which is significant in its market for capital goods will encounter a rising supply price and this will slow down its expansion. There are some subtleties here. A single competitive firm may suppose that it can buy any number of 'bricks' for delivery, however rapid or slow, at a fixed price per brick. But if many firms in the economy (or in an industry facing a rising supply curve) were to order above normal quantities of 'bricks' for quick delivery, some of them would have to be disappointed. To get these 'bricks' quickly, they would have to pay higher prices. It is possible that each of the expanding firms would fail to realize this and would *plan* its expansion path as if the price of 'bricks', even for immediate delivery, were to remain what it has been before the start of general expansion. These plans must then, in a continuous model, be continuously altered, because at all times the price of 'bricks' would be changing away from the value that, in their planning, the firms individually took to be fixed. Actual behaviour, then, ever based on a false assumption, would not be optimal, and our model would not describe this behaviour. But if the individual competitive firms, *in their planning*, took correct account of the effects of general expansion of factor prices, they would see that it is more expensive to expand sooner rather than later because factor prices would be highest at the beginning of the general expansion (when marginal profitability of plant size is highest) and would subsequently decline (as marginal profitability declines with expanding plant). Our assumption that competitive firms take account of a speed premium function $c_2(ds/dt, t)$ at a time of general expansion does not entail our supposing that each firm imagines that *its* expansion affects factor prices, but only that each firm has reasonable expectations about the effects of the *general* expansion on the expansion costs that it confronts. It is difficult to generalize about how these expectations will show up in the function $c(ds/dt, t)$. If each firm assumes simply that the start of general expansion will see higher factor prices, but that those prices will decline as the rate of general expansion abates, then (in the absence of *internal* speed-premium costs), the expansion-cost function will be $c = k(t) \cdot ds/dt$, where $k(t)$ is the price of a unit increment of plant and declines over time. (We consider this case in greater detail later on.) If, however, each firm supposes that it will not confront a perfect market, but may have to pay premiums to get more rather than fewer 'bricks' by a given date, or that it may have to tap more costly or inferior sources of supply to get all it decides it wants by a given date, the expansion-cost function will have to be written in the more general form $c = c(ds/dt, t)$.

These problems of aggregation and of the (ir?-) reconciliation of the parametric character of factor prices in the competitive model with 'rational' expectations and optimal plan fulfillment deserve further analysis. It is admittedly a bold stroke for us to regard the individual firm of our model as a miniature of an entire industry or of the economy. But this we do. We suppose that in a tight market for capital goods, individual firms have realistic expectations that price premiums must be paid both for earlier and larger deliveries. This means that expansion cost is an increasing function of the rapidity and promptness of expansion. Moreover, for the model firm we may reasonably assume, as we have, that this function is continuous, because we may think of capital goods as flowing out of the supplying industry to the expanding industry more or less rapidly depending on the demand price for capital of the expanding industry and on the length of time that has elapsed since the expansion began. [...]

Returning to the specific model just treated (in which $\partial^2 c/\partial(ds/dt)\partial t = 0$), we want next to ask how an increase in desired capital stock will be translated into investment over a period of time. (We here make contact with the distributed lag models.) This is to ask what determines the ratio of investment in successive periods. This is given by

$$ds/dt|_{\tau+1} + ds/dt|_{\tau} = \frac{\lambda_2 \left(s_0 - \dfrac{\alpha - rk}{\beta} \right) e^{\lambda 2(\tau+1)}}{\lambda_2 \left(s_0 - \dfrac{\alpha - rk}{\beta} \right) e^{\lambda 2\tau}} = e^{\lambda 2}$$

$e^{\lambda 2}$ is therefore the common ratio of investment at dates one unit (year or quarter) apart. According to our model, then, the coefficients of lagged differences between the desired and actual stocks of capital will constitute a declining geometric series. This provides a rationale for the distributed lag formulation of Koyck, which in his work has been proposed largely as a statistically convenient formulation to fit to empirical data.

Others ... have also proposed that distributed lag coefficients should decline in a geometrical series, having come to this proposition quite directly from the assumption that the decision maker adjusts his stock to a new level of equilibrium stock demand by adding to stock a fixed proportion of the difference between desired and actual stock each time period. This is an *ad hoc* proposition which we have now adduced from theoretical considerations— plus some *ad hoc* simplification of the forms of the functions considered.

How does the common ratio $e^{\lambda 2}$ change as the rate of time discount (what would correspond to the market rate of interest in a perfect capital market) changes? That is, what is the sign of

$$\frac{de^{\lambda_2}}{dr} = e^{\lambda_2} \cdot \frac{d\lambda_2}{dr} = e^{[r-\sqrt{(r^2+2\beta/\gamma)}]/2}(1/2)\left[1-(r^2+2\beta/\gamma)^{-1/2}r\right] =$$

$$(1/2)e^{[r-\sqrt{(r^2+2\beta/\gamma)}]/2}\left[1-\sqrt{\left(\frac{r^2}{r^2+2\beta/\gamma}\right)}\right]?$$

The bracketed factor is necessarily positive, as is the other factor so that e^{λ_2} increases with an increase in the rate of interest. This means that investment tends to be spread out more uniformly, the higher the interest rate, *ceteris paribus*, as one would expect; or, in other words, that a rise in the interest rate delays investment. [...]

3.3 The Acceleration Principle*

[...]

To start, it will be assumed that we are dealing with a single firm that moves smoothly from one position of equilibrium to another with perfect foresight. We rule out all problems of availability of credit, nonhomogeneity and indivisibilities of capital equipment, inaccurate expectations, excess capacity, or full employment of capital goods industries. These drastic assumptions for a tool of business cycle analysis are made to facilitate a simple demonstration of the acceleration principle.

In Figure 3.4 the equal-product curves derived from the firm's production function, involving the use of two factors only, capital and labor, are represented by the heavy curved lines convex to the origin. Each equal-product line represents the various proportions in which capital and labor can be combined by this firm to produce the outputs x, $x+1$, $x+2$, etc.

The lighter lines in Figure 3.4 are equal-expenditure lines representing the various amounts of capital and labor which could be purchased at the constant costs e_0, e_1, e_2, etc. If the firm has no excess capacity and wishes to increase its output, say, from x to $x+1$ and wants to minimize its costs in doing so, the well-known theory of the firm requires it to use additional capital and labor in a combination that is indicated by the tangency of an equal-expenditure line e_1, with the equal-product line $x+1$. Satisfaction of this geometrical requirement is equivalent to the condition that the ratio of the marginal physical productivities of the two factors be equal to the ratio of their market prices.

The purpose of reverting to this elementary theory of the firm is to obtain a clear picture of the meaning of the accelerator under simple assumptions which, it is hoped, will provide some insights under more complicated conditions. Figure 3.4 indicates that, if the firm decides to increase its output from x to $x+1$, or by Δx_1, it will increase its use of labor from L_0 to L_1, or by ΔL_1, and its use of capital from K_0 to K_1, or by ΔK_1. Expressing the

*From R. S. Eckaus, 'The Acceleration Principle Reconsidered', *Quarterly Journal of Economics* (Harvard University), May 1953.

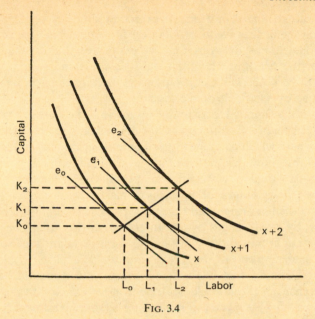

FIG. 3.4

increase in capital ΔK_1 as some factor, β_1, times Δx_1, the increase in output, we can obtain the following statement of the acceleration principle for the firm under these extremely simplified conditions.

$$\Delta K_1 = \beta_1 \cdot \Delta x_1, \tag{1}$$

where β_1 is now the acceleration coefficient. If Δx_1, the change in output, is considered to be a unit change, or $\Delta x_1 = 1$, then

$$\Delta K_1 = \beta_1. \tag{2}$$

Thus, in this case the accelerator for the firm, β_1, is equal in numerical value to the increase in capital required to increase output by one unit from x to $x+1$.

If the firm should further expand its output by one unit from $x+1$ to $x+2$, there would again be additional capital required and again a coefficient, β_2, which could be called an accelerator; and so on for further increases in output. The line drawn through the points of tangency is the firm's 'expansion path'.[...]

The major points resulting directly from this analysis can now be made quickly. Even more special assumptions would have to be added to all those already made for the firm's accelerator to be constant. For example, under the assumptions of constant returns to scale, if the factor price ratios remained constant, then $\beta_1 = \beta_2 = \ldots$, and the accelerator would be constant. Or if the assumption of constant coefficients of production were added to that of constant returns to scale, the accelerator would remain constant even if the factor price ratios changed, or if the firm exercised some degree of monopsony in purchasing the factors. With production functions of a type other than linear and homogenous functions it can be easily seen that it would be quite unlikely that the firm's accelerator would be constant as it increased its output. But there would still be an expansion path for the firm which could be summarized by a variable accelerator.

If the drastically simplifying assumptions made at the start of this analysis are dropped, a host of difficulties come flooding back. The firm still will have an expansion path which could be plotted on a diagram with coordinates as in Figure 3.4, but now this path would be irreversible. Each point on the expansion path would now be affected by all the influences previously assumed away: e.g., failure of business firms to try to minimize costs, stringencies in the financing of additional capital, indivisibilities and so on. Over sufficiently small ranges of output the expansion might be approximated by a straight line and a constant accelerator might still be utilized. With larger changes in output, the acceleration coefficient itself would change, and if the acceleration principle is to be meaningful it should be able to explain such changes. If this could be done, Kaldor's answer to the question which he poses, 'In what sense can it be assumed that investment is a simple (and linear!) function of the *change* in the level of output?' would not have to be the one which he gives: '*as between alternative positions of long-period equilibria*'.[1] (His italics.) Limiting the applicability of the acceleration principle to long-run analysis would not overcome the problem of the variability of the accelerator. On the other hand, if the accelerator is explicitly considered a parameter whose variations require an independent explanation, use of the acceleration principle need not be limited to long-run analysis.

As it now stands then the acceleration principle claims that, if excess capacity is at the lowest level desired by the firm, new investment is equal to some parameter times the increase in its output and that variations in the parameter must be explained separately. As a variable parameter the accelerator concept retains more general validity, I believe. Indeed, if one believed, for example, that there was capital deepening in the upward phases of the cycle, or increasing or decreasing returns to scale, the accelerator could be used to describe these different types of production functions and the growth of capital equipment during an expansion of output.[2] But an explanation of the variations in the accelerator must be given if the acceleration principle is to be meaningful.

---

[1] N. Kaldor, 'Mr. Hicks on the Trade Cycle', *Economic Journal*, 1951, pp. 837–8.

[2] This can, perhaps, be seen more readily with another diagram derived from Figure 3.4. Suppose Figure 3.4 is converted into a three dimensional surface by having an output axis rise vertically out of the page from the junction of the other two axes. Then project on the capital stock-output plane the outline of a curve running along the surface from one of the points of tangency to another. This would develop a curve something like the adjoining. The acceleration coefficient for the increase in output from x to $x+1$ is now seen to be the tangent of

CRITICAL APPRAISAL OF THE ACCELERATION PRINCIPLE

If the validity of the acceleration principle is confined to the realm of abstraction, it can hardly be useful for business cycle theory. Having gone back to fundamentals to show the basic justification for the acceleration principle, it is now necessary to consider further to what extent the principle is vitiated by the qualifications which must be imposed, and to what extent it retains some usefulness for business cycle analysis in its flexible or nonlinear form.

The criticisms of the acceleration principle as descriptive of a firm's investment behaviour are well known and numerous. Many of the qualifications the acceleration principle requires, which its critics stressed in the 1930's and again recently, were recognized by its early proponents. Clark, in his original paper, discussed briefly the amendments to the theory necessitated if excess capacity existed, and the unsymmetrical operation of the accelerator on the downward phase of the cycle. He also mentioned other barriers to the action of the acceleration principle which have been stressed in recent writings: (1) the limitations imposed by the separate problems of financing additional capital equipment; (2) prohibitive changes in the relative prices of capital and other factors; (3) uncertainty of producers regarding permanency of an increase in demand leading to unwillingness to undertake capital expansion; (4) possible delay in acquiring additional capital stock due to lack of idle capacity in producers' goods industries. In addition to the limitations mentioned by Clark a number of further qualifications are important of which the following list is meant to be more representative than exhaustive. Some of these were also at least touched on by Clark. Briefly, additional qualifications are: (1) Business firms do not always follow profit maximizing behaviour or even act in such a way as to maintain their share of the market due to lack of motivation or knowledge of opportunities; (2) the existence of discontinuities or indivisibilities in the production function prevents smooth and continuous adjustments; (3) a separate and distinct influence is exerted by

---

the angle α_1. If there are increasing returns to scale, for example, α_2 will be less than α_1, and the tan α_2 will also be smaller than the tan α_1.

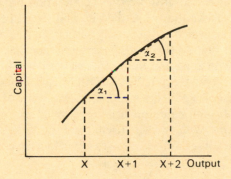

expectations based on factors other than demand for output, such as group psychological buoyancy or depression; (4) changed methods of production modify the reactions of firms to changes in demand for output; (5) changes in profits may exert an influence on businessmen's investment decisions in a way which is, to some extent, distinct and different from the influence of changes in output.

The process of generalizing the acceleration principle from the level of a partial explanation of the investment behavior of the firm to a macro-economic relation involves further possible pitfalls. In addition to the fore-going qualifications the macro-economic accelerator will also be modified by changing relations between the various sectors of the economy. For example, since the various sectors of the economy do not fluctuate simultaneously, variations in the size of the macro-economic accelerator will be introduced owing to the differences in the ratios of investment to changes in output in the various sectors. Moreover, nonrecurring shifts in the relative contribution of different sectors of the economy to total output and differential technological changes will again introduce variations in the acceleration principle. [...]

Among the critics of the acceleration principle there has been an interesting amount of agreement as to a more suitable relation for the determination of investment. The replacement for the acceleration principle which has been suggested quite often in various forms is a relation in which the rate of investment is made to depend on the rate of output and the level of capital stock. This particular type of replacement for the acceleration principle will be considered now in order to place both the criticism of the acceleration principle and the formula suggested in its stead in a better perspective.

Although the relations were generally derived by different methods there is a strong 'family resemblance' among the investment-determining relations developed by Tinbergen, Klein, Kalecki, Kaldor, Chenery, and Goodwin. Insamuch as it is the type of investment relation developed by these men which has gained wide support as a superior replacement for the acceleration principle, some of the various formulae will be presented briefly for comparison. I shall then show that by a simple restatement the acceleration principle can be made to contain very similar features.

Klein, one of the recent critics of the acceleration principle, has followed an approach much like that of Tinbergen and developed several types of investment relations which are generally similar. In Klein's relations investment is sometimes made a function of profits rather than output. The stock of capital enters with a lag and the profits or output variables are either or both current and lagged terms. Effects of other variables such as the interest rate or a price index of capital are also included in some of Klein's investment relations. The following equation will serve as an example of the type of investment relation with which Klein works. In his book, *Economic Fluctuations in the United States, 1921–1941*,[3] Klein develops three models in

[3] (New York, 1950), p. 87.

the first of which the investment relation is

$$I = \beta_0 + \beta_1 \frac{pX - E}{q} + \beta_2 \left(\frac{pX - E}{q}\right)_{-1} + \beta_3 K_{-1} + \beta_4 t + u_2. \qquad (3)$$

I is net investment in constant dollars; pX is the value of privately produced output; E stands for excise tax payments; K_{-1} is the stock of capital at the end of the previous year in constant dollars; q is the price of producer goods; t is time, introduced as a specific allowance for trend. The β's are constants, and u_2 is a random disturbance.

The general form of the investment relations developed by Tinbergen and Klein is in turn similar to that developed by Kalecki, as was noted by Klein with particular respect to the model from which equation (3) was drawn. One such investment relation of Kalecki's which contains modifications of an earlier formula, though omitting some other refinements, is

$$2\varepsilon \frac{dI_{t+\varepsilon}}{dt} = a \frac{dP_t}{dt} - (b+c)I_t. \qquad [4] \qquad (4)$$

In this equation I is the rate of investment; P is profits and t is time. The letters a, b and c stand for parameters reflecting respectively the influence on investment of changes in the price of capital goods, the repressive influence on new investment of the existing capital stock, and the effects of risk, market imperfections and the degree of indebtedness of entrepreneurs. ε is the total lag of a change in the rate of investment behind changes in the level of profits. If equation (4) is integrated, an equation for the level of investment is obtained as follows:

$$I_{t+\varepsilon} = \frac{a}{2\varepsilon}P_t - \frac{(b+c)}{2\varepsilon}K_t + \text{a constant.} \qquad (5)$$

Kaldor did not derive an investment relation in an explicitly algebraic form in his 'Model of the Trade Cycle' paper.[5] Although he devoted an appendix to an explanation of the differences between himself and Kalecki on this matter, Kaldor has also testified as to the extent of agreement between them with respect to the important variables in the investment relation and the manner in which they affect investment. Thus, Kaldor, too, believes that the level of output and the level of capital stock are the important determinants of new investment.[6]

The examples which have been given of investment relations in which the rate of output or profits and the level of capital stock with appropriate lags

---

[4] M. Kalecki, *Studies in Economic Dynamics* (London, 1943), p. 68.

[5] *Economic Journal*, Vol. L (1940), pp. 78–92.

[6] *Ibid.*, p. 89ff. As has been indicated above the acceleration principle was one of Kaldor's main targets for criticism in his review of Hicks's book. In this review the investment relation $I_{t+1} = Y_t f(Y_t/C_t)$ was recommended as avoiding most of the difficulties inherent in the acceleration principle. Here again I is investment; Y is output and C is capacity. 'Mr. Hicks on the Trade Cycle', *Economic Journal*, Vol. LXI (Dec. 1951), p. 840.

are the important variables could probably be extended at length. Two more examples should be mentioned here at least briefly in order to indicate the ubiquity of this type of relation and the further modifications which are possible: the 'capacity principle' of Chenery and the 'flexible accelerator' of Goodwin. Neither Chenery nor Goodwin could be described as hostile to the general idea behind the acceleration principle, and each separately developed a modification in a form similar to the examples given above. Chenery's final modification of the acceleration principle[7] is written

$$\Delta K_{t+\theta} = b(\beta X_t - \lambda K_t). \tag{6}$$

K is capital stock so that ΔK is investment. X is output and t is time. β is the accelerator; b is a 'reaction coefficient', and λ is a 'capacity factor' indicating the optimum degree of utilization of plant at any particular time. Approaching from a quite different theoretical direction, Goodwin arrived at a very similar expression. By successive modifications of the theory of the marginal efficiency of capital Goodwin[8] derived the flexible accelerator in the form

$$K = \frac{1}{\xi}(\kappa y + \phi - K). \tag{7}$$

In this relation the notation is similar to that of Chenery's above with K now the time rate of change of capital stock, or investment. ϕ is an 'innovational shift function'; $1/\xi$ is a constant similar to Chenery's b, and κ is the accelerator. This relation, although written in terms of differentials instead of differences, has the same family characteristics as the preceding examples in which investment is also made to depend primarily on the level of income and capital stock. The investment relations derived by Chenery and Goodwin are unique, however, as compared with the previous examples, in that they are intended to make the acceleration principle operate as a feedback mechanism. That is, the rate of investment is made to depend upon differences between the actual level of capital stock and the ideal level desired.

It is the type of investment relation as exemplified by the equations (3) to (7) in which the levels of output and capital stock play the most important roles, which I will call for convenience the velocity principle. In various forms it is this type of relation which has often been suggested recently as the most likely replacement for the acceleration principle. It is now interesting to revert to the acceleration principle, which depends on the rate of change of output, and ask how different it is from the velocity principle. For this purpose a diagram such as that of note 2 above will be used. The ordinate of this diagram is the level of capital stock and the abscissa is the level of output. The curve KK' drawn on this coordinate system indicates the aggregated capital equipment

[7] H. B. Chenery, 'Overcapacity and the Acceleration Principle', *Econometrica*, 1952.
[8] R. M. Goodwin, 'The Nonlinear Accelerator and the Persistence of Business Cycles', *Econometrica*, 1951. [See Reading 6.2 below—Ed.]

which businessmen would desire for each level of output. Time is implicit in the diagram which will be considered to be irreversible. Price changes, uncertainty, indivisibilities, and other factors affecting investment decisions may all be assumed to be reflected in the curve.

If initially, K_0, the level of capital stock, was in the aggregate exactly that desired to produce an output X_0, then K_1 indicates the higher level needed if output rises at time t_1 to output X_1 under some (changing) set of price and outlook influences. This line aa' is drawn through points 0 and 1 on the curve KK'. α_1 is the angle with the horizontal made by aa'.

It can be seen readily that the investment $K_1 - K_0$ necessary to raise output from X_0 to X_1 is

$$I_1 = K_1 - K_0 = (\tan \alpha_1)(X_1 - X_0). \qquad (8)$$

This is the acceleration principle, and in this form $\tan \alpha_1$ is the accelerator. Rewriting equation (8), it can be put in the form

$$I_1 = (\tan \alpha_1) X_1 - K_0 + a. \qquad (9)$$

Thus, the acceleration principle can be rewritten as the velocity principle. The resemblance of equation (9) to the examples given above of the investment relations developed by, say, Klein and Kalecki, in which the levels of output and capital were the important variables, is clear.

It is not mere coincidence that the relation in equation (9) derived from the acceleration principle looks so much like Klein's and Kalecki's relations. The acceleration principle and these other relations are derived from quite similar conceptions of investment by the firm. From each point of view the firm compares the future output which it wants to produce with its existing productive capacity, and invests if added productive capacity is needed to make up the difference. The future output which the firm wants to be able to produce is a decision based on expectations created by recent experiences of output and/or profits. Present productive capacity can be measured either by the existing stock of capital, as in, say, Klein's relations, or by current output with an appropriate adjustment if not all the capital stock is being used, as is done in the acceleration principle. The question now is really whether there is any difference between the acceleration principle and the velocity principle. The difference, I believe, is only in that the velocity principle includes in the formula for investment an allowance for the effect of the initial amount of capital equipment. In using the acceleration principle the effect of the initial stock of capital must be specified as a condition.

The diagram in Figure 3.5 can be used further to indicate how the acceleration principle can be adjusted to make allowances for certain other qualifications and show even closer similarity to the equations of Klein, Kalecki, Chenery, and Goodwin. Should the initial level of capital not be just at K_0, the aggregate amount desired by businessmen to produce X_0, then equation (9) can take account of this by use of a parameter in front of K_0.

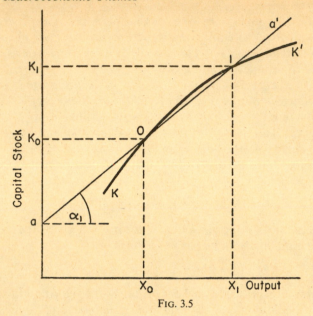

Fig. 3.5

The investment relation would then read

$$I_1 = (\tan \alpha_1)X_1 - cK_0 + a. \tag{10}$$

The similarity in form of equation (10), a restatement of the acceleration principle, and Kalecki's relation in equation (5) does not necessarily imply that they are now equally useful. Kalecki's relation has a temporary advantage in that it assigns to each of the coefficients particular roles in allowing for price changes, effects of risk, etc. However, it would be possible by analysis of the factors influencing the shape of the curve KK' in Figure 3.5 and thus of the economic significance of the coefficients of equation (10) also to make allowance for similar forces and, perhaps, in a manner as definite as in Kalecki's relation.

Figure 3.5 could be exploited still further to show how the acceleration principle can be put in a form very similar to that of Klein's investment relation in which current as well as lagged income and the lagged level of capital stock are the important variables. This could be done by substituting for the constant a a function of X. Further manipulation of terms could also produce a relation similar to Tinbergen's 'profit principle' except that it would be in terms of output. By additional assumptions modifications could be achieved with respect to lags and the effects of other variables. Multiplying the right hand side of equation (10) by an appropriate coefficient would produce a relation which could be interpreted similarly to Chenery's and Goodwin's investment functions.

One of the important qualifications to the simple acceleration principle is that it would give misleading results when applied to situations of decreasing output. As a result it is considered to apply only to the upward phase of the cycle. Hick's use of the principle was, for example, subject to this consideration. Equation (10) provides another way of seeing how the acceleration principle will give an indication of when it should be 'turned off'. When $(\tan \alpha_1) X_1 < cK_0 + a$ then I_1 would be negative. Since the rate of disinvestment is limited by other factors than those in the equation, the occurrence of a negative figure for I_1 can be used as a signal for the suspension of the action of the acceleration principle.

This section has shown that, rewritten in a slightly different form, the acceleration principle correctly stated becomes the velocity principle and actually allows for the influence of the level of capital stock, the supposed neglect of which is one of the major criticisms often made against it. In this modified form of the velocity principle other qualifications can be imposed on the acceleration principle and it can take on a form quite similar to the investment relations which some of its critics have proposed in its stead. A summarization should, perhaps, be confined to the limited observation that there is often more than one way of coming to the same conclusion. But even this bare observation is useful in counteracting some of the excessive criticism of the acceleration principle and in defining its range of usefulness. The acceleration principle, though it must be used carefully and with judicious qualifications, does, I believe, contain an important core of truth. This final section, by showing the connection of the acceleration principle to other forms of investment relations, has helped to demonstrate this truth.

3.4 The Neoclassical Theory of Investment*

[...]

In providing a framework for the theory of investment behavior, the first problem is to choose an appropriate basis for the theory. Two alternative possibilities may be suggested. First, the theory of investment could be based on the neoclassical theory of optimal capital accumulation. There are three basic objections to this possibility, the first of which is that a substantial body of noneconometric work on the motivation of business firms, mainly surveys of businessmen, suggests that 'marginalist' considerations are largely irrelevant to the making of business decisions. This evidence has been subjected to careful scrutiny by White,[1] who concludes that the data accumulated by the surveys are so defective, even by the standards of noneconometric empirical work, that no reliance can be placed on conclusions based on them. A second objection is that previous attempts to base the

*From D. W. Jorgenson, 'The Theory of Investment Behavior', in R. Ferber (ed.), *Determinants of Investment Behavior* (New York: National Bureau of Economic Research, 1967).
[1] W. H. White, 'Interest Inelasticity of Investment Demand', *American Economic Review*, September 1956, pp. 565–587.

study of investment on neoclassical economic theory have been unsuccessful,[2] but this argument will not withstand critical scrutiny. First, none of the tests of the neoclassical theory reported in the early literature was based on a fully rigorous statement of the theory. Secondly, the assumptions made about the lag between changes in the demand for capital services and actual investment expenditures were highly restrictive. Frequently, the lag was assumed to be concentrated at a particular point or to be distributed over time in a very simple manner. Tests of the neoclassical theory were carried out prior to the important contribution of Koyck to the analysis of distributed lags and investment behavior.[3] Despite these deficiencies, the pioneering tests of the neoclassical theory reported by Tinbergen reveal substantial effects for the price of investment goods, the change in this price, and the rate of interest.[4] Similarly, tests reported by Roos reveal substantial effects for the price of investment goods and rate of interest.[5] Klein's studies of investment in the railroad and electric power industries reveal substantial effects for the rate of interest.[6]

A third and more fundamental objection has recently been restated by Haavelmo, who argues that a demand schedule for investment goods cannot be derived from neoclassical theory:[7]

What we should reject is the naive reasoning that there is a demand schedule for investment which could be derived from a classical scheme of producers' behavior in maximizing profit. The demand for investment cannot simply be derived from the demand for capital. Demand for a finite addition to the stock of capital can lead to any rate of investment, from almost zero to infinity, depending on the additional hypothesis we introduce regarding the speed of reaction of capital-users. I think that the sooner this naive, and unfounded, theory of the demand-for-investment schedule is abandoned, the sooner we shall have a chance of making some real progress in constructing more powerful theories to deal with the capricious short-run variations in the rate of private investment.

We will show that it is possible to derive a demand function for investment goods based on purely neoclassical considerations. While it is true that the conventional derivation of such a demand schedule, as in Keynes's construction of the marginal efficiency of investment schedule,[8] must be dis-

---

[2] J. Meyer and E. Kuh, *The Investment Decision*, Cambridge, Mass., pp. 7–14.

[3] L. M. Koyck, *Distributed Lags and Investment Analysis*, Amsterdam, 1954.

[4] Tinbergen, *Stastical Testing*, see also the discussion of Tinbergen's results by T. Haavelmo, 'The Effect of the Rate of Interest on Investment: A Note', *Review of Economic Statistics*, February 1941, pp. 49–52.

[5] C. F. Roos and V. S. Von Szeliski, 'The Demand for Durable Goods', *Econometrica*, April 1943, pp. 97–112; Roos, 'The Demand for Investment Goods', *American Economic Review*, May 1948, pp. 311–320; Roos, 'Survey of Economic Forecasting Techniques', *Econometrica*, October 1955, pp. 363–395.

[6] L. R. Klein, 'Studies in Investment Behavior', in *Conference on Business Cycles*, New York, National Bureau of Economic Research, 1951.

[7] Haavelmo, *Theory of Investment*, p. 216.

[8] J. M. Keynes, *The General Theory of Employment, Interest and Money*, New York, 1936, esp. Chapter 11, pp. 135–146.

missed as naive, there is a sense in which the demand for investment goods can be taken to depend on the cost of capital; such a theory of investment behavior can be derived from the neoclassical theory of optimal capital accumulation. [...]

OPTIMAL CAPITAL ACCUMULATION

To develop the theory of investment behavior in more detail, we must first define the present value of the firm. For simplicity, we limit the analysis to a production process with a single output, a single variable input, and a single capital input. Where Q, L, and I represent levels of output, variable input, and investment in durable goods and p, w, and q represent the corresponding prices, the flow of net receipts at time t, say $R(t)$, is given by:

$$R(t) = p(t)Q(t) - w(t)L(t) - q(t)I(t). \tag{1}$$

Present value is defined as the integral of discounted net receipts; where $r(s)$ is the rate of time discount at time s, net worth (W) is given by the expression:

$$W = \int_0^\infty e^{-\int_0^t r(s)ds} R(t)dt. \tag{2}$$

For purposes of the following discussion, we may assume that the time rate of discount is a constant without loss of generality. Accordingly, the present value of the firm may be represented in the simpler form:

$$W = \int_0^\infty e^{-rt} R(t)dt.$$

Present value is maximized subject to two constraints. First, the rate of change of the flow of capital services is proportional to the flow of net investment. The constant of proportionality may be interpreted as the time rate of utilization of capital stock, that is, the number of units of capital service per unit of capital stock. We will assume that capital stock is fully utilized so that this constant may be taken to be unity. Net investment is equal to total investment less replacement; where replacement is proportional to capital stock, this constraint takes the form:

$$\dot{K}(t) = I(t) - \delta K(t) \tag{3}$$

where $\dot{K}(t)$ is the time rate of change of the flow of capital services at time t. This constraint holds at each point of time so that $\dot{K}$, K, and I are functions of time; to simplify notation, we will use K in place of $K(t)$, I in place of $I(t)$, and so on. Secondly, levels of output and levels of labor and capital services are constrained by a production function:

$$F(Q, L, K) = 0. \tag{4}$$

We assume that the production function is twice differentiable with positive marginal rates of substitution between inputs and positive marginal productivities of both inputs. Furthermore, we assume that the production function is strictly convex.

To maximize present value (2) subject to the constraints (3) and (4), we consider the Lagrangian expression:

$$\mathscr{L} = \int_0^\infty [e^{-rt}R(t) + \lambda_0(t)F(Q, L, K) + \lambda_1(t)(\dot{K} - I + \delta K)]dt, \qquad (5)$$

$$= \int_0^\infty f(t)dt,$$

where:

$$f(t) = e^{-rt}R(t) + \lambda_0(t)F(Q, L, K) + \lambda_1(t)(\dot{K} - I + \delta K).$$

The Euler necessary conditions for a maximum of present value subject to the constraints (3) and (4) are:

$$\frac{\partial f}{\partial Q} = e^{-rt}p + \lambda_0(t)\frac{\partial F}{\partial Q} = 0, \qquad (6)$$

$$\frac{\partial f}{\partial L} = -e^{-rt}w + \lambda_0(t)\frac{\partial F}{\partial L} = 0,$$

$$\frac{\partial f}{\partial I} = -e^{-rt}q - \lambda_1(t) = 0,$$

$$\frac{\partial f}{\partial K} - \frac{d}{dt}\frac{\partial f}{\partial \dot{K}} = \lambda_0(t)\frac{\partial F}{\partial K} + \delta\lambda_1(t) - \frac{d}{dt}\lambda_1(t) = 0,$$

and also:

$$\frac{\partial f}{\partial \lambda_0} = F(Q, L, K) = 0, \qquad (7)$$

$$\frac{\partial f}{\partial \lambda_1} = \dot{K} - I + \delta K = 0.$$

Combining the necessary conditions for labor and output, we obtain the marginal productivity condition for labor services:

$$\frac{\partial Q}{\partial L} = \frac{w}{p}. \qquad (8)$$

Of course, output, labor, wages and prices are all functions of time. The difference between this marginal productivity condition and the corresponding condition of the 'static' theory of the firm is that condition (8) holds at every point of time over the indefinite future whereas the marginal productivity condition of the 'static' theory of the firm holds only at a single point in time. A similar marginal productivity condition for capital services may be derived. First, solving the necessary conditions (6) for $\lambda_1(t)$:

$$\lambda_1(t) = -e^{-rt}q,$$

the necessary condition for capital services may be written:

$$\lambda_0(t)\frac{\partial F}{\partial K} - \delta e^{-rt}q - re^{-rt}q + e^{-rt}\dot{q} = 0.$$

Combining this condition with the necessary condition for output, we obtain the marginal productivity condition for capital services:

$$\frac{\partial Q}{\partial K} = \frac{q(r+\delta)-\dot{q}}{p} = \frac{c}{p}, \tag{9}$$

where:

$$c = q(r+\delta)-\dot{q}. \tag{10}$$

Again, output, capital, prices, and the rate of time discount are functions of time so that these conditions hold at every point of time over the indefinite future. [...]

The complete neoclassical model of optimal capital accumulation consists of the production function (4) and the two marginal productivity conditions (8) and (9):

$$F(Q,K,L) = 0, \quad \frac{\partial Q}{\partial L} = \frac{w}{p}, \quad \frac{\partial Q}{\partial K} = \frac{c}{p},$$

and the two side conditions (3) and (10):

$$I = \dot{K} + \delta K,$$

$$c = q(r+\delta)-\dot{q}.$$

The production function and marginal productivity conditions hold at each point of time. The side conditions are differential equations also holding at each point of time. Combined, these conditions determine the levels of output, labor input, and capital input, together with the level of investment and the shadow price for capital services. [...]

THE THEORY OF INVESTMENT BEHAVIOR

Beginning with the neoclassical model of optimal capital accumulation, we may derive differentiable demand functions for labor and capital services and a differentiable supply function for output, say:

$$L = L(w,c,p), \tag{11}$$

$$K = K(w,c,p),$$

$$Q = Q(w,c,p).$$

The problem of deriving the demand for investment goods as a function of the rate of interest is a subtle one. Haavelmo expresses the view that the demand for investment goods cannot be derived from the profit maximizing theory of the firm. This is a consequence of his interpretation of the demand function for capital services and condition (3) determining the level of investment from replacement and the rate of change of demand for capital services. According to this interpretation, finite variations in the rate of interest with all other prices held constant result in finite changes in the demand for capital services. As the rate of interest varies, demand for investment goods assumes only three possible values—negatively infinite, positively infinite, or the value obtained where the initial level of capital services is precisely equal to the demand for capital services. Investment demand has a finite value for only one rate of interest. In this interpretation, the demand function for capital services is analyzed by means of comparative statics, that is, by comparing alternative production plans at a given point of time. Any attempt to derive the demand for investment goods as a function of the rate of interest by such comparisons leads to nonsensical results, as Haavelmo correctly points out.

However, an alternative interpretation of the demand function for capital services and condition (3) determining the level of investment is possible. Under the hypothesis that the firm is following an optimal path for capital accumulation and that the optimal path is continuous, the initial level of capital is always equal to the demand for capital services. By imposing this condition at the outset, the demand for investment goods as a function of the rate of interest at any point of time may be analyzed by means of comparative dynamics, that is, by comparing alternative paths of capital accumulation, each identical up to that point of time and each continuous at that point. The demand for investment goods is given by condition (3):

$$I = \dot{K} + \delta K,$$

where the level of capital services, K, is fixed; but from the demand function for capital services (11), this condition implies that for fixed values of the price of output and the price of labor services, the implicit price of capital services must remain unchanged. Holding the price of investment goods constant, the rate of change of the price of investment goods must vary as the rate of interest varies so as to leave the implicit price of capital services unchanged. Formally, the condition that variations in the rate of interest leave the implicit price of capital services unchanged may be represented as:

$$\frac{\partial c}{\partial r} = 0;$$

holding the price of investment goods constant, this condition implies that the own-rate of interest on investment goods, $r - \dot{q}/q$. must be left unchanged by variations in the rate of interest.

We assume that all changes in the rate of interest are precisely compensated by changes in the rate of change of the price of current and future investment goods so as to leave the own-rate of interest on investment goods unchanged. Under this condition the discounted value of all future capital services, which is equal to the current price of investment goods, is left unchanged by variations in the time path of the rate of interest. The condition that the time path of the own-rate of interest on investment goods is left unchanged by a change in the time path of the rate of interest implies that forward prices or discounted future prices of both investment goods and capital services are left unchanged by variations in the rate of interest. For a constant rate of interest, this condition may be represented in the form:

$$\frac{\partial^2 e^{-rt}c(t)}{\partial r \partial t} = 0.$$

Like the previous condition, this condition holds at every point of time.

To derive the demand for investment goods as a function of the rate of interest, we first differentiate the demand for capital services with respect to time, obtaining:

$$\dot{K} = \frac{\partial K}{\partial w} \cdot \frac{\partial w}{\partial t} + \frac{\partial K}{\partial c} \cdot \frac{\partial c}{\partial t} + \frac{\partial K}{\partial p} \cdot \frac{\partial p}{\partial t}.$$

For simplicity, we consider only the case in which $\partial w/\partial t = \partial p/\partial t = 0$, that is, the price of output and the price of labor services are not changed. In this case, we obtain:

$$\dot{K} = \frac{\partial K}{\partial c} \cdot \frac{\partial c}{\partial t}.$$

Differentiating the implicit price of capital services with respect to time, we have:

$$\frac{\partial c}{\partial t} = \frac{\partial q}{\partial t}(\delta + r) + q\frac{\partial r}{\partial t} - \frac{\partial^2 q}{\partial t^2}. \tag{12}$$

To derive the demand for investment goods, we combine expression (12) for the rate of change of capital services with condition (3) for the rate of investment, obtaining:

$$I = \frac{\partial K}{\partial c}\left[\frac{\partial q}{\partial t}(\delta + r) + q\frac{\partial r}{\partial t} - \frac{\partial^2 q}{\partial t^2}\right] + \delta K,$$

which depends on the rate of interest and the price of investment goods through the rate of change of capital services. Differentiating this investment demand function with respect to the rate of interest, we obtain:

$$\frac{\partial I}{\partial r} = \frac{\partial^2 K}{\partial c^2} \cdot \frac{\partial c}{\partial r} \cdot \frac{\partial c}{\partial t} + \frac{\partial K}{\partial c}\frac{\partial^2 c}{\partial t \partial r} + \delta\frac{\partial K}{\partial c} \cdot \frac{\partial c}{\partial r}.$$

But $\partial c/\partial r = 0$, since changes in the rate of interest are compensated ·by changes in the rate of change of the price of investment goods so as to leave the implicit price of capital services unchanged. This condition implies that:

$$\frac{\partial^2 q}{\partial t \partial r} = q.$$

Secondly, $\partial^2 e^{-rt} c(t)/\partial r \partial t = 0$, since changes in the time path of the rate of interest leave the time path of forward or discounted prices of capital services unchanged. This condition implies that:

$$\frac{\partial^2 c}{\partial t \partial r} = c.$$

Combining these two conditions, we obtain:

$$\frac{\partial I}{\partial r} = \frac{\partial K}{\partial c} \cdot c < 0,$$

so that the demand for investment goods is a decreasing function of the rate of interest.

We conclude that it is possible to derive the demand for investment goods as a function of the rate of interest on the basis of purely neoclassical considerations. However, the demand for investment goods depends on the rate of interest through a comparison of alternative paths of capital accumulation, each continuous and each depending on a time path of the rate of interest. Although this conclusion appears to be the reverse of that reached by Haavelmo, his approach to the demand for investment goods is through comparative statics, that is, through comparison of alternative production plans at a given point of time. The demand function for investment goods cannot be derived by means of such comparisons. As a proposition in comparative statics, any relation between variations in the rate of investment and changes in the rate of interest is nonsensical.

To summarize, the complete neoclassical model of optimal capital accumulation consists of the production function (4), the two marginal productivity conditions (8) and (9), and the side condition (10). An alternative form of this model consists of the demand functions for capital and labor services, the supply function for output:

$$L = L(w, c, p),$$

$$K = K(w, c, p),$$
$$Q = Q(w, c, p);$$

and the demand function for investment goods:

$$I = \frac{\partial K}{\partial c} \frac{\partial c}{\partial t} + \delta K,$$

$$= I\left(w, c, p, \frac{\partial c}{\partial t}\right).$$

The demand for investment goods depends on the change in the demand for capital with respect to a change in the implicit price of capital services, the time rate of change in the price of capital services, and the level of replacement demand. Where the time rates of change of the price of labor services and the price of output are not zero, the demand function for investment goods may be rewritten:

$$I = \frac{\partial K}{\partial w}\frac{\partial w}{\partial t} + \frac{\partial K}{\partial c}\frac{\partial c}{\partial t} + \frac{\partial K}{\partial p}\cdot\frac{\partial p}{\partial t} + \delta K,$$

$$= I\left(w, c, p, \frac{\partial w}{\partial t}, \frac{\partial c}{\partial t}, \frac{\partial p}{\partial t}\right).$$

[...]

4. Money

Introductory Note

To have a chapter devoted to 'money' may seem rather odd, since there is clearly a case for arguing that the influence of monetary phenomena pervades virtually the whole of macroeconomic analysis. However, the Readings in this chapter are concerned with issues which are, broadly speaking, purely monetary, while interactions of monetary and 'real' phenomena are dealt with in a variety of contexts in other chapters: in the context of general macroeconomics in Chapters 1 and 9, and in connection with growth, cycles, and inflation in Chapters 5–7; monetary policy is discussed in Chapter 10.

Readings 4.1 and 4.2 represent attempts to provide firmly based theoretical justifications for the two major elements of the demand for money proposed by Keynes—the transactions demand and the speculative demand.

Baumol [Reading 4.1] notes that the demand for a stock of cash in order to finance a flow of transactions has close analogies with producers' demands for inventories (or raw materials, work-in-progress, or finished goods). In both cases, stocks are held in order to avoid dislocations, and in both cases, there is a cost to holding stocks which rational decision-makers will wish to minimize. Abstracting from uncertainty (which will be reflected in precautionary and speculative demands for money), assume that transactions occur at a rate of T pounds (dollars, etc.) per year. Suppose that cash is withdrawn from an investment in lots of £C evenly spaced over the year. There are two costs attached to the procedure: a charge on each withdrawal, and the loss of interest on the average cash balance held of £$C/2$. The number of withdrawals in the year will be T/C and, assuming a charge per withdrawal of £b and an interest rate i, the cost of holding the transactions balance will be

$$b \cdot \frac{T}{C} + i \cdot \frac{C}{2}.$$

To minimize this, differentiate with respect to C and set the result equal to zero:

$$\frac{\delta}{\delta C}\left(\frac{bT}{C} + \frac{iC}{2}\right) = \frac{-bT}{C^2} + \frac{1}{2} = 0$$

from which

$$C = \sqrt{\frac{2bT}{i}}.$$

The average cash balance, $C/2$, is thus equal to $\sqrt{(bT/2i)}$ and it follows that the demand for transactions balances will vary directly with the square-root of the value of transactions in a period, and inversely with the square-root of the interest rate. This may be contrasted with simple accounts of the transactions demand which generally assume that the demand will vary proportionately with the value of transactions, and will not be affected by changes in the interest rate.[1]

The rationale of the second major component of the demand for money—the speculative demand—is explored by Tobin [Reading 4.2]. Like Keynes, Tobin assumes that there is only one monetary asset other than cash: consols (or bonds) of fixed face value yielding a fixed sum per year (the 'coupon') in perpetuity. It follows that the price of bonds will fluctuate inversly with the going rate of interest. The return over a year on £1 invested in bonds will be the interest yield, r, plus (or minus) the expected capital gain (or loss), g, which is equal to $(r/r_e) - 1$.[2] Thus the investor will hold bonds if $r + g$ is positive, cash if $r + g$ is negative. The decision therefore depends on whether $r + (r/r_e) - 1$ is positive or negative, that is, on whether $r1 + (1/r_e) \gtrless 1$ or $r \gtrless r_e/(1 + r_e)$. In practice, the expected rate of interest is unlikely to be completely independent of the current rate, but, provided that expectations are 'sticky', there will always be some critical value of the current level of the interest rate such that above that rate bonds are held, below it cash.

This all-or-nothing decision for each investor raises several problems. First, it is necessary (though no doubt reasonable) to assume differing expectations among investors if the aggregate liquidity preference (or speculative demand) schedule is to slope smoothly downwards. Secondly, even then, it can be argued that in long-run equilibrium expectations will settle down, so that the aggregate curve will become discontinuous. And, finally, common sense suggests that even individual investors may hedge their bets by generally holding both cash and bonds, though in varying proportions.

It is this latter observation which leads Tobin to suggest that liquidity preference must be based essentially on *uncertainty* in the mind of each investor about future rates of interest. Suppose that this uncertainty means that an investor expects a zero capital gain or loss, but recognizes that there is an equal chance of gain or loss. If he holds a proportion A_1, of his portfolio in cash and A_2 in bonds, his expected return is $\mu_R = A_2 r$. Given a measure of the dispersion of the expectation of capital gain or loss (reflecting the degree of uncertainty), σ_g, the dispersion of his expected return will be

---

[1] Baumol proceeds to argue (pp. 162–3) that if the money supply is increased without affecting speculative balances, it follows that the value of transactions will rise with the square of the increase, suggesting a very powerful 'quantity theory' effect. But it is not explained why speculative balances should be unaffected, and the implicit reversal of the direction of causality seems illegitimate.

[2] If the coupon is C per bond, the price of the bond will be C/r. The capital gain on each bond will be $(C/r_e) - (C/r)$. The number of bonds per £1 invested is $1/(C/r) = r/C$. Hence the capital gain per £1, g, is equal to $r/C[(C/r_e) - (C/r)] = (r/r_e) - 1$.

$\sigma_R = A_2\sigma_g$. From these two expressions, it follows that $\mu_R = r \cdot \sigma_g/\sigma_R$. In other words, given the current rate of interest, r, and a given level of uncertainty, σ_g, then the lower is σ_R (the risk of capital gain or loss on the portfolio) the lower is the expected return μ_R. The investor chooses his distribution between cash and bonds by balancing risk against expected return, so that one can postulate indifference curves between the two. The point of tangency with the line $\mu_R = r \cdot \sigma_g/\sigma_R$ represents the optimal choice.

Clearly, everything depends on the shape of these indifference curves. Tobin distinguishes two basic types of investor—risk-averters and risk-lovers. Risk-lovers have indifference curves which always slope downwards: a lower expected return is always accepted in order to have a higher chance of capital gain. Such an investor will always reach his optimal possible position by holding all his portfolio in bonds. Risk-averters, in contrast, have indifference curves which slope upwards: they will not accept greater risk unless this is compensated by a greater expected return. In general, the indifference curves will be convex downwards, indicating that at high levels of risk a given increase in risk requires a greater compensating increase in expected return than at low risk levels. The optimal point for such risk-averters will normally be somewhere along the line $\mu_R = r \cdot (\sigma_R/\sigma_g)$ rather than at either extreme, so that the portfolio will contain both cash and bonds: the investor is a diversifier.[3] For such investors, a rise in the interest rate will raise the expected return on existing portfolio and, in normal circumstances, this will allow the investor to tolerate a greater over-all risk and so to increase his holding of bonds. Liquidity preference will thus decline with a rise in the rate of interest.

Tobin's rationale of liquidity preference has two significant advantages over earlier formulations. First, it allows for both expectations and uncertainty, and secondly it accounts for the observation that investors typically do hold cash balances (in excess of transactions needs) as well as bonds—that is, for the phenomenon of diversification.

So far, we have been concerned with only one choice—that between cash and (undated) bonds. But even ignoring equities and other corporate securities and concentrating only on the bond market, it is clear that a good deal of importance must be attached to the differences between the rate of return on short-, medium-, and long-dated government stock—that is to the *term structure* of interest rates.

The paper by Modigliani and Sutch [Reading 4.3] examines the behaviour of the divergence between long-run and short-run rates in the context of a particular attempt by the U.S. monetary authorities to alter this gap ('Operation Twist', in the early 1960s). The aim was to lower the long-run

---

[3] Under rather special assumptions concerning the utility function underlying the indifference curves, there may be a class of investors whose curves, although sloping upwards, are not convex downwards. Thus these investors will be risk-averters, but will find their optimal position at one or other extreme point, and will thus hold either all cash or all bonds—they are 'plungers'.

rate in order to stimulate investment, and to raise the short-run rate in order to attract foreign funds and thus strengthen the balance of payments.

Three basic hypotheses concerning the term structure of interest rates can be distinguished. The traditional or *expectations* theory is based on the assumption that investors seek simply to maximize the yield on their portfolios and are prepared to shift completely freely between long and short securities in order to do so. In a world of perfect certainty, where all future short rates are known, this implies that the long-run rate of interest will be a geometric average of the intervening short-run rates. More realistically, if future rates are not known with certainty, the long rate will be the average of *expected* short rates. This has three direct implications. First, the long rate will be determined by expected short rates, so that any policy to control the long rate can only be carried out by operating at the short end of the market. Secondly, the yield gap between long rates and short rates will be determined simply by whether short rates are expected to rise or fall. If short rates are expected to rise, the long rate will be higher than the short rate, and vice versa if short rates are expected to fall. Finally, fluctuations in the current short rate will (because of the averaging process) have only a damped influence on the long rate: short rates will thus generally be less stable than long rates.

The *liquidity* or *risk-premium* theory adds to the expectations theory the notion that borrowers and lenders will differ in their respective attitudes to long and short loans. *Ceteris paribus*, lenders will prefer to lend short, borrowers to borrow long. Thus for equilibrium a special inducement must be offered in the long market as compared with the short market in order to persuade lenders to lend long. Hence long rates will tend to be higher than short rates, though this bias may of course be offset if short rates are expected to fall substantially. Lenders' preference for liquidity presumably reflects uncertainty about their future cash needs.

The *market segmentation* theory rejects the traditional theory by denying shiftability, and hence the link between the long rate and expected short rates, but retains the notion of a preference for relatively short commitments of funds by lenders. Borrowers are assumed to have a strong preference for matching their assets and liabilities so as to be certain of meeting future obligations. Thus, for example, discount houses will tend to operate only at the short end of the market, and life assurance offices only at the long end. Rates of return in each such 'segment' of the market will thus be determined independently by supply and demand. Because demand in each segment is likely to be very stable, it is changes in the *supply* of funds which will change the term structure. The normal tendency for long rates to exceed short rates thus reflects excess supply at the short end, attributable to lenders' preference for liquidity.

Modigliani and Sutch point out that all these factors may play a part in determining the term structure. If traders are not rigidly tied to market segments, but merely have 'preferred habitats', then expectations will still have a part to play, albeit a weakened one, in determining relative interest rates which are no longer completely independent, and lenders' preference for liquidity will still account for the tendency, other things being equal, for long rates to stand above short rates. The empirical results presented suggest that the link between expected short rates and the long rate is fairly strong—vindicating the expectations theory—but that the authorities' actions in altering the relative supplies of short- and long-term securities did have a mild effect on the yield gap, suggesting that there is some evidence of traders' reluctance to move from their preferred habitats in response to changes in other habitats.

Readings 4.4 and 4.5 are concerned with two aspects of the supply of money. Tobin [Reading 4.4] argues that the existence of non-bank financial intermediaries—for example, savings banks, finance companies, and building societies (savings and loan associations in U.S. parlance)—significantly modifies the conventional view of commercial banks as creators of money and, consequently, the narrow definition of 'money' as notes and coin in circulation together with commercial banks' demand deposits.

The conventional view can be summarized formally as follows. At the root of the banking system lies currency plus the commercial banks' required deposits with the central bank (together known as the 'monetary base' or 'high-powered' money, H). This is directly controlled by the authorities. The money supply, M, consists of currency, C, together with bank demand deposits, D. If the required reserve ratio is r, then commercial banks' reserves at the central bank are $rD = r(M-C)$. Thus the monetary base is

$$H = C + r(M-C)$$

from which

$$M = \frac{H - C(1-r)}{r} = \frac{H-C}{r} + C.$$

From this expression it can be seen that an increase in the high-powered money stock achieved by a reduction in reserve requirements (i.e. in increase in H with C constant) will raise the money supply by a multiple $1/r$ of the reduction:

$$\frac{\partial M}{\partial H} = \frac{1}{r}.$$

And, of course, if $r =$ zero (no legal reserve requirement), the commercial banks' ability to create money is virtually unlimited.

Lying behind this analysis, however, is the assumption that an expansion of bank lending is fully matched by an expansion of bank deposits: A borrows from his bank and pays B, who deposits the money with his own bank. But in practice, non-bank financial intermediaries compete for deposits with the banks (whose own time-deposit accounts also compete with demand-deposit accounts.) The *convenience* of the means-of-payment function of demand-deposits can thus be offset by the positive yield on alternatives. The 'leakage' of bank advances in this way reduces the extent to which commercial banks can create money—quite apart from the existence of reserve requirements—and the fact that the extent of the leakage depends upon individuals' portfolio choices and institutions' decisions about interest rates offered makes the connection between changes in the monetary base and changes in the money supply relatively loose. Furthermore, the fact that the central bank will always, as 'lender of last resort', lend to the commercial banks means that the latter can, if it is 'profitable', always avoid the pressure of reserve requirements. Again, this reduces the sureness with which the authorities can control the money supply through the lever of the monetary base. The main point is that, in the end, the behaviour of both commercial banks and non-bank financial intermediaries is governed by profitability. Since this depends on the whole structure of both lenders' and borrowers' portfolios, and thus on the whole structure of interest rates, the 'money supply' as conventionally defined becomes to a considerable degree endogenous, rather than an exogenous quantity controlled by the authorities. And once the special nature of demand deposits—their acceptability as a means of payment—is recognized as not of overwhelming and fundamental significance, it is evident that it is the control of 'liquidity' in a general sense, rather than of narrowly defined 'money', which is important for monetary policy.

A different aspect of the significance of financial intermediation is discussed by Gurley and Shaw [Reading 4.5]. One of the neoclassical responses to Keynes's analysis of underemployment equilibrium was to elevate the 'Pigou effect' to a position of central importance (see Chapter 1 above). A deflationary policy which resulted in falling wages and prices would, if pursued far enough, stimulate aggregate demand through the effect of the increased real value of wealth on private expenditure. But Gurley and Shaw point out that this effect cannot work if the assets in question are the liabilities of another agent within the private sector—if the assets are 'inside' money. For then the effect of falling prices on the value of the wealth of the creditor is balanced by the increase in the real burden of debt of the debtor: the only net effect will be that which follows from the consequential redistribution of real wealth within the private sector. If, however, the debtor is the government, and if it is assumed that the government does not reduce its expenditure as the real burden of its debt rises, there will be an increase in private sector expenditure—the case of 'outside' money. If the increased burden of servicing government interest-bearing debt is taken into account, 'inside money' in the relevant sense consists simply of currency—the Pigou effect becomes Patinkin's real balance effect (see Readings 1.5–1.7 above).

The validity of the inside/outside distinction has been questioned;[4] this

[4] For a review of the controversy, see H. G. Johnson, 'Inside Money, Outside Money, Income, Wealth and Welfare in Contemporary Monetary Theory', *Journal of Money, Credit and Banking*, Feb. 1969.

debate and the debate about the significance of non-bank financial inter-mediaries reflect the trend in recent monetary theory away from the dis-cussion of individual assets and towards a more general approach in terms of widely diversified portfolios considered in the context of a highly complex monetary system.

4.1 The Transactions Demand for Cash*

[...]

A stock of cash is its holder's inventory of the medium of exchange, and like an inventory of a commodity, cash is held because it can be given up at the appropriate moment, serving then as its possessor's part of bargain in an exchange. We might consequently expect that inventory theory and monetary theory can learn from one another. This note attempts to apply one well-known result in inventory control analysis to the theory of money.

A SIMPLE MODEL

We are now interested in analyzing the transactions demand for cash dictated by rational behaviour, which for our purposes means the holding of those cash balances that can do the job at minimum cost. To abstract from precautionary and speculative demands let us consider a state in which transactions are perfectly foreseen and occur *in a steady stream*.

Suppose that in the course of a given period an individual will pay out T dollars in a steady stream. He obtains cash either by borrowing it, or by withdrawing it from an investment, and in either case his interest cost (or interest opportunity cost) is i dollars per dollar per period. Suppose finally that he withdraws cash in lots of C dollars spaced evenly throughout the year, and that each time he makes such a withdrawal he must pay a fixed 'broker's fee' of b dollars.[1] Here T, the value of transactions, is predetermined, and i and b are assumed to be constant.

* From W. J. Baumol, 'The Transactions Demand for Cash: An Inventory Theoretic Approach', *Quarterly Journal of Economics* (Harvard University), Nov. 1952.

[1] The term 'broker's fee' is not meant to be taken literally. It covers all non-interest costs of borrowing or making a cash withdrawal. These include opportunity losses which result from having to dispose of assets just at the moment the cash is needed, losses involved in the poor resale price which results from an asset becoming 'secondhand' when purchased by a non-professional dealer, administrative costs, and psychic costs (the trouble involved in making a withdrawal) as well as payment to a middleman. So conceived it seems likely that the 'broker's fee' will, in fact, vary considerably with the magnitude of the funds involved, contrary to assumption. However, *some* parts of this cost will not vary with the amount involved—e.g. postage cost, bookkeeping expense, and, possibly, the withdrawer's effort. It seems plausible that the 'broker's fee' will be better approximated by a function like $b + kC$ (where b and k are constants), which indicates that there is a part of the 'broker's fee' increasing in proportion with the amount withdrawn. As shown in a subsequent footnote, however, our formal result is completely unaffected by this amendment.

We must also extend the meaning of the interest rate to include the value of protection against loss by fire, theft, etc., which we obtain when someone borrows our cash. On the other hand, a premium for the risk of default on repayment must be deducted. This protection obtained by

In this situation any value of C less than or equal to T will enable him to meet his payments equally well provided he withdraws the money often enough. For example, if T is $100, he can meet his payments by withdrawing $50 every six months or $25 quarterly, etc.[2] Thus he will make T/C withdrawals over the course of the year, at a total cost in 'brokers' fees' given by bT/C.

In this case, since each time he withdraws C dollars he spends it in a steady stream and draws out a similar amount the moment it is gone, his average cash holding will be $C/2$ dollars. His annual interest cost of holding cash will then be $iC/2$.

The total amount the individual in question must pay for the use of the cash needed to meet his transaction when he borrows C dollars at intervals evenly spaced throughout the year will then be the sum of interest cost and 'brokers' fees' and so will be given by

$$\frac{bT}{C}+\frac{iC}{2}. \tag{1}$$

Since the manner in which he meets his payments is indifferent to him, his purpose only being to pay for his transactions, rationality requires that he do so at minimum cost, i.e. that he choose the most economical value of C. Setting the derivative of (1) with respect to C equal to zero we obtain[3]

$$-\frac{bT}{C^2}+\frac{i}{2} = 0,$$

i.e.

$$C = \sqrt{\frac{2bT}{i}}. \tag{2}$$

Thus the simple situation here considered, the rational individual will, given the price level,[4] demand cash in proportion to the square root of the value of his transactions. [...]

---

lending seems to be mentioned less frequently by theorists than the risk, yet how can we explain the existence of interest free demand deposits without the former?

[2] In particular, if cash were perfectly divisible and no elapse of time were required from withdrawal through payment he could make his withdrawals in a steady stream. In this case he would never require any cash balances to meet his payments and C would be zero. However, as may be surmised, this would be prohibitive with any b greater than zero.

[3] This result is unchanged if there is a part of the 'broker's fee' which varies in proportion with the quantity of cash handled. For in this case the 'broker's fee' for each loan is given by $b+kC$. Total cost in 'broker's fees' will then be

$$\frac{T}{C}(b+kC) = \frac{T}{C}b+kT.$$

Thus (1) will have the constant term, kT, added to it, which drops out in differentiation.

[4] A doubling of *all* prices (including the 'broker's fee') is like a change in the monetary unit, and may be expected to double the demand for cash balances.

SOME CONSEQUENCES OF THE ANALYSIS

I shall not labor the obvious implications for financial budgeting by the firm. Rather I shall discuss several arguments which have been presented by monetary theorists, to which our result is relevant.

The first is the view put forth by several economists, that in a stationary state there will be no demand for cash balances since it will then be profitable to invest all earnings in assets with a positive yield in such a way that the required amount will be realized at the moment any payment is to be made. According to this view no one will want any cash in such a stationary world, and the value of money must fall to zero so that there can really be no such thing as a truly static monetary economy. Clearly this argument neglects the transactions costs involved in making and collecting such loans (the 'broker's fee').[5] Our model is clearly compatible with a static world and (2) shows that it will generally pay to keep some cash. The analysis of a stationary monetary economy in which there is a meaningful (finite) price level does make sense.

Another view which can be re-examined in light of our analysis is that the transactions demand for cash will vary approximately in proportion with the money value of transactions. This may perhaps even be considered the tenor of quantity theory though there is no necessary connection, as Fisher's position indicates. If such a demand for cash balances is considered to result from rational behaviour, then (2) suggests that the conclusion cannot have general validity. On the contrary, the square root formula implies that demand for cash rises less than in proportion with the volume of transactions, so that there are, in effect, economies of large scale in the use of cash.

The magnitude of this difference should not be exaggerated, however. The phrase 'varying as the square' may suggest larger effects than are actually involved. Equation (2) requires that the average transaction velocity of circulation vary exactly in proportion with the quantity of cash, so that, for example, a doubling of the stock of cash will *ceteris paribus*, just double velocity.[6]

A third consequence of the square root formula is closely connected with the second. The effect on real income of an injection of cash into the system may have been underestimated. For suppose that (2) is a valid expression for the general demand for cash, that there is widespread unemployment, and that for this or other reasons prices do not rise with an injection of cash.

---

[5] It also neglects the fact that the transfer of cash takes time so that in reality we would have to hold cash at least for the short period between receiving it and passing it on again.

It is conceivable, it is true, that with perfect foresight the difference between money and securities might disappear since a perfectly safe loan could become universally acceptable. There would, however, remain the distinction between 'real assets' and the 'money-securities'. Moreover, there would be a finite price for, and non-zero yield on the former, the yield arising because they (as opposed to certificates of their ownership) are not generally acceptable, and hence not perfectly liquid, since there is trouble and expense involved in carrying them.

[6] Since velocity equals $(T/C) = (i/2b)C$ by (2).

Suppose, moreover, that the rate of interest is unaffected, i.e. that none of the new cash is used to buy securities. Then so long as transactions do not rise so as to maintain the same proportion with the square of the quantity of money, people will want to get rid of cash. They will use it to demand more goods and services, thereby forcing the volume of transactions to rise still further. For let ΔC be the quantity of cash injected. If a proportionality (constant velocity) assumption involves transactions rising by $k\Delta C$, it is easily shown that (2) involves transactions rising by more than twice as much, the magnitude of the excess increasing with the ratio of the injection to the initial stock of cash. More precisely, the rise in transactions would then be given by[7]

$$2k\Delta C + \frac{k}{C}\Delta C^2.$$

Of course, the rate of interest would really tend to fall in such circumstances, and this would to some extent offset the effect of the influx of cash, as is readily seen when we rewrite (2) as

$$T = C^2 i/2b. \tag{3}$$

Moreover, prices will rise to some extent,[8] and, of course, (3) at best is only an approximation. Nevertheless, it remains true that the effect of an injection of cash on, say, the level of employment, may often have been underestimated. For whatever may be working to counteract it, the force making for increased employment is greater than if transactions tend, *cateris paribus*, toward their original proportion to the quantity of cash.

Finally the square root formula lends support to the argument that wage cuts can help increase employment, since it follows that the Pigou effect and the related effects are stronger than they would be with a constant transactions velocity. Briefly the phenomenon which has come to be called the Pigou effect[9] may be summarized thus: General unemployment will result in reduction in the price level which must increase the purchasing power of the stock of cash provided the latter does not itself fall more than in proportion with prices.[10] This increased purchasing power will augment demand for commodities or investment goods (either directly, or because it is used to buy securities and so forces down the rate of interest.) In any case, this works for a reduction in unemployment.

[7] This is obtained by setting $k = C(i/2b)$ in (3), below, and computing ΔT by substituting $C + \Delta C$ for C.

[8] Even if (2) holds, the demand for cash may rise only in proportion with the money value of transactions when all prices rise exactly in proportion, the rate of interest and transactions remaining unchanged. For then a doubling of all prices and cash balances leaves the situation unchanged, and the received argument holds. The point is that b is then one of the prices which has risen.

[9] See A. C. Pigou, 'The Classical Stationary State', *Economic Journal*, Vol. LIII, December 1943.

[10] Presumably the 'broker's fee' will be one of the prices which falls, driven down by the existence of unemployed brokers. There is no analogous reason for the rate of interest to fall, though it will tend to respond thus to the increase in the 'real stock of cash'.

Now the increase in the purchasing power of the stock of cash which results from fallen prices is equivalent to an injection of cash with constant prices. There is therefore exactly the same reason for suspecting the magnitude of the effect of the former on the volume of transactions has been underestimated, as in the case of the latter. Perhaps this can be of some little help in explaining why there has not been more chronic unemployment or runaway inflation in our economy.

4.2 Liquidity Preference*

[...]

One of the basic functional relationships in the Keynesian model of the economy is the liquidity preference schedule, an inverse relationship between the demand for cash balances and the rate of interest. This aggregative function must be derived from some assumptions regarding the behavior of the decision-making units of the economy, and those assumptions are the concern of this paper. Nearly two decades of drawing downward-sloping liquidity preference curves in textbooks and on classroom blackboards should not blind us to the basic implausibility of the behavior they describe. Why should anyone hold the non-interest bearing obligations of the government instead of its interest bearing obligations? The apparent irrationality of holding cash is the same, moreover, whether the interest rate is 6%, 3% or $\frac{1}{2}$ of 1%. What needs to be explained is not only the existence of a demand for cash when its yield is less than the yield on alternative assets but an inverse relationship between the aggregate demand for cash and the size of this differential in yields.[1]

TRANSACTIONS BALANCES AND INVESTMENT BALANCES

Two kinds of reasons for holding cash are usually distinguished: transactions reasons and investment reasons.

Transactions balances: size and composition

No economic unit—firm or household or government—enjoys perfect synchronization between the seasonal patterns of its flow of receipts and its flow of expenditures. The discrepancies give rise to balances which accumulate temporarily, and are used up later when expenditures catch up. Or, to put the same phenomenon the other way, the discrepancies give rise to the

---

* From J. Tobin, 'Liquidity Preference as Behaviour Towards Risk', *Review of Economic Studies*, Feb. 1958.

[1] '...in a world involving no transaction friction and no uncertainty, there would be no reason for a spread between the yield on any two assets, and hence there would be no difference in the yield on money and on securities...in such a world securities themselves would circulate as money and be acceptable in transactions; demand bank deposits would bear interest, just as they often did in this country in the period of the twenties.' Paul A. Samuelson, *Foundations of Economic Analysis* (Cambridge: Harvard University Press, 1947), p. 123. The section, pp. 122–124, from which the passage is quoted makes it clear that liquidity preference must be regarded as an explanation of the existence and level not of the interest rate but of the differential between the yield on money and the yields on other assets.

need for balances to meet seasonal excesses of expenditures over receipts. These balances are *transactions balances*. The aggregate requirement of the economy for such balances depends on the institutional arrangements that determine the degree of synchronization between individual receipts and expenditures. Given these institutions, the need for transactions balances is roughly proportionate to the aggregate volume of transactions.

The obvious importance of these institutional determinants of the demand for transactions balances has led to the general opinion that other possible determinants, including interest rates, are negligible.[2] This may be true of the size of transactions balances, but the composition of transactions balances is another matter. Cash is by no means the only asset in which transactions balances may be held. Many transactors have large enough balances so that holding part of them in earning assets, rather than in cash, is a relevant possibility. Even though these holdings are always for short periods, the interest earnings may be worth the cost and inconvenience of the financial transactions involved. Elsewhere[3] I have shown that, for such transactors, the proportion of cash in transactions balances varies inversely with the rate of interest; consequently this source of interest-elasticity in the demand for cash will not be further discussed here.

Investment balances and portfolio decisions

In contrast to transactions balances, the investment balances of an economic unit are those that will survive all the expected seasonal excesses of cumulative expenditure over cumulative receipts during the year ahead. They are balances which will not have to be turned into cash within the year. Consequently the cost of financial transactions—converting other assets into cash and vice versa—does not operate to encourage the holding of investment balances in cash.[4] If cash is to have any part in the composition of investment balances, it must be because of expectations or fears of loss on other assets. It is here, in what Keynes called the speculative motives of investors, that the explanation of liquidity preference and of the interest-elasticity of the demand for cash has been sought.

The alternatives to cash considered, both in this paper and in prior discussions of the subject, in examining the speculative motive for holding

[2] The traditional theory of the velocity of money has, however, probably exaggerated the invariance of the institutions determining the extent of lack of synchronization between individual receipts and expenditures. It is no doubt true that such institutions as the degree of vertical integration of production and the periodicity of wage, salary, dividend, and tax payments are slow to change. But other relevant arrangements can be adjusted in response to money rates. For example, there is a good deal of flexibility in the promptness and regularity with which bills are rendered and settled.

[3] 'The Interest Elasticity of the Transactions Demand for Cash', *Review of Economics and Statistics*, Vol. 38 (August 1956), pp. 241–247.

[4] Costs of financial transactions have the effect of deterring changes from the existing portfolio, whatever its composition; they may thus operate against the holding of cash as easily as for it. Because of these costs, the *status quo* may be optimal even when a different composition of assets would be preferred if the investor were starting over again.

cash are assets that differ from cash only in having a variable market yield. They are obligations to pay stated cash amounts at future dates, with no risk of default. They are, like cash, subject to changes in real value due to fluctuations in the price level. In a broader perspective, all these assets, including cash, are merely minor variants of the same species, a species we may call monetary assets—marketable, fixed in money.value, free of default risk. The differences of members of this species from each other are negligible compared to their differences from the vast variety of other assets in which wealth may be invested: corporate stocks, real estate, unincorporated business and professional practice, etc. The theory of liquidity preference does not concern the choices investors make between the whole species of monetary assets, on the one hand, and other broad classes of assets, on the other. Those choices are the concern of other branches of economic theory, in particular theories of investment and of consumption. Liquidity preference theory takes as given the choices determining how much wealth is to be invested in monetary assets and concerns itself with the allocation of these amounts among cash and alternative monetary assets.

Why should any investment balances be held in cash, in preference to other monetary assets? We shall distinguish two possible sources of liquidity preference, while recognizing that they are not mutually exclusive. The first is inelasticity of expectations of future interest rates. The second is uncertainty about the future of interest rates. These two sources of liquidity preference will be examined in turn.

INELASTICITY OF INTEREST RATE EXPECTATIONS

Some simplifying assumptions

To simplify the problem, assume that there is only one monetary asset other than cash, namely consols. The current yield of consols is r per 'year'. \$1 invested in consols today will purchase an income of \$$r$ per 'year' in perpetuity. The yield of cash is assumed to be zero; however, this is not essential, as it is the current and expected differentials of consols over cash that matter. An investor with a given total balance must decide what proportion of this balance to hold in cash, A_1, and what proportion in consols, A_2. This decision is assumed to fix the portfolio for a full 'year'.[5]

[5] As noted above, it is the costs of financial transactions that impart inertia to portfolio composition. Every reconsideration of the portfolio involves the investor in expenditure of time and effort as well as of money. The frequency with which it is worth while to review the portfolio will obviously vary with the investor and will depend on the size of his portfolio and on his situation with respect to costs of obtaining information and engaging in financial transactions. Thus the relevant 'year' ahead for which portfolio decisions are made is not the same for all investors. Moreover, even if a decision is made with a view to fixing a portfolio for a given period of time, a portfolio is never so irrevocably frozen that there are no conceivable events during the period which would induce the investor to reconsider. The fact that this possibility is always open must influence the investor's decision. The fiction of a fixed investment period used in this paper is, therefore, not a wholly satisfactory way of taking account of the inertia in portfolio composition due to the costs of transactions and of decision making.

Fixed expectations of future rate

At the end of the year, the investor expects the rate on consols to be r_e. This expectation is assumed, for the present, to be held with certainty and to be independent of the current rate r. The investor may therefore expect with certainty that every dollar invested in consols today will earn over the year ahead not only interest $\$r$, but also a capital gain or loss g:

$$g = \frac{r}{r_e} - 1 \tag{1}$$

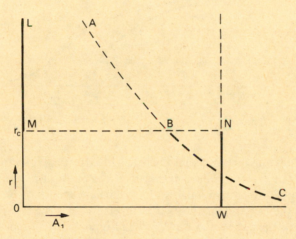

FIG. 4.1. Individual demand for cash assuming certain but inelastic interest rate expectations

For this investor, the division of his balance into proportions A_1 of cash and A_2 of consols is a simple all-or-nothing choice. If the current rate is such that $r+g$ is greater than zero, then he will put everything in consols. But if $r+g$ is less than zero, he will put everything in cash. These conditions can be expressed in terms of a critical level of the current rate r_c, where:

$$r_c = \frac{r_e}{1+r_e} \tag{2}$$

At current rates above r_c, everything goes into consols; but for r less than r_c, everything goes into cash. [...]

Differences of opinion and the aggregate demand for cash

According to this model, the relationship of the individual's investment demand for cash to the current rate of interest would be the discontinuous step function shown by the heavy vertical lines *LMNW* in Figure 4.1. How then do we get the familiar Keynesian liquidity preference function, a smooth, continuous inverse relationship between the demand for cash and the rate of interest? For the economy as a whole, such a relationship can be derived from individual behaviour of the sort depicted in Figure 4.1 by assuming that individual investors differ in their critical rates r_c. Such an aggregate relationship is shown in Figure 4.2.

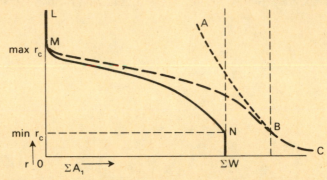

Fig. 4.2. Aggregate demand for cash assuming differences among individuals in interest rate expectations

At actual rates above the maximum of individual critical rates the aggregate demand for cash is zero, while at rates below the minimum critical rate it is equal to the total investment balances for the whole economy. Between these two extremes the demand for cash varies inversely with the rate of interest r. Such a relationship is shown as $LMN\Sigma W$ in Figure 4.2. The demand for cash at r is the total of investment balances controlled by investors whose critical rates r_c exceed r. Strictly speaking, the curve is a step function; but, if the number of investors is large, it can be approximated by a smooth curve. Its shape depends on the distribution of dollars of investment balances by the critical rate of the investor controlling them; the shape of the curve in Figure 4.2 follows from a uni-modal distribution.

Capital gains or losses and open market operations

In the foregoing analysis the size of investment balances has been taken as independent of the current rate on consols r. This is not the case if there are already consols outstanding. Their value will depend inversely on the current rate of interest. Depending on the relation of the current rate to the previously fixed coupon on consols, owners of consols will receive capital gains or losses. Thus the investment balances of an individual owner of consols would not be constant at W but would depend on r in a manner illustrated by the curve ABC in Figure 4.1.[6] Similarly, the investment balances for the whole economy

---

[6] The size of their investment balances, held in cash and consols may not vary by the full amount of these changes in wealth; some part of the changes may be reflected in holdings of assets other than monetary assets. But presumably the size of investment balances will reflect at least in part these capital gains and losses.

would follow a curve like *ABC* in Figure 4.2, instead of being constant at
ΣW. The demand for cash would then be described by *LMBC* in both
figures. Correspondingly the demand for consols at any interest rate would be
described by the horizontal distance between *LMBC* and *ABC*. The value of
consols goes to infinity as the rate of interest approaches zero; for this
reason, the curve *BC* may never reach the horizontal axis. The size of
investment balances would be bounded if the monetary assets other than cash
consisted of bonds with definite maturities rather than consols.

According to this theory, a curve like *LMBC* depicts the terms on which a
central bank can engage in open-market operations, given the claims for the
future payments outstanding in the form of bonds or consols. The curve tells
what the quantity of cash must be in order for the central bank to establish a
particular interest rate. However, the curve will be shifted by open market
operations themselves, since they will change the volume of outstanding
bonds or consols. For example, to establish the rate at or below *min* r_c, the
central bank would have to buy all outstanding bonds or consols. The size
of the community's investment balances would then be independent of the
rate of interest; it would be represented by a vertical line through, or to the
right of, *B*, rather than the curve *ABC*. Thus the new relation between cash
and interest would be a curve lying above *LMB*, of the same general contour
as *LMNΣW*.

Keynesian theory and its critics

I believe the theory of liquidity preference I have just presented is essentially
the original Keynesian explanation. The *General Theory* suggests a number of
possible theoretical explanations, supported and enriched by the experience
and insight of the author. But the explanation to which Keynes gave the
greatest emphasis is the notion of a 'normal' long-term rate, to which investors
expect the rate of interest to return. When he refers to uncertainty in the
market, he appears to mean disagreement among investors concerning the
future of the rate rather than subjective doubt in the mind of an individual
investor.[7][...]

Keynes's use of this explanation of liquidity preference as a part of his
theory of underemployment equilibrium was the target of important criticism
by Leontief and Fellner. Leontief argued that liquidity preference must necessarily be zero *in equilibrium*, regardless of the rate of interest. Divergence
between the current and expected interest rate is bound to vanish as
investors learn from experience; no matter how low an interest rate may be,

[7] J. M. Keynes, *The General Theory of Employment, Interest, and Money* (New York:
Harcourt Brace, 1936), Chapters 13 and 15, expecially pp. 168–172 and 201–203. One quotation
from p. 172 will illustrate the point: 'It is interesting that the stability of the system and its
sensitiveness to changes in the quantity of money should be so dependent on the existence of a
variety of opinion about what is uncertain. Best of all that we should know the future. But if not,
then, if we are to control the activity of the economic system by changing the quantity of money,
it is important that opinions should differ.'

it can be accepted as 'normal' if it persists long enough. This criticism was a part of Leontief's general methodological criticism of Keynes, that unemployment was not a feature of equilibrium, subject to analysis by tools of static theory, but a phenomenon of disequilibrium requiring analysis by dynamic theory.[8] Fellner makes a similar criticism of the logical appropriateness of Keynes' explanation of liquidity preference for the purposes of his theory of underemployment equilibrium. Why, he asks, are interest rates the only variables to which inelastic expectations attach? Why don't wealth owners and others regard pre-depression price levels as 'normal' levels to which prices will return? If they did, consumption and investment demand would respond to reductions in money wages and prices, no matter how strong and how elastic the liquidity preference of investors.[9]

These criticisms raise the question whether it is possible to dispense with the assumption of stickiness in interest rate expectations without losing the implication that Keynesian theory drew from it. Can the inverse relationship of demand for cash to the rate of interest be based on a different set of assumptions about the behaviour of individual investors? This question is the subject of the next part of the paper.

UNCERTAINTY, RISK AVERSION, AND LIQUIDITY PREFERENCE

The locus of opportunity for risk and expected return

Suppose that an investor is not certain of the future rate of interest on consols; investment in consols then involves a risk of capital gain or loss. The higher the proportion of his investment balance that he holds in consols, the more risk the investor assumes. At the same time, increasing the proportion in consols also increases his expected return. In the upper half of Figure 4.3 the vertical axis represents expected return and the horizontal axis risk. A line such as OC_1 pictures the fact that the investor can expect more return if he assumes more risk. In the lower half of Figure 4.3, the left-hand vertical axis measures the proportion invested in consols. A line like OB shows risk as proportional to the share of the total balance held in consols.

The concepts of expected return and risk must be given more precision.

The individual investor of the previous section was assumed to have, for any current rate of interest, a definite expectation of the capital gain or loss g (defined in expression (1) above) he would obtain by investing one dollar in consols. Now he will be assumed instead to be uncertain about g but to base his actions on his estimate of its probability distribution. This probability distribution, it will be assumed, has an expected value of zero and is independent of the level of r, the current rate on consols. Thus the investor

[8] W. Leontief, 'Postulates: Keynes' General Theory and the Classicists', Chapter XIX in S. Harris, editor, *The New Economics* (New York: Knopf, 1947), pp. 232–242. Section 6, pp. 238–239, contains the specific criticism of Keynes' liquidity preference theory.

[9] W. Fellner, *Monetary Policies and Full Employment* (Berkeley: University of California Press, 1946), p. 149.

considers a doubling of the rate just as likely when rate is 5% as when it is 2%, and a halving of the rate just as likely when it is 1% as when it is 6%.

A portfolio consists of a proportion A_1 of cash and A_2 of consols, where A_1 and A_2 add up to 1. We shall assume that A_1 and A_2 do not depend on the absolute size of the initial investment balance in dollars. Negative values of A_1 and A_2 are excluded by definition; only the government and the banking system can issue cash and government consols. The return of a portfolio R is:

$$R = A_2(r+g) \qquad 0 \leqslant A_2 \leqslant 1 \qquad (3)$$

Since g is a random variable with expected value zero, the expected return on the portfolio is:

$$E(R) = \mu_R = A_2 r. \qquad (4)$$

The risk attached to a portfolio is to be measured by the standard deviation of R, σ_R. The standard deviation is a measure of the dispersion of possible returns around the mean value μ_R. A high standard deviation means, speaking roughly, high probability of large deviations from μ_R, both positive and negative. A low standard deviation means low probability of large deviations from μ_R; in the extreme case, a zero standard deviation would indicate certainty of receiving the return μ_R. Thus a high-σ_R portfolio offers the investor the chance of large capital gains at the price of equivalent chances of large capital losses. A low-σ_R portfolio protects the investor from capital loss, and likewise gives him little prospect of unusual gains. Although it is intuitively clear that the risk of a portfolio is to be identified with the dispersion of possible returns, the standard deviation is neither the sole measure of dispersion nor the obviously most relevant measure.

The standard deviation of R depends on the standard deviation of g, σ_g, and on the amount invested in consols:

$$\sigma_R = A_2 \sigma_g \qquad 0 \leqslant A_2 \leqslant 1. \qquad (5)$$

Thus the proportion the investor holds in consols A_2 determines both his expected return μ_R and his risk σ_R. The terms on which the investor can obtain greater expected return at the expense of assuming more risk can be derived from (4) and (5):

$$\mu_R = \frac{r}{\sigma_g} \sigma_R \qquad 0 \leqslant \sigma_R \leqslant \sigma_g \qquad (6)$$

Such an *opportunity locus* is shown as line OC_1 (for $r = r_1$) in Figure 4.3. The slope of the line is r_1/σ_g. For a higher interest rate r_2, the opportunity locus would be OC_2; and for r_3, a still higher rate, it would be OC_3. The relationship (5) between risk and investment in consols is shown as line OB in the lower half of the Figure. Cash holding $A_1 (\, = 1 - A_2)$ can also be read off the diagram on the right-hand vertical axis.

Loci of indifference between combinations of risk and expected return

The investor is assumed to have preferences between expected return μ_R and risk σ_R that can be represented by a field of indifference curves. The investor is indifferent between all pairs (μ_R, σ_R) that lie on a curve such as I_1 in Figure 4.3. Points on I_2 are preferred to those on I_1; for given risk, an investor always prefers a greater to a smaller expectation of return. Conceivably, for some investors, *risk-lovers*, these indifference curves have negative slopes. Such individuals are willing to accept lower expected return in order to have the chance of unusually high capital gains afforded by high values of σ_R. *Risk-averters*, on the other hand, will not be satisfied to accept more risk unless they can also expect greater expected return. Their indifference curves will be positively sloped. Two kinds of risk-averters need to be distinguished. The first type, who may be called *diversifiers* for reasons that will become clear below, have indifference curves that are concave upward, like those in Figure 4.3. The second type, who may be called *plungers*, have indifference curves that are upward sloping, but either linear or convex upward.

We can now examine the consequences of a change in the interest rate r, holding constant the investor's estimate of the risk of capital gain or loss. An increase in the interest rate will rotate the opportunity locus OC to the left. How will this affect the investor's holdings of cash and consols? [...]

In Figure 4.3 OC_1, OC_2, and OC_3 represent opportunity loci for successively higher rates of interest. The indifference curves I_1, I_2, and I_3 are drawn so that the points of tangency T_1, T_2, and T_3, correspond to successively higher holdings of consols A_2. In this diagram, the investor's demand for cash depends inversely on the interest rate. [...]

The theory of risk-avoiding behaviour has been shown to provide a basis for liquidity preference and for an inverse relationship between the demand for cash and the rate of interest. This theory does not depend on inelasticity of expectations of future interest rates, but can proceed from the assumption that the expected value of capital gain or loss from holding interest-bearing assets is always zero. In this respect, it is a logically more satisfactory foundation for liquidity preference than the Keynesian theory described earlier. Moreover, it has the empirical advantage of explaining diversification—the same individual holds both cash and 'consols'—while the Keynesian theory implies that each investor will hold only one asset.

The risk aversion theory of liquidity preference mitigates the major logical objection to which ... the Keynesian theory is vulnerable. But it cannot completely meet Leontief's position that in a strict stationary equilibrium liquidity preference must be zero unless cash and consols bear equal rates. By their very nature consols and, to a lesser degree, all time obligations contain a potential for capital gain or loss that cash and other demand obligations lack. Presumably, however, there is some length of experience of constancy in the interest rate that would teach the most stubbornly timid investor to ignore that potential. In a pure stationary state, it could be argued, the interest

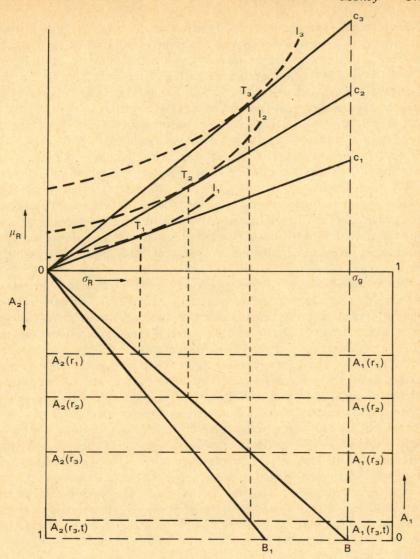

FIG. 4.3. Portfolio selection at various interest rates and before and after taxation

rate on consols would have been the same for so long that investors would unanimously estimate σ_g to be zero. So stationary a state is of very little interest. Fortunately the usefulness of comparative statics does not appear to be confined to comparisons of states each of which would take a generation or more to achieve. As compared to the Keynesian theory of liquidity preference, the risk aversion theory widens the applicability of comparative statics in aggregative analysis; this is all that need be claimed for it.

The theory, however, is somewhat ambiguous concerning the direction of relationship between the rate of interest and the demand for cash. For low interest rates, the theory implies a negative elasticity of demand for cash with respect to the interest rate, an elasticity that becomes larger and larger in absolute value as the rate approaches zero. This implication, of course, is in accord with the usual assumptions about liquidity preference. But for high interest rates, and especially for individuals whose estimates σ_g of the risk of capital gain or loss on 'consols' are low, the demand for cash may be an increasing, rather than a decreasing, function of the interest rate. However, the force of this reversal of direction is diluted by recognition ... that the size of investment balances is not independent of the current rate of interest r. ... [W]e have considered the proportionate allocation between cash and 'consols' on the assumption that it is independent of the size of the balance. An increase in the rate of interest may lead an investor to desire to shift towards cash. But to the extent that the increase in interest also reduces the value of the investor's consol holdings, it automatically gratifies this desire, at least in part.

The assumption that investors expect on balance no change in the rate of interest has been adopted for the theoretical reasons explained earlier rather than for reasons of realism. Clearly investors do form expectations of changes in interest rates and differ from each other in their expectations. For the purposes of dynamic theory and of analysis of specific market situations, the two theories ... are complementary rather than competitive. The formal apparatus of the preceding section will serve just as well for a non-zero expected capital gain or loss as for a zero expected value of g. Stickiness of interest rate expectations would mean that the expected value of g is a function of the rate of interest r, going down when r goes down and rising when r goes up. In addition to the rotation of the opportunity locus due to a change in r itself, there would be a further rotation in the same direction due to the accompanying change in the expected capital gain or loss. At low interest rates expectation of capital loss may push the opportunity locus into the negative quadrant, so that the optimal position is clearly no consols, all cash. At the other extreme, expectation of capital gain at high interest rates would increase sharply the slope of the opportunity locus and the frequency of no cash, all consols positions. ... The stickier the investor's expectations, the more sensitive his demand for cash will be to changes in the rate of interest.

4.3 The Term Structure of Interest Rates*

This paper is an examination of the success, or we should say lack of success, of the policy launched at the beginning of 1961 by the incoming Kennedy Administration, which has become known as 'Operation Twist'. This was an attempt to twist the maturity structure of interest rates by raising yields on securities with short term to maturity while simultaneously lowering, or at

* From F. Modigliani and R. Sutch, 'Innovations in Interest Rate Policy', *American Economic Review (Papers and Proceedings)*, May 1966.

least holding the line on, long-term rates. Higher short-term rates were expected to contribute significantly toward stemming the outflow of capital and thus helping the United States balance-of-payments problem, while low long-term rates were considered desirable to stimulate the economy by increasing the flow of private investment. We are not concerned, however, with the broad issue of whether Operation Twist contributed to improving the balance of payments while sustaining domestic activity. Our focus is, rather, on Operation Twist per se. We direct ourselves to a review of the techniques used by the government and Federal Reserve to affect the term structure and attempt to asses how far they succeeded in achieving the stated goal of twisting the yield curve.

As far as we can see there were two main actions aimed directly at such a twisting:

1. Federal Reserve open market operations and Treasury debt management operations directed toward shortening the average term to maturity of the outstanding government debt held by the public. An increase in the relative supply of short-term securities were expected to exert upward pressure on short-term rates, while the corresponding decrease in the availability of long-term securities should have tended to lower long-term yields, thus twisting the term structure in the desired direction.

2. Beginning in January, 1962, the successive increases in the structure of ceiling rates payable on commercial banks' time and saving deposits under Regulation Q. According to the *Economic Report of the President* of January, 1962, this 'action was taken to promote competition for saving and to encourage retention of foreign funds by member banks and thus moderate pressures on this country's balance of payments' [3, p. 88, Table 8]. Also under this heading one should include the recent acquiescence by the Federal Reserve Board to the issuance of unsecured notes and debentures by commercial banks.[1] [...]

RECENT THEORETICAL DEVELOPMENTS IN THE ANALYSIS OF THE MATURITY STRUCTURE

There is by now general agreement that in an ideal world of no transaction costs or taxes, rational behavior and certainty (about future rates), the maturity structure of yields must be controlled by the simple principle that all

---

[1] Other tools were brought to bear on the problem but were not designed to twist yield curves; rather, they were policies that were intended to change the reaction of the economy to a given yield curve. These can be broadly summarized under two headings: (1) Measures directly aimed at reducing capital exports for a given structure of long- and short-term rates: these measures include primarily (a) the interest equalization tax and (b) the Johnson Administration program of voluntary restraint in bank lending to foreigners and to domestic firms for foreign operations, and in direct foreign investments. (2) Fiscal measures aimed at increasing the rate of domestic long-term investments for a given level of long-term rates: these measures include (a) the Internal Revenue Department's revised depreciation guide lines and (b) the investment credit provisions. An assessment of these policies is beyond the province of this study, which will concentrate only on those techniques designed to change the shape of the yield curve.

outstanding instruments, regardless of maturity, must produce identical returns over any given interval of time—where the return is defined as the sum of cash payments plus any increase (or minus any decrease) in the market value of the instrument. This principle in turn implies that at any date t the spread between the yield of an n period bond and the short rate, $S(n, t) = R(n, t) - R(1, t)$, is equal to minus the capital gain from holding the n period instrument. The capital gain in turn is inversely related to the change in yield: $\Delta R(n, t) = R(n-1, t+1) - R(n, t)$. Consequently, $R(n, t)$ can be expressed in terms of the current short rate $R(1, t)$ and the future long rate $R(n-1, t+1)$. Moreover, since $R(n-1, t+1)$ can in turn be expressed in terms of $R(1, t+1)$ and $R(n-2, t+2)$, and so on, recursively, it is readily apparent that $R(n, t)$ can also be expressed in terms of the current and future rates for one period loans prevailing in each of the n periods to maturity, $R(1, t)$, $R(1, t+1), \ldots R(1, t+n-1)$, although the precise form of the functional relation will depend on the shape of the stream of cash payments promised by the bond until maturity. Finally, because the return to the lender and the cost to the borrower over any interval will be the same regardless of the maturity of the instrument held or issued, neither would have a special incentive to match the maturity structure of his assets or liabilities to the length of time for which he intends to remain a creditor or debtor.

There is unfortunately much less agreement as to the determinants of the yield structure in the 'real' world. The prevailing points of view may be summarized as follows.

1. At one end of the spectrum is the Pure Expectation Hypothesis, which holds that the certainty model provides an adequate approximation to the real world, except that the equality of returns of the certainty world must now be replaced by the equality of 'expected' returns, where the expected returns may be thought of as the mean value (or some other analogous measure of central tendency) of the subjective probability distribution of possible returns. In particular, for every n, $R(n, t)$ must equal $R(1, t)$ minus the expected capital gain, determined by the expected change in the n period rate, say $\Delta R^e(n, t)$. For otherwise holders of bonds with lower expected returns would try to sell them, bidding down their price and raising their yield, and to acquire higher yielding instruments, bidding up their price and reducing their yields, until the postulated relation would come to hold.

2. A variant of the expectation hypothesis, of Keynesian inspiration [10] but articulated largely by Hicks [8], which has wide support at the present, may be labeled the Risk Premium Model. It basically accepts the view that yields on various maturities are related to each other by the expectations of future long rates, and hence also short rates, but it calls attention to differences in the degree of uncertainty which attaches to the expected return to be obtained, in the short run, from holding securities of different length. While the return on short-term securities is certain (since the value of the principal is guaranteed by repayment at the end of the period), the return

on longer maturities is not guaranteed because of the uncertainty of future rates and hence of the end of period market value of the bond. Furthermore, the uncertainty tends to be greater the longer the maturity, since a given change in the long rate tends to produce a greater variation in terminal value the longer the remaining life to maturity. If, then, investors are prevailingly risk averters, as a good deal of other evidence suggests, one should expect that if the expected return were the same on all maturities, they would tend to prefer the safer short-term instruments. Hence, in order to induce the market to hold the longer-term maturities supplied by long-term borrowers, the expected return on these maturities must exceed that on shorter-term instruments by an expected risk or liquidity premium. According to this view, the yield curve will tend to rise more than the curve implied by the pure expectation hypothesis because of the increasing risk premium as the term to maturity increases. The size of these risk premiums might be expected to depend on the relative supplies of longer maturities and the strength of investors' risk aversion.

3. Finally, there is the view that might be labeled the Market Segmentation Hypothesis. The proponents of this approach suggest that both lenders and borrowers have definite preferences for instruments of a specific maturity, and for various reasons, partly due to institutional factors and regulations constraining financial intermediaries, will tend to stick to securities of the corresponding maturity, without paying attention to rates of return on other maturities.[2] Hence the rates for different terms to maturity tend to be determined, each in its separate market, by their independent supply and demand schedules. The rates so set might well imply wide differences in the expected return obtainable in the current period, or over some sequence of periods, by investing in different maturities, but such differences, it is argued, would not induce traders to move out of their preferred maturity—or maturity habitat, as we shall call it—except possibly when the discrepancies become extreme and glaring.

In our view, each of the three models has its merits, but also suffers from shortcomings. We propose, therefore, an alternative model which, in essence, blends the previous three, and which we label the Preferred Habitat Theory. This model shares with the Hicksian approach the notion that the yield structure is basically controlled by the principle of the equality of expected returns, but modified by the risk premiums. Yet it differs from it in one fundamental respect. The Hicksian model assumes that all traders are concerned with the short period return and that, therefore, anybody going long is bearing the risk associated with the uncertainty of the short period return from longer-term instruments. But this view would be correct only if we could assume that every lender desires to turn his portfolio back into cash at the end of the short period; i.e. that he has a short habitat (cf. Meiselman [14]). In reality, however, different transactors are likely to have different

---

[2] This view has been stressed by a number of authors, in particular Culbertson [3].

habitats, as the segmentation theory points out. Suppose that a person has an n period habitat; that is, he has funds which he will not need for n periods and which, therefore, he intends to keep invested in bonds for n periods. If he invests in n period bonds, he will know exactly the outcome of his investments as measured by the terminal value of his wealth (this being only approximately true if he were to invest in a conventional loan and precisely true for a pure n period loan; that is, a loan that was issued on a discount basis). If, however, he stays short, his outcome is uncertain, as it will depend on the future course of the short rates in periods 2, 3,..., n-1. Furthermore, he is likely to have to incur greater transaction costs. Thus, if he has risk aversion, he will prefer to stay long unless the average of the expected short rates exceeds the long rate by an amount sufficient to cover extra transaction costs and to compensate him for the extra risk of going short. Similarly, if he should invest in maturities longer than n, he would also be exposing himself to risk, this time to the Hicks-Keynesian uncertainty as to the price he can fetch for his not-yet-matured bonds. Thus, risk aversion should not lead investors to prefer to stay short but, instead, should lead them to hedge by staying in their maturity habitat, unless other maturities (longer or shorter) offer an expected premium sufficient to compensate for the risk and cost of moving out of one's habitat. Similar considerations will clearly apply, *mutatis mutandis*, to the borrower's side of the market.

Under this model the rate for a given maturity, n, could differ from the rate implied by the Pure Expectation Hypothesis by positive or negative 'risk premiums', reflecting the extent to which the supply of funds with habitat n differs from the aggregate demand for n period loans forthcoming at that rate. If the n period demand exceeded the funds with n period habitat, there would tend to arise a premium in the n period maturity, and conversely.[3] Such premiums or discounts would tend to bring about shifts in funds between different maturity markets, both through the 'speculation' of investors tempted out of their natural habitat by the lure of higher expected returns and through 'arbitrage' by intermediaries induced to 'take a position' by borrowing in the maturity range where the expected return is low, and lending where the expected return is high.

In summary, then, the Habitat Model implies that the spread $S(n, t)$ between the long rate $R(n, t)$ and the short rate $R(1, t)$ should depend primarily on the expected change in the long rate, $\Delta R^e(n, t)$. But it suggests that the spread could also be influenced by the supply of long- and short-term securities by primary borrowers (i.e. by borrowers other than arbitrageurs) relative to the corresponding demand of primary lenders, to an extent reflecting prevailing risk aversion, transaction costs, and facilities for effective arbitrage operations.

---

[3] This is only approximately true, for under risk aversion, funds of habitat n would not be indifferent as to where they would move but would tend to spill, preferably into neighboring maturities where the risk would tend to be smaller.

These conculsions can be conveniently summarized in the following equations.

Expected current return on an n period bond
$$\equiv R(n,t) + \text{Expected capital gain}$$
$$= R(1,t) + F_t$$

where F_t stands for the net effect of relative supply factors and could in principle be positive or negative. Solving for $R(n,t)$, and taking the Expected Capital Gain as proportional to the expected fall in the long rate, i.e. to $-\Delta R^e(n,t)$, we can also write

$$R(n,t) = R(1,t) - \text{Expected capital gain} + F_t$$
$$= R(1,t) + \beta \Delta R^e(n,t) + F_t \tag{1}$$

AN OPERATIONAL FORMULATION OF THE HABITAT MODEL

Before we can test our hypothesis we must recast equation (1) into an operational form suitable for empirical estimation. This entails specifying both a theory of how expectations are formed and a functional form for the summary term 'F'. For a model of expectations we draw on the highly imaginative approach of Frank de Leeuw [4] who synthesized two currently held views as to the determinants of the expected change in long-term rates.[4]

One widely held hypothesis associated with Keynes [11] holds that the market expects the interest rate to regress toward a 'normal' level based on past experience. Modifying slightly De Leeuw's formulation, we approximate this normal level, denoted by $\bar{R}_t$, by some average of the long rates for the past m periods and a constant which could be thought of as a very long-run normal level. Thus:

$$\bar{R}_t = v \sum_{i=1}^{m} \mu_i R_{t-i} + (1-v)c \qquad 0 < v < 1$$

where R_t is used hereafter as a symbol for the long-term rate and the μ_i's are weights adding up to one. Since the recent experience should be more salient we should expect the μ_i's to decline towards zero as i rises from one to m. This regressive hypothesis can thus be formalized as

$$\Delta R_t^e{}^6 = \alpha_1 (\bar{R}_t - R_t) = \alpha_1 \left[v \sum_{i=1}^{m} \mu_i R_{t-i} + (1-v)c - R_t \right]^5 \tag{2}$$

where α_1 is a measure of the speed with which R_t is expected to return to $\bar{R}$.

A quite different hypothesis, advanced by James Duesenberry, suggests that

[4] Meiselman [14] and Kessel [9] have also made important contributions in this area, but while their work provides impressive support for the expectations model, their approach is not directly applicable to our problem.

[5] This hypothesis could also be derived by replacing the notion of a normal level with the notion of a normal range (cf., Malkiel [13]).

expectations might be extrapolative: 'a rise in rates [leading] to and expectation of a further rise and vice versa' ([5], p. 318). De Leeuw suggests that the recent trend in rates might be approximated by the difference between the current rate and some weighted average of recent past rates and accordingly express the extrapolative hypothesis as

$$\Delta R_t^6 = \alpha_2 \left(R_t - \sum_{i=1}^{n} \delta_i R_{t-i} \right); \qquad \alpha_2 > 0 \tag{3}$$

where n should be appreciably smaller than m and the weights, δ_i, would probably decline rather rapidly.

Now, as De Leeuw rightly points out, it is quite credible that both hypotheses contain an important element of truth—that expectations contain both extrapolative and regressive elements. If so, we can combine the right-hand side of (2) and (3) to obtain

$$\Delta R_t^e = -aR_t + \sum_{i=1}^{m} b_i R_{t-i} + dc \tag{4}$$

where $a = (\alpha_1 - \alpha_2)$, $b_1 = \alpha_1 v \mu_i - \alpha_2 \delta_i$, with δ_i defined to be zero for $i > n$, and $d = \alpha_1(1-v)$. Since the term in the summation now represents the difference of two lag structures, we can no longer expect it to be of a simple geometric form. Indeed, if the extrapolative element is at all significant (i.e. α_2 is not zero or small compared with $\alpha_1 v$) we should find that initially, since δ_i falls faster than μ_i, b_i rises (possibly even from negative values), reaching a peak in the neighborhood of n and then declines back toward zero.

We are ready now to substitute equation (4) into the basic hypothesis (1) which yields

$$R_t = r_t - \beta a R_t + \sum_{i=1}^{m} \beta b_i R_{t-i} + \beta dc + F_t$$

where r_t is used hereafter to denote the short rate $R(1,t)$. As it now stands, this equation involves the current long rate on both sides; but this can be readily handled by solving the equation for R_t, obtaining finally

$$R_t = Ar_t + \sum_{i=1}^{m} B_i R_{t-i} + C + F_t' + \dot{\varepsilon}_t \tag{5}$$

where

$$A = \frac{1}{1 + \beta a}, \quad B_i = \frac{\beta}{1 + \beta a} b_i, \quad C = \frac{\beta dc}{1 + \beta a} \text{ and } \varepsilon_t \text{ is the error term.}$$

We note that, since β and a are supposed to be positive, the coefficient A should be positive but distinctly below unity, and that, since the lag coefficients, B_i, are proportional to the b_i of (4), our earlier inferences about the b_i's—which define the lag structure—applies equally to the B_i's.

As is well known, an equation in the form of (5) implies that R_t can also be expressed as a function only of r_t and a weighted sum of all previous short rates, r_{t-i}. This result can be derived by using equation (5) to express R_{t-1} in terms of r_{t-1}, and R_{t-2} to R_{t-m-1}, and so on, recursively. The final result involves only r_{t-j}, with j extending indefinitely into the past, but with the coefficients of the far removed r_{t-j} approaching zero. Hence, to à first approximation R_t can be expressed as an average of a finite and reasonably small number of lagged values of r:

$$R_t = \alpha + \beta_0 r_t + \sum_{i=1}^{m} \beta_i r_{t-i} + \eta_t \tag{6}$$

This equation is very similar to (5), from which it differs only because the distributed lag on the long rate is replaced by a distributed lag on the short rate. This substitution is in essence equivalent to hypothesizing that the expected long rate R_t^e can be approximated as a weighted average of past short rates rather than past long rates.

Lags of between two and seven years were tested with the most satisfactory results obtained for lags of around four years. The 16-quarter lag produced lower standard errors, smaller serial correlation, and the most sensible lag structure, although the multiple correlation and *DW* statistics[6] were not very sensitive to the length of lag, at least beyond four years. The result can be summarized as follows, omitting for the moment variables besides the short rate:

$$S_t = 1 \cdot 239 - 0 \cdot 684 r_t + \sum_{i=1}^{16} \beta_i r_{t-i} \tag{7}$$
$$\quad\;\; (0 \cdot 028)\; (0 \cdot 030)$$

$$R^2 = \cdot 975 \qquad S_e = \cdot 093 \qquad DW = 1 \cdot 42$$

The expression

$$\sum_{i=1}^{16} \beta_i R_{t-i}$$

represent the finite lag. [...]

These results are rather striking. The coefficient of r_t has the predicted sign and order of magnitude, the lag structure has the predicted shape, and its initial rising segment provides impressive support for the hypothesis that expectations involve significant extrapolative as well as the widely recognized regressive elements. The multiple correlation is quite high and the standard error remarkably low, less than 10 base points. (This, incidentally, is a vast improvement over De Leeuw's original model, which for the same period, even with additional significant variables has a standard error of 34 base points and a *DW* of ·79.)

---

[6] The symbol *DW* denotes the Durbin–Watson statistic, a measure of the estimated first order serial correlation of the residual error [6].

To see what light the Habitat Theory can shed on the nature of the mechanism, we note once more that the rather large constant term in (7) suggests that during the postwar period the expected return from long-term bonds tended to exceed the short rate by a positive premium. According to the Habitat model the prevalence of such a positive premium would indicate a systematic tendency for the primary supply of funds to exceed the primary demand in the short market and to fall short of the primary demand in the long market. We have further seen that under these conditions the size of the premium on longs would depend, among other things, on the 'facilities for effective arbitrage operations'. In particular, we should expect that any significant impediment to arbitrage, such as a curtailment of the ability of a certain class of would-be arbitrageurs to attract short-term funds with a rate as high as they would otherwise be prepared to pay, would tend to raise the premium. Among such potential arbitrageurs one presumably would include commercial banks, hence the Regulation Q ceiling on time deposit rates (if sufficiently low to be effective) would be a force creating an artificially large premium. Thus, we would presume that increases in the ceiling rate would tend to reduce the spread by allowing banks to arbitrage away part of this premium.

This theoretical formulation suggests that to measure the effect of Regulation Q we need to introduce a variable which (1) should treat the successive lifting of the ceilings, not as positive forces contributing to twist, but rather as the removal of an interference with normal arbitrage operations; and (2) should lay the largest role when other short-term rates are very close to or above ceiling; while it should cease to have effect once the ceiling is sufficiently above these rates. Beyond that level, changes in the ceiling should no longer affect the spread. Thus we define a variable, Q, as follows:

$$Q_t = r_t - (q_t - a) \quad \text{if positive, zero otherwise}$$

where q_t is the ceiling rate under Regulation Q and $(r_t + a)$ is a threshold level such that any higher ceiling would be irrelevant at time t. Just how high the gap, a, should be is hard to guess a priori, and depends in a large measure upon what rate is used for r_t. Since we are dealing with the market for government securities it seems sensible to use the treasury bills rate itself for r_t. For a we assumed somewhat arbitrarily a value of one hundred base points.[7]

When we fit our regression model, including the variable Q, for the entire period from 1952 to mid-1965, we find that the coefficient of the variable Q has the expected positive sign, although it is on the border-line of statistical significance.[8] It is also rather small, as it implies that when r_t equals the ceiling,

[7] We use the ceiling rate q_t rather than the average rate actually offered by banks because q_t is the policy variable whose effect we wish to estimate. See also footnote 8.

[8] Nearly identical results are obtained if Q is entered with a one-quarter lag, raising the possibility that a short distributed lag on Q might improve the results, although we have not investigated this approach. It was also found that if the threshold level, a was chosen to be 50 base points rather than 100, the same qualitative results were obtained.

the premium is only ten base points higher than it would be in the absence of an effective ceiling. The marginal statistical significance and the small magnitude of the coefficient estimated for Q raises the possibility that other events in the period after 1961 are causing a spurious effect. One such major development, and one that could have affected the ability of commercial banks to attract short-term funds, was the introduction in 1961 of negotiable Time Certificates of Deposit (CD's). To be sure, the spectacular growth of this instrument after 1962 could not have occurred had not the ceiling been raised that year, so that banks could offer CD's at rates competitive with other short-term instruments. Nonetheless, the CD must be regarded as a true financial innovation which could have enhanced the capacity of banks to arbitrage even if Regulation Q had never existed.[...]

REFERENCES

1. S. Almon, 'The Distributed Lag Between Capital Appropriations and Expenditures', *Econometrica*, Jan., 1965.
2. *Brookings Quarterly Econometric Model of the United States Economy*, J. Duesenberry, G. Fromm, L. Klein, E. Kuh, eds. (Rand McNally and North Holland, 1965).
3. J. Culbertson, 'The Term Structure of Interest Rates', *Q.J.E.*, Nov., 1957.
4. F. de Leeuw, 'A Model of Financial Behavior', Chap. 13 in [2].
5. J. Duesenberry, *Business Cycles and Economic Growth* (McGraw-Hill, 1958).
6. J. Durbin and G. Watson, 'Testing for Serial Correlation in Least Squares Regression, II', *Biometrika*, June, 1951.
7. Z. Griliches, 'A Note on Serial Correlation Bias in Estimates of Distributed Lags', *Econometrica*, Jan., 1961.
8. J. Hicks, *Value and Capital* (Oxford Univ. Press, 1939).
9. R. Kessel, *The Cyclical Behavior of the Term Structure of Interest Rates* (N.B.E.R., Occasional Paper 91, 1965).
10. J. Keynes, *A Treatise on Money*, Vol. II (Harcourt, Brace and Co., 1930).
11. *The General Theory of Employment, Interest and Money* (Harcourt, Brace and Co., 1936).
12. N. Liviatan, 'Consistent Estimation of Distributed Lags', *Int. Econ. Rev.* Jan., 1963.
13. B. Malkiel, 'Expectations, Bond Prices and the Term Structure of Interest Rates', *Q.J.E.*, May, 1962.
14. D. Meiselman, *The Term Structure of Interest Rates* (Prentice-Hall, 1962).
15. R. Solow, 'On a Family of Lag Distributions', *Econometrica*, Apr., 1960.

4.4 Financial Intermediation and the Supply of Money*
[...]

THE OLD VIEW

Perhaps the greatest moment of triumph for the elementary economics teacher is his exposition of the multiple creation of bank credit and bank deposits. Before the admiring eyes of freshmen he puts to rout the practical

* From J. Tobin, 'Commercial Banks as Creators of "Money"', in D. Carson (Ed.), *Banking and Monetary Studies* (Homewood, Illinois: Richard D. Irwin, 1963). Richard D. Irwin, Inc.,© 1963. Reprinted with permission.

banker who is so sure that he 'lends only the money depositors entrust to him.' The banker is shown to have a worm's-eye view, and his error stands as an introductory object lesson in the fallacy of composition. From the Olympian vantage of the teacher and the textbook it appears that the banker's dictum must be reversed: depositors entrust to bankers whatever amounts the bankers lend. To be sure, this is not true of a single bank; one bank's loan may wind up as another bank's deposit. But it is, as the arithmetic of successive rounds of deposit creation makes clear, true of the banking system as a whole. Whatever their other errors, a long line of financial heretics have been right in speaking of 'fountain pen money'—money created by the stroke of the bank president's pen when he approves a loan and credits the proceeds to the borrower's checking account.

In this time-honored exposition two characteristics of commercial banks— both of which are alleged to differentiate them sharply from other financial intermediaries—are intertwined. One is that their liabilities—well, at least their demand deposit liabilities—serve as widely acceptable means of payment. Thus, they count, along with coin and currency in public circulation, as 'money'. The other is that the preferences of the public normally play no role in determining the total volume of deposits or the total quantity of money. For it is the beginning of wisdom in monetary economics to observe that money is like the 'hot potato' of a children's game: one individual may pass it to another, but the group as a whole cannot get rid of it. If the economy and the supply of money are out of adjustment, it is the economy that must do the adjusting. This is as true, evidently, of money created by bankers' fountain pens as of money created by public printing presses. On the other hand, financial intermediaries other than banks do not create money, and the scale of their assets is limited by their liabilities, i.e. by the savings the public entrusts to them. They cannot count on receiving 'deposits' to match every extension of their lending.

The commercial banks and only the commercial banks, in other words, possess the widow's cruse. And because they possess this key to unlimited expansion, they have to be restrained by reserve requirements. Once this is done, determination of the aggregate volume of bank deposits is just a matter of accounting and arithmetic: simply divide the available supply of bank reserves by the required reserve ratio.

The foregoing is admittedly a caricature, but I believe it is not a great exaggeration of the impressions conveyed by economics teaching concerning the roles of commercial banks and other financial institutions in the monetary system. In conveying this mélange of propositions, economics has replaced the naive fallacy of composition of the banker with other half-truths perhaps equally misleading. These have their root in the mystique of 'money'—the tradition of distinguishing sharply between those assets which are and those which are not 'money', and accordingly between those institutions which emit 'money' and those whose liabilities are not 'money'. The persistent strength of this tradition is remarkable given the uncertainty and controversy over where to draw the dividing line between money and other assets. Time was when only currency was regarded as money, and the use of bank deposits was regarded as a way of economizing currency and increasing the velocity of money. Today scholars and statisticians wonder and argue whether to count commercial bank time and savings deposits in the money supply. And if so, why not similar accounts in other institutions? Nevertheless, once the arbitrary line is drawn, assets on the money side of the line are assumed to possess to the full properties which assets on the other side completely lack. For example, an eminent monetary economist, more candid than many of his colleagues, admits that we don't really know what money is, but proceeds to argue that, whatever it is, its supply should grow regularly at a rate of the order of 3 to 4 per cent per year.[1]

THE 'NEW VIEW'

A more recent development in monetary economics tends to blur the sharp traditional distinctions between money and other assets and between commercial banks and other financial intermediaries; to focus on demands for and supplies of the whole spectrum of assets rather than on the quantity and velocity of 'money'; and to regard the structure of interest rates, asset yields, and credit availabilities rather than the quantity of money as the linkage between monetary and financial institutions and policies on the one hand and the real economy on the other.[2] In this essay I propose to look briefly at the implications of this 'new view' for the theory of deposit creation, of which I have above described or caricatured the traditional version. One of the incidental advantages of this theoretical development is to effect something of a reconciliation between the economics teacher and the practical banker.

According to the 'new view', the essential function of financial intermediaries, including commercial banks, is to satisfy simultaneously the portfolio preferences of two types of individuals or firms.[3] On one side are borrowers, who wish to expand their holdings of real assets—inventories, residential real estate, productive plant and equipment, etc.—beyond the

[1] E. S. Shaw, 'Money Supply and Stable Economic Growth', in *United States Monetary Policy* (New York: American Assembly, 1958), pp. 49–71.

[2] For a review of this development and for references to its protagonists, see Harry Johnson's survey article, 'Monetary Theory and Policy', *American Economic Review*, Vol. LII (June, 1962), pp. 335–84. I will confine myself to mentioning the importance, in originating and contributing to the 'new view', of John Gurley and E. S. Shaw (yes, the very same Shaw cited in the previous footnote, but presumably in a different incarnation). Their viewpoint is summarized in *Money in a Theory of Finance* (Washington, D.C.: The Brookings Institution, 1960).

[3] This paragraph and the three following are adapted with minor changes from the author's paper with William Brainard, 'Financial Intermediaries and the Effectiveness of Monetary Controls', *American Economic Review*, Vol. LIII (May, 1963), pp. 384–86.

limits of their own net worth. On the other side are lenders, who wish to hold part or all of their net worth in assets of stable money value with negligible risk of default. The assets of financial intermediaries are obligations of the borrowers—promissory notes, bonds, mortgages. The liabilities of financial intermediaries are the assets of the lenders—bank deposits, insurance policies, pension rights.

Financial intermediaries typically assume liabilities of smaller default risk and greater predictability of value than their assets. The principal kinds of institutions take on liabilities of greater liquidity too; thus, bank depositors can require payment on demand, while bank loans become due only on specified dates. The reasons that the intermediation of financial institutions can accomplish these transformations between the nature of the obligation of the borrower and the nature of the asset of the ultimate lender are these: (1) administrative economy and expertise in negotiating, accounting, appraising, and collecting; (2) reduction of risk per dollar of lending by the pooling of independent risks, with respect both to loan default and to deposit withdrawal; (3) governmental guarantees of the liabilities of the institutions and other provisions (bank examination, investment regulations, supervision of insurance companies, last-resort lending) designed to assure the solvency and liquidity of the institutions.

For these reasons, intermediation permits borrowers who wish to expand their investments in real assets to be accommodated at lower rates and easier terms than if they had to borrow directly from the lenders. If the creditors of financial intermediaries had to hold instead the kinds of obligations that private borrowers are capable of providing, they would certainly insist on higher rates and stricter terms. Therefore, any autonomous increase—for example, improvements in the efficiency of financial institutions or the creation of new types of intermediaries—in the amount of financial intermediation in the economy can be expected to be, *ceteris paribus*, an expansionary influence. This is true whether the growth occurs in intermediaries with monetary liabilities—i.e. commercial banks—or in other intermediaries.

Financial institutions fall fairly easily into distinct categories, each industry or 'intermediary' offering a differentiated product to its customers, both lenders and borrowers. From the point of view of lenders, the obligations of the various intermediaries are more or less close, but not perfect, substitutes. For example, savings deposits share most of the attributes of demand deposits; but they are not means of payment, and the institution has the right, seldom exercised, to require notice of withdrawal. Similarly there is differentiation in the kinds of credit offered borrowers. Each intermediary has its specialty—e.g. the commercial loan for banks, the real-estate mortgage for the savings and loan association. But the borrowers' market is not completely compartmentalized. The same credit instruments are handled by more than one intermediary, and many borrowers have flexibility in the type of debt they incur. Thus, there is some substitutability, in the demand for credit by borrowers, between the assets of the various intermediaries.[4]

The special attention given commercial banks in economic analysis is usually justified by the observation that, alone among intermediaries, banks 'create' means of payment. This rationale is on its face far from convincing. The means-of-payment characteristic of demand deposits is indeed a feature differentiating bank liabilities from those of other intermediaries. Insurance against death is equally a feature differentiating life insurance policies from the obligations of other intermediaries, including banks. It is not obvious that one kind of differentiation should be singled out for special analytical treatment. Like other differentia, the means-of-payment attribute has its price. Savings deposits, for example, are perfect substitutes for demand deposits in every respect except as a medium of exchange. This advantage of checking accounts does not give banks absolute immunity from the competition of savings banks; it is a limited advantage that can be, at least in some part for many depositors, overcome by differences in yield. It follows that the community's demand for bank deposits is not indefinite, even though demand deposits do serve as means of payment.

THE WIDOW'S CRUSE

Neither individually nor collectively do commercial banks possess a widow's cruse. Quite apart from legal reserve requirements, commercial banks are limited in scale by the same kinds of economic processes that determine the aggregate size of other intermediaries.

One often cited difference between commercial banks and other intermediaries must be quickly dismissed as superficial and irrelevant. This is the fact that a bank can make a loan by 'writing up' its deposit liabilities, while a savings and loan association, for example, cannot satisfy a mortgage borrower by crediting him with a share account. The association must transfer means of payment to the borrower; its total liabilities do not rise along with its assets. True enough, but neither do the bank's, for more than a fleeting moment. Borrowers do not incur debt in order to hold idle deposits, any more than savings and loan shares. The borrower pays out the money, and there is of course no guarantee that any of it stays in the lending bank. Whether or not it stays in the banking system as a whole is another question, about to be discussed. But the answer clearly does not depend on the way the loan was initially made. It depends on whether somewhere in the chain of transactions initiated by the borrower's outlays are found depositors who wish to hold new deposits equal in amount to the new loan. Similarly, the outcome for the savings and loan industry depends on whether in the

---

[4] These features of the market structure of intermediaries, and their implications for the supposed uniqueness of banks, have been emphasized by Gurley and Shaw, *op. cit*. An example of substitutability on the deposit side is analyzed by David and Charlotte Alhedeff, 'The Struggle for Commercial Bank Savings', *Quarterly Journal of Economics*, Vol. LXXII (February, 1958), pp. 1–22.

chain of transactions initiated by the mortgage are found individuals who wish to acquire additional savings and loan shares.

The banking system can expand its assets either (a) by purchasing, or lending against, existing assets; or (b) by lending to finance new private investment in inventories or capital goods, or buying government securities financing new public deficits. In case (a) no increase in private wealth occurs in conjunction with the banks' expansion. There is no new private saving and investment. In case (b), new private saving occurs, matching dollar for dollar the private investments or government deficits financed by the banking system. In neither case will there automatically be an increase in savers' demand for bank deposits equal to the expansion in bank assets.

In the second case, it is true, there is an increase in private wealth. But even if we assume a closed economy in order to abstract from leakages of capital abroad, the community will not ordinarily wish to put 100 per cent of its new savings into bank deposits. Bank deposits are, after all, only about 15 per cent of total private wealth in the United States; other things equal, savers cannot be expected greatly to exceed this proportion in allocating new savings. So, if *all* new savings is to take the form of bank deposits, other things cannot stay equal. Specifically, the yields and other advantages of the competing assets into which new saving would otherwise flow will have to fall enough so that savers prefer bank deposits.

This is *a fortiori* true in case (a) where there is no new saving and the generation of bank liabilities to match the assumed expansion of bank assets entails a reshuffling of existing portfolios in favor of bank deposits. In effect the banking system has to induce the public to swap loans and securities for bank deposits. This can happen only if the price is right.

Clearly, then, there is at any moment a natural economic limit to the scale of the commercial banking industry. Given the wealth and the asset preferences of the community, the demand for bank deposits can increase only if the yields of other assets fall. The fall in these yields is bound to restrict the profitable lending and investment opportunities available to the banks themselves. Eventually the marginal returns on lending and investing, account taken of the risks and administrative costs involved, will not exceed the marginal cost to the banks of attracting and holding additional deposits. At this point the widow's cruse has run dry.

BANKS AND OTHER INTERMEDIARIES COMPARED

In this respect the commercial banking industry is not qualitatively different from any other financial intermediary system. The same process limits the collective expansion of savings and loan associations, or savings banks, or life insurance companies. At some point the returns from additional loans or security holdings are not worth the cost of obtaining the funds from the public.

There are of course some differences. First, it may well be true that commercial banks benefit from a larger share of additions to private savings than other intermediaries. Second, according to modern American legal practice, commercial banks are subject to ceilings on the rates payable to their depositors—zero in the case of demand deposits. Unlike competing financial industries, commercial banks cannot seek funds by raising rates. They can and do offer other inducements to depositors, but these substitutes for interest are imperfect and uneven in their incidence. In these circumstances the major readjustment of the interest rate structure necessary to increase the relative demand for bank deposits is a decline in other rates. Note that neither of these differences has to do with the quality of bank deposits as 'money'.

In a world without reserve requirements the preferences of depositors, as well as those of borrowers, would be very relevant in determining the volume of bank deposits. The volume of assets and liabilities of every intermediary, both nonbanks and banks, would be determined in a competitive equilibrium, where the rate of interest charged borrowers by each kind of institution just balances at the margin the rate of interest paid its creditors. Suppose that such an equilibrium is disturbed by a shift in savers' preferences. At prevailing rates they decide to hold more savings accounts and other nonbank liabilities and less demand deposits. They transfer demand deposits to the credit of nonbank financial institutions, providing these intermediaries with the means to seek additional earning assets. These institutions, finding themselves able to attract more funds from the public even with some reduction in the rates they pay, offer better terms to borrowers and bid up the prices of existing earning assets. Consequently commercial banks release some earning assets—they no longer yield enough to pay the going rate on the banks' deposit liabilities. Bank deposits decline with bank assets. In effect, the nonbank intermediaries favored by the shift in public preferences simply swap the deposits transferred to them for a corresponding quantity of bank assets.

FOUNTAIN PENS AND PRINTING PRESSES

Evidently the fountain pens of commercial bankers are essentially different from the printing presses of governments. Confusion results from concluding that because bank deposits are like currency in one respect—both serve as media of exchange—they are like currency in every respect. Unlike governments, bankers cannot create means of payment to finance their own purchases of goods and services. Bank-created 'money' is a liability, which must be matched on the other side of the balance sheet. And banks, as businesses, must earn money from their middleman's role. Once created, printing press money cannot be extinguished, except by reversal of the budget policies which led to its birth. The community cannot get rid of its currency supply; the economy must adjust until it is willingly absorbed. The 'hot potato' analogy truly applies. For bank-created money, however, there is an economic mechanism of extinction as well as creation, contraction as well as expansion. If bank deposits are excessive relative to public preferences, they will tend to decline; otherwise banks will lose income. The burden of adaptation is not placed entirely on the rest of the economy.

THE ROLE OF RESERVE REQUIREMENTS

Without reserve requirements, expansion of credit and deposits by the commercial banking system would be limited by the availability of assets at yields sufficient to compensate banks for the costs of attracting and holding the corresponding deposits. In a régime of reserve requirements, the limit which they impose normally cuts the expansion short of this competitive equilibrium. When reserve requirements and deposit interest rate ceilings are effective, the marginal yield of bank loans and investments exceeds the marginal cost of deposits to the banking system. In these circumstances additional reserves make it possible and profitable for banks to acquire additional earning assets. The expansion process lowers interest rates generally—enough to induce the public to hold additional deposits but ordinarily not enough to wipe out the banks' margin between the value and cost of additional deposits.

It is the existence of this margin—not the monetary nature of bank liabilities—which makes it possible for the economics teacher to say that additional loans permitted by new reserves will generate their own deposits. The same proposition would be true of any other system of financial institutions subject to similar reserve constraints and similar interest rate ceilings. In this sense it is more accurate to attribute the special place of banks among intermediaries to the legal restrictions to which banks alone are subjected than to attribute these restrictions to the special character of bank liabilities.

But the textbook description of multiple expansion of credit and deposits on a given reserve base is misleading even for a régime of reserve requirements. There is more to the determination of the volume of bank deposits than the arithmetic of reserve supplies and reserve ratios. The redundant reserves of the thirties are a dramatic reminder that economic opportunities sometimes prevail over reserve calculations. But the significance of that experience is not correctly appreciated if it is regarded simply as an aberration from a normal state of affairs in which banks are fully 'loaned up' and total deposits are tightly linked to the volume of reserves. The thirties exemplify in extreme form a phenomenon which is always in some degree present: the use to which commercial banks put the reserves made available to the system is an economic variable depending on lending opportunities and interest rates.

An individual bank is not constrained by any fixed quantum of reserves. It can obtain additional reserves to meet requirements by borrowing from the Federal Reserve, by buying 'Federal Funds' from other banks, by selling or 'running off' short-term securities. In short, reserves are available at the discount window and in the money market, at a price. This cost the bank must compare with available yields on loans and investments. If those yields are low relative to the cost of reserves, the bank will seek to avoid borrowing reserves and perhaps hold excess reserves instead. If those yields are high relative to the cost of borrowing reserves, the bank will shun excess reserves and borrow reserves occasionally or even regularly. For the banking system as a whole the Federal Reserve's quantitative controls determine the supply of unborrowed reserves. But the extent to which this supply is left unused, or supplemented by borrowing at the discount window, depends on the economic circumstances confronting the banks—on available lending opportunities and on the whole structure of interest rates from the Fed's discount rate through the rates on mortgages and long-term securities.

The range of variation in net free reserves in recent years has been from −5 per cent to +5 per cent of required reserves. This indicates a much looser linkage between reserves and deposits than is suggested by the textbook exposition of multiple expansion for a system which is always precisely and fully 'loaned up'. (It does not mean, however, that actual monetary authorities have any less control than textbook monetary authorities. Indeed the net free reserve position is one of their more useful instruments and barometers. Anyway, they are after bigger game than the quantity of 'money'!)

Two consequences of this analysis deserve special notice because of their relation to the issues raised earlier in this paper. First, an increase—of, say, a billion dollars—in the supply of unborrowed reserves will, in general, result in less than a billion-dollar increase in required reserves. Net free reserves will rise (algebraically) by some fraction of the billion dollars—a very large fraction in periods like the thirties, a much smaller one in tight money periods like those of the fifties. Loans and deposits will expand by less than their textbook multiples. The reason is simple. The open-market operations which bring about the increased supply of reserves tend to lower interest rates. So do the operations of the commercial banks in trying to invest their new reserves. The result is to diminish the incentives of banks to keep fully loaned up or to borrow reserves, and to make banks content to hold on the average higher excess reserves.

Second, depositor preferences do matter, even in a régime of fractional reserve banking. Suppose, for example, that the public decides to switch new or old savings from other assets and institutions into commercial banks. This switch makes earning assets available to banks at attractive yields—assets that otherwise would have been lodged either directly with the public or with the competing financial institutions previously favored with the public's savings. These improved opportunities for profitable lending and investing will make the banks content to hold smaller net free reserves. Both their deposits and their assets will rise as a result of this shift in public preferences, even though the base of unborrowed reserves remains unchanged. Something of this kind has occurred in recent years when commercial banks have been permitted to raise the interest rates they offer for time and savings deposits.

CONCLUDING REMARKS

The implications of the 'new view' may be summarized as follows:

1. The distinction between commercial banks and other financial intermediaries has been too sharply drawn. The differences are of degree, not of kind.

2. In particular, the differences which do exist have little intrinsically to do with the monetary nature of bank liabilities.

3. The differences are more importantly related to the special reserve requirements and interest rate ceilings to which banks are subject. Any other financial industry subject to the same kind of regulations would behave in much the same way.

4. Commercial banks do not possess, either individually or collectively, a widow's cruse which guarantees that any expansion of assets will generate a corresponding expansion of deposit liabilities. Certainly this happy state of affairs would not exist in an unregulated competitive financial world. Marshall's scissors of supply and demand apply to the 'output' of the banking industry, no less than to other financial and nonfinancial industries.

5. Reserve requirements and interest ceilings give the widow's cruse myth somewhat greater plausibility. But even in these circumstances, the scale of bank deposits and assets is affected by depositor preferences and by the lending and investing opportunities available to banks.

I draw no policy morals from these observations. That is quite another story, to which analysis of the type presented here is only the preface. The reader will misunderstand my purpose if he jumps to attribute to me the conclusion that existing differences in the regulatory treatment of banks and competing intermediaries should be diminished, either by relaxing constraints on the one or by tightening controls on the other.

4.5 Inside and Outside Money*

[...]

'INSIDE' MONEY AND 'OUTSIDE' MONEY

In a rudimentary economy ... money was government debt, issued in payment for governmental purchases of goods and services or in transfer payments. It was a claim held by consumers and firms against government. From the standpoint of the private sectors, it was a net external or outside claim. Given the nominal amount of this outside money, its real value varied inversely with the price level, and each such change in its real value represented a wealth transfer between the private sectors and government. This wealth transfer affected private demands for money, goods, and labor but it was assumed not to affect government demand. Therefore, the wealth transfer, due to a change in the price level, had a net effect on aggregate

* From J. G. Gurley and E. S. Shaw, *Money in a Theory of Finance* (Washington, D.C.: Brookings Institution, 1960), Chapter 3. © 1960 by the Brookings Institution, Washington, D.C., U.S.A. Reprinted by permission.

demands for money, goods, and labor. The conclusion followed that only one price level was appropriate to general equilibrium in any particular real context; any other price level would produce imbalance on all markets. The price level, in other words, was determinate in the rudimentary economy.

In the second model, money is still government debt, but it is issued in payment for government purchases of private securities. It is a claim of consumers and firms against the world outside the private sectors, but it is counterbalanced by private debt to the world outside, that is, to government in this model. It is based on internal debt, so we refer to it as 'inside' money.

Given the nominal amount of inside money, its real value varies inversely with the price level. The governmental monetary system neither loses nor gains in real terms by such variation in the real amount of its debt because there is an equal change in the real value of its claims against firms. And the two private sectors together do not lose real wealth to government as the price level rises nor gain real wealth as the price level falls. That is, a change in the price level does not result in a wealth transfer between the private economy and government when money is inside money. Instead it results merely in a wealth transfer between consumers and firms, the former gaining and the latter losing in our second model when the price level falls. This transfer is a distribution effect of price-level instability that we are pledged, by neo-classical rules of static analysis, either to treat as a short-run phenomenon or to neglect.

Since a change in the price level, when money is inside money, does not affect government's behavior and has no net effect on total wealth in the private economy, is the price level determinate in our second model? Is only one price level appropriate in any particular real context, or will any price level do?

The traditional answer would be that the price level is not determinate, and that any price level would be compatible with general equilibrium. On this view, the second model is a barter economy, moneyless and bound by Say's Law of Markets. Our own conclusion ... is that price changes do have net effects other than distribution effects which point to one and only one price level as 'right' for general equilibrium in a given complex of real variables and nominal money.

The proof that our second model, with only inside money, is really a money economy and not simply a barter economy can be put in a homely, intuitive way. Although the private economy issues bonds, and so can adapt the nominal stock of bonds to any price level in order to maintain some one real stock of bonds, it has no control over nominal money. Hence it cannot adapt the nominal stock of money to any price level in order to maintain the desired real stock of money. Given nominal money, there is only one price level that provides to consumers the desired portfolio mix of real bonds and real money and to firms the desired proportion of real money to real debt. Change in the price level from an equilibrium position has no net effect, it is true, on aggregate private wealth, but it does have effects on the composition of this wealth that will tend to drive the price level back to its starting point. Price inflation and deflation have no net effect on aggregate wealth; the distribution effects between private debtors and creditors we are pledged to put aside; but there is still a portfolio-mix or diversification effect that makes the price level determinate.

To illustrate our point, imagine an initial equilibrium with a price level of 100, nominal and real bonds in consumer portfolios of $90, nominal and real money of $10. Total nominal and real bonds are $100, with $90 of them in consumer portfolios and $10 of them in the monetary system. In the private sectors, the bond-money ratio of 9–1 is appropriate to the interest rate on bonds in equilibrium. Now imagine that the price level doubles to 200 and that nominal bonds are also doubled (to $200) by business firms, to avoid distribution effects. Given the monetary system's nominal bonds of $10 and hence nominal money of $10, consumer portfolios of nominal bonds rise to $190. At the higher price level, real business debt is still $100 but consumers hold $95 in real bonds, and real money balances are only $5. The bond money ratio has risen, in real terms, from 9–1 at the price level of 100 to 19–1 at the price level of 200. The latter ratio is inappropriate to the initial bond rate, real income, and real wealth. At the new price level, then, there will be excess real demand for money, excess real supply of bonds and goods, so that the system is destined to grope its way back to the initial level of prices and initial stock of nominal bonds.

A COMBINATION OF INSIDE AND OUTSIDE MONEY

Now we imagine that nominal money consists no longer of inside money alone, as in the basic version of our second model where it was created exclusively on the basis of domestic business bonds in the monetary system's portfolio, or of outside money alone, as in our rudimentary economy where it was a net claim of the private sectors against government. Instead, nominal money is now composed of a combination of inside and outside money, the latter created, say, on the basis of gold in the monetary system's portfolio. This change in specifications certainly makes the second model more realistic, but it does more than that. The important result is that monetary policy ceases to be trivial or neutral and that some nominal stock of money is uniquely right for each state of general equilibrium.

Suppose that stationary equilibrium prevails. Firms are in their desired financial position, with net debt bearing the appropriate relationship to tangible assets and gross debt properly adjusted to net debt. Consumers are also satisfied, with financial assets in the correct relationship to income and properly diversified between money and business bonds. In this stagnant context the Banking Bureau increases nominal money, inside variety, by an open-market buying operation. Are there *real* effects of this easy-money policy?

The answer is clearly 'yes'. The outside money, backed by gold, is not matched by domestic business bonds in the Banking Bureau's portfolio. Hence, if the open-market operation increases total nominal money by, say, 10 per cent, it adds to the Bureau's bond holdings by more than 10 per cent, assuming gold holdings are constant. This means that the open-market operation increases the proportion of money balances to business bonds held by consumers and of money balances to net debt for business firms, for the Banking Bureau has increased its share of total business bonds. At the initial price level, the open-market operation achieves a real transfer of bonds from private sectors to the monetary system, changing portfolio composition for private spending units. At a price level increased in proportion to nominal money, with nominal bonds of business adjusted in the same degree, the real composition of private portfolios would still be more heavily weighted with money than before the monetary system took action. The impact of the open-market operation on portfolio balance cannot be nullified by a proportional increase in the price level, money wage rate, and nominal bonds of business. The increase in money, relative to bonds, in private portfolios is acceptable to the private sector only at a lower rate of interest. And the ultimate equilibrium will also involve, as the result of monetary expansion, a larger real stock of capital, a higher level of real income, and a price level that is higher but proportionally less so than the increase in nominal money.

Money has ceased to be neutral, and monetary policy is trivial no longer in the second model. Open-market buying by the monetary system touches off growth in real wealth and income, at the expense of some inflation. Open-market selling by the monetary system depresses real wealth and income, with accompanying deflation. These are the conclusions for the case of stationary equilibrium.

They can be illustrated as follows. Assume an initial position of equilibrium with price level of 100, nominal and real money of $20, consisting of $10 of inside money based on business bonds held by the Banking Bureau and $10 of outside money based on gold. Total business debt is $100 of which $10 is held by the Banking Bureau and $90 by consumers. Equilibrium is now disturbed by an open-market buying operation in business bonds of $20, which doubles nominal money. Equilibrium cannot be restored in quantity-theory fashion by doubling nominal bonds and the price level, since then the initial portfolio mix of bonds-to-money for private spending units of $90–$20 is reduced, in real terms, to $85–$20. With nominal money, nominal bonds, and the price level doubled, the Banking Bureau has raised its real bond holdings from $10 to $15. In the private sector, real bonds have become less plentiful relative to real money so that one element in a new equilibrium will be a reduced rate of interest. This in turn raises the equilibrium real stock of capital and the real level of income.

Similar conclusions regarding the neutrality of money apply under conditions of growth. Imagine that balanced growth is occurring at some rate n in all real and nominal stocks and flows, with relative prices and the absolute price level stable. The stock of money has both inside and outside components, with each increasing at rate n. If the monetary system doubles the rate of expansion for total nominal money and both of its elements, the only effect is doubling of other nominal variables including the price level. But if the monetary system doubles the rate of expansion in nominal money solely by accelerating purchases of business bonds, there are real effects. Then the monetary system absorbs a larger share of real bond issues, leaving a smaller share for private investors. The adjustment in private portfolio-balance requires some decline in the rate of interest, some increase in the growth rate of capital and income, and an increase in the price level proportionally smaller than the rise in rate of monetary expansion. Conversely, if the monetary system takes up a smaller proportion of real bond issues, expanding outside money rather than inside money, the real effects begin with a rise in the bond rate and restraint on real growth.

Growth involves expansion in financial assets of which our model provides two varieties—a homogeneous bond and money. It is the real value of financial assets which influences behavior of consumers and firms on all markets. Any combination of circumstances, such as a money stock with both inside and outside components, which makes it possible for the second model's monetary system to manipulate the proportion of real money to real bonds, empowers the monetary system in some degree to regulate the real value and real composition of private portfolios. Then the monetary system can play the role of financial intermediary, in real terms, and can vary its participation in the risks of growth. By intermediating a little more, it relieves private spending units of some risk in bond-holding. By intermediating a little less, it intensifies private risks. The result is some reduction in the bond rate in the first case, some increase in the bond rate in the second case. And the change in this one relative price affects the whole contour of real growth.

MONETARY POLICY AND THE NEO-CLASSICAL RULES

We have come to the conclusion, first, that out model is a money-economy in which nominal stocks of money and bonds and the price level have a job to do in maintaining equilibrium in the markets for goods and labor, in assuring equality between investment desired by firms, as deficit spenders, and saving desired by consumers for release to firms. Our second conclusion has been that monetary policy is trivial, and money neutral, in the second model as first formulated: that real demand for money can be satisfied equally well by price deflation or nominal monetary expansion; and that the private sectors can transfer real saving and maintain portfolio balance with or without intervention by the monetary system. The third conclusion is that monetary policy may be significant, and money non-neutral, if the money stock is not exclusively inside or outside money.

These conclusions are valid under the neo-classical specifications we have built into the second model—absence of money illusion, freedom from distribution effects of change in the price level and bond rate, stability of expectations regarding the price level and bond rate, perfect competition and flexibility of prices on markets for labor, goods, and (except for intervention by the monetary system) for bonds. The conclusions are valid for analysis of the model in terms of static equilibrium for the stationary state or in balanced growth. That is to say, they are valid under circumstances in which money is least likely to matter and is most likely to be merely a veil over the real aspects of economic behavior. These are the circumstances in which the private sectors are most efficient in manipulating real money and real bonds by adjustments in the price level and nominal bonds.

Money's role becomes more pivotal in real behavior if our model is lifted out of its context of neo-classical, static equilibrium analysis. Anything one does to reduce the efficiency of a change in the price level, relative to a change in nominal money, as a means of adapting the stock of money to its desired quantity, enhances the real significance of monetary policy. Any obstructions to adapting nominal primary debt to changes in the price level make it more important for the monetary system to operate continuously on the markets for bonds and money.

Price deflation cannot create real money, to satisfy incremental demand for it, if prices and money wage rates are inflexible. And price deflation cannot accommodate demand for money if, because of money illusion, it is nominal rather than real money that spending units want. Again, price deflation that excites expectations of further deflation and so intensifies demand for money is a poor substitute for expansion of nominal money.

In the second model, distribution effects of price-level instability result, in any short run, from the partitioning of the private sector into debtors and creditors. If real growth brings about endemic incremental demand for money, the persistent downward pressure on the price level tends constantly to transfer wealth from debtor firms to creditor consumers. The real effect of such a transfer is to depress saving and investment, retard growth in real capital, and inhibit growth in output. Distribution effects are avoided if the endemic incremental demand for money is satisfied at a stable price level by nominal monetary expansion.

Static neo-classical analysis averts distribution effects of movements in the price level by perfectly flexible refunding of nominal bonds. The number of bonds outstanding is corrected for movements in the price level and simultaneously with movements in the price level. As one leaves such a frictionless world, the more convinced one must be about the real costs of price-level instability in terms of short-period disturbances to the rate of saving and investment and to allocation of saving among investment opportunities. It is easy to visualize a world without distribution effects, but such a world is remote from our own. Continuous intermediation by the monetary system is a necessary crutch for the private sectors to lean upon in directing real saving to investment and in maintaining portfolio balance.

SUMMARY

In the rudimentary economy, there were three markets: for labor services, current output, and money. The feature of our second economy is the addition of a fourth market, that for primary securities. These securities are gilt-edged, homogeneous perpetuities (bonds) of business firms. There continue to be three sectors: consumers, business firms, and government. However, government has no income and no spending on income and product account; it is the monetary system, composed as before of a Policy and a Banking Bureau. The two private sectors transact on all markets, while the government transacts only on the two financial markets. The Banking Bureau, on orders of the Policy Bureau, purchases or sells primary securities and creates or destroys money. The financial profile of the economy is that business firms issue the only form of primary security and acquire money, the only form of indirect security; government purchases primary securities and issues money; and consumers acquire either primary securities or money or both.

Business firms may sell their primary securities directly to consumers or they may sell them to the Banking Bureau. The first is direct finance, in which consumers acquire primary securities; the second is indirect finance, in which consumers and firms acquire money balances.

The real demand for money balances emanates from consumers and business firms. Both sectors increase their real demand for money when their real incomes rise. The real demand for money increases, too, when consumers acquire additional real holdings of financial assets (bonds and money) and when firms acquire real capital relative to real debt. A lower rate of interest on bonds stimulates private real demand for money, while a lower marginal real rental rate works in the same direction for firms. The nominal stock of money is once again determined by the Policy Bureau in the context of its policy aims and of private sectors' real demand for money. The Banking Bureau makes this stock available without hesitation or protest.

The nominal stock of money in the rudimentary economy was entirely 'outside' money; that is, it was a net claim by the private sectors on an 'outside' sector—the government. The nominal stock of money in our second economy is wholly of the 'inside' variety; that is, it is based on private internal debt, and it is entirely counterbalanced by business primary debt. Hence, in contrast to the rudimentary economy, any change in the price level now results in wealth transfers only between the two private sectors, one gaining and the other losing by equal amounts. Neo-classical rules ignore the effect of such wealth transfers on aggregate demands for labor services, current output, and money. It would seem, therefore, that any price level is compatible with given aggregate real demands. Nevertheless, the price level is determinate in the second economy as it was in the first. This is because the private sectors desire a diversified financial position. Given the normal stock of money, there is only one price level that achieves the desired mix between real primary securities and real money.

Within the neo-classical framework, monetary policy has neutral effects on the real variables of the economy when all money is of the inside variety— as it did when all money was of the outside variety in the rudimentary economy. A change in nominal money has no other effect than to change proportionally prices and money wage rates. In the same way as before, moreover, monetary policy ceases to be neutral if there is rigidity of prices, if price expectations are not of unitary elasticity, if there is money illusion, or if we admit distribution effects of wealth transfers.

Even within a strict neo-classical framework, however, monetary policy may not be neutral on real variables when there exists a combination of inside and outside money; that is, when the Banking Bureau holds both business bonds and 'foreign' securities or gold behind its monetary liabilities. Then an increase in nominal money, owing to the Banking Bureau's purchase of business bonds, increases the Bureau's holdings of real bonds proportionally more than its real monetary liabilities. This means that private sectors' real holdings of business bonds are reduced relative to their real holdings of money. Hence, the equilibrium interest rate is lower, and other real variables in the economy will adjust. A combination of inside and outside money, then, permits the monetary authority to get a grip on levels of real income and wealth.

5. Economic Growth

Introductory Note

Despite the fact that economic growth—albeit at an unsteady rate—had been taking place in industrial countries for as long as statistics could show, the revival of interest in the theory of economic growth had to wait until the main analytical tools of the Keynesian revolution had been assimilated. Post-Keynesian growth theory can be regarded as starting from Harrod's seminal 1939 paper on dynamic theory [Reading 5.1], whose fundamental purpose was to argue for a 'new method of approach—indeed, a mental revolution (p. 208) in thinking about economic growth and cycles, for the conventional comparative statics methodology simply could not deal with the problem.

Harrod begins by marrying together the acceleration principle and the theory of the multiplier. The acceleration coefficient (or 'capital–output ratio'), C, is defined as 'the value of the capital goods required for the production of a unit increment of output'; its particular size will depend 'on the state of technology and the nature of the goods constituting the increment of output. It may be expected to vary as income grows and in different phases of the trade cycle; it may be somewhat dependent on the rate of interest.'[1] Now, as an accounting identity, investment in any period must be equal to saving, which Harrod takes as a fixed proportion, s, of the value of output. And the actual rate of growth of output in a period, G, is equal to $\Delta Y/Y$, where Y is output. Thus

$$I \equiv sY$$

and thus

$$\frac{I}{\Delta Y} \equiv \frac{s}{G}.$$

But $I/\Delta Y$ is the *actual* increment in the capital stock divided by the *actual* increment of output, which Harrod denotes by C_p. Thus we can write

$$G \equiv \frac{s}{C_p}.$$

Now if C_p happens to be equal to C, the capital–output ratio 'warranted' by technological and other conditions, then the actual rate of growth, G, is

[1] These considerations are important, for they indicate that the textbook 'Harrod–Domar' model is more rigid than is warranted by Harrod's own discussion.

equal to the rate which the circumstances of the economy warrants, $G_w \equiv s/C$, and the economy is growing at an equilibrium rate.

The question immediately arises: what happens if the actual rate of growth is not equal to the warranted rate? Harrod provides two examples. First, suppose that for some reason (for example, a general increase in confidence), the actual growth rate exceeds the warranted rate. Then C_p, the actual ratio of investment to the increment of output, will be less than C, the investment ratio *appropriate* to that increment. Producers will feel themselves short of capital, investment will rise, and there will be a further stimulus to expansion, and the actual rate of growth, G, will move still further from the warranted rate. Or suppose that s, the propensity to save, rises. The warranted rate of growth will thus rise and the actual rate of growth will now be lower than the warranted rate. But the increase in saving is a depressing influence on demand: producers, instead of increasing production, will reduce it (in relative terms), and the actual growth rate will fall still further below the warranted rate. The dynamic equilibrium represented by the warranted rate of growth is thus highly unstable.

Harrod points out, however, that the degree of instability depends on the rigidity with which the acceleration principle and the savings relation are employed. In particular, a good deal of investment will be uninfluenced by current changes in the rate of growth, but will be governed by much longer-run expectations or by technical innovations. Financial factors and the state of confidence will also play a part. The existence of investment of this kind will both depress the warranted growth rate and reduce the degree of instability of the system.

Finally, Harrod draws attention to the fact that labour has so far been neglected. But there is clearly a 'natural' rate of growth allowed by the increase in the labour supply and by technological progress which increases the productivity of labour. There is no connection between the natural rate and the warranted rate and, in particular, no inherent tendency for them to coincide. Thus if the warranted rate exceeds the natural rate (starting from a position of unemployment), full employment must eventually be reached. The actual rate must then fall below the warranted rate and the instability of the system will produce a chronic tendency to depression. Harrod suggests that since C is likely to be influenced by interest rates, monetary policy might appropriately be used in such a case to hold interest rates down, raising C and reducing the warranted rate to bring it into line with the natural rate. Variations in public expenditure could then be used to combat purely cyclical fluctuations in the rate of growth.

Despite Harrod's emphasis on the factors which might alter the value of C, and on the existence of investment of a kind insensitive to short-run changes in demand, the supposed 'rigidity' of the incremental capital–output ratio and the consequential supposed 'knife-edge' instability of the model provoked voluminous criticism. The most fundamental attack was from writers of the 'neoclassical' school, beginning with Solow [see Reading 5.2].[2] Solow rejects the notion of lack of substitutability between capital and labour (and hence the assumption of a fixed capital–output ratio), arguing that in long-run analysis, the 'short-run' tools of analysis—the multiplier and the accelerator—must be replaced by 'marginal' analysis. This is perhaps a more contentious assertion than Solow makes it appear, but it naturally has far reaching consequences.

Solow retains the assumption of a proportional savings ratio, but introduces a production function relating output to inputs of labour and capital, and in which labour and capital can be substituted in varying proportions to produce a given level of output. The labour supply is assumed to grow at a given proportional rate n, and full employment is assumed. Then it can be shown that the economy will always settle down to a capital–labour ratio such that output grows at the same rate as the labour force (that is, the warranted rate adjusts, through changes in the ratio of capital to labour in production, to the natural rate). We here follow, and slightly modify, Solow's 'less formal' analysis [pp. 226–7]. Denote the capital–labour ratio, K/L, by r. Then the proportional change in r will be the difference between the proportional changes in K and L:

$$\frac{\dot{r}}{r} = \frac{\dot{K}}{K} - \frac{\dot{L}}{L}.$$

Now, given that $\dot{K} = I = S = sY$, and that $\dot{L}/L = n$, we can write

$$\frac{\dot{r}}{r} = \frac{sY}{K} - n$$

or

$$\dot{r} = \frac{sY}{K} \cdot \frac{K}{L} - nr = \frac{sY}{L} - nr.$$

This is a simplified form of Solow's eqn. (6), which is graphed as Figure 5.2. It shows the determinants of the change in the capital–labour ratio. But its economic significance is not very clear: although an economic meaning can be given to the first term on the right-hand side—average savings per head—the term nr has no such simple economic meaning. The preceding expression, however,

$$\frac{\dot{r}}{r} = \frac{sY}{K} - n$$

---

[2] A second critique—though more of a development than an attack—pointed out that changes in the warranted rate could be engineered by changes in the savings propensity such as could occur if the propensities to save out of profits and wages differed and if there were a shift in the distribution of income between wages and profits. For a brief account of this contention, and for Harrod's own response, see Joan Robinson, 'Harrod after Twenty-one Years', *Economic Journal*, 1970, and the following exchange.

can be interpreted quite simply: the capital–labour ratio r will rise if the rate of growth of investment (= savings) in relation to the capital stock exceeds the proportional rate of growth of the labour force, and vice versa. This function can be graphed once we know how Y/K varies with r. Now as r increases (that is, the ratio of capital to labour increases), at a given level of output the ratio of output to capital must fall. Furthermore, as r reaches higher and higher levels, the *rate* of fall of Y/K must diminish. Thus the shape of the Y/K (and hence the sY/K) locus is downward sloping and convex downwards. The growth rate of the labour force is, of course, invariant with respect to r (Figure 5.1).

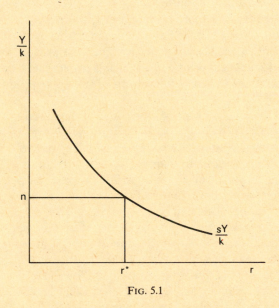

Fig. 5.1

At r^*, the rates of growth of capital and labour are equal, and (given constant returns) equal to the rate of growth of output. To the right of the point of intersection ($r > r^*$), labour is growing faster than capital, and r will tend to fall; conversely to the left of r^*, r will tend to rise. Thus not only is there always an equilibrium capital–labour ratio, the equilibrium is *stable*: 'whatever the initial capital–labour ratio, the system will develop *towards* a state of balanced growth at the natural rate'. It can readily be seen that the system will respond in a similarly stable way to a *change* in the natural rate of growth.

To assess this analysis, it is necessary to explain the process in purely economic terms. Suppose that there is an increase in the natural rate of growth. Then, by assumption, the rate of growth of output must increase so as to maintain full employment. But at the *initial* levels of investment and capital stock, the rate of growth of capital is less than that of labour, so that K/L falls. But as we saw earlier, as K/L falls, Y/K rises. Hence sY/K rises, and since investment is equal to savings, I/K rises, and this process will continue until $\dot{Y}/Y = \dot{K}/K = \dot{L}/L = n$.

It is thus clear that the result depends on two crucial assumptions: first, that full employment persists throughout, and secondly, that investment is determined by the amount of saving. It is of course possible to build on to the simple neoclassical model mechanisms which will ensure that these two conditions are met;[3] alternatively, one might adopt a 'weak' version of the approach by saying simply that, given flexibility in the capital–labour mix (and hence in the capital–output ratio), there will generally be an attainable warranted rate equal to the natural rate, but without maintaining that there are endogenous forces which will *automatically* ensure such adjustment. But in the absence of either of these modifications, the model is dependent on two very questionable suppositions—that full-employment output is some-how always maintained and that the volume of savings determines the volume of investment.

As Eisner [Reading 5.3] points out, the neoclassical growth model's starting-point—flexibility in the capital–output ratio—was chosen largely in order to avoid the apparent 'knife-edge' instability of the Harrod–Domar model. But, as we have seen, it is something of a caricature of Harrod's own presentation (as it is of Domar's) to regard the capital–output ratio as completely rigid; for the existence of long-range investment, the influence of the state of business confidence, and financial factors, all reduce the 'rigidity' of the model. Of course, limits to profitable investment opportunities, or a Keynesian 'liquidity trap' floor to the rate of interest may mean that there are limits to the possible adjustment of the capital–output ratio, and thus to the warranted rate of growth, which are not allowed for in the neoclassical model. Eisner concludes that, if the neoclassical interpretation of the Harrod–Domar model was too rigid, the neoclassical model itself is too flexible.

The neoclassical model so far discussed is broadly in real terms, taking no account of the influence of money whether in a 'Keynesian' or a 'quantity theory' way. Johnson [Reading 5.4] offers a rather stylized account of the influence of money in a neoclassical framework. Money is currency, treated by the public as net wealth ('outside' money), all wages and prices are flexible, and money is neutral in the sense that fluctuations in the supply of money about its growth trend will affect prices but not real output. But it does *not* follow that money is neutral in the sense that a change in the growth trend of the money supply will have no effect on the rate of growth of output. A more rapid rate of growth of the money supply will, *ceteris paribus*, increase the rate of price inflation, and it is through this channel that the rate of growth of output can be influenced.

[3] In general, by adding labour and financial markets.

The argument turns on the role played by real money balances. On the one hand, *disposable* income per head at any time is said to be equal to actual output per head *plus* the growth of real balances. But the growth of real balances must itself be financed by saving. The addition to savings (via the increase in disposable income) on the first count—$sbgy$ (where s is the propensity to save, b is the ratio of real balances to output, and g is the growth rate of output, y)—is more than offset by the savings required for the increase in real balances—bgy. Thus the higher the demand for real balances (represented by b), the lower the amount of savings available to finance investment and, with the neoclassical assumption that savings determine investment, the lower will be the ratio of investment to output. Now, other things being equal, the demand for cash balances will be lower the more rapid is the rate of price inflation, since the inflation rate represents the (negative) return on holding cash. And this rate of price change is, as we have seen, governed by the rate of expansion of the money supply. Thus the more rapid is monetary expansion, the faster is the rate of price inflation, the lower the demand for real balances, the higher the level of 'available' savings and thus of investment, and the more rapid the rate of growth of the economy.

Another line of development of growth models has reflected the recognition of technical progress as a major—even dominating—source of growth in output per head, rather than increased capital per head. The simplest way of allowing for the contribution of technical progress, particularly in empirical work, is to treat it as 'disembodied', that is, taking place at a rate unconnected with the rate of accumulation of capital or the growth of the labour supply. Using, for example, the Cobb–Douglas production function [see Chapter 8], we may write

$$X_t = aL_t^\alpha K_t^{(1-\alpha)} e^{\lambda t}.$$

On taking logarithms

$$\log X_t = \log a + \alpha \log L_t + (1-\alpha) \log K_t + \lambda t,$$

and differentiating with respect to time,

$$\frac{1}{X_t}\frac{dX_t}{dt} = \alpha \frac{1}{L_t}\frac{dL_t}{dt} + (1-\alpha)\frac{1}{K_t}\frac{dK_t}{dt} + \lambda$$

or

$$g_x = \alpha g_1 + (1-\alpha)g_k + \lambda,$$

where g_x is the percentage rate of growth of output, g_1 of labour, and g_k of capital. Thus output growth is a weighted average of capital and labour, together with a 'residual' rate, λ, reflecting technical progress, which is assumed to take place at a constant percentage rate.

Solow [Reading 5.5] points out that, despite its convenience, the assumption that technical progress is disembodied is simply inconsistent with the common-sense observation that innovations must generally be embodied in new investments. But this means that 'capital' can no longer be treated as a homogeneous aggregate: in particular, capital of different ages, or 'vintages', must be treated separately. If technical progress still takes place at a steady rate, each vintage will embody technical progress up to the date at which it was brought into use, but no further improvement will take place. Thus the production function can be applied separately to each vintage:

$$X_v(t) = aL_v(t)^{\alpha}K_v(t)^{(1-\alpha)}e^{\lambda v},$$

where K_v is the addition to capital—gross investment—at time v. Depreciation at a proportional rate σ means that the average life of capital is $1/\sigma$ and thus the amount of capital of vintage v remaining at time t is

$$K_v(t) = K_v(v)e^{-\alpha(t-v)} = I(v)e^{-\alpha(t-v)},$$

where $I(v)$ is gross investment at time v.

Essentially all that remains is to aggregate the investments of different vintages remaining, and to use the resulting sum to replace 'the' capital stock in the production function:

$$X(t) = aL(t)^{\alpha}J(t)^{(1-\alpha)}e^{-\alpha(1-\alpha)t}$$

where

$$J(t) = \int_{-\infty}^{t} e^{[\alpha + \lambda|(1-\alpha)]v}I(v)dv.$$

The problem now is to estimate the parameters of the new production function—especially λ, the rate of embodied technical progress. Evidently, the higher is λ, the more productive will be new capital compared with older capital and the greater the scope for raising the growth rate by increasing the rate of investment. Solow finds λ to be about 3 per cent per annum, and suggests that, for an advanced economy, doubling the rate of investment might increase output at the end of a decade by 26 per cent, while if technical progress were wholly disembodied, doubling the rate of investment would yield only 14 per cent by the end of the decade.

5.1 The Rate and Stability of Economic Growth

1. The following pages constitute a tentative and preliminary attempt to give the outline of a 'dynamic' theory. Static theory consists of a classification of terms with a view to systematic thinking, together with the extraction of such knowledge about the adjustments due to a change of circumstances as is yielded by the 'laws of supply and demand'. It has for some time appeared to me that it ought to be possible to develop a similar classification and system of axioms to meet the situation in which certain forces are operating

* From R. F. Harrod, 'An Essay in Dynamic Theory', *Economic Journal*, 1939.

steadily to increase or decrease certain magnitudes in the system. The consequent 'theory' would not profess to determine the course of events in detail, but should provide a framework of concepts relevant to the study of change analogous to that provided by static theory for the study of rest.

The axiomatic basis of the theory which I propose to develop consists of three propositions—namely, (1) that the level of a community's income is the most important determinant of its supply of saving; (2) that the rate of increase of its income is an important determinant of its demand for saving, and (3) that demand is equal to supply. It thus consists in a marriage of the 'acceleration principle' and the 'multiplier' theory, and is a development and extension of certain arguments advanced in my *Essay on the Trade Cycle*.[1]

2. Attempts to construct a dynamic theory have recently been proceeding upon another line—namely, by the study of time lags between certain adjustments. By the introduction of an appropriate lag the tendency of a system to oscillate can be established. In these studies there is some doubt as to the nature of the trend on which the oscillation is superimposed. Supposing damping measures could be introduced, to counteract the oscillation caused by the lag, would the system be stationary or advancing? And at what rate? Dynamic theory in my sense may throw some light upon this.

Moreover it is possible, and this the following argument seeks to establish, that the trend of growth may itself generate forces making for oscillation. This, if so, would not impair the importance of the study of the effect of lags. But it may be that the attempt to explain the trade cycle by *exclusive* reference to them is an unnecessary *tour de force*. The study of the operation of the forces maintaining a trend of increase and the study of lags should go together.

3. The significance of what follows should not be judged solely by reference to the validity or convenience of the particular equations set forth. It involves something wider: a method of thinking, a way of approach to certain problems. It is necessary to 'think dynamically'. The static system of equations is set forth not only for its own beauty, but also to enable the economist to train his mind upon special problems when they arise. For instance, an economist may pose to himself the question, What would be the effect on the system of an increase of exports or of a labour-saving invention? By reference to the state equations, he then proceeds to work out the new equilibrium position supposing the new higher level of exports to be maintained in

[1] Especially in Ch. 2, secs. 4–5. The 'Acceleration Principle' was there designated the 'Relation'. There is an objection to the use of the term acceleration in this connection. The study of the condition in which demand and supply are flowing at an unaltered rate has long been known as Static Theory: this implies that the equilibrium of prices and quantities resulting therefrom is regarded as analogous to a state of rest. By analogy, therefore, a steady rate of increase of demand, which is our first matter for consideration in dynamic theory, and a major effect of which is expressed by the 'Relation', should be regarded as a velocity. Acceleration would be a rate of change in this.

However, the use of the expression Acceleration Principle in the sense of my relation is rapidly accelerating in current literature, and I reluctantly bow to the *force majeure* of usage.

perpetuity or the labour-saving invention to be incorporated in the productive technique once for all.

But let the question be: Suppose the level of exports begins and continues to increase steadily, or suppose its rate of increase to increase, or suppose labour-saving inventions begin to be made in a steady or growing stream; then the static method will not suffice. The static theorist may hope to reduce this supposed steady increase to a succession of steps up, each having the same effect. But if the following argument is correct, the effect on the moving equilibrium of advance may often be in the opposite direction to the effect on the static equilibrium produced by each of the steps considered singly. A new method of approach—indeed, a mental revolution—is needed.

Once the mind is accustomed to thinking in terms of trends of increase, the old static formulation of problems seems stale, flat and unprofitable. This is not to deny to static theory its own appropriate sphere. It will become apparent which kind of problem belongs to each branch of study.

4. I now propose to proceed directly to the Fundamental Equation, constituting the marriage of the acceleration principle and the multiplier theory. This probably gives too much importance to the acceleration principle, and the necessary modification is introduced subsequently.

Let G stand for the geometric rate of growth of income or output in the system, the increment being expressed as a fraction of its existing level. G will vary directly with the time interval chosen—e.g., 1 per cent per annum = $\frac{1}{12}$ per cent per month. Let G_w stand for the warranted rate of growth. The warranted rate of growth is taken to be that rate of growth which, if it occurs, will leave all parties satisfied that they have produced neither more nor less than the right amount. Or, to state the matter otherwise, it will put them into a frame of mind which will cause them to give such orders as will maintain the same rate of growth in being, the equilibrium is, for reasons to be explained, a highly unstable one. I use the unprofessional term warranted instead of equilibrium, or moving equilibrium, because, although every point on the path of output described by G_w is an equilibrium point in the sense that producers, if they remain on it, will be satisfied, and be induced to keep the same rate of growth in being, the equilibrium is, for reasons to be explained, a highly unstable one.

If x_0 is output in period 0 and x_1 output in period 1, $G = (x_1 - x_0)/x_0$. Since we suppose the period to be short, x_0 or x_1 may alternatively stand in the denominator

x_0 and x_1 are compounded of all individual outputs. I neglect questions of weighting. Even in a condition of growth, which generally speaking is steady, it is not to be supposed that all the component individuals are expanding at the same rate. Thus even in the most ideal circumstances conceivable, G, the actual rate of growth, would diverge from time to time from G_w, the warranted rate of growth, for random or seasonal causes.

Let s stand for the fraction of income which individuals and corporate bodies choose to save. s is total saving divided by x_0 or x_1. This may be expected to vary, with the size of income, the phase of the trade cycle, institutional changes, etc.

Let C stand for the value of the capital goods required for the production of a unit increment of output. The unit of value used to measure this magnitude is the value of the unit increment of output. Thus, if it is proposed in month 1 to raise the output of shoes, so that in month 1 and all subsequent months output is one pair higher than in month 0, and the machine required to do this—neglecting all other capital that may be required—has a value 48 times the value of a pair of shoes, C per month = 48. The value of C is inversely proportional to the period chosen. C per annum = 4 in this case.[2] The value of C depends on the state of technology and the nature of the goods constituting the increment of output. It may be expected to vary as income grows and in different phases of the trade cycle; it may be somewhat dependent on the rate of interest.

Now, it is probably the case that in any period not the whole of the new capital is destined to look after the increment of output of consumers' goods. There may be long-range plans of capital development or a transformation of the method of producing the pre-existent level of output. These facts will be allowed for in due course. For the moment let it be assumed that all new capital goods are required for the sake of the increment of output of consumers' goods accruing.

Reserving proof for the next paragraph, we may now write the Fundamental Equation in its simplest form:[3]

$$G_w = \frac{s}{C} \tag{1}$$

It should be noticed that the warranted rate of growth of the system appears here as an unknown term, the value of which is determined by certain 'fundamental conditions'—namely, the propensity to save and the state of technology, etc. Those who define dynamic as having a cross-reference to two points of time may not regard this equation as dynamic; that particular definition of dynamic has its own interest and field of reference. I prefer to define dynamic as referring to propositions in which a rate of growth appears as an unknown variable. This equation is clearly more fundamental than those expressing lags of adjustment.

[2] If a month is the unit, the number of shoes added per period is 1, if a year 144. The value of G per annum is 12 times as great as that of G per month, since the numerator of G per annum is 144 times as great and the denominator 12 times as great as the numerator and denominator respectively of G per month. The number of machines added per month is $1 \equiv 48$ shoes $\equiv 48$ units of increment of output. C per month = 48. The number of machines added per year is $12 \equiv 48 \times 12$ shoes. Thus the value in shoes of the annual increment of capital required to produce an annual increment of 144 shoes is 48×12 units. Therefore C per annum = $(48 \times 12)/144 = 4 = 1/12$ of C per month.

[3] Since the value of G_w varies directly and that of C inversely with the unit period chosen, and the value of s is independent of the unit, the validity of the equation is independent of the unit period chosen.

5. The proof is as follows. Let C_p stand for the value of the increment of capital stock in the period divided by the increment of total output. C_p is the value of the increment of capital per unit increment of output actually produced. Circulating and fixed capital are lumped together.

$$G = \frac{s}{C_p} \tag{1a}$$

is a truism, depending on the proposition that actual saving in a period (excess of the income in that period over consumption) is equal to the addition to the capital stock. Total saving is equal to sx_0. The addition to the capital stock is equal to $C_p(x_1 - x_0)$. This follows from the definition of C_p. And so,

$$sx_0 = C_p(x_1 - x_0)$$

$$\therefore \frac{s}{C_p} = \frac{x_1 - x_0}{x_0} = G$$

G is the rate of increase in total output which actually occurs; C_p is the increment in the stock of capital divided by the increment in total output which actually occurs. If the value of the increment of stock of capital per unit increment of output which actually occurs, C_p, is equal to C, the amount of capital per unit increment of output required by technological and other conditions (including the state of confidence, the rate of interest, etc.) then clearly the increase which actually occurs is equal to the increase which is justified by the circumstances. This means that, since C_p includes all goods (circulating and fixed capital), and is in fact production minus consumption per unit increment of output during the period, the sum of decisions to produce, to which G gives expression, are on balance justified—i.e., if $C = C_p$, then $G = G_w$, and (from (1a) above)

$$G_w = \frac{s}{C}$$

This is the fundamental equation, stated in paragraph 4, which determines the warranted rate of growth. To give numerical values to these symbols, which may be fairly representative of modern conditions: if 10 per cent of income were saved and the capital coefficient per annum (C) were equal to 4, the warranted rate of growth would be $2\frac{1}{2}$ per cent per annum.

It may be well to emphasize at this point that no distinction is drawn in this theory between capital goods and consumption goods. In measuring the increment of capital, the two are taken together; the increment consists of total production less total consumption. Some trade-cycle theorists concern themselves with a possible lack of balance between these two categories; no doubt that has its importance. The theory here considered is more fundamental or simple; it is logically prior to the considerations regarding lack of balance, and grasp of it is required as a preliminary to the study of them.

6. To use terminology recently employed by distinguished authorities, C_p is an *ex post* quantity. I am not clear if C should be regarded as its corresponding *ex ante*. C is rather that addition to capital goods in any period, which producers regard as ideally suited to the output which they are undertaking in that period. For convenience the term *ex ante* when employed in this article will be used in this sense.

The truism stated above, (1a), gives expression to Mr. Keynes' proposition that saving is necessarily equal to investment—that is, to *ex post* investment. Saving is not necessarily equal to *ex ante* investment in this sense, since unwanted accretions or depletions of stocks may occur, or equipment may be found to have been produced in excess of, or short of, requirements.

If *ex post* investment is less than *ex ante* investment, this means that there has been an undesired reduction of stocks or insufficient provision of productive equipment, and there will be a stimulus to further expansion of output; conversely if *ex post* investment exceeds *ex ante* investment. If *ex post* investment is less than *ex ante* investment, saving is less than *ex ante* investment. In his *Treatise on Money* Mr. Keynes formulated a proposition, which has been widely felt to be enlightening, though experience has led him subsequently to condemn the definitions employed as more likely to be misconstrued than helpful. He said that if investment exceeded saving, the system would be stimulated to expand, and conversely. If for the definitions on which that proposition was based, we *substitute* the definition of *ex ante* investment given above, it is true that if *ex ante* investment exceeds saving, the system will be stimulated, and conversely. This truth may account for the feeling of satisfaction which Mr. Keynes' proposition originally evoked and the reluctance to abandon it at his behest. In many connections we are more interested in *ex ante* than in *ex post* investment, the latter including as it does unwanted accretions of stocks. Mr. Keynes' proposition of the *Treatise* may still be a useful aid to thinking, if we substitute for 'Investment' in it *ex ante* investment as defined above

7. Two minor points may be considered before we proceed with the main argument.

(i) It may be felt that there is something unreal in this analysis, since the increase in capital which producers will regard as right in period 1 is in the real world related not to the increase of total output in period 1, but to prospective increases in subsequent periods. This objection may be divided into two parts. (*a*) In view of the fact that much of the outlay of capital is connected with long-range planning, it may be held that the fundamental equation gives too much weight to the short-period effect of the acceleration principle. This objection is freely admitted and allowed for in the subsequent modification of the equation. (*b*) It may further be objected that even in the sphere in which the acceleration principle holds there must be some lag between the increased provision of equipment (and stocks?) and the increased flow of output which they are designed to support. There may be some force in this. But the point is deliberately neglected in this part of the argument, along with all questions of lags. The study of these lags is of undoubted importance, but a division of labour in analysis is indispensable, and in this case the neglect is necessary in order to get the clearest possible view of the forces determining the trend and its influence as such. Moreover, the lag referred to in this sub-heading (*b*) may properly be regarded as unimportant, since, in the event of a *steady* advance (*G*) being maintained, the difference between $x_1 - x_0$ and $x_2 - x_1$ will be of the second order of small quantities. In other words, it matters not whether we regard the increment of capital as required to support the increment of total output in the same period or in the one immediately succeeding it.

8. (ii) In the demonstration given above (paras. 6 and 7) reference was made to the distinction between the *ex post* and the *ex ante* increase of capital goods. No reference was made to the distinction between *ex post* and *ex ante* saving.[4] Suppose that *G* is not equal to G_w might not the discrepancy show itself on the other side of the equation, not in any divergence of C_p from *C*, but in *ex post* saving not being equal to *ex ante* saving?

I have no very clear view as to possible causes likely to operate in a systematic way to distort *ex post* from *ex ante* saving, or of the probable importance of such distortions. It is said, for instance, that in a time of rising prices, fixed-income classes will not adapt their modes of life simultaneously, and so may save less than they would be disposed to do had they clearly foreseen the impending rise. *Per contra* variable-income classes may not foresee their own rise of income, and so spend less than they would have been disposed to do.

This question of the possible divergence of *ex post* from *ex ante* saving must be kept entirely distinct from that of the variations in *s* in the different phases of the trade cycle, which not only are admitted, but also play a part in the argument. *s* may vary because the level of income or of profit is abnormally swollen or depressed.

The neglect of these possible divergences has no importance for the argument, since they will have the same effect on growth as the divergences of C_p from *C* for which they may serve as substitute. Thus if *G* exceeds G_w, the right-hand side of the equation must exceed *s/C*. If the whole of this effect is found in C_p it will be *less* than C, and this is a stimulus to expansion.[5] Firms finding themselves short of stock or equipment will increase their orders. If, on the other hand, the whole of this effect is found in a divergence of *ex post s* from *ex ante s*, *ex post s* will be *greater* than *ex ante s*. Savers will find that they have saved more than they would have done had they

---

[4] Be it noted that *ex ante* is here used of saving in a sense analogous to that defined in the expression *ex ante* investment; it is the saving which savers would choose to make in any period, were they able to adapt expenditure simultaneously with the changing circumstances of the period.

[5] The reader who is surprised that an excess of *G* over G_w is stimulating will find the explanation in the next paragraph.

foreseen their level of income or the level of prices correctly. Consequently they will be stimulated to expand purchases, and orders for goods will consequently be increased. Throughout the following pages the reader, whenever he finds a reference to the excess or deficiency of C_p compared with C, may substitute, if he prefers it, a supposed deficiency or excess of *ex post* saving compared with *ex ante* saving, without affecting the course of the argument.

9. We now come to a point of major importance, constituting the difference between the dynamic equilibrium (warranted rate of growth) and the static equilibrium. Normally the latter is stable and the former unstable. This gives a *prima facie* reason for regarding the dynamic analysis as a necessary propaedeutic to trade-cycle study.

Some recent writers have been disposed to urge that the static equilibrium is not so stable as is sometimes claimed. Suppose that an increased output of a commodity, constituting a departure from equilibrium, is tried, so that its supply stands at a point at which the supply curve is above the demand curve. It is argued that, instead of a relapse at once occurring, reducing supply to the point of intersection of the supply and demand curves—this showing the stability of the old equilibrium—the upshot depends on how all parties now proceed. It is suggested that there may be a tendency to waltz round the point of intersection or, more broadly, that in the backward adjustment there may be wide repercussions disturbing the whole system. It is even held that the whole question of the stability of the static equilibrium, in the sense of the tendency of a relapse to it when a random departure occurs, is itself a dynamic problem, which cannot be looked after by the system of static equations. I have the impression that this type of criticism exaggerates the importance of this problem, and constitutes to some extent a failure to see the wood for the trees, and that on its own ground the theory of static equilibrium is well able to hold its own.

But when we look at the dynamic equilibrium, new vistas are opened. The line of output traced by the warranted rate of growth is a moving equilibrium, in the sense that it represents the one level of output at which producers will feel in the upshot that they have done the right thing, and which will induce them to continue in the same line of advance. Stock in hand and equipment available will be exactly at the level which they would wish to have them. Of course what applies to the system in general may not apply to each individual separately. But if one feels he has over-produced or over-ordered, this will be counterbalanced by an opposite experience of an equal importance in some other part of the field.

But now suppose that there is a departure from the warranted rate of growth. Suppose an excessive output, so that G exceeds G_w. The consequence will be that C_p, the actual increase of capital goods per unit increment of output, falls below C, that which is desired. There will be, in fact, an undue depletion of stock or shortage of equipment, and the system will be stimulated to further expansion. G, instead of returning to G_w, will move farther from it in an upward direction, and the farther it diverges, the greater the stimulus to expansion will be. Similarly, if G falls below G_w, there will be a redundance of capital goods, and a depressing influence will be exerted; this will cause a further divergence and a still stronger depressing influence; and so on. Thus in the dynamic field we have a condition opposite to that which holds in the static field. A departure from equilibrium, instead of being self-righting, will be self-aggravating. G_w represents a moving equilibrium, but a highly unstable one. Of interest this for trade-cycle analysis!

Suppose an increase in the propensity to save, which means that the values of s are increased for all levels of income. This necessarily involves, *ceteris paribus*, a higher rate of warranted growth. But if the actual growth was previously equal to the warranted growth, the immediate effect is to raise the warranted rate above the actual rate. This state of affairs sets up a depressing influence which will drag the actual rate progressively farther below the warranted rate. In this as in other cases, the movement of a dynamic determinant has an opposite effect on the warranted path of growth to that which it has on its actual path. How different from the order of events in static theory!

The reader may have some difficulty in the expression 'stimulus to expansion'. What is the significance of this, in view of the fact that some growth is assumed as a basic condition? It must be remembered that the value of G depends on aggregates x_0 and x_1. These are sums of numerous quantities for which individuals are responsible. It must be supposed that at all times some individuals are jogging on at a steady level, others are risking an increase of orders or output, others are willy-nilly curtailing. G is the resultant of their separate enterprises. Some are in any event likely to be disappointed. If G is equal to G_w, it is to be supposed that the general level of enterprise undertaken in period 0, including in sum a certain increase over that in the preceding period, is found to be satisfactory. Those running short of stock balance those with surpluses. This justifies further action on similar lines, though the individuals increasing orders for stock in trade or planning new equipment in period 1 may not be identical in person with those doing so in period 0. If an expansive force is in operation, more individuals, or individuals having greater weight, will be induced by their trading position to venture increases than did so in the preceding period. Conversely if a depressing force is in operation.

The dynamic theory so far stated may be summed up in two propositions. (i) A unique warranted line of growth is determined jointly by the propensity to save and the quantity of capital required by technological and other considerations per unit increment of total output. Only if producers keep to this line will they find that on balance their production in each period has been neither excessive nor deficient. (ii) On either side of this line is a 'field' in which centrifugal forces operate, the magnitude of which varies directly as the distance of any point in it from the warranted line. Departure from the warranted line sets up an inducement to depart farther from it. The moving equilibrium of advance is thus a highly unstable one.

The essential point here may be further explained by reference to the expressions over-production and under-production. The distinction between particular over-production and general over-production is well known. In the event of particular over-production, there will normally be a tendency to reduce production of the particular line, and so equilibrium will be restored. We may define general over-production as a condition in which a majority of producers, or producers representing in sum the major part of production, find they have produced or ordered too much, in the sense that they or the distributors of their goods find themselves in possession of an unwanted volume of stocks or equipment. By reference to the fundamental equation it appears that this state of things can only occur when the actual growth has been *below* the warranted growth—i.e., a condition of general over-production is the consequence of producers in sum producing too little. The only way in which this state of affairs could have been avoided would have been by producers in sum producing more than they did. Over-production is the consequence of production below the warranted level. Conversely, if producers find that they are continually running short of stocks and equipment, this means that they are producing above the warranted level.

But the condition of over-production, or, as we should perhaps call it, apparent over-production, will lead to a curtailment of production or orders, or a reduction in the rate of increase on balance, and consequently, so long as the fundamental conditions governing the warranted rate are unchanged, to a larger gap between actual and warranted growth, and so to an intensification of the evils which the contraction was intended to cure.

It must be noted that a rate of growth lying on either side of the warranted rate is regarded here as unwarranted. If the actual rate exceeds the warranted rate, producers on balance will not feel that they have produced or ordered too much; on the contrary, they will be running short of stocks and/or equipment. Thus they will not feel that they have produced the warranted amount plus something; on the contrary, they will feel that everything which they have produced has been warranted, and that they might warrantably have produced something more. None the less, we define their production as unwarrantably large, meaning by that that they have produced in excess of the unique amount which would leave them on balance satisfied with what they had done and prepared to go forward in the next period on similar lines.

10. The foregoing demonstration of the inherent instability of the moving equilibrium, or warranted line of advance, depends on the assumption that the values of s and C are independent of the value of G. This is formally correct. The analysis relates to a single point of time. s is regarded as likely to vary with a change in the size of income, but a change in the rate of growth at a given point of time has no effect on its size. C may also be expected to vary with the size of income, e.g., owing to the occurrence of surplus capital capacity from time to time, but the same argument for regarding it as independent of the rate of growth at a particular point of time applies.

It may be objected, however, that this method of analysis is too strict to be realistic, since the discovery that output is excessive or deficient, and the consequent emergence of a depressing or stimulating force, takes some time, and in the interval required for a reaction to be produced an appreciable change in s or C may have occurred.

Consider this with reference to an experimental increase in G above a warranted level. According to the theory of instability, any such experiment will be apparently over-justified, stocks or equipment running short in consequence of it. Is it possible that if resulting changes in the values of s or C are taken into account, this doctrine will have to be modified?

In order to justify modifying the doctrine, it would be necessary to show that, in consequence of the experimental increase, s was substantially increased or C reduced. It is unlikely that C would be reduced. The capital coefficient may often stand below the level appropriate to the technological conditions of the age, owing to the existence of surplus equipment. If this were so, the higher rate of output consequent upon the experimental increase would tend to raise C. A smaller proportion of firms would come to find their capacity redundant, and a larger proportion would have to support a greater turnover by ordering extra equipment.

With saving the case is different. An expansion of activity might increase the proportion of income saved. What increase of saving is required for a modification of the instability theory?

This can be shown simply. Let x_e be an experimental increase of output above the warranted level. Let s_m stand for the fraction of the consequential income saved. The instability principle requires that

$$Cx_e > s_m x_e$$

i.e., that
$$s_m < C$$

$$< \frac{s}{G_w}$$

This condition needs interpretation. Since C and G_w do not both appear in the equation, it is necessary to define the period by which G_w is measured. This should be done by reference to the reaction time mentioned above— namely, the time required for an undue accretion or depletion of capital goods to exert its influence upon the flow of orders. If this reaction time is six months, then G_w must be measured as growth per six months.

Thus the instability condition requires that the fraction of marginal income saved shall not be more than the fraction of total income saved multiplied by the total income and divided by the increment of warranted income per six months. Thus if the warranted growth is $2\frac{1}{2}$ per cent per annum, or $1\frac{1}{4}$ per cent per six months, the instability principle requires that the fraction of marginal income saved must be less than eighty times the fraction of average income saved. Supposing that the high figure of 50 per cent is taken as the fraction of marginal income saved, the fraction of total income saved must be greater than five-eighths of 1 per cent. Thus for any normal warranted rate of growth and level of saving, the instability principle seems quite secure.

The force of this argument, however, is somewhat weakened when long-range capital outlay is taken into account. It will then appear that the attainment of a neutral or stable equilibrium of advance may not be altogether improbable in certain phases of the cycle.

11. It should be noticed that the instability theory makes the empirical verification of the acceleration principle more arduous. For it leads to the expectation that in the upward phase of the cycle the actual rate will tend to run above the warranted rate, and the accretion of capital to be less than that required by the acceleration principle; and conversely in the downward phase. Thus a finding that the volume of investment fluctuates less than is required by direct computation from the acceleration principle is consistent with the theory here set forth, in which, none the less, the acceleration principle is presented as a leading dynamic determinant.

12. It is now expedient to introduce further terms into our equation to reduce the influence of the acceleration principle. Some outlays of capital have no direct relation to the current increase of output. They may be related to a prospective long-period increase of activity, and be but slightly influenced, if at all, by the current increase of trade. Or they may be induced by new inventions calculated to cheapen production or change consumers' modes of spending their income, so that they are not related to increments of output, but are designed to revolutionize the methods for producing some portion of already existing output or to substitute one line of goods for another in the consumers' budget. There are doubtless numerous factors, including the state of confidence and the rate of interest affecting the volume of such outlay. It may suffice for the purpose in hand to divide it into two parts.

One part, K, is conceived to be quite independent both of the current level of income and its current rate of growth. The other, expressed as a fraction of income, k, is conceived to vary with the current level of income, as distinct from its rate of growth. This seems a reasonable assumption. Long-period anticipations are bound to be influenced by the present state of prosperity or adversity: even public authorities are apt to reduce the volume of public works in a slump. Companies may relate their expenditure on long-range plans to the current state of their profit account.

Having regard to the principle that the total increase of capital is equal to the total saving in the period, our fundamental equation may be modified as follows:

$$G_w = \frac{s - k - \dfrac{K}{x}}{C}. \tag{2}^6$$

$$\therefore \frac{s - k - \dfrac{K}{x_0}}{C_p} = \frac{x_1 - x_0}{x_0} = G$$

$$\therefore G_w = \frac{s - k - \dfrac{K}{x_0}}{C}.$$

It must be noticed that C and C_p now stand not for the total increase of capital (desired and actual, respectively) per unit increment of output, but only for the net increase of capital after the capital represented by k and K has been subtracted.

It may be noticed that the larger the volume of outlay which will be sustained independently of the current rate of growth, the *smaller* is the warranted rate of growth. A larger part of savings being absorbed in such outlay, there will be a smaller part to be looked after by the acceleration principle.

13. In the following pages the expression long-range capital outlay will be used for the magnitude denoted by $xk + K$. This must not be supposed to cover all investment in durable fixed equipment; for much of that is related to, and directly governed by, the current output of consumption goods. It refers only to that part of the output of fixed equipment the production of which is not governed by the current demand for consumption goods.

If long-range capital outlay were large by comparison with that required to support the current increase in turnover of consumable goods, the peculiar conditions defined in §10 for the invalidity of the instability principle might in certain circumstances be realised. For the fraction of total income saved *and* devoted to the finance of the increase of current output might be very small compared with the fraction of marginal income saved. It is not, however, to be supposed that it would normally be small enough to invalidate the instability principle. For, with normal growth at $2\frac{1}{2}$ per cent, saving at 10 per cent, marginal saving at 50 per cent and the reaction time 6 months, this would mean that fifteen-sixteenths of capital would normally be devoted to long-range capital outlay and only one-sixteenth would be directly associated with the current increase of output (cf. §10). But such a situation might well arise in certain phases of the trade cycle, especially when capital capacity was redundant and saving low. In that case a stable equilibrium of advance might for a time be achieved.

$^6\, s x_0 = C_p(x_1 - x_0) + k x_0 + K$

14. To complete the picture, foreign trade must be taken into account. It is reasonable to measure exports, including invisible exports and the earnings of foreign investments, in absolute terms. The value of income which may be earned in this way may be conceived to be independent both of the level of activity at home and of its growth (though in so far as the trade cycle is worldwide, its value will be *de facto* related to income). Let E stand for this value. Imports, on the other hand, are better taken as a fraction, i, of the current level of income. We than have, by parity of reasoning,

$$G_w = \frac{s+i-k-\dfrac{K}{x}-\dfrac{E}{x}}{C} \tag{3}[7]$$

i need not be equal to E/x; the difference represents an international movement of capital. The influence of the various magnitudes on the warranted rate of growth is shown by the equation.

15. The fundamental dynamic equation has been used to demonstrate the inherent tendency of the system to instability. Space forbids an application of this method of analysis to the successive phases of the trade cycle. In the course of it the values expressed by the symbols on the right-hand side of the equation undergo considerable change. As actual growth departs upwards or downwards from the warranted level, the warranted rate itself moves, and may chase the actual rate in either direction. The maximum rates of advance or recession may be expected to occur at the moment when the chase is successful.

For the convenience of the reader who may be tempted to experiment with this tool, it must be observed that C is always positive. Being the total quantity of capital required in connection with increments (or decrements) of current output divided by the increment (or decrement) of that output, when the latter is negative the former is negative also, and the coefficient remains positive. C_p, on the other hand, may be negative; it is not negative whenever there is a depletion of capital goods, but only when the amount of capital goods outstanding is moving in the opposite direction to the level of total output.

The formula is not well adapted to dealing with the case of zero growth. But that matter is quite simple. Zero growth is only warranted when the amount of saving is equal to the amount required for long-range capital outlay. If the amount of saving exceeds this, there will be a tendency for output to decline, and conversely.

It may be well to make one point with regard to a downward departure

---

[7] The principle now is that saving plus income expended on imports must be equal to the increase of capital in the country plus income derived from abroad. This is deducible from the fact that income derived from the sale of home made goods to consumers at home is equal to the income devoted to their purchase. Thus:

$$sx_0 + ix_0 = C_p(x_1 - x_0) + kx_0 + K + E$$

from the warranted position of sufficient importance to outlive one reaction time and bring the system within the field where the centrifugal forces have substantial strength. The downward lapse will then continue until the warranted rate, determined by the values on the right-hand side of the equation, itself moves down. This will happen when the numerator falls or the denominator rises. But in a phase of declining rate of growth the capital coefficient is not in general likely to rise. And so long as there is still some positive growth, albeit at a declining rate, the fraction of income saved is not likely to fall. Therefore, once the rate of growth is driven downwards from the warranted level, the warranted level is not itself likely to fall, or the downward movement therefore to be checked until the rate of growth becomes negative and the level of income recedes. Now, if the actual rate is standing below the warranted rate, the centrifugal force will continue to operate, driving the actual rate progressively downwards, unless or until the warranted rate itself falls to a level as low as the actual rate. But, since the actual rate is now negative, this cannot happen until the numerator of the right-hand side of the equation becomes negative—that is, until saving falls below the level required for long-range capital outlay.

16. Alongside the concept of warranted rate of growth we may introduce another, to be called the natural rate of growth. This is the maximum rate of growth allowed by the increase of population, accumulation of capital, technological improvement and the work/leisure preference schedule, supposing that there is always full employment in some sense.

There is no inherent tendency for these two rates to coincide. Indeed, there is no unique warranted rate; the value of warranted rate depends upon the phase of the trade cycle and the level of activity.

Consideration may be given to that warranted rate which would obtain in conditions of full employment; this may be regarded as the warranted rate 'proper' to the economy. *Prima facie* it might be supposed healthier to have the 'proper' warranted rate above than below the natural rate. But this is very doubtful.

The system cannot advance more quickly than the natural rate allows. If the proper warranted rate is above this, there will be a chronic tendency to depression; the depressions drag down the warranted rate below its proper level, and so keep its average value over a term of years down to the natural rate. But this reduction of the warranted rate is only achieved by having chronic unemployment.

The warranted rate is dragged down by depression; it may be twisted upwards by an inflation of prices and profit. If the proper rate is below the natural rate, the average value of the warranted rate may be sustained above its proper level over a term of years by a succession of profit booms.

Thus each state of affairs has its appropriate evils. There is much to be said for the view that it is better that the proper warranted rate should be lower rather than higher than the natural rate.

17. In order fully to grasp the dynamic principle, it is necessary to bear in mind that changes in fundamental conditions have opposite effects on the actual rate and the warranted rate. An increased amount of long-range capital outlay, an increase in the capital coefficient, an increase in the propensity to consume, and an increase in the active balance on international account, or a decline in the passive balance, are all properly thought to have a stimulating effect on the system. But they all tend, as may readily be seen from the equation, to reduce the warranted rate. This paradox may be readily explained.

Suppose that one of these stimulants begins to operate when the actual rate is equal to the warranted rate. By depressing the warranted rate, it drags that down below the actual rate, and so automatically brings the actual rate into the field of centrifugal forces, driving it away from the warranted rate—that is, in this case, upwards. Thus the stimulant causes the system to expand.

It must not be inferred that these stimulants are only of temporary benefit. For it may be healthy for an economy to have its proper warranted rate reduced. This is likely to be so when its proper warranted rate is tending to be above the natural rate.[8] The long-run value of the stimulant can only be assessed if it is known whether, in its absence, the proper warranted rate is running above or below the natural rate.

It is often felt that a high propensity to save should warrant a great increase in the output of wealth, and this induces an extreme aversion to accept Mr. Keynes' view that excessive saving in the modern age is hostile to prosperity. The feeling is justified to the extent that higher propensity to save does, in fact, *warrant* a higher rate of growth. Trouble arises if the rate of growth which it warrants is greater than that which the increase of population and the increase of technical capacity render permanently possible. And the fundamental paradox is that the more ambitious the rate *warranted* is, the greater the probability that the actual output will from time to time, and even persistently fall below that which the productive capacity of the population would allow.

18. Policy in this field is usually appraised by reference to its power to combat tendencies to oscillation. Our demonstration of the inherent instability of the dynamic equilibrium confirms the importance of this. But there are two points to be noticed in this connection. 1. The nature of the measures suitable for combating the tendency to oscillate may depend on whether the natural rate is above or below the proper warranted rate. 2. In addition to dealing with the tendency to oscillation when it occurs, it may be desirable to have a long-range policy designed to influence the relation between the proper warranted rate of growth and the natural rate.

[8] This may be the most fundamental rational explanation of the common view that it is dangerous for an old country to be a large importer of capital. For this involves a high warranted rate of growth, and it is dangerous to have a high warranted rate when the natural rate is low. *Per contra* for a young country, whose natural rate is high, it is considered healthy and proper to have a large import of capital.

If, in the absence of interference, the proper warranted rate is substantially above the natural rate, the difficulties may be too great to be dealt with by a mere anti-cycle policy. In the first place, there is the probability of a slump occurring before full employment is reached, since during the revival the warranted rate may be dangerously near the actual rate, and liable at any time to overpass it, thus generating depression. Secondly, there is an acute problem if the actual rate reaches the ceiling of full employment and is depressed to the natural rate, and therefore below the warranted rate. An attempt may then be made to drag down the warranted rate below its normal level by increasing public works (K). But the difficulty of the proper warranted rate being above the natural rate will be chronic, and this means that only by keeping in being a large and growing volume of public works can the slump be prevented. In fine, the anti-cycle policy has to be converted into a permanent policy for keeping down the proper warranted rate.

19. The ideal policy would be to manipulate the proper warranted rate so that it should be equal to the natural rate. If this could be achieved—but in fact only a rough approximation would be possible—an anti-cycle policy would none the less be an indispensable supplement. For the warranted rate is bound to be disturbed by the varying incidence of inventions and fluctuations in the foreign account. An anti-cycle policy would be necessary to combat the run-away forces which come into being as soon as a substantial change occurs in the warranted rate.

20. A low rate of interest makes for a low warranted rate of increase, by encouraging high values of K and C and, possibly also, by having a depressing influence on s. Since the effects of changes in the rate of interest are probably slow-working, it may be wise to use the rate of interest as a long-range weapon for reducing the warranted rate of growth, and to reserve *suitable* public works for use against the cycle. It is not suggested, however, that a low rate of interest has sufficient power of its own to keep down the warranted rate without the assistance of a programme of public works to be kept permanently in operation.

If permanent public works activity and a low long-term rate availed to bring the proper warranted rate into line with the natural rate, variations in the short-term rate of interest might come into their own again as an ancillary method of dealing with oscillations.

21. This essay has only touched in the most tentative way on a small fraction of the problems, theoretical and practical, of which the enunciation of a dynamic theory suggests the formulation. In the last paragraph it was implicitly hinted that our present situation is one of a relatively high proper warranted rate. The evidence for this comes from inside and outside the dynamic theory itself. According to the dynamic theory, the tendency of a system to relapse into depression before full employment is reached in the boom suggests that its proper warranted rate exceeds its natural rate. Outside evidence includes the known decline in the growth of population, which involves a decline in the natural rate. More controversial points are the tendency of a more wealthy population to save a larger fraction of its income (high value of s involves high warranted rate), and the tendency of modern progress to depress rather than elevate the value of C (low value of C involves high warranted rate).

The main object of this article, however, is to present a tool of analysis, not to diagnose present conditions.

5.2 The Neoclassical Growth Model*
[...]

INTRODUCTION

All theory depends on assumptions which are not quite true. That is what makes it theory. The art of successful theorizing is to make the inevitable simplifying assumptions in such a way that the final results are not very sensitive. A 'crucial' assumption is one on which the conclusions do depend sensitively, and it is important that crucial assumptions be reasonably realistic. When the results of a theory seem to flow specifically from a special crucial assumption, then if the assumption is dubious, the results are suspect.

I wish to argue that something like this is true of the Harrod–Domar model of economic growth. The characteristic and powerful conclusion of the Harrod–Domar line of thought is that even for the long run the economic system is at best balanced on a knife-edge of equilibrium growth. Were the magnitudes of the key parameters—the savings ratio, the capital–output ratio, the rate of increase of the labor force—to slip ever so slightly from dead center, the consequence would be either growing unemployment or prolonged inflation. In Harrod's terms the critical question of balance boils down to a comparison between the natural rate of growth which depends, in the absence of technological change, on the increase of the labor force, and the warranted rate of growth which depends on the saving and investing habits of households and firms.

But this fundamental opposition of warranted and natural rates turns out in the end to flow from the crucial assumption that production takes place under conditions of *fixed proportions*. There is no possibility of substituting labor for capital in production. If this assumption is abandoned, the knife-edge notion of unstable balance seems to go with it. Indeed it is hardly surprising that such a gross rigidity in one part of the system should entail lack of flexibility in another.

A remarkable characteristic of the Harrod–Domar model is that it consistently studies long-run problems with the usual short-run tools. One usually thinks of the long run as the domain of the neoclassical analysis, the land of the margin. Instead Harrod and Domar talk of the long run in terms

* From R. Solow, 'A Contribution to the Theory of Economic Growth', *Quarterly Journal of Economics* (Harvard University), 1956.

of the multiplier, the accelerator, 'the' capital coefficient. The bulk of this paper is devoted to a model of long-run growth which accepts all the Harrod–Domar assumptions except that of fixed proportions. Instead I suppose that the single composite commodity is produced by labor and capital under the standard neoclassical conditions. The adaptation of the system to an exogenously given rate of increase of the labor force is worked out in some detail, to see if the Harrod instability appears. The price-wage-interest reactions play an important role in this neoclassical adjustment process, so they are analyzed too. Then some of the other rigid assumptions are relaxed slightly to see what qualitative changes result: neutral technological change is allowed, and an interest-elastic savings schedule. Finally the consequences of certain more 'Keynesian' relations and rigidities are briefly considered.

A MODEL OF LONG-RUN GROWTH

There is only one commodity, output as a whole, whose rate of production is designated $Y(t)$. Thus we can speak unambiguously of the community's real income. Part of each instant's output is consumed and the rest is saved and invested. The fraction of output saved is a constant s, so that the rate of saving is $sY(t)$. The community's stock of capital $K(t)$ takes the form of an accumulation of the composite commodity. Net investment is then just the rate of increase of this capital stock dK/dt or $\dot{K}$, so we have the basic identity at every instant of time:

$$\dot{K} = sY. \tag{1}$$

Output is produced with the help of two factors of production, capital and labor, whose rate of input is $L(t)$. Technological possibilities are represented by a production function

$$Y = F(K,L). \tag{2}$$

Output is to be understood as net output after making good the depreciation of capital. About production all we will say at the moment is that it shows constant returns to scale. Hence the production function is homogeneous of first degree. This amounts to assuming that there is no scarce non-augmentable resource like land. Constant returns to scale seems the natural assumption to make in a theory of growth....

Inserting (2) in (1) we get

$$\dot{K} = sF(K,L). \tag{3}$$

This is one equation in two unknowns. One way to close the system would be to add a demand-for-labor equation: marginal physical productivity of labor equals real wage rate; and a supply-of-labor equation. The latter could take the general form of making labor supply a function of the real wage, or more classically of putting the real wage equal to a conventional subsistence level. In any case there would be three equations in the three unknowns K, L, real wage.

Instead we proceed more in the spirit of the Harrod model. As a result of exogenous population growth the labor force increases at a constant relative rate n. In the absence of technological change n is Harrod's natural rate of growth. Thus:

$$L(t) = L_0 e^{nt}. \tag{4}$$

In (3) L stands for total employment; in (4) L stands for the available supply of labor. By identifying the two we are assuming that full employment is perpetually maintained. When we insert (4) in (3) to get

$$\dot{K} = sF(K, L_0 e^{nt}) \tag{5}$$

we have the basic equation which determines the time path of capital accumulation that must be followed if all available labor is to be employed.

Alternatively (4) can be looked at as a supply curve of labor. It says that the exponentially growing labor force is offered for employment completely inelastically. The labor supply curve is a vertical line which shifts to the right in time as the labor force grows according to (4). Then the real wage rate adjusts so that all available labor is employed, and the marginal productivity equation determines the wage rate which will actually rule.[1]

In summary, (5) is a differential equation in the single variable $K(t)$. Its solution gives the only time profile of the community's capital stock which will fully employ the available labor. Once we know the time path of capital stock and that of the labor force, we can compute from the production function the corresponding time path of real output. The marginal productivity equation determines the time path of the real wage rate. There is also involved an assumption of full employment of the available stock of capital. At any point of time the pre-existing stock of capital (the result of previous accumulation) is inelastically supplied. Hence there is a similar marginal productivity equation for capital which determines the real rental per unit of time for the services of capital stock. The process can be viewed in this way: at any moment of time the available labor supply is given by (4) and the available stock of capital is also a datum. Since the real return to factors will adjust to bring about full employment of labor and capital we can use the production function (2) to find the current rate of output. Then the propensity to save tells us how much of net output will be saved and invested. Hence we know the net accumulation of capital during the current period. Added to the already accumulated stock this gives the capital available for the next period, and the whole process can be repeated.

POSSIBLE GROWTH PATTERNS

To see if there is always a capital accumulation path consistent with any rate of growth of the labor force, we must study the differential equation (5) for the qualitative nature of its solutions. Naturally without specifying the

[1] The complete set of three equations consists of (3), (4) and $[\partial F(K, L)/\partial L] = w$.

exact shape of the production function we can't hope to find the exact solution. But certain broad properties are surprisingly easy to isolate, even graphically.

To do so we introduce a new variable $r = K/L$, the ratio of capital to labor. Hence we have $K = rL = rL_0 e^{nt}$. Differentiating with respect to time we get

$$\dot{K} = L_0 e^{nt}\dot{r} + nrL_0 e^{nt}.$$

Substitute this in (5):

$$(\dot{r} + nr)L_0 e^{nt} = sF(K, L_0 e^{nt}).$$

But because of constant returns to scale we can divide both variables in F by $L = L_0 e^{nt}$ provided we multiply F by the same factor. Thus

$$(\dot{r} + nr)L_0 e^{nt} = sL_0 e^{nt} F\left(\frac{K}{L_0 e^{nt}}, 1\right)$$

and dividing out the common factor we arrive finally at

$$\dot{r} = sF(r, 1) - nr. \tag{6}$$

Here we have a differential equation involving the capital-labor ratio alone.

This fundamental equation can be reached somewhat less formally. Since $r = K/L$, the relative rate of change of r is the difference between the relative rates of change of K and L. That is:

$$\frac{\dot{r}}{r} = \frac{\dot{K}}{K} - \frac{\dot{L}}{L}.$$

Now first of all $\dot{L}/L = n$. Secondly $\dot{K} = sF(K, L)$. Making these substitutions:

$$\dot{r} = r\frac{sF(K, L)}{K} - nr.$$

Now divide L out of F as before, note that $L/K = 1/r$ and we get (6) again.

The function $F(r, 1)$ appearing in (6) is easy to interpret. It is the total product curve as varying amounts r of capital are employed with one unit of labor. Alternatively it gives output per worker as a function of capital per worker. Thus (6) states that the rate of change of the capital-labor ratio is the difference of two terms, one representing the increment of capital and one the increment of labor.

When $\dot{r} = 0$, the capital-labor ratio is a constant, and the capital stock must be expanding at the same rate as the labor force, namely n. (The warranted rate of growth, warranted by the appropriate real rate of return to capital, equals the natural rate.) In Figure 5.2, the ray through the origin with slope n represents the function nr. The other curve is the function $sF(r, 1)$. It is here drawn to pass through the origin and convex upward: no output unless both inputs are positive, and diminishing marginal productivity of capital, as would be the case, for example, with the Cobb–Douglas function. At the point of intersection $nr = sF(r,1)$ and $\dot{r} = 0$. If the capital-labor ratio r^* should ever be established, it will be maintained, and capital and labor will grow thenceforward in proportion. By constant returns to scale, real output will

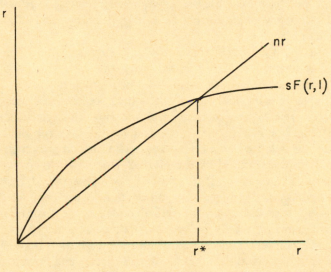

Fig. 5.2

also grow at the same relative rate n, and output per head of labor force will be constant.

But if $r \neq r^*$, how will the capital-labor ratio develop over time? To the right of the intersection point, when $r > r^*$, $nr > sF(r,1)$ and from (6) we see that r will decrease toward r^*. Conversely if initially $r < r^*$, the graph shows that $nr < sF(r,1)$, $\dot{r} > 0$, and r will increase toward r^*. Thus the equilibrium value r^* is *stable*. Whatever the initial value of the capital-labor ratio, the system will develop *toward* a state of balanced growth at the natural rate. The time path of capital and output will not be exactly exponential except asymptotically.[2] If the initial capital stock is below the equilibrium ratio, capital and output will grow at a faster pace than the labor force until the equilibrium ratio is approached. If the initial ratio is above the equilibrium value, capital and output will grow more slowly than the labor force. The growth of output is always intermediate between those of labor and capital. [...]

[2] There is an exception to this. If $K = 0$, $r = 0$ and the system can't get started; with no capital there is no output and hence no accumulation. But this equilibrium is unstable: the slightest windfall capital accumulation will start the system off toward r^*.

5.3 The Neoclassical Growth Model: A Critique*

[...]

In recent journals several respected economists have joined the attack on growth-cyclical models of the Harrod–Domar–Hicks variety. I submit that these models are such, in their inspiration and assumptions, that the attacks can be successful only with the inclusion of an apparently unintended target — Keynes. I propose to make clear the Keynesian content of the growth models and to redress somewhat the current balance by defending and building upon the Keynesian heritage.

The banners of the attackers are strikingly similar. James Tobin rebels against the concept of 'straight and narrow paths from which the slightest deviation spells disaster'.[1] Kenneth Boulding ridicules the 'H–D–H' or 'Hiccup' dynamic with its 'dismal', 'gloomy', 'masochistic' prophecies.[2] Robert Solow rejects 'the characteristic and powerful conclusion of the Harrod–Domar line of thought ... that even for the long run the economic system is at best balanced on a knife-edge of equilibrium growth'.[3] All three see the basic problem raised by the Harrod–Domar–Hicks growth model enthusiasts as the unique result of (arbitrary and unwarranted) assumptions of fixed proportions of the factors of production. More completely, in the words of Tobin, 'Contemporary theoretical models of the business cycle and of economic growth typically possess two related characteristics: (1) they assume production functions that allow for no substitution between factors and (2) the variables are all real magnitudes; monetary and price phenomena have no significance' (p. 103). Generally, the attackers argue that with consideration of variable-factor proportions and flexible prices, *unlike* in the Harrod–Domar–Hicks models, not one but a variety of warranted rates of growth become possible and the economy will be free to adjust to whatever rate is appropriate for full employment.

WHAT HARROD, DOMAR AND HICKS REALLY SAID

It can be shown quickly that the growth models *did* encompass variable factor proportions and reasonable operation of the money–price mechanism. First, in Harrod's formulation, G_w, the warranted or self-sustaining rate of growth, depends upon s, the proportion of income saved (or that proportion remaining after saving is utilized in 'autonomous' investment and export balances), C_r, the 'required' or equilibrium, current capital–output ratio which leaves entrepreneurs satisfied, and d^* (for 'deepening'),[4] the proportion

* From R. Eisner, 'On Growth Models and the Neo-Classical Resurgence', *Economic Journal*, 1958.

[1] 'A Dynamic Aggregative Model', *Journal of Political Economy*, Vol. LXIII (April 1955), 103–15.

[2] 'In Defense of Statics', *Quarterly Journal of Economics*, Vol. LXIX (November 1955), especially pp. 492–5.

[3] 'A Contribution to the Theory of Economic Growth', *Quarterly Journal of Economics*, Vol. LXX (February 1956), 65–94.

[4] Harrod used the symbol d to denote deepening; we have changed this to d^* in order to avoid confusion with the differential and derivative symbol, d.

of output absorbed in lengthening the production process or increasing the capital–output ratio. Algebraically,

$$G_w = \frac{s - d^*}{C_r} \tag{1}$$

or
$$G_w C_r + d^* = s \tag{1.1}$$

In this latter form the above equation expressed directly the condition of equality between the proportion of output for which there is investment demand $(G_w C_r + d)$ and the proportion of output saved (s).[5] If the actual rate of growth is less than the warranted rate, investment demand must then be less than saving, and the rate of growth of output and (eventually) the rate of output must turn down. But if G_n, the '*natural*' rate of growth or maximum rate of growth of which the economy is capable under conditions of full employment, is less than G_w, then the *actual* rate at full employment would have to be less than G_w. It follows that investment demand would have to be less than saving at full employment. Thus full employment could at best represent a momentary position of disequilibrium. A critical aspect of the problem, then, can be formulated as how to prevent G_w from exceeding G_n. One way to do this is to have deepening—a positive value of d^*. Harrod states explicitly, 'd may have a positive value because of the nature of the inventions occurring. It may also have a positive value because the rate of interest is falling. Our aim should be to get such a progressive reduction in the rate of interest that

$$G_w C_r = s - d = G_n C_r.'$$

Harrod adds, 'If d is positive, C_r will increase through time, and may eventually become so great as to enable us to dispense with d.'

[5] If we write capital as

$$K = Y \cdot \frac{K}{Y} \tag{1.2}$$

investment can be written

$$I = \frac{dK}{dt} = \frac{K}{Y}\frac{dY}{dt} + Y\frac{d(K/Y)}{dt} \tag{1.3}$$

and the ratio of investment to income is

$$\frac{I}{Y} = \frac{d \log Y}{dt} \cdot \frac{K}{Y} + \frac{d(K/Y)}{dt} \tag{1.4}$$

For the equilibrium condition described by the warranted rate of growth it is presumed that K/Y, the actual, current capital-output ratio, is the ratio currently *demanded*, and therefore equals C_r. Then if $d(K/Y)/dt$, or 'deepening', is taken as the time rate at which entrepreneurs *demand* (*desire*) that the capital-output ratio change, I/Y is the ratio of investment *demand* to output. The warranted rate of growth is that value of $d \log Y/dt$ (Harrod's G) for which

$$\frac{d \log Y}{dt} \cdot \frac{K}{Y} + \frac{d(K/Y)}{dt} = \frac{I}{Y} = s = \frac{S}{Y}, \tag{1.5}$$

or that value which makes investment demand equal saving.

Now, increasing capital intensity stemming from lower interest rates implies changing factor proportions and indeed, with linear, homogenous production functions (as assumed by Solow and Tobin), changes in the capital–output ratio must mean changes in factor proportions. Thus Harrod is saying that factor proportions *may* change so much—the economy *may* get so capital intensive—that the rate of growth necessary to absorb saving (the 'warranted' rate, G_w) will be reduced to an acceptable level. But, Harrod continues, 'The question we now have to ask is whether there will be any natural tendency for the rate of interest to come down sufficiently. *This is the crux of the matter* [emphasis added, R. E.], the crux, perhaps, of that modern economic situation to which we shall revert, when the post-war shortages cease.' I submit that there can be no doubt that in Harrod's model factor proportions are quite variable and the money–price mechanism is free to operate as it will; there is no uneconomic, arbitrary, technological constraint. However, as more capital is used, other things remaining equal, the return on capital must fall. The difficulty is that this fall may conflict with the Keynesian floor to the rate of interest or, more generally, with the rate of return on capital which entrepreneurs will find acceptable.

Domar, similarly, is clear in pointing out that the crucial issue is not whether capital–output ratios are fixed but rather whether they are free to adjust in such a manner as to eliminate 'The Problem of Capital Accumulation'. Raising the question of the American economy's ability to continue indefinitely absorbing new capital at its rapid post-war rate, Domar writes:

> Implicit in this worry is the belief that the possibilities of the so-called deepening of capital (in the sense of an increasing ratio of capital to output) are limited. Therefore the amount of capital that the economy can absorb, at a given income level and over a given period of time, is limited as well. ... We have thus assumed, at least for the purpose of this discussion, that there exists a fairly stable ratio between annual output (or national income) and the capital stock needed for its production, this ratio to be indicated by the letter *s*. While, strictly speaking, we shall treat *s* as a given constant, it need not be so. It is certainly not the same among various firms and industries. The national average (if such exists) can be made a function of time, interest rate, or of something else. *But it must have some stability, because if s can be anything, our argument falls through and we are back at the Knight–Simons Position* [that 'investment opportunities are practically unlimited'].

Finally, Hicks would have cyclical fluctuations about a growth trend develop with any of a wide variety of capital–output ratios (as well as saving ratios and lags). Hicks argues that any values of the accelerator above the 'Upper Point' will generate a 'strong' cycle when equilibrium is disturbed, values merely above the 'Middle Point' will lead the system into strong cycles, and even values merely above the 'Lower Point' will contribute to some (damped) cyclical fluctuations. And Hicks devotes much space in his 'inspection of the ceiling' and his analysis of 'the monetary factor' to a consideration of whether the forces that transform the accelerator or the desired capital–output ratios are likely to eliminate the troublesome instability and departures from full employment which the H–D–H models all suggest. Hicks' answer, of course, is not encouraging. But again, the difficulty is due to incapacities of adjustment of the monetary framework and of the economic system generally and not an arbitrary assumption of (technologically determined) corners in the production isoquants.

'A DYNAMIC AGGREGATIVE MODEL' WITH SOME KEYNESIAN PARAMETERS

The issues may be fairly joined by constructing a model which draws heavily upon the elegant presentations of two of the critics, Solow and Tobin, and utilises such a model to consider conditions or assumptions sufficient to give the peculiar or particular Harrod–Domar–Hicks results. We shall consider first the factor-proportion question, assuming initially that private saving equals the change in physical capital and is some constant ratio of output. Later we shall enlarge the area of debate by introducing a more general saving function, complete with a 'Pigou effect' and a new 'dynamic Pigou theorem'.

The Production Function, Factor Proportions and the Rate of Profit

Let us assume, with Solow and Tobin, that net output is a linear, homogeneous function of capital and labour:

$$Y = F(K,L) \tag{2}$$

and that output consists of only one good, which may be consumed or retained as capital (invested). Writing $r = K/L$ for the capital–labour ratio, we may, on the basis of the homogeneity assumption, factor out L and rewrite the production function:

$$Y = L \cdot F(r,1) \tag{3}$$

We may further assume diminishing marginal returns to each factor of production, throughout the economically relevant range of factor proportions, so that, in particular,

$$\frac{d^2 F}{dr^2} < 0 \tag{4}$$

But since in equilibrium the rate of profit, i, is presumed to equal the net marginal product of capital, we may write

$$i = F_K \equiv F_r \tag{5}$$

and, consequently, substituting in (4),

$$\frac{di}{dr} < 0 \tag{6}$$

In words, i must be a monotonic, decreasing function of r; an increase in the capital–labour ratio must mean a decrease in the rate of profit.

Taking Harrod's system as representative for our purposes, we may express his symbols as

$$C_r = \frac{K}{Y} = r\frac{L}{Y} = \frac{r}{F(r,1)} \tag{7}$$

and

$$d* = \frac{d(K/Y)}{dt} = \frac{dC_r}{dr} \cdot \frac{dr}{dt} \tag{8}$$

where r is the capital–labour ratio corresponding to the equilibrium capital–output ratio, C_r, and

$$\frac{dC_r}{dr} = \frac{F(r,1) - rF_r}{[F(r,1)]^2} \tag{9}$$

Hence, substituting in (1) and simplifying terms, and denoting $F(r,1)$ by F,

$$G_w = \left(\frac{d \log Y}{dt}\right)_w = \frac{s}{r} \cdot F - \frac{d \log r}{dt} + \frac{d \log F}{dt} \tag{10}[6]$$

But since $F(r,1)$ is total output per unit of labour and rF_r is the return to capital per unit of labour, for all economically relevant values of r (where the share of capital is less than unity) we obtain from (9) the condition that

$$\frac{dC_r}{dr} > 0 \tag{11}$$

or that Harrod's C_r, the capital–output ratio, varies in the same direction as

[6] Noting that

$$\frac{d \log F}{dt} = \frac{d \log Y/L}{dt} = \frac{d \log Y}{dt} - \frac{d \log L}{dt} \tag{10.1}$$

we may write the actual rate of growth of output

$$\frac{d \log Y}{dt} = \frac{d \log K}{dt} - \left(\frac{d \log K}{dt} - \frac{d \log L}{dt}\right) + \frac{d \log F}{dt} \tag{10.2}$$

Since saving is presumed to be realised (whether consistent with entrepreneurial equilibrium or not),

$$\frac{s}{r} \cdot F = \frac{sL \cdot F}{K} = \frac{1}{K}\frac{dK}{dt} = \frac{d \log K}{dt} \tag{10.3}$$

so that, substituting in (10.2),

$$\frac{d \log Y}{dt} = \frac{s}{r} \cdot F - \left(\frac{d \log K}{dt} - \frac{d \log L}{dt}\right) + \frac{d \log F}{dt} \tag{10.4}$$

But then, where

$$\frac{d \log K}{dt} - \frac{d \log L}{dt} = \frac{d \log r}{dt} \tag{10.5}$$

(10.4) becomes identical with (10): the actual rate of growth of output equals the warranted rate when the capital-labour ratio is actually changing at the rate $d \log r/dt$ consistent with entrepreneurial equilibrium.

the capital–labour ratio. From (8) and (11),

$$d^* \gtreqless 0 \text{ as } \frac{dr}{dt} \gtreqless 0 \tag{12}$$

or deepening depends upon an increase in the capital–labour ratio: more-over,

$$\frac{dd^*}{d\left(\frac{dr}{dt}\right)} > 0 \tag{13}$$

i.e., deepening is a monotonically increasing function of the rate of change of the capital–labour ratio. Now, dismissing negative values of C_r, as economically irrelevant, and negative values of $s-d^*$ as unlikely and un-interesting in the present context, we see from (1) that

$$\partial G_w = \frac{\partial G_w}{\partial C_r} < 0 \tag{14}$$

and

$$\frac{\partial G_w}{\partial d^*} < 0 \tag{15}$$

Then, combining (14) and (11),

$$\frac{\partial G_w}{\partial r} = \frac{\partial G_w}{\partial C_r} \cdot \frac{dC_r}{dr} < 0 \tag{16}$$

and combining (15) and (13),

$$\frac{\partial G_w}{\partial\left(\frac{dr}{dt}\right)} = \frac{\partial G_w}{\partial d} \cdot \frac{dd^*}{d\left(\frac{dr}{dt}\right)} < 0 \tag{17}[7]$$

[7] These results may also be obtained directly in terms of r. Again denoting $Y/L = F(r,1)$ by F, we may write

$$C_r = \frac{K}{L} \cdot \frac{L}{Y} = \frac{r}{F} \tag{16.1}$$

Then, substituting in (1),

$$G_w = (s-d^*)\frac{F}{r} \tag{16.2}$$

The partial derivative of G_w with respect to r, assuming s and d^* constant, is then

$$\frac{\partial G_w}{\partial r} = -(s-d^*)\frac{(F-rF_r)}{r^2} \tag{16.3}$$

As explained above in regard to (11), we may take $F-rF_r$, the relative share of labour, as positive. Hence, where

$$s-d^* = \text{constant} > 0, \quad \frac{\partial G_w}{\partial r} < 0 \tag{16.4}$$

And the partial derivative of G_w with respect to d^*, with s and r assumed unchanged, is

$$\frac{\partial G_w}{\partial d^*} = -\frac{F}{r} > 0 \tag{17.1}$$

In words again, Harrod's warranted rate of growth may be reduced by an increase in the capital–labour ratio (16) as well as by an increase in the rate of change of the capital–labour ratio (17).

But now we shall introduce some reasonable parameters into our production function. Critics of the growth models deal with functions which implicitly or explicitly (like the Cobb–Douglas illustration Solow employs) imply the assumption that the marginal net product of capital is always positive, regardless of how high the capital–labour ratio rises; barring demand problems it must always pay to invest. This, indeed, is one of the 'crucial' assumptions[8] on which the growth model *critiques* rest. It embodies again the optimistic notion of unlimited investment opportunities; it should not be surprising that it yields optimistic conclusions. Let us, however, in curiously more classical vein, recognize that in any given period, or with a given production function, there is a limit to the extent to which greater round-aboutness of production will pay for itself. All we are arguing is that with a given quantity of labour there is some finite amount of capital at which the diminishing *net* marginal return to capital will reach zero. With more than that amount of capital the marginal net product of capital will be negative; additional capital will not realize, and hence should not be expected to realize, sufficient returns during its life-time to pay for itself. We thus add the further description of our production function,

$$F_K \gtreqless 0 \text{ as } K \gtreqless K_0, \ L = L_0 \tag{18}$$

or utilizing the homogeneity assumption and defining $r_0 = K_0/L_0$,

$$i = F_K \equiv F_r \gtreqless 0 \text{ as } r \gtreqless r_0 \tag{19}$$

Now the existence of r_0, a limit to the profitable extensibility of the capital–labour ratio, will prove sufficient to admit the possibility of the 'H–D–H' difficulties,[9] but, if we wish to get more Keynesian, we can add a liquidity trap at say i_1, where $i_1 > 0$ and is the rate of return equal to the floor to the rate of interest. To i_1 will correspond some capital–labor ratio, say r_1, where $r_1 < r_0$ and

$$i = F_K \equiv F_r \gtreqless i_1 \text{ as } r \gtreqless r_1 \tag{20}$$

---

[8] Solow warns that: 'A "crucial" assumption is one on which the conclusions do depend sensitively, and it is important that crucial assumptions be reasonably realistic. When the results of a theory seem to flow specifically from a special crucial assumption, then if the assumption is dubious, the results are suspect' (*loc. cit.*, p. 65). But he charges this to the Harrold-Domar model.

[9] The simplifying assumption of linear homogeneity of the production function enables us to meet the Solow-Tobin type *critiques* on their own ground, but it is a stronger assumption than we require. The Harrod–Domar–Hicks problem may be exhibited by any production function in which, with the given (presumably exogenous) growth of labour supply and the rate of capital accumulation consistent with the saving function, the marginal net product of capital is declining, and has no non-negative lower bound.

Hence there is an upper limit to the value of r, which may be denoted by r_0 or r_1, depending upon whether we wish to assume that the rate of (net) profit can fall to zero or only to some value above zero. Since from (16) it can be seen that G_w is a monotonically decreasing function of r, for any given values of s and d^* (e.g., $d^* = 0 = dr/dt$), there is then a lower limit to G_w. If this lower limit is still higher than the actual or maintainable rate of growth the economy in in for the H–D–H maladies.

But what if there is deepening, that is, d^* and dr/dt are positive? Here we are referring not to a *higher* but to an *increasing* capital–labour ratio. As we noted in (17), the greater the rate of increase of the capital–labour ratio, other things equal, the less the warranted rate of growth. Thus we may concede that if the warranted rate of growth is too high there is always some rate of change of factor proportions which will be sufficient to make the warranted rate of growth any necessary lower figure. We are not, however, out of the woods. For, in accordance with (6), an increasing value of r must mean a decreasing rate of profit. But since $i \geq 0$ or $i \geq i_1$, eventually (with $dr/dt > \varepsilon; \varepsilon > 0$),

$$\text{as } r \gtreqqless r_0 \text{ or as } r \gtreqqless r_1, \frac{di}{dt} \gtreqqless 0 \tag{21}$$

Then, writing

$$\frac{dr}{dt} = \frac{dr}{dF_r} \cdot \frac{dF_r}{dt} \tag{22}$$

we can see that since, as stated in (5), in equilibrium, the rate of profit equals the marginal product of capital or $i = F_r$, as

$$\frac{di}{dt}\left(= \frac{dF_r}{dt} \right) \gtreqqless 0, \frac{dr}{dt} \gtreqqless 0 \quad \text{unless} \quad \frac{dr}{dF_r} \gtreqqless -\infty$$

and, substituting $di = dF_r$, in (22) and (22) in (8), we derive,

$$d^* = \frac{dC_r}{dr} \cdot \frac{dr}{di} \cdot \frac{di}{dt} \tag{24}$$

To paraphrase our equations once more, where the capital–labour ratio is increasing $(dr/dt > 0)$, deepening is taking place $(d^* > 0)$, and then, as Harrod (among others) points out, the warranted rate of growth is reduced and thereby relief is found. But deepening $(d^* > 0)$ requires a falling marginal net product of capital, and hence a falling rate of profit $(dF_r/dt = di/dt < 0)$. There is a limit to how far the rate of profit can fall, and hence, unless the marginal net product of capital falls asymptotically to this limit (so that $dr/dF_r \to -\infty$, the unlimited investment opportunities argument again), there is a limit to how long any given rate of deepening (any given positive value of $d*$) can be maintained. Thus we should observe that the rate of deepening is curbed not only by price and money rigidities and direct institutional constraints on the rate of fall of the equilibrium rate of return on investment (di/dt); whatever the freedom from constraints, as long as there is a lower limit to i (even if only at $i = 0$), i cannot fall fast for long withour hitting bottom.

Our system has been endowed explicitly with the neo-classical complements of variable factor proportions, flexible prices, cash-balance effects and a *fixed* linear, homogeneous production function (thus ruling out the employment of capital-using innovations like a *Deus ex machina* to set the plot straight). By way of summary, we shall describe the operation of this system when confronted with a rate of growth in the labour supply (ultimately Harrod's 'natural rate of growth') less than the 'proper' full-employment rate warranted by the supply of saving. And by way of simplification of exposition we shall consider the case (suggested by Tobin) where the supply of labour is 'completely inelastic... with respect to the real wage and with respect to time'.

Since the rate of saving is (by hypothesis) positive, the ratio of capital to labour must increase continuously and the rate of profit must fall continuously. As the rate of profit falls the community becomes disposed to take larger and larger proportions of increments of wealth in the form of money. With a fixed stock of money, successive increments of wealth will then require successive declines in the level of prices. But as the rate of profit approaches the value of i at which M_i approaches minus infinity we find the community approaching a situation where no further increase in the stock of capital and decline in the rate of profit is consistent with portfolio balance, regardless of the decline in the price level (or alternately, increase in the quantity of money). The rate of profit cannot (in equilibrium) fall below the point of infinite elasticity of the demand for money because the community stops accepting further increases in capital (which is what lowers the value of i) as i reaches that lower limit. But this means that positive saving can take place only in the form of the increased cash balances stemming from falling prices. And it is only thus that the relatively too large (positive) warranted rate of growth is reducible to equality with the natural rate.

There is no assurance that such a solution, of perpetually falling prices, would prove dynamically stable when we admit the role of expectations. For price declines generating expectations of further price declines would increase the relative attractiveness of money as compared to physical capital, and might leave no point of equilibrium as long as there were physical capital of which individuals might dispose. I shall not attempt to explore further the difficulties along these lines, but, in any event, it is on this solution of perpetually *falling* prices—a 'dynamic Pigou theorem'—that a rejection of the *possibility* of the growth model problems would have to rest.

CONCLUSION

The implications of recent models of economic growth and fluctuation of the Harrod–Domar–Hicks variety have been challenged as the consequence of arbitrary assumptions of rigid technological relationships and/or rigid price relationships. This challenge is unfounded.

For the Harrod–Domar–Hicks models require no more in the way of a production function than most of us would be willing to grant as reasonable. Specifically, they do require a schedule of *net* marginal productivity of capital declining in such a way that there is a limit to the capital–labour (or capital–output) ratio which is economically feasible. This limit may be reached at the point where the marginal efficiency of investment equals the rate of interest set by the Keynesian liquidity trap. It may even be reached only at the point where the marginal net product of capital is zero (and the marginal efficiency of investment also zero if expectations are founded on reality). But limit there must be.

And if there must be an *upper* limit to the capital–output ratio, there must, for any saving ratio, be a *lower* limit to the rate of growth of output (or labour) which will be consistent with the saving forthcoming. This minimum 're-quired' rate of growth can then be reduced only to the extent the saving ratio can be reduced. If the saving ratio will not adjust automatically, via interest-rate changes or 'Pigou effects', to whatever value is consistent with whatever rate of growth of output obtains, then there remains some minimum 'warranted', 'equilibrium' or 'full-employment' rate of growth. This rate of growth is thus determined jointly by the upper limit to the automatic, free adjustment of the capital–output ratio and the lower limit to the automatic free adjustment of the saving ratio. If we do not obtain this rate of growth we are in some kind of trouble—an underemployment trouble which the models merely seek to explain, not create.

We are not always in this kind of trouble. We may not always face a problem of capital–output ratios and saving ratios determined by free economic forces being inconsistent with underlying determinants of economic growth such as population and the development of additional natural resources. The problem may become remote for substantial periods of time because of various social or governmental pressures (intended or unintended) upon these ratios. But whether or not the problem is at any moment of time crying for solution, it does exist. And in view of the historical record of cyclical instability, uneven growth and recurring periods of unemployment in the (private-profit-motivated) capitalistic economies we have known, the problem seems important. It is perhaps a mark of the technological backwardness of economic theory that the 'H–D–H dynamic' arrived so late. It will certainly (in the view of this observer) be a mistake to hasten to discard it.

5.4 Money in a Neoclassical Growth Model*
[...]

EXTENSIONS TO A MONETARY ECONOMY

Assumptions and Problems

The model of economic growth developed in preceding sections is a 'real' model, in which the only asset available for holding by the public is material capital; this section extends the model to take account of the existence of money. To do so, it is assumed that money exists in the form of non-interest-bearing currency (fiat money) issued by a government or issuing agency ('the monetary authority'), additions to the money supply being effected by the printing of additional currency and the distribution of it to the public. The public is assumed to regard money as net wealth; in technical terms, the model is an 'outside money' model. It should be emphasized that the assumptions that money is non-interest-bearing and that it is treated as net wealth are crucial to the analysis.

Following the classical tradition of monetary theory, it is assumed that wages and prices are perfectly flexible, in the specific sense that the real value of the public's holdings of money is instantaneously adjusted to the desired level of real cash balances. The desired level of real cash balances per person is assumed to be a function, first, of the level of per capita income or per capita wealth, either non-human or total non-monetary wealth (in the present model this is a matter of indifference, since in the absence of technical change income per head, capital per head, and the capitalized value of human labour services are uniquely correlated); second, of the rate of return on material capital; and third, of the expected rate of return on money balances. For simplicity, it is assumed that, *ceteris paribus*, the desired level of real cash balances bears a fixed ratio to whichever scale variable, income or the two definitions of wealth, is assumed to determined monetary and saving behaviour, so that this ratio is a function of the two rate of return variables. The rate of return on capital, on the assumption that capital is the same stuff as output and lasts forever, is the marginal product of capital. The expected rate of return on money balances is the negative of the expected rate of change of prices, being negative when prices are expected to rise, zero when prices are expected to remain constant, and positive when prices are expected to fall. It is assumed that the expected rate of change of prices is equal to the actual rate of change of prices; the actual rate of change of prices, in its turn, is determined by the rate of growth of real output, and the rate of growth of the money supply provided by the monetary authority. Whatever the monetary authority does with the supply of money, the desired level of

* From H. G. Johnson, *Essays in Monetary Economics* (London: George Allen & Unwin Ltd., 1967; Cambridge, Mass.: Harvard University Press, 1969), Ch. 4: 'Money in a Neo-Classical One-Sector Growth Model'. Reprinted by permission of the publishers, © Harry G. Johnson, 1967, 1969.

real balances will be secured by an appropriate movement of the price level; but the required price level change will determine the rate of return on real balances, and hence influence desired real balances and through them the growth of the economy. Further, the increase in real balances secured in this way will influence the accumulation of real capital, the mechanism depending on the theory of saving employed.

Three alternative assumptions about saving will be explored, two being variants of the Keynesian assumption of a constant ratio of saving to income and the third being that saving behaviour is governed by a desired ratio of wealth to real output. The two variants respectively ignore and take account of the utility yield of real balances as an item of real income influencing saving. The analysis based on the first assumption includes some remarks on the Keynesian problem of a possible minimum to the rate of return at which real investment will be undertaken.

The main emphasis of the analysis is placed on two related problems: the 'neutrality' of money in the context of economic growth, and the possibility of using monetary policy to influence the growth of the economy. In all three models, money is by assumption 'neutral' in the comparative-statics sense that a once-for-all change in the quantity of money, superimposed on a trend rate of growth of the money supply maintained by the monetary authority, would produce a once-for-all change in the price level with no real effects on the economy. In the context of growth theory, however, the question arises whether money is 'neutral' in the more relevant sense that a difference in the rate of change of the money supply maintained by the monetary authority would make no difference to the speed with which the economy approaches its equilibrium growth path, and, most fundamentally, that a difference in the rate of change of the money supply would make no difference to the output and consumption per head characteristic of the equilibrium growth path. If money is not neutral in the former sense, monetary policy can accelerate or retard the economy's approach to long-run equilibrium growth, and if it is not neutral in the latter sense, monetary policy can influence the characteristics of equilibrium growth.

For analytical simplicity, the monetary authority is assumed, not to fix the rate of growth of the money supply, but to govern the rate of increase of the money supply so as to achieve a target rate of price inflation or deflation, a higher rate of inflation or a lower rate of deflation requiring a higher rate of monetary expansion *ceteris paribus*. This assumption implies that, if the economy starts below its long-run equilibrium ratio of capital to output, the money supply is expanded at a declining rate as capital accumulates, the rate of expansion converging on the rate of growth of population plus the monetary authority's target rate of price change (which may be negative). Also, the policy question of whether the monetary authority can influence the characteristics of the equilibrium growth path is cast in terms of whether it can shift the economy towards the golden rule path. Though, as previously argued, there is no real justification for regarding such an objective as desirable, this formulation of the problem seems consistent with the spirit of growth theory.

The Keynesian Constant Savings Ratio Model

On the assumption that aggregate saving is a constant proportion of aggregate income, the growth of real balances as the economy grows, whether by increasing capital per worker or by growth in the number of workers at a constant ratio of capital to labour only, appears as an addition to current real output in the reckoning of the current income from which savings are made, and therefore raises the ratio of saving to output. However, the growth of real balances also absorbs saving, since the additional real balances must be held, so that the net effect is a reduction in the ratio of savings invested in the creation of material capital to output, as compared with the ratio that would obtain in a pure barter economy. Given the rate of growth of aggregate output, the absolute increase of real balances will be greater, and therefore the reduction in the ratio of real capital investment to output will be greater, the greater is the desired ratio of real balances to output. Actually, the rate of growth of aggregate output cannot be taken as given, but will be interdependent with the ratio of real investment to output; but it is intuitively evident and can be proved that, allowing for this relationship, the ratio of real investment to output will vary inversely with the ratio of real balances to output.[1]

Since the rate of return on real capital is fixed by the capital to labour ratio (or the level of output per head) the desired ratio of real balances to output will vary inversely with the rate of increase of prices maintained by the monetary authority. Thus the ratio of material capital investment to output will vary directly with the rate of increase of prices maintained by the monetary authority. This in turn implies that the more expansionary is

[1] Output per head is $y = f(k)$. Let disposable income per head be $y' = y(1+bg)$ where b is the ratio of real balances to output demanded and g is the growth rate. Saving will be sy', from which must be deducted savings devoted to increasing real balances bgy, leaving real savings

$$s'(y) = sy\left[1 - bg\left(\frac{1}{s}-1\right)\right].$$

Now

$$\frac{f'}{y}s'(y) = f's - f'bg(1-s) = \frac{f's}{1+f'b(1-s)}.$$

Hence

$$s'(y) = sy\left[1 - \frac{bf'(1-s)}{1+bf'(1-s)}\right],$$

and it is evident that

$$\frac{\partial s'(y)}{\partial b} < 0.$$

monetary policy, the faster will the economy grow (starting from any level of output per head below the equilibrium level for a barter economy), and the higher will be the level of capital per head at which the economy arrives on its long-run equilibrium growth path.

The mechanics of the model are illustrated in Figure 5.3 ... $O \cdot y'$ is disposable income *per capita*; it is the sum (*per capita*) of output and the current increment of real balances, the latter being determined by output, the ratio

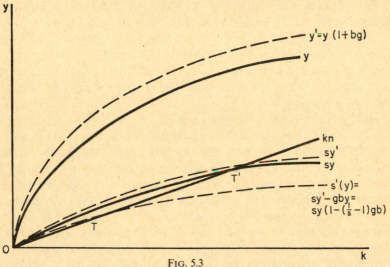

FIG. 5.3

NOTE: y is output per worker, k is capital per worker, Sy is saving per worker, Rn (where n is the rate of growth of population) shows the investment required to maintain capital per head as the labour force grows.

of real balances to output (earned income) b, and the current rate of growth g. Total saving is $O \cdot sy'$ and the saving available for investment in real capital is

$$O \cdot s'(y) = O \cdot sy\left[1 - \left(\frac{1}{s} - 1\right)gb\right].$$

It should be noted that g is itself a function of $s'(y)$, so that one cannot simply shift the $O \cdot y'$ curve to represent the effects of varying the level of b; however, the proof previously mentioned ensures that this heuristic procedure gives the correct answer. Moreover, the prime concern of the analysis is with the equilibrium at the point T at which $O \cdot s'(y)$ crosses the capital requirements curve $O \cdot kn$, and here the rate of growth of output must be $g = n$.[2] The relation between $O \cdot y'$ and $O \cdot y$ is governed by the following conflicting factors. As y rises, the rate of return on real capital must fall, tending to raise

[2] The dynamics of the process of adjustment to the long-run equilibrium growth path, in both this and the models presented subsequently, are complex and raise awkward problems which cannot be readily handled diagrammatically.

the desired ratio of real balances to income and the ratio of y' to y; on the other hand, an increase in y means a decline in the growth rate, for a constant savings ratio, since it implies a higher capital to output ratio and therefore a smaller proportionate 'deepening' of capital per unit of output; and this implies a reduction in the ratio to income of the additional real balances required by growth, and therefore of y' to y. The magnitude of b, the desired ratio of real balances to income, will (*ceteris paribus*) be greater the smaller the target rate of price increase or greater the target rate of price decrease maintained by the monetary authority. Hence the intersection at T of $O \cdot s'(y)$ with $O \cdot kn$ must be farther to the right of the diagram, the lower the target rate of price deflation or higher the target rate of price inflation set by the monetary authority. An upper limit is set by the point T', which would imply a rate of inflation great enough to reduce the desired real balance ratio to negligibility.[3]

In this model, therefore, money is neutral neither in the sense that the rate of convergence on the equilibrium growth path is independent of the rate of monetary expansion, nor in the more fundamental sense that the characteristics of the equilibrium path are independent of monetary policy. It follows that within limits monetary policy in this model can be used to move the economy towards fulfilment of the golden rule conditions. If the economy's saving behaviour causes it to overshoot the golden rule ratio of real investment (accumulation of material capital) to output, this can be counteracted by contraction of the money supply to generate a deflationary price trend. There may be a limit on the application of such a deflationary policy, however; if material capital is desired only for its yield, while money yields utility services, there would be a presumption that investment in real capital would cease if the rate of return on money accruing from deflation exceeded the rate of return on real investment. (In a more general portfolio-balance model, with risk attaching to both assets and risk-aversion, there would be no such presumption.) If, on the other hand, the economy's saving behaviour causes it to fall short of the golden rule ratio of real investment to output, it can be nudged towards that position by an increase in the rate of expansion of the money supply. The extreme limit of such a policy would be a rate of inflation that reduced the ratio of real balances to income to negligibility and raised the ratio of real investment to output to the economy's savings ratio; this ratio might still fall short of that ratio required by the golden rule for maximizing consumption per head.

In this model, as in neo-classical growth models generally, it is assumed that the real savings produced by the savings ratio get invested in capital goods, regardless of the rate of return earned thereon. Keynesian economists frequently assume that investors demand a certain minimum rate of return on real investment, and that rather than take less they will accumulate saving

---

[3] This assumes that the public is precluded from issuing monetary debt to the monetary authority, an assumption that would be less reasonable in a fiscal policy model.

in the form of cash. In this model, the results of such behaviour would be an increase in the real value of cash balances through deflation, until real balances had risen to the level per head required to reduce the ratio of real savings to output to that required for the economy to grow at its long-run equilibrium rate, with an equilibrium capital–labour ratio such as to yield the required minimum rate of return on real investment. This result could be achieved alternatively without deflation by sufficient expansion of the money supply. The assumed investor behaviour, however, is arbitrary, in that it rests on the implicit Keynesian assumption that the (actual and expected) rate of return on money balances is precisely zero; if, instead, it is assumed that the (actual and expected) return on money balances varies inversely with the rate of inflation, and that investors demand a minimum premium of the rate of return on real investment over the rate of return on cash balances, it follows that the long-run growth equilibrium of the economy would involve a rate of return on real investment equal to the required premium, plus the equilibrium growth rate of population, minus the rate of growth of the money supply (the difference between the last two being the rate of return on the money supply); and the monetary authority could, subject to the limits discussed in the previous paragraph, offset the demands of investors for a premium by operating on the rate of growth of the money supply.

To conclude the discussion of this model, it should be noted that the analysis can readily be extended to include Harrod-neutral technical progress, by redefining labour in efficiency-units. [...]

5.5 Technical Progress, Investment, and Economic Growth*

AGGREGATE PRODUCTION FUNCTIONS AND TECHNICAL CHANGE

In a series of papers ... over the last few years, a number of authors have suggested an interesting and important proposition: that by far the larger part of the observed increase in output per head is a consequence of 'technical progress' rather than of increased capital per head. The methods used are not all the same. In particular, some authors have made explicit use of an aggregate production function and others have on the surface avoided this device. Still, I think it fair to say that explicitly or implicitly the model underlying this work may be represented thus: $Q(t) = F(K(t), L(t); t)$ or more specifically

$$Q(t) = B(t)f(K(t), L(t)). \tag{1}$$

* From R. M. Solow, 'Investment and Technical Progress', in K. J. Arrow, S. Karlin, and P. Suppes (Eds.), *Mathematical Methods in the Social Sciences* (Stanford University Press, 1959). Excerpted with the permission of the publishers, Stanford University Press.© 1960 by the Board of Trustees of the Leland Stanford Junior University.

Here, Q, K, and L stand respectively for aggregate output and inputs of physical capital and labor services at time t. One may describe this as an aggregate production function shifting through time. The second and considerably more restrictive representation amounts to the assumption that shifts in the production function are 'neutral' or 'uniform'. There is not much evidence for or against this assumption; since it is a great convenience it will be adopted without comment.

Three other specializations of (1) are sometimes made. The first is to postulate that the production function exhibits constant returns to scale, that is, the F or f is homogeneous of first degree in K and L. A nineteenth-century follower of Malthus and Ricardo would be inclined to believe that since land and other irreplaceable natural resources are implicitly being held constant, a tendency to diminishing returns would show itself. But over historical time few observers would claim to have found this the case, at least not in aggregates that give a heavy weight to manufacturing and other non-extractive industries. Against this, an even older tradition might expect to find increasing returns to scale, as a consequence of an ever-finer division of labor. A delicate empirical question arises here. Over long periods of time one observes a continuing trend increase in K and L. Presumably $B(t)$ is also an increasing function of time. Thus the effects of technical progress and of increasing returns to scale are confounded in the data. If K and L each double and Q increases by 110 per cent, the extra 10 per cent may be due to either effect or to both, and the time series do not provide enough independent variation to settle the allocation with confidence. Once again I will follow the dictates of custom and convenience and assume constant returns to scale.

Secondly, I have stated my belief that the particular functional form adopted for f is a matter of no great consequence. Over the range of K/L actually observed in the United States almost any function of two variables with positive partial derivatives and the right curvature will do fairly well. The time-hallowed favorite is the constant-elasticity Cobb–Douglas function, and I adopt it in what follows. I think this is a safe procedure as long as it is taken frankly as an approximation and no deep distributive meaning is read into the results. My calculations could be carried out in principle with any choice of a production function; the Cobb–Douglas function enables me to carry them out in practice.

Finally, if we approximate $B(t)$ by an exponential, equation (1) is reduced to

$$Q(t) = Be^{\lambda t}L(t)^{\alpha}K(t)^{1-\alpha} \tag{2}$$

In this form the model has been used ... on Norwegian, ... on Finnish, and ... on American data. My own earlier paper can be interpreted in this way ... although my primary purpose at the time was to find a way to avoid the restrictive assumptions and to deal instead with (1) or something even more general.

For the more complicated problem I want to treat now, I have not found any way to improve upon (2).

AN OBJECTION TO THE USUAL FORMULATION

There are other criticisms that can be leveled against any attempt to interpret aggregate economic statistics in terms of (2). There are index-number problems involved in the measurement of each of the variables. In the same vein it may be argued that the aggregate production function is itself a dubious tool. Even waiving all this, it is true that the notion of time-shifts in the function is a confession of ignorance rather than a claim to knowledge; they ought to be analyzed further into such components as improvements in the skill and quality of the labor force, returns to investment in research and education, improvements in technique within industries, and changes in the industrial composition of input and output, etc.

But in this paper I want to take up only one difficulty with (2), a rather different one. It is an implication of (2) that 'technical change' is peculiarly disembodied. It floats down from the outside. If K and L are held constant, equation (2) predicts that output will increase anyway, approximately exponentially at rate λ. If K and L both increase exponentially at rate γ, then output will simply increase at rate $\gamma + \lambda$. In particular, the pace of investment has no influence on the rate at which technique improves. It is as if all technical progress were something like time-and-motion study, a way of improving the organization and operation of inputs without reference to the nature of the inputs themselves. The striking assumption is that old and new capital equipment participate equally in technical change. This conflicts with the casual observation that many if not most innovations need to be embodied in new kinds of durable equipment before they can be made effective. Improvements in technology affect output only to the extent that they are carried into practice either by net capital formation or by the replacement of old-fashioned equipment by the latest models, with a consequent shift in the distribution of equipment by date of birth.

My objective is to reconstruct the model to make allowance for this aspect of reality.

AN ALTERNATIVE MODEL

To this end, it becomes necessary to distinguish capital equipment of different dates of construction or vintages. Let $K_v(t)$ represent the number of machines or units of capital of vintage v (i.e., produced at time v) still in existence at time $t \geqslant v$. At time t, the surviving stock of capital of vintage v will be worked by a certain quantity of labor, $L_v(t)$. If $L(t)$ is the total supply of labor, to be allocated over capital of all vintages, we have

$$L(t) = \int_{-\infty}^{t} L_v(t)\, dv. \tag{3}$$

My assumption is that all technical progress is uniform and approximately exponential over time, and that capital goods at their moment of construction embody all the latest knowledge but share not at all in any further improvements in technology.[1] If $Q_v(t)$ stands for the output produced at time t using equipment of vintage v, then

$$Q_v(t) = Be^{\lambda v} L_v(t)^{\alpha} K_v(t)^{1-\alpha}. \tag{4}$$

Thus the Cobb–Douglas function applies for output produced with capital of given vintage,[2] but it is also evident the multiplicative improvement factor turns itself off the moment that the capital goods take shape.

For $Q(t)$, the total output at time t, we have

$$Q(t) = \int_{-\infty}^{t} Q_v(t) \, dv. \tag{5}$$

The quantity $K_v(v)$ stands for gross investment, the output of capital goods at time v. Call it $I(v)$. I shall make the simplest possible assumption about depreciation, that is, that capital goods are exposed to a constant force of mortality δ. Thus the average length of life of capital is $1/\delta$ and

$$K_v(t) = K_v(v)e^{-\delta(t-v)} = I(v)e^{-\delta(t-v)} \tag{6}$$

The picture is one of a continuum of capital goods of various vintages and corresponding productivity, subject to an exponential life table. At each moment of time the labor force is reshuffled over the existing capital goods. Total output is determined by integrating over all layers of capital stock.

If there is competition in the labor market, all homogeneous labor must receive the same wage regardless of the age of the capital on which it operates. Hence the allocation of labor to capital of various vintages must equalize the marginal productivity of labor in all uses. This will also have

---

[1] It would not be difficult to allow simultaneously for a component of progress that does diffuse equally over old and new capital.

[2] One special feature of (4) depends critically on the multiplicative form of the Cobb-Douglas function. Suppose I write $Q_v(t) = BL_v(t)^{\alpha}[e^{\lambda t/(1-\alpha)}K_v(t)]^{1-\alpha}$. Formally, all technological progress appears as a steady improvement in the quality of capital goods at rate $\lambda/(1-\alpha)$; this accounts for the important role this number will turn out to play. On the surface it seems that by grouping terms differently I could make it appear that only the quality of the labor force improves. But it is not really so. Shortly I shall require the marginal productivity of labor to be equal regardless of the vintage of the capital on which it works. This condition reveals that labor is viewed as homogeneous. Of course I could *completely* reverse the roles of L and K, and then it would be legitimate to speak of sucessive generations of workers as more efficient than their forbears. Or if I were to treat B as a non-constant function of time, I could think of it as representing either pure know-how or improvement in the labor force, irrespective of date of birth. But all this is possible only because the production function is multiplicative. For other production functions that are homogeneous of first degree, one cannot translate a multiplicative shift of the whole function into improvement factors for individual inputs one at a time. (Of course, trivially a multiplicative shift can be thought of as an identical shift in all factors.)

the effect of maximizing the output obtainable from the given total labor force and the given stock of capital goods. Naturally, this does not mean that the marginal product of labor is constant over time, but rather that it is a function of time and independent of v for each t. Let $m(t)$ be the marginal product of labor at time t; then from (4) we have

$$m(t) = \frac{\partial Q_v(t)}{\partial L_v(t)} = \alpha B e^{\lambda v} L_v(t)^{\alpha-1} K_v(t)^{1-\alpha}. \tag{7}$$

Substitute for $K_v(t)$ from (6), solve for $L_v(t)$, and write $\sigma = \delta + \lambda/(1-\alpha)$; the result is

$$L_v(t) = (\alpha B)^{1/(1-\alpha)} e^{-\delta t} m(t)^{1/(\alpha-1)} e^{\sigma v} I(v) = h(t) e^{\sigma v} I(v). \tag{8}$$

If desired, $m(t)$ can then be determined from (3), since

$$L(t) = (\alpha B)^{1/(1-\alpha)} e^{-\delta t} m(t)^{1/(\alpha-1)} \int_{-\infty}^{t} e^{\sigma v} I(v) dv = h(t) \int_{-\infty}^{t} e^{\sigma v} I(v) dv. \tag{9}$$

Substitution of (8) in (4) and simplification yields $Q_v(t) = B e^{-\delta(1-\alpha)t} h(t)^{\alpha} e^{\sigma v} I(v)$ and, from (5), we have

$$Q(t) = B e^{-\delta(1-\alpha)t} h(t)^{\alpha} \int_{-\infty}^{t} e^{\sigma v} I(v) dv. \tag{10}$$

Together, (9) and (10) give

$$Q(t) = B e^{-\delta(1-\alpha)t} L(t)^{\alpha} J(t)^{1-\alpha}, \tag{11}$$

where

$$J(t) = \int_{-\infty}^{t} e^{\sigma v} I(v) dv.$$

This is the equation that replaces the earlier formulation (2). The surface similarity hides some real differences, since $J(t)$ has a more complicated structure than the earlier $K(t)$. But a bit of similarity is regained when one remembers that in (2) the function $K(t)$ must represent net capital stock in the sense of machinery that is still in existence and productive. If we make the exponential life-table assumption, we have

$$K(t) = e^{-\delta t} \int_{-\infty}^{t} e^{\delta v} I(v) dv, \tag{6'}$$

and (2) and (11) will coincide when $\lambda = 0$ and differ otherwise, as differ they must.

If an economy characterized by (2) and (6') and one characterized by (11) and (6) have forever experienced the same rate of gross investment and the same input of labor, and $\lambda \neq 0$, then of course the second economy will have a lower output than the first, and in general a different rate of growth of output. One curiosity does arise. If the two economies have both grown exponentially since the beginning of time, that is, if $L(t)$ and $I(t)$ have both been proportional to $e^{\gamma t}$, then while the second system will still have a lower output than the first, the outputs will remain in proportion and both will grow at the same rate, $\gamma + \lambda$. [...]

ECONOMIC SIGNIFICANCE

When the aggregate production function (2) is estimated from time series for advanced economies, λ always comes out to be around $\cdot 015$ and α to be about $\cdot 75$. From this flows an important conclusion: that the possibility of speeding up economic growth by faster accumulation of capital is extremely limited. This follows because (2) implies

$$\frac{1}{Q}\frac{dQ}{dt} = \lambda + \alpha \frac{1}{L}\frac{dL}{dt} + (1-\alpha)\frac{1}{K}\frac{dK}{dt}.$$

If we take the numerical values suggested and assume the labor force to grow at 1 per cent per year and the capital–output ratio to be about 3, output will grow at about 3 per cent per year if 10 per cent of the national product is invested. If the investment quota is doubled from 10 per cent to 20 per cent, the rate of increase of output rises only to just under 4 per cent. This seems like a meager reward for what is after all a revolution in the speed of accumulation of capital.

The alternative model developed in this paper redresses the balance somewhat and attributes greater importance to capital investment. The reason is, of course, that capital formation is a vehicle for carrying technical change into effect. A numerical illustration of this point will also suggest how deceptive it may be to traffic exclusively in exponential rates of growth, as many economists have come to do.

Let me make this last point first, and then proceed to a more useful comparison of the two models. In (2), suppose that both $L(t)$ and $I(t)$ have always grown exponentially at rate γ. Then Q has grown and will grow at rate $\gamma + \lambda$. Now turn to (11); make the same assumptions and precisely the same conclusions emerge. Output will grow in the form $e^{(\gamma + \lambda)t}$. *But*, in the first place, (2) yields an output that has a ratio of

$$\left(\frac{\sigma + \gamma}{\delta + \gamma}\right)^{1-\alpha} : 1.$$

to the output of (11). Thus the absolute gap in output between the two models itself grows exponentially, the ratio remaining fixed. As one would expect, (2) is more optimistic than (11), and possibly substantially more so. Since

$$\left(\frac{\sigma + \gamma}{\delta + \gamma}\right)^{1-\alpha} = \left(1 + \frac{\lambda}{(1-\alpha)(\delta + \gamma)}\right)^{1-\alpha},$$

we observe that the relative optimism of (2) increases in direct proportion to λ and in inverse proportion to γ, both of which conclusions confirm common sense.

In the second place, it seems to me that calculations of this kind may be quite misleading. It is not hard to generate paradoxes by juggling exponentials. If investment has been growing exponentially forever, then the capital stock is composed overwhelmingly of extremely new items. This is what enables (11) to make output grow at the same rate as (2): the drag of obsolete capital is relatively small. But the practical question is really a different one: if the rate of capital formation is stepped up now, how much will it influence output over the next decade?

Suppose that gross investment has always been constant, equal to I_0, up until $t = 0$, and that at $t = 0$ it jumps to and remains at $(1+h)I_0$. For simplicity, assume that employment remains constant after $t = 0$. Then calculate the ratio of GNP at time t to GNP at time 0. From (2) we get

$$\frac{Q(t)}{Q(0)} = e^{\lambda t}[1+h(1-e^{-\delta t})]^{1-\alpha}.$$

From (11) we get

$$\frac{Q(t)}{Q(0)} = e^{\lambda t}[1+h(1-e^{-\sigma t})]^{1-\alpha}.$$

Remember that this is not the whole story. The $Q(0)$ derived from (2) is itself larger than the $Q(0)$ derived from (11) in the ratio

$$\left(1+\frac{\lambda}{(1-\alpha)\delta}\right)^{1-\alpha}.$$

Let us put $\lambda = \cdot 015$, $\alpha = \cdot 7$, and $\delta = \cdot 05$, so that $\sigma = 10$, and ask what the picture is at $t = 10$. To make things substantial, imagine that $h = 1$, that is, that the historical rate of gross capital formation was suddenly doubled at $t = 0$. Then (2) would imply that $Q(10)/Q(0) = 1\cdot 28$, while (11) would make $Q(10)/Q(0) = 1\cdot 35$. If h were zero, that is, if the additional investment were not undertaken at all, the ten-year increase would be 16 per cent in both cases. Thus (2) suggests that the doubling of gross investment brought about an additional 12 per cent increase in output, while (11) attributes to the new capital formation a 19 per cent increase in output over a decade. The difference is not staggering, but neither does it seem to me negligible.

Similar calculations can be made for the hypothetical case in which investment has been constant until $t = 0$, at which time it begins to increase at 5 per cent per year. The results are not qualitatively different from the above. The $Q(t)/Q(0)$ ratios are about $1\cdot 19$ and $1\cdot 25$ respectively, and since as before the ratio would be $1\cdot 16$ with no change in investment policy, we may say that (2) attributes a 3 per cent increase in output to the new capital formation, while (11) imputes 9 per cent.

All this is with $\lambda = \cdot015$, as in the earlier studies. Since my tentative empirical calculations suggest that λ is closer to $\cdot03$, let me rework my first case above using this value. With $\lambda = \cdot03$, σ becomes $\cdot15$, with all other constants having the same value as before. Then the model (2) gives $Q(10)/Q(0) = 1\cdot49$ and (11) gives $Q(10)/Q(0) = 1\cdot61$. Now if $h = 0$, the ten-year increase in output would be 35 per cent. Thus (2) attributes to the doubling of gross investment an additional 14 per cent increase in output, while according to (11) the extra capital formation is responsible for a 26 per cent increase in output over the decade. In other words, (11) makes the extra capital formation and technical progress share almost equally in the increase of output. This somewhat understates the difference between the two models, since (11) asserts what (2) denies; that if gross investment were to fall to zero, technical progress would cease. [...]

6. Business Cycles

Introductory Note

Almost all industrial countries have experienced fluctuations in their long-run pattern of economic growth. Although there has been much dispute about the degree of regularity of these fluctuations, in respect of both amplitude and frequency, there has been a measure of agreement that there is enough observed regularity to suggest the need for a theory of these variations, even though it is admitted that upheavals such as wars, bursts of innovations, and so on, may have partially obscured their pattern.

The most formal theory of the cycle is undoubtedly that which results from the interaction of the multiplier with the accelerator theory of investment. An early paper by Samuelson,[1] following work by Hansen, showed that if investment depended on the *lagged* change in income, then the interaction with the multiplier produced a relationship between current income and income of the previous two periods which had well-known mathematical properties—notably, that of producing, under certain conditions, a *cyclical* path for the level of income over time. Thus if investment depends on the lagged change in income:

$$I_t = v(Y_{t-1} - Y_{t-2})$$

(where v is the accelerator coefficient), and if saving is proportional to current income:

$$S_t = sY_t,$$

then:

$$sY_t = v(Y_{t-1} - Y_{t-2}),$$

or

$$Y_t = \frac{v}{s}Y_{t-1} - \frac{v}{s}Y_{t-2}.$$

Informally, the fact that income depends positively on last period's income, but negatively on the income of two periods ago means that it is no longer

[1] P. A. Samuelson, 'Interactions Between the Multiplier Analysis and the Principle of Acceleration', *Review of Economics and Statistics*, 1939.

clear that income must always grow steadily.[2] In fact for certain plausible values of v and s, an oscillatory path for Y results.

This, then, is the beginning of a formal theory of the cycle, but two difficulties remain. Firstly, except by chance the fluctuations which result will either have a steadily increasing violence, or they will conversely be damped and eventually die out. If the parameters v and s (and the lags involved) are such as to produce explosive cycles, then an explanation of how they are contained within the observed limits must be added. If damped cycles are produced, there must be an explanation of how the business cycle nevertheless persists. Secondly, the simple multiplier-accelerator theory can procude *either* fluctuations *or* steady growth in income, but not both. An explanation of the observed phenomenon of fluctuations about in rising trend in output is therefore required.

The paper by Hicks [Reading 6.1], subsequently elaborated and extended in his *A Contribution to the Theory of the Trade Cycle*, begins by noting that the combination of the multiplier and the *unlagged* accelerator can only produce steady growth, and that this is a possible interpretation of Harrod's growth theory. He then points out (a) that the theory would produce a less unstable result if it were 'braked' in some way, by the introduction of lags, and (b) that it is 'not really reasonable' not to introduce such lags, for that implies that current investment should depend on the increment of output in the same period.[3] Attention is drawn to the mathematical properties of the resulting mathematical equation which we have already noted, but Hicks

---

[2] Formally, the second-order difference equation with fixed coefficients,

$$Y_t - \frac{v}{s}Y_{t-1} + \frac{v}{s}Y_{t-2} = 0,$$

has a general solution

$$Y^t = A_1 P_1^t + A_2 P_2^t$$

where A_1 and A_2 are constants and P_1, P_2 are the roots of the auxiliary equation

$$sp^2 - vp + v = 0.$$

Thus

$$P_1, P_2 = \frac{v}{2s} \pm \sqrt{\left[\frac{v}{s}\left(\frac{v}{4s} - 1\right)\right]}$$

The roots are real, and one root is greater than one, if $v \geqslant 4s$. In this case, Y does grow steadily. But if $v \leqslant 4s$, the roots are complex, leading to an oscillatory solution. The oscillations will be damped if $v < s$ and explosive if $s < v < 4s$. Only in the special case $s = v < 4s$ will an oscillation of constant amplitude and period result. The only *equilibrium* solution in all cases is $Y_t = 0$, all t.

[3] It is arguable that this is a fundamentally different use of the accelerator relation from that employed by Harrod. For Harrod (see pp. 206–23 above), the relation $I_t = c(Y_t - Y_{t-1})$ is a relation between a given level of investment and the increment of output which would 'warrant' (i.e. justify) that level. But Hicks interprets the relation *casually*—a certain change in output leads to a certain level of investment—and, reasonably, he then points out that this must be a lagged response.

points out that it remains true that the *equilibrium* solution of such equations is still $Y = 0$.

More satisfactory progress can be made, according to Hicks, if there is some long-range investment which is independent of short-run cyclical fluctuations in output, but which is related to the long-run trend ('natural') rate of growth of the economy. It is evident that the 'equilibrium' path of output is then dependent on this long-range investment. Now assume that investment induced by the operation of the accelerator remains a destabilizing influence but that (a) there is some maximum ratio of actual output to the equilibrium level of output ('full employment' output) which cannot be exceeded but which of course grows at the same rate as equilibrium output, and (b) that the accelerator ceases to operate when output falls, since net investment (except in stocks) cannot be significantly negative (that is, the rate of decline of the stock of capital is limited to the rate at which existing equipment is scrapped). A plausible pattern of cyclical growth now emerges. In the up-swing, a limit is reached at full employment (F). The rate of growth of output declines, induced investment falls, and the downswing begins. But there is also a floor (L) to output—the output consequential on long-range investment. As this floor is reached, its growth leads to a positive increment of output and the accelerator comes back into operation: the next upswing begins. There is an equilibrium path for output (E) which depends on long-range investment and the accelerator-induced investment which would occur at that rate of growth, and fluctuations about this level, although endemic, are contained within growing limits.

Goodwin's model of cyclical growth [Reading 6.2] represents a further extension and elaboration of the multiplier-accelerator model of the trade cycle. He recognizes the value of Hicks's attempt to combine the phenomena of growth and cycles, but argues that Hicks's introduction of growth by means of exponentially-growing autonomous investment is not really adequate. Instead, the central elements of economic growth are taken to be the growth of the labour force and improvements in technique. These lead to persistent growth in the productive *capacity* of the economy, but not necessarily to an equivalent growth in demand. Adequate demand is achieved only inter-mittently, through bursts of innovational (and accelerator-caused) invest-ment; after each such burst, output and employment fall, though to succes-sively higher levels because each expansion generates an increase in fixed or quasi-fixed outlays which break the fall at higher levels in each downswing.

Because Goodwin rejects the simple proportionality of capital and output, capital stock is taken as the central variable. The behaviour of income can always be traced from the behaviour of investment. A 'flexible' version of the accelerator is employed: the desired capital stock, K^*, is related both to the level of income and to the rate of innovation, $\beta(t)$:

$$K^* = vY + \beta(t).$$

Investment is then related to the gap between desired and actual capital stock, subject to two important non-linearities: first, as in Hicks's model, there is a lower limit (set by the rate at which capital can be scrapped) to the rate of disinvestment, and, secondly, there is a maximum rate set by the capacity of the investment goods industry.[4] Between these two limits, investment is taken to be proportional to the gap between desired and actual capital stocks:

$$I = \lambda(K^* - K).$$

This copes with the supply side of the model; demand is given by the multiplier:

$$Y = f(I)$$

where variability in the propensity to save (and hence in the size of the multiplier) is admitted. In particular, the propensity to save is likely to be rather small (high multiplier) in the downswing since expenditure is difficult to cut back in the face of declining income.

Combining these three equations, and eliminating K^* and Y:

$$I = \lambda[vY + \beta(t) - K]$$
$$= \lambda[vf(I) + \beta(t) - K],$$

from which

$$K = vf(I) - \frac{1}{\lambda}I + \beta(t).$$

Now in the upturn, if we assume $\beta(t)$ to be constant, capital accumulation proceeds at the maximum rate until the desired capital stock is reached. Investment then slackens but this, taken with the large multiplier in the downswing, causes output to fall so fast that the desired capital stock falls faster than the acutal stock: there is no halt to this process until gross investment falls to zero. A prolonged depression ensues, until the capital stock falls below the low level required in the depression. Short sharp booms are thus interspersed with prolonged depressions.

This ignores, however, the sources of 'natural' growth—the rises in the quantity and productivity of the labour force. The consequential rise in the full-employment ceiling which takes place during the boom prolongs the boom by delaying the point at which the actual capital stock outstrips the desired stock, while the greater expenditures and associated fixed outlays associated with the boom raise the 'floor' and hence the extent to which the desired capital stock needs to fall. Thus booms are lengthened and depressions shortened. Finally, when it is recognized that innovation, as well as raising labour productivity, will generally require extra investment—$\beta(t)$—we come still closer to reality. A steady rise in $\beta(t)$ will further prolong the boom and shorten the depression, while variations in $\beta(t)$ may account for differences between cycles both over time and between countries.

[4] This corresponds to the 'full-employment' level of output, since otherwise the latter could never be achieved.

Both Hicks's and Goodwin's models presuppose an economy whose behaviour is characterized by a tendency towards explosive oscillations, which must therefore be constrained by 'ceilings' and/or 'floors' if cycles of reasonably regular amplitude are to be accounted for. But suppose that the economy's inherent tendency is towards damped cycles: how then can persistent cycles be explained? Broadly speaking, the only theoretical answer which has been offered (see the classic paper by Frisch)[5] is in terms of persistent though random shocks to the system—erratic variations in any or all of the variables, whether exogenous or endogenous. Informally, such shocks keep the system in motion and prevent its settling down to a stable equilibrium, but the frequency of the cycles which the system follows is governed by the multiplier/accelerator interaction. There is some tentative empirical evidence (see Chapter 11) that this is indeed a plausible view to take of the generation of business cycles.

An entirely different account of the genesis of business cycles is given by Friedman and Schwartz [Reading 6.3]. They begin from the fact that the historical data for the U.S. show a high correlation between cyclical movements in the economy at large and cyclical movements in the money stock. The basic question concerns the direction of causality—it is admitted that statistical correlation alone cannot settle this question, and that there must be a causal linkage from the general level of activity to the stock of money. What is at issue is whether there is *also* a significant causal linkage running from money to economic activity. In support of the latter proposition, Friedman and Schwartz adduce evidence from particular historical episodes which suggests, first, that changes in activity have always been accompanied by changes in the money stock, while there have not been (major) disturbances in the money stock which have not been accompanied by changes in activity; and secondly, changes in the stock of money can be attributed to specific historical events rather than systematically to changes in activity.

These propositions raise two interrelated questions: to what extent is the 'monetary theory' of disturbances in opposition to 'conventional' theories and, if there is a distinctively monetarist theory, what is the transmission mechanism?

For Friedman and Schwartz (and for other monetarists), the first question is answered by contrasting the 'money multiplier'—the statistical relationship between changes in money and changes in income—with the supposedly analogous alternative, the 'Keynesian' investment multiplier in which investment is taken as wholly autonomous. The apparently greater stability of the money multiplier as compared with the investment multiplier is taken as prima facie evidence in favour of the monetarist explanation.

---

[5] R. Frisch, 'Propagation Problems and Impulse Problems in Dynamic Economics', in R. Gordon and L. Klein (Eds.), *Readings in Business Cycles* (American Economic Association, 1966). This paper originally appeared in 1933.

This is not the place to embark on a résumé of the 'monetarist v. Keynesian' debate (which is touched on in Chapter 9 below), but three lines of objection to this procedure have been advanced. First, since it is of the essence of Keynesian economics that investment is at least partially affected by monetary factors, the money multiplier and the investment multiplier cannot be treated as simple alternative summaries of the macroeconomic process. Secondly, the Keynesian multiplier is the relationship between total 'autonomous' expenditures—including, for example, government expenditure and exports—and income; this relationship involves leakages into taxation and imports as well as saving. It is thus highly improbable that the relationship between investment and income will be at all stable—but this is not evidence against the over-all analysis. Thirdly, there is the question of whether the fact that major disturbances in the money supply have preceded major changes in income is evidence of causality of a kind at variance with Keynesian analysis. On the one hand, it is not necessary to give overwhelming importance to monetary factors in order to believe that large exogenously-caused increases or decreases in liquidity can have marked expansionary or contractionary effects on some kinds of expenditure—notably on durable assets. On the other hand, the importance of expectations in economic behaviour suggests that monetary adjustments may well take place in advance of the movements in expenditure with which they are associated, without this reflecting causality in the monetarist direction: thus, for example, banks may make funds available in advance of the investment expenditures by companies which they are intended to finance.

Finally, there is the question of the transmission mechanism. Friedman's account runs in terms of portfolio adjustment, where portfolios are broadly conceived as comprising a whole spectrum of assets from money through financial assets and equities to durable producer and consumer goods. An increase at the liquid end of this spectrum will diffuse throughout, ultimately raising the demand for goods and services. Thus exogenous fluctuations in the money supply will induce fluctuations in the demand for goods and services. In addition, an endogenous cycle may be set up: a rise in demand will tend to raise prices and, if there is a lag in the adjustment of (real) money balances to the new price level, the initial portfolio adjustment will tend to be overdone. The initial rise in demand will thus be followed by a fall in demand, and a damped cycle is likely to result.

To summarize, the major questions in the analysis of business cycles are very largely empirical: the relative importance of monetary and real determinants of expenditure, the sensitivity to changes in output of different kinds of investment, the lengths of lags, the size of the multiplier, and so on. A certain amount of empirical evidence is available from the study of econometric models of actual economies; some of this evidence is presented in Chapter 11.

6.1 The Multiplier-Accelerator Model of the Trade Cycle* [...]

I

The central feature of Mr. Harrod's theory is a certain equation which (modifying Mr. Harrod's notation a little) I will write in the form $gc = s$. s is saving, expressed as a proportion of income (or output); g is the rate of growth of output (increment of output expressed as a proportion of output); c is the ratio of investment to the increment of output. Those whose minds (like my own) find it difficult to think in terms of these ratios will prefer to multiply up by income or output (Y). gY is then identifiable as the increment of output during the period, which could be written dY/dt. The equation thus becomes $c(dY/dt) = sY$. This is recognisable as our old friend, the equation of Saving and Investment. (Y, it should be understood, is measured in terms of goods, not in terms of money or of 'wage-units'.)

The reason why Mr. Harrod prefers to write a familiar equation in this unfamiliar form is that he is anxious to stress the dependence of investment on the rate of change of output—the 'Relation' which other economists have called the 'acceleration principle'. In given conditions of technique, and with a given rate of interest, the ratio (c) between *ex-ante* investment and the change in income may perhaps be properly regarded as more or less constant. If this is so, and if the saving ratio s may also be regarded as constant, then the fundamental equation $c(dY/dt)/Y = sY$ can be treated as a differential equation, and solved as such. The solution is $Y = Y_0 e^{gt}$, where Y_0 is the level of income at time zero, which must be supposed to be given, and g is now *defined* as s/c, where both s and c are now to be taken as given constants. The economic meaning of this solution is, of course, that the economy expands at a constant rate g.

The solution is got by assuming that the economy is all the time in a state of Keynesian equilibrium, with *ex-ante* investment equal to *ex-ante* saving. The path defined by the solution is therefore not the path which will actually be followed; it is the path which would be followed if the system remained continually in this sort of equilibrium. (Mr. Harrod calls it the 'warranted' rate of growth.) And that means, as we shall see, very little more than that it is a *possible* path of development.

The use of the concept of equilibrium in such matters as this is very tricky. In the Keynesian system, we were first told that the savings-investment equation determined the level of output; then it became clear that it only determined the equilibrium level of output; the actual level, at any particular time, might depart from the equilibrium level. This was an important qualification, with many consequences not yet all of them fully appreciated; but it did not in itself seriously affect the usefulness of the Keynesian construction, because the Keynesian equilibrium is *stable*. If *ex-ante* saving exceeds *ex-ante* investment (under Keynesian or near-Keynesian assump-

* From J. R. Hicks, 'Mr. Harrod's Dynamic Theory', *Economica*, 1949.

tions) output will tend to fall, thus tending to restore equilibrium. And *vice versa*. Because there are these stabilising forces tending to hold the system to an equilibrium position (or, as we might say, more dynamically, to hold it on an equilibrium path), it is probable that divergences from a Keynesian equilibrium would be limited. Great divergences must be short lived. Thus, in so far as the Keynesian system is valid, it does not only explain 'tendencies'; it does, at least in a rough sort of way, explain the facts. If it is valid, then it is a first approximation to what does actually happen. It has this property in virtue of its mathematical *stability*. The ordinary supply and demand theory for a single commodity has the same property for the same reason.

Mr. Harrod's equilibrium path—his 'warranted rate of growth'— does not have this property. His system is mathematically unstable. A rise in the rate of saving (*s*) raises the warranted rate of growth (*g*), thus causing the equilibrium path to slope more steeply upwards. There is sense in this. With the demand for the use of savings coming from the increase in output, an increased supply of savings can only be absorbed if output increases more rapidly than before. But an increase in *s* will not cause the economy to move on to this new path. Just as in the Keynesian case a rise in *s* causes *ex-ante* saving to exceed *ex-ante* investment, and therefore tends to diminish output. But this means (under Mr. Harrod's assumptions) that the system tends at once to move away from its equilibrium rate of advance. Instead of expanding as it 'ought' to do, it starts to contract.

Mr. Harrod is, of course, well aware of this instability; he draws a number of interesting conclusions from it, some of them, I think, very important conclusions. In a sense he welcomes the instability of his system, because he believes it to be an explanation of the tendency to fluctuation which exists in the real world. I think, as I shall proceed to show, that something of this sort may well have much to do with the tendency to fluctuation. But mathematical instability does not in itself elucidate fluctuation. A mathematically unstable system does not fluctuate; it just breaks down. The unstable position is one in which it will *not* tend to remain. That is all that the condition of mathematical instability tells us. But, on being barred from that position, what will it do? What path will it follow? Mere knowledge of the unstable position does not tell us....

II

Faced with this difficulty, I have been tempted to go beyond the ordinary functions of a reviewer, and to enquire whether it is not possible, by some modification of Mr. Harrod's assumptions, to overcome the deficiency. The prize is a great one, for no one can study Mr. Harrod's work at all deeply without feeling that results of really great significance are just round the corner. What we have to do is to introduce just sufficient frictions to give the model mathematical stability, while not sacrificing the economic instability on which the substance of the argument depends. Can this be done?

It can be done as soon as we are allowed to make some use of lags. It is not generally realised (Mr. Harrod has certainly failed to realise it) that the great function of lags in this sort of dynamic theory is to impart just that measure of stability in the small—day-to-day stability we might call it—as is required in order to make the movement of the system economically determinate. The lags are needed to hold the system to a given path. Mr. Harrod's theory, in the form he has given it, may be regarded as an indirect proof of this; because he will have no lags, his system explodes out of the time dimension. A dynamic system which is economically unstable, having a high propensity to fluctuate, cannot be efficiently studied unless some of the variables are lagged.

The easiest way to introduce lags is to work in terms of period analysis. Instead of treating time as continuous, we break it up into successive periods. The increment of output, which formerly appeared as dY/dt, will now appear as $Y_n - Y_{n-1}$. If there are are no lags, the basic equation will then have to be written

$$c(Y_n - Y_{n-1}) = sY_n \tag{1}$$

the properties of which are substantially the same as those of Mr. Harrod's equation.

But as soon as the equation is written in this form, it does at once look decidedly queer. It is not really reasonable to assume that current investment should depend upon the increment of output *in the same period* (especially if periods are fairly short), and still less is it reasonable to assume that saving depends wholly upon the income of the same period. If we make the simplest possible lagging assumptions, we shall make investment depend upon the increment of income in the preceding period, and *consumption* upon the income of the preceding period. Current saving would then equal $Y_n - (1-s)Y_{n-1}$, so that the basic difference equation becomes

$$c(Y_{n-1} - Y_{n-2}) = Y_n - (1-s)Y_{n-1}$$

or

$$Y_n = (1-s+c)Y_{n-1} - cY_{n-2} \tag{2}$$

An equation of this kind is completely stable in the short run, for an increase in s reduces Y_n as it should. It can therefore be used to trace out a path which is such that an economy might possibly follow it.

The properties of such paths have been widely studied by mathematical economists. Without going into detail, the following general conclusions may be mentioned. s and c being given, the path is completely determined when *two* initial positions (say Y_0 and Y_1) are given. Associated with any particular difference equation, there will be a 'full equilibrium' position, which is such that it can be maintained indefinitely if it is once fully established. For very low values of c, the system approximates to the Keynesian type, and therefore moves steadily towards its full equilibrium. For very large values of c, the system tends away from full equilibrium. For intermediate values, it oscillates about the equilibrium position, the oscillations having a diminishing amplitude if c is less than 1, and an increasing amplitude if c is greater than 1. These are the results for the 'second-order' equation, in which Y_n depends upon its *two* previous values. Similar, but mathematically much more complex, results appear to hold for difference equations of higher orders.

These results have attracted much attention because they seem to show that on quite simple assumptions a system may be constructed which has an automatic tendency to develop fluctuations. But the more one works with this structure, interesting as it is, the more one feels that its fluctuations are really too simple. They do not take account of some of the most elementary features of the real problem, which must surely find a place, and a central place, in a realistic theory. The mathematical economists do seem to have got hold of a part of the mechanism, but there are other things which they have left out which need to be brought in.

Now Mr. Harrod has got some of these other things. Although his system will not do in the small, it is better than theirs in the large. Is it impossible to build up a construction which will combine the merits of each?

III

The reader may have noticed that the lagged Harrod equation (2) would, in itself, be unsatisfactory for the purposes of the mathematical theory which we have just described. For if we seek to determine its full equilibrium level of output (which can always be determined from a difference equation by putting its various Ys equal to one another) the answer must clearly come out as $Y = 0$. This would not perhaps worry Mr. Harrod very much, because he is seeking to analyse a dynamic process, not an equilibrium situation. He does not want his system to settle down to 'equilibrium'.

But this means that the only solution of the difference equation in which he will be interested is that which occurs when c is relatively large, so that the system becomes 'explosive'. He is quite ready for his system to explode provided that it does not explode too fast!

Nevertheless, since the system is to fluctuate, having down-tracks as well as up-tracks, it is important that the down-tracks should be checked somewhere. After all, slumps do have bottoms; something has to be introduced to stop the slump tending to an 'equilibrium' with no output at all.

The only provision which Mr. Harrod makes to meet this need is the suggestion that some part of the investment of a period may be 'long-range'— so that its 'worthwhileness is not deemed to have any relation to current requirements'. I believe that this is the solution; but by treating this long-range investment as a fraction (presumably in principle a constant fraction) of current income, Mr. Harrod makes it impossible for it to give him any really substantial help. For whether the long-range investment depends upon Y_n, Y_{n-1} or Y_{n-2}, its introduction in this guise only affects the coefficients in the difference equation; and no juggling with the coefficients will prevent an equation of the form

$$\alpha Y_n + \beta Y_{n-1} + \gamma Y_{n-2} = 0$$

from having its equilibrium solution at zero output.

I believe that the readiest way out is to make the long-range investment depend, not upon current output, but upon the trend value of output. Evidently we must not treat long-range investment as a constant; for if we did so, though we should get a bottom to our slumps, we should lose the possibility of the upward trend, on the introduction of which into the model Mr. Harrod sets so much store. If, however, we make the assumption that the long-range investment depends, other things being equal, upon the natural growth of the economy (in productivity and perhaps population), we can get a bottom to our slumps and still retain the general progressive movement.

I would therefore suggest that we introduce a term $H(1+g)^n$ for the long-range investment, where H is a constant, and g (also a constant) is now Mr. Harrod's *natural* rate of growth. The introduction of this term certainly seems to be worth trying, and it proves to have the most interesting effects.

IV

On introducing this term, the difference equation (2) is transformed into

$$H(1+g)^n + c(Y_{n-1} - Y_{n-2}) = Y_n - (1-s)Y_{n-1} \tag{3}$$

This equation is just a shade harder to handle than (2), but in fact by a simple device we can reduce it to an equivalent form.

The nearest thing to an equilibrium solution which is possible for this new equation is that which gives a steady advance at the *natural* rate. At such a steady advance, we should have $Y_n = E(1+g)^n$, where E is a constant. Substituting this trial solution in (3), we find

$$H(1+g)^n = E(1+g)^n - (1-s+c)E(1+g)^{n-1} + cE(1+g)^{n-2}$$

whence

$$E = \frac{H(1+g)^2}{(1+g)(s+g) - cg} \tag{4}$$

If, as we may properly assume, there is enough saving to look after the investment engendered in the steady advance, E will be positive.

Now write $Y_n = E(1+g)^n(1+y_n)$, so that y_n is the proportion by which actual income in the nth period exceeds (or, if y_n is negative, falls short of) its *moving* equilibrium value. Substituting this value in (3) and using (4), we get

$$y_n - \frac{1-s+c}{1+g}y_{n-1} + \frac{c}{(1+g)^2}y_{n-2} = 0 \tag{5}$$

which is a simple difference equation of exactly the same type as (2). Its full equilibrium solution is at $y_n = 0$; but this no longer corresponds to zero output, but to the output which gives a steady advance.

What we have now found is that in our revised model, the proportional divergences from the moving equilibrium output will obey the same laws as were obeyed by the level of output itself in the simple model (2). Thus if $c/(1+g)^2$ is small, any displacement from the moving equilibrium will be followed by a steady movement back to the equilibrium. The moving equilibrium can then be regarded as stable. For larger values of c, we should get fluctuations about the moving equilibrium, which (as c increased) would first be damped, and would then become 'explosive'. Finally, for very large values of c, we should get a steady divergence from equilibrium as the result of any chance displacement.

Now it is, I think, these latter possibilities (relatively neglected by the econometrists) to which Mr. Harrod seeks to draw our attention. In order to study them conveniently, we may perhaps fix our attention upon one particular value of c, which makes the difference equation more than usually easy to handle. This is the minimum value which gives a steady divergence from equilibrium, without there being any fluctuations induced by the difference equation itself. It can be calculated to be $c = (1 + \sqrt{s})^2$. Substituting this value of c in (5), we get

$$y_n - 2\lambda y_{n-1} + \lambda^2 y_{n-2} = 0 \tag{6}$$

where $\lambda = (1 + \sqrt{s})/(1 + g)$. It is obviously safe to assume that $\lambda > 1$.

The solution of equation (6) is $(nA + B)\lambda^n$, where A and B are constants, depending on the initial positions. Thus if we start from a position which is such that A is positive, y will steadily increase (at least after a limited number of initial periods), and if we start from a position in which A is negative, y will steadily diminish (subject to the same proviso). We have therefore verified that we are dealing with an 'explosive' equation; and we may be sure that for higher values of c we should get cases which would be still more explosive.

If we start from an equilibrium position, with $y_0 = 0$, we are bound to have $B = 0$, since by putting $n = 0$, we see that $y_0 = B$. A is determined by the value of y in period 1, being equal to y_1/λ when $B = 0$. Applying the general formula, we see that $y_n = n\lambda^{n-1} y_1$. Thus if we began with an upward displacement, so that y_1 was positive, y_n would increase from period to period in a ratio which at first exceeded λ, but gradually approached the limiting value λ as n became large.

V

Thus the difference equation tells us that if there chances to be an upward displacement from the equilibrium level, y will expand indefinitely. But y cannot expand indefinitely! For y, it will be remembered, is not the equilibrium level of output, which *can* expand indefinitely, given sufficient time;

it is the proportion in which actual output exceeds the moving equilibrium output, and in that moving equilibrium the natural growth of the system has already been allowed for. It is therefore reasonable to assume that there is some maximum level which y cannot exceed—something which we may call the Full Employment level. Until that limit is reached, output can expand, both by natural growth and by a reduction in the percentage of unemployed resources. Once, however, the limit is reached, only natural growth is possible. And that means that y has reached its maximum value.

Let us write the full employment limit of y as f. Then if we have started, as before, from the moving equilibrium, and have encountered the full employment ceiling in the nth period after the initial divergence, we have the following situation. $y_{n-2} = (n-2)\lambda^{n-3}y_1$; $y_{n-1} = (n-1)\lambda^{n-2}y_1$; but y_n does not equal $n\lambda^{n-1}y_1$, but is kept down to the lower value f. What then happens to y_{n+1}? In order to discover this, we have to go back to the difference equation (6), for there is no reason why it should not continue to hold.

$$y_{n+1} = 2\lambda f - \lambda^2 y_{n-1}$$

This may be greater or less than f, but if it is greater than f, it will have to be replaced by f, since f is its greatest possible value. We pass on to y_{n+2}. Applying the difference equation to this, we see that its maximum possible value is $2\lambda f - \lambda^2 f = f[1-(\lambda-1)^2]$. This is definitely less than f; so that, *having reached its full employment limit, the system must begin to turn round again and output to go down, at least relatively to the trend.*

This conclusion is quite generally true. If we go back to the more general equation (5), we see that two successive ys which are equal and positive must be followed by a third which is lower than they are. This follows from the same inequality as gave us our fundamental condition that the (moving) equilibrium level of output should be positive.

What happens next? Effectively we are now starting from two successive ys which are both equal to the same positive magnitude f. We have to use the difference equation to work out the ensuing path. It is not difficult to show that successive ys will continue to fall, and that a point must be reached at which output does not merely fall relatively to its moving equilibrium, but falls absolutely.

When this happens, I think that we must reconsider our difference equation. If the system continued on the path determined by the same difference equation, output would ultimately fall to zero; our model, having agreed with experience quite well up to this point, would therefore at this point begin to diverge sharply. Can we see why? The induced investment, on which so much has depended, is investment induced by an *expansion* in output; if we maintained the same difference equation on the downswing as on the upswing, we should be letting it go into reverse and becoming negative when output began to fall. This does not look right. It is true that there are some sorts of investment (investment in working capital) for which a construction of this sort might be plausible. Increases in output induce investment in working capital, of the sort which we have so far taken into account; and it is reasonable to suppose that reductions in output will cause entrepreneurs to find their working capital excessive, so that they will take steps to reduce their excessive stocks. So far as fixed capital is concerned, however, this is not possible. There does therefore seem to be a changed situation in the downswing from what there was in the upswing, and it is reasonable to allow for this change by changing the form of the difference equation. Let us say, as a first approximation, that when output turns absolutely downwards, the induced investment term $c(Y_{n-1} - Y_{n-2})$ simply drops out. It becomes zero, but does not become negative. Suppose this occurs, what happens?

The difference equation now takes the form

$$H(1+g)^n = Y_n - (1-s)Y_{n-1} \tag{7}$$

instead of the form expressed in equation (3). This is a much easier equation to handle than equation (3), but it will be convenient to set out its solution in similar form. It will have a similar moving equilibrium, which we may write $L(1+g)^n$, and the value of the constant L can be determined by a similar substitution. We get

$$H(1+g)^n = L(1+g)^n - (1-s)L(1+g)^{n-1}$$

or

$$L = \frac{1+g}{s+g}H \tag{8}$$

Comparing this with the expression previously got for E ([4] above), we see that L will always be less than E, so that the new moving equilibrium will always be lower than the old.

Now write $Y_n = L(1+g)^n(1+z_n)$, so that z_n is the proportion in which actual income exceeds the new (lower) moving equilibrium level. Substituting this in (7) and using (8) we get

$$z_n = \frac{1-s}{1+g}z_{n-1}$$

The coefficient $(1-s)/(1+g)$ is necessarily positive and less than unity. Starting, therefore, from a given value of z_0, the successive zs get smaller and smaller, in geometrical progression. By what is essentially the Kahn convergent series, the system tends towards its lower moving equilibrium $L(1+g)^n$.

But it will not get there. For once z has fallen so far as to become less than a certain ratio (which, as can readily be verified, is the not particularly small ratio g/s), the fall in the proportion z by which actual output exceeds the lower moving equilibrium output becomes less than the rate at which that moving equilibrium is itself rising; and once this happens, actual output will begin to rise. The original difference equation should then come back into operation, and that will start a new expansion *relatively to the natural growth*.

The simplest way of proving that this must be so is the following. Suppose, for a moment, that there is no induced investment until the lower equilibrium has actually been reached. Then the system will start taking up successive positions which are actually on the lower equilibrium line. In these positions the ys (measured, as before, from the upper equilibrium) are negative and equal. Now if y_0 and y_1 are both equal to $-a$, we shall have [by (6)]$y_2 = -2\lambda a + \lambda^2 a$, so that $y_2 - y_1 = (\lambda - 1)^2 a$, which is certainly positive. It can further be shown, by the usual methods, that $y_n - y_{n-1} = (n-1)\lambda^{n-2} \times (\lambda - 1)^2$, which will always be positive. The same result can be shown to hold for the more general case, in which we assume a larger value for c.

Thus, if the system actually hits its lower equilibrium, it will then be bound to start an upward expansion. If induced investment appears before it has hit the lower equilibrium, that is simply a further expansionary influence. The output so generated will then be greater, for each period, than that which we have just calculated. The expansion is therefore demonstrated *a fortiori*.

VI

Our model is now complete; and by our algebraic method, we have shown its internal consistency. For further discussion, it will be convenient to have a graphical representation.

Fig. 6.1 represents ... time on the horizontal axis, and on the vertical the logarithm of output (or investment). Steady progress is therefore represented by a straight line which slopes upwards, and steady progress at the 'natural rate of growth' by a straight line of given slope. There are four such lines which play a part in our model. First, there is the Full Employment line F. Secondly, there is the 'upper equilibrium' line E; and thirdly there is the 'lower equilibrium' line L. Finally, there is the 'long-range investment' line H, the upward slope of which is responsible for the upward slopes of E and L. It should again be emphasized that output is being measured in real terms, so that F may slope upwards, on account of an upward trend in productivity, even if population is constant. H slopes upwards at the natural rate of growth, because, by assumption, it is geared to the trend. E and L slope upward because they depend on H.

We know that L must lie above H, because of the Keynesian multiplier argument. We know that E must lie above L, because E includes the multiplier effect of induced investment (at the natural rate of growth of output) as well as the multiplier effect of the long-range investment. We shall assume for the present that E lies below F, though it should be noticed that we have not proved that it must do so.

The E line is such that the economy could possibly advance along it in a smooth manner without fluctuation. But it will do so only if it is held to it in some manner, for any chance divergence in either direction will set up a movement away from the equilibrium E. Suppose that there is a chance divergence in an upward direction. Output then begins to grow at more than its natural rate of growth, and though there may be some tendency for the actual rate of growth to slow up after some time has elapsed, the actual rate will always exceed the natural rate (at least according to the value which we have given to *c*). And that means that the actual path AB must hit the ceiling F sooner or later. But when it hits the ceiling, the rate of increase in output

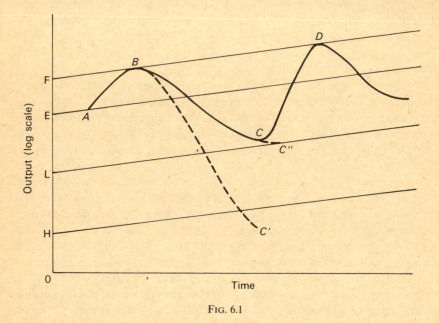

FIG. 6.1

is slowed up, and therefore (in the next period) induced investment is cut down. But the induced investment, which corresponds to an increase in output at the natural rate (which is all that is allowed by the ceiling F) is only sufficient to engender a level of output which approximates to the E line, not one which goes along the F line. Output therefore tends to move back, on the course BC', towards the E line. But as output moves back, the rate of increase in output falls below the natural rate, and in consequence actual output tends to fall below the E line. The track which would be generated, on this principle, after the 'upper turning-point' B had been passed, would plunge downwards indefinitely, tending towards an output of zero. I show it on the diagram by the dotted line BC'.

It was, however, at this point that we felt it necessary to introduce our second complication. A downward movement in actual output, when it becomes an absolute fall, not merely a fall relatively to the natural rate of growth, should not be thought of as causing induced investment to become negative (or at least as only doing so to a minor extent). The path BC′ is therefore too pessimistic. If zero is the lowest point to which induced investment can fall, then on the down-track we have a situation in which the only investment occurring is that which is represented by H. And L is the equilibrium to which the system will tend when the only investment is that represented by H. The system will therefore move along a path BC″, which is determined by the familiar multiplier theory of Keynes (or Kahn). This path will merge into the L line at a point C″.

But since the L line is upward sloping, the path BC″ will have begun to turn upwards at a point C, which precedes C″. At this point the 'accelerator' comes back into gear. It must then bring about a positive induced investment, which will cause the actual path to diverge from CC″ in an upward direction. The rate of growth will then soon be in excess of the natural rate, and the path CD must therefore intersect the E line sooner or later. When it does so, it will still have a rate of growth in excess of the natural rate, and will therefore keep on rising. Finally, it must hit the F line, and when it does so, it is bound to turn down as before, for exactly the same reason as before.

There has thus been engendered a complete cycle, and a cycle which is completely self-perpetuating. It must turn down when it gets to the top, and when it approaches the bottom it must turn up. So long as the fundamental data remain unchanged, actual output must fluctuate between the limits L and F, and will do so indefinitely.

VII

Further, what has been accomplished is something more than the making of a special model, which happens to show a fluctuation, something like the observed sort, for certain values of its parameters. We have used special values for purposes of illustration, but the cycle which has been engendered does not depend on the special values chosen. All that is necessary is (1) that the relations between income and consumption, on the one hand, and between investment and changes in income, on the other, should be such as to impart a rather strong tendency to instability in the level of output; (2) that the system should have an upward trend, and that some investment should be geared to that upward trend; (3) that the supply of resources, at any given time, should not be inexhaustible; (4) that falls in output should not induce disinvestment, in the way that rises in output induce investment, except (possibly) to a minor extent. These conditions are certainly not at all restrictive; all of them (except possibly the first) are things which we should naturally expect to be true. And the first condition, though its validity is certainly far from self-evident, is not intrinsically unplausible. We do therefore seem to have shown that a cycle, which is strongly reminiscent of that which we experience, can be explained on the basis of a minimum number of hypotheses, each of which is very reasonable in itself. It is hardly possible for a *theory* of the Cycle to do more than that.

Besides, from this point we can again go forward. The next thing to do should be to reconsider the very simple difference equation on which our formal analysis (though not the real essence of our argument) has been based. It is, as a matter of fact, most unlikely that the two relations (between income and consumption, and between investment and change in income) are as simple in form as we have assumed them to be. We have taken a simple form, in order to keep our main difference equation down to the second order; but there can be little doubt that the equation we thereby got is over-simplified, though it should be noticed that the mathematical difficulties accumulate very rapidly when we introduce additional complications in this direction. There is, however, one generalisation which can be made without incurring these mathematical difficulties. We can allow for the probability that a part of consumption will depend upon current income as well as a part on previous income; an amendment in this direction makes the system *more* liable to fluctuate. This has a bearing on the weakest of the four assumptions listed in the previous paragraph. It will probably have been noticed that in order to get our model to work, we did apparently need a rather large value for the capital coefficient c; it looked as if it had to be distinctly larger than unity. So large a value for c is not altogether unplausible (Mr. Harrod is evidently prepared to accept a value of this order of magnitude); nevertheless when we remember that 'long-range' investment is being otherwise allowed for, a doubt must remain whether so large a value of c is realistic. It is therefore useful to notice that if only a part of consumption is lagged, we can manage to work our model with much smaller values of c. The value of c can be appreciably less than unity, and we can still get the required instability in the level of output.

Such things evidently need much further enquiry; but the way to that enquiry is now open. It will then be of great importance to study the changes in the model which may occur through changes in the sizes of some of the parameters, and to enquire whether they have any correspondence with observed changes in the behaviour of the actual economy through various cycles. If it could be shown that there is such correspondence, the theory would receive striking confirmation. I am in fact inclined to think that some of this confirmation can be sighted without looking very far. One thing which clearly could happen would be that the value of c was not large enough for the upward swing (AB or CD in Fig. 6.1) to hit the Full Employment ceiling. If this were to happen, the boom would turn down before it hit the ceiling; but the rest of the cycle could apparently go on as before. Does not this look very like the case of the boom which 'peters out'? Mr. Harrod has done some useful work on the factors determining the size of c; by using his researches on this point, and concentrating on the effects of changes in his factors in this direction, it does look as if the theory we have been advancing should be capable of some indirect verification.

Again, it is clearly not realistic to assume that the 'height' of the H line (the long-range investment) will, as we have drawn it, be constant in all circumstances. Such things as wars and their aftermaths (and maybe other disturbances too) must be thought of as causing 'autonomous' fluctuations in long-range investment. The effects of such fluctuations could be analysed. A considerable upward hump in the H line could, for instance, push the corresponding E *above* the Full Employment line. If this happened, there would be no tendency for output to turn down when it reached the Full Employment level. Let us consider the matter, for instance, in terms of equation (6). We saw that in a system which was 'driven' by that equation, two successive ys which were both equal to f would be succeeded by a third which was equal to $f-(\lambda-1)^2 f$; if f is positive, this must be smaller than f. But if f is negative, as in the case we are considering, the third y will be *larger* than f; being above the Full Employment level, it will then have to be replaced by f. Thus the system can remain in Full Employment as long as the hump in the H-curve lasts.

This is itself a highly suggestive result; one further modification, which can be introduced into our structure, not only without damage but with benefit, makes it more suggestive still. It is not quite right to treat 'Full Employment', as we have done hitherto, as a rigid barrier; it is better to regard it as a zone which, if penetrated, calls forth rapidly increasing resistances to the expansion of output, but in which some increase of output can, up to a point, still be attained. This modification makes no real difference to the structure of our theory; the slowing-up of expansion, due to the resistances, will still cause output to turn downwards once the zone is fairly penetrated, so long as the equilibrium level E is lower than the level at which the resistances begin. But if we allow that the resistances begin (as I think they do) at a level of output which is short of that where there is a tendency to define inflation, we get another important result. We can see why it is that the ordinary commercial boom, carried by induced investment, is most unlikely to penetrate through the resisting medium so far as to cause any serious inflation; the resistances will cause it to turn downwards before it gets to that point. It is only when there is a big hump in the H-curve, pushing the equilibrium level well into the Full Employment zone, that the system can have enough 'steam' in it to carry it to the inflationary point. The ordinary commercial boom is unlikely to do that. Our theory therefore affords a ready explanation of another well-established practical generalisation, which was previously rather out of touch with theory; it shows why it is that inflation is so liable to occur in conditions of war and post-war reconstruction, but rarely (if ever) results from a purely commercial boom.

I should, however, not like it to be inferred from these arguments that a continued boosting of the H-curve, so as to keep E above F, is a desirable solution of the cycle problem. For what is bound to happen, in this 'over-employment' situation, is that induced investment is kept steadily below its normal relation to current output. And since, on the whole, the induced investment is *needed* in order to enable output to be produced efficiently, its repression (certainly its continued repression) is bound to have adverse effects on the efficiency of production. Thus even if the danger of open inflation can be somehow averted, this 'solution' can cure the cycle only at the price of a severe loss in efficiency. The true object of policy should be to keep the equilibrium line as near as possible to the Full Employment mark, but not to push beyond it. If this is done, it will also be necessary to have measures at hand to correct the downward divergences from equilibrium, which are then liable to occur. This policy is much harder than its alternative; but if it can be achieved, its results will be infinitely preferable.

6.2 Growth and Cycles*
[...]

THE STRUCTURE AND FUNCTIONING OF THE MODEL

First, we may go over in outline the structure and functioning of the model. The indispensable growth elements are improvements in techniques and the increase in the labour force, both of which are taken as given and more or less continuously growing. Innovational investment characteristically does not require increased output but, on the other hand, both greater employment and greater productivity mean larger output which will, with given techniques, call for more capital. The possibility of greater output is not the same as its realization, and for the answer to this we appeal to the Kahn-Keynes multiplier. The existence of a cycle means that aggregate demand is not always adequate to realize the full productive capacities of capitalism, and at first sight we might be tempted to wonder that they are ever realized. In general, new techniques require heavy investment outlays which swell demand, so that both the increased output per labourer and the increased number of labourers are absorbed. When the economy has achieved its new higher levels of output and capital it cannot hold them, because the great burst of investment (both innovational and accelerational) is necessary to create the effective demand, and, when it ceases, demand and output drop, thus creating unemployed capital and unemployed labour. Therefore we have a dynamic, but not a static, breakdown theory. Just as output rises each time to new heights, it also does not fall to its previous low, because the expansion generates fixed outlays which break the fall at higher levels on each swing. The revival awaits the accumulation of sufficient pressure for innovational investment. In the first approximation no lags are introduced, with the result that we have a two-phase cycle, full employment and deep depression. It is assumed throughout that the structural coefficients are such as to give explosive behaviour. Therefore investment, once begun, carries the economy to full employment, and this upper limit rises rapidly with the accumulation of capital, which allows the realization of the technological advance.

*From R. M. Goodwin, 'A Model of Cyclical Growth', in E. Lundberg (Ed.), *The Business Cycle in the Post-War World* (London: Macmillan, 1955). Reprinted by permission of the International Economic Association and Macmilian, London and Basingstoke.

In simple terms the economy is strongly expansionist in both output and demand. It is always straining to get to the full employment limit, but, by the mere fact of being there for a time, it is projected downward again. To think of a mechanical analogy, we may picture a gas-filled balloon underneath a stairway. A slight draught carries it steadily forward and it rises until it hits the ceiling, but then it bumps downward. After a time it begins to rise again, yet, having moved forward, it now passes the old level and rises until it hits the bottom of the next step. Thus it is essentially non-oscillatory, but is converted, by successive steps, into an intermittent upward drift. The central feature of the analogy is the parallelism between stair steps and full employment ceilings: it is these limits which control the character of the growth. It seems to me that full employment must, in some fairly intimate manner, guide the long-range behaviour of the model, otherwise it is difficult to see why we would not find that the model would predict, after a time, a cycle around a level of 50 or 150 per cent of full employment, which is unrealistic. The concept of full employment I employ uncritically, and I do not think the many reservations required make any serious difficulties.

Throughout the argument capital stock will be taken as the central explanatory variable. Since the behaviour of capital is taken to be the main feature of the cycle this seems logical. The reason why I have not followed Professor Hicks and Mr. Harrod in taking income as the dependent variable, is that once we break the simple proportionality between capital and income, the behaviour of income no longer tells us anything conclusive about the behaviour of investment. To see this we must juxtapose actual stock to the desired stock of capital, and in view of this it seems preferable to work throughout with capital stock. Upon doing this we quickly realize how utterly hopeless it is to explain the lower turning point in terms of the necessity for replacement of a wasting capital stock.

There are more serious objections against the use of the quantity of capital than against the use of the quantity of output. Capital has never been satisfactorily defined quantitatively, and it is doubtful whether we can attach any useful meaning to the concept of variations in the stock of capital. However, at the cruder level of approach used here there is perhaps no very serious objection. Capital is taken to mean the stock of equipment, in the broadest sense, that is used in production, so that an increase in output calls for more capital, and a decrease for less. It is useful to pretend that capital stock is the sum of all past net investments, but since it is output and not capital that really matters, we need not worry if the resulting quantity of capital is partly fictitious. This problem arises sharply in the case of innovational investment which, in our system, means an unequivocal addition to capital stock. But our crude aggregative model ignores the fact that innovational investment also destroys capital, so that in fact we cannot be sure whether there has been an increase or a decrease.

Throughout I shall use the 'flexible accelerator' as the explanatory principle for investment. ... According to this principle, net investment will be under-taken as long as desired capital is greater than existing capital, and disinvestment in the contrary case. Desired capital, ξ, I shall assume to be determined by

$$\xi = vy + \beta(t), \qquad (1)$$

where v is the acceleration coefficient, y is the output, and $\beta(t)$ is a parameter to be associated primarily with changes in technique. Thus innovation means that more capital is desired with a given output, and the accelerator means more capital is desired only with increased output.

It is to be noted that, even if we ignore $\beta(t)$, this is not the acceleration principle, which assumes a perfect adjustment of capital to output at all times. On the contrary, it is assumed here that with a given stock of capital we can produce more (by overtime, etc.) than it was designed to produce, and, obviously, also less. Furthermore, in designed capacity, there is usually some stand-by or peak-load capacity which can be used. The point is that this high-level operation involves higher variable costs, strain on staff and equip-ment, delays, etc., all of which create a pressure to expand capital and capacity. Therefore the short-run is characterized by a failure to exemplify the acceleration principle, but it is also dominated by efforts to attain the accelerational quantity of capital. The assumption here is that entrepeneurs behave on homeostatic principles as exemplified by servo-mechanisms. We sidestep the question of expectations, although the rate at which investment proceeds in response to a given excess or deficiency of capital is a kind of measure of confidence in the continuation of current rates of output.

For the sake of simplicity, we assume that the pressure to expand is pro-portional to the difference between ξ and k, subject to two crucial non-linearities. The lower one is set by the rate of wastage of capital at zero gross investment, and the upper one by the maximum output of new capital goods obtainable with given capital and labour supply. The picture is as drawn in Fig. 6.2, and we may write it for convenience as,

$$g(\dot{k}) = \xi - k. \qquad (2)$$

Beyond this, I assume that full employment in the capital goods trades tends to coincide with full employment generally. A little reflection shows that it must be so, else we should either never attain full employment, or else have violent inflation in all booms. In general this result may come about in the following way: as the boom proceeds we may tend to hit capacity limits in the instrumental trades before general full employment; these trades, facing a backlog in any case, will divert some of their output to enlarging their own capacity; this process will continue so long as there is unemployed labour available. Thus we arrive, if not initially, finally, at simultaneous full capacity output in both producers' and consumers' goods industries. Beyond this point it is dangerous for the former to go, since it would mean sharply rising costs along with falling output in consumption goods. There is a tendency to moderate inflation in most booms, and it could be assumed that the maximum output in durable goods lies slightly above the general limit so that the investment trades often try to bid resources away from the others.

If this relation between capital goods output and general output is to be maintained it follows that, with full employment, further growth in output must be split between the two in the proportion given by the secular multiplier. Thus, if the multiplier is 5, a rise of 10 in total output will include a rise of 2 in the output of new capital. The assumption is clearly necessary to the proper functioning of the model, but it is bound to appear somewhat arbitrary unless we assume some equilibrating mechanism behind the scenes.

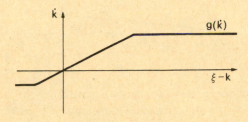

FIG. 6.2

There remains the stimulating question whether or not innovations, which continually increase the amount of desired capital, raise the acceleration coefficient. ... The point is that new methods of production almost always require additions to capital stock, but they also destroy capital, sometimes by making it obsolete, sometimes by reducing the cost of replacing it. Therefore we may be continually adding to our capital autonomously but find that, after many years, a routine addition to output requires the same addition to capital stock as before.

In the absence of any information, or grounds for believing one effect or the other to predominate, it is simplest to assume that the acceleration coefficient v remains unchanged, and this I shall do. It seems much better not to lump this problem with the much more identifiable one of whether or not innovations are capital using or capital saving. Whereas Mr. Harrod defines capital using in terms of v, I prefer to define it in terms of the increase or decrease of $\beta(t)$. The important point is 'that major innovations and also many minor ones entail construction of New Plant (and equipment)....'[1] The fact that net investment with constant output need not make industry 'more capitalistic' is only paradoxical, because we are dealing with aggregates which suppress all structural interdependence.

To incorporate a theory of effective demand and the generation of income, we may follow well-established Keynesian lines and write

$$y = f(\dot{k} + \gamma(t)), \tag{3}$$

[1] J. A. Schumpeter, *Business Cycles*, New York, 1939, Vol. i, p. 93.

where $\gamma(t)$ is 'public spending' suitably defined, and everything is in constant prices. I shall not discuss government anti-cyclical policy, and hence I shall suppress $\gamma(t)$, but the reader will find no difficulty in introducing it.

The slope of this function is the multiplier, and its inverse is the aggregate savings function (all lags are ignored and the equality of savings and investment is assumed). The uniqueness of this function has been one of the first central Keynesian doctrines to waver. Following Professor Duesenberry[2] we may represent the shape of this function as in Fig. 6.3. When going down we

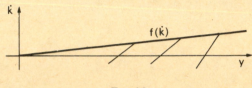

Fig. 6.3

follow the steeper slope, and only when we venture again into new, higher ranges of income does saving again grow only slowly. The necessity for some such contrast between short- and long-run phenomena is clear, but the explanation of this anomalous savings function is not quite so well established.

Professor Duesenberry has advanced an ingenious explanation, and I should like to suggest some further considerations which also may help. Fundamentally, it may be an expression of the familiar Marshallian distinction between the long and the short period. The long period is much longer in the downward than in the upward direction. Thus, as the scale of output is expanded, all outlays go up easily, but a part of them 'freeze' and become 'fixed' and cease to be quickly reducible in the event of a fall in output. We can think not only of 'fixed' interest but stable dividend policies, irreducible managerial, maintenance, sales and research staffs. Many workers also are not discharged, but many are and cease to be a cost to the firm. But to society they remain a fixed charge, and they continue to consume, though at a lower rate, whether through savings, charity, credit or public relief. Similarly, as Professor Duesenberry has shown, the consumer finds that his outlay is fairly easily variable in the upward direction, but is awkwardly rigid downward. In the long run, this would cease to be so. Finally, it is almost a law of political science, as well as a political slogan, that government outlays expand easily but resist contradiction to an extraordinary degree. A related though distinct phenomenon is the fact ... that in the early stages of the boom there is a large increase in output before there is much increase in capacity, leading to large profits which are mostly saved. As the prosperity continues the accumulation of capital may lead to a fall in profits and hence in savings. This could generate

[2] J. S. Duesenberry, *Income, Saving and the Theory of Consumer Behavior*, Cambridge (Mass.), 1949.

the kind of savings function shown in Fig. 6.3, for in depression there is no significant decumulation, and hence the savings function will not be reversible. Here again aggregates conceal the real problem, for we must appeal to a classical competitive behaviour to explain why entrepreneurs undertake investment which *lowers* profits.

THE COMPLETE MODEL

We are now in a position to assemble the various parts into a working model. Combining equations (1), (2) and (3) we get

$$\xi - k = vf(k) + \beta(t) - k = g(k),$$

or, rearranging,

$$k = vf(k) - g(k) + \beta(t). \tag{4}$$

The function $vf(k)$ is the same as $f(k)$ only much flatter, and therefore the situation at any point of time is as shown in Fig. 6.4.

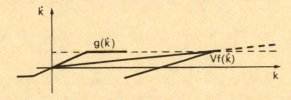

FIG. 6.4

If we subtract $g(k)$ from $vf(k)$, call it $\phi(k)$, and add $\beta(t)$ to it, we get the result shown in Fig. 6.5. It is evident that an increase in $\beta(t)$ simply shifts the $\phi(k)$ curve to the right. All our relations are satisfied if we remain on the curve. All lags have been abstracted from in the interest of simplicity, and with the conviction that these are of secondary rather than of primary importance for the cycle.

To begin with, let us consider the case of a completely unprogressive economy with $\beta(t)$ constant, no increases in productivity and no growth in the labour force. If we begin at the upturn, we have capital k_1, and start accumulating at the peak rate. This means peak output, and a much larger amount of capital is desired than the existing stock. The capital goods fill this backlog at the maximum attainable rate until we reach the amount k_3. At this point entrepreneurs would begin to slacken in their rate of new investment, but this proves impossible because the more they slacken the investment the lower is income and output, and hence the lower is desired capital by a multiple. There is no feasible position short of zero gross investment, below which point they cannot go and to which they instantaneously jump. This instantaneous jump from full boom to deep depression is a direct consequence of abstracting from lags, and we shall at a later point drop this assumption.

In consequence of zero gross investment output is now low, and the existing stock of capital, k_3, is greatly in excess of desired capital. Capital is now decumulated at the maximum possible rate until k_1 is reached, and then the process is begun all over again. If, as a result of a war or some such large disturbance, capital is slightly in excess of the equilibrium amount, k_2, combined with a low rate of net investment, we get an accelerated rise to k_3. This behaviour corresponds rather closely to the familiar 'multiplier-accelerator process', but it is executed by this model only under exceptional circumstances.

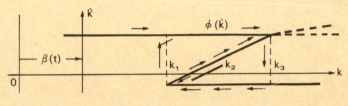

FIG. 6.5

The model is completely unrealistic in its depression behaviour. Even under favourable circumstances it would remain depressed much longer than in boom. The curve of Fig. 6.5 probably much over-estimates any actually achieved rate of physical wastage of capital assets. Our model identifies two things which are in fact not the same. Zero gross investment means the non-spending of depreciation allowances, and hence determines the lower level of income as represented. But unfortunately this does not represent actual disappearance of capital goods, especially since, following a boom, their age composition will be abnormal and actual disappearance quite small. Some reduction there will be, and also a general ageing which will be conducive to investment, but these effects will be weak. It should be admitted that this is a shortcoming both in this model and in that of Professor Hicks.

THE SOURCES OF GROWTH

There are two sources of growth and these may be conveniently considered in turn. In the first place there is the rise in the full employment level, both because the size of the labour force increases and because the productivity of labour rises through innovation. The organic connection between cycle and trend will be most sharply emphasized if we assume that all growth in the full employment ceiling occurs only during booms. Thus, at the end of a depression there will have been some attrition in capital stock, but this may be roughly counterbalanced by the growth in the labour stock, so that we may plausibly assume that the full employment level is about the same at the end of the depression as it was at the beginning. In the ensuing boom full employment output may rise rapidly, because the capital is being accumulated to equip with newest techniques the expanded labour force. But this output rises above the previous peak and carries us into the range of the large secular multiplier. This time the acceleration coefficient gives us the large additions to desired capital which the rising output entails. The achieved rate of rise in full employment output, say of 4 per cent or 5 per cent per year, fixes the rate of growth of desired capital, and this, in combination with the slowly accelerating capital stock, determines the length of the boom.

If we continue along the top horizontal curve we eventually reach the termination of the boom. With secular progress the full employment limit rises, and the peak output of capital goods rises in a fixed proportion to it. This means that the flat top to $\phi(k)$ slowly rises, which raises the required

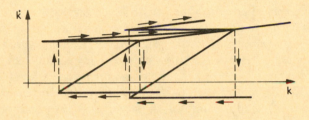

FIG. 6.6

capital and prolongs the boom. Therefore we move along a horizontal curve which is steadily rising, so that in fact we follow a slowly rising curve as is shown in Fig. 6.6. This postpones, but does not avoid, the final accumulation of sufficient capital to induce a slackening of investment and the consequent end to the boom. Whereas the boom is prolonged, the slump is shortened, because the 'fixed' outlays which have become swollen during the boom now place a higher 'floor' to output, and hence to desired capital. Therefore it is not necessary to carry out the absurdly unrealistic task of decumulating, by wear and tear, all of the capital accumulated during the preceding boom. It remains true, however, that realistic figures still give a depression that lasts longer than the boom.

The economy surges forward and plunges down, but it does not go back to its old low. There is no 'progress' during depression; it all occurs during the boom, or at least it is all 'realized' during the boom. Therefore there would be no meaning to drawing any smooth trend line through the time series of national income. Finally, it should be noted that secular growth takes place without any autonomous or innovational outlays.

We have already taken account of the results of innovation in increasing productivity; it remains only to include the fact that they ordinarily mean additional investment outlay. We therefore allow $\beta(t)$ to rise, more or less smoothly, which implies that there has been in capitalism a continuous stream of ideas for new methods of production which have required additional capital outlays. These may occur slowly at some times and rapidly at others, but $\beta(t)$, being the resultant of many small events cumulated, is likely to be fairly continuous.

Making no more definite assumptions than this we get the Schumpeterian result that the steady accumulation of potential 'new combinations' is converted into bursts of development which eventually exhaust themselves and relax into depressions. They may sometimes come as a result of his isolated, pioneer entrepeneur, but they need not. In this way we make a closer mutual conditioning between the state of trade and innovating activity.

The effect of a steadily rising $\beta(t)$ is a steady shifting of the $\phi(k)$ curve to the right. Thus it is not necessary to await the slow wasting of capital, for desired capital rises to overtake the existing stock. Therefore, depending on the given historical rapidity of growth of new methods of production, the depression may be so short as to amount only to a 'crisis', or it may drag on for many years awaiting significant technological advance. Contrariwise, the advance of $\beta(t)$ postpones the end of the boom by increasing capital requirements, so that under favourable conditions the boom may be much lengthened. Since the model, like capitalism itself, is dominated by vigorous growth, we may use variations in $\beta(t)$ to account for, in part at least, the enormous variation from cycle to cycle and country to country. Thus we can account for snap depressions like 1907, or prolonged stagnation as in the 1870's or 1930's. Again, a long boom like the 1920's can be fitted in. The current post-war boom can be explained by the steady accumulation of possibilities during the great depression and the war, and by the length of time needed to accumulate the capital to exploit these as well as to equip the considerably increased labour force.

A questionable feature of this model lies in the fact that it lumps together the accelerational and innovational demands for new capital. Yet this has much to recommend it, for the new methods and forms of capital will be most readily installed when rising demand requires additional capital in any case. Probably most new types of capital are installed during booms, and so innovational investment is hopelessly mixed with accelerational investment. Also, while not necessary, a high and rising demand is favourable to innovational outlays.

THE LOWER TURNING POINT

Even allowing for the vigorously expansionist nature of capitalism, the lower turning point remains a difficulty for a model built solely on capital requirements. There are numerous factors which alleviate the problem and I shall allude to three. Throughout we have taken no account of the distinction between working and fixed capital. As is well known there is no serious technical limit to the rate of disinvestment in the former, and hence the excessive stock of working capital may be quickly dissipated. As has been shown by Professors Lundberg and Metzler this leads to a rise in investment and output. The resultant increase in desired capital may well ignite a general boom much earlier than we would expect from the 'fixed' capital model. Second, as has been pointed out by Mr. Harrod, the aggregative model completely misses the vital fact of the heterogeneity of capital goods. Thus some capital wears out quickly and requires gross investment to maintain output. As the depression persists, there will be rising gross investment even though a vast amount of capital is still redundant. This means rising output and capital requirements, which rise to meet the declining stock. In fact, this dispersion in the durability of different capital goods must be a large part of the explanation of the failure of gross investment to fall to zero in deep depression. Finally, we should mention the possibility that government outlays for relief, war or public works may lift the economy enough to set off the boom. This point has been so completely discussed that it seems uneccessary to go into it.

6.3 Money and Business Cycles*

SOME PLAUSIBLE INTERPRETATIONS OF THE FACTUAL EVIDENCE

The stock of money displays a consistent cyclical behavior which is closely related to the cyclical behavior of the economy at large. This much the factual evidence summarized above puts beyond reasonable doubt.

That evidence alone is much less decisive about the direction of influence. Is the cyclical behavior of money primarily a reflection of the cyclical behavior of the economy at large, or does it play an important independent part in accounting for the cyclical behavior of the economy? It might be, so far as we know, that one could marshal a similar body of evidence demonstrating that the production of dressmaker's pins has displayed over the past nine decades a regular cyclical pattern; that the pin pattern reaches a peak well before the reference peak and a trough well before the reference trough; that its amplitude is highly correlated with the amplitude of the movements in general business. It might even be demonstrated that the simple correlation between the production of pins and consumption is higher than the simple correlation between autonomous expenditures and consumption; that the partial correlation between pins and consumption—holding autonomous expenditures constant—is as high as the simple correlation; and that the correlation between consumption and autonomous expenditures—holding the production of pins constant—is on the average zero. We do not, of course, know that these statements are valid for pins and, indeed, rather doubt that they are but, even if they were demonstrated beyond a shadow of doubt, they would persuade neither us nor our readers to adopt a pin theory of business cycles.

* From M. Friedman and Anna Schwartz, 'Money and Business Cycles', *Review of Economics and Statistics (Supplement)*, 1963.

If the only decisive statistical evidence for money were comparable to the items just cited for pins, it would correspondingly not justify the acceptance of a monetary theory of business cycles. At the same time, it is worth noting that, even then, the monetary theory and the pin theory would by no means be on all fours. Most economists would be willing to dismiss out of hand the pin theory even on such evidence; most economists would take seriously the monetary theory even on much less evidence, which is not by any means the same as saying that they would be persuaded by the evidence. Whence the difference? Primarily, the difference is that we have other kinds of evidence. We know that while pins are widely used and occasionally of critical importance, taken as a whole, they are a minor, if not trifling, item in the economy. We expect the effect to be in rough proportion to the cause, though this is by no means always the case—a rock can start a landslide. We can readily conceive of an economy operating without pins yet experiencing cycles like those of history; we can readily conceive of large autonomous changes occurring in the production of pins, but we cannot readily conceive of any channels through which such autonomous changes could have wide-reaching effects on the rest of the economy. Men who have thought about and studied these matters have never been led to suggest the pin industry as a prime mover in the cyclical process. In all these respects, the monetary theory is on a wholly different footing. We know that money is a pervasive element in the economy; that the stock of money is sizable compared with other aggregate economic magnitudes; that fluctuations of the kind we call business cycles have apparently occurred only in an economy in which 'economic activities are...carried on mainly by making and spending money'.[1] We not only can conceive of the money stocks being subject to large autonomous changes, but we can also readily conceive of channels through which such changes could have far-reaching effects on the rest of the economy. Men who have thought about and studied these matters have been led to give money a critical role in their theories.

One more preliminary observation. The key question at issue is not whether the direction of influence is wholly from money to business or wholly from business to money; it is whether the influence running from money to business is significant, in the sense that it can account for a substantial fraction of the fluctuations in economic activity. If the answer is affirmative, then one can speak of a monetary theory of business cycles or—more precisely—of the need to assign money an important role in a full theory of business cycles. The reflex influence of business on money, the existence of which is not in doubt in light of the factual evidence summarized above, would then become part of the partly self-generating mechanism whereby monetary disturbances are transmitted. On the other hand, if the influence from money to business is minor, one could speak of a cyclical theory of monetary

[1] Wesley C. Mitchell, *Business Cycles: the Problem and Its Setting*, New York, NBER, 1927, Chapter II, and p. 62.

fluctuations but not a monetary theory of business cycles. To illustrate again with pins: Changes in business conditions doubtless affect the production of pins, and no doubt there is some feedback effect of changes in the production of pins on general business. But, whereas the first effect may well be large relative to the total fluctuations in pin production, the feedback effect is almost certainly trivial relative to the fluctuations in business. Hence we are ready to accept a business cycle theory of pin production but not a pin theory of business cycles.

The factual evidence summarized above goes beyond the list of items we conjectured for pins and contains some bits that are relevant to the key question at issue. The most important is the fact that the relation between money and business has remained largely unchanged over a period that has seen substantial changes in the arrangements determining the quantity of money. During part of the period, the United States was on an effective gold standard, during part, on an inconvertible paper standard with floating exchange rates, during part, on a managed paper standard with fixed exchange rates. The commercial banking system changed its role and scope greatly. The government arrangements for monetary control altered, the Federal Reserve System replacing the Treasury as the formal center of control. And the criteria of control adopted by the monetary authorities altered. If the predominant direction of influence had been from business to money, these changes might have been expected to alter the relation between business changes and monetary changes, but the relation has apparently remained much the same in both timing and amplitude. Yet this evidence is by no means decisive. Cagan has shown that the public's decisions about the proportion in which it divides its money balances between currency and deposits is an important link in the feedback mechanism whereby changes in business affect the stock of money. The changes in monetary arrangements have affected greatly the trends in the deposit-currency ratio but appear not to have affected its cyclical behavior. Hence this part of the supply mechanism has been roughly constant and has played a roughly constant role over the whole period.

In our view, the most convincing evidence supporting the idea that money plays an important independent part is not the evidence summarized in the first part of this paper but evidence of a rather different kind—that garnered from study of the historical circumstances underlying the changes that occurred in the stock of money. This evidence is much more clear cut for major movements than for minor.

Major economic fluctuations

Major movements in U.S. history include the deep depressions used here to distinguish deep from mild depression cycles in our classification of historical reference cycles; ... the substantial inflations which have occurred primarily during wartime; and a few long-continued movements in one direction, such as the generally rising level of money income and prices from 1896 to 1913. With respect to these events, the historical record justifies two important generalizations.

1. There is a one-to-one relation between monetary changes and changes in money income and prices. Changes in money income and prices have, in every case, been accompanied by a change in the rate of growth of the money stock, in the same direction and of appreciable magnitude, and there are no comparable disturbances in the rate of growth of the money stock unaccompanied by changes in money income and prices.

2. The changes in the stock of money cannot consistently be explained by the contemporary changes in money income and prices. The changes in the stock of money can generally be attributed to specific historical circumstances that are not in turn attributable to contemporary changes in money income and prices. Hence, if the consistent relation between money and income is not pure coincidence, it must reflect an influence running from money to business.

Inflationary Episodes. The second generalization requires little more than its statement to be recognized as true for the inflationary episodes. During periods of U.S. engagement in wars, the increased rate of growth of the money stock stemmed from use of the printing press, in more or less subtle ways, to help finance government military expenditures. During our neutrality in World War I from 1914 to early 1917, it had its origin in use by the Allies of their gold reserves to finance war purchases here. During those war years, the reflex influence of the rising tide of business on the stock of money was in the opposite direction to the actual movement in the money stock, since business expansion of itself tended to produce a worsening in the balance of payments and hence an outflow of gold or a decreased inflow.

The situation is equally clear from 1896 to 1913. The rise in the stock of money reflected predominantly an increase in the U.S. gold stock, which was part of a worldwide growth of the gold stock emanating from the discovery of new mines and improvements in techniques of extracting gold from low-grade ore. The domestic expansion alone would have made for gold outflows. The feedback was therefore counter to the main current.

For the wartime episodes, the evidence is equally consistent with a different theory, that the independent force was a major shift in government spending propensities; that the shift in spending propensities would have had the same effect on income and prices if it had been financed wholly by borrowing from the public at large with an unchanged money stock, rather than being financed in part by the use of monetary reserves (as it was in the early years of World War I) or by government creation of money (as in the other war years); that it was not financed wholly by borrowing because resort in part to use of monetary reserves and the printing press was politically easier and perhaps financially cheaper.

Evidence from the study by Friedman and Meislman (discussed in the subsection on the relative roles of money and investment, page 279, above)[2] rather decisively contradicts this alternative explanation. In any event, the alternative explanation will not hold for the 1896–1913 inflation, since there was no obvious independent shift of major magnitude in spending propensities. The only immediate factor producing such a shift that comes to mind is the income earned from gold production. However, although the increase in the stock of gold over that period was large compared to the gold stock at the start and was capable of producing large increases in the stock of money via a multiplicative effect on other kinds of money, the gold stock itself was a small fraction of the total money stock, and the increase in the money stock only a fraction of the increase in money income. Hence, the value of gold production was a small fraction indeed of the increase in income. The increased gold production could hardly have produced the observed increase of money income through any spending multiplier effect. But any effect it might have had must have been through its effect on the stock of money.

Deep depressions. For deep depressions, the historical evidence justifying our second generalization is as clear as for the inflationary episodes, though less well known and hence less self-evident. A summary statement of the proximate source of the change in the money stock will in most instances enable the reader to judge for himself the extent to which the decline in the stock of money can be explained by the contemporary change in money, income, and prices.

1875–78:   Political pressure for resumption led to a decline in high-powered money, and the banking crisis in 1873 and subsequent bank failures to a shift by the public from deposits to currency and to a fall in the deposit-reserve ratio.

1892–94:   Agitation for silver and destabilizing movements in Treasury cash produced fears of imminent abandonment of the gold standard by the United States and thereby an outflow of capital which trenched on gold stocks. Those effects were intensified by the banking panic of 1893, which produced a sharp decline, first in the deposit-currency ratio and then in the deposit-reserve ratio.

1907–08:   The banking panic of 1907 led to a sharp decline in the deposit-currency ratio and a protective attempt by banks to raise their own reserve balances, and so to a subsequent fall in the deposit-reserve ratio.

1920–21:   Sharp rises in Federal Reserve discount rates in January 1920 and again in June 1920 produced, with some lag, a sharp contraction in Federal Reserve credit outstanding, and thereby in high-powered money and the money stock.

[2] [Not reprinted here—Ed.]

1929–33:   An initial mild decline in the money stock from 1929 to 1930, accompanying a decline in Federal Reserve credit outstanding, was converted into a sharp decline by a wave of bank failures beginning in late 1930. Those failures produced (1) widespread attempts by the public to convert deposits into currency and hence a decline in the deposit-currency ratio, and (2) a scramble for liquidity by the banks and hence a decline in the deposit-reserve ratio. The decline in the money stock was intensified after September 1931 by deflationary actions on the part of the Federal Reserve System, in response to England's departure from gold, which led to still further bank failures and even sharper declines in the deposit ratios. Yet the Federal Reserve at all times had power to prevent the decline in the money stock or to increase it to any desired degree, by providing enough high-powered money to satisfy the banks' desire for liquidity, and almost surely without any serious threat to the gold standard.

1937–38:   The doubling of legal reserve requirements in a series of steps, effective in 1936 and early 1937, accompanied by Treasury sterilization of gold purchases led to a halt in the growth of high-powered money and attempts by banks to restore their reserves in excess of requirements. The decline in the money stock reflected largely the resultant decline in the deposit-reserve ratio.

A shift in the deposit-currency ratio and the accompanying bank crises played an important role in four of these six episodes. This ratio, as we have seen, has a systematic cyclical pattern which can be regarded as a feedback effect of business on money. However, in each of those episodes, the shift in the deposit-currency ratio represented a sharp departure from the typical cyclical response and, in at least two (1875–78 and 1892–94), represented a subsequent reaction to an initial monetary disturbance that had no such close link with contemporary changes in money income and prices. Moreover, in two episodes (1920–21 and 1937–38), neither a shift in the deposit-currency ratio nor bank failures played any role. And such a shift has played no important role in any of the large expansions in the stock of money. A fractional reserve banking structure susceptible to runs is an institutional feature that renders the stock of money sensitive to autonomous deflationary changes; hence runs may frequently play an important role in sharp declines. This feature, however is clearly not essential for a large economic change to be accompanied by a large monetary change in the same direction.

The 1907–08 episode is a particularly nice example of the intermixture of autonomous monetary disturbances and a feedback. The failure of the Knickerbocker Trust Company in the fall of 1907 converted what had been a mild decline in the money stock as a result of gold exports and a consequent decline in high-powered money into a severe decline as a result of bank runs and a consequent decline in the deposit-currency ratio. The accompanying sharp rise in short-term interest rates and a premium on currency produced a large gold inflow. The accompanying sharp intensification in the business decline worked in the same direction by its effect on the balance of inter-national payments. Since the runs were prevented from producing widespread bank failures through the concerted suspension by banks of convertibility of deposits into currency, these feedback effects fairly promptly reversed the money decline and, along with the reversal, the business decline came to an end.

Conclusions for Major Movements. The factors that produced the changes in the stock of money are autonomous only in the sense of not being directly attributable to the contemporary cyclical changes in money income and prices. In a broader context, each of course has its origins and its explanation, and some are connected fairly clearly with longer-term economic developments. There can be no doubt, for example, that the silver agitation was intensified by prior declining agricultural prices, or that the financial boom in the early 1900's encouraged financial activities which laid the basis for Knickerbocker Trust's failure, or that the worldwide declining price trend of the 1870's and 1880's encouraged exploration for gold and improvement of refining techniques.

The narrower sense is, however, important for our purpose. The question at issue is whether the one-to-one relation between monetary change and major economic change can be explained by a relation running from economic change to money, as a one-to-one relation between changes in pin production and in economic activity could be explained if it existed. Such an explanation would require that the changes in money be connected rather rigidly with either the contemporary changes in economic conditions or more basic factors that could account alike for the course of economic events and for the changes in the stock of money. The demonstration that the major changes in the stock of money have been attributable to a variety of sources, many of which are connected directly neither with contemporary business develop-ments nor with earlier business developments—which themselves can be regarded as determining the contemporary course of business—therefore contradicts any such explanation of the one-to-one relation between economic change and monetary change.

There seems to us, accordingly, to be an extraordinarily strong case for the propositions that (1) appreciable changes in the rate of growth of the stock of money are a necessary and sufficient condition for appreciable changes in the rate of growth of money income; and that (2) this is true both for long secular changes and also for changes over periods roughly the length of business cycles. To go beyond the evidence and discussion thus far presented: our survey of experience leads us to conjecture that the longer-period changes in money income produced by a changed secular rate of growth of the money stock are reflected mainly in different price behavior rather than in different rates of growth of output; whereas the shorter-period changes in the rate of growth of the money stock are capable of exerting a sizable influence on the rate of growth of output as well.

These propositions offer a single, straightforward interpretation of all the historical episodes involving appreciable changes in the rate of monetary growth that we know about in any detail. We know of no other single suggested interpretation that is at all satisfactory and have been able to construct none for ourselves. The character of the U.S. banking system—in particular, for most of its history, the vulnerability of the system to runs on banks—can come close to explaining why sizable declines in money income, however produced, should generally be accompanied by sizable declines in the stock of money; but this explanation does not hold even for all declines, and it is largely irrelevant for the rises. Autonomous increases in government spending propensities plus the irresistible political attraction of the printing press could come close to providing a single explanation for wartime inflations, accounting for the coincidence of rising incomes and rising stock of money without any necessary influence running from money to income; but this explanation cannot account for peacetime inflations, in which the growth of the money stock has reflected a rise in specie rather than in government-issued money; and it is not even a satisfactory explanation for the wartime episodes, since price rises in different wartime episodes seem more closely related to the concurrent changes in the stock of money than to the changes in government expenditure.

It is perhaps worth emphasizing and repeating that any alternative interpretation must meet two tests: it must explain why the major movements in income occurred when they did, and also it must explain why such major movements should have been uniformly accompanied by corresponding movements in the rate of growth of the money stock. The monetary interpretation explains both at the same time. It leaves open the reasons for the change in the rate of growth of the money stock and, indeed, at this point is highly eclectic, taking account of the fact that historically there have been many different reasons.

We have emphasized the difficulty of meeting the second test. But even the first alone is hard to meet except by an explanation which asserts that different factors may from time to time produce large movements in income, and that these factors may operate through diverse channels—which is essentially to plead utter ignorance. We have cited several times the apparently widespread belief in investment as the prime mover. The alternative explanation for times of war, suggested above, is a special application of this theory, with investment broadened to mean 'autonomous expenditures' and government spending included in the same category. But even for the first test alone, we find it hard to accept this theory as a valid general explanation: can a drastic collapse in autonomous investment explain equally 1873–79, 1892–94, 1920–21, 1929–33, 1937–38? Capital formation at the end of the seventies was apparently one and one-half times its level at the beginning and seems not to have slumped seriously at any time during the decade ... The 1890's saw some decline, but the following decade was marked by a vigorous and sustained rise. The 1920–21 episode was destined to be followed by a construction and investment boom. If the experience of 1920–21 is to be interpreted as a result of an investment collapse, that decline must have been a consequence of the decline in government expenditures and the subsequent collapse of inventory speculation before fixed capital expenditures had developed to take their place. But why, then, did the sharp decline in government expenditures after World War II not produce a subsequent economic collapse? Emphasis on inventory speculation involves a highly episodic interpretation, since it characterizes few of the other episodes. Surely, one cannot adduce that in World War I, slow using up of investment opportunities—often implicitly or explicitly called on to explain why, from time to time, there is allegedly a collapse of investment or a position of stagnation—was responsible for the 1920–21 recession. This is an equally implausible explanation for 1937–38 and, as already implied, for earlier episodes as well.

Of course, in most or all of these contractions, the incentive to invest and the actual amount spent on investment declined. The question at issue, however, is whether the decline was a consequence of the contemporary economic collapse—triggered, we would say, by monetary changes—or the ultimate working out of autonomous elements of weakness in the demand for investment that themselves triggered the contraction.

Even if all these episodes of contraction can somehow be interpreted as reflecting an autonomous decline in investment, is a sharp increase in investment opportunities a satisfactory explanation for the worldwide 1897–1913 rise in money income? If money is not a critical link but only a passive accompaniment of change, how is it that China escaped the early years of the Great Depression? We would say thanks to being on a silver standard and hence having a floating exchange rate vis-à-vis gold currencies, whereas all countries linked to gold were enmeshed in the depression. And how is it that China had the most severe contraction of all in the years from 1933 to 1936, when our silver purchase program drained silver from China and caused a sharp decline in its money stock, whereas the rest of the world was in a period of business expansion? And we could extend this list of embarrassing questions without difficulty.

We feel as if we are belaboring the obvious and we apologize to any reader who shares that feeling. Yet repeated experience has led us to believe that it is necessary to do so in order to make clear how strong is the case for the monetary explanation of major movements in money income.

Of course, it is one thing to assert that monetary changes are the key to major movements in money income; it is quite a different thing to know in any detail what is the mechanism that links monetary change to economic change; how the influence of the one is transmitted to the other; what sectors of the economy will be affected first; what the time pattern of the impacts will be, and so on. We have great confidence in the first assertion. We have little confidence in our knowledge of the transmission mechanism, except in such broad and vague terms as to constitute little more than an impressionistic representation rather than an engineering blueprint. Indeed, this is the challenge our evidence poses: to pin down the transmission mechanism in specific enough detail so that we can hope to make reasonably accurate predictions of the course of a wide variety of economic variables on the basis of information about monetary disturbances. In the section below on the relation between variations in income and money, we outline one part of the transmission mechanism which can account for the greater amplitude of variation in income than in money and on which we have some empirical evidence; in the last section, we sketch in a much more tentative way the major channels through which monetary fluctuations might be able to account for economic fluctuations, both the major movements we have so far been considering, and the minor movements to which we now turn. [...]

A TENTATIVE SKETCH OF THE MECHANISM TRANSMITTING MONETARY CHANGES

However consistent may be the relation between monetary change and economic change, and however strong the evidence for the autonomy of the monetary changes, we shall not be persuaded that the monetary changes are the source of the economic changes unless we can specify in some detail the mechanism that connects the one with the other. Though our knowledge is at the moment too meager to enable us to do this at all precisely, it may be worth sketching very broadly some of the possible lines of connection, first, in order to provide a plausible rationalization of our empirical findings; second, to show that a monetary theory of cyclical fluctuations can accommodate a wide variety of other empirical findings about cyclical regularities; and third, to stimulate others to elaborate the theory and render it more specific.

Let us start by defining an Elysian state of moving equilibrium in which real income per capita, the stock of money, and the price level are all changing at constant annual rates. The relation between these rates depends on whether real income is rising or falling, whether wealth is remaining constant as a ratio to income or is rising or falling relative to income, on the behavior of relative rates of return on different forms of wealth, and on the wealth elasticity of demand for money. To simplify, let us suppose that all interest rates in real terms (i.e. adjusted for the rate of change in prices) and also the ratio of wealth to income are constant, so that the wealth elasticity of demand for money can be approximated by the elasticity of demand for money with respect to permanent income. If real income is rising at the rate of a_y per year, the stock of money demanded will then be rising at the rate of δa_y per year, where δ is the income elasticity of demand for money, and prices will be rising at the rate of $a_P = a_M - \delta a_y$, where a_M is the rate of rise in the nominal stock of money per capita. For example, if income per capita is rising at 2 per cent per year, the stock of money at 4 per cent a year, and δ is 3/2, then prices would be rising at 1 per cent a year.[3] If δ and a_y were to be the same, and the stock of money were to rise at, say, 10 per cent a year, prices would be rising at the rate of 7 per cent a year; if the stock of money were to be declining at 10 per cent a year, prices would be falling at the rate of 13 per cent a year.[4]

Let us now suppose that an unexpected rise to a new level occurs in the rate of change in the money stock, and it remains there indefinitely—a single shock, as it were, displacing the time path of the money stock. In tracing the hypothetical effects of the higher rate of growth of the money stock, there will be some difference in detail depending on the source of the increase— whether from gold discoveries, or central bank open-market purchases, of government expenditures financed by fiat money, or a rise in the deposit-currency ratio, or a rise in the deposit-reserve ratio. To be definite, therefore, let us suppose it comes from an increased rate of open-market purchases by a central bank.

Although the initial sellers of the securities purchased by the central bank were willing sellers, this does not mean that they want to hold the proceeds in money indefinitely. The bank offered them a good price, so they sold; they added to their money balances as a temporary step in rearranging their portfolios. If the seller was a commercial bank, it now has larger reserves than it has regarded before as sufficient and will seek to expand its investments and its loans at a greater rate than before. If the seller was not a commercial bank, he is not likely even temporarily to want to hold the proceeds in currency but will deposit them in a commercial bank, thereby, in our fractional reserve system, adding to the bank's reserves relative to its deposits. In either case, therefore, in our system, commercial banks become more liquid. In the second case, in addition, the nonbank seller has a higher ratio of money in his portfolio than he has had hitherto.

Both the nonbank seller and commercial banks will therefore seek to re-adjust their portfolios, the only difference being that the commercial banks will in the process create more money, thereby transmitting the increase in high-powered money to the total money stock. The interposition of the commercial bank in the process means that the increase in the rate of growth

[3] These are roughly the actual values of a_y, a_p, and a_M over the 90 years 1870–1960 in the U.S. They yield a rather smaller value of δ (1·5) than we estimate by multiple regression techniques (roughly 1·8).

[4] It may seem strange that a 1 percentage point difference in the rate of change in the stock of money produces precisely a 1 percentage point difference in the rate of change of prices regardless of the magnitude of the rate of change of money. Will there not, it is tempting to say, be a flight from money as the rate of change in prices and hence the cost of holding money rises? The answer is that we are comparing states of equilibrium, not the transition from one state to another. In a world in which prices are rising at 7 per cent a year, the stock of money will be smaller relative to income (i.e. velocity will be higher) than it would in a world in which prices are falling at 13 per cent a year. But, in both, velocity will be *changing* only in response to the change in real income, which is by assumption the same in the two worlds. Of course, it is possible that δ is different at different levels of cost of holding money; but that would be an effect of a rather subtler kind.

of the money stock, which initially was less than in high-powered money, will for a time be greater. So we have here already a mechanism working for some overshooting.

It seems plausible that both nonbank and bank holders of redundant balances will turn first to securities comparable to those they have sold, say, fixed-interest coupon, low-risk obligations. But as they seek to purchase these they will tend to bid up the prices of those issues. Hence they, and also other holders not involved in the initial central bank open-market transactions, will look farther afield: the banks, to their loans; the nonbank holders, to other categories of securities—higher-risk fixed coupon obligations, equities, real property, and so forth.

As the process continues, the initial impacts are diffused in several respects: first, the range of assets affected widens; second, potential creators of assets now more in demand are induced to react to the better terms on which they can be sold, including business enterprises wishing to engage in capital expansion, house builders or prospective homeowners, consumers who are potential purchasers of durable consumer goods—and so on and on; third, the initially redundant money balances concentrated in the hands of those first affected by the open-market purchases become spread throughout the economy.

As the prices of financial assets are bid up, they become expensive relative to nonfinancial assets, so there is an incentive for individuals and enterprises to seek to bring their actual portfolios into accord with desired portfolios by acquiring nonfinancial assets. This, in turn, tends to make existing nonfinancial assets expensive relative to newly constructed nonfinancial assets. At the same time, the general rise in the price level of nonfinancial assets tends to raise wealth relative to income, and to make the direct acquisition of current services cheaper relative to the purchase of sources of services. These effects raise demand curves for current productive services, both for producing new capital goods and for purchasing current services. The monetary stimulus is, in this way, spread from the financial markets to the markets for goods and services.

Two points need emphasis at this stage. The first is that the terms 'financial markets', 'assets', 'investment', 'rates of interest' and 'portfolio' must, in order to be consistent with the existing empirical evidence, be interpreted much more broadly than they often are. It has been common to restrict attention to a small class of marketable financial securities and the real capital it finances, to regard 'the' rate of interest as the market yield on such securities, and the 'investment' which is affected by changes in the rate of interest as solely or mainly the items classified as 'capital formation' in national income accounts. Some of the empirical results summarized earlier are inconsistent with this view. To rationalize the results, it is necessary to take a much broader view, to regard the relevant portfolios as containing a much wider range of assets, including not only government and private fixed-interest and equity securities traded on major financial markets, but also a host of other assets, even going so far as to include consumer durable goods, consumer inventories of clothing and the like and, maybe also, such human capital as skills acquired through training, and the like. Similarly, it is necessary to make 'rate of interest' an equally broad construct, covering explicit or implicit rates on the whole spectrum of assets.

The second point is to note how readily these tentative lines on our sketch accommodate some of the documented regularities of business cycles. The cyclical counterpart to our assumed initial shock is the rise in the rate of growth of the money stock that generally occurs early in contraction. On the basis of the sketch so far, we should expect it to have its first impact on the financial markets, and there, first on bonds, and only later on equities, and only still later on actual flows of payments for real resources. This is of course the actual pattern. The financial markets tend to revive well before the trough. Historically, railroad bond prices have risen very early in the process. Equity markets start to recover later but still generally before the business trough. Actual expenditures on purchases of goods and services rise still later. The consistent tendency for orders to lead actual purchases would of course be expected on this theory, but it would follow simply from the mechanics of the production process. Hence it gives no definite support to this or any other theory. It is simply a stage in the way any impulse, however generated, will be transmitted. The tendency for the prices of financial assets to rise early in the pattern is quite a different matter. If the initial impulse were generated by an autonomous increase in spending on final goods and services, it would be plausible to expect the timing to be the reverse of what it actually is. Of course, on the theory being sketched, the precise timing will depend on the source of the initial monetary impulse. However, under the banking structure of the United States and other financially developed countries, whatever the initial impulse, commercial banks will play a key role in transforming it into an increased rate of growth in the money stock, and this will impose a large measure of uniformity on the outcome.

One other feature of cyclical experience that our sketch may be able to rationalize and that is worthy of special note is the behaviour of the deposit-currency ratio. The initial monetary impulse is concentrated among holders of financial assets and is then diffused to the rest of the community. But this means, as we have noted, that the redundant balances are initially in the hands of asset holders with a high ratio of deposits to currency. As the redundant balances are diffused, they spread to more nearly a representative group in the population. Consistently with this sequence, the ratio of deposits to currency starts to rise early in contraction, not very far removed in time from the trough in the rate of rise in the money stock; the deposit-currency ratio continues to rise during the rest of contraction and early expansion but then reaches a peak around mid-expansion, and falls. The turning point, on this sketch, reflects the point at which the net tide of redundant balances has shifted from the financial community to the rest of the community.

To return to our sketch, we had reached the stage at which the demand for the services of factors of production was rising, which means, of course, a rise in money incomes. This will tend to be partly reflected in a rise of the prices of resources and of final goods; at the same time, the prices of non-financial assets will already have been rising as demand shifted to them from financial assets. These price rises themselves tend to correct portfolios by making the real value of monetary assets less than they otherwise would be. The result is to reduce the relative redundancy of monetary assets, which sets the stage for a rise in the structure of interest rates in place of the prior decline. The exact sequence of rises in prices, whether it affects first prices of final products, and only later prices of factors and so shifts profit margins—and so on—depends on the structure of the product and factor markets. Like the relation between new orders and production, this is part of the transmission mechanism common to all theories and tells little or nothing about the generating impulse. This does not mean it is unimportant. On the contrary, it may well determine the sequence of events once the stage is reached at which income is rising, as well as the time duration of subsequent reactions.

However, the important point for our purposes is very different. It is that the process we have described will tend to overshoot the mark; it will not simply produce a smooth movement to the new path consistent with the new rate of growth of the money stock assumed to prevail. There are two classes of reasons embodied in our analysis that explain why the process will over-shoot. One, and in our view the more basic theoretically, has to do with the demand for money. At the higher rate of price rise that is the new ultimate equilibrium, the amount of money demanded will be less in real terms than it was initially, relative to wealth and hence income. But this means that, in the process of going from the initial to the new equilibrium, prices must rise at a faster rate than their ultimate rate. Hence the rate of price rise must overshoot. This effect is reinforced by that embodied in the subsection, 'Conclusions for Major Movements'. In the initial stages of the process, money holders overestimate the extent of monetary redundancy, since they evaluate money stocks at unduly low levels of prices; they are slow, that is to revise their estimates of permanent prices upward, hence they initially seek more radical readjustments in their portfolios than will ultimately turn out to be required. (If this analysis is applied to a cyclical process rather than to our special case of a shift from one moving equilibrium to another, a second element from that part of the section would also enter to produce over-shooting—a slow revision of estimates of permanent real income.) The second class of reasons for overshooting has to do with feedback effects through the monetary mechanism. Two of these have already been mentioned. First, the effect of the initial assumed shock is to cause a greater rate of rise in high-powered money than in the money stock as a whole. But since there is nothing about the shock that will permanently alter the ratio of money to high-powered money, it follows that the money stock must for a time grow faster than ultimately in order to catch up. Second, there is reason for the deposit-currency ratio to rise in the initial stages of the process above its long-run equilibrium level. In addition to these two classes of reasons for overshooting, which derive from the specifically monetary elements in our sketch, there may of course be those arising from the other elements of the transmission mechanism common to almost any theory.

The tendency to overshoot means that the dynamic process of transition from one equilibrium path to another involves a cyclical adjustment process. Presumably, these cyclical adjustments will be damped, though no merely verbal exposition can suffice to assure that the particular mechanism described will have that property. Presumably also, the extent of overshooting will not be negligible relative to the disturbance, though again no merely verbal exposition can suffice to assure that the mechanism described will have that property.

The passage from this analysis of a single displacement of the rate of growth of money to a monetary theory of partly self-generating cyclical fluctuations is direct and has in large part been embodied in the preceding statement. It may be worth noting, however, that it would be rather more plausible to suppose a shock to take the form of an unusually high or low rate of growth of the stock of money for some time, with a reversion to a previous level rather than a shift to a permanently new level. Such a shock is equivalent to two shocks of the kind we have been considering—but shocks in opposite directions. Hence the shock itself gives rise to a cyclical movement in addition to the cyclical adjustment to each shock separately. The fact that in the cycle there is never that complete adjustment to the existing state of affairs that is present in the assumed initial Elysian state of moving equilibrium is of no decisive importance. It merely means that one state of incomplete adjustment succeeds another and that successive widenings and narrowings of discrepancies between actual and desired portfolios replace the introduction of a discrepancy and the correction of it. As noted parenthetically earlier, of somewhat more moment are the fluctuations in real income and employment over the cycle, which introduce an important reason for overshooting.

The central element in the transmission mechanism, as we have outlined it, is the concept of cyclical fluctuations as the outcome of balance sheet adjustments, as the effects on flows of adjustments between desired and actual stocks. It is this interconnection of stocks and flows that stretches the effect of shocks out in time, produces a diffusion over different economic categories, and gives rise to cyclical reaction mechanisms. The stocks serve as buffers or shock absorbers of initial changes in rates of flow, by expanding or contracting from their 'normal' or 'natural' or 'desired' state, and then slowly alter other flows as holders try to regain that state.

In this stock-flow view, money is a stock in a portfolio of assets, like the stocks of financial assets, or houses, or buildings, or inventories, or people, or skills. It yields a flow of services as these other assets do; it is also subject to increase or decrease through inflows and outflows, also as the other assets are. It is because our thinking has increasingly moved in this direction that it has become natural to us to regard the rate of change in the stock of money as comparable to income flows and to regard changes in the rate of change as a generating force in producing cyclical fluctuations in economic activity. [...]

7. Inflation

Introductory Note

Prior to the Second World War, little attention was paid to the problem of price inflation—the phenomenon of a persistent and perceptible rise in the general level of prices. This was partly, no doubt, due to the fact that the 1930s had been a period of stable, if not falling, prices, while in earlier periods price movements had shown considerable cyclical swings but little or no secular upward tendency. Particular episodes of rising prices—including periods of hyperinflation—could generally be attributed to particular circumstances, often of a monetary nature. Even Keynes's own analysis, in *How To Pay for the War* (1940), was particularized in the sense of being addressed to the special circumstances of the war, in which massive excess effective demand was attributable to the huge expansion of government spending and reduction in the production of goods and services for private use. 'Unless we establish iron regulations limiting what is to be sold and establishing maximum prices for every article of consumption, with the result that there is nothing left to buy and the consumer goes home with the money burning his pocket, there are only two alternatives. Some means must be found for withdrawing purchasing power from the market; or prices must rise until the available goods are selling at figures which absorb the increased quantity of expenditure—in other words the method of inflation.'[1]

Hansen [Reading 7.1] provides a straightforward formalization of excess demand inflation which is explicitly dynamic in assuming that both prices and wages will respond to excess demand pressures in their respective markets. The analysis begins with the assumption of a fixed actual level of employment and consequently of output, which we may conveniently think of as the full-employment level. *Planned* production, however, will vary positively with the ratio of prices to wages: the higher this ratio, the more profitable will production be and the higher the level which will be planned. However, the higher are profits (with given real income), the lower are real wages and hence, assuming a higher consumption for workers than for capitalists, the lower will be consumption demand. Assuming all other demands—notably investment demand—constant, there will thus be an inverse relationship between planned total demand and the ratio of prices to wages. Suppose that these two schedules—of planned production and

[1] Keynes, op. cit., p. 8.

planned demand—intersect to the right of the full-employment level of output (see Figure 7.1, p. 301). Suppose that the going price/wage ratio is $(p/w)_0$. Then there is excess demand, $Q_d^0 - Q_f$, since actual output is restricted to Q_f. Prices will tend to rise. But similarly, planned production Q_p^0 is greater than possible production Q_f, so that there is excess demand for labour and a tendency for wages to rise. Somewhere between $(p/w)_1$ and $(p/w)_2$, there will be a dynamic equilibrium with prices and wages rising at the same rate. This is easily seen. At $(p/w)_1$, there is no excess demand, but there is excess planned production, and hence excess demand for labour: the wage rate rises and p/w falls. Conversely, at $(p/w)_2$, there is no excess demand for labour but there is excess demand for goods: the price level, and hence p/w, rises. Somewhere between these two points is an equilibrium characterized by equal rates of increase of prices and wages. (Note that this equilibrium need not be at the intersection of the Q_d and Q_p schedules: equal volumes of excess demand for goods and excess planned production do not entail equal rates of increase of prices and wages.)

The solution to inflation in this excess demand model is to shift the demand schedule downwards, by cutting investment or the budget deficit, until it passes through the intersection of Q_p with Q_f at A. At that point, both excess demands are zero and price and wage stability will result.[2]

A second strand in the explanation of inflation came from the recognition that, in practice, businessmen often claimed to set prices on some sort of 'cost-plus' basis. An influential, though unpublished, paper by Godley [Reading 7.2] explored the short-run behaviour of prices in the U.K. between 1950 and 1957 against the background of this suggestion, and introduced the important concept of 'normal cost' pricing. Godley notes that purely arithmetically, it is possible to view prices as a weighted sum of profits, wage costs per unit of output, and materials and fuel prices. But this is not to say that one can immediately predict the effect of a change in, say, output on prices, for any of the other elements could also be affected by the change in output.

Suppose that profits are a constant proportional mark-up on wage and import costs per unit of output. Then an index of prices should closely follow an index of costs (Godley weights imports and wages according to their relative shares in value-added, and allows for a six-month lag in adjusting prices). A fairly close correspondence is in fact found, but there is a striking pattern about the deviations between changes in unit costs and changes in prices: the change in price is greater than the change in costs when output rises rapidly, and less than the change in costs when output stagnates. This

---

[2] Note the analogy with the 'balanced wage/price deflation' discussed by Patinkin (pp. 50 ff. above). It could be argued, in parallel fashion, that the operation of the real balance effect makes A the full equilibrium point. In the Hansen equilibrium described above, prices and wages rise at the same rate. But this results in declining real balances which will reduce consumption and shift the Q_d schedule downwards. This will continue until point A is reached.

suggests that prices are set not according to *actual* unit costs, but the unit costs calculated on the basis of the 'normal', or trend, increase in output. Thus 'normal' costs rise less than actual costs when output stagnates, and prices rise less than the rise in actual costs would suggest; profit margins are correspondingly squeezed. And vice versa in periods of rapid expansion of output. Since prices are set according to 'normal' costs, short-run fluctuations in demand and output will have no significant effect on prices.

As Godley stresses, all this takes the wage bill as given. But this would vary itself with demand; it is the connection between wage rates and the demand for labour (itself derived from the demand for goods) to which we now turn. Phillips's original celebrated article[3] was largely empirical; Lipsey [Reading 7.3] attempts to provide a theoretical explanation of the 'Phillips curve' in terms of conventional market behaviour.

There are two basic elements in this account. First, it is suggested that not only will price (in this case the wage rate) rise when excess demand is present, but the *rate* of increase will vary directly with the degree of excess demand. Secondly, there is the question of the shape of the relationship between excess demand for labour (which is not observable) and unemployment (which is). To take this latter question first, it is suggested that the relationship is highly non-linear. When excess demand for labour is zero, there will still be some unemployment of a purely frictional kind. As excess demand increases, unemployment falls; but since unemployment cannot fall below zero, ever-increasing excess demand will only reduce unemployment towards zero. Excess supply, however, increases the unemployment rate proportionately. The relationship between (proportional) excess demand for labour and the unemployment rate thus has the shape shown in Figure 7.2(c), p. 310. If the relationship between the rate of change of wages and the excess demand for labour is one of simple proportionality, then the Phillips curve relationship for this market between unemployment and the rate of change of wage rates will have precisely the same shape. Lipsey points out that there is a problem in aggregating from individual markets to a macroeconomic Phillips curve because of this non-linearity. Suppose there are two markets, both with unemployment at U_a, so that there is no wage inflation. Now suppose that unemployment falls in one market and rises in the other, the over-all level of unemployment constant. Then the fall in unemployment in one market will cause wages to rise faster than the rate at which they fall in the other market: there is an over-all increase in wages despite constant unemployment. In general, the macro-curve will lie above the micro-curves, and will rise further the greater the dispersion of unemployment between different markets in the economy.

Finally, it is noted that this theory of the Phillips curve cannot provide an answer to the question of whether changes in the rate of wage-inflation

[3] A. W. Phillips, 'The Relation Between Unemployment and the Rate of Change of Money Wage Rates in the U.K., 1861–1957', *Economica*, 1958.

are attributable to demand or to supply factors: a change in excess demand could result from either a shift in the demand schedule or a shift in the supply schedule. The theory is thus neutral as between 'cost push' and 'demand pull' theories of wage inflation.

Later development of the Phillips curve took account of two things: the role of price inflation as a factor in wage bargaining, and the advent in both Britain and the U.S. of various forms of prices and incomes policy. Laidler [Reading 7.4] points out that while 'orthodox' analysis of the labour market is in terms of real wages, the Phillips curve is an hypothesis about the determination of money wages. We now have the beginnings of a theory of the 'wage–price spiral': if prices are set in a cost-plus way, then an increase in money wages in excess of productivity growth will increase prices. But if wage bargains take account of price inflation—either by compensating for past price inflation or by allowing for expected price inflation where expectations are extrapolated from part experience—there will be a further induced rise in wage-rates ... and so on. Laidler shows, using an 'expectations' account of wage bargaining, that in general this situation will produce a long-run Phillips curve significantly steeper than the short-run curve. Algebraically, if

$$\dot{w} = f(u) + \dot{p}_e$$

where $\dot{w}$ is the proportional rate of change of money wages and $\dot{p}_e$ is the proportional rate of change of expected prices, with $\dot{p}_e = \delta\dot{p}$, i.e. expected price inflation is some proportion δ of actual inflation, and if

$$\dot{p} = \dot{w} - \dot{q}$$

where $\dot{q}$ is the rate of growth of productivity, then

$$\dot{p} = \frac{f(u) - \dot{q}}{(1 - \delta)}.$$

Thus the trade-off between prices (and money wages) and unemployment is steeper the greater is δ, the sensitivity of price expectations to current experience. Algebraically, it is of course possible for the rates of price and wage inflation to become indeterminate: $\delta = 1$. This possibility must, however, be surrounded with a number of caveats. Firstly, most accounts of the generation of expectations suggest that they are formed on the basis of a weighted average of past experience, so that the response to current changes is damped. Secondly, and perhaps more importantly, wage costs are only a part of total costs so that a given increase in wage costs per unit of output will normally result in a less than proportionate increase in prices. On the other hand, under a progressive income-tax system, gross wages must rise more than in proportion to prices if real disposable income is to be maintained. It is probably fair to say that there is as yet no firm empirical consensus on the values of these parameters which determine whether or not the wage–price spiral is stable. Laidler draws attention to the fact that an exogenously-induced change in price expectations, such as an incomes policy might attempt, could restrain wage–price inflation at a lower cost in unemployment than would otherwise have been needed.

It is perhaps worth noting that a number of monetarist writings presuppose a one-for-one adjustment of expected price inflation to actual inflation. There is then one rate of unemployment (the 'natural' rate) at which the *real* wage is constant but at an indeterminate rate of money wage/price inflation, and above (below) which there must be accelerating inflation (disinflation). Since, even at the 'natural' rate of unemployment, the inflation rate is indeterminate, the rate of change of the money supply comes into its own as the determinant of the rate of inflation.

A gradual, though persistent, rise in the level of prices is one thing: hyperinflation is quite another. Cagan's paper, of which Reading 7.5 is the conclusion, is based on a study of seven hyperinflations of varying degrees of severity. Thus, to take two examples, at the peak of the German hyperinflation of 1923 (in October) prices were rising at a rate of 32,400 per cent a month, or doubling every $3\frac{1}{2}$ days, while in Hungary in July 1946, prices were rising nearly seven times every day. Cagan's explanation is, not surprisingly, purely monetary. The cost of holding money in a hyperinflation is effectively the rate of depreciation of the currency. Willingness to hold cash will depend on the expected rate of price inflation; the expected rate of inflation is assumed to be a weighted average of previous actual rates with recent experience having the greatest influence. Cagan observes that a change in the demand for real cash balances (the ratio of the quantity of money to the price level) can only be achieved, given the nominal amount of money in circulation, by a change in the price level. Finally, the demand for real balances is related statistically to the expected rate of price inflation; the statistical fit is found to be very good. Thus the hyperinflationary process is explained as follows: the crucial variable is the demand for real balances; this demand is determined by expected price inflation, itself a product of previous rates of inflation; with an exogenously given quantity of money, the price level (which adjusts so as to procure the desired level of *real* balances) thus depends on the supply of money and on previous rates of change of prices. But, similarly, previous price levels depended on the supply of money and on yet earlier rates of inflation. By repeated substitution, there emerges a dynamic relationship in which the level of prices depends only on current and past changes in the supply of money: hyperinflation is thus wholly attributable to rapid increases in the money supply.

It is clear that the degree to which an analysis of this kind could be adapted to circumstances of the much more moderate inflations which have (so far) been experienced in recent years in the industrialized countries depends on the plausibility of the central assumption that, under inflationary conditions, the only significant cost of holding money is its expected rate of depreciation. Another crucial question concerns the point at which govern-ments lose the power to finance budgetary deficits without dangerously large increases in the money supply. This latter point depends on two con-siderations: the rate of inflation itself and the time-lag between the govern-ment's expenditure and the accrual of the income on which its tax revenue is based. Thus an economy in which direct taxes are collected a year in arrears will, *ceteris paribus*, find under inflationary conditions a greater gap between its current income and current expenditure to be financed than one whose direct taxes are collected with a shorter lag.

7.1 Demand Inflation*
[...]

A SIMPLE DYNAMIC MODEL FOR INFLATION

We assume that there is perfect competition in all markets unless some-thing is said to the contrary, and that the expectations are that the prices of the moment will persist in the future. It is further assumed that only one commodity is produced, for which only one (variable) factor, labour-services, is used. The quantity of labour-services per unit of time is a given magnitude, and there is thus a given actual production, which is called Q_1;

$$Q_1 = \text{constant.} \tag{1}$$

With given equipment and technique and with expectations as described above, the volume of planned production Q_0 is a function of the relation between price p and wage-rate w, (p/w), such that the higher the price is relative to the wage-rate, the larger is the attempted (= planned = optimum) pro-duction.

$$Q_0 = \varphi\left(\frac{p}{w}\right), \tag{2}$$

$$\varphi' > 0. \tag{3}$$

Since we are at present considering only the case of inflation in which the total real income is constant (at a maximum), the demand for consumer-goods may be regarded as a function of the price–wage ratio, such that the higher the price is relative to the wage-rate, the less is the demand for consumer-goods. This is due to the fact that the higher (p/w) is, the greater is the capitalists' share of the total national income, and that the capitalists' consumption-ratio is less than the workers'; and we neglect the possibility ... that the expected income of the capitalists increases so strongly when prices rise, that demand increases with rising price–wage ratio. The demand for investment commodities is taken to be constant (for example, determined by

* From Bent Hansen, *A Study in the Theory of Inflation* (London: George Allen and Unwin, Ltd., 1951), chapter 7: 'On Open Inflation: Simple Model'.

a given rate of interest), and the state's demand for commodities (and 'production of commodities' = demand for labour-services) is taken to be constant (fixed by the budget), and we therefore find the total quantitative planned demand for commodities, D_0, to be given by

$$D_0 = \Phi\left(\frac{p}{w}\right), \tag{4}$$

$$\Phi' < 0. \tag{5}$$

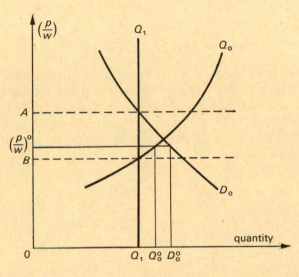

Fig. 7.1

In Figure 7.1, with the quantity of commodities as abscissa and the price–wage ratio as ordinate, the actual production, the planned production and the planned demand for commodities are indicated.

We now have, reading horizontally, that

$$D_0 - Q_1 = \text{(quantitative) inflationary gap} \atop \text{in the commodity-markets,} \tag{6}$$

$$Q_0 - Q_1 = \text{unrealizable production} = \text{index for} \atop \text{the factor-gap (quantitative).} \tag{7}$$

So it can be seen that, if there is monetary pressure of inflation, the point of intersection of Q_0 and D_0 lies to the right of Q_1, since otherwise it would not be possible with given (p/w) to have a positive inflationary gap in the commodity-markets and positive factor-gap simultaneously, and further, a monetary pressure of inflation exists only when the price–wage ratio is in the closed interval between A and B. When $(p/w) > A$, the inflationary gap in the commodity-markets < 0, and when $(p/w) < B$, the index for the factor-gap, and the factor-gap along with it, is negative.

$(Q_0 - Q_1)$, which is taken as index for the factor-gap, is connected with the factor-gap in a way given by the shape of the marginal cost curve. $(Q_0 - Q_1)$ is thus an unambiguous index for the factor-gap, since $(Q_0 - Q_1) = 0$ implies that the factor-gap is zero, and larger $(Q_0 - Q_1)$ always implies a larger factor-gap, and *vice versa*. This is all we need to know in what follows.

If the equations (1), (2), and (4), and in addition the two conditions of equilibrium:

$$D_0 - Q_1 = 0, \tag{8}$$

$$Q_0 - Q_1 = 0, \tag{9}$$

are considered as a static equilibrium system in the magnitudes Q_1, Q_0, D_0 and (p/w), the system obviously is overdetermined and inconsistent. This is nothing to be downhearted about, however, since we do not wish to treat the system statically.

Equations (8) and (9) are thus not to be used, but we introduce two dynamical equations, firstly

$$\frac{dp}{dt} = f(D_0 - Q_1), \tag{10}$$

where

$$f(0) = 0 \tag{11}$$

and

$$f' > 0, \tag{12}$$

and secondly

$$\frac{dw}{dt} = F(Q_0 - Q_1), \tag{13}$$

where

$$F(0) = 0 \tag{14}$$

and

$$F' > 0, \tag{15}$$

t denoting time.

Equations (10) and (13) with the properties described have often been used in the literature. ... Yet it should be remarked that (13) should really have the form $dw/dt = G(g(Q_0 - Q_1))$, since $Q_0 - Q_1$ is only an index for the factor-gap, so that the factor-gap $= g(Q_0 - Q_1)$, but since the function g may be supposed to have similar properties to the function G (namely $g(0) = 0$ and $g' > 0$), $G(g(Q_0 - Q_1))$ may be replaced by $F(Q_0 - Q_1)$, a monotone function of a monotone function being itself a monotone function, and $G(g(0))$ being equal to 0 from $G(0) = 0$ and $g(0) = 0$. The function F thus preserves the properties which are characteristic of G.

For the price–wage ratio we have

$$\frac{d\left(\dfrac{p}{w}\right)}{dt} = \frac{w \cdot \dfrac{dp}{dt} - p \cdot \dfrac{dw}{dt}}{w^2} = \frac{f(D_0 - Q_1) - \left(\dfrac{p}{w}\right) \cdot F(Q_0 - Q_1)}{w}, \tag{16}$$

from which it follows that the condition for the ratio of price to wage-rate to be constant, that is, for

$$\frac{d\left(\dfrac{p}{w}\right)}{dt} = 0, \tag{17}$$

is that

$$\left(\frac{p}{w}\right) = \frac{f(D_0 - Q_1)}{F(Q_0 - Q_1)}, \tag{18}$$

assuming $F(Q_0 - Q_1) \neq 0$ and also p and $w \neq 0$ and positive.

Equation (18) may now be used as a condition of what in the following will be called *quasi-equilibrium*, so we now have the quasi-equilibrium system given by:

$$Q_1 = \text{constant} \tag{1}$$

$$Q_0 = \varphi\left(\frac{p}{w}\right) \tag{2}$$

$$D_0 = \Phi\left(\frac{p}{w}\right) \tag{4}$$

$$\left(\frac{p}{w}\right) = \frac{f(D_0 - Q_1)}{F(Q_0 - Q_1)} \tag{18}$$

in the four unknowns Q_1, Q_0, D_0 and (p/w). With the help of (10) and (13) we next find the speed of the rise in the price, dp/dt, and the speed of the rise in the wage-rate, dw/dt. From (18) it is at once evident that, in quasi-equilibrium,

$$\frac{p}{w} \cdot \frac{dw}{dp} = 1, \tag{19}$$

i.e., the wage-elasticity of the price, or, if preferred, the price-elasticity of the wage-rate, is equal to 1.

On considering the functions φ, Φ, f and F, restricted according to (3), (5), (11), (12), (14), and (15), it is not difficult to see that there is one and only one solution of the system; and the value of (p/w) given by the solution is in the open interval AB. It follows directly from this that both the excess demand for commodities and the excess demand for factors are positive, so that both price and wage-rate will follow a persistent upward trend. Since there is accordingly a quasi-equilibrium solution for this system, it may be shown that this quasi-equilibrium is stable in the sense that, whatever price–wage relation we start with, there will be forces at work which tend to bring the system back to the quasi-equilibrium position.

We will call the quasi-equilibrium values of (p/w), D_0 and Q_0 respectively $(p/w)^0$, D_0^0 and Q_0^0, and we then get

$$\frac{d\left(\frac{p}{w}\right)^0}{dt} = \frac{f(D_0^0 - Q_1) - \left(\frac{p}{w}\right)^0 \cdot F(Q_0^0 - Q_1)}{w} = 0. \tag{20}$$

We now wish to show that when $(p/w) < (p/w)^0$, then $d(p/w)/dt > 0$, and conversely, when $(p/w) > (p/w)^0$, then $d(p/w)/dt < 0$, for these are the conditions that any movement away from the quasi-equilibrium position is always accompanied by a tendency to return to that position.

It is now assumed that $(p/w)^1 < (p/w)^0$, and we have that D_0^1 is the demand and Q_0^1 is the planned production at $(p/w)^1$, and accordingly

$$\frac{d\left(\frac{p}{w}\right)^1}{dt} = \frac{f(D_0^1 - Q_1) - \left(\frac{p}{w}\right)^1 \cdot F(Q_0^1 - Q_1)}{w} > \frac{d\left(\frac{p}{w}\right)^0}{dt} = 0 \tag{21}$$

because $f(D_0^1 - Q_1) > f(D_0^0 - Q_1)$, $(p/w)^1 < (p/w)^0$, $F(Q_0^1 - Q_1) < F(Q_0^0 - Q_1)$ and lastly w, whose numerical value is admittedly undetermined, is positive. In the same way it may be seen that when $(p/w) > (p/w)^0$, $d(p/w)/dt < 0$. We have thus shown that the quasi-equilibrium is stable.

In Figure 7.1 the quasi-equilibrium position is indicated by $(p/w)^0$, the excess demand in the commodity-market being $D_0^0 - Q_1$, and the excess demand in the labour-market being $Q_0^0 - Q_1$ (index). It is evident that this quasi-equilibrium position need in no way coincide with the point of intersection of the curve for demand, D_0, and the curve for supply, Q_0. Therefore, although the system does certainly tend to a fixed relation between excess demand for commodities and excess demand for labour-services, it is not such that the excess demand for labour-services 'corresponds' to the excess demand for commodities in the sense that there is just such an excess demand for labour-services as would be necessary to produce the amount of the excess demand for commodities. The planned production which cannot be carried out, $Q_0^0 - Q_1$, may be greater than or smaller than the excess demand for commodities, depending on whereabouts in the interval AB the quasi-equilibrium price–wage ratio is, and the quasi-equilibrium position is itself a matter depending on the functions f, F, φ, and Φ.

It is also intuitively evident that the system must move towards such a quasi-equilibrium position. If we consider Figure 7.1 and begin with a price–wage ratio *A*, the excess demand for commodities at this price–wage ratio will be zero, whereas the excess demand for labour-services will be positive. The price will consequently be constant, while the wage-rate tends to rise, which means that the price–wage ratio at *A* tends to fall. When the price–wage ratio has become a little lower, an excess demand for commodities will begin to appear, while the excess demand for labour-services simultaneously decreases. The price therefore begins to rise, and the speed of the rise in the wage-rate is retarded, which retards the fall in the price–wage ratio. In this way the price–wage ratio will fall—increasingly slowly—to a level where the excess demand for commodities 'corresponds' to the excess demand for factors in the sense that the percentage rise of the wage-rate per unit time which is thus brought about is equal to the percentage rise of the price per unit time. Corresponding reasoning could be put forward if we started from the price–wage ratio *B* instead.

When we prefer to speak about quasi-equilibrium instead of equilibrium, it is of course because this quasi-equilibrium is no static equilibrium, since both price and wage-rate rise without interruption and excess demands are not zero. There is equilibrium only in the sense that the price–wage ratio, excess demand for commodities and for labour-services, and along with them the speeds of the rise in the price and the wage-rate are constant.

That the system moves towards such a quasi-equilibrium may be taken as a dynamic proof for the Keynesian proposition that the ratio of prices to wages tends to be constant, so that a certain rise in money-wages is accompanied by a corresponding rise in prices, that is, so that the real wages of the workers tend to remain constant, despite possible attempts to raise them by raising the money wages. But this result applies here only in respect of a tendency which does not have effect until quasi-equilibrium is reached. And the movement towards quasi-equilibrium takes time, depending on the functions *f* and *F*. Therefore, if we suppose that a position of dynamic quasi-equilibrium has been attained with price–wage ratio $(p/w)^0$ and constant speeds for the rise in the price and the rise in the wage-rate, and further suppose that the wage-rate at some moment suddenly increases with a jump faster than the value of the speed of the rise in the wage-rate which follows from the given excess demand for labour-services, (we thus suppose that a spontaneous wage-rise occurs, which is superimposed on the induced (continuous) increase in wages, (p/w) will be displaced downwards below the quasi-equilibrium value $(p/w)^0$. This will lead to a fall in the excess demand for labour-services and a rise in the excess demand for commodities; the new price–wage ratio immediately begins to rise again, (the price-elasticity of the wage-rate becomes < 1), so that it approaches the old quasi-equilibrium position after a time, but until quasi-equilibrium is reached, the workers evidently have the benefit of a rise in the real wage. [...]

7.2 Costs, Prices and Demand in the Short Run*

As a piece of arithmetic it is the case that in any period

$$P = a\pi + b\frac{W}{X} + cM$$

where

P = prices
π = unit profits
W = wage bill
X = output
M = materials and fuel prices.

It is obviously not legitimate to argue that measures which will change the individual terms on the right-hand side of the equation (or spontaneous change, in any of them) will have such and such an affect on the price level without considering the effect they will also have on the other side.

A rather crude form of this argument, which is quite often found in commentaries on the economic situation, states categorically that a rapid increase in output is the best way of keeping prices stable. This is a paradoxical view, since it implies that the faster demands rise, the slower prices will rise; it is also in direct conflict with the doctrine underlying U.K. economic policy between 1955 and 1958, which has avowedly been trying to keep prices stable by restraining demand and output. The fact that it is paradoxical and contrary to Government doctrine does not make it wrong; but the view is by no means obviously correct, since any measures designed to increase X will probably also increase π, W, and M and it is, prima facie, plausible to imagine that these changes will offset one another. A good instance of this type of view is to be found in the March 1959 *Economic Review* by the N.I.E.S.R. 'The prospects for prices', it says, 'depend considerably on how much output and productivity recover and how quickly the benefits are passed on to the consumer.' In a purely arithmetical sense this is, of course, true, simply because X is a term in the equation. But if it is intended to tell us something about the way prices actually will behave, it must mean something of the kind that prices will rise less if productivity rises 6 per cent in the next year than if it rises 2 per cent. But what would happen to profits, the wage bill, and material prices in the former case?

We may first ask whether there has in the past been any close short-term correlation between costs and prices. In Table 1 we deduce an index of the price of total final output on the assumption that it equals after a lag of six months the change in labour costs and import prices appropriately weighted.

* From W. A. H. Godley, 'Costs, prices and demand in the short run' (previously unpublished, 1959).

There is a striking feature about the discrepancies between the calculated and actual price indices in this calculation. It is immediately obvious that whenever the increase in output is particularly small (or negative) (for example 1952, 1953, or 1957) the increase in prices has been overestimated, and when it has been particularly large (for example, 1954 and 1955) the increase in prices has been underestimated. This pattern of divergence can be made more precise. Let us take the annual average rate of increase in output between 1949 and 1955 (3·2 per cent p.a.) as being 'normal'. We can then say that (with no significant exception) whenever output has risen by less

Table 1

	1949	1950	1951	1952	1953	1954	1955	1956	1957
1. Income from employment	100·0	106·0	115·1	125·6	133·8	142·1	153·5	167·3	179·8
2. Total final output	100·0	103·7	108·2	110·4	111·9	116·8	122·0	125·9	128·2
3. Unit labour costs	100·0	102·2	106·4	113·8	119·6	121·7	125·8	132·9	140·2
4. Import prices	100	109	133	146	136·5	130	133	136	136
5. 3 weighted	77	78·7	81·9	87·6	92·1	93·7	96·9	102·3	107·9
6. 4 weighted	23	25·1	30·6	33·6	31·4	29·9	30·6	31·3	31·3
7. Total costs	100·0	103·8	112·5	121·2	123·5	123·6	127·5	133·6	139·2
8. Index of total final output prices	100·0	103·7	115·1	122·0	122·4	124·0	128·3	135·2	139·8
9. Annual % change in 7		+3·8	+8·4	+7·7	+1·9	+0·1	+3·1	+4·8	+4·2
10. Annual % change in 8		+3·7	+11·0	+6·0	+0·3	+1·3	+3·5	+5·4	+3·4

than the 'normal' amount the increase in prices has been overestimated and vice versa. The exceptions are 1949/50 and 1955/56; in neither of these cases is the divergence of the change either of normal from actual output nor of the calculated from actual prices very large. This consistent pattern of divergence tends to suggest that with exceptional changes in output (that is, exceptionally large or small) there is a movement in profit margins which at least partially counteracts the supposed 'pressure' of labour costs on prices. Table 2 tests the hypothesis that prices are fixed on the assumption that output rises at the 'normal' rate (as defined above) whether in fact it does so or not.

The close correspondence between the changes in the actual and calculated indices in Table 2, together with the absence of bias in the divergences, give prima facie support to the view that when output rises faster than the long-term trend there is an increase in profit margins which exactly offsets the 'benefit' which might be expected from relatively reduced labour costs; vice versa, when output rises less than the long-term trend (or falls) a cut in profit margins exactly offsets the rise in labour costs above the long-term trend. At the very least these calculations show that a much better explanation and forecast of prices could in the past have been made by assuming that

Table 2

	1949	1950	1951	1952	1953	1954	1955	1956	1957
1. Income from employment	100·0	106·0	115·1	125·6	133·8	142·1	153·5	167·3	179·8
2. Total final output 'normalized'	100·0	103·4	106·9	110·5	114·2	118·1	122·1	126·2	130·5
3. 'Normal' unit wage costs	100·0	102·5	107·7	113·7	117·2	120·3	125·7	132·6	137·8
4. Import prices	100	109	133	146	136·5	130	133	136	136
5. 3 weighted	77·0	78·9	82·9	87·5	90·2	92·6	96·8	102·1	106·1
6. 4 weighted	23·0	25·1	30·6	33·6	31·4	29·9	30·6	31·3	31·3
7. Total 'costs'	100·0	104·0	113·5	121·1	121·6	122·5	127·4	133·4	137·4
8. Index of total final output prices	100·0	103·7	115·1	122·0	122·4	124·0	128·3	135·2	139·8
9. Annual % change in 7		+4·0	+9·1	+6·7	+0·4	+0·7	+4·0	+4·7	+3·0
10. Annual % change in 8		+3·7	+11·0	+6·0	+0·3	+1·3	+3·5	+5·4	+3·4

fluctuations in profit margins exactly offset exceptional movements in costs, than by assuming that prices move in the same way as costs.

When the pressure of demand falls, businessmen are immediately faced with two opposing forces with regard to prices. On the one hand there is an upward pressure on the cost side, but there is also a downward pressure on demand side, and expert opinion has, in fact, been divided as to which of these two forces will gain the upper hand. The evidence presented here tends to the conclusion that *given the change in the wage and salary bill*, the two forces exactly cancel one another out. In other words in the short term (which here means at least two years) the pressure of demand makes no difference to the price level.

The rate of change in the wage and salary bill is, however, itself sensitive among other things to the pressure of demand, through its effect on wage rates, wage drift, hours worked, and employment, though almost certainly very much less so than the rate of change in output. Therefore a fall in the pressure of demand even though it causes unit costs to rise (above what they would be if the pressure of demand had not fallen) may nevertheless result in prices rising less fast.

The view advanced here, that short-term fluctuations in demand about its long-term trend make very little difference to the price level, is not really a paradoxical one. It implies that businessmen have in their minds an idea about what the long-term trend of output is and fix their prices on the basis of the costs implied by this trend, and keep them there when output in fact fluctuates about the trend, so profit margins rise when output rises faster and fall when output rises less fast, or declines.

This view, however, is of little use for considering what the outcome would be if changes in the pressure of demand caused output to diverge from its trend for a prolonged period of time. After a certain point businessmen would certainly revise their opinion about what constitutes a normal rate of increase; they would and could not *for ever* allow in their prices for a 3·2 per cent increase in output if no increase in fact took place. It cannot, however, from this be inferred that an increase in prices (above what they would have been if output *had* risen at 3·2 per cent) must *eventually* take place. The failure of output to rise at its long-term rate will be accompanied by a continuous fall in the pressure of demand. This itself is something which cannot *for ever* continue; but even if it continues for a rather lengthy period it is plausible to suppose that it will have a cumulative effect (through unemployment etc.) on the rate of increase in the wage and salary bill. It is therefore most unclear as to whether the result will be to raise prices or lower them.

7.3 The Phillips Curve*
[...]

THE RELATION BETWEEN $\dot{W}$ AND U

We shall consider this relationship, first, for a single market, and then for the whole economy, using lower-case letters to refer to the single market variables and capitals to refer to the corresponding macro-variables.

We might analyse the market for any commodity since the argument at this stage is quite general. Since, however, the subject of the present article is the labour market we shall use the terminology appropriate to that market. The usual argument merely states that when there is excess demand, for example *ij* in Figure 7.2(a), wage rates will rise, while, when there is excess supply, for example *mn* in Figure 7.2(a), wage rates will fall. Nothing is said about the speed at which the adjustment takes place. We now introduce the dynamic hypothesis that the rate at which *w* changes is related to the excess demand, and specifically, the greater is the proportionate disequilibrium, the more rapidly will wages be changing.[1] Thus the hypothesis is $\dot{w} = f\{(d-s)/s\}$ which says that the speed at which wages change depends on the excess demand as a proportion of the labour force. Figure 7.2(b) illustrates a simple form of this relation, $\dot{w} = \alpha\{(d-s)/s\} \cdot 100$ according to which if we start with excess demand of, for example, $Oc(= gh/w'g$ in Figure 7.2(a)), wages will be rising at the rate *cd*, but, if the excess demand increases to $Oa(= ij/w''j$ in Figure 7.2(a)), wages will be rising at the rate *ab*.

There are a number of advantages in including the relations illustrated in Figure 7.2(b) in one's theory rather than having only the ones illustrated in Figure 7.2(a). If it is known that both of the curves of Figure 7.2(a) are shifting

---

* From R. G. Lipsey, 'The Relation Between Unemployment and Wage Ratio', *Economica*, 1960.

[1] This is Phillips' hypothesis. It is also used extensively, for example, by Bent Hansen, *The Theory of Inflation*, London, 1951. [See Reading 7.1 above—Ed.].

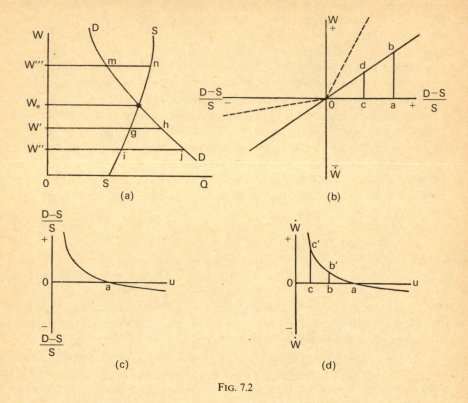

Fig. 7.2

continuously (e.g. the demand curve due to cyclical variations in income, and the supply curve due to exogenous changes in the labour force), then no two price-quantity observations will lie on the same curve. It will then be difficult to discover by observation the *ceteris paribus* relations either between supply and price or between demand and price. For the relation in Figure 7.2(b) to be observed it is necessary only that there be an unchanging *adjustment mechanism* in the market, i.e., that a given excess demand should cause a given rate of change of price *whatever the reason for the excess demand*— whether demand shift, a supply shift, or a combination of both. The rate of change of price can be observed directly and, to obtain the relation shown in Figure 7.2(b), it is only necessary to know demand and supply *at the existing market price*; it is not necessary to know what would be demanded and supplied at other prices.

Now if excess demand for labour were directly observable there would be no need to go any further. Unfortunately, this is not the case ... and it is necessary to relate excess demand to something that is directly observable, in this case the percentage of the labour force unemployed.

Figure 7.2(c) shows the relation between $(d-s)/s$ and the percentage of the labour force unemployed, u. When demand is equal to supply (wage rate

Ow_e in Figure 7.2(a)), there will be jobs available for all those who wish to work at the going wage rate. This is *not* equivalent to saying that there will be no one unemployed, but rather that the number of unemployed will be matched by an equal number of unfilled vacancies. Given that workers change jobs for any reason whatever, and that a finite time is taken to change, zero excess demand must be accompanied by some positive amount of *frictional unemployment*. From this it follows that, when the wage rate is stable (at Ow_e in Figure 7.2(a)), there will be some quantity of unemployment (Oa in Figure 7.2(c)), the exact quantity being determined by the amount of movement and the time taken to move. Now consider points to the left of a in Figure 7.2(c). The larger is the excess demand the easier will it be to find jobs, and the less will be the time taken in moving between jobs. Thus, unless there is a completely offsetting increase in numbers of persons moving between jobs, an increase in excess demand will cause a reduction in u. It is, however, impossible that u could be reduced below zero so that as $(d-s)/s$ approaches infinity, u must approach zero (or some small value > 0) asymptotically. Now consider points to the right of a. Any increase in excess supply brings an equal increase in the number of persons unemployed. Therefore, to the right of point a, there will be a linear relation between $(d-s)/s$ and u.

Now in order to obtain the relation between the two observable quantities, $\dot{w}$ and u, we need merely combine Figures 7.2(b) and 7.2(c) to obtain the relation illustrated in Figure 7.2(d). The relation between $\dot{w}$ and $(d-s)/s$ (Figure 7.2(b)) is assumed to be linear throughout. The relationship between $\dot{w}$ and u, however, is non-linear to the left of the point a because of the non-linear relation over that range between u and $(d-s)/s$ (Figure 7.2(c)) while the relation between $\dot{w}$ and u is linear to the right of a because of the assumed linear relation over that range between u and $(d-s)/s$ (Figure 7.2(c)). The relation illustrated in Figure 7.2(d) shows the *speed at which prices adjust to a disequilibrium* and we shall call it an *adjustment function*.

This relationship between $\dot{w}$ and u is an extremely simple one, and it holds considerable promise for empirical testing. The relation is, however, easily misinterpreted and it may be worth considering some examples. Consider, first, a case in which a market is observed over three successive time periods at the points a, b' and c' in Figure 7.2(d). This means that the demand and/or the supply curves have shifted over the period in such a way as to increase the disequilibrium in spite of the increase in wage rates. For example, the demand curve may have shifted so quickly to the right that the equilibrating movements in w were more than offset. Now consider a case in which the market is observed first at c', then at b' and finally at a. This is consistent with many market changes, two of which will be mentioned by way of illustration. First, both the demand and supply curves might be stable while the increase in wages restores equilibrium. Second, even though the demand curve is shifting to the right, the rate of increase in wages is fast enough to reduce the excess demand. When we observe either of these time sequences (*a* to *b'* to *c'* or *c'* to *b'* to *a*) we do not know what shifts in the curves have occurred but only that, in the first case, the shifts were such as to increase the disequilibrium in spite of equilibrating movements in *w* while, in the second case, any shifts that did occur either were not sufficient to offset the equilibrating changes in *w* or actually helped to remove the disequilibrium. If, to take a final example, the market is observed at *b'* over several successive periods, then we know that rightward shifts in demand and/or leftward shifts in supply were sufficient just to offset the equilibrating effects of changes in *w*, leaving excess demand constant.

It must be emphasized that knowledge of the shape of the adjustment function does not allow one to distinguish between *causes* of disequilibrium. Consider a market that is observed at *a* at time 0, at *b'* at $t = 1$, at *c'* at $t = 2$, at *b'* at $t = 3$, and finally at *a* at $t = 4$. All we know is that there was an increasing disequilibrium associated with ever faster increases in *w*, but after a while the disequilibrium lessened until, at $t = 4$, it is completely eliminated. Now these observations are consistent with either a rightwards shift in the demand curve, first at an increasing rate and then at a decreasing rate, or with a leftwards shift in the supply curve, indicating first a rapid withdrawal of labour supplies and then a slower withdrawal.

The relation also raises the problem of the influence of unions, but, in fact, tells us very little about their influence on the market processes. There are a number of points to notice here. First, the observation of the postulated relation is quite consistent with changes in wages caused by union-induced shifts in the labour supply curve. For, as illustrated in the previous paragraph, shifts in the supply curve would give rise to observations lying on the adjustment function. Second, unions might influence the speed of the dynamic adjustment illustrated in Figure 7.2(b). They might, for example, cause a faster increase of wages in response to excess demand and a slower fall in response to excess supply than would otherwise occur. In other words, they might shift the adjustment function to the shape illustrated by the dotted line in Figure 7.2(b). If a completely stable relation between $\dot{w}$ and *u* is observed over time, all that can be said is that, whatever is the influence of the union on the market, this influence has remained *relatively stable* over that time period.

We must now consider the effect of aggregating a number of markets each with the same relation between $\dot{w}$ and *u* in order to obtain a relation between $\dot{W}$ (the rate of change of a national index of wage rates) and *U* (the percentage of the whole labour force unemployed). The main problems can be illustrated in the case of two markets, α and β, *with identical relation functions* of the sort illustrated in Figure 7.2(d). We assume for simplicity in exposition that the labour force is divided equally between the two markets so that

$$U = \frac{u_\alpha + u_\beta}{2} \quad \text{and} \quad \dot{W} = \frac{\dot{w}_\alpha + \dot{w}_\beta}{2}.$$

Consider, first, what would happen if both markets always had identical levels of unemployment. Since the percentage of the labour force unemployed would be the same in both markets, the national index of percentage unemployment would be the same as the figure for the two markets ($u_\alpha = u_\beta = U$). Also, since both markets would be showing identical rates of change of money wage rates, the national index would show the same rate of change ($\dot{w}_\alpha = \dot{w}_\beta = \dot{W}$). If the level of unemployment then were allowed to vary in exactly the same way in both markets (so that $u_\alpha = u_\beta$ and $\dot{w}_\alpha = \dot{w}_\beta$), it follows that the observed relation between $\dot{W}$ and U would be identical with the relation between $\dot{w}$ and u in each of the individual markets.

Consider, second, what would be observed if aggregate unemployment were held constant at say $0a$ per cent $[(u_\alpha + u_\beta)/2 = 0a]$, while the distribution of this unemployment were varied as between markets (say $u_\alpha < u_\beta$). Since the relation between $\dot{w}$ and u is non-linear to the left of the point a, wages will be increasing faster in the market with excess demand (α) than they will be falling in the market with excess supply (β). Therefore the national index of wage rates will be rising $[\dot{W} = (w_\alpha + \dot{w}_\beta)/2 > 0]$ in spite of the fact that the overall unemployment percentage remains unchanged at $0a$. Furthermore, as the distribution of U between the two markets is made less equal, $\dot{W}$ will take on larger and larger values since, when u_α is reduced by the same amount by which u_β is increased, $\dot{w}_\alpha$ will be increased by more than the amount by which $\dot{w}_\beta$ will be decreased.

Finally, consider what would happen if the two markets were kept in the same relation to each other (e.g. $u_\alpha = k \cdot u_\beta$, where $k < 1$) while the total level of employment $[(u_\alpha + u_\beta)/2 = U]$ were allowed to vary. As U varies, a relation between U and W will be traced out. We will call this curve A_m for *macro-adjustment curve* and distinguish it from the curves a_i for *individual market adjustment curves*. By the reasoning in the last paragraph, this relation between $\dot{W}$ and U will lie above the individual market adjustment curves. Now consider increasing the degree of inequality between two markets (i.e. reduce the value of k). Because of the non-linearity in the individual market relations between $\dot{w}$ and u, this will increase $\dot{w}_\alpha$ by more than it will reduce $\dot{w}_\beta$. Therefore $\dot{W}$ for the whole economy will be increased. It should be noted, however, that because of the linear relation to the right of a, this upward displacement will not occur if there is excess supply in both markets (u_α and $u_\beta > 0a$).

This analysis leads to a number of important conclusions about the relation between the individual adjustment functions (the a_i's) and the macro-curve (A_m). (1) The macro-function can never lie below the individual market functions. (2) The macro-function will coincide with the individual (identical) a_i's only if there is an identical percentage of the labour force unemployed in each market at all levels of aggregate unemployment. (3) Whenever there is any degree of inequality in the distribution of unemployment combined with excess demand in at least one market ($u < 0a$ for some markets), the macro-observations will lie above the individual market curves for corresponding levels of unemployment. (4) The greater is the degree of inequality between markets, the further will the macro-observations be above the individual market curves, and thus the greater will be the degree of upward displacement of the observed macro-function. The macro-function relating $\dot{W}$ and U will be *linear* only if there is excess supply in all markets (i.e. if *all* markets are in the range where the relation between $\dot{w}$ and u is linear). In all other cases it will be non-linear.

These conclusions have a number of interesting real-world implications: (1) If one wishes to predict the rate of change of money wage rates ($\dot{W}$), it is necessary to know not only the level of unemployment but also *its distribution between the various markets of the economy*. It follows immediately that the observed macro-function need not be accepted as immutable even if the individual functions are. The macro-relation may be shifted by a policy designed to change the degree of inequality existing between the individual markets; if the distribution of U were made more even the macro-curve would shift downwards, thus increasing the downward flexibility of the overall wage level. (2) Because of the upward displacement of the macro-observations, the observed macro-relation between $\dot{W}$ and U will always tend to overstate the upward flexibility and to understate the downward flexibility of wage rates to be found in a typical individual market. (3) Thus, given non-linear a_i's, if a stable macro-relation between $\dot{W}$ and U *is* observed over a large number of cycles, it is implied that in both the upswing and the downswing roughly the same degree of inequality of unemployment has existed as between cycles. (4) Finally, great caution must be exercised in trying to infer from a statistically fitted relation between $\dot{W}$ and U what would happen to wage rates if unemployment were held constant at any level for a long time. If unemployment were held constant, we would expect the degree of inequality in its distribution between markets to change substantially. We would thus expect the macro-adjustment function to shift. [...]

7.4 Expectations and the Phillips Curve*

[...]

The simple theory of the Phillips curve, ... and its apparent policy implications, were absorbed with remarkable speed into the generally accepted corpus of macro-economics, and though the early and mid-1960s generated a large enough literature on the topic, in my judgement at least, nothing of basic importance was added by this literature to the fundamental contributions of Phillips and Lipsey.

It was not until the late 1960s that two circumstances were to produce

* From David Laidler, 'The Phillips Curve, Expectations and Incomes Policy', in H. G. Johnson and A. R. Nobay (Eds.), *The Current Inflation* (London: Macmillan & Co. Ltd., 1971; New York: St. Martin's Press, Inc., 1971).

both new academic interest in the Phillips curve and genuine intellectual advance in our understanding of it. In Britain, the attempt by the late Government to influence the rate of inflation by way of a prices and incomes policy, whether or not it was prompted by a conscious effort to by-pass the inflation–unemployment trade-off implicit in the Phillips curve, was certainly amenable to interpretation and analysis as such. Incomes policy seems an important subject for study and the Phillips curve a natural tool to use in the course of that study. In the United States an important role in the resurgence of interest in monetary economics was played by the analysis, both positive and normative, of the relationships between expectations about the rate of inflation and the behaviour over time of the velocity of circulation of money. The variable proved particularly powerful in dealing with data drawn from inflationary situations. It was again a natural, not to say fruitful, extension of the analysis of price expectations to look at their role in the determination of the rate of money wage inflation.

Now in empirically analysing recent British experience, Parkin has shown that it is helpful to deal simultaneously with the effects of incomes policy and inflationary expectations; both seem to have played a role in generating the relevant data so that the effects of both have had to be allowed for when the data are analysed. However, the two phenomena are analytically distinct, and it will be convenient initially to treat them separately here.

There is ... an element of ambiguity in Lipsey's analysis of the labour market behaviour that produces the Phillips curve. It starts from two propositions: that the supply and demand for labour determine the equilibrium wage level, and that the rate of change of the wage level in disequilibrium will depend upon the extent of the disequilibrium as measured by the excess demand for labour. Now the Phillips curve is an hypothesis about the behaviour of *money* wages while orthodox supply and demand analysis of the labour market is about the behaviour of *real* wages, and the two concepts are only interchangeable in conditions of price-level stability. If the excess demand for labour is inversely related to the level of unemployment and positively related to the rate of change of the *real* wage, then we may predict that there will exist a stable inverse relationship between the rate of change of *real* wages and the level of unemployment. However, this relationship is not the Phillips curve; to get from it to the Phillips curve we must introduce the expected rate of price inflation into our model.

We need the expected rate of inflation and not its actual current rate because individual wage bargains are struck at discrete intervals and, for any particular bargain, it is not the current price level that matters in determining the real wage that is being aimed at but the level of prices that is expected to rule over the period for which the bargain is being struck. Thus the rate at which the money wage rate will change between any two bargains will be influenced by how price expectations have changed between the times at which the two bargains are struck, and not *directly* by how the price level

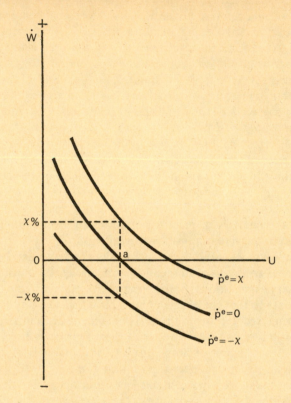

FIG. 7.3. A family of Phillips curves

itself has changed over the same interval; though in practice one would expect expectations to be based at least to some extent upon actual recent experience. In any case, merely to keep the real wage constant when prices are rising will result in money wages rising at the expected rate of price inflation, and attempts to increase real wages will result in money wages rising faster than the expected rate of price inflation.

Once we insist that the supply of and demand for labour determine the real wage, and once we note that wage bargains get struck at discrete intervals so that it is expected and not current prices that enter into the determination of the relevant real wage, we find that ... there is a different Phillips curve for every expected rate of price inflation (p^e). Representatives of a family of such curves are drawn in Figure 7.3, and they have the characteristic implied by the above analysis that each level of unemployment corresponds to a unique rate of change of the *real* wage rate.

Now the foregoing argument implies much more than that there exists a variable, changes in whose value can shift the Phillips curve. Causation does not run only one way from the expected rate of price inflation to the rate of

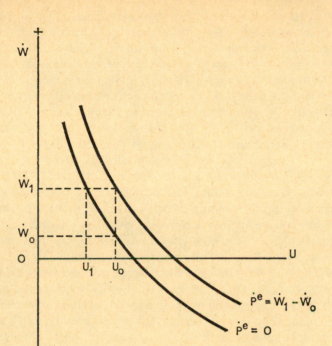

Fig. 7.4. Short- and long-run response of unemployment to the rate of wage inflation

wage inflation. This becomes clear the moment one considers the way in which these variables are likely to interact over time, and, as we shall now see, the nature of their interaction is such as to lead to the conclusion that the trade-off between wage inflation and the level of unemployment implied by the Phillips curve is mainly a short-run phenomenon. Indeed, the strict logic of the argument that follows implies that the trade-off is *solely* a short-run phenomenon—that the 'long-run' Phillips curve is vertical—but this latter proposition, though it is the most contentious one in current academic debates about the role of price expectations in the Phillips curve, is not in my judgement fundamental to any of the implications of the analysis for anti-inflationary policy. The fact that the trade-off becomes steeper with the passage of time is what is important from this point of view, and everyone involved in these debates seems to agree that it does so.

Why this should be the case is best seen by way of an example. Let Figure 7.4 depict the situation in an economy in which there is price stability—and expected price stability—and in which U_0 yields a rate of wage inflation W_0 which is just compensated for by rising labour productivity.

Now if the authorities in this economy were to decide that U_0 was too high a level of unemployment, that U_1 was preferable, they could initially achieve this level of unemployment by policies which would also lead to a rate of wage inflation of $\dot{W}_1$. However, with no change in productivity growth prices would begin to rise at a rate equal to $\dot{W}_1 - \dot{W}_0$. Now so long as people form their expectations about inflation on the basis of current and past behaviour of prices, the price inflation thus induced would begin to become anticipated. It would continue at the same rate so long as the authorities pursued policies to maintain wage inflation at a rate of $\dot{W}_1$, and the longer it continued at that rate the closer to the actual rate of inflation would the expected rate move. Thus, the closer to its ultimate location (at $p^e = \dot{W}_1 - \dot{W}_0$) would the short-run Phillips curve shift and the closer to U_0 would the level of unemployment compatible with the rate of wage inflation $\dot{W}_1$ become.

There have been a number of empirical investigations of the kind of wage–price spiral implied in the above example, and there seems to be abundant evidence that wage inflation which proceeds sufficiently fast to involve price inflation does lead the public to form expectations about price inflation that shift the traditional (what I am now calling the 'short-run') Phillips curve upwards. In the long run the trade-off between inflation and unemployment vanishes completely only if actual inflation becomes perfectly anticipated, and there does seem to be doubt. as to whether the mechanism involved works quite as perfectly in practice as it does in the foregoing fairly abstract piece of economic analysis; nevertheless there is no disagreement that the trade-off becomes considerably less acute as time passes and people permit current inflation to influence their expectations. This is an extremely important discovery from the point of view of the design of anti-inflationary policy, as we shall now see.

The Phillips curve as originally conceived presented policy-makers with a simple trade-off indeed: more unemployment for less inflation. The introduction of expectations into the analysis complicates the trade-off. Again an example is the best way to see this. Suppose the 'long-run' Phillips curve is such as is depicted in Figure 7.5, and I have drawn it with a slope to emphasize the independence of what I have to say of extreme assumptions about perfect learning mechanisms being embodied in the model, and suppose we begin at point X on that curve with a given rate of inflation and a given level of unemployment. Suppose the Government of the day finds point X uncongenial and prefers point Y; how is it to get there? There are many routes, but a comparison of two of them will suffice to illustrate the nature of the policy trade-off involved in choosing a route.

First, suppose the Government attempts to attain at once the rate of inflation compatible with Y. This would involve taking policy steps to contract the excess demand for labour to such an extent that initially the economy would move to Y' on the short-run Phillips curve that passes through X. Clearly the actual rate of inflation would then be below that expected on the short-run Phillips curve passing through X and, as expectations were revised downwards, this short-run Phillips curve would shift to the left until point Y was reached.

Alternatively the authorities could choose to move immediately to the level of unemployment compatible with ultimate equilibrium at Y. This would involve shifting the economy to point Y'' on the short-run Phillips curve. Again, the actual inflation rate would fall below the expected one, and again the constant revision of expectations in the light of experience

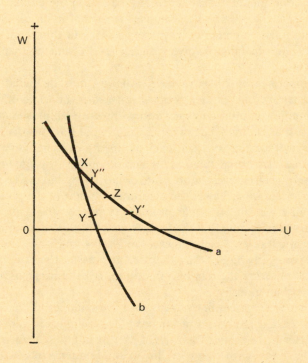

FIG. 7.5. Long- and short-run Phillips curves
a. Short-run curve   b. Long-run curve

would eventually result in the economy reaching Y. However, inasmuch as people learn about the likely future rate of inflation from current experience, the bigger is the discrepancy between experience and expectations, the faster are expectations likely to be revised. This is a well-tested proposition and in the present context it implies that the first route from X to Y considered will be a more rapid one than the second.

Now the decision to start the foregoing analytic example from a point of equilibrium on the long-run Phillips curve was a matter of expositional convenience only. In Britain at the moment, both the rate of inflation and the level of unemployment are high by standards of recent history. Phillips's original analysis suggested that a level of unemployment of just under $2\frac{1}{2}$ per cent combined with productivity growth in the region of 2–3 per cent per annum would lead to virtual price stability! This fact suggests that the current British situation is best represented by a point on a short-run Phillips curve to the right of the long-run one, a point such as Z. Indeed, if inflation expectations are still catching up with experience the point Z, far from being static, might actually be moving upwards. However, this does not mean that the foregoing analysis is irrelevant. If the basic mechanism sketched out above is a good model of the effects of inflation in the labour market, it is still true that we may expect to reduce the rate of inflation only slowly if we maintain unemployment at its present level, and that if we seek a rapid end to inflation this must involve a higher level of unemployment than we have at present.

This comparison of routes whereby inflation may be ended is of course merely illustrative of a general proposition about the trade-offs implied by the introduction of inflation expectations into the Phillips curve, and that proposition is as follows. The more rapidly is the rate of inflation reduced, the higher will be the average level of unemployment while it is being reduced. One can bring inflation to a halt quickly by having more unemployment for a relatively short time, or slowly by having less unemployment for a longer time. This is the qualitative nature of the policy trade-off. I do not think we can yet say anything very precise about its quantitative nature other than to note that the experience of both Britain and the United States over the last few years suggests that, if unemployment rates are to be kept from rising any higher than they are at present, then the timetable for significantly reducing the rate of inflation must be conceived of in terms of years rather than months.

Indeed we need not confine ourselves to the evidence of the last few years on this matter. The analysis we have been discussing leads to the conclusion that any attempt to reduce the current rate of inflation below its expected rate will lead to an increase in the unemployment rate which, though 'transitory', may nevertheless endure for an uncomfortably lengthy period. There is no reason to suppose that this conclusion applied only to situations in which the relevant inflation rates are positive, and once this is grasped, the events of the later 1920s and 1930s in Britain and those of the 1930s in the United States may also be regarded as evidence of the consequences of rapid reductions in the rate of inflation relative to its expected level. One might also note that when viewed in this broader perspective, modern theories of the Phillips curve come to look like more general versions of Keynes's hypothesis about the downward rigidity of money wages. They predict, after all, that the rate of change of money wages is rigid downwards relative to the expected rate of price inflation, and a special case of this is a downward rigidity in the level of money wages when the expected rate of inflation is zero.

Now the analysis of the last few paragraphs assumes that price-level expectations are only influenced by data generated within a 'wage-price spiral', and that the workings of the labour market are not interfered with so as to alter the manner in which wages respond to market forces. Some form of incomes policy is frequently put forward as a means of breaking into the mechanism described above in such a way as to enable the economy to by-pass the sacrifices of output inherent in the unemployment generated by reducing the rate of inflation by conventional methods.

There are two distinct ways in which incomes policy might break into this spiral. It might influence the way in which real wages respond to shifts in the supply of and demand for labour, or it may influence expectations about inflation independently of the current behaviour of prices. As we shall see in a moment, incomes policy as practised in the past seems to have been effective in interfering with the supply and demand mechanism in the labour market — not always with the results anticipated — but I must confess to having doubts about according any unique role to incomes policy as a means of influencing expectations; since I know of no study either published or unpublished on this particular issue, however, these doubts are not as firmly based as they might be.

There is no question that it would be highly desirable to have a tool with which expectations about inflation could be damped independently of a fall in the actual rate of inflation. In terms of Figure 7.5 such a tool would shift the 'short-run' Phillips curve downwards and to the left independently of the wage–price mechanism described above and hence enable the rate of inflation to be reduced at a lower cost in unemployment than otherwise.

This shift of the short-run Phillips curve would not, in and of itself, reduce the rate of inflation of course. There is nothing in the foregoing analysis to suggest that changing expectations alone will have any influence on the rate of inflation; it simply suggests that if expectations about inflation can be changed independently of the influence of information transmitted by market forces, then a given rate of inflation will be attainable at a lower cost in transitory unemployment than otherwise. The Phillips curve analysis is, as I noted at the outset, silent and neutral on the appropriate policies with which to achieve a given rate of inflation. [...]

7.5 A Monetary Theory of Hyperinflation*
[...]
FLUCTUATIONS IN REAL CASH BALANCES
The evidence given in the preceding sections verifies the hypothesis that these fluctuations result from changes in the variables that determine the demand for real cash balances. With a change in demand, individuals cannot

* From P. Cagan, 'The Monetary Dynamics of Hyperinflation', in M. Friedman (ed.), *Studies in the Quantitive Theory of Money* (University of Chicago Press, 1956).

alter the nominal amount of money in circulation, but they can alter the real value of their collective cash balances by spending or hoarding money, and so bid prices up or down, respectively. Only one of the variables that determine this demand has an amplitude of fluctuation during hyper-inflation as large as that of the balances and could possibly account for large changes in the demand. That variable is the cost of holding money, which during hyperinflation is for all practical purposes the rate of depreciation in the real value of money or, equivalently, the rate of rise in prices.

To relate the rate of price rise to the demand for the balances, it is necessary to allow for lags. There are two lags that could delay the effect of a change in this rate on the demand. First, there will be a lag between the expected and the actual rate of price rise; it may take some time after a change in the actual rate before individuals expect the new rate to continue long enough to make adjustments in their balances worthwhile. Second, there will be a lag between the desired and the actual level of the balances; it may take some time after individuals decide to change the actual level before they achieve the desired level. The method used to take account of these lags relates actual real cash balances to an average of past rates of price change, weighted by an exponential curve, so that price changes more recent in time are given greater importance. The weights never fall to zero, but past price changes sufficiently distant in time receive too small a weight to have any influence on the weighted average. The steepness of the weighting pattern indicates the length of period over which most of the weight is distributed. This method of allowing for the two lags does not distinguish between them. However, the period of time required for adjusting the balances to desired levels seems negligible compared with the past period of time normally reviewed in forming expectations. For this reason I have assumed that the actual level of real cash balances always equals desired levels and that the weighted average of past rates of price change measures only the 'expected rate of price change'. But there is no direct evidence on the relative importance of the two lags, and the name given to the weighted average may be lacking somewhat in descriptive accuracy.

The specific form of the hypothesis, restated to allow for lags, asserts that variations in the expected rate of price change account for variations in real cash balances during hyperinflation, where the expected rate is an exponentially weighted average of past rates. The hypothesis was tested by fitting a least-squares regression to time series for the balances and the expected rate. The regression fits the data for most months of the seven hyperinflations with a high degree of accuracy, and thus the statistical results strongly support the hypothesis.

The regression functions derived from these fits provide good approximations to the demand function for the balances and so reveal certain characteristics of this demand during hyperinflation. The elasticity of demand with respect to the expected rate of price change increases in absolute value as this expected rate rises. This contradicts the often stated view that the degree to which individuals can reduce their holdings of a depreciating currency has a limit. The demand elasticity indicates that they reduce their holdings by an increasing proportion of each successive rise in the expected rate. Indeed, the reason why issuing money on a grand scale does not almost immediately lead to extreme flight from the currency is not due to inelasticity in the demand for it but to individuals' lingering confidence in its future value. Their confidence maintains the lag in expectations, whereby the expected rates of price change do not at first keep pace with the rapidly rising actual rates. However, the weighting pattern for the lag appears to become much steeper in the later months, indicating that the lag in the expected behind the actual rates tends to shorten in response to continual inflation.

Thus the large changes in the balances during hyperinflation correspond to large changes in the rate of price change with some delay, not simultaneously. The demand function that expresses this correspondence can be be interpreted to represent a dynamic process in which the course of prices through time is determined by the current quantity of money and an exponentially weighted average of past rates of change in this quantity. The process implies that past and current changes in the quantity of money cause the hyperinflation of prices. This link between changes in prices and money is only broken when the absolute value of the slope of the demand function is especially high or the lag in expectations is especially short. In that event price increases become self-generating. What this means is that the rise in prices immediately produces a proportionately greater decline in real cash balances. Then the effect of percentage changes in prices and the balances on each other does not diminish, as a stable moving equilibrium of prices requires, but grows. Such a process sends up the *percentage* change in prices at no less than an exponential rate, even if the quantity of money remains constant. Apparently the demand slope and the lag never reached the critical level in the seven hyperinflations, for none had self-generating price increases. Instead of running away on their own, price increases remained closely linked to past and current changes in the quantity of money and could have been stopped at any time, as they finally were, by tapering off the issue of new money.

THE TREMENDOUS INCREASE IN MONEY AND PRICES

If in fact price increases were not self-generating, what accounted for their tremendous size? The above explanation of their behaviour in terms of large increases in the quantity of money only raises the further question, 'Why did this quantity increase so much?' Clearly, issuing money on a large scale serves as a major source of funds for government expenditures. The inflation resulting from new issues places a tax on cash balances by depreciating the value of money. The revenue in real terms raised by this tax is the product of the rate of rise in prices (the tax rate) and real cash balances (the tax base). By setting the rate of increase in the quantity of money, the note-issuing authorities indirectly determine the rate of tax through the process implied by the demand function. The simplicity of administering this tax undoubtedly explains why governments resorted to continual issues of money in the difficult periods after the two world wars. An explanation of why those issues became so large, however, is found in the response of the tax base to the tax rate.

If the tax rate remains constant, the tax base and, therefore, the revenue ultimately become constant. Among all constant rates, there is one that yields a maximum ultimate revenue. With a tax rate that increases rapidly enough, however, the revenue forever exceeds this maximum amount for a constant rate because of delays in adjusting the tax base produced by the lag in expectations. In the beginning and closing months of the seven hyper-inflations, the authorities successfully pursued a policy of inflating at increasing tax rates to take advantage of this lag and collected more revenue thereby than they could have obtained with any constant rate. This policy led to actual rates far above the constant rate that would have maximized ultimate revenue and produced the tremendous increases in money and prices characteristic of hyperinflation.

In the middle months the rate of increase in the money supply tapered off, for what reason it is not entirely clear, and the revenue temporarily decreased. As a result, the revenue collected with the actual tax rates was not greater on the average than the amount that could have been obtained with a constant rate. The resumption of increasing rates in the closing months restored the revenue to amounts at least as large as those in the beginning months. In order to compensate for the low level to which the tax base fell after many months of hyperinflation, the tax rates rose to astronomical heights. This explosion of the rates in the final months completely disrupted the economy and forced the government to substitute a traditional tax program for a policy of printing money.[...]

The model used has definite limitations: it only applies accurately to large price increases, and it fails to describe the closing months in four of the hyperinflations. In the closing months real cash balances sometimes rose when the model indicates they should have fallen. This limitation likely results from expectations that current price increases would not last very long. Such expectations are not related in any direct or obvious way to past changes in prices. To take account of this limitation of the model does not seem to require revisions that would contradict the premise of this study that domestic monetary factors alone explain hyperinflations.

Many prevailing theories of economic disturbances emphasize external monetary factors like the foreign-exchange rate, as well as real factors like the level of employment and real income, the structure of trade unionism, the rate and extent of capital formation, and so on. These factors are prominent primarily in discussions of depression. Yet they also enter into discussions of inflation. The theory of the cost-price spiral, which borrows its concepts and framework from theories of income and employment common in discussions of depression, has been applied to inflation with the suggestion, sometimes explicit, that it applies to hyperinflation as well. Closely related and often identical to the theory of the cost-price spiral is the explanation of hyperinflation in terms of the depreciation of the foreign-exchange rate.

These theories postulate that a rise in prices results from increases in wages or prices of imported goods and precedes increases in the quantity of money. This study points to the opposite sequence and indicates that an extreme rise in prices depends almost entirely on changes in the quantity of money. By implication, the rise in wages and the depreciation of the foreign-exchange rate in hyperinflations are effects of the rise in prices. Extreme changes in a short period of time in exchange rates will primarily reflect variations in the real value of the currency. It is perfectly true that the public might well expect depreciation of the currency to show up more accurately in depreciation of exchange rates than in any set of readily available commodity prices and so follow these rates in adjusting their balances. Circumstances are easy to imagine in which *for a short time* the exchanges might depreciate faster than prices rise and so appear to move in advance of prices. But this result would not mean that the rise in prices had become the effect rather than the cause of exchange depreciation. Real cash balances would be related to this depreciation only so long as it remained a good indicator of price changes.

The model suggests in addition that the spiral theory places emphasis on the wrong factors. *Hyper*inflation at least can be explained almost entirely in terms of the demand for money. This explanation places crucial importance on the supply of money. While the monetary authorities might capitulate to pressures for sustaining wage increases, as the spiral theory presumes, they will typically attend to many other considerations. The most important of these in hyperinflation is the revenue raised by issuing money, which was analysed above. More precise analysis than this of the determinants of the money supply goes beyond a mechanistic account of the inflationary process and involves the motives of governments, with whom the authority to open and close the spigot of note issues ultimately lies.

8. The Distribution of Income

Introductory Note

The determination of the distribution of the national income between the owners of the various factors of production is one of the oldest questions in economics, and one which has, not surprisingly, attracted a wide variety of answers. Much of the dispute has been given added piquancy by the suggestion—not universally accepted—that factor shares, however determined, have been quite amazingly constant over long periods of time and in the face of sweeping changes in techniques and levels of production.

Perhaps the simplest account is the 'marginalist' or 'neoclassical' theory. For the sake of simplicity, assume only two factors of production, labour and capital. Then money national income is divided between wages and profits. In particular, the share of wages, λ say, is equal to the wage bill divided by income:

$$\lambda = \frac{W}{Y} = \frac{wL}{pX}$$

where w is the wage rate, L the volume of employment, p the price level, and X real output. Now under perfectly competitive conditions, w/p, the real wage, is equal to the marginal product of labour (MPL) while X/L is by definition the average product of labour (APL). Thus

$$\lambda = \frac{\text{MPL}}{\text{APL}}.$$

What then determines MPL and APL? The answer, in general, is the amounts of labour and capital available, and the technique of production, summarized in the production function

$$X = f(L, K).$$

If this function—which represents purely *technical* considerations—can be specified, the average and marginal products of factors can be found. To take a well-known example, the Cobb-Douglas production function has the form:

$$X = aL^z K^\beta$$

or, if constant returns to scale are assumed:[1]

$$X = aL^{\alpha}K^{1-\alpha}.$$

Now the marginal product of labour is equal to

$$\frac{\partial K}{\partial L} = {}^{\alpha}aL^{\alpha-1}K^{1-\alpha} = \frac{\alpha aL^{\alpha}K^{1-\alpha}}{L} = \alpha\frac{X}{L}.$$

And thus labour's share, λ, is

$$\lambda = \frac{\text{MPL}}{\text{APL}} = \alpha\,\frac{X}{L}\bigg/\frac{X}{L} = \alpha.$$

The share of capital, similarly, is equal to the rate of profit multiplied by the amount of capital, divided by the value of output:

$$k = \frac{\rho K}{pL} = \frac{\partial K}{\partial K}\cdot\frac{L}{K} = 1-\alpha.$$

Thus, if the technology of the economy can be described by a Cobb-Douglas production function, and if competitive conditions ensure that factors are paid their real marginal products, factor shares will be constant over time no matter how the relative quantities of labour and capital change. This implies that any change in the ratio of capital to labour is exactly offset (in terms of income shares) by a change in their marginal productivities and thus in their rewards: the elasticity of substitution between labour and capital is unity.

This is a beguiling result. There are enormous difficulties in calculating the shares of labour and capital in the national product—for example, how should the incomes of the self-employed be allocated, or how should the growth of non-operatives (or 'white collar' workers) be treated—but a large number of economists have been satisfied that, as a working approximation, the relative shares of labour and capital have been remarkably constant over long periods of time and in the face of tremendous changes in techniques of production and in the growth of capital—exactly as the Cobb–Douglas function suggests.

Criticism of the use of the Cobb–Douglas function has taken a variety of forms. Most fundamentally, it has been argued (most forcibly by Joan Robinson) that there cannot logically be a way of arriving at an aggregate value of capital, K, which can be used in a 'production function' in order to explain the return on capital. This is because capital, *once in existence*, must be valued in terms of its expected future earnings. But these earnings them-

---

[1] In technical terms, if the function is homogeneous of degree one: equal proportionate increases in the inputs of labour and capital raise output in the same proportion. Thus if the proportionate increase is γ, the new level of output is:

$$X' = a(\gamma L)^{\alpha}(\gamma K)^{\beta} = a\gamma^{\alpha+\beta} = a\gamma^{\alpha+\beta}L^{\alpha}K^{\beta} = \gamma^{\alpha+\beta}X = \gamma X$$

only if $\alpha+\beta = 1$, or $\beta = (1-\alpha)$.

selves depend on the rate of profit. Thus in order to value capital, the rate of profit must be known. To use the capital stock so arrived at in order to explain the rate of profit thus involves complete circularity of argument.

Another fundamental objection is that the value of α, on which everything depends, is totally unexplained. Unlike, say, the propensity to consume, it is not a parameter which can be given direct economic significance—for example, why should α not vary over time, and why does it apparently vary from country to country?

Both these objections can be made to any aggregate production function which relates output to inputs of labour and capital in a fixed way. A specific objection to the Cobb–Douglas form is that the elasticity of substitution between labour and capital is restricted to unity. This led to the formulation of a more general production function having a constant (but not necessarily unit) elasticity of substitution—the C.E.S. production function. An elasticity of substitution of less than one means that a rise in the relative price of a factor is less than offset by a fall in the relative quantity employed, so that its relative share rises, or, to put it the other way round, the relatively rapidly growing factor (generally capital) will experience a declining share of income.

The first problem, then, in providing a 'marginalist' or neoclassical theory of distribution is to decide how stable relative shares have been or, what comes to the same thing, how close to one the elasticity of substitution has been.

Solow [Reading 8.1] points out that, as a matter of statistical theory, if relative shares in the different sectors of the economy fluctuate independently, the aggregate shares will be much more stable: since marginalist theories are essentially micro-economic, aggregate stability is thus irrelevent if it hides micro-variability. Solow finds that for year-to-year changes this is indeed the case—in fact, given variability within industries, the aggregate wage share actually varied more, rather than less, than might have been expected. For the longer term trend in relative shares, Solow suggests that there has actually been some upward movement in the wage share, and that this is consistent, given the rates of growth of capital and labour, with an elasticity of substitution of less than one—of about $\frac{2}{3}$, in fact. Attention is finally drawn to the fact that labour as well as capital is difficult to measure—an unknown fraction of wage and salary payments represents payment to 'human capital', the result of investment in education, health, training, and so on—so that the observed upward movement in labour's share may itself be an illusion.

Bronfenbrenner [Reading 8.2] develops further the point about the relative insensitivity of factor shares to alternative assumptions about the elasticity of substitution. Provided only that the elasticity is not well below unity, relative shares will be fairly constant even in the face of quite marked changes in the capital–labour ratio.

Marginalist theories, then, which assume a production function character-ized by an elasticity of substitution of or somewhat below unity are consistent with the evidence of a stable or slightly rising share of labour. The argument can, however, be inverted: production functions fit the data rather well *because* relative shares have been quite stable. If this possibility is admitted, of course, we need an alternative theory of distribution.

Kaldor [Reading 8.3] provides such an alternative by marrying the Keynesian savings function with the assumptions of different propensities to save out of wages and out of profits. We thus have the aggregate savings function

$$S = s_p P + s_w W = s_p P + s_w(Y - P)$$

(where s_p and s_w are the propensities to save out of profits, P, and wages, W). Equating savings with investment gives

$$I = (s_p - s_w)P + s_w Y.$$

On dividing through by Y and rearranging:

$$\frac{P}{Y} = \frac{1}{s_p - s_w}\frac{I}{Y} - \frac{s_w}{s_p - s_w};$$

the share of profits is related to the share of investment.

This expression is, of course, an identity. In order to interpret it as a theory of the determination of the share of profits, in the first place an explanation of how the investment/income ratio is determined must be provided. This Kaldor does by recourse to the Harrod–Domar growth model—or rather, to the simple accelerator theory of investment. Then

$$I = v\Delta Y$$

and

$$\frac{I}{Y} = \frac{v\Delta Y}{Y} = vG_w;$$

the investment ratio is given by the capital/output ratio multiplied by the warranted rate of growth. But we are immediately in trouble: for long-run equilibrium the warranted rate of growth must be equal to the natural rate; as Kaldor notes (p. 346), the warranted rate can be made to adjust to the natural rate by a variation in P/Y and hence in s and I/Y. But the direction of causality has now been reversed—I/Y depends on P/Y and not vice versa; we no longer have a theory of distribution.

Similar difficulties are encountered if we consider the effects of a change in one or other of the savings propensities. Suppose that s_w rises. Then, with I/Y given, the share of profits falls just far enough to compensate for the workers' extra savings, since $I/Y = s$, the over-all propensity to save is constant. But it is difficult to see why profits should fall in this way. It is more plausible to assume that the initial effect is simply a reduction in demand and hence in output, leading to a rise in I/Y. With depressed demand, certainly, the share of profits may fall, tending to effect the rise in I/Y, but what is more important is that the investment ratio cannot be taken as fixed. This suggests that the identity should be expressed as

$$\frac{I}{Y} = (s_p - s_w)\frac{P}{Y} + s_w.$$

This simply reflects the fact that value of the multiplier (Y/I) will depend on the distribution of income if the propensities to save out of profits and out of wages differ.

Tobin [Reading 8.4] satirizes the Kaldorian theory by showing that it can be generalized to any number of categories of income and any number of kinds of expenditure. Kaldor's response [Reading 8.5] suggests that this is formally true but economically nonsense. It is interesting to note, though, that Tobin's approach makes much more economic sense if we replace the Kaldorian dependence of income distribution on the investment ratio by the 'Keynesian' dependence of the value of the multiplier on the distribution of income. In the latter case, it might well make perfectly good sense to examine the savings propensities of a large number of classes of income receives rather than just two—classified either by type or by level of income—if there were grounds for expecting noticeable variation in savings propensities across these classes.

Joan Robinson [Reading 8.6] draws together a variety of distribution theories: the marginalist theory, the degree-of-monopoly theory, the Kaldorian theory, and the 'relative bargaining power' theory. In the short run, the second and third of these can readily be reconciled: when there is spare capacity, margins are squeezed and consumption and total income are higher for a given rate of investment. The investment ratio and thus the profit share are relatively low. This argument can be put the other way round, of course: lower margins give a lower profit share, a higher over-all propensity to consume and thus a higher multiplier, increasing income for a given rate of investment.

The situation is somewhat complicated when workers' bargaining power is brought into the picture. Below full employment, increases in money wages will probably not be fully reflected in prices; demand and employment rise with real wages. As full employment is reached, however, further money-wage increases will be merely inflationary.

Only when we move into the long run do marginalist considerations become important, for the stock of capital can no longer be taken as fixed. If two economies, confronting the same technology, are compared, the one with the more capital-intensive methods of production will have the higher real wage—either because for a given money wage rate prices must be lower to raise output to capacity, or because monopoly power is lower. But it does not follow that the *share* of wages will be higher—whether it is or not depends on whether the 'elasticity of substitution' of capital for labour is less or greater than one.

This is to compare two economies at the same time, but in considering changes in relative shares over time, the rate of investment must be brought into the picture. *Provided* that full employment is maintained, that savings propensities are unchanged, that technical progress and the growth of demand are neutral, that the degree of monopoly is constant, and that there is steady growth, the rates of growth of capital and output will be the same, the investment ratio unchanging, and the rate of profit on capital and relative shares will be constant over time.

Any comprehensive analysis of the movements of relative shares must thus be highly eclectic. It is worth noting finally that under conditions of wage-push inflation, the existence of a lag in adjusting prices to unit wage costs will introduce a relationship between changes in the rate of inflation and in the share of profits. A rise in the rate of wage inflation will, before prices adjust, depress the profit share. If the new, higher, rate of wage inflation is maintained, the profit share will stabilize, but at a lower level.

8.1 How Constant are Relative Shares?[*]

Ever since the investigations of Bowley and Douglas it has been widely believed that the share of the national income accruing to labor is one of the great constants of nature, like the velocity of light or the incest taboo. Keynes called it 'a bit of a miracle'. Even if it is sometimes observed that the pattern of distributive shares shows long-run shifts or short-run fluctuations, the former can be explained away and the latter neglected on principle. The residual belief remains that, apart form a slight (and questionable) upward trend and a countercyclical movement, the share of wages in the privately produced national income is unexpectedly stable. Much effort is devoted to exploiting and explaining this fact.

The object of this paper is to suggest that, like most miracles, this one may be an optical illusion. It is not clear what exactly is meant by the phrase: 'The wage share in national income is relatively stable' or 'historically almost constant'. The literature does not abound in precise definitions, but obviously literal constancy is not in question. In any case, what I want to show is that for one internally consistent definition of 'relatively stable', the wage share in the United States for the period 1929–1954 (or perhaps longer) has not been relatively stable.

If this contention is accepted, it is not without some general implications for economic theory. Beginning with Ricardo there have been sporadic revivals of interest in macroeconomic theories of distribution. Now it is possible to have an aggregative distribution theory without believing in the historical constancy of relative shares, but the belief certainly reinforces the desire for such a theory. After all, a powerful macroeconomic fact seems to

[*] From R. M. Solow, 'A Skeptical Note on the Constancy of Relative Shares', *American Economic Review*, 1958.

call for a macroeconomic explanation. It need not have one, but that is beside the point. As Kaldor says:

...no hypothesis as regards the forces determining distributive shares could be intellectually satisfying unless it succeeds in accounting for the relative stability of these shares in the advanced capitalist economies over the last 100 years or so, despite the phenomenal changes in the techniques of production, in the accumulation of capital relative to labor and in real income per head.[1]

But if, in fact, relative stability of distributive shares is at least partially a mirage, one may feel freer to seek intellectual satisfaction elsewhere. There is still a lot to be explained.

HOW TO BE CONSTANT THOUGH VARIABLE

Table 1 shows the share of compensation of employees in a number of different aggregate income totals, so that the reader can see what kind of variability occurs, over the business cycle and over longer periods.

What does an economist mean when he says that the wage share has been relatively stable? Since he does not mean that it has been absolutely constant, he must mean that in some sense or other it has been more nearly constant than one would ordinarily expect. The sentence already quoted from Kaldor suggests that since technique, real capital and real income per head have all changed 'phenomenally', you would normally expect distributive shares to have changed 'a lot', but they have only changed 'a little' and this requires a special explanation. Not to split verbal hairs, it is evident that this is no definition at all. One must have some standard by which to judge whether some particular series of observations has fluctuated widely or narrowly.

Such standards of comparison can arise in a variety of ways. A tight theory may itself provide a benchmark. For example, the fraction of males among live births in a well-defined animal population is subject to statistical fluctuations from year to year. But the theory of sex determination, although perhaps not complete, gives some indication of how variable one ought normally expect the series to be. To say that the series is relatively stable could then simply mean that the observed variance is significantly less than the variance expected from the theory. Something like this does appear to be in the back of some authors' minds when they refer to the stability of the wage share. Take as a starting-point the neoclassical general equilibrium theory of distribution, which is formulated in terms of production functions, input-ratios, and the like. These quantities fluctuate over time. Ought not the pattern of distributive shares to show comparable variability, according to the theory?

But there is a world of difference between this case and the genetic illustration. The general equilibrium theory is in the first instance a micro-economic one. Between production functions and factor-ratios on the one hand, and aggregate distributive shares on the other lies a whole string of

[1] N. Kaldor, 'Alternative Theories of Distribution', *Review of Economic Studies*, Feb. 1956, p. 84.

Table 1. *Share of Compensation of Employees in Various Income Totals, 1929–1955*

Year	As Per Cent of National Income	As Per Cent of Privately Produced Income	As Per Cent of Income Originating in Corporate Business	As Per Cent of Income Originating in Manufacturing
1929	58·2	55·6	74·6	74·2
1930	61·8	57·3	78·7	76·7
1931	66·5	63·2	87·9	88·0
1932	73·2	69·3	101·0	108·0
1933	73·4	69·5	101·6	104·7
1934	70·0	69·6	88·3	89·4
1935	65·3	60·8	83·8	82·6
1936	66·1	61·3	80·0	78·3
1937	65·1	61·0	79·9	78·7
1938	66·6	61·8	83·0	83·3
1939	66·1	61·6	80·9	79·9
1940	63·8	59·5	76·2	73·4
1941	61·9	57·6	72·7	69·0
1942	61·9	56·8	71·7	71·1
1943	64·4	57·6	72·2	73·4
1944	66·4	58·8	73·8	74·8
1945	68·0	59·8	77·0	77·3
1946	65·5	60·6	79·9	78·8
1947	65·3	61·7	77·5	75·9
1948	63·6	60·0	74·8	72·9
1949	65·2	61·2	75·7	73·5
1950	64·3	60·4	73·6	70·8
1951	65·1	60·8	74·0	71·1
1952	67·2	62·8	76·7	75·4
1953	68·9	64·5	78·5	77·5
1954	64·4	65·0	79·6	79·3
1955	68·9	64·7	77·4	76·5

Source: Department of Commerce, *Surv. Curr. Bus., National Income* Supplement, 1954, and July 1956.

intermediate variables: elasticities of substitution, commodity-demand and factor-supply conditions, markets of different degrees of competitiveness and monopoly, far-from-neutral taxes. It is hard to believe that the theory offers any grip at all on the variability of relative shares as the data change—in fact this may be viewed by some as a symptom of its emptiness. A license to speculate, maybe, but hardly a firm standard. As a matter of speculation, the theory might be taken to imply that the aggregate shares come about through a kind of averaging process, in which many approximately independently changing parameters intervene. From this view would follow an expectation of 'relative stability', if anything.

A second possible source of a standard of variability is suggested by the analogy of statistical quality control. There the problem is also one of detecting 'excessive' variability (or sometimes even deficient variability). But in the absence of some outside specification, the standard is usually given by the past behavior of the process itself. Clearly if the wage share had once oscillated between 50 and 80 per cent and now moved only in the range from 60 to 70 per cent, we could speak of relative stability. But it is not claimed that this is the case.

Third, the contrast between micro- and macroeconomic theories suggests that it might be possible to formulate an *internal* standard of variability. A hint in that direction is contained in a remark of Phelps Brown and Hart: 'Yet it still remains true that the changes in the share of wages in national incomes are not so great as we should expect when we look at the often wide swings of the corresponding shares within particular industries, and this relative stability also calls for explanation.' Indeed it does; if the calorie contents of breakfast, lunch, and supper each varies widely, while the 24-hour total remains constant, we at once suspect a master hand at the controls. Similarly if wide swings within industries yield only narrow swings in the aggregate, this points to some specifically interindustrial or macroeconomic force.

But relative shares have denominators as well as numerators. However we subdivide the economy, the over-all share will be a weighted average, not a sum, of the respective shares for the subdivisions. This does not automatically entail that the over-all share will have a smaller variance than the sector shares. That all depends on the intersector correlations, i.e., on the macro-economic forces. Note an interesting consequence: it is *negative* correlations between sectors which reduce the variance of the weighted average.

Here we have something empirically testable. Suppose, to take the simplest possible case, the economy is divided into k equal-sized sectors, in each of which the wage share is equally variable through time. Then if the sector shares fluctuate independently, the aggregate wage share will have a variance only $1/k$ times the common sector variance. If this were in fact the picture, it would be hard to claim that the relative stability of the aggregate shares required a specifically macroeconomic explanation. It might still be claimed that the aggregate share is more stable than it ought to be on this hypothesis, but now the explanation would have to be sought in the excessive stability of the individual sector shares. I suppose it could be plausibly argued that there are macroeconomic reasons for such microeconomic stability, but this is not the form that current theories take.

The more general case is no more complicated. Suppose there are k sectors, with shares $S_1, \ldots, S_k$ and weights in the aggregate $w_1, \ldots, w_k$. If the S_i represent the share of wages in the sector value-added, the w_i will represent the share of the sector value-added in the total. Let σ_i^2 be the variance of S_i through time, and let symbols without subscripts represent the aggregate share and its variance. Then in the null case of independence among sectors we would find:

$$\sigma^2 = \sum_1^k w_i^2 \sigma_i^2, \tag{1}$$

and in any case we would have

$$S = \sum_{1}^{k} w_i S_i. \tag{2}$$

Predominantly positive correlations among sectors will yield a larger σ^2 and negative correlations a smaller σ^2. [...]

EMPIRICAL RESULTS

The sector shares in Table 2 were calculated from the 1954 *National Income Supplement to the Survey of Current Business* (pp. 176–79). In each case they represent the ratio of 'compensation of employees' to 'national income originating'. [...]

Table 2. *Share of compensation of employees in income originating in selected sectors of the economy for selected years, 1929–1953*

Sector	Weight	1929	1935	1937	1939	1941	1947	1951	1953	Variance
Agriculture, etc.	·113	·170	·134	·153	·185	·162	·170	·162	·206	·0004
Mining	·031	·751	·813	·715	·761	·705	·733	·704	·740	·0013
Contract Construction	·056	·667	·709	·704	·710	·733	·727	·759	·766	·0010
Manufacturing	·441	·742	·826	·787	·799	·690	·759	·711	·711	·0021
Wholesale and Retail Trade	·230	·702	·726	·691	·701	·624	·633	·650	·670	·0013
Transportation	·084	·725	·800	·812	·785	·717	·840	·805	·815	·0018
Communications and Public Utilities	·044	·541	·540	·560	·550	·543	·697	·619	·604	·0030
Total (Current Weights)		·647	·658	·656	·675	·613	·653	·631	·696	·0007
Fixed-Weight Total		·652	·702	·677	·688	·613	·666	·642	·678	·0008

The table shows both the current-weighted over-all labor share and a fixed-weight series using the weights of 1941. In only one year does the use of fixed weights result in a change in the aggregate share of more than 2 percentage points, and the variability, as measured by the variance, is affected hardly at all. In part this is because the weights do not change radically, the main shift being a decrease in the relative weights of Agriculture and Transportation between 1929 and 1953, with Manufacturing gaining.

The last column shows the variance of each sector share and of the two aggregate-share series. The fixed-weight aggregate has a variance of ·0008. If formula 1 is used to calculate a theoretical variance on the assumption that the sector shares moved independently in a statistical sense, it turns out to be ·0005. This difference is almost certainly not statistically significant. We would have to conclude that the aggregate share varied just about as much as it would vary if the individual sector shares fluctuated independently, with positive and negative intercorrelations approximately offsetting each other. If anything, the aggregate share fluctuated a bit *more* than the hypothesis of independence would indicate. Anyone who believes that the aggregate share over this period was unexpectedly stable must believe the same of the sector shares and presumably seek the explanation there. [...]

There are various ways of explaining the facts. Perhaps it is a fair idealization that the several industries buy their labor and capital inputs in the same or similar markets, so they can be imagined to face the same factor prices. If it is further assumed that each industry produces a single commodity with a technology describable by a smooth production function, then everything will depend on the distribution of elasticities of substitution among industries. If nearly all elasticities of substitution are on the same side of unity, then the wage shares will go up and down together in nearly all industries and there will be strong positive correlation. If elasticities of substitution are evenly divided on both sides of unity, there will be two groups of industries whose wage shares will move in opposed phase. Whether the net result is to increase or reduce the variance of the aggregate wage share as compared with the hypothetical zero-correlation value will depend in a complicated way on the arrangement of weights and elasticities. [...]

It must be admitted that none of this is very informative. It is all too static, too inattentive to technical change, too free with unknown and unknowable parameters—in a word, too neoclassical. It would be nice to have a single aggregative bulldozer principle with which to crash through the hedge of microeconomic interconnections and analogies. It is not inconceivable that the bulldozer may yet clank into view; but it is by no means inevitable either. [...]

In general, the data we have examined suggest the following: if by the 'historical constancy' of labor's share it is meant that the share of the total social product imputed to wages has shown a marked absence of fluctuation as compared with the fluctuations of its industrial components, then this belief is probably wrong. Whatever exceptional stability there has been in the pattern of relative shares appears attributable to the components. This in turn suggests that there is no need for a special theory to explain how a number of unruly microeconomic markets are willy-nilly squeezed into a tight-fitting size ·65 strait-jacket. A theory which wishes to produce the magic number among its consequences may have to say something about the component sectors among its premises.

THE CHARACTER OF TRENDS

There are still some interesting problems to be found among the sectors and in the aggregates. One such—and some economists would no doubt prefer to phrase the whole 'historical constancy' question in these terms—is the mildness of the observable trends in the sector shares and in the aggregate relative shares. The history of western capitalism is supposed to be characterized by a long-run accumulation of capital relative to labor. We expect this trend to result in *some* trend in the distribution of the product. Why do we not observe a stronger one?

First, let us look at the orders of magnitude involved. No great accuracy is possible because of the difficulty of finding a reasonable measure of capital stock, because no two available time series are conceptually identical, and finally because of the imputation problem involved. Roughly speaking, during the first half of this century the capital/labor ratio for the private non-farm sector rose by about 60 per cent. But most or all of the increase took place before 1929. Between 1929 and 1949 there was little change, possibly even a decline. In manufacturing the contours were broadly similar, although the initial increase in the capital/labor ratio during the period 1909–1929 was considerably greater.

So far as distributive shares are concerned, it is generally accepted that there has been a slight tendency for the labor share to increase secularly. But before 1929 the trend was approximately horizontal (with some short-run movements); between 1929 and 1949 there is a more pronounced upward tilt in the wage and salary share as Table 1 shows.

What lends mystery to this picture is that in the first quarter-century, when capital accumulates much more rapidly than the labor force grows, the distributive share picture shows little or no trend. But in the second quarter-century, when the growth of capital relative to labor slows down or ceases, the wage share begins to rise. It seems likely that the difference between the two periods may be tied up with a slightly higher rate of technical progress in the years since 1929.

But let us accept the notion that economic history shows us a strong tendency for capital to grow relative to labor. We are then led to expect a strong trend in relative shares. But which way? The neoclassical answer is that this depends on 'the' elasticity of substitution, or rather on the distribution of elasticities of substitution on either side of unity.

Here we run up against the same kind of verbal question that occupied us earlier. What is a 'strong' trend in relative shares? And what constitutes an elasticity of substitution 'substantially' different from unity in terms of common-sense expectations? And how different from unity need the elasticity of substitution be in order that it convert a strong trend in the capital/labor ratio into a strong trend in relative shares? For the case of a two-factor, constant-returns-to-scale production function, it is not hard to calculate that the elasticity of the labor share with respect to the capital/labor ratio is $-S_K\{1-(1/\tau)\}$ where S_K is the share of property in income and τ is the elasticity of substitution. Is an elasticity of substitution of $\frac{2}{3}$ substantially different from unity? It means that a 10 per cent change in the relative costs of capital and labor services will induce a 6·7 per cent change in the capital/labor ratio. If $\tau = \frac{2}{3}$ and $S_K = ·30$, the elasticity of the labor share with respect to the capital/labor ratio is ·15. Thus if the capital/labor ratio rises by 60 per cent (with $\tau = \frac{2}{3}$) the labor share should rise by 9 per cent. And since the labor share hovers around ·70, this means a rise of about 6 or 7 percentage points. But this is just the order of magnitude observed!

I don't mean to conclude from this example that yet another problem evaporates. But before deciding that observation contradicts expectation, there is some point in deciding what it is we expect. In this case what needs precision is the notion of substitutability, and the problem is complicated further by the need to consider changes occurring over varying periods of time.

There are even more fundamental obstacles to a clear evaluation of the argument about trends. An unknown fraction of society's capital takes the form of the improvement of human abilities and skills. Casual observation suggests that this fraction has been increasing over time. Correspondingly an unknown fraction of what we call wages, even 'production workers' wages', no doubt constitutes a rent on that human capital. So the true quantitative picture is far from clear. If it were possible to separate out the part of nominal wages and salaries which is really a return on investment, the share of property income in the total might be found to be steadily increasing. An alternative way of looking at it is to say that investment in education, training, public health, etc., has the effect of increasing the efficiency of the human agent, so that a measurement in man-hours underestimates the rate at which the labor force grows as properly measured in efficiency units. In this case it might be found that the accumulation of nonhuman capital does not proceed at a faster rate than the labor force grows. These are intrinsically difficult distinctions to draw empirically, but they hold much theoretical and practical importance.

There are of course still other discrepancies between the data we have and the analytical concepts to which we pretend they correspond. The problem of imputing to a labor a proper share of the income of unincorporated enterprises has received some attention. But even in the corporate sector possibilities exist for converting what is 'really' property income into nominal labor income, and vice versa, and there are often tax reasons for doing so. If this were a random effect in time it would do no great harm, but in fact it may behave more systematically than that.

To complete the catalog of uncertainties about trends, I ought to mention the intrusion of technical change between the simple facts of factor ratios and factor rewards. About the incidence of historical changes in techniques little is known, and without this it is difficult to know what residual remains to be accounted for.

8.2 Relative Shares and the Elasticity of Substitution*

Microeconomic or marginalist distribution theory has for a generation explained relative share changes largely by the elasticity of substitution

* From M. Bronfenbrenner, 'A Note on Relative Shares and the Elasticity of Substitution', *Journal of Political Economy*, 1960.

between inputs in production.[1] Constancy of relative shares requires a value
of unity. If the elasticity of substitution is less than unity, an input's relative
share rises if its quantity falls (relative to the quantities of other inputs). The
reverse is true if the elasticity of substitution exceeds unity.

This theory has been attacked as an inadequate explanation for the
observed degree of constancy in the relative shares of labor and capital in
developed capitalist countries, particularly the Commonwealth countries and
the United States. Such a degree of constancy, argue the critics, requires a
unitary elasticity of substitution over all. There is no outside evidence that
it actually has this value.[2] To quote Kaldor, formulator of an important rival
macroeconomic theory of distribution: 'Existing theories are unable to
account for such constanc[y] except in terms of particular hypotheses
(unsupported by any independent evidence) such as the unity-elasticity of
substitution between Capital and Labour.'[3]

The principal rebuttal to date has been by Solow,[4] whose main stress is
on the residual variability of the distributive shares both within and between
various industry groups. He applies the standard statistical formula for the
standard error of the arithmetic mean to show that the over-all variability of
the labor share is no lower than one would expect from its (substantial)
variability within each industry group and the number of such groups within
the economy.

This note will develop an alternative rebuttal. It will derive a relation or
formula among relative shares, share shifts, and the elasticity of substitution.
This relation or formula will show a high degree of constancy of relative
shares as a mathematical consequence over a wide range of values of the
elasticity of substitution, given reasonable values for other coefficients. For
low values of this elasticity, however, it will show shares shifting with input
prices—at once a common-sense and a suggestive result.

To derive our basic relation or formula, we shall begin by assuming two
main groups of inputs or factors of production. Call them a and b (labor and
capital), with prices p_a and p_b. The share of a (labor), or simply s, is by
definition $[ap_a/(ap_a+bp_b)]$. It follows that

$$\frac{ap_a}{bp_b} = \frac{s}{1-s} = \frac{(a/b)}{p_b/p_a}.\tag{1}$$

[1] The concept of elasticity of substitution was introduced into the literature almost simultaneously by Professor Hicks and Mrs. Robinson in the early 1930's (J. R. Hicks, *Theory of Wages* [London: Macmillan & Co., 1932], pp. 114–20, 244–47; Joan Robinson, *Economics of Imperfect Competition* [London: Macmillan & Co., 1933], pp. vii, 256, 330).

[2] The production function generally used in empirical testing of marginal distribution theory is the Cobb-Douglas function. In this function the elasticity of substitution between capital and labor is unitary regardless of the values of any statistically fitted coefficients.

[3] Nicholas Kaldor, 'A Model of Economic Growth', *Economic Journal*, December, 1957, p. 592.

[4] Robert M. Solow, 'A Skeptical Note on the Constancy of Relative Shares', *American Economic Review*, September, 1958, pp. 618–31. For a more recent statistical study see I. B. Kravis, 'Relative Income Shares in Fact and Theory', *American Economic Review*, December, 1959, pp. 917–49. The Solow article anticipates briefly some part of my own argument as well (pp. 629–30). [See Reading 8.1 above—Ed.]

If we define our units of a and b such that their prices in some base period are equal, as we may do without loss of generality, the ratio (a/b) is in these units also equal to $[s/(1-s)]$.

The expression $[s/(1-s)]$ may be set up as a dummy variable z. To show how the labor share s changes with the labor-capital ratio (a/b) when the price ratio (p_b/p_a) is also dependent upon (a/b), we employ the following relationships which use the dummy variable:[5]

$$\frac{ds}{d(a/b)} = \frac{dz}{d(a/b)} \div \frac{dz}{ds} \quad \frac{dz}{d(a/b)} = \frac{1}{p_b/p_a} - \left[\frac{(a/b)}{(p_b/p_a)^2} \frac{d(p_b/p_a)}{d(a/b)} \right].$$

The elasticity of substitution between a and b is written σ and defined as[6]

$$\frac{d(a/b)}{(a/b)} \div \frac{dr}{r},$$

but r, the marginal rate of substitution between a and b, equals (p_b/p_a) under competitive conditions. (This equating of r with $[p_b/p_a]$ is, incidentally, the only point at which this derivation supplements mathematical identities with conventional economic theory.)

We can now solve for $[dz/d(a/b)]$ in terms of the elasticity of substitution thus defined:

$$\frac{dz}{d(a/b)} = \frac{1}{(p_b/p_a)} \left(1 - \frac{1}{\sigma} \right) = \frac{p_a}{p_b} \left(\frac{\sigma-1}{\sigma} \right).$$

The derivative (dz/ds) is simply $[1/(1-s)^2]$. If we divide $[dz/d(a/b)]$ by this result, we obtain the desired expression for the change of the labor share with respect to the labor-capital ratio

$$\frac{ds}{d(a/b)} = \frac{(1-s)^2(p_a/p_b)(\sigma-1)}{\sigma}. \tag{2}$$

Expression (2) can be converted easily to elasticity terms:[7]

$$\frac{Es}{E(a/b)} = \frac{ds}{d(a/b)} \frac{(a/b)}{s} = \frac{(1-s)^2(ap_a/bp_b)(\sigma-1)}{s\sigma} = \frac{(1-s)(\sigma-1)}{\sigma}. \tag{3}$$

Both (2) and (3) are clearly zero when the elasticity of substitution is unitary. In other words, a unit value of σ implies complete constancy of relative shares. When σ takes on other values, however, (2) and (3) do not vary greatly from zero, particularly if σ becomes greater than unity. To show

---

[5] The first relationship applies the 'function of a function' rule of elementary calculus. The second relationship follows from the differentiation of eq. (1).

[6] Cf. R. G. D. Allen, *Mathematical Analysis for Economists* (London: Macmillan & Co., 1938), p. 341.

[7] A similar result was reached by Solow (*op. cit.*, p. 629). In deriving it, the reader should remember that, by eq. (1), $(ap_a/bp_b) = s/(1-s)$.

this, we may differentiate equations (2) and (3) partially with respect to σ:

$$\frac{\partial}{\partial \sigma}\left[\frac{ds}{d(a/b)}\right] = \frac{p_a}{p_b}\left[\frac{(1-s)}{\sigma}\right]^2$$

and

$$\frac{\partial}{\partial \sigma}\left[\frac{Es}{E(a/b)}\right] = \frac{1-s}{\sigma^2}.$$

These expressions are both clearly small for large relative shares (s close to unity) or for large values of the elasticity of substitution (σ greater than unity).

Another demonstration of the insensitivity of the labor share is furnished by substituting realistic values in equation (2). Let the labor share s be two-thirds, a not unrepresentative value for the United States. Let the units of labor and capital be chosen as before so as to make p_a and p_b equal. In other words, let the base-period price of a unit of labor be equal to the base-period price of a unit of capital services. The base-period labor-capital ratio (a/b) must be 2:1 in these arbitrary units to give the postulated labor share of two-thirds. Making these substitutions, equation (2) reduces to

$$\frac{ds}{d(a/b)} = \frac{(1/3)^2(\sigma-1)}{\sigma} = \frac{1}{9} - \frac{1}{9\sigma}. \qquad (4)$$

If we postulate that a change in s must be five percentage points in either direction before we can regard it as significant in view of the vagaries of our

Table 1. *Changes in labor-capital ratio required for a five-point increase in the labor share*

Elasticity of substitution (σ)	Change in labor-capital ratio (a/b)	
	Absolute	Relative
0·25.......	−0·150	−0·075
0·50.......	−0·450	−0·225
0·75.......	−1·350	−0·675
1·00.......	Infinite	Infinite
1·50.......	1·350	0·675
2·00.......	0·900	0·450
3·00.......	0·675	0·338
5·00.......	0·563	0·281

statistics, the required numerical change in the labor-capital ratio can be computed for any elasticity of substitution:

$$d\frac{a}{b} = \frac{0·050}{(0·333)^2}\frac{\sigma}{\sigma-1} = \frac{0·450\sigma}{\sigma-1}. \qquad (5)$$

The required percentage change can be obtained by dividing these results by 2, since our units have been chosen so as to set the base-period labor-capital ratio equal to that figure.

The results with reference to a five-point *increase* in the labor share are given in Table 1. A reversal of signs in the last two columns would give the figures for a five-point *decrease*. No special skill is required to draw up similar tables for other relative shares, elasticities of substitution, or thresholds of significance.

For example, with an elasticity of substitution equal to 2, a rise of the labor-capital ratio from 2·00 to 2·90 would be required for a five-point rise in the labor share; a fall from 2·00 to 1·10 would be required for a five-point fall. For an elasticity of substitution equal to one-half, the labor-capital ratio would have to fall from 2·00 to 1·55 for a five-point rise in the labor share or rise from 2·00 to 2·45 for a five-point fall. [...]

[The] table ... shows that, even for elasticities considerably removed from unity, changes such as will produce even five-point changes in relative shares are unrealistically high for the short or the intermediate run. This is especially true for elasticities greater than unity. For these, the right side of equation (4) never falls below 0·450 (absolute); the corresponding minimum relative change in the labor·capital ratio is 0·225.

We may conclude that conventional marginal distribution theory does in fact imply considerable constancy of relative shares, provided only that the elasticity of substitution between capital and labor is not well below unity. This constancy is perfect only when the elasticity of substitution is unitary, but it is high for other values as well. Conversely, a high degree of constancy in relative shares is consistent with a wide range of elasticities of substitution. Relative shares are insensitive to changes in elasticities of substitution, much as the Lorenz curve coefficient of concentration is insensitive to many types of change in the personal income distribution.

The constancy of relative shares may be complete, as argued by Kaldor, or incomplete, as argued by Kravis. Whether complete or incomplete, this constancy does not argue against marginalist distribution theory. Allegations to the contrary are simply wrong, despite the weight of authority which supports them. Neither, of course, does such constancy argue in favor of marginal theory against rival formulations which imply similar results. Whether complete or incomplete, the constancy of relative shares is not a satisfactory 'crucial experiment' for choosing between the marginal theory and its alternatives. [...]

8.3 A Keynesian Theory of Distribution*

[...]

Keynes, as far as I know, was never interested in the problem of distribution as such. One may nevertheless christen a particular theory of distribution as 'Keynesian' if it can be shown to be an application of the specifically

* From N. Kaldor, 'Alternative Theories of Distribution', *Review of Economic Studies*, 1955–6.

Keynesian apparatus of thought and if evidence can be adduced that at some stage in the development of his ideas, Keynes came near to formulating such a theory.[1] The principle of the Multiplier (which in some way was anticipated in the *Treatise* but without a clear view of its implications) could be alternatively applied to a determination of the relation between prices and wages, if the level of output and employment is taken as given, or the determination of the level of employment, if distribution (i.e., the relation between prices and wages) is taken as given. The reason why the multiplier-analysis has not been developed as a distribution theory is precisely because it was invented for the purpose of an employment theory—to explain why an economic system can remain in equilibrium in a state of under-employment (or of a general under-utilization of resources), where the classical properties of scarcity-economics are inapplicable. And its use for the one appears to exclude its use for the other. If we assume that the balance of savings and investment is brought about through variations in the relationship of prices and costs, we are not only bereft of a principle for explaining variations in output and employment, but the whole idea of separate 'aggregate' demand and supply functions—the principle of 'effective demand'—falls to the ground; we are back to Say's Law, where output as a whole is limited by available resources, and a fall in effective demand for one kind of commodity (in real terms) generates compensating increases in effective demand (again in real terms) for others. Yet these two uses of the Multiplier principle are not as incompatible as would appear at first sight: the Keynesian technique, as I hope to show, can be used for both purposes, provided the one is conceived as a short-run theory and the other as a long-run theory—or rather, the one is used in the framework of a static model, and the other in the framework of a dynamic growth model.

We shall assume, to begin with, a state of full employment (we shall show

[1] I am referring to the well-known passage on profits being likened to a 'widow's cruse' in the *Treatise on Money*, Vol. 1, p. 139. 'If entrepreneurs choose to spend a portion of their profits on consumption (and there is, of course, nothing to prevent them from doing this) the effect is to *increase* the profit on the sale of liquid consumption goods by an amount exactly equal to the amount of profits which have been thus expended...Thus however much of their profits entrepreneurs spend on consumption, the increment of wealth belonging to entrepreneurs remains the same as before. Thus profits, as a source of capital increment for entrepreneurs, are a widow's cruse which remains undepleted however much of them may be devoted to riotous living. When on the other hand, entrepreneurs are making losses, and seek to recoup these losses by curtailing their normal expenditure on consumption, i.e. by saving more, the cruse becomes a Danair jar which can never be filled up; for the effect of this reduced expenditure is to inflict on the producers of consumption-goods a loss of an equal amount. Thus the diminution of their wealth, as a class is as great, in spite of their savings, as it was before.' This passage, I think, contains the true seed of the ideas developed in the *General Theory*—as well as showing the length of the road that had to be traversed before arriving at the conceptual framework presented in the latter work. The fact that 'profits', 'savings' etc. were all defined here in a special sense that was later discarded, and that the argument, specifically refers to expenditure on consumption goods, rather than entrepreneurial expenditure in general, should not blind us to the fact that here Keynes regards entrepreneurial incomes as being the resultant of their expenditure decisions, rather than the other way round—which is perhaps the most important difference between 'Keynesian' and 'pre-Keynesian' habits of thought.

later the conditions under which a state of full employment will *result* from our model) so that total output or income (Y) is given. Income may be divided into two broad categories, Wages and Profits (W and P), where the wage-category comprises not only manual labour but salaries as well, and Profits the income of property owners generally, and not only of entrepreneurs; the important difference between them being in the marginal propensities to consume (or save), wage-earners' marginal savings being small in relation to those of capitalists.[2]

Writing S_w and S_p for aggregate savings out of Wages and Profits, we have the following income identities:

$$Y \equiv W + P$$

$$I \equiv S$$

$$S \equiv S_w + S_p.$$

Taking investment as given, and assuming simple proportional saving functions $S_w = s_w W$ and $S_p = s_p P$, we obtain:

$$I = s_p P + s_w W = s_p P + s_w (Y - P) = (s_p - s_w)P + s_w Y$$

Whence

$$\frac{I}{Y} = (s_p - s_w)\frac{P}{Y} + s_w \tag{1}$$

and

$$\frac{P}{Y} = \frac{1}{s_p - s_w}\frac{I}{Y} - \frac{s_w}{s_p - s_w}. \tag{2}$$

Thus, given the wage-earners' and the capitalists' propensities to save, the share of profits in income depends simply on the ratio of investment to output.

The interpretative value of the model (as distinct from the formal validity of the equations, or identities) depends on the 'Keynesian' hypothesis that investment, or rather, the ratio of investment to output, can be treated as an independent variable, invariant with respect to changes in the two savings propensities s_p and s_w. (We shall see later that this assumption can only be true within certain limits, and outside those limits the theory ceases to hold.) This, together with the assumption of 'full employment', also implies that the level of prices in relation to the level of money wages is determined by demand: a rise in investment, and thus in total demand, will raise prices and profit margins, and thus reduce real consumption, whilst a fall in investment, and thus in total demand, causes a fall in prices (relatively to the wage level) and thereby generates a compensating rise in real consumption. Assuming

---

[2] This may be assumed independently of any skewness in the distribution of property, simply as a consequence of the fact that the bulk of profits accrues in the form of company profits and a high proportion of companies' marginal profits is put to reserve.

flexible prices (or rather flexible profit margins) the system is thus stable at full employment.

The model operates only if the two savings propensities differ and the marginal propensity to save from profits exceeds that from wages, i.e. if:

$$s_p \neq s_w$$

and

$$s_p > s_w$$

The latter is the stability condition. For if $s_p < s_w$, a fall in prices would cause a fall in demand and thus generate a further fall in prices, and equally, a rise in prices would be cumulative. The degree of stability of the system depends on the *difference* of the marginal propensities, i.e., on $1/(s_p - s_w)$ which may be defined as the 'coefficient of sensitivity of income distribution', since it indicates the change in the share of profits in income which follows upon a change in the share of investment in output.

If the difference between the marginal propensities is small, the coefficient will be large, and small changes in I/Y (the investment/output relationship) will cause relatively large changes in income distribution P/Y; and *vice versa*.

In the limiting case where $s_w = 0$, the amount of profits is equal to the sum of investment and capitalist consumption, i.e.:

$$P = \frac{1}{s_p} I.$$

This is the assumption implicit in Keynes' parable about the widow's cruse—where a rise in entrepreneurial consumption raises their total profit by an *identical* amount—and of Mr. Kalecki's theory of profits which can be paraphrased by saying that 'capitalists earn what they spend, and workers spend what they earn'.

This model (i.e., the 'special case' where $s_w = 0$) in a sense is the precise opposite of the Ricardian (or Marxian) one—here wages (not profits) are a residue, profits being governed by the propensity to invest and the capitalists' propensity to consume, which represent a kind of 'prior charge' on the national output. Whereas in the Ricardian model the ultimate incidence of all taxes (other than taxes on rent) fall on profits, here the incidence of all taxes, taxes on income and profits as well as on commodities, falls on wages.[3] Assuming however that I/Y and s_p remain constant over time, the share of

---

[3] The ultimate incidence of taxes can only fall on profits (on this model) in so far as they increase s_p, the propensity to save out of *net* income after tax. Income and profits taxes, through the 'double taxation' of savings, have of course the opposite effect: they reduce s_p, and thereby make the share of *net* profits in income larger than it would be in the absence of taxation. On the other hand, discriminatory taxes on dividend distribution, or dividend limitation, by keeping down both dividends and capital gains, have the effect of raising s_p. (All this applies, of course, on the assumption that the Government *spends* the proceeds of the tax—i.e. that it aims at a balanced budget. Taxes which go to augment the budget surplus will lower the share of profits in much the same way as an increase in workers' savings.)

wages will also remain constant—i.e., real wages will increase automatically, year by year, with the increase in output per man.

If s_w is positive the picture is more complicated. Total profits will be reduced by the amount of workers' savings, S_w; on the other hand, the sensitivity of profits to changes in the level of investment will be greater, total profits rising (or falling) by a greater amount than the change in investment, owing to the consequential reduction (or increase) in workers' savings.[4]

The critical assumption is that the investment/output ratio is an independent variable. Following Harrod, we can describe the determinants of the investment/output ratio in terms of the rate of growth of output capacity (G) and the capital/output ratio, v:

$$\frac{I}{Y} = Gv. \tag{3}$$

In a state of continuous full employment G must be equal to the rate of growth of the 'full employment ceiling', i.e., the sum of the rate of technical progress and the growth in working population (Harrod's 'natural rate of growth'). For Harrod's second equation:

$$\frac{I}{Y} = s$$

we can now substitute equation (1) above:

$$\frac{I}{Y} = (s_p - s_w)\frac{P}{Y} + s_w.$$

Hence the 'warranted' and the 'natural' rates of growth are not independent of one another; if profit margins are flexible, the former will adjust itself to the latter through a consequential change in P/Y.

This does not mean that there will be an *inherent* tendency to a smooth rate of growth in a capitalist economy, only that the causes of cyclical movements lie elsewhere—not in the lack of an adjustment mechanism between s and Gv. As I have attempted to demonstrate elsewhere[5] the causes of cyclical movements should be sought in a disharmony between the entrepreneurs' *desired* growth rate (as influenced by the degree of optimism and the volatility of expectations) which governs the rate of increase of output capacity (let us call it G') and the natural growth rate (dependent on technical progress and the growth of the working population) which governs the rate of growth in

---

[4] Thus if $s_p = 50\%$, $s_w = 10\%$, $I/Y = 20\%$, P/Y will be 15%; but a rise in I/Y to 21% would raise P/Y to 17·5%. If on the other hand $s_w = 0$, with $s_p = 50\%$, P/Y would become 40%, but an increase in I/Y to 21% would only increase P/Y to 42%. The above formulae assume that average and marginal propensities are identical. Introducing constant terms in the consumption functions alters the relationship between P/Y and I/Y, and would reduce the *elasticity* of P/Y with respect to changes in I/Y.

[5] *Economic Journal*, March 1954, pp. 53–71.

output. It is the excess of G' over G—not the excess of s over Gv—which causes periodic breakdowns in the investment process through the growth in output capacity outrunning the growth in production.[6]

Problems of the trade cycle however lie outside the scope of this paper; and having described a model which shows the distribution of income to be determined by the Keynesian investment-savings mechanism, we must now examine its limitations. The model, as I emphasized earlier, shows the share of profits P/Y, the rate of profit on investment P/vY, and the real wage rate W'/L, as functions of I/Y which in turn is determined independently of P/Y or W/L. There are four different reasons why this may not be true, or be true only within a certain range.

1. The first is that the real wage cannot fall below a certain subsistence minimum. Hence P/Y can only attain its indicated value, if the resulting real wage exceeds this minimum rate, w'. Hence the model is subject to the restriction $W/L \geqslant w'$, which we may write in the form:

$$\frac{P}{Y} \leqslant \frac{Y - w'L}{Y}. \tag{4}$$

2. The second is that the indicated share of profits cannot be below the level which yields the minimum rate of profit necessary to induce capitalists to invest their capital, and which we may call the 'risk premium rate', r. Hence the restriction:

$$\frac{P}{vY} \geqslant r. \tag{5}$$

3. The third is that apart from a minimum rate of profit on capital there may be a certain minimum rate of profit on turnover—due to imperfections of competition, collusive agreements between traders, etc., and which we may call m, the 'degree of monopoly' rate. Hence the restriction:

$$\frac{P}{Y} \geqslant m. \tag{6}$$

It is clear that equations (5) and (6) describe *alternative* restrictions, of which the higher will apply.

4. The fourth is that the capital/output ratio, v, should not in itself be influenced by the rate of profit, for if it is, the investment/output ratio Gv will itself be dependent on the rate of profit. A certain degree of dependence

[6] I/Y will therefore tend to equal $G'v$, not Gv. It may be assumed that taking very long periods G' is largely governed by G but over shorter periods the two are quite distinct, moreover G itself is not independent of G', since technical progress and population growth are both stimulated by the degree of pressure on the 'full employment ceiling', which depends on G'. The elasticity of response of G to G' is not infinite however: hence the greater G', the greater will be G (the *actual* trend-rate of growth of the economy over successive cycles) but the greater also the ratio G'/G which measures the strength of cyclical forces.

follows inevitably from the consideration, mentioned earlier, that the value of particular capital goods in terms of final consumption goods will vary with the rate of profit, so that, even with a *given technique* v will not be independent of P/Y. (We shall ignore this point.) There is the further complication that the relation P/Y may affect v through making more or less 'labour-saving' techniques profitable. In other words, at any given wage-price relationship, the producers will adopt the technique which maximizes the rate of profit on capital, P/vY; this will affect (at a given G) I/Y, and hence P/Y. Hence any rise in P/Y will reduce v, and thus I/Y, and conversely, any rise in I/Y will raise P/Y. If the sensitiveness of v to P/Y is great, P/Y can no longer be regarded as being determined by the equations of the model; the *technical* relation between v and P/Y will then govern P/Y whereas the savings equation (equation (2) above) will determine I/Y and thus (given G) the value of v.[7] To exclude this we have to assume that v is invariant to P/Y,[8] i.e.:

$$v = \bar{v}. \tag{7}$$

If equation (4) is unsatisfied, we are back at the Ricardian (or Marxian) model. I/Y will suffer a shrinkage, and will no longer correspond to Gv, but to, say, αv where $\alpha < G$. Hence the system will not produce full employment; output will be limited by the available capital, and not by labour; at the same time the classical, and not the Keynesian, reaction-mechanism will be in operation: the size of the 'surplus' available for investment determining investment, not investment savings. It is possible however that owing to technical inventions, etc., and starting from a position of excess labour and underemployment (i.e., an elastic total supply of labour) the size of the surplus will grow; hence I/Y and α will grow; and hence α might rise above G (the rate of growth of the 'full employment ceiling', given the technical progress and the growth of population) so that in time the excess labour becomes absorbed and full employment is reached. When this happens (which we may call the stage of *developed* capitalism) wages will rise above the subsistence level, and the properties of the system will then follow our model.

If equations (5) and (6) are unsatisfied, the full employment assumption breaks down, and so will the process of growth; the economy will relapse into a state of stagnation. The interesting conclusion which emerges from these equations is that this may be the result of several distinct causes.

[7] This is where the 'marginal productivity' principle would come in but it should be emphasized that under the conditions of our model where savings are treated, not as a constant, but as a function of income distribution, P/Y, the sensitiveness of v to changes in P/Y would have to be very large to overshadow the influence of G and of s_p and of s_w on P/Y. Assuming that it is large, it is further necessary to suppose that the value of P/Y as dictated by this technical relationship falls within the maximum and minimum values indicated by equations (4)–(6).

[8] This assumption does not necessarily mean that there are 'fixed coefficients' as between capital equipment and labour—only that technical innovations (which are also assumed to be 'neutral' in their effects) are far more influential on the chosen v than price relationships.

'Investment opportunities' may be low because G' is low relatively to G, i.e., the entrepreneurs' expectations are involatile, and/or they are pessimistic; hence they expect a lower level of demand for the future than corresponds to potential demand, governed by G. On the other hand, 'liquidity preference' may be too high, or the risks associated with investment too great, leading to an excessive r. (This is perhaps the factor on which Keynes himself set greatest store as a cause of unemployment and stagnation.) Finally, lack of competition may cause 'over-saving' through excessive profit margins; this again will cause stagnation, unless there is sufficient compensating increase in v (through the generation of 'excess capacity' under conditions of rigid profit margins but relatively free entry) to push up Gv, and hence I/Y.

If however equations (2)–(6) are all satisfied there will be an inherent tendency to growth and an inherent tendency to full employment. Indeed the two are closely linked to each other. Apart from the case of a developing economy in the immature stage of capitalism (where equation (4) does not hold, but where $\gamma < G$), a tendency to continued economic growth will only exist when the system is only stable at full employment equilibrium—i.e. when $G' \geqslant G$.

This is a possible interpretation of the long-term situation in the 'successful' capitalist economies of Western Europe and North America. If G' exceeds G, the investment/output ratio I/Y will not be steady in time, even if the *trend* level of this ratio is constant. There will be periodic breakdowns in the investment process, due to the growth in output capacity outrunning the possible growth in output; when that happens, not only investment, but total output will fall, and output will be (temporarily) limited by effective demand, and not by the scarcity of resources. This is contrary to the mechanics of our model, but several reasons can be adduced to show why the system will not be flexible enough to ensure full employment in the short period.

1. First, even if 'profit margins' are assumed to be fully flexible, in a downward, as well as an upward, direction the very fact that investment goods and consumer goods are produced by different industries, with limited mobility between them, will mean that profit margins in the consumption goods industries will not fall below the level that ensures full utilization of resources in the consumption goods industries. A *compensating* increase in consumption goods production (following upon a fall in the production of investment goods) can only occur as a result of a transfer of resources from the other industries, lured by the profit opportunities there.

2. Second, and more important, profit-margins are likely to be inflexible in a downward direction in the short period (Marshall's 'fear of spoiling the market') even if they are flexible in the long period, or even if they possess short period flexibility in an upward direction.

This applies of course not only to profit margins but to real wages as well, which in the short period may be equally inflexible in a downward direction at the *attained* level, thus compressing I/Y, or rather preventing an *increase* in I/Y following upon a rise in the entrepreneurs' desired rate of expansion G'. Hence in the short period the shares of profits and wages tend to be inflexible for two different reasons—the downward inflexibility of P/Y and the downward inflexibility of W/L—which thus tend to reinforce the long-period stability of these shares, due to constancy of I/Y, resulting from the long period constancy of Gv and $G'v$. [...]

I am not sure where 'marginal productivity' comes in in all this—except that in so far as it has any importance it does through an extreme sensitivity of v to changes in P/Y.

8.4 A General Kaldorian Theory of Distribution*

If Mr. Kaldor is going to transform the Keynesian theory of employment into a Keynesian theory of distribution,[1] should he not aspire to a *General Theory of Distribution*? For all the flaws that Mr. Kaldor detects in it, neo-classical distribution theory is general; it will divide up the national product among 3 or 101 factors as well as or badly as between 2. Mr. Kaldor's substitute should not do less. In limiting his contesting factors to Capital and Labor, he has been unduly modest. The purpose of the present note is to sketch the manner of generalization.

First, a brief review of Mr. Kaldor's two factor theory: Full employment national output is divided into two fractions, Investment y_1 and Consumption y_2, $(y_1 + y_2 = 1)$, in proportions that are independent of the distribution of output between Capitalists' share, s_1, and Labor's share, s_2, $(s_1 + s_2 = 1)$. Capitalists divide their income as follows: a fraction b_{11} for investment, a fraction b_{12} $(= 1 - b_{11})$ for consumption. For Laborers the corresponding fractions are b_{21} and b_{22}. The following two equations can be solved for the shares s_1 and s_2:

	Capital	Labor
Investment	$b_{11}s_1$	$+ b_{21}s_2 = y_1$
Consumption	$b_{12}s_1$	$+ b_{22}s_2 = y_2$

The solution is: $s_1 = \dfrac{y_1 - b_{21}}{b_{11} - b_{21}}$ $s_2 = \dfrac{b_{11} - y_1}{b_{11} - b_{21}}$

Assuming, as Mr. Kaldor does, that in a state of nature $b_{11} > y_1 > b_{21}$, the solution gives positive shares for both factors.[2] If the economists for

* From J. Tobin, 'Towards a *General* Kaldorian Theory of Distribution', *Review of Economic Studies*, 1959–60.

[1] N. Kaldor, 'Alternative Theories of Distribution', this *Review*, 1955–56, XXIII (2), 94–100. [See Reading 8.3—Ed.]

[2] In addition to imposing the restriction that both shares must be non-negative, Mr. Kaldor warns us that there are narrower limits (classical or neoclassical?) set by means of subsistence for Labor and the minimum tolerable rate of profit for Capital.

trade union federations and capitalists' clubs are on the ball, the state of nature may not last. Assuming that the capitalists are asleep, Labor can raise its share by hoisting b_{21}, Labor's average and marginal propensity to save, towards y_1, difficult as it may be for union leaders hardened to bargaining tables and picket lines to shift their energies to thrift campaigns among their own members. But if the unions slumber while the capitalists are roused by the financial press, Capital will reduce its propensity to save b_{11}; investment in yachts and caviar will yield handsome returns.

Alas, if both sides take the theory seriously, their manoeuvres will destroy it. There will be no longer any protection against singular matrices and other embarrassments, and the whole theory of distribution will have to be surrendered to the game theorists.

Meanwhile, however, let us proceed to the n-factor theory. Final output must be divided into n categories: e.g., Aspirin, Binoculars, Cadillacs, Dress suits, Electronic calculators, Football pools, Goose livers, Harrows, ... Newspapers. Likewise, the population must be split into n mutually exclusive classes. Call them 'factors' if you like, but the distinctive advantage of the theory is that the groups need have nothing at all to do with supplying productive services. Let the classes be, for example, Actors, Bird-watchers, Conservative peers, Dons, Executives, Farmers, Gourmets not elsewhere classified, Hoopers, ... Nuclear physicists. Class i has income share s_i and divides it in proportions $b_{i1}, b_{i2}, \ldots b_{in}$ ($\sum y_j = \sum s_i = 1$). Kindly suppress any neoclassical atavisms that suggest that the output of Cadillacs might depend on Executives' share, the output of Goose-livers on the income of Gourmets n.e.c., the production of Harrows on Farmers' fortunes, and so on. The assumption that they don't is just an extension of the two-factor assumption that the division of output between Investment and Consumption is independent of Profits and Wages. The equations that determine the shares s_i are as follows:

	Actors	Bird-watchers	Conser. peers	....	Nuclear physicists
Aspirin	$b_{11}s_1 +$	$b_{21}s_2 +$	$b_{31}s_3 +$	.... $+$	$b_{n1}s_n = y_1$
Binoculars	$b_{12}s_1 +$	$b_{22}s_2 +$	$b_{32}s_3 +$	.... $+$	$b_{n2}s_n = y_2$
Cadillacs	$b_{13}s_1 +$	$b_{23}s_2 +$	$b_{33}s_3 +$	.... $+$	$n_{n3}s_n = y_3$
....		....			
....		....			
Newspapers	$b_{1n}s_1 +$	$b_{2n}s_2 +$	$b_{3n}s_n +$	.... $+$	$b_{nn}s_n = y_n$

Now if the Dons will just hurry to make their marginal propensities conform to the fractions in which output is divided (the vector $b_{41}, b_{42}, b_{43} \ldots b_{4n}$ to equal $y_1, y_2, y_3 \ldots y_n$), centuries of public neglect of education and educators will be avenged.

8.5 Against a General Kaldorian Theory of Distribution*
[. . .]

Professor Tobin's paper raises two separate issues. The first concerns the justification of 'aggregating' output into two categories, Consumption and Investment, and 'aggregating' incomes into two types, residual and contractual, or Profits and Wages. This, clearly, is a fundamental question which goes far beyond the confines of the Keynesian distribution theory; it raises the whole issue of the raison d'être of the 'macro-economic' approach. The basic assumption of all Keynesian theory is that Investment—i.e., expenditure charged to a capital account, and not an income account—is determined independently of current savings. But since in equilibrium, savings must be equal to investment, it is the decisions concerning capital expenditure which will determine the level and/or the distribution of incomes, and not the other way round. Assuming an excess supply of labour, the profit margins on the sale of output must be taken as given, and an increase in investment will cause incomes and employment to expand until savings increase sufficiently to match the higher level of investment. But assuming 'full employment', and hence a given real income, an increase in Investment (which also involves in this case a higher *ratio* of Investment to Consumption) will cause profit margins to increase until the savings-investment equilibrium is restored.

Professor Tobin is free to reject this 'independence-assumption' either in the under-employment case or in the full-employment case, though if he wished to differentiate between them and reject it in the one whilst accepting it in the other, his readers, I am sure, would be grateful if he would show his hand and reveal his true reasons. But he is not free simply to ridicule the whole macro-proceeding by saying, in effect, why bunch everything into two categories, instead of 50 or 500? Macro-economic models, for all their shortcomings, attempt to do something rather more subtle than just aggregating production into two arbitrary categories, *A* and *B*, and incomes into two equally arbitrary categories *X* and *Y*—the division in each case is justified by fundamental behavioural properties of the capitalist system. Investment is picked out, because expenditures debited to a capital account are independent of the current income flow in a way in which expenditures on income account are not; Profits are picked out, because any change in aggregate demand relatively to aggregate supply affects residual incomes in a contrary direction to contractual incomes and also because in any reasonably stable system the proportion of profit saved is very much greater than savings out of contractual incomes of *all* kinds. Of course it would be nonsense to suggest that it is the decision to produce Goose Livers on a certain scale which determines the incomes of Gourmets, instead of the other way round. But it is just as nonsensical to imply that the assumption that

* From N. Kaldor, 'A Rejoinder to . . . Professor Tobin', *Review of Economic Studies*, 1959–60.

the division of output between Investment and Consumption is independent of Profits and Wages is equally far-fetched.

Professor Tobin's second point is that the theory only works so long as there is no collusion between members of each of the two groups, in raising or lowering their propensities to consume so as to influence their share of the product; and if there is collusion on both sides, there will be all the horrors of bilateral monopoly. With all this I heartily agree. But may I remind him that the same can be equally said of the neo-classical theory or indeed any other theory such as the Ricardian or the Marxian? As Wicksell, in particular, never tired of emphasizing, once capitalists acted in collusion the marginal productivity theory of interest and wages goes out of the window.

8.6 The Theory of Distribution: A Synthesis*

The theory of the distribution of the product of industry between wages and profits which is knocking about in current economic teaching consists of a number of propositions, each of which seems quite unexceptionable in itself, but none of which bears any relation to the rest. We cannot be satisfied with this state of affairs, and we must try to fit the pieces together into a coherent whole.

I am confining the present discussion to a closed economy (without international trade) abstracting from government operations and from scarce factors of production. There is a two-class society, in which wages and profits account for the national income.

The first proposition is ancient and respectable. It is that the relative shares of wages and profits are governed by the supplies of factors and the elasticity of substitution between them. A high ratio of capital to labour is associated with a low rate of profit, high real wages and a high degree of mechanization of methods of production.

The second proposition was derived by Michal Kalecki from the analysis of imperfect competition. It is that, because in manufacturing industry under-capacity working is normal and competition is never perfect, gross profit margins (the excess of prices over prime costs) are governed by the price-policy of firms. The relation of prices to money-wage rates determines real-wage rates. Thus, grouping all the influences that play on gross margins (when there is surplus capacity) under the title of the degree of monopoly, the share of wages in product is determined by how great the degree of monopoly is.

The third proposition, again, is due to Kalecki and is to be found less sharply stated also in Keynes. It is that the relative shares are governed by the rate of investment and the propensity to consume of each class. The share

* From Joan Robinson, 'The Theory of Distribution', in *Collected Economic Papers, Volume II* (Oxford: Basil Blackwell & Mott, 1960).

of wages tends to be greater the greater the proportion of saving out of profits and of saving out of wages. Given the propensity to consume of each class, the share of wages is lower the greater the ratio of investment to the value of total output.

The rate of investment in turn can be accounted for in two ways which do not seem to be connected with each other. Investment is determined, in one sense, by profit expectations, the 'animal spirits' of entrepreneurs which incline them to take the risks of investment, and the state of supply of finance, which may be subsumed under the head of the level of interest rates.

In another sense, the rate of investment that can be maintained over the long run depends on technical conditions and the supply of labour.[1] According to this view, the rate at which the effective supply of labour is growing, allowing for increasing output per man-hour due to inventions and improvements in methods of production, limits the rate at which capital can accumulate, because there would be no point in bringing capital goods into existence when there is not going to be labour to operate them.

The fourth proposition is mere common sense. It is that the relative shares depend upon the relative bargaining strength of workers and employers.

I

Each of these propositions seems, on the face of it, to contain an important element of truth. How are they to be reconciled with each other?

Let us begin in a short-period situation with given productive capacity in existence. A certain rate of gross investment in capital equipment is going on. In so far as this represents new productive capacity coming into use, it is accompanied by an appropriate rate of investment in working capital and stocks. Thus, the rate of outlay on capital goods of all sorts is given. The flow of money demand for consumption goods and services, or *commodities* for short, is equal to the wages bill *minus* workers' net savings *plus* the outlay of rentiers (that is, of capitalists, including recipients of dividends, looked at in their capacity as passive owners of wealth, as opposed to their capacity as active entrepreneurs) *plus* any unemployment allowances which are not at the expense of other consumption.

Saving out of wages and unemployment allowances complicate exposition very much, though they do not introduce any difficulty of principle. We may simplify by assuming them away for the moment. The total flow of money demand for commodities is then the wages bill *plus* rentier expenditure.

The outlay of workers engaged on producing commodities provides just enough receipts to the firms concerned to cover their wages bill. Gross profits, therefore, are equal to the wages bill for gross investment *plus* rentier expenditure. The value of gross investment (including profit on the sale of capital goods) is matched partly by the amortization of capital (at whatever rate, rightly or wrongly, it is being allowed for) and partly by the savings

[1] This is the idea expressed by Harrod's 'natural rate of growth', *Towards a Dynamic Economics*.

of rentiers. The balancing item which equates the value of net investment to net saving is the undistributed profits of firms. There are all sorts of metaphysical problems involved in this item, concerning the division of gross profit between amortization and net profit, and the notional value to be attached to capital goods produced within a firm for its own use, but these need not concern us. We are interested only in the interchange of actual money transactions between entrepreneurs, workers and rentiers. The global total of gross profit on the sale of commodities is equal to the wages bill for gross investment *plus* rentier expenditure, and these are not metaphysical concepts, but actual money flows. So much for the global total of gross profit. How is it distributed over the flow of output of commodities?

When output is determined by the capacity of equipment in existence the answer is simple. The stream of money demand encounters a flow of output limited by capacity, and prices are set at the level which equates demand to supply. Here the degree of monopoly has nothing to say, for prices would be just as high under perfect competition. Output, and therefore the wages bill at any given level of money-wage rates, is fixed by the brute facts of productive capacity; the average level of profit margins is simply the ratio of the global gross profits (fixed by investment and rentier consumption) to the wages bill (fixed by employment at capacity), the distribution of profit margins over particular markets being set by the pattern of supply and demand, and the division of output between stages of production. But this situation is found only in extreme conditions of a seller's market. Normally, the level of utilization of plant depends partly on the price-policy of the firms concerned and the degree of monopoly has to be brought into the question of the determination of margins. [...]

Whether margins are governed by supply and demand or by the price-policy of firms, it is evident that, with a given rate of investment going on, the level of employment and the output of commodities is lower the higher is the level of profit margins, for a given flow of money-wages provides purchasing power for less commodities when prices are higher, and a given global profit is recovered from a smaller output when profit per unit of output is greater. [...]

This is no more than a restatement of the familiar Keynesian proposition that, given the rate of investment, the level of employment will be lower the smaller is the propensity to consume in the economy as a whole. A smaller share of a given output going to the workers entails a lower propensity to consume for the economy as a whole, because the propensity to consume out of profits is less than out of wages.

We can now see how to reconcile the view that, with given propensities to consume of each class, the share of wages in national income is determined by the ratio of investment to income, with the view that (when there is surplus capacity) it is determined by the degree of monopoly. The share of profit in income is determined by the *ratio* of investment to income, but the amount of income associated with a given *rate* of investment in influenced by the amount of capacity in existence and the degree of monopoly. The lower is the level of margins the larger is the output of consumption goods accompanying a given *rate* of investment, and therefore the lower is the *ratio* of investment to income. The proposition that the share of profits in income is a function of the ratio of investment to income is perfectly correct, but capacity and the degree of monopoly have to be brought in to determine what income it is that profits are a share of, and investment is a ratio to.

To illustrate the influence of the degree of monopoly, let us consider an economy in which there is both unemployment and surplus capacity and inquire what would happen of there was an outbreak of competitive price-cutting, assuming (though, of course, this is quite arbitrary) that the rate of investment remains unchanged in money terms.

Let us suppose that rentier outlay in money terms has sufficient inertia to keep it constant for some time, whatever happens, and that workers' total expenditure is equal to wages. Then (with an unchanged rate of investment going on) the total of gross profits in money terms is unaffected, in the first instance, by price-cutting. Taking one with another, firms in the consumption sector are receiving the same total sums, in excess of their total wages bill, as before. Employment, the wages bill and the rate of output are increased, and the same global total of margins as before is spread over a larger volume of sales. Prices have fallen and the real-wage rate has risen.

In time, rentier consumption will react one way or the other to the change in prices and increase or reduce profits accordingly. In so far as rentiers spend less when prices are lower (or if the mere fear that price-cutting is going to lower profits reduces the amount of dividends distributed, and rentiers respond by reducing money expenditure), the total of gross profits in money terms is correspondingly reduced. Similarly, if there is a non-transfer element in unemployment allowances which falls as men are taken into work (or if workers save more as the total of wages rises), gross profits in money terms fall. But these are minor reactions. Looking at it by and large, the cut in prices raises real wage rates without appreciably reducing profits.

By the same token, an increase in monopoly raising profit margins reduces real wages without appreciably increasing profits.

This is the appropriate place to consider the fourth proposition, and bring bargaining power into the argument. Suppose that money wages are raised in an industry supplying markets where profit margins were fairly high. The group of firms concerned were working below capacity in the situation that we have assumed, and they will not raise prices fully in proportion to the rise of wages. Indeed, for a moderate rise they may prefer to keep prices constant if the over-all elasticity of demand for their output is appreciable, for otherwise sales would fall further below capacity output. The additional demand due to the expenditure of the additional money wages increases demand for wage goods of all kinds while prices remain more or less constant, for producers generally prefer to meet additional demand, up to capacity, rather than to raise prices. The workers then attack somewhere else, and the story repeats itself. All round, prices may be raised, but less than in proportion to the all-round rise in money wages. Thus the exercise of bargaining strength playing against monopolistic power raises real wages and increases employment.

When either of these influences, or a combination of them, has carried the economy up to the point of full capacity in a large number of lines, any further increase in money outlay raises prices, as demand strikes against the barrier of rising marginal costs. The degree of monopoly having been eroded by price-cutting or wage-bargaining, the physical limitations upon output come into action to defend profit margins from a further fall. We are back in the situation of a seller's market that we began by discussing.

When full employment is reached before full capacity, the consumption sector may try to draw labour away from investment, but in the prevailing situation investment in all kinds of labour-saving equipment appears highly profitable and the capital-good industries are unwilling to part with workers. On the assumption that the investment sector maintains its employment, the total output of commodities reaches a maximum when full employment is attained.

Beyond this the exercise of bargaining power by the workers loses itself in a vicious spiral which persists as long as investment and rentier consumption in real terms are maintained.

Real wages can then be increased only by an increase in the workers' own saving, by a reduction in rentier consumption (whether due to a spontaneous increase in saving, or enforced by the rise in prices relatively to money income) or by a reduction in the rate of investment.

This is a situation with which we have lately grown familiar.

The sad moral of this tale is that, when there is unemployment (combined with excess capacity), a rise in money-wage rates raises real wages and increases prosperity all round, whereas when there is already full employment it yields, at best, an advantage to the workers at the expense of the rentiers and at worst disrupts the whole economy. Yet raising money wages in the face of unemployment is very difficult and in the face of full employment only too easy.

The argument so far can be summed up as follows. The share of wages in full-employment income tends to be lower the higher the level of investment and the lower the level of thriftiness. Given the propensities to consume and the rate of investment, there is a certain level of profit margins that is compatible with full employment in any given short-period situation. Full employment without inflationary pressure is attainable only if there is adequate capacity. For any level of capacity above this minimum there is one level of profit margins that will just secure full employment. If interaction of the degree of monopoly and the state of bargaining power have failed to set profit margins at the right level, there is either unemployment or inflationary pressure, as the case may be.

All this applies to differences in the degree of monopoly with a given rate of investment. Now consider the effect of a difference in the rate of investment in given short-period conditions, with constant money-wage rates. With a lower level of employment in the investment sector (compared to a higher level), effective demand for commodities is less. In general, we should expect prices to be lower, partly because marginal cost (including user cost) is lower and partly because competition is likely to be more active when the degree of excess capacity is greater. If so, the relative share of wages is higher. The matter is not quite so simple as it is made to appear in some trade cycle models, for history comes in. The same rate of investment to-day, if it has been approached from a higher level in the recent past (we are going down into a slump), is likely to be associated with higher profit margins than if it has been approached from below (we are ascending towards a boom); for in the intervening depression there may have been price-cutting by 'weak sellers', and even if rings have been tightened up in consequence, they may have only been able to prevent further price-cutting without restoring margins to their pre-slump level. It is a case where the distance from A to B is not the same as the distance from B to A.

But the behaviour of relative shares over the trade cycle, and its influence upon the course of the cycle, requires a paper to itself.

To sum up so far, in a short-period situation, with given productive capacity, the share of wages in the value of output is the resultant of three independent sets of influences. (1) It tends to be greater the lower the rate of investment. (2) It tends to be less the greater the degree of monopoly, which results from the interaction of the price-policy of firms and the bargaining position in the labour market. (3) It tends to be greater the lower the propensity to consume of individuals and the propensity of firms to distribute profits. We now turn to the long-period aspects of the question.

II

So far we have taken the stock of capital in existence as an arbitrary datum, and looked only at short-period situations. We must now consider differences in the ratio of capital to labour and inquire how the first of our four propositions, that the levels of wages and profits are governed by the supplies of the factors, fits in with the rest.

Since we have now moved into the sphere of long-period concepts we must take profit margins net of amortization and investment net of replacements. Let us agree to lock this tiresome skeleton firmly into its cupboard by assuming that, in the economy as a whole, amortization allowances and current replacements are in gear with each other.

The best approach to the question of differences in the factor ratio is by means of comparing economies endowed by past history with different amounts of productive capacity. We first compare economies with different amounts of equipment for producing consumer goods embodying the same techniques of production.

One economy, say Alaph, has a considerably larger productive capacity than another, Beth. The propensities to consume are the same in each economy, money-wage rates are the same, and we arbitrarily assume that the same rate of net investment per annum (measured in money-wage units) is going on in each; then if profit margins were also the same in each, the rate of output of commodities would be the same, and Alaph, with the greater stock of capital, would have a large amount of idle capacity. But capacity would not have been maintained in the long run (beyond a small margin to give elbow room) if it could not be used. Therefore, Alaph must have a lower level of prices.

To account for the difference we have to delve into past history. Was it that capacity somehow came into existence in Alaph and led to the erosion of profit margins through competition and pressure from the workers? Or is it that a higher degree of monopoly in Beth (combined with lower bargaining power of workers) causing effect demand to be lower has restrained investment in the past, and is the cause of Beth having less productive capacity? In either case, a higher ratio of capital to labour is associated with a lower degree of monopoly and a larger relative share of wages.

Here we assumed the techniques of production in the two economies were identical, though the wage rates differed; in short, there was no substitutability of factors. Where there is a range of possible techniques to choose from, each individual producer will be inclined to organize production so that the less labour is required per unit of output, the greater is the cost of labour to him in terms of his own product. Thus a higher level of real wages, which means a higher ratio of money wages to prices all round, leads to the use of more mechanized techniques of production in any given state of technical knowledge. At the same time, the relative prices of commodities of which output per head is low for technical reasons tend to be higher the higher the level of real wages, and in so far as demands are elastic to price, less of them is consumed.

Comparing two economies in the same phase of technical development, one with higher real wages than the other (whether because the degree of monopoly in the past has been lower and the bargaining power of workers greater, or because the urge to accumulate capital has been greater), the economy with higher real wages is using more mechanized methods of production and consuming more relatively capital-intensive products. High wages, therefore, are associated with high output per man employed. It follows that when techniques are malleable we cannot say, in general, that an economy with a higher rate of real wages has a higher share of wages in income. Higher wages are associated with higher output per head, and relative shares may go either way.

This is sometimes expressed by saying that the elasticity of substitution between labour and capital may be greater or less than unity. That is not a very helpful way of putting the point, but the idea that the 'elasticity of substitution' is trying to express is an important element in the theory of relative shares.

We must now reconcile the proposition that the relative shares are determined by the conditions of substitutability of factors with the proposition that they are a function of the ratio of investment to income.

The ratio of net investment to the value of the stock of capital (given the propensities to consume) determines the rate of profit on capital. Where the technical conditions are such that a high *rate* of profit is associated with a high *share* of profit they are such that output per unit of value of capital is low, and for that very reason the ratio of investment to income is high. Where a high *rate* of profit is associated with a low *share* of profit, output per unit of capital is high, and for that very reason the ratio of investment to income is low. These are purely formal relationships. The operative forces, in a comparison between economies with the same technical knowledge and different factor endowments are: the amount of accumulation that has taken place up to date (which has affected and been affected by the degree of monopoly and bargaining power of workers over the past), and the technical conditions of substitutability of factors and the pattern of demand, which together with the amount of accumulation determine the amount and the form of productive capacity in the existing situation; the interplay of monopoly and bargaining power in the existing situation, which governs the level of utilization of productive capacity; and the propensities to consume and the rate at which investment is going on, which govern the shares of wages and profits in the output so determined.

III

So far we have taken the rate of investment as an arbitrary datum. We must now attempt to reconcile the two views of what governs investment—that it depends upon animal spirits and the supply of finance and that it is determined over the long run (ignoring the trade cycle, and comparing boom to boom and slump to slump) by the real forces of population growth and technical progress. When the animal spirits of the entrepreneurs incline them to a rate of investment higher than the real forces justify, then they must either speed up technical progress (perhaps at the same time giving it a capital-using bias) so that the real forces expand to make room for them, or they will force up the cost of labour against themselves by raising wage rates relatively to productivity, lower the general rate of profit and find a vent for accumulation in raising the degree of mechanization.

Since a falling rate of profit is associated with rising capital per unit of output, relative shares once more may go either way. The greater the substitutability between factors in production and between commodities in demand the more accumulation can be absorbed with a given long-run fall in the level of the rates of profit on capital, and the greater the tendency for the relative share of profits to rise.

When animal spirits are deficient or the interest rates fail to fall with rates of profit, while the degree of monopoly is rigid, the economy sinks into the state of stagnation depicted by Keynes. Investment fails to keep up with the pace set by the real forces, and chronic unemployment sets in.

In conditions of under-employment we cannot make any simple generalizations about the behaviour of relative shares through time. They will wobble along somehow or other, as the various influences that we have discussed play upon them.

The theory of relative shares with full employment, and a rate of accumulation governed by the real forces, can be summarized as follows: the rate of accumulation together with the thriftiness conditions determine the rate of profit on capital, and so, in conjunction with technical conditions, the equilibrium ratio of capital to labour and the relative shares.

Provided that it is possible for accumulation to keep up with the real forces—that is to say, that they do not require such a high ratio of investment to full employment income as to drive wages below the tolerable minimum, and that over the long run the real forces establish a steady rate of growth; that the animal spirits of entrepreneurs, in conjunction with the conditions of supply of finance, are just sufficient to keep up with the real forces; that technical progress is neutral, without bias in the capital-saving or capital-using direction, and that the development of demand is neutral as between less and more capital-intensive products; that the interplay of the degree of monopoly and bargaining power, having been such as to allow full employment in the first place, maintain it by keeping real wages rising in step with productivity; and that the propensities to consume remain constant; then the value of capital per unit of output remains constant through time, and so does the general rate of profit on capital. The relative shares, therefore, remain constant at whatever level they were when the story began.

This direct approach to the constancy of the shares through time is all that is necessary in such a case, but there is no difficulty in seeing that it agrees with our four propositions. The postulate of neutrality means that the conditions of substitutability are not altering. The degree of monopoly and wage-bargaining are continuously adapting themselves to the growth of capacity so as to preserve full employment, and since the ratio of net investment and of income to the value of the stock of capital are both constant, their ratio to each other is also constant. Thus, all four propositions are satisfied by the constancy of relative shares.

When technical progress and the development of demand are biased in the capital-saving direction, and accumulation slows down so as to keep the rate of profit constant, the relative share of profits falls accordingly. If the capital-saving bias is compensated by an increase in the degree of mechanization, the rate of profit falls. The opposing effects of a capital-saving bias in technical progress and of an increase in the degree of mechanization tend to keep the ratio of capital to income more or less constant, so that, with a falling rate of profit, there is a presumption that the share of profits falls also in this case. Conversely, a capital-using bias tends to raise the share of profits. But in this case it is important to remember the proviso that the rate of accumulation required to provide equipment for all available labour is not so great as to drive real wages below the tolerable level.

A bias in technical progress can be expressed in terms of the first proposition, as a change in the conditions of substitutability favourable or adverse to labour, while the movements of investment and of income relatively to the stock of capital can be expressed in terms of their ratio to each other, so that there is no conflict between a statement of the effects of biased progress in terms of the rate of profit and the capital/income ratio and a statement in terms of our four propositions.

All this concerns the analysis of relative shares under conditions of full employment. But full employment is a postulate, not a result of the theory. In various circumstances the degree of monopoly may be too high (and bargaining power too weak) to permit of full employment at the rate of investment which the animal spirits of the entrepreneurs decree, accumulation may fail to keep pace with the growth of the effective supply of labour, or the bargaining power of the workers may be so strong as to generate a disruptive inflation. It is at the points where the theory breaks down that it begins to become interesting.

9. Current Controversies

Introductory Note

In addition to continuing argument in particular areas of macroeconomics, two more general controversies have provoked a good deal of attention in recent years. These have concerned the 'neo-monetarist' school, of which Professor Friedman is a leading proponent, and the reappraisal of 'Keynesian' macroeconomics offered by, for example, Professors Clower and Leijonhufvud.

The general tenor of the neo-monetarist approach is clear from Reading 6.3 by Friedman and Schwartz on business cycles. Put crudely, their argument was based very largely on the empirical analysis of changes in the money stock and changes in the level of economic activity. It was suggested that the historical evidence showed a unique correlation between changes in the former and subsequent changes in the latter, while no such systematic relationship could be found between changes in autonomous expenditure and changes in income such as the 'Keynesian' multiplier would entail.

In two important articles published in 1970–1 [Reading 9.1], Friedman attempted to set out the theoretical framework for the neo-monetarist analysis, and to compare and contrast it both with the classical quantity theory and with the Keynesian approach. The Keynesian approach, it is claimed, contains three crucial propositions: that unemployment equilibrium is possible, that prices are rigid in the short run, and that the velocity of circulation of money is unstable. The first proposition, it is said, has been demonstrated to be false because it ignores the real balance effect (see Readings 1.5–1.7 above). The second and third, taken together, imply that if the 'Cambridge' or 'income' version of the quantity theory equation is written

$$M = kPy$$

(where M is the money supply, P the price level, y real income, and k the income velocity of circulation), a change in M will cause changes in k and/or y but not (below full employment) in P. Friedman prefers to retain the possibility of flexibility in the price level. The difficulty is that the addition of the extra variable, P, means that 'conventional' macroeconomic models now have a 'missing equation'—there is one more variable than there are equations. (This incomplete model is set out on pp. 375–7). Three possible solutions are explored. The simple quantity theory (the 'classical' theory with which Chapter 1 was partly concerned) takes real income as given, and drops income from the consumption equation. The interest rate equates savings and investment (and thus, given income, fixes consumption), and the supply of money determines the price level. The simple income-expenditure theory takes the price level as fixed; the remainder of the system is then simultaneously determinate in the way familiar from the IS–LM analysis.

Friedman's own preferred solution is to ignore the division of nominal income between prices and real income. This seems satisfactory so far as the monetary side of the model is concerned, but it does raise problems for the consumption function (p. 380). The solution is to introduce a distinction between real and nominal rates of interest— the real rate being the nominal rate less the rate of price inflation. Assuming that the nominal rate r, differs from the 'permanent' or 'anticipated' rate, p^*, by the 'permanent' rate of price change, then

$$r = p^* + (\dot{p}/p)^*$$

where $\dot{p}/p$ is the proportional rate of price change. Since the rate of price change is equal to the rate of change of nominal income less the rate of change of real income,

$$\begin{aligned} r &= p^* - (\dot{y}/y)^* + (\dot{Y}/Y)^* \\ &= p^* - g^* + (\dot{Y}/Y)^* \\ &= k_0 + (\dot{Y}/Y)^* \end{aligned} \tag{1}$$

where the gap between the permanent real interest rate and the trend rate of growth of real income, g^*, is taken to be constant. Friedman takes the *anticipated* rate of change of nominal income as given (by past experience); there is thus a self-contained monetary sector which fully determines the level of nominal income, for equation (1) determines the rate of interest, r, and, with a given money supply and interest rate, the demand for money is uniquely dependent on Y. This is pure quantity theory except that (i) the supply of money determines nominal income rather than the price level, and (ii) the velocity of circulation *does* depend on the interest rate—but the interest rate is exogenously determined in the somewhat bizarre way described above.

What Friedman would like (p. 384) is a further self-contained 'real' sector, based on the multiplier, which would account for real consumption, real investment, and real income. With nominal income determined by the money supply and real income by the multiplier, their ratio would give the price level. But, for various reasons—notably the need to account for changes in the real interest rate in the investment and savings functions, and the importance of price changes and of permanent income in the consumption function—this is thought unsatisfactory: the saving-investment sector is regarded as 'unfinished business'!

As Tobin [Reading 9.2] points out, if the real interest rate is given, Friedman's short-run model implies that the level of real income is wholly determined by the multiplier. Given the expected rate of price inflation, the nominal interest rate is fixed and the money supply then determines the level of nominal income and thus the price level.[1] Thus with a fixed money supply, fiscal policy has unlimited potency in apportioning the resulting level of nominal income between real income and the level of prices.

The crux of the matter is of course the way in which real and nominal interest rates are determined. Friedman requires both that the 'permanent' real rate should be virtually constant, and that the short-run divergences of nominal and real rates should reflect *only* the expected rate of inflation, which is exogenously given by past experience. It is not necessary, of course, to be a neo-monetarist in order to believe in *some* connection between the expected rate of inflation and the level of nominal interest rates. Inflationary expectations, *ceteris paribus*, raise the real cost of holding cash balances but also reduce the real yield and potential gain from holding bonds, which are denominated in money terms. The reduction in the demand for bonds, and consequential fall in their prices, will raise nominal rates of return—but there is no reason to suppose that this process must continue until the supposedly stable real rate is re-established. Friedman attributes to Keynesian economics a neglect of the determination of the price level which renders the analysis incomplete. But Keynes did not neglect the price level, nor has modern analysis—though modern treatments have concentrated on 'Phillips curve' approaches. Friedman's alternative rests on an analysis of the determination of real and nominal rates of interest which is theoretically unsupported and, in the short run at least, empirically implausible.

Hahn [Reading 9.3] offers a wider-ranging critique of Friedman's views in reviewing the latter's *The Optimum Quantity of Money and Other Essays*, published in 1969. It is first pointed out that Friedman wishes to treat money as one among many goods for which a utility-maximizing agent will have a demand function. But it is difficult to see any theoretical reason why this demand function should be assumed to have a stability which other demand functions—for example the consumption function—do not possess. Yet the stability of the demand for money function as compared with the consumption function (and thus of the 'money multiplier' as compared with the 'investment multiplier') is Friedman's most basic tenet (cf. Reading 6.3 above). Even as a partly empirical matter, Hahn notes that it is relationships between 'permanent' variables rather than actual variables for which stability is claimed, and that no convincing explanation is given of why behaviour should be governed by 'permanent' rather than actual quantities. And when 'permanent' variables are explained as lagged functions of actual variables, the hypotheses become indistinguishable from simple habit-influenced accounts of behaviour (cf. the permanent income hypothesis of consumption behaviour discussed in Chapter 2 above).

Leaving these objections aside, Hahn passes on to Friedman's broad propositions concerning the effects on the economy of changes in the supply of money. These are that in the long run monetary policy is 'neutral', that is,

[1] Cf. Cagan's monetary analysis of hyperinflation in Reading 7.5 above.

it cannot affect the real equilibrium of the economy, while in the short run fluctuations in the supply of money play a dominant role in producing cyclical fluctuations in both real income and prices.

Hahn first points out that it cannot be true that an increase in the supply of money has the same effect whether the increase is scattered from a helicopter or results from open-market purchases of bonds. Depending on which method is used, there must be a difference in the ratio of money to bonds which cannot be affected by changes in the price level. There must, therefore, be some difference in portfolios and thus ultimately in the real long-run equilibria of the economy.

Short-run changes in the money supply similarly must have their 'real' effects through portfolio adjustments. Open-market purchases of bonds must raise bond prices if sales are to be made, and this leads to portfolio adjustment across the board: the demand for other assets must rise—notably demand for non-financial assets such as investment goods. The effect will be more powerful, at any rate in the short run, if money is scattered from a helicopter since there will be a real balance effect on consumption in addition to a portfolio imbalance reflecting excessive liquidity.

The difficulty is that the portfolio readjustment is wholly 'Keynesian': an increase in the money supply raises bond prices, lowers interest rates, and stimulates the demand for investment goods. Perhaps Friedman simply believes this to be a 'very' powerful effect—possibly spilling over to consumption demand. In that case, the issue is purely empirical. But there are further problems: if the link from money to real income is via investment, why is investment so poorly correlated with income? And if there is also an effect on consumption, ought not Friedman to find the absence of a strong correlation between investment and consumption as much evidence against the monetarist as against the multiplier analysis? It is evident that Friedman's views have not reached a steady state. As Hahn points out, in *The Optimum Quantity of Money*, everything depends on the steepness of the LM curve—on the efficacy, in a conventionally Keynesian sense, of monetary policy. For the Friedman of *A Theoretical Framework for Monetary Analysis*, as Tobin shows, the exogeneity of the interest rate concedes a powerful role to fiscal policy. At every point, it is hard to find a theoretical issue on which the neo-monetarist view differs except in emphasis from that of an eclectic post-Keynesian. Perhaps it is simply the 'unearthly mystical element in Friedman's thought' detected by Joan Robinson which accounts for the continued ability of neo-monetarism to excite controversy.[2]

A second recent area of debate has been concerned with the validity of the way in which the Keynesian revolution was reconciled with neoclassical thought to produce the 'neoclassical synthesis' with which much of Chapter 1 dealt. That synthesis purported to show that an unemployment equilibrium was only possible if a 'rigidity' in the system—rigid wage-rates, or the

[2] J. Robinson, *Economic Heresies* (London: Macmillan, 1971), p. 87.

liquidity trap, for example—prevented the free flexibility of all wages and prices. Given such flexibility, it was argued, there would always be an attainable set of prices consistent with full-employment equilibrium. The importance of the Keynesian analysis was its practical significance in the real world, where rigidities of one sort or another were inevitable, but as a matter of pure theory the Keynesian analysis was held to be a special case, while the neoclassical analysis of adjustment through price changes remained the general case.

Clower [Reading 9.4] mounts a fundamental attack on this neoclassical attempt to subsume the Keynesian revolution, which he terms the 'Keynesian counter-revolution'. Attention is first drawn to the precise 'classical' propositions which Keynes accepted in the *General Theory*, and to his reasons for rejecting the classical analysis. In brief, Keynes accepted the notions of profit-maximizing entrepreneurs and rational utility-maximizing consumers. What he rejected was the application of orthodox price theory based on their rational behaviour to situations which departed from full-employment equilibrium. Under orthodox price theory, it is assumed that individual transactors, whether firms or households, base their sale and purchase plans only on prevailing market prices. If, in any market, supply differs from demand, prices will adjust until equilibrium is reached. The difficulty is that this analysis runs only in terms of planned transactions. If trading at disequilibrium prices does take place, firms' and households' incomes will not be at their equilibrium (= full employment) levels, and the market imbalances which emerge may not take the economy towards the full-employment equilibrium—hence the need in orthodox price theory to avoid such trading at 'false' prices by means of devices such as a hypothetical auctioneer, or re-contracting, or *tâtonnement*.

The argument can be expressed in a simplified fashion if we assume that the economy consists of a large number of identical firms and identical households. Firms, which have identical transformation curves, employ labour (*l*) at the going money wage (*w*) to produce a homogeneous product (*q*) which is sold at the going price (*p*); profits (*π*) are maximized:

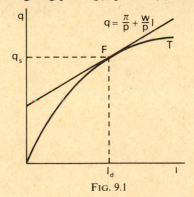

FIG. 9.1

Since $pq = \pi + wl$ (the value of output is equal to profits plus wages), or $q = (\pi/p) + (w/p) \cdot l$, production is pushed to the point at which, given the real wage w/p, this cost line is tangential to the transformation curve, T. At this point, F, profits (the intercept on the q-axis, in real terms) are maximized, the supply of commodities is q_s and the demand for labour is l_d.

Households have identical indifference maps between work and leisure; they supply labour and purchase goods at the going wage and price levels, they receive some distributed profits, π', and maximize utility:

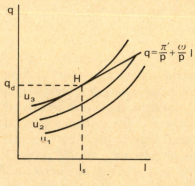

FIG. 9.2

Expenditure is equal to income, so that the budget constant is $pq = \pi' + wl$, or, in real terms, $q = (\pi'/p) + (w/p) \cdot l$. Households move along this budget line to the point H at which the highest possible indifference curve is reached. Demand for goods is q_d and labour offered is l_s.

If we assume for simplicity that all profits are distributed to households, then the firms' cost line and households' budget line are identical. Full-employment equilibrium is then reached at the point of tangency between the transformation curve and an indifference curve:

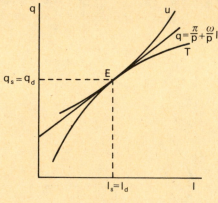

FIG. 9.3

The equilibrium real wage is given by the common slope at *E*, or, if the money wage is given, this slope fixes the 'right' price level. Both commodity and labour markets clear: there is full employment.

What happens, though, if the going price is 'too low', so that the real wage is higher than the full-employment level? The common cost/budget line now has a steeper slope, labour supply exceeds demand, and there is apparently excess demand in the commodity market:

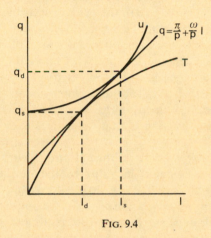

Fig. 9.4

There is unemployment, $l_s - l_d$, but the apparent excess demand for goods should push prices up, so that the real wage falls and full-employment equilibrium will be regained at *E*.

The difficulty is that q_d in Figure 9.4 is not *actual* demand for goods, but what *would* be demanded if households were in fact employed to the level desired at the going real wage, l_s. But actual employment is only l_d: households cannot move along their budget line beyond *F*, at which point the economy is stuck. Households' income is determined by the demand for labour, not the supply, and their 'constrained' demand for goods is thus forced to be equal to the supply at *F*. Thus although 'notional' excess demand for goods exists, there is no 'effective' excess demand, and therefore no upward pressure on prices, no tendency for the real wage to fall, and no tendency towards full employment—*despite the assumption of price flexibility*.

This is, of course, a highly schematic résumé of Clower's argument, still more of Keynes's. But it brings out the central importance of the consumption function in Keynesian analysis, and gives the answer to the question which should perhaps have been at the back of anyone's mind after absorbing the Keynesian approach—why do we speak of '*effective* demand' and not just of 'demand'?

Leijonhufvud's *On Keynesian Economics and the Economics of Keynes* is a thorough re-examination of the whole of Keynes's analysis and its interpretation and misinterpretation by later authors. In the brief extract reproduced here [Reading 9.5], Leijonhufvud explores Keynes's analysis of unemployment situations, starting from Clower's demonstration that when trading takes place at disequilibrium prices, the price system will generally fail to provide 'correct' information—that is, to move the economy to full employment. For example, suppose, beginning from a situation of full employment, entrepreneurs' expectations become less optimistic. The demand for investment goods falls and, correspondingly, there is a fall in the issue of securities. The consequential rise in the price of securities depresses yields and the rate of interest, increasing the demand for money. The fall in investment demand, magnified by the operation of the multiplier, reduces output and, in consequence, the demand for money. A new equilibrium is reached when the excess supply of goods and excess demand for money have been eliminated, at a lower level of output and employment. But no change in the money wage has been assumed: in this sense, the money wage ruling in the new unemployment situation is that 'appropriate' to full-employment equilibrium.

The formal analysis of general equilibrium price theory still applies: the excess supply of labour is equal in value to the increased demand for commodities which would result if the involuntarily unemployed workers were re-employed. But unemployed workers offer labour in return for money, not goods. Faced with deficient (and, as the multiplier process operates, falling) demand, producers cannot see that hiring more workers will ultimately, though indirectly, increase the demand for their own output and 'justify' their decision. Equally, employers facing deficient demand will not hire more labour in response to a cut in real wages.

An exactly analogous difference between Keynesian and neoclassical approaches can be seen in the analysis of the savings-investment problem. For neoclassical theorists, an autonomous increase in savings, which reflects a decision to consume less now in order to consume more in the future, should be matched by a switch by firms from production of consumption goods into investment so as to provide for the higher *future* demand for consumption goods. But, again, the market cannot provide the relevant information which would cause firms to behave in this way. Producers see the decline in current effective demand, but cannot see the rise in future demand, and so the rise in the propensity to save is not matched by a rise in the investment ratio: output simply declines.

Once stated, these propositions seem obvious. What, then, explains their apparent absence from the 'neoclassical synthesis'? The answer seems to be that the formal tools available to Keynes, and the formal models of the 'Keynesian system', were essentially tools of comparative statics, while the underlying analysis of the *General Theory* was of a dynamic disequilibrium. In comparing two equilibria, as the formal models tend to do, it seems natural to compare the two sets of prices (including wage- and interest-rates) and then to infer that the unemployment 'equilibrium' is prevented from turning into the full-employment equilibrium simply because one or other of the prices is not 'free' to adjust. The lesson of the recent reappraisal is that price flexibility is a necessary but not a sufficient condition for such an adjustment to take place. Prices must not only be free to adjust, but there must also be endogenous forces at work to procure the required adjustment. But pressures on prices result from actual, or effective, excess demands, not from the notional excess demands calculated from the gaps between full- and under-employment levels of variables. General equilibrium analysis throws up the prices which would rule at full-employment equilibrium; Keynesian analysis shows that market forces will not, in general, produce a tendency towards that price set.

9.1 A Theoretical Framework for Monetary Analysis*

THE KEYNESIAN CHALLENGE TO THE QUANTITY THEORY

The income-expenditure analysis developed by John Maynard Keynes in his *General Theory* (Keynes 1936) offered an alternative approach to the interpretation of changes in nominal income that emphasized the relation between nominal income and investment or autonomous expenditures rather than the relation between money income and the stock of money.

Keynes's basic challenge to the reigning theory can be summarized in three propositions that he set forth:

1. As a purely *theoretical* matter, there need not exist, even if all prices are flexible, a *long-run equilibrium* position characterized by 'full employment' of resources.

2. As an *empirical* matter, prices can be regarded as rigid—an institutional datum—for *short-run economic fluctuations*; that is, for such fluctuations, the distinction between real and nominal magnitudes that is at the heart of the quantity theory is of no importance.

3. The demand function for money has a particular empirical form—corresponding to absolute liquidity preference—that makes velocity highly unstable much of the time, so that changes in the quantity of money would, in the main, simply produce changes in V in the opposite direction. This proposition is critical for both propositions (1) and (2), though the reasons for absolute liquidity preference are different in the long run and in the short run. Absolute liquidity preference at an interest rate approaching zero is a necessary though not a sufficient condition for proposition (1). Absolute liquidity preference at the 'conventional' interest rate explains why Keynes

* From M. Friedman, *A Theoretical Framework for Monetary Analysis* (New York: National Bureau of Economic Research Inc., 1971). This monograph puts together two articles published in the *Journal of Political Economy* in 1970 and 1971.

regarded the quantity equation, though perfectly valid as an identity, as largely useless for policy or for predicting short-run fluctuations in nominal and real income (identical by proposition [2]). In its place, Keynes put the income identity supplemented by a stable propensity to consume.

(a) Long-Run Equilibrium

The first proposition can be treated summarily because it has been demonstrated to be false. Keynes's error consisted in neglecting the role of wealth in the consumption function—or, stated differently, in neglecting the existence of a desired stock of wealth as a goal motivating savings. All sorts of frictions and rigidities may interfere with the attainment of a hypothetical long-run equilibrium position at full employment; dynamic changes in technology, resources, and social and economic institutions may continually change the characteristics of that equilibrium position; but there is no fundamental 'flaw in the price system' that makes unemployment the natural outcome of a fully operative market mechanism.

(b) Short-Run Price Rigidity

Alfred Marshall's distinction among market equilibrium, short-period equilibrium, and long-period equilibrium was a device for analyzing the dynamic adjustment in a particular market to a change in demand or supply. This device had two key characteristics. One, the less important for our purposes, is that it replaced the continuous process by a series of discrete steps—comparable with approximating a continuous function by a set of straight-line segments. The second is the assumption that prices adjust more rapidly than quantities, indeed, so rapidly that the price adjustment can be regarded as instantaneous. An increase in demand (a shift to the right of the long-run demand curve) will produce a new market equilibrium involving a higher price but the same quantity. The higher price will, in the short run, encourage existing producers to produce more with their existing plants, thus raising quantity and bringing prices back down toward their original level, and, in the long run, attract new producers and encourage existing producers to expand their plants, still further raising quantities and lowering prices. Throughout the process, it takes time for output to adjust but no time for prices to do so. This assumption has no effect on the final equilibrium position, but it is vital for the path to equilibrium.

This Marshallian assumption about the price of a particular product became widely accepted and tended to be carried over unthinkingly to the price level in analyzing the dynamic adjustment to a change in the demand for or supply of money. As noted above, the Cambridge cash-balances equation $[M = kPy]$ lends itself to a demand-supply interpretation along Marshallian lines. So interpreted, a change in the nominal quantity of money (a once-for-all shift in the supply schedule) will require a change in one or more of the variables on the right-hand side of [the] equation—k, or P, or y—in order to reconcile demand and supply. In the final full equilibrium, the adjustment will, in general, be entirely in P, since the change in the nominal quantity of money need not alter any of the 'real' factors on which k and y ultimately depend. As in the Marshallian case, the final position is not affected by relative speeds of adjustment.

There is nothing in the logic of the quantity theory that specifies the dynamic path of adjustment, nothing that requires the whole adjustment to take place through P rather than through k or y. It was widely recognized that the adjustment during what Fisher, for example, called 'transition periods' would in practice be partly in k and in y as well as in P. Yet this recognition was not incorporated in formal theoretical analysis. The formal analysis simply took over Marshall's assumption. In this sense, the quantity theorists can be validly criticized for having 'assumed' price flexibility—just as Keynes can be validly criticized for 'assuming' that consumption is independent of wealth, even though he recognized in his asides that wealth has an effect on consumption.

Keynes was a true Marshallian in method. He followed Marshall in taking the demand-supply analysis as his framework. He followed Marshall in replacing the continuous adjustment by a series of discrete steps and so analyzing a dynamic process in terms of a series of shifts between static equilibrium positions. Even his steps were essentially Marshall's, his short-run being distinguished from his long-run by the fixity of the aggregate capital stock. However, he tended to merge the market period and the short-run period, and, true to his own misleading dictum, 'in the long run we are all dead', he concentrated almost exclusively on the short run.

Keynes also followed Marshall in assuming that one variable adjusted so quickly that the adjustment could be regarded as instantaneous, while the other variable adjusted slowly. Where he deviated from Marshall, and it was a momentous deviation, was in reversing the roles assigned to price and quantity. He assumed that, at least for changes in aggregate demand, quantity was the variable that adjusted rapidly, while price was the variable that adjusted slowly, at least in a downward direction. Keynes embodied this assumption in his formal model by expressing all variables in wage units, so that his formal analysis—aside from a few passing references to a situation of 'true' inflation—dealt with 'real' magnitudes, not 'nominal' magnitudes (Keynes 1936, pp. 119, 301, 303). He rationalized the assumption in terms of wage rigidity arising partly from money illusion, partly from the strength of trade unions. And, at a still deeper level, he rationalized wage rigidity by proposition (1): under conditions when there was no full-employment equilibrium, there was also no equilibrium nominal price level; something had to be brought in from outside to fix the price level; it might as well be institutional wage rigidity. Put differently, flexible nominal wages under such circumstances had no economic function to perform; hence they might as well be made rigid.

However rationalized, the basic reason for the assumption was undoubtedly the lack of concordance between observed phenomena and the implications of a literal application of Marshall's assumption to aggregate magnitudes. Such a literal application implied that economic fluctuations would take the form wholly of fluctuations in prices with continuous full employment of men and resources. Clearly, this did not correspond to experience. If anything, at least in the decade and a half between the end of World War I and the writing of *The General Theory*, economic fluctuations were manifested to a greater degree in output and employment than in prices. It therefore seemed highly plausible that, at least for aggregate phenomena, relative speeds of adjustment were just the reverse of those assumed by Marshall.

Keynes explored this penetrating insight by carrying it to the extreme: all adjustment in quantity, none in price. He qualified this statement by assuming it to apply only to conditions of underemployment. At 'full' employment, he shifted to the quantity-theory model and asserted that all adjustment would be in price—he designated this a situation of 'true inflation'. However, Keynes paid no more than lip service to this possibility, and his disciples have done the same; so it does not misrepresent the body of his analysis largely to neglect the qualification.

Given this assumption, a change in the nominal quantity of money means a change in the real quantity of money. In [the Cambridge] equation we can divide through by P, making the left-hand side the real quantity of money. A change in the (nominal and real) quantity of money will then be matched by a change in k or in y.

Nothing up to this point seems to prevent Keynes from having a purely monetary theory of economic fluctuations, with changes in M being reflected entirely in y. However, this conflicted with Keynes's interpretation of the facts of the Great Depresssion, which he regarded, I believe erroneously, as showing that expansive monetary policy was ineffective in stemming a decline. Hence, he was inclined to interpret changes in M as being reflected in k rather more than in y. This is where his proposition (3) about liquidity preference enters in.

Indeed, in the most extreme, and I am tempted to say purest, form of his analysis, Keynes supposes that the whole of the adjustment will be in k. And, interestingly enough, this result can also be regarded as a direct consequence of his assumption about the relative speed of adjustment of price and quantity. For k is not a numerical constant but a function of other variables. It embodies liquidity preference. In Keynes's system, the main variable it depends on is the interest rate. This too is a price. Hence, it was natural for Keynes to regard it as slow to adjust, and to take, as the variable which responds, the real quantity of money people desire to hold.

If changes in M do not produce changes in y, what does? Keynes's answer is the need to reconcile the amount some people want to spend to add to the stock of productive capital with the amount the community wants to save to add to its stock of wealth. Hence Keynes puts at the center of his analysis the distinction between consumption and saving, or more fundamentally, between spending linked closely to current income and spending that is largely independent of current income.

As a result of both experience and further theoretical analysis, there is hardly an economist today who accepts Keynes's conclusion about the strictly passive character of k, or the accompanying conclusion that money (in the sense of the quantity of money) does not matter, or who will explicitly assert that P is 'really' an institutional datum that will be completely unaffected even in short periods by changes in M.

Yet Keynes's assumption about the relative speed of adjustment of price and quantity is still a key to the difference in approach and analysis between those economists who regard themselves as Keynesians and those who do not. Whatever the first group may say in their asides and in their qualifications, they treat the price level as an institutional datum in their formal theoretical analysis. They continue to regard changes in the nominal quantity of money as equivalent to changes in the real quantity of money and hence as having to be reflected in k and y. And they continue to regard the initial effect as being on k. The difference is that they no longer regard interest rates as institutional data, as Keynes in considerable measure did. Instead, they regard the change in k as requiring a change in interest rates which in turn produces a change in y. Hence, they attribute more significance to changes in the quantity of money than Keynes and his disciples did in the first decade or so after the appearance of *The General Theory*. [...]

A SIMPLE COMMON MODEL

We can summarize the key points of the preceding sections of this paper, and lay a groundwork for the final sections, by setting forth a highly simplified aggregate model of an economy that encompasses both a simplified quantity theory and a simplified income-expenditure theory as special cases. In interpreting this model, it should be kept in mind that the same symbols can have very different empirical counterparts, so that the algebraic statement can conceal a difference as fundamental as that described in the preceding four paragraphs.

For the purpose of this summary, we can neglect foreign trade, by assuming a closed economy, and the fiscal role of government, by assuming that there are neither government expenditures nor government receipts. We can also neglect stochastic disturbances. What I shall concentrate on are the division of national income between induced and autonomous expenditures and the adjustment between the demand for and supply of money.

The simple model is given by six equations:

$$\frac{C}{P} = f\left(\frac{Y}{P}, r\right);\tag{1}$$

$$\frac{I}{P} = g(r);\tag{2}$$

$$\frac{Y}{P} = \frac{C}{P} + \frac{I}{P}\left(\text{or, alternatively, } \frac{S}{P} = \frac{Y-C}{P} = \frac{I}{P}\right);\tag{3}$$

$$M^D = P \cdot l\left(\frac{Y}{P}, r\right);\tag{4}$$

$$M^S = h(r);\tag{5}$$

$$M^D = M^S.\tag{6}$$

The first three equations describe the adjustment of the flows of savings and investment; the last three, of the stock of money demanded and supplied. Equation (1) is a consumption function (Keynes's 'marginal propensity to consume') expressing real consumption (C/P) as a function of real income ($Y/P = y$) and the interest rate (r). For simplicity, wealth is omitted, although, if the model were to be used to illustrate Keynes's proposition (1), and why it is fallacious, wealth would have to be included as an argument in the function.

Equation (2) is an investment function (Keynes's marginal efficiency of investment) which expresses real investment (I/P) as a function of the interest rate. Here again, consistent with both Keynes and subsequent literature, both the total stock of capital and real income could be included as arguments. However, in Keynes's spirit, the model refers to a short period in which the capital stock can be regarded as fixed. For a longer-period model, the capital stock would have to be included and treated as an endogenous variable, presumably defined by an integral of past investment. The inclusion of income in the equation, as an independent variable, would confuse the key point of the distinction between C and I. As a theoretical matter, the relevant distinction is not between consumption and investment but between expenditures that are closely linked to current income ('conditional' on income would, from this point of view, be a better mnemonic for $\bar{C}$ than consumption, though the term usually used is 'induced') and expenditures that are autonomous, that is, independent (a better mnemonic for I than investment), of income. The identification of these categories with consumption and investment is an empirical hypothesis. For theoretical purposes, any part of investment spending that is conditional on current income should be included with C.

Equation (3) is typically referred to as the income identity. As the parenthetical transformation makes clear, it can also be regarded as a market-clearing or adjustment equation specifying that saving is to be equal to investment.

Equation (4) is the demand function for nominal money balances (Keynes's liquidity preference function). [It simply] expresses the real quantity of money demanded (M^D/P) as a function of real income and the interest rate. Here again, as in equation (1), wealth could properly be included but is omitted for simplicity.

Equation (5) is the supply function of nominal money. To be consistent with the literature, the interest rate enters as a variable. However, no purpose for which we shall use the model would be affected in any way by treating M^S as simply an exogenous variable, determined, say, by the monetary authorities.

Equation (6) is the counterpart of equation (3), a market-clearing or adjustment equation specifying that money demanded shall equal money supplied.

These six equations would be accepted alike by adherents of the quantity theory and of the income-expenditure theory. On this level of abstraction, there is no difference between them. However, while there are six equations, there are seven unknowns: C, I, Y, r, P, M^D, M^S. There is a missing equation. Some one of these variables must be determined by relationships outside this system.

THE MISSING EQUATION: THREE APPROACHES

The difference between the quantity theory and the income-expenditure theory is the condition that is added to make the equations determinate.

The simple income-expenditure theory adds the missing equation in one form. Different versions of the quantity theory add it in two other forms. Of these, the missing equation that has been generally regarded in the literature as defining the simple quantity theory is discussed in this section. The missing equation supplied by an alternative version of the quantity theory that is implicit in much recent literature but has not heretofore been made explicit is discussed in the following section. I shall designate the alternative version of the quantity theory as the monetary theory of nominal income.

The simple quantity theory adds the equation

$$\frac{Y}{P} = y = y_0;\tag{7}$$

that is, real income is determined outside the system. In effect, it appends to this system the Walrasian equations of general equilibrium, regards them as independent of these equations defining the aggregates, and as giving the value of Y/P, and thereby reduces this system to one of six equations determining six unknowns.

The simple income-expenditure theory adds the equation

$$P = P_0; \tag{8}$$

that is, the price level is determined outside the system, which again reduces the system to one of six equations in six unknowns. It appends to this system a historical set of prices and an institutional structure that is assumed either to keep prices rigid or to determine changes in prices on the basis of 'bargaining power' or some similar set of forces. Initially, the set of forces determining prices was treated as not being incorporated in any formal body of economic analysis. More recently, the developments symbolized by the 'Phillips curve' reflect attempts to bring the determination of prices back into the body of economic analysis, to establish a link between real magnitudes and the rate at which prices change from their initial historically determined level.

For the quantity theory specialization, given that $Y/P = y_0$, equations (1), (2), and (3) become a self-contained set of three equation in three unknowns: C/P, I/P, and r. Substituting (1) and (2) into (3), we have

$$y_0 - f(y_0, r) = g(r), \tag{9}$$

or a single equation which determines r. Let r_0 be this value of r. From equation (5), this determines the value of M, say M_0 which, using equation (6), converts equation (4) into

$$M_0 = P \cdot l(y_0, r_0), \tag{10}$$

which now determines P.

Equation (10) is simply the classical quantity equation, as can be seen by multiplying and dividing the right-hand side by y_0 and replacing $l(y_0, r_0)/y_0$ by its equivalent, $1/V$. If we drop the subscripts, this gives,

$$M = \frac{Py}{V}, \tag{11}$$

or

$$P = \frac{MV}{y}. \tag{12}$$

For the income-expenditure specialization, setting $P = P_0$ does not in general permit of a sequential solution. Substituting equations (1) and (2) into equation (3) gives

$$\frac{Y}{P_0} - f\left(\frac{Y}{P_0}, r\right) = g(r), \tag{13}$$

an equation in two variables, Y and r. This is the *IS* curve of Hicks's famous

IS–LM analysis. Substituting equations (4) and (5) into equation (6) gives

$$h(r) = P_0 \cdot l\left(\frac{Y}{P_0}, r\right),\tag{14}$$

a second equation in the same two variables, Y and r. This is Hicks's *LM* curve. The simultaneous solution of the two determines r and Y.

Alternatively, solve equation (13) for Y as a function of r, and substitute in equation (14). This gives a single equation which determines r as a function of the demand for and supply of money. This can be regarded as the Keynesian parallel to equation (10), which determines P as a function of the demand for and supply of money.

A simpler sequential analysis, faithful to many textbook versions of the analysis and to Keynes's own simplified model, is obtained by supposing either that Y/P is not an argument in the right-hand side of equation (4) or that absolute liquidity preference holds so that equation (4) takes the special form:

$$M^D = 0 \text{ if } r > r_0\tag{4a}$$

$$M^D = \infty \text{ if } r < r_0.$$

In either of these cases, equations (4) or (4a), (5), and (6) determine the interest rate, $r = r_0$ (just as in the simple quantity approach, equations [1], [2], and [3] do); substituting the interest rate in equation (2) determines investment, say at $I = I_0$ and in equation (1) makes consumption a function solely of income, so that real income must then be determined by the requirement that it equate saving with investment.

If we approximate the function $f(Y/P, r_0)$ by a linear form, say,

$$\frac{C}{P} = C_0 + C_1 \frac{Y}{P},\tag{15}$$

substitute equation (15) in equation (3), and solve for Y/P, we get

$$\frac{Y}{P} = \frac{C_0 + I_0}{1 - C_1},\tag{16}$$

or the simple Keynesian multiplier equation, with $C_0 + I_0$ equalling autonomous expenditure and $1/(1 - C_1)$ equalling the multiplier.

THE MISSING EQUATION:
THE THIRD APPROACH EXAMINED

A third form of the missing equation involves bypassing the breakdown of nominal income between real income and prices and using the quantity theory to derive a theory of nominal income rather than a theory of either prices or real income.

(a) Demand for Money

As a first step, assume that the elasticity of the demand for money with respect to real income is unity. We can then write (4) in the equivalent form:

$$M^D = Y \cdot l(r), \tag{4b}$$

where the same symbol l is used to designate a different functional form. This enables us to eliminate prices and real income separately from the equations of the monetary sector.

This assumption cannot, so far as as I am aware, be justified on theoretical grounds. There is no reason why the elasticity of demand for money with respect to per capita real income should not be either less than one or greater than one at any particular level of income, or why it should be the same at all levels of real income. However, much empirical evidence indicates that the income elasticity is not very different from unity. The empirical evidence seems to me to indicate that the elasticity is generally larger than unity, perhaps in the neighborhood of 1·5 to 2·0 for economies in a period of rapid economic development, and of 1·0 to 1·5 for other circumstances. Other scholars would perhaps set it lower. More important, the present theory is for short-term fluctuations during which the variation in per capita real income is fairly small. Given that the elasticity is unlikely to exceed 2·0, no great error can be introduced for such moderate variations in income by approximating it by unity.

(b) Savings and Investment Functions

As a second step, it is tempting to make a similar assumption for the savings and investment functions, i.e., to write:

$$C = Y \cdot f(r), \tag{1a}$$

or,

$$C = Y \cdot f(r, Y), \tag{1b}$$

and

$$I = Y \cdot g(r), \tag{2a}$$

which would eliminate any separate influence of prices and real income from the savings-investment sector also. However, this is an unattractive simplification on both theoretical and empirical grounds. Theoretically, it dismisses Keynes' central point: the distinction between expenditures that are independent of current income (autonomous expenditures) and expenditures dependent on current income (induced expenditures). Empirically, much evidence suggests that the ratio of consumption to income over short periods is not independent of the level of measured income [equation (1a)], or of the division of a change in income between prices and output [equation (1b)]. The extensive literature on the consumption function rests on this evidence.

(c) Interest Rates

A more promising route is to combine a key idea of Keynes' with a key idea of Irving Fisher's.

The idea that we take over from Keynes is that the current market interest rate (r) is largely determined by the rate that is expected to prevail over a longer period (r^*).

Carrying this idea to its limit gives:

$$r = r^*. \tag{17}$$

The idea that we take over from Fisher is the distinction between the nominal and the real rate of interest:

$$r = \rho + \left(\frac{1}{P}\frac{dP}{dt}\right), \tag{18}$$

where ρ is the real rate of interest and $(1/P)(dP/dt)$ is the percentage change in the price level. If the terms r and $(1/P)(dP/dt)$ refer to the observed nominal interest rate and observed rate of price change, ρ is the realized real interest rate. If they refer to 'permanent' or 'anticipated' values, which we shall designate by attaching an asterisk to them, then ρ^* is likewise the 'permanent' or 'anticipated' real rate.

Combine equation (17) and the version of (18) that has asterisks attached to the variables. This gives:

$$r = \rho^* + \left(\frac{1}{P}\frac{dP}{dt}\right)^*, \tag{19}$$

which can be written as:

$$r = \rho^* + \left(\frac{1}{Y}\frac{dY}{dt}\right)^* - \left(\frac{1}{y}\frac{dy}{dt}\right)^* = \rho^* - g^* + \left(\frac{1}{Y}\frac{dY}{dt}\right)^* \tag{20}$$

where $g^* = [(1/y)(dy/dt)]^* =$ 'permanent' or 'anticipated' rate of growth of real income, i.e., the secular or trend rate of growth.

Let us now assume that

$$\rho^* - g^* = k_o, \tag{21}$$

i.e., that the difference between the anticipated real interest rate and the anticipated rate of real growth is determined outside the system. This equation is the counterpart of the full employment and rigid price assumptions [equations (7) and (8)] of the simple quantity theory and the simple Keynesian income-expenditure theory.

There are two ways that assumption (21) can be rationalized: (1) that over a time interval relevant for the analysis of short-period fluctuations, ρ^* and g^* can separately be regarded as constant; (2) that the two can be regarded as moving together, so the difference will vary less than either. Of course, in both cases, what is relevant is not absolute constancy, but changes in $\rho^* - g^*$ that are small compared to changes in $[(1/P)(dP/dt)]^*$, and hence in r.

1. The stock of physical capital, the stock of human capital, and the body of technological knowledge are all extremely large compared to annual additions. Physical capital is, say, of the order of three to five years' national income; annual net investment is of the order of $\frac{1}{10}$ to $\frac{1}{5}$ of national income or 2 to 8 per cent of the capital stock. Let the capital *stock* be subject even to very rapidly diminishing returns and the real yield will not be much affected in a few years time. Similar considerations apply to human capital and technology.

If we interpret g^* as referring to growth potential, then a roughly constant yield on capital, human and nonhuman, and a slowly changing stock of capital imply a slowly changing value of g^* as well.

Empirically, a number of pieces of evidence fit in with these assumptions. We have interest rate data over very long periods of time, and these indicate that rates are very similar at distant times, if the times compared have similar price behavior. More recently, the Federal Reserve Bank of St. Louis has been estimating the 'real rate', and their estimates are remarkably stable despite very large changes in nominal rates.

Similarly, average real growth has differed considerably at any one time for different countries—compare Japan in recent decades with Great Britain—but for each country has been rather constant over considerable periods of time.

2. Let s^* = the fraction of permanent income which is invested. Then the permanent rate of growth of income as a result of this investment alone will be equal to $s^*\rho^*$. Empirically, the actual rate of growth tends to be larger than this product, if s^* refers only to what is recorded as capital formation in the national income accounts. One explanation, frequently suggested, is that recorded capital formation neglects most investment in human capital and in improving technology and that allowance for these would make the relevant s^* much higher than the 10 or 20 per cent that is the fraction estimated in national income accounts, both because it would increase the numerator of the fraction (investment) and decrease the denominator (income) by requiring much of what is commonly treated as income to be treated as expenses of maintaining human capital and the stock of technology. In the limit, as s^* approaches unity, ρ^* approaches g^*, so $\rho^* - g^* = 0$. Without going to this extreme,

$$\rho^* - g^* = (1 - s^*)\rho^*. \tag{22}$$

The preceding argument suggests that ρ^* is fairly constant, and subtracting g^* decreases the error even further.

Empirically, it does seem to be the case that ρ^* and g^* tend to vary together, though in the present state of evidence, this is hardly more than a rough conjecture.

(d) The Alternative Model

If we substitute equation (4b) for equation (4), keep the original equations (5) and (6), and substitute equation (21) in equation (20) to replace the remaining equations of the initial simple model, we have the following system of four equations:

$$M^D = Y \cdot l(r) \tag{4b}$$

$$M^S = h(r) \tag{5}$$

$$M^D = M^S \tag{6}$$

$$r = k_o + \left(\frac{1}{Y}\frac{dY}{dt}\right)^*. \tag{23}$$

At any point of time, $[(1/Y)(dY/dt)]^*$, the 'permanent' or 'anticipated' rate of growth of nominal income is a predetermined variable, presumably based partly on past experience, partly on considerations outside our model. As a result, this is a system of four equations in the four unknowns, M^D, M^S, Y, and r.

Prices and quantity do not enter separately, so the set of equations constitutes a model of nominal income.

It will help to clarify the essence of this third approach to simplify it still further by assuming that the nominal money supply can be regarded as completely exogenous, rather than a function of the interest rate, and to introduce time explicitly in the system. Let $M(t)$ be the exogenously determined supply of money. We then have from equations (4b), (5), and (6)

$$Y(t) = \frac{M(t)}{l(r)}, \tag{24}$$

or

$$Y(t) = V(r) \cdot M(t), \tag{25}$$

where V stands for velocity of circulation. This puts the equation in standard quantity theory terms, except that it does not try to go behind nominal income to prices and quantities. Equations (23) and (25) then constitute a two-equation system for determining the level of nominal income at any point in time. To determine the path of nominal income over time, there is needed in addition some way to determine the anticipated rate of change of nominal income. I shall return to this below.

Although the symbolism in the demand equation for money [(4b) or (25)] is the same as in the two other specializations of the general model, there is an important difference in substance. Both the simple quantity theory and the income-expenditure theory implicitly define equilibrium in terms of a stable price level, hence real and nominal interest rates are the same. The third approach, based on a synthesis of Keynes and Fisher, abandons this limitation. The equations encompass 'equilibrium' situations in which prices may be rising or falling. The interest rate that enters into the demand schedule for money is the nominal interest rate. So long as we stick to a single interest rate, that rate takes full account of the effect of rising or falling prices on the demand for money.

(e) *The Saving-Investment Sector*

What about equations (1) to (3), which we have so far completely by-passed? Here the interest rate that is relevant, if a single rate is used, is clearly the real not the nominal rate. If we replace r by ρ, these equations become

$$\frac{C}{P} = f\left(\frac{Y}{P}, \rho\right) \tag{1$'$}$$

$$\frac{I}{P} = g(\rho) \tag{2$'$}$$

$$\frac{Y}{P} = \frac{C}{P} + \frac{I}{P}. \tag{3}$$

If we were to accept a more restricted counterpart of equations (17) and (21), namely

$$\rho = \rho^* = \rho_o, \tag{26}$$

i.e., the realized real rate of interest is a constant, then these equations would be a self-contained consistent set of five equations in the five variables, C/P, I/P, Y/P, ρ, ρ^*. Equations (26) would give the real interest rate. Equation (2)$'$ would give real investment and equations (1)$'$ and (3), real income. The price level would then be given by the ratio of the nominal income obtained from equations (23) and (25) to the real income given by equations (1)$'$, (2)$'$, (3), and (26). The two sets of equations combined would be a complete system of seven equations in seven variables determining both real and nominal magnitudes.

Such a combination, if it were acceptable, would be intellectually very appealing. Over a decade ago, during the early stages of our comparison of the predictive accuracy of the quantity theory and the income-expenditure theory, my hopes were aroused that such a combination might correspond with experience. Some of our early results were consistent with the determination of the real variables by the multiplier, and the nominal variables by velocity. However, later results shattered the hope for this outcome. The unfavorable empirical findings, moreover, are reinforced by theoretical considerations.

The major theoretical objections are twofold. First, it seems entirely satisfactory to take the anticipated real interest rate (or the difference between the anticipated real interest rate and the secular rate of growth) as fixed for the demand for money. There, the real interest rate is at best a supporting actor. Inflation and deflation are surely center stage. Suppressing the variations in the real interest rate (or the deviations of the measured real rate from the anticipated real rate) is unlikely to introduce serious error. The situation is altogether different for saving and investment. Omitting the real interest rate in that process is to leave out Hamlet. Second, the consumption function (1)′ is highly unsatisfactory, especially once we take inflation and deflation into account. Wealth, anticipations of inflation, and the difference between permanent and measured income are too important and too central to be pushed off stage completely.

Hence for both empirical and theoretical reasons, I am inclined to reject this way of marrying the real and the nominal variables and to regard the saving-investment sector as unfinished business, even on the highly abstract general level of this paper. [...]

9.2 Friedman's Theoretical Framework*

Milton Friedman has earned our gratitude by the two articles setting forth his theoretical framework.[1] He has certainly facilitated communication by his willingness to express his argument in a language widely used in macro-economics, the Hicksian *IS-LM* apparatus. He undoubtedly hoped that use of a common theoretical apparatus would reduce the controversy about the roles of monetary and fiscal policies to an econometric debate about empirical magnitudes. If the monetarists and the neo-Keynesians[2] could agree as to which values of which parameters in which behavior relations imply which policy conclusions, then they could concentrate on the evidence regarding the values of those parameters. I wish that these articles had brought us closer to this goal, but I am afraid they have not. I have been very surprised to learn what Professor Friedman regards as his crucial theoretical differences from the neo-Keynesians.

* From J. Tobin, 'Friedman's Theoretical Framework', *Journal of Political Economy*, 1972. Reprinted by permission of the University of Chicago Press.
[1] [See Reading 9.1—ed.].
[2] I do not know what to call those of us who take an eclectic nonmonetarist view. 'Neo-Keynesian' will do, I guess, but so would 'neoclassical'. The synthesis of the last twenty-five years certainly contains many elements not in *The General Theory* (Keynes 1936). Perhaps it should be called Hicksian, since it derives not only from his *IS-LM* article but, more importantly, from his classic paper on money (Hicks 1935). One thing the nonmonetarists should *not* be called is 'fiscalists'. The debate is not symmetrical. Whereas neo-Keynesians believe that *both* monetary and fiscal policies affect nominal income, monetarists believe that only monetary policies do so. At least, I *think* that is the distinctive and characteristic message that monetarists have been conveying to the profession and the public. Friedman agrees that this gives 'the right flavor of our conclusions'.

MONEY, INCOME, AND PRICES IN
SHORT-RUN EQUILIBRIUM

First, let me explain what I thought the main issue was. In terms of the Hicksian language of Friedman's two articles, I thought (and I still think) it was the shape of the LM locus. This locus is for given stock of money M and price level p, the combinations of real income Y and interest rate r that satisfy $M/p = L(Y,r)$.[3] It will be vertical if the demand for money is wholly insensitive to interest rates. This assumption leads to the following characteristic monetarist propositions:

a) Y can be changed only if M/p is changed. Or, if one prefers a relation between nominal magnitudes, pY can be changed only if M is changed. The link may or may not be one of proportionality, and it may of course involve lags and leads and stochastic terms.

b) In particular, a shift of the IS locus, whether due to fiscal policy or to exogenous change in consumption and investment behavior, cannot alter Y.

c) If Y is supply-determined, then M/p is determined and both the price level p and money income pY are proportionate to M.

The neo-Keynesian view is that the LM locus is upward sloping, because $\partial L/\partial \dot{Y}$ is positive and $\partial L/\partial r$ is not zero but negative. Assuming that there is also some interest sensitivity of investment and/or consumption, we have the following characteristic neo-Keynesian propositions:

d) If Y is not uniquely determined by the supply equations of the system, it can be changed *either* by shifts in the IS curve, whether they stem from policy or other exogenous shocks, *or* by shifts in the LM locus, whether due to monetary policy or exogenous shocks.

e) In particular, an increase in the nominal stock of money M will be absorbed partly in an increase in Y, partly in an increase in p, and partly in a reduction in velocity due to a decline in the interest rate r.

f) Even with Y supply-determined, price level and money income are not uniquely related to the nominal money supply M. They also depend on the interest rate and thus on fiscal policy. For example, an expansionary fiscal policy or any other upward shift in the IS locus will raise r, lower the stock

[3] To minimize misunderstanding, I should point out that imagining an LM curve in (Y,r) space for a given price level p does *not* mean that p is taken to be an exogenous variable in the complete system of which the LM relation is only a part. Even if M is exogenously given, there is a whole family of LM curves, one for each possible value of p. (Indeed, there may be other endogenous variables, including actual or expected rate of change of p, which help to determine the position of the LM curve.) In system-wide equilibrium, the economy must be on that LM curve which corresponds to a value of p that satisfies the other relations of the system, notably including those that describe the labor market. The crucial issue is the shape of a typical member of the LM family. Because of the way in which p enters the equation $M/p = L$, all members of the family have essentially the same shape, which depends on the partial derivatives of the demand for money function L. The monetarist-Keynesian differences listed in the text depend on whether $\partial L/\partial r$ is zero, so that a typical LM curve is vertical, or negative, so that a typical LM curve has positive slope.

of real balances demanded, and raise the price level corresponding to any nominal money stock.[4]

All this is the stuff of macroeconomics courses all over the country. Friedman, however, explicitly disavows belief that the demand for money is independent of interest rates and denies that his propositions depend on any such assumption. May we, therefore, assume that he accepts propositions *d*, *e*, and *f* and rejects *a*, *b*, and *c*?

Friedman shifts attention to the supply side of the model, the short-run relation of *Y* and *p*. I was certainly amazed to find this relationship—which he calls the 'missing equation'—identified as the crux of the controversy. I had thought that both monetarists and neo-Keynesians agreed that short-run variations of money income (*pY* or *MV*), however caused, were generally divided between changes in output and changes in price. The common view, I thought, was that the proportions in which an increment in aggregate nominal demand go into output increase and price increase depend on the degree of pressure on existing labor and capital resources. There is plenty of qualitative empirical evidence for such a proposition, though plenty of theoretical and statistical doubt about its precise specification.

Anyway, it is a caricature of the monetarist position to identify it with the notion that *Y* is wholly supply-determined in the short run. We know that Friedman himself has not assumed that. He summarizes his own view as follows: 'I regard the description of our position as "money is all that matters for changes in *nominal* income and for *short-run* changes in real income" as an exaggeration but one that gives the right flavor of our conclusions.'

It is equally a caricature of the neo-Keynesian view to say that *p* is an 'institutional datum' in the short run. Keynes certainly did not make this assumption, nor did Hansen—and neither has any careful version of a complete neo-Keynesian macroeconomic model. Nor is it at all necessary for proposition (*d*). As long as *Y* is not wholly supply-determined, as long as prices are not completely flexible in the short run, the monetary authorities can change the *real* supply of money, not just the nominal stock. As long as *Y* is not wholly supply-determined, any analysis of the consequences of changes in the real supplies of monetary assets is relevant and legitimate. Once again, just as in the debate over the shape of the money demand function, Friedman has tried to saddle his opponents and critics with an extreme assumption and to claim the entire middle ground for himself. In both cases, the truth is that it is his propositions, not theirs, which depend on a special polar case.

His second article is, if possible, more surprising than the first. The 'missing equation'—apportioning changes in money income between price and output—is no longer the crux of the matter. Instead, we are asked to

[4] None of these propositions depends on absolute liquidity preference (the trap) or, Friedman to the contrary, on any 'tendency to regard *k* or velocity as passively adjusting to changes in the quantity of money'.

assume that in the short run both the real interest rate and the nominal interest rate are fixed. The real rate, which is relevant to real investment and saving decisions, is identified with the net marginal productivity of capital along a normal growth path. This yield changes very slowly, if at all. The nominal rate is simply the real rate plus the anticipated rate of inflation, which is taken to be firmly predetermined by past experience and other considerations.

Friedman invokes the memory of Keynes, as well as that of Fisher, as inspiration for this construction. The Keynesian touch is that speculators

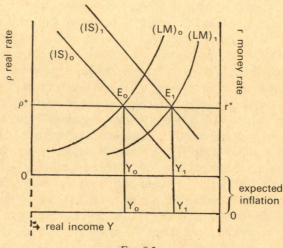

Fig. 9.5

keep the actual nominal rate at its proper value. But it is important to note that these are not Keynesian 'liquidity preference' speculators between money and bonds. They are Fisherian speculators between goods, or equities in goods, and bonds. The nominal interest rate is not in a liquidity trap. There is indeed, for every M/p, a normally shaped LM curve in the nominal interest rate and real income. But the only point on it that matters is the one that corresponds to the exogenously determined interest rate.

The level of real income is determined wholly by the IS (or multiplier) equations, once the real rate of interest is given. Given $M/p = L(r, Y)$, the fixing of both r and Y determines M/p and leads to a short-run quantity theory of both price level and money income.

The system is illustrated in figure 9.5. Given the $(IS)_0$ locus and the real rate ρ^*, the equilibrium E_0 is determined with real income Y_0. The nominal rate is measured on the right-hand vertical axis, displaced from the left-hand, real rate, axis by the expected rate of inflation. There is a family of LM curves, connecting real income and the nominal rate, of which two are shown: $(LM)_1$ corresponds to a greater real stock of money M/p than $(LM)_0$.

The only LM locus that can coexist with $(IS)_0$ is $(LM)_0$. If the authorities try to shift $(LM)_0$ to the right by increasing M, their efforts will be frustrated by an offsetting rise in p.

Fiscal policy, however, can control real income. Indeed, an increase in real government purchases will have the full multiplier effect—for example, shifting the IS locus to $(IS)_1$ and real income to Y_1. The LM curve will follow along, shifting to $(LM)_1$; this will require a reduction of p if the nominal stock of money is kept constant or increased insufficiently. So deficit spending increases output and employment and lowers prices and money wages. Prices are completely flexible, not because output is supply-determined but because it is multiplier-determined.

As this result suggests, the model is bizarre, and it is hard to imagine that it is seriously intended. Critics have complained that the constant-velocity assumption of monetarism ignores interest-rate effects on the demand for money. It is indeed difficult to persist in maintaining that they are negligible while simultaneously stressing the importance of the rate of price inflation both for nominal interest rates and for velocity. So here is a model that acknowledges the interest sensitivity of the demand for money but preserves the quantity theory by the simple expedient of fixing interest rates. But the cost of this expedient is to concede fiscal policy more control over output and employment than virtually any Keynesian would claim.

The author himself offers this model as tentative and expresses serious doubts. He doubts that the real rate should really be regarded as a constant in the short run, and he is surely justified. The rate of investment depends, on the one hand, on estimates of the future stream of quasi-rents from the ownership of capital and, on the other, on the discount rate at which this stream is converted to present value for comparison with the cost of capital goods. Both of these determinants are subject to short-run changes connected with departures from the long-run growth path of the economy. Securities markets provide a somewhat exaggerated index of these fluctuations, in the ratio of the market value of claims on business income to the reproduction cost of business assets. The sensitivity of this ratio to short-run changes in business activity and the sensitivity of investment to this ratio are important determinants of the short-run stability or instability of the economy.

Friedman finds it easy to accept the assumption of his model that the only short-run fluctuations of nominal interest rates relevant to the demand for money are those associated with the inflation premium. This is not consistent with his acknowledgment that real rates relevant for investment and saving decisions vary in the short run. Nor is it consistent with the ample empirical evidence of rapid interest-rate gyrations. When the Treasury bill rate falls 350 basis points and the corporate bond rate 150 basis points in seven months, as happened July 1970–February 1971, it strains credulity to attribute the decline to a change in inflationary expectations, the more so when inflation continued unabated and when in any case Friedman has taught us that these expectations are a slowly changing derivative of past experience.

Friedman's ostentatious discovery of the problem of 'the missing equation' may give innocent readers the idea that macroeconomics has neglected or fudged an important relationship, without which its models are logically and empirically incomplete. This is not true. Keynes certainly included in his system a relationship between real output and the price level, derived from a theory of labor demand and supply. All careful expositions, mathematical or verbal, of the Keynesian model have done likewise. In postwar macroeconomics, the price variable has slipped one derivative, and the 'missing equation' is the complex of price-wage-employment-output relations summarized partially in 'Okun's law' and partially in 'Phillips curves' for wages and prices. A large fraction of the profession is pre-occupied with theoretical and empirical investigations of these matters. [...]

9.3 Friedman's Views on Money*
[...]
Friedman writes: 'The quantity theorist accepts the empirical hypothesis that the demand for money is highly stable—more stable than functions such as the consumption function ...'. He emphasizes that it is the functional dependence of money on parameters, and not the demand for money or the money income ratio, for which this superior stability is claimed. If this claim is correct it must either be taken to mean that the 'empirical hypothesis' refers to a relative lack of success in discovering correct consumption functions or it constitutes a theoretical challenge of great importance, not only for Keynesians but also for Friedman. For his methodology rests firmly on the agent of traditional theory maximizing under constraint. This methodology is justifiable if (a) we can specify the variable of the objective function, and if (b) this objective function is relatively stable. But if the objective function is stable and the constraints have been properly specified, then so should be all the optimal policy functions of the agent. If the objective function is volatile, then either one abandons the approach as useless or one argues that it has been wrongly specified. In the latter event, Friedman is of course right in noting the vacuity of a procedure of attempting to find stable functions by incorporating more and more variables. But my point is that in his theoretical guise he proceeds traditionally, i.e. with a stable objective function, and that he must then explain why one policy function should be more volatile than another. The same arguments apply when functions aggregated over individuals are at stake. From the fact that Friedman evidently does not consider these matters pertinent I conclude that the 'empirical hypothesis' in question is nothing more than the claim

* From F. H. Hahn, 'Professor Friedman's Views on Money', *Economica*, 1971 [an article reviewing Friedman's *The Optimum Quantity of Theory and Other Essays* (1969)—Ed.].

that empirically established demand functions for money have behaved 'better' than empirically established consumption functions. It is puzzling that such a claim should be the basis of a school of economic thought. It is also possible that I have misunderstood him when he claims that the analysis of the demand for money is substantively different from the analysis of the demand for consumption and that he has in mind a well-founded theoretical framework to explain the different performances of the two functions. If so, it really is rather important that he should produce it. In its absence, the view that 'the proof of this pudding is in the eating' is of course quite worthless.

But there is further trouble since the demand function for money is not well behaved in the natural observable variables:

Over long periods, *real* income and velocity tend to move in opposite directions; over reference cycles, in the same direction. Over long periods, changes in the nominal stock of money dominate, at least in a statistical sense, the swings in *money* income, and the inverse movements in velocity are of minor quantitative importance; over reference cycles, changes in velocity are in the same direction as changes in the nominal stock of money and are comparable in quantitative importance in accounting for changes in money income.

To reconcile these findings, permanent income and permanent prices are introduced as arguments of the demand function for money.[1] In a rather obvious way one may then maintain that the 'permanent velocity', unlike the measured velocity, behaves no differently over the cycle than it does in the long run which is taken to give us points on the true demand curve for money. Similarly the behaviour of 'permanent balances', i.e. money balances deflated by permanent prices, can be taken as generated by the 'true' demand curve. The new variables allow one to maintain that the demand function for money is a stable one.

There is here displayed the ingenuity we have come to associate with Friedman; but I do not find the story convincing. First note that there are other commonsense ways of reconciling the secular and cyclical behaviour of velocity. For instance, it may well be argued that the variance of the distribution of events for which precautionary balances are held is for obvious reasons smaller in the boom than in the depression. Or, to invoke another methodology, the probability of certain 'disasters' is less in the upswing than it is in the downswing. If Friedman, instead of having adopted his portmanteau utility-function approach, had undertaken an analysis of the agent's actions in the face of uncertainty, his demand function for money would have had to include parameters representing this uncertainty and there might then

---

[1] No precise definition of these 'permanent' variables is given. When there are many assets, permanent income in the strict sense of the consumption-function literature is difficult to define. Permanent prices, I suppose, are the prices expected to rule over the average. For the moment, the important point is that permanent magnitudes change by less than actual ones.

have been no need for any reconciliation as far as velocity is concerned. However, I do not wish to propound a new theory, but rather note some of the difficulties with the one here offered.

Firstly, permanent income in the strict sense depends, of course, on the portfolio policy (and work policy) of the agent and is not an independent variable. Friedman himself uses the concept more like 'normal income' and we shall do the same. But he considers money 'as a durable consumer good held for the services it renders and yielding a flow of services proportional to the stock', and also argues that among these services the 'precautionary' one is the most important. Yet the precautionary services rendered by a unit of money depend on the calculation of abnormal and not normal events. Granted that the demand for these services depends on normal income, it is surely surprizing that the quantity of such services yielded by a unit of money should be independent of whether matters are 'normal' or not. Second, for the same reasons, it cannot be the case that at any moment of time it is the money stock deflated by permanent or 'normal' prices that is an adequate index for the precautionary services rendered by money at that moment of time. Third, it must be supposed that the agent is concerned with pre-cautionary services and not with the asset which yields them, and it is odd that the relative power to yield such services of different assets should be taken as invariant. Fourth, what are these precautionary services anyway? One interpretation surely is that the holding of money reduces the variance in consumption. But on this interpretation, transaction costs apart, the portfolio decision is taken myopically.[2] Of course, one cannot in general separate the decision of the composition from the decision of the volume of assets, and to that extent all future expected events exert some influence on the current demand for assets. However, it remains true that anything consumed has irrevocably disappeared while a portfolio decision is binding (ignoring transaction costs) for as short a period as it is sensible to take, and to that extent one would expect the present and immediate future to be much more important than the distant or normal future. Fifth, it is odd that while Friedman makes so much of normal prices and income he makes nothing of the normal prices of other assets which have played an important role in the Keynesian literature. If in booms the interest rate is higher than the level taken as normal, we should expect the velocity to behave as it does (as Friedman himself notes).[3] But, what is important, we might also expect

---

[2] The point here is this: the saving decision will in general depend on expected magnitudes of variables over the more or less distant future. In the absence of transaction costs, the composition of assets will depend only on current values and those expected for the more or less immediate future. On these grounds one would not expect 'permanent', i.e. long-run, values to be very important, relatively to current values and myopic expectations, in explaining the demand for money balances.

[3] If in the boom, say, interest rates rise, but are expected to fall again, and *vice versa* in the depression, this will reinforce the expected effect of cyclical variations in interest rates and asset prices on velocity.

those other assets to be better carriers of security services than they were hitherto.

Taking a leaf out of Friedman's book, I do not regard these objections as 'decisive'. Rather they are a strong indication that a proper formulation of the theory should be attempted. A model in which the expected utility of consumption over the indefinite future is the objective does not seem capable of generating Friedmanesque results. Of course, he has money in the utility function, but I doubt that that will serve. I do not know whether it is permanent or current prices which are to be included in the utility function, but the indications are that it is the former. Of that I can make no sense. Precautionary services rendered to be by money now can have nothing to do with 'the quantity of goods and services to which these balances are equivalent ... over an ... indefinite period'.

But there are also indications that I have been taking the whole business too seriously and that all that is meant is that people notice, and adjust to, current events with a lag. Certainly on this interpretation one could make a good case for the importance of variables which formally look like the 'permanent' ones. Indeed, in the empirical work the 'permanent' variables are simple expected values. Clearly none of the above objections apply to a proposition that at any moment of time agents are adjusted to what they expected the world to look like at that moment of time. In that case we also do not require all the paraphernalia about the services of money, etc.; and the empirical results are no test of any such theory.

The empirical work, if not taken as a test of a theory, is certainly interesting and, as Friedman says, suggestive. He finds that the cyclical behaviour of the residual of the demand for money not explained by expected income or prices can be explained by changes in the relative profitability of other assets. However, it is claimed that the behaviour of the total velocity could not be explained in this way. It would be interesting to know whether this would still be the case if 'permanent' as well as 'current' yields of those assets were used in the regressions. Friedman finds the interest elasticity of demand for money to be low, but one is worried by the inclusion of interest-bearing deposits at the bank in the definition of money, which in this connection may be important. However, he is perfectly correct in his assertion that no point of outstanding theoretical importance is at stake here (unless it is claimed that the interest elasticity should be infinite). Some of his critics have been wrong, for instance, in their claim that a zero interest elasticity necessarily implies the 'classical dichotomy'. Of course, policy judgments are indeed affected should the low interest elasticity be a correct finding.

Although I am leaving matters of statistical technique to others more competent, I must take note of the obvious difficulties of identification posed by Friedman's single-equation method. I have already quoted his declaration of faith—he calls it an 'empirical hypothesis'—that the demand function for money is stable, so that he has no doubt that his estimates are estimates of demand and not of supply. If one does not share his faith, one should like much more evidence than he gives. It is true that in other connections, for example in the monetary history of wars and gold discoveries, Friedman can argue convincingly that changes in the monetary supply were autonomous, although even here one must suppose it to have had endogenous components. As far as I can judge, it is not sufficient to attribute part of a change in the monetary stock to exogenous events to be sure that the single-equation estimate is one of the demand, rather than of the supply, function of money. Friedman is aware of the difficulty but has not resolved it, especially as far as cyclical estimates are concerned. To resolve the disputed causal mechanism he appeals, among other things, to a lead in the monetary stock, but agrees that this is not decisive and recently has reiterated a kind of biased agnosticism. In any event I cannot at the moment see why the equation of the demand for money could not also be taken as one of supply. Clearly much more sophisticated techniques, and in particular a good many more equations, will be required to settle the matter. As Friedman himself notes, the demand for money is more important than the demand for pins; by the same token, a single-equation estimate of the demand for pins is much more acceptable than it is of the demand for money. I return to some of these matters below.

To sum up so far. Friedman has a lazy man's theory of the demand for money in that he explains it by unanalysed utility and productive services. A consequence of this is, for instance, that he looks for no indicators of uncertainty nor for independent evidence on money as a 'factor of production' in his empirical work. The claim of the superior stability of the demand function for money in the absence of a theoretical explanation seems to me at best to constitute an inducement to engage on more research on the other functions. The theoretical foundations of the permanent income and price hypothesis are not given and its intuitive appeal is not high. The single-equation time series estimates may be suggestive, but by Friedman's own standards, hardly persuasive. [...]

I now turn to the most difficult and most important problem raised by Professor Friedman's work. The good correlation which he finds between changes in the money stock and changes in money income and prices, all variously dated and sometimes represented by new variables such as permanent prices, leads him to claim an important causal role for the actions of the monetary authorities in changing important economic variables. This is to be taken as an 'anti-Keynesian' result (a) because he finds changes in investment expenditures to be a poor explanatory variable, and (b) because Keynesians are supposed to hold the view that money does not matter and are committed to fiscal policy. In addition he asserts that the evidence substantiates a Quantity Theory in generalized form, and in particular that, since the interest elasticity of demand for money is low, one may do very well in predicting money income by using the money multiplier derived from the stable money income ratio. Lastly, it is part of the doctrine that the authorities cannot control real balances so that the long-run equilibrium of the economy cannot be affected by monetary policy. This is so whether money is, say, dropped by helicopter or increased through open-market operations.

One of the main reasons why all these claims raise the difficulties they do is that Friedman has only the most rudimentary causal stories to support him and, as already argued before both by me and by him, one is not convinced until one is told. There is the further awkward fact that the most casual theorizing is combined with such abstraction as the complete and accurate capitalizing by all agents of the tax burden of servicing public debt.

I start with the claim that long-run equilibrium cannot be affected by monetary policy.

First let me make a pedantic point which would be very awkward nonetheless for a theorist. Everyone knows that in the general equilibrium models we have been discussing for the past twenty years the real equilibrium values of the volume of monetary assets can be determined, but not their nominal values. Unfortunately, however, the conditions for such an equilibrium to be unique are rather stringent. If there are many equilibria they will not all be stable for any adjustment theory we choose to use. It then follows that there is nothing in these models as such to allow one to conclude that the final equilibrium is independent of initial conditions and of monetary policy in particular.

But this is only the most obvious of the difficulties the reader encounters in this connection. Suppose it to have been met. Friedman seems to hold the view that the long-run result of a once-over change in the money stock does not depend on whether money has been dropped from a helicopter or whether it has entered the system through open-market operations.[4] The argument is consistent with the assumption that government debt, if taxes to service it are properly capitalized, is always of zero net value to the economy. It is like private debt; your claim to interest is exactly counterbalanced by my tax obligation. Once again let us accept this extreme idealization and ask whether the conclusions will follow in the context of the Walrasian model which is somewhere in the background of all of Friedman's work.

There is an obvious difficulty in discussing long-run equilibrium which is never defined or specified. I return to this almost at once. But we may notice straight away that, if this is Friedman's position, it must be incorrect. It implies that the long-run supply of government debt can be anything at all. For instance, it is higher when the nominal stock of money has been increased by helicopter than when it is increased by open-market operations.

---

[4] Friedman admits that the 'detail' of adjustment may depend upon the source of monetary change (p. 230). But throughout the book the source of monetary change is not a relevant variable. If the view I ascribe to him is not the one he holds, then ch. 5 and much of the empirical work are rather mysterious.

Suppose the debt to be serviced by lump-sum taxation. Of course, for the individual the purchase of a bond yields the usual return since his tax payments are independent of his actions. We now have exactly the situation studied by Lange and Patinkin: the real value of bonds is not an argument of any demand function. They both showed, and their demonstration is perfectly compatible with Friedman's portfolio theory, that the demand function for real bond holdings is homogeneous of degree zero in prices and money. Anyone can look up the simple demonstration. Hence if the long-run equilibrium is indeed unique, the required real bonds are uniquely given. Hence an alteration of the ratio in which the two assets are available would make long-run equilibrium impossible and the economy would follow a path depending on the manipulation of this ratio. Alternatively if different long-run real bond holdings are compatible with long-run equilibrium, then these equilibria will differ from one another. [...]

Since it would appear that monetary policy can affect long-run equilibrium values ... a good many positions taken up by Friedman can be answered in this simple way. But of course it is his contention that while the long run is inviolate to monetary management, the short run, and in particular whether we can ever reach the long run, is not. Indeed, monetary changes are among the most powerful autonomous changes working for good or ill. The central contention here is that 'the stock of money is much more closely and systematically related to income over business cycles than is investment or autonomous expenditures', and that history teaches us 'a lesson of the most profound importance ... that monetary policy can prevent money itself from being a major source of economic disturbance'. Let me therefore turn to the short run. [...]

Consider an unexpected rise in the rate of change in the monetary stock to a permanently higher level by means of a permanently higher rate of open-market purchases by the central bank. Friedman writes that 'although the initial sellers of the securities purchased by the Central Bank were willing sellers, this does not mean they want to hold the proceeds in money indefinitely', and adds that the sale is only a 'temporary step in rearranging their portfolio'. The only sense I can make of this view of Friedman's own portfolio analysis is that to persuade people to sell securities, their price must be raised; and that this price then leads to a rearrangement of the whole portfolio with the consequence that the prices of other assets rise also. This, except for the acknowledged exceptional case of the liquidity trap, is pure Keynes. Should there be a liquidity trap nothing will happen.

But suppose that the demand for non-financial assets, for example investment, is very insensitive to such changes in the rates of return on financial assets and that the saving decision is also insensitive. The story Friedman tells would come to a full stop. The rates of return on financial assets would have adjusted themselves in such a manner as to make people content to hold the larger stock of money. I do not claim that this will happen. What I do claim is that it is the sensitivity of demand for non-financial reproducible assets which is the vital link not only for traditional economies but for Friedman. But then is it not odd that changes in investment demand should be such a bad explanatory variable?

Equally puzzling is the view that nothing essential would have been changed in the 'short period' story had we employed the helicopter instead of open-market operations. Had we indeed used the helicopter, not only would people have found themselves with too much money but they would undoubtedly have been wealthier. Even if real asset demands were interest-inelastic, the story would not have stopped there. That is one vital difference. Even if asymptotically the same state is reached, it might take quite different time spans. The helicopter is like Keynesian pump-priming; open-market operations are not. The puzzle then is this. The course of events is governed by changes in interest rates and asset prices and by the sensitivity of real decisions to such changes. But the investment and consumption functions are, according to Friedman, very unstable. How does this unstable and vital link between monetary and real changes permit the 'close and systematic' relation between monetary and real changes?

Let me discuss the same problem inaccurately, but perhaps more clearly, in textbook language. For the textbook Keynesian open-market operations may make no difference because *LL* is perfectly flat. This may be due either to a very high interest elasticity of demand for money or, as Kaldor would argue, to a high elasticity of the supply of money. (I do not suggest that Kaldor would mean infinite elasticity). For Friedman *LL* could still be pretty flat in spite of the low interest elasticity of demand for money, if the elasticity of supply is high enough (and in this matter I find both his evidence and remarks ambiguous). But suppose *LL* to be steep. It cannot be vertical, else no open-market operations are possible. Also, the steeper it is, the greater is the effect of open-market operations on interest rates. But if *IS* is moving all over the place, then our predictions from money changes to real changes will also be rather bad, although the steeper *LL*, the less will be the error in income change forecasts for any given variability of *IS*. But in any case once a very steep *LL* is granted, Friedman need not appeal to the instability of the Keynesian expenditure functions: shifts in *IS* can have little effect on income. The alleged instability of *IS* is really a red herring; everything follows from a very steep *LL*, but the latter is by no means a logical consequence of a low interest elasticity of the demand for money even if this much disputed claim is true. Put in yet another way, if *LL* is as steep as Friedman requires, the instability of the consumption function, say, should be no obstacle to accurate forecasts of the effects of autonomous expenditure changes on income: they will be negligible. On the other hand the steep *LL* implies very violently fluctuating interest rates. I simply do not believe in it.

While generally predicting a return to the same steady state in his experiment, Friedman wants the path to be cyclical. He finds the necessary wherewithal in the following consideration. Initially the actions of agents and of banks were geared to the present price level and its present rate of change. However, in the final equilibrium prices will have to be rising at a higher rate (since the money stock is increasing at a higher rate), and 'the amount of money demanded will be less in real terms than it was initially, relative to wealth and hence income'. Hence at some stage prices must be rising faster than at their ultimate rate. In addition, there are lags in expectations and the actions of financial institutions to be taken into account.

The first of these explanations, which is the one to which Friedman attaches the most importance, is rather odd for him. If real cash balances are lower while real wealth is the same, households must be holding more of some other asset. If that is capital, real interest rates will be lower. Monetary prices seem to have been able to affect long-run real equilibrium values contrary to the views expressed, for instance, in his presidential address. In any case the whole cyclical story requires far deeper analysis than he gives it; and I do not find helpful comments like: 'Presumably, these cyclical adjustments will be damped, though no merely verbal exposition can suffice to assure that the particular mechanism described will have that property ...'. The 'monetary lead' part of the story is now very much played down.

Nor can the famous policy prescription be given much justification in the absence of a well formulated cyclical theory. A steady state is a steady state, and if we are in one we had better increase monetary assets at a steady rate. On Friedman's own views, a departure from this blissful state is ascribable to the 'money side'. But surely this may be just as much due to fluctuations in the demand (not the demand functions) for money as in its supply. Suppose the future becomes more or less uncertain, for instance; then the policy will give violent fluctuations in interest rates and certainly more instability than would be the case if at the prevailing (steady-state rates) we gave them as much money as they wished to hold. In any case I have simply not been able to piece together an argument from what Friedman writes which would support his policy recommendations. It should be noted that he himself writes: 'Clearly, the view that monetary change is important does not preclude the existence of other factors that affect the course of business or that account for the quasi-rhythmical character of business fluctuations'. This is pretty agnostic and leaves the policy question wide open, especially since it is unlikely that the operation of these other factors is independent of monetary policy.

So far I have not discussed price changes, and Friedman's discussion of the relation between monetary changes and price level changes has some interesting and valuable features. For instance, his distinction between expected and unexpected price change is excellent and he makes good use of it in dealing with money wages. No doubt he is also right in arguing that elementary textbook Keynesians pay far too little attention to prices, although it is hard to maintain that Keynes was guilty of this. But the habit of, say, analysing the effects of a shift in autonomous expenditure by shifting the *IS* curve to the right and forgetting all about *LL* is fairly widespread and lamentable. Indeed, one must agree that vulgarized Keynes can be very bad economics.

For Friedman the connexion between monetary changes and changes in money income is so direct because he takes velocity to be very interest-inelastic. Even when this is granted, rather formidable difficulties remain if this is to be translated into a quantity theory of prices. For instance, when the money stock is lower as a result of open-market operations, the consequent higher interest rate will reduce the demand for goods and services. The extent to which this causes a reduction in prices and a fall in output depends on many factors which have nothing whatever to do with the portfolio decision. It depends on the conditions of production, the degree of competition, money wage flexibility, etc. Without studying these in their own right nothing of much value can be said.

But we may take this case as a test case. A Keynesian analysis of the rise in interest rates consequent on the monetary operation might go something as follows. The higher monetary rates will cause a fall in productive invest-ment, in the demand, indeed, for all producible durable goods. This will lead to a multiplier contraction. If money wages do not fall in the face of increased unemployment, the new short-run equilibrium will be one of lower real income with somewhat higher real wages and possibly higher interest rates. The higher real wages arises from diminishing marginal productivity of labour in the short run, and of course we would not wish to insist on this. The higher interest rate may be required in order to induce agents to hold the stock of money there is. The multiplier itself is not $1/s$, but the resultant solving the two simultaneous relations; the excess demand for goods and excess demand for money. One cannot easily predict what will happen to money wages, and in the long run we are all dead. This I believe would be a 'Keynesian' story with the *caveat* in the background that, should the contemplated exogenous monetary change cause a significant shift in expectations, the story might be different in detail and possibly even in direction. As far as prices are concerned, the behaviour of money wages is probably the crucial variable, with marginal productivity considerations a poor second.

The Friedman 'short run' story, if I understand him correctly, differs mainly in that he simply speaks of a fall in demand leading to lower prices, and does not distinguish between the price of labour and that of goods. In the present volume no theoretical analysis or empirical evidence is presented on money wages. He is completely specialized to equations in money, money income and money prices. The debate on real wages and profit margins over the cycle is not of interest to him. But there is nothing to lead me to suppose that he disagrees with the above Keynesian sketch, except that he must be taking money wages as much more flexible (whatever that means precisely) than Keynesians do and that he treats 'the long run' as if he, or we, knew what it meant. But then I have already argued repeatedly, it is these relations of wage flexibility, interest elasticity of real demand, production and competitive conditions which must be studied.

Friedman writes continually as if non-Friedmanites are committed to the view that changes in the quantity of money do not matter. The popularity of the *IS–LL* apparatus is enough to contradict this. Moreover, the inventor of this expository device emphasized that the horizontal piece of *LL* should be taken as reasonable for deep depressions only. A reading of the *General Theory* will show that Keynes did not build his revolution on the liquidity trap. The 'real balance effect' he neglected; however, this is of academic interest only, and must be particularly unimportant when money balances change through open-market operations and people act on 'permanent prices'. But what Keynesians have argued is that it is the changes in interest rates in the first instance and wage flexibility in the second which are the phenomena of importance. I can see nothing wrong in that. What is more important, there is nothing in this book to persuade one that stability is better served by the possible large fluctuations in interest rates which may accompany Friedman's policy than it would be by a policy designed perhaps not to peg but to reduce fluctuations in interest rates. [...]

9.4 Keynes and the Keynesians: A Theoretical Appraisal*

Twenty-five years of discussion and controversy have produced a large and surprisingly harmonious literature on Keynes and the Classics. Although the series still has not converged to a point of universal agreement, the domain remaining open to dispute has contracted steadily with the passage of time. On one essential issue, however, contemporary opinion is still largely undecided: precisely what are the purely formal differences, if any, between Keynes and the Classics? Perhaps the clearest symptom of our uncertainty is the continued lack of an explicit integration of price theory and income analysis. Equally significant, however, is the ambivalence of professional economists towards the Keynesian counter-revolution launched by Hicks in 1937 and now being carried forward with such vigour by Patinkin and other general equilibrium theorists (1—6).[1] The elegance and generality of this literature makes it most alluring. At the same time, one can hardly fail to

---

* From R. W. Clower, 'The Keynesian Counter-revolution: A Theoretical Appraisal', in F. Hahn and F. Brechling, *The Theory of Interest Rates* (London: Macmillan, 1965), as reprinted in a slightly revised version in R. W. Clower (ed.), *Monetary Theory* (Harmondsworth: Penguin, 1969).

[1] The 'counter-revolution' to which I refer is clearly not a conscious revolt against Keynesian economics, for all of the writers involved are, in a practical sense, strong supporters of what they conceive to be the Keynesian revolution. It is another question whether the same people are Keynesians in a theoretical sense. That is one of the issues on which this paper is intended to shed some light.

be impressed—and disturbed—by the close resemblance that some of its central doctrines bear to those of orthodox economics.

I do not presume at this late date either to improve the views of previous writers on Keynes and the Classics or to transform equivocations into certainties. Things are not that simple. However, I shall attempt to show that the same highly special theoretical presuppositions which led to Keynes' original attack on orthodox economics continue to pervade contemporary price theory and that the Keynesian counter-revolution would collapse without them. Unlike Keynes, who had to deal with doctrines of which no authoritative account had ever been given, we now have an extremely clear idea of the orthodox content of contemporary theory.[2] We thus have a distinct advantage over Keynes in describing what has been said. However, our basic problem is to discover and describe what has not but should have been said—and here we are on all fours with Keynes. Like Keynes, therefore, I must begin by asking 'forgiveness if, in the pursuit of sharp distinctions, my controversy is itself too keen' (7).

KEYNES AND TRADITIONAL THEORY

Our first task is to express in modern idiom those aspects of orthodox economics which were of special concern to Keynes. This may be accomplished most conveniently by considering a two-sector economy comprising households on one side and firms on the other. Corresponding to this division into sectors, we distinguish two mutually exclusive classes of commodities: (a) those which are supplied by firms and demanded by households; (b) those which are supplied by households and demanded by firms. Commodities in class (a) will be distinguished by numerical subscripts $i = 1, \ldots, m$, those in class (b) by numerical subscripts $j = m+1, \ldots, n$. Thus, quantities supplied and demanded by firms are denoted, respectively, by variables $s_1, \ldots, s_m, d_{m+1}, \ldots, d_n$, while quantities demanded and supplied by households are denoted, respectively, by variables $d_1, \ldots, d_m, s_{m+1}, \ldots, s_n$. Prevailing market prices (expressed in units of commodity n) are then represented by symbols $\mathbf{p}_1, \mathbf{p}_2, \ldots, \mathbf{p}_{n-1}(\mathbf{p}_n \equiv 1)$, or, in vector notation, $\mathbf{P}$.[3]

For ease of exposition, we shall ignore aggregation problems and suppose that the preferences of all households in the economy are adequately characterized by a community utility function, $U(d_1, \ldots, d_m; s_{m+1}, \ldots, s_n)$. Similarly, we shall assume that technical conditions confronting all business firms in the economy are adequately characterized by an aggregate transformation function $T(s_1, \ldots, s_m; d_{m+1}, \ldots, d_n) = 0$. Needless to say, the functions U and T are assumed to possess all continuity and curvature

---

[2] For this, we have mainly to thank the counter-revolutionists, since it is their writings which have revived interest in general equilibrium theory.

[3] Here and throughout the remainder of the paper, boldface symbols will invariably be used to refer to magnitudes that are to be regarded as given parameters from the standpoint of individual transactors.

properties needed to ensure the existence of unique extrema under circumstances to be specified below.

Dealing first with the orthodox theory of the firm, we obtain sector supply and demand functions, $\bar{s}_i(\mathbf{P})$, $\bar{d}_i(\mathbf{P})$ as solutions of the problem:
maximize

$$r = \sum_i^m \mathbf{p}_i s_i - \sum_j^n \mathbf{p}_j d_j,^4$$

subject to

$$T(s_1, \ldots, s_m; d_{m+1}, \ldots, d_n) = 0.^5$$

Underlying both sets of solutions are transactor equilibrium conditions of the form

$$\mathbf{p}_k + \frac{\lambda \partial T}{\partial \bar{v}_k} = 0 \quad (\bar{v} = \bar{d}, \bar{s}; k = 1, 2, \ldots, n).$$

In particular, if $n = 2$ and we interpret s_1 as goods and d_2 as labour, we easily establish Keynes' classical postulate I, namely, 'the [real] wage is equal to the marginal product of labour'. (*General Theory*, p. 5.)

In a similar fashion, the demand and supply functions of the household sector are obtained as solutions, $\bar{d}_i(\mathbf{P},\mathbf{r})$, $\bar{s}_i(\mathbf{P},\mathbf{r})$, of the problem
maximize

$$U(d_1, \ldots, d_m; s_{m+1}, \ldots, s_n),$$

subject to

$$\sum_i^m \mathbf{p}_i d_i - \sum_j^n \mathbf{p}_j s_j - \mathbf{r} = 0,$$

the profit variable $\mathbf{r}$ being treated as a fixed parameter in this context.[6]

Underlying these solutions are transactor equilibrium conditions of the form

$$\frac{\partial U}{\partial \bar{v}_k} + \gamma \mathbf{p}_k = 0 (\bar{v} = \bar{d}, \bar{s}; k = 1, \ldots, \boldsymbol{n}).$$

Thus, if we consider the case $n = 2$ and adopt an appropriate interpretation of the variables d_1 and s_2, we readily derive Keynes' classical postulate II, namely, 'The utility of the [real] wage when a given volume of labour is employed is equal to the marginal disutility of that amount of employment.' (*General Theory*, p. 5.)

[4] The symbols $\sum_i^m$ and $\sum_j^n$ denote, respectively, the operations $\sum_{i=1}^m$ and $\sum_{j=m+1}^n$.

[5] Since $\mathbf{p}_n \equiv 1$ by assumption, we have not shown it as an explicit divisor of the price variables included in the vector $\mathbf{P}$; but it is there all the same. Thus, the demand and supply functions of the business sector are homogeneous of order zero in the n price variables $\mathbf{p}_1, \ldots, \mathbf{p}_n$. Provided $d_n \neq 0$, however, the same functions are not in general homogenous in the $n-1$ *numéraire* prices which are contained in the vector $\mathbf{P}$.

[6] The household demand-and-supply functions are homogeneous of order zero in the $n+1$ variables $\mathbf{p}_1, \ldots, \mathbf{p}_n$ and $\mathbf{r}$, but not in the n variables $\mathbf{p}_1, \ldots, \mathbf{p}_{n-1}$ and $\mathbf{r}$ (provided $s_n \neq 0$).

So much for the basic ideas of the orthodox theory of transactor behaviour. Let us turn next to the theory of price formation, again seeking to express matters as Keynes might have expressed them had he been less steeped in Marshallian habits of thought.

At least since the time of Adam Smith, the market mechanism has been regarded by economists as an ingenious device for reconciling the freedom of individuals to trade as they please with the ultimate necessity for individuals in the aggregate to buy neither more nor less of any commodity than is offered for sale. To accomplish this feat, the mechanism must be supplied with information about individual sale and purchase plans, which is precisely what is supposed to be furnished by the supply-and-demand functions of orthodox theory.

Assuming that all business profits accrue to accounts in the household sector, we may assert first of all that the sale and purchase plans of individual transactors at any given instant of time[7] depend only on prevailing market prices.[8] We may then argue as follows.

If prevailing prices are such that demand differs from supply in any market, this means that individual trading plans, taken as a whole, are mutually inconsistent, which in turn, means that at least some individual plans cannot be carried into effect at prevailing market prices. In these circumstances, it is plausible to suppose that prevailing prices tend to vary over time, rising in markets where demand exceeds supply, falling in markets where supply exceeds demand. Accordingly, the economy may be said to be in a state of disequilibrium. On the other hand, if prevailing market prices at any given instant happen to be such that demand is equal to supply in every market simultaneously, this means that individual trading plans, considered as a whole, are mutually consistent; hence, that all transactions planned at prevailing prices can, in principle, actually be carried out. In these circumstances, it is plausible to suppose that there are no extraneous forces at work tending to alter either individual trading plans or prevailing market prices, and the economy may be said to be in a state of equilibrium.

The only snag in this argument is the familiar one about the number of equations being one greater than the number of prices to be determined.

---

[7] I have chosen to regard 'time' as a continuous rather than a discrete variable, and to confine discussion to current values of all magnitudes, in order to discourage both myself and readers from playing meretricious games with alternative lag assumptions. No part of the present or subsequent argument is affected in any essential way if time is made discrete, lags are introduced, etc.

[8] Since we are performing market rather than individual experiments (Patinkin, 1, p. 15), the parameter **r** which appears in the household demand and supply functions is now replaced by the function the value of

$$\bar{r} = \sum_i^m \mathbf{p}_i \bar{s}_i - \sum_j^n \mathbf{p}_j \bar{d}_j,$$

which depends only on the price vector **P**.

From the theory of household behaviour, however, we know that

$$\sum_i^m \mathbf{p}_i \bar{d}_i - \sum_j^n \mathbf{p}_j \bar{s}_j - \mathbf{r} = 0, \tag{1}$$

and from the theory of business behaviour, we know that

$$\sum_i^m \mathbf{p}_i \bar{s}_i - \sum_j^n \mathbf{p}_j \bar{d}_j - \bar{r} = 0. \tag{2}$$

Subtracting (2) from (1), therefore, we have

$$\sum_{k=1}^n \mathbf{p}_k [\bar{d}_k - \bar{s}_k] \equiv \mathbf{r} - \bar{r}. \tag{3}$$

Since in general the variables $\mathbf{r}$ and $\bar{r}$ refer to completely independent individual experiments, we cannot assume that $\mathbf{r} \equiv \bar{r}$. In the case of market experiments, however, it does seem plausible to suppose that $\mathbf{r} = \bar{r}$ provided that the variables $s_1, \ldots, s_m$ and $d_{m+1}, \ldots, d_n$ have assumed their equilibrium values. If this is granted, then (3) leads immediately to Walras' law (in the sense of Lange, 8, pp. 49–68).[9]

$$\sum_{k=1}^n \mathbf{p}_k [\bar{d}_k(\mathbf{P}) - \bar{s}_k(\mathbf{P})] \equiv 0. \tag{4}$$

Walras' law obviously implies that the *numéraire* value of one of the excess demands can be inferred from the values of the others, which rids us of the extra supply-and-demand equation. Rewritten in the form

$$\sum_k \mathbf{p}_k \bar{s}_k \equiv \sum_k \mathbf{p}_k \bar{d}_k,$$

Walras' law might also be said to assert that 'supply creates its own demand' (cf. *General Theory*, p. 18)—and we shall hear more of this in the sequel. For the time being, however, it may merely be remarked that Walras' law must be valid under the circumstances assumed here.

This account of orthodox doctrine accords well enough, I think, both with modern analysis and with Keynes' conception of classical theory. For the special case $n = 2$, in particular, it is apparent that Keynes' views, as expressed in chapter 2 of the *General Theory*, are exactly equivalent to what is presented above. Granted that this is so, we may reasonably assert that orthodox economics provides a general theory of equilibrium states—that is, an adequate account of the factors determining equilibrium prices and equilibrium transaction plans in a market economy. Moreover, the same analysis may be said to provide the beginnings of a theory of disequilibrium prices and disequilibrium transaction plans. Clearly, however, orthodox analysis does not provide a general theory of disequilibrium states: firstly, because

---

[9] The distinction drawn by Lange between Walras' law and Say's law is not relevant here; from a formal point of view, the two propositions are equivalent.

it yields no direct information about the magnitude of *realized* as distinct from *planned* transactions under disequilibrium conditions; secondly, because it tacitly assumes that the forces tending at any instant to change prevailing market prices are independent of realized transactions at the same moment (this includes as a special case the assumption, made explicitly in all 'tâtonnement', 'recontract' and 'auction' models, that no disequilibrium transactions occur).[10]

It is instructive to compare these views with those of Keynes, as represented by the following assortment of quotations (not all of them torn out of context):

I shall argue that the postulates of the classical theory are applicable to a special case only and not to the general case ... (*General Theory*, p. 3).

The question ... of the volume of the *available* resources, in the sense of the size of the employable population, the extent of natural wealth and the accumulated capital equipment, has often been treated descriptively [in orthodox writings]. But the pure theory of what determines the *actual employment* of the available resources has seldom been examined in any detail. ... I mean, not that the topic has been overlooked, but that the fundamental theory underlying it has been deemed so simple and obvious that it has received, at the most, a bare mention. (*General Theory*, pp. 4–5.)

A theory cannot claim to be a *general* theory, unless it is applicable to the case where (or the range within which) money wages are fixed, just as much as to any other case. Politicians are entitled to complain that money wages *ought* to be flexible; but a theorist must be prepared to deal indifferently with either state of affairs. (*General Theory*, p. 276.)

... the classical theory ... is wholly unable to answer the question what effect on employment a reduction in money wages will have. For it has no method of analysis wherewith to attack the problem. (*General Theory*, p. 260.)

Clearly, there is nothing very novel in any of this; up to this point, at least, the belief that Keynes is 'saying nothing new' need not be confined to those '... who are strongly wedded to ... the classical theory' (cf. *General Theory*, p. v). Like us, Keynes does not in any way deny the generality of orthodox equilibrium analysis; he only denies that orthodox economics provides an adequate account of disequilibrium phenomena.

II. THE KEYNESIAN INDICTMENT OF ORTHODOX ECONOMICS

Grounds for theoretical controversy first begin to emerge when we come to the stage in Keynes' argument (*General Theory*, chapter 2) at which he seeks to isolate specific instances in orthodox economics of 'lack of clearness and of generality' (*General Theory*, p. v).

The first item in his bill of particulars is embedded in a lengthy discussion

[10] J. R. Hicks (3), note to ch. 9, pp. 127ff. Also Patinkin (1) supplementary note B, pp. 377–85.

of wage bargains between entrepreneurs and workers (*General Theory*, pp. 1–15). Outwardly, this item represents little more than a vigorous attack on orthodox preconceptions about the stability of a market economy. For the burden of his argument seems to be that if labour is ever forced to move 'off its supply curve' it may be unable to get back on again. If this is an accurate interpretation, we may say immediately that Keynes' criticisms are not of fundamental theoretical significance, for there is no reason to suppose that Keynes was more expert at stability analysis than his orthodox predecessors. However, the same argument might also be interpreted as a direct attack on the orthodox theory of household behaviour. This would certainly put labour off its supply curve and would also explain Keynes' categorical rejection of classical postulate II. But if this is what Keynes intended, i.e. to deny the validity of the orthodox theory of household behaviour, one can only say that he was singularly unsuccessful in providing a rationale for his attack.

The second item in Keynes' bill of particulars is essentially the same as the first: classical theory is charged with failure to recognize the existence of involuntary unemployment (*General Theory*, pp. 15–18). Again, the basic question is: Are 'involuntary unemployment' and 'chronic disequilibrium' synonymous terms for the same objective phenomenon, or is 'involuntary unemployment' a special kind of disequilibrium peculiarly associated with the breakdown of the orthodox theory of household behaviour? Here there is somewhat clearer evidence that Keynes believes his objections to orthodox analysis go very deep indeed:

... if the classical theory is only applicable to the case of full employment, it is fallacious to apply it to the problems of involuntary unemployment—if there be such a thing (and who will deny it?). The classical theorists resemble Euclidean geometers in a non-Euclidean world who, discovering that in experience straight lines apparently parallel often meet, rebuke the lines for not keeping straight—as the only remedy for the unfortunate collisions which are occurring. Yet, in truth, there is no remedy except to throw over the axiom of parallels and to work out a non-Euclidean geometry. Something similar is required today in economics. We need to throw over the second postulate of the classical doctrine and to work out the behavior of a system in which involuntary unemployment in the strict sense is possible. (*General Theory*, pp. 16–17.)

Again, however, we are given no compelling theoretical reason to think that the proposed reconstruction of orthodox economics is really necessary.

The third and final item in Keynes' indictment is a denial of the relevance of Walras' law (*General Theory*, pp. 18–21). Most later writers (e.g. Ohlin, 4, p. 230, footnote; Goodwin, 9; Patinkin, 1, p. 249) have argued either that this portion of Keynes' indictment is wrong, or that the proposition which Keynes attacks is not in fact the one he thought he was attacking. Most economists have opted for the second explanation (10, especially p. 113),[11]

[11] But see H. Rose's note on Walras' law and the reply by Patinkin (11, 12).

partly in deference to Keynes' acknowledged intellectual powers, partly because they recognize that if Keynes seriously meant to question the validity or relevance of Walras' law, he would have to reject the orthodox theory of household behaviour and propose an acceptable alternative—and the alternative would have to include orthodox theory as a special case, valid under conditions of full employment. Walras' law is not, after all, an independent postulate of orthodox analysis; it is a theorem which is susceptible of direct proof on the basis of premises which are typically taken as given in contemporary as well as classical price theory.

III. THE POST-KEYNESIAN DILEMMA

The conclusion which I draw from all this may be put in one phrase: *either Walras' law is incompatible with Keynesian economics, or Keynes had nothing fundamentally new to add to orthodox economic theory.* This may seem an unnecessarily brutal way to confront one sacred cow with another. But what other conclusion is possible? In Keynes' mind, at least, the three items in his bill of particulars 'all amount to the same thing in the sense that they all stand and fall together, any one of them logically involving the other two' (*General Theory*, p. 22). As we have already seen, he could hardly hold this view seriously unless he regarded each of the three items as an attack on the orthodox theory of household behaviour. But suppose that this is not in fact Keynes' view; suppose that Walras' law is both unreservedly valid, relevant and compatible with Keynesian economics. In this event, the recent literature on monetary theory makes it perfectly evident that Keynes may be subsumed as a special case of the Hicks–Lange–Patinkin theory of *tâtonnement* economics, which differs from orthodox theory only in being more detailed and precise. We would then have to conclude that Keynes added nothing fundamentally new to orthodox economic theory.

Thus, we are caught on the horns of a dilemma. If Keynes added nothing new to orthodox doctrine, why have twenty-five years of discussion failed to produce an integrated account of price theory and income analysis? If Keynes did add something new, the integration problem becomes explicable; but then we have to give up Walras' law as a fundamental principle of economic analysis. It is precisely at this point, I believe, that virtually all previous writers have decided to part company with Keynes. I propose to follow a different course. I shall argue that the established theory of household behaviour is, indeed, incompatible with Keynesian economics, that Keynes himself made tacit use of a more general theory, that this more general theory leads to market excess-demand functions which include quantities as well as prices as independent variables and, except in conditions of full employment, the excess-demand functions so defined do not satisfy Walras' law. In short, I shall argue that there has been a fundamental misunderstanding of the formal basis of the Keynesian revolution.

IV. DISEQUILIBRIUM SYSTEMS:
A PRELIMINARY VIEW

Before attempting to deal directly with the issues raised above, we must say something more about the mechanics of disequilibrium states. In our earlier discussion of orthodox analysis, it was pointed out that the whole of traditional price theory rests on the tacit assumption that market excess demands are independent of current market transactions. This implies that *income magnitudes do not appear as independent variables in the demand or supply functions of a general equilibrium model*; for incomes are defined in terms of quantities as well as prices, and quantity variables never appear explicitly in the market excess-demand functions of traditional theory. To be sure, income variables could be introduced by taking factor supplies as given parameters; but this would preclude the formulation of a general equilibrium model containing supply functions of all marketable factor services.[12] The importance of these propositions for Keynesian economics can hardly be over-emphasized, for they imply directly that the Keynesian consumption function and other market relations involving income as an independent variable cannot be derived explicitly from any existing theory of general equilibrium.[13]

The most lucid account of the role which current transactions *might* play in general equilibrium theory has been presented by Professor Hicks in *Value and Capital* (3, pp. 119ff.). The following passages are especially significant in the present connexion (pp. 127–9):

Since, in general, traders cannot be expected to know just what total supplies are available on any market, nor what total demands will be forthcoming at particular prices, any price which is fixed initially can be only a guess. It is not probable that demand and supply will actually be found to be equated at such a guessed price; if they are not, then in the course of trading the price will move up or down. Now if there is a change of price in the midst of trading, the situation appears to elude the ordinary apparatus of demand-and-supply analysis, for, strictly speaking, demand curves and supply curves give us the amounts which buyers and sellers will demand and supply respectively at any particular price, if that price is fixed at the start and adhered to throughout. Earlier writers, such as Walras and Edgeworth, had therefore supposed that demand-and-supply analysis ought strictly to be confined to such markets as

[12] This was apparently overlooked by Patinkin when he formulated his 'general theory' of macroeconomics (*Money, Interest and Prices*, ch. 9). It is instructive to notice that this chapter is not supplemented by a mathematical appendix. Some of the consequences of this oversight are evident in the later discussion, see especially the argument beginning at p. 216, including the footnotes to pp. 218 and 220. I do not mean to suggest that authors may not put such variables as they please into their models. My point is that such variables as can be shown to be functionally dependent on others should not then be manipulated independently.

[13] Cf. Lange, *Price Flexibility and Employment* (5, ch. 9, p. 53). Lange's usage of the phrase 'propensity to consume' is perfectly legitimate, but the concept invoked by him is not in any sense a consumption function of the sort Keynes worked with since, except on the Keynesian definition, it is not possible to talk about changes in consumption in response to changes in income without at the same time talking about changes in prices.

permitted of 'recontract'; i.e. markets such that if a transaction was put through at a 'false' price ... it could be revised when the equilibrium price was reached. Since such markets are highly exceptional, their solution of the problem (if it can be called one) was not very convincing.

> ... in the general case ... gains and losses due to false trading only give rise to income effects—effects, that is, which are the same kind as the income effects which may have to be considered even when we suppose equilibrium prices to be fixed straight away. We have seen again and again that a certain degree of indeterminateness is nearly always imparted by income effects to the laws of economic theory. All that happens as a result of false trading is that this indeterminateness is somewhat intensified. How much intensified depends, of course, upon the extent of the false trading; if very extensive transactions take place at prices very different from equilibrium prices, the disturbance will be serious. But I think we may reasonably suppose that the transactions which take place at *very false* prices are limited in volume. If any intelligence is shown in price-fixing, they will be.

It is heartening to know that income effects can be ignored if they are sufficiently unimportant to be neglected; but this is hardly a solution to the problem at issue. The essential question is whether the supply-and-demand functions of traditional analysis are in any way relevant to the formation of market prices in situations where disequilibrium transactions *cannot* be ignored.

To answer this question, we must first define explicit theoretical measures of disequilibrium transaction quantities. Perhaps the simplest way to define such measures is to suppose that actual transactions in any given market are always dominated by the 'short' side of the market; that is to say, market transactions are equal to planned market supply if demand is greater than supply, to planned market demand if supply is equal to or greater than demand (13, p. 203; 14; 1, pp. 157–8). This is, of course, the procedure which has been followed by all previous writers, in so far as they have said anything at all on the subject.

Taken by itself, this addendum to traditional theory has no logical implications; but it opens the way for further analysis. For example, some writers have suggested the desirability of supposing that actual transactions exert a more or less direct influence on price adjustment via 'spillover' effects—changes in prevailing supply and demand conditions to reflect current discrepancies between planned and realized purchases and sales. The most recent expression of this view has been voiced by Patinkin (1, p. 157).[14] His suggestion is to redefine the usual price adjustment functions to make the rate of change of price in one market a function not of excess demand in that market alone, but also of excess demand in all other markets. That this is not an entirely satisfactory vehicle for expressing his basic views, however, is indicated by three considerations.

Firstly, it is not consistent with established preference analysis to suppose

---

[14] Also see Hansen (15) and Enthoven (16).

that transactors alter their sale and purchase plans before prevailing market prices have already varied in response to the pressure of excess demand somewhere in the economy. Secondly, the supposition that price movements in one market are governed by excess-demand conditions in all markets is logically equivalent to the supposition that individual traders respond not merely to absolute levels of prevailing prices but also to current rates of change of prices. This implies some basic changes in established preference analysis to allow prices as seen by transactors to differ from current market prices (17). Thirdly, from Walras' law (obviously applicable in this instance), the 'money' value of potential 'spillover' from any given market is measured by the aggregate 'money' value of the market excess supply of all other commodities. Thus, if 'spillover' effects from a given market are *fully* reflected in other markets, we are left with effective excess demand in the given market (and, by induction, in all other markets also) identically equal to zero; which is to say that prices never vary. Patinkin does not go to this extreme; he relies instead on a proposition of Samuelson (18, p. 42)[15] and supposes that 'spillover' effects in any given market are only partially reflected in transfers of demand to other markets. But this is simply *ad hoc* theorizing—inventing a solution to a problem which has actually been evaded rather than resolved.

A more promising way to bring current transactions into general equilibrium theory is by way of so-called stock-flow models. Unless we suppose that all commodities traded in the economy are highly perishable, it is clearly plausible to argue that goods will accumulate or decumulate (or both) somewhere in the economic system during periods of market disequilibrium. This forces us to consider possible extensions of traditional theory to deal explicitly with asset-holding phenomena.

There is now a reasonably adequate theoretical literature on this subject, including a number of recent papers on monetary theory and at least one important book on the theory of investment.[16] I think it fair to say, however, that this literature has made little impression on the profession at large; which is perhaps another way of remarking that the equilibrium properties of stock-flow models are essentially the same as those of traditional pure-flow models and that few economists are deeply concerned with anything else. Here, therefore, I shall merely observe that the explicit introduction of asset-holding phenomena into traditional theory entails a re-

---

[15] In fairness to Samuelson, it should be added that his discussion does not refer to spillover effects, but instead to what I have elsewhere called 'dynamical interdependence' among market excess-demand functions. See Bushaw and Clower (19, ch. 4, pp. 82ff.).

[16] Vernon L. Smith, *Investment and Production* (20). This book includes a comprehensive bibliography on the 'real' part of the stock-flow literature. For further details of the 'monetary' part, see George Horwich, 'Money, prices and the theory of interest determination' (21). The latest in this series is the article by Archibald and Lipsey (22, October 1958), the related 'Symposium on monetary theory' (22, October 1960), and Baumol's 'Stocks, flows and monetary theory' (23). The general theory underlying such models is developed at perhaps excessive length in Bushaw and Clower (19).

definition of market excess-demand functions to include asset as well as price arrays among the relevant independent variables and, along with this, an extension of the usual equation systems to include stock-adjustment functions. As a consequence, actual transaction quantities influence market adjustment indirectly, via their impact on existing asset stocks—which creates certain new sources of potential instability (24; 18, pp. 170–71). Even in this type of model, however, current transactions exercise an influence only after a certain time delay. As in more usual general equilibrium models, therefore, current incomes never appear as independent variables. Thus, this potential road to the *General Theory* also turns out to be a blind alley.

The preceding discussion probably does not exhaust the list of possible ways of introducing current transactions into excess-demand functions, but we have now gone far enough to appreciate that the problem is by no means so transparent as some writers might have us believe. At this point, therefore, let us return to the route which Keynes apparently travelled before us.

V. SAY'S PRINCIPLE AND WALRAS' LAW

In our earlier account of the theory of household behaviour, we did not distinguish between planned and realized magnitudes because to have done so would not in fact have been a meaningful procedure in the context of orthodox equilibrium analysis. However, if we adopt the view that states of transactor disequilibrium are, in principle, just as admissible as states of transactor equilibrium (and how can we do otherwise?) (1, pp. 237–8; 14, pp. 318ff.), the distinction between plans and realizations becomes both meaningful and theoretically relevant. In the discussion that follows, we shall adopt just this point of view; accordingly, we shall henceforth interpret boldface symbols $\mathbf{d}$, $\mathbf{s}$ and $\mathbf{r}$ as realized or actual magnitudes (hence, given parameters from the standpoint of individual transactors); planned or notional magnitudes will be denoted, as before, by such symbols as d, $\bar{s}$, r, etc.

For any individual household (here, we are informally modifying our discussion to recognize that the household sector comprises a multitude of independent decision units), we may clearly assume that the realized *numéraire* value of actual purchases during any given interval of time is identically equal to the aggregate *numéraire* value of realized sales and realized profit receipts during the same interval:

$$\sum_{k=1}^{n} \mathbf{p}_k [\mathbf{d}_k - \mathbf{s}_k] - \mathbf{r} \equiv 0. \tag{5}$$

Indeed, this is just a tacit definition of the concept of a transactor, since what it asserts is that commodities are acquired through market exchange rather than theft, gifts, heavenly favours, etc. The familiar household budget constraint, although similar in form to the truism, equation (5) asserts the rather different proposition that no transactor consciously *plans* to purchase units of any commodity without at the same time *planning* to finance the purchase either from profit receipts or from the sale of units of some other commodity. For later reference, I shall call the last and very general proposition *Say's principle*. This is essentially a rational planning postulate, not a book-keeping identity nor a technical relation. Unlike the market principle known as Walras' law, moreover, Say's principle does not depend on the tacit assumption that values are calculated in terms of current market prices or on the equally tacit assumption that market prices are independent of individual purchases and sales. Neither does it presuppose that individual behaviour is in any sense optimal. Thus, Say's principle may indeed be regarded as a fundamental convention of economic science, akin in all relevant respects to such basic ideas of physical science as the second law of thermodynamics. Say's principle is not true in the nature of things; but unless we presuppose something of the sort, we have absolutely nothing upon which to build an account of individual decision processes.

Suppose now that we carry through the usual utility maximization procedure to arrive at household demand and supply functions, $\bar{d}_i(\mathbf{P}, \mathbf{r})$, $\bar{s}_j(\mathbf{P}, \mathbf{r})$, interpreting Say's principle to mean what it usually means in this context, namely,

$$\sum_i^m \mathbf{p}_i d_i - \sum_j^n \mathbf{p}_j s_j - \mathbf{r} = 0.$$

Must we then assert that any reasonable definition of market demand and supply magnitudes will necessarily make use of the functions $\bar{d}_i$, $\bar{s}_j$ so defined? Not necessarily, for the definition of these functions tacitly presupposes something more than Say's principle, namely, that every household expects to be able to buy or sell any desired quantity of each and every commodity at prevailing market prices (24, p. 232ff.).

Now, the rationale of the last presupposition is hardly self-evident. Keynes has been scoffed at on more than one occasion for his dichotomized account of spending and saving decisions (see *General Theory*, p. 166). As far as I can see, the only reason for making humorous comments about this view is that established preference analysis tacitly presupposes that selling, buying and saving plans are all carried out simultaneously. But what if one does not happen to consider the presuppositions of established preference analysis, tacit or otherwise, to be the final word on this subject? (25, 26.) I suggest that the question will bear further examination.

The notion that all household decisions are accomplished at a single stroke seems to be an analytically convenient and intuitively plausible procedure as long as we consider each household to be an isolated performer of conceptual experiments. When households are considered to be part of a connected market system, however, the same notion assumes a rather different aspect. What is then presupposed about planned sales and purchases cannot possibly be true of realized sales and purchases, unless the system as a whole is always in a state of equilibrium; that is to say, not every household can buy and sell just what it pleases if supply exceeds demand somewhere in the economy. Do we nevertheless suppose that the facts of life never intrude upon the thought experiments of households?

The answer to this is, I think, that the matter is not of much theoretical significance if, as is usually true when we deal with competitive supply-and-demand models, we are primarily interested in comparative-statics propositions. In this event, differences between realized and planned purchases and sales of individual households may properly be supposed to occur more or less at random. If we entertain the notion of developing market models that will have practical application to situations of chronic disequilibrium, however, we must surely question the universal relevance of the 'unified decision' hypothesis and, by the same token, question whether the usual households supply and demand functions provide relevant market signals.

VI. THE DUAL-DECISION HYPOTHESIS

For the moment, let us imagine ourselves to be involuntarily unemployed in the sense of Keynes. Specifically, imagine that we have a strong wish to satisfy our champagne appetites but that the demand for our services as economic consultants does not in fact allow us to gratify this desire without doing serious damage to our household finances. How do we communicate our thirstiness to producers of champagne; how can they be made aware of our willingness to solve their market research problems in exchange for copious quantities of their excellent beverage?

The answer is that we do so indirectly. We offer more favourable terms to potential buyers of our services (these may include some champagne merchants), leaving it to the market to provide us more employment and income and, in due time, more booze. Do we also signal our craving directly by drawing on money balances and savings accounts and sending our children out to work? In short, do we drink more even before we work more? Or do we become, at least temporarily, involuntarily abstemious and postpone our satisfaction to financially more propitious times? Clearly, this is to pose the question in a highly misleading way, for the issue is not, 'Which do we do?', but 'How much do we do of each?'

But if even this much is granted, we thereby affirm that the demand functions of orthodox theory do not provide relevant market signals. For if realized current receipts are considered to impose any kind of constraint on current consumption plans, planned consumption as expressed in effective market offers to buy will necessarily be less than desired consumption as given by the demand functions of orthodox analysis.

A formal statement of the problem will clarify matters at this point. Following the usual procedure of traditional theory, suppose that the preference function $U(d_1, \ldots, d_m; s_{m+1}, \ldots, s_n)$ is maximized subject to the budget constraint

$$\sum_i^m \mathbf{p}_i d_i - \sum^n \mathbf{p}_j s_j - \mathbf{r} = 0,$$

and the resulting first-order conditions are used to define the notional demand and supply functions $\bar{d}_i(\mathbf{p},\mathbf{r})$ and $\bar{s}_j(\mathbf{p},\mathbf{r})$. Provided that realized current income is not less than notional current income, i.e. provided

$$\sum_j^n \mathbf{p}_j s_j \geqslant \sum_j^n \mathbf{p}_j \bar{s}_j,$$

we may suppose that the functions $\bar{d}_i$ and $\bar{s}_j$ constitute relevant market signalling devices. For this is just to say that current income receipts do not impose an operative constraint on household spending decisions.[17]

In contrary case, however, i.e. if

$$\sum_j^n \mathbf{p}_j s_j < \sum_j^n \mathbf{p}_j \bar{s}_j,$$

a second round of decision making is indicated: namely, maximize

$$U(d_1, \ldots, d_m; s_{m+1}, \ldots, s_n),$$

subject to the modified budget constraint

$$\sum_i^m \mathbf{p}_i d_i - \sum^n \mathbf{p}_j s_j - \mathbf{r} = 0.$$

Solving this problem, we obtain a set of *constrained* demand functions,

$$\hat{d}_i(\mathbf{P}, \mathbf{Y}) \qquad (i = 1, \ldots, m),$$

where, by definition,

$$\mathbf{Y} \equiv \sum^n \mathbf{p}_j s_j + \mathbf{r}.$$

The values of the constrained functions, $\hat{d}_i$, will then be equal to those of the corresponding notional functions, $\bar{d}_i$, if and only if

$$\sum_j^n \mathbf{p}_j (s_j - \bar{s}_j) = 0.$$

Except in this singular case,[18] however, the constrained demand functions

[17] More generally, we might argue that an excess of current income over desired income does affect current expenditure directly; compulsory overtime might be considered a case in point. But we shall not deal with situations of that kind here. In effect, we suppose that individuals are never forced to sell more factor services than they want to sell, though they may be forced for lack of buyers to sell less than they desire.

[18] The constrained demand functions are not even defined, of course, when realized income *exceeds* desired income.

$\bar{d}_i(\mathbf{P}, \mathbf{Y})$ and the notional supply functions $\bar{s}_j(\mathbf{P}, \mathbf{r})$, rather than the notional functions $\bar{d}_i$ and $\bar{s}_j$, are the relevant providers of market signals.

Here and elsewhere in the argument, it may be helpful if the reader imagines that a central 'market authority' is responsible for setting all prices (using the nth commodity as an accounting unit), and that this 'authority' maintains continual surveillance over all sale and purchase orders communicated to it by individual transactors to ensure that no purchase order is 'validated' unless it is offset by a sale order that has already been executed (i.e. purchase orders are simply 'cancelled' unless the transactor has a positive balance of 'book credit' with the market authority sufficient to cover the entire value of the purchase order). It must be assumed that the market authority communicates continuously with each transactor to inform it of the precise level of its current credit balance, and further informs each transactor of the precise rate at which previously validated purchase orders currently are being executed. Sale orders are 'validated' automatically, but the rate at which such orders are executed is governed by prevailing demand conditions. It is implicit in this entire line of argument that, at some 'initial' stage in the evolution of market trading arrangements, the market authority advances a nominal quantity of book credit to one or more transactors to set the trading process in motion (without such initial advances, no sale order could ever be executed since no purchase order would ever be validated).

Established preference analysis thus appears as a special case—valid in conditions of full employment—of the present *dual-decision theory*. Considered from this point of view, the other side of involuntary unemployment would seem to be involuntary under-consumption, which should have considerable intuitive appeal to those of us who really do have unsatisfied champagne appetites.

It is worth remarking explicitly that *the dual-decision hypothesis does not in any way flout Say's principle*. It would be more accurate to say that this hypothesis assigns greater force to the principle by recognizing that current income flows may impose an independent restriction on effective demand, separate from those already imposed by prevailing market prices and current transfer receipts. Indeed, it is this theory which is invariably presented in geometrical classroom expositions of the theory of consumer behaviour. It is only in mathematical versions of preference analysis that we lose sight of realized current income as an operative constraint on effective demand.

It is another question whether Keynes can reasonably be considered to have had a dual-decision theory of household behaviour at the back of his mind when he wrote the *General Theory*. For my part, I do not think there can be any serious doubt that he did, although I can find no direct evidence in any of his writings to show that he ever thought explicitly in these terms. But indirect evidence is available in almost unlimited quantity: in his treatment of the orthodox theory of household behaviour, his repeated discussions of 'Say's law', his development of the consumption function concept, his account of interest theory, and his discussions of wage and price determination. It is also significant, I believe, that a year after the appearance of the *General Theory*, Keynes' own evaluation of the theoretical significance of the consumption function concept still differed sharply from that of his reviewers (28):

This psychological law was of the utmost importance in the development of my own thought, and it is, I think, absolutely fundamental to the theory of effective demand as set forth in my book. But few critics or commentators so far have paid particular attention to it.

Finally, it is important to notice that unless the orthodox approach to household behaviour is modified (tacitly if not explicitly) to recognize the dual-decision hypothesis, the Keynesian notion of an aggregate consumption function does not make sense, the distinction between transactions and speculative balances is essentially meaningless, the liquidity-preference theory of interest is indistinguishable from the classical theory of loanable funds, fluctuations in the demand for physical assets cannot be supposed to have more impact on output and employment than fluctuations in the demand for securities, and excess supply in the labour market does not diminish effective excess demand elsewhere in the economy. In short, Keynes either had a dual-decision hypothesis at the back of his mind, or most of the *General Theory* is theoretical nonsense.

VII. FROM THE CLASSICS TO KEYNES

We remarked above that the dual-decision hypothesis already has an established position in the oral tradition of established preference analysis. We have also argued that it plays an important (if tacit) role in income analysis. Thus, it is only when we turn to contemporary general equilibrium theory that no trace of the hypothesis is anywhere to be found. Yet it is precisely in this area that the dual decision approach is most clearly relevant—and most damaging to orthodoxy.

Referring to our previous account of traditional analysis (Part I, above), we recall that the business sector supply and demand functions may, from a market point of view, be so defined as to depend solely on the price vector $\mathbf{P}$, permitting us to write Walras' law in the form

$$\sum_i^m \mathbf{p}_i[\bar{d}_i(\mathbf{P}) - \bar{s}_i(\mathbf{P})] + \sum_j^n \mathbf{p}_j[\dot{\bar{d}}_j(\mathbf{P}) - \bar{s}_j(\mathbf{P})] \equiv 0.^{19}$$

In the context of the present discussion, the most interesting implication of Walras' law is obtained by calling the commodities $1, \ldots, m$ 'goods' and the commodities $m+1, \ldots, n$ 'factors'. We may then assert that excess supply of factors necessarily implies the simultaneous existence of excess demand for

---

[19] Cf. equation (4) above.

goods. More generally, we may assert that in any disequilibrium situation, there is always an element of excess demand working directly on the price system to offset prevailing elements of excess supply.

According to the dual-decision hypothesis, however, the market relevance of the household functions $\bar{d}_i(\mathbf{P})$ and $\bar{s}_j(\mathbf{P})$ is contingent on the satisfaction of the condition that realized current income be not less than planned income.[20] Suppose, however, that

$$\sum_j^n \mathbf{p}_j[\bar{d}_j - \bar{s}_j] < 0;$$

i.e. suppose that notational aggregate demand for factors is less than aggregate supply (in the sense indicated). Then involuntary unemployment may be said to exist since realized factor income cannot exceed the aggregate money value of planned demand for factor inputs, that is to say,

$$\sum^n \mathbf{p}_j[\bar{d}_j - \mathbf{s}_j] \geqslant 0.$$

In this situation, the dual-decision hypothesis requires that we replace the usual household demand functions, $\bar{d}_i$, by the constrained demand functions $\hat{d}_i(\mathbf{P}, \mathbf{Y})$, which, by definition, satisfy the condition

$$\sum_i^m \mathbf{p}_i \bar{d}_i(\mathbf{P}) \geqslant \sum_i^m \mathbf{p}_i \hat{d}_i(\mathbf{P}, \mathbf{Y});$$

i.e. the aggregate money value of constrained demand for goods is at most equal to the aggregate money value of planned demand for goods in the sense of traditional preference analysis. It follows immediately that, in a state of involuntary unemployment, Walras' law must be replaced by the more general condition

$$\sum_i^m \mathbf{p}_i[\hat{d}_i(\mathbf{P}, \mathbf{Y}) - \bar{s}_i(\mathbf{P})] + \sum_i^n \mathbf{p}_j[\bar{d}_j(P) - \bar{s}_j(\mathbf{P})] \leqslant 0;$$

i.e. *the sum of all market excess demands, valued at prevailing market prices, is at most equal to zero.* Indeed, since the equality sign applies with certainty only in the absence of factor excess supply, the dual-decision hypothesis effectively implies that Walras' law, although valid as usual with reference to *notional* market excess demands, is in general irrelevant to any but full employment situations. *Contrary to the findings of traditional theory, excess demand may fail to appear anywhere in the economy under conditions of less than full employment.*

[20] Profit receipts do not concern us since we are still proceeding on the assumption that the condition $\mathbf{r} = \bar{r}$ is satisfied (this is no longer essential to the argument, but is very convenient). What we are supposing, in effect, is that household receivers of profit income have perfect information about profit prospects (they may even be producer-consumers) and react to this information precisely as if corresponding amounts of *numéraire* profit were actually being received.

The common sense of the preceding analysis may be clarified by a simple geometrical illustration. Let the curve T in the accompanying figure represent the business sector transformation function, let U_1 and U_2 represent alternative household sector indifference curves, and let $L(\mathbf{p}_f/\mathbf{p}_g)$ represent, simultaneously, the profit function of firms and the budget constraint of households. In the situation illustrated, the real wage at time t, $\mathbf{p}_f/\mathbf{p}_g$, is such that $\bar{s}_f > \bar{d}_f$; hence, factors are in excess supply. Moreover, since $\bar{d}_g > \bar{s}_g$, goods are simultaneously in a state of notional excess demand. If the real wage rate is assumed to vary inversely with notional excess demand for goods (as is assumed to be the case in orthodox analysis),

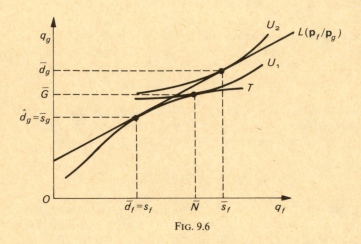

Fig. 9.6

$\mathbf{p}_f/\mathbf{p}_g$ will tend to fall over time at time t, and the system may therefore be said to tend towards full employment (defined by reference to the point $(\bar{N}, \bar{G})$). However, if the real wage rate is assumed to vary inversely with 'effective' excess demand for goods, no adjustment of the real wage rate will tend to occur at time t since, as indicated, constrained demand for goods, $\hat{d}_g$, is equal to planned supply of goods at prevailing price and income levels.[21]

This illustration of how effective excess demand may be insufficient to induce price adjustment, despite the obvious sufficiency of notional excess demand, says nothing, of course, about the stability of full employment equilibrium under alternative adjustment hypotheses. For example, if the real wage rate varies in response *either* to constrained excess demand for goods *or* excess demand for factors, then in the situation illustrated the system may still tend towards full employment equilibrium. The point of the example is merely to illustrate that, *when income appears as an independent variable in the market excess-demand functions—more generally, when trans-*

[21] Compare Keynes' discussion of the same model, *General Theory* (7, p. 261).

actions quantities enter into the definition of these functions—traditional price theory ceases to shed any light on the dynamic stability of a market economy.[22]

This line of analysis might be carried a good deal further; but I think enough has been said to justify such conclusions as are germane to the present argument:

Firstly, orthodox price theory may be regarded as a special case of Keynesian economics, valid only in conditions of full employment.

Secondly, an essential formal difference between Keynesian and orthodox economics is that market excess demands are in general assumed to depend on current market transactions in the former, to be independent of current market transactions in the latter. This difference depends, in turn, on Keynes' tacit use of a dual-decision theory of household behaviour and his consequent rejection of Walras' law as a relevant principle of economic analysis.

Thirdly, chronic factor unemployment at substantially unchanging levels of real income and output may be consistent with Keynesian economics even if all prices are flexible; this problem has yet to be investigated within the context of a Keynesian model of market price formation.

VIII. CONCLUSION

My original intention in writing this paper was simply to clarify the formal basis of the Keynesian revolution and its relation to orthodox thought. This I think I have done. In a line, Keynesian economics brings current transactions into price theory whereas traditional analysis explicitly leaves them out. Alternatively, we may say that Keynesian economics is price theory without Walras' law,[23] and price theory with Walras' law is just a special case of Keynesian economics. The bearing of my argument on the

---

[22] In an unpublished article 'A Keynesian market equilibrium model', my colleague Mitchell Harwitz considers a more general version of the rigid wages case with results that go far to anticipate the dual-decision hypothesis on which the present argument places so much weight. The following passage (Harwitz, p. 40), is particularly significant:

'Suppose one market is permanently restrained from full adjustment. What does this mean terms of the individual participants in the market? *It means that some or all of them face a binding constraint in addition to the budget constraint.* For concreteness, consider the Keynesian labour market. A worker, faced with a certain real wage, can sell *less* labour than is consistent with the usual constrained maximum. In effect, he is in equilibrium, but at a boundary [position] imposed by a quantity constraint on the labour he can sell.... It must be granted that these positions are equilibria by our definition; but their stability is a more delicate question. ... A complete answer would require a theory of the dynamical behaviour of economic units both in and out of equilibrium.'

[23] It is vacuously true, of course, that a proposition similar to Walras' law holds even in Keynesian economics if we *define* the difference between desired sales and realized sales as an excess demand for 'money income'. But the proposition then becomes an empirically meaningless tautology. In conventional value theory, the total value of commodities (goods and money) offered for sale is always equal to the total value of commodities (goods and money) demanded for purchase because all purchase orders are presumed to be effective regardless of prevailing demand-and-supply conditions. But in the present discussion, purchase orders are not validated automatically, sale orders thus do not necessarily generate effective demand for other commodities (effective demands are constrained by purchase orders *executed*, not purchase orders *placed*).

Keynesian counter-revolution is correspondingly plain; contemporary general equilibrium theories can be maintained intact only if we are willing to barter Keynes for orthodoxy.

This is not the end of the matter, for there is a choice to be made. No one can deny that general equilibrium analysis, as presently constituted, is a useful instrument for thinking about abstract economic problems, and this would hardly be so if it did not omit many realistic frills. The danger in using this instrument to think about practical problems is that, having schooled ourselves so thoroughly in the virtues of elegant simplicity, we may refuse to recognize the crucial relevance of complications that do not fit our theoretical preconceptions. As Keynes has put it, 'The difficulty lies, not in the new ideas, but in escaping from the old ones, which ramify, for those brought up as most of us have been, into every corner of our minds' (*General Theory*, p. viii).

I shall be the last one to suggest that abstract theory is useless; that simply is not so. At the same time, I am convinced that much of what now passes for useful theory is not only worthless economics (and mathematics), but also a positive hindrance to fruitful theoretical and empirical research. Most importantly, however, I am impressed by the worth of Keynesian economics as a guide to practical action, which is in such sharp contrast to the situation of general price theory. As physicists should and would have rejected Einstein's theory of relativity, had it not included Newtonian mechanics as a special case, so we would do well to think twice before accepting as 'useful' or 'general', doctrines which are incapable of accommodating Keynesian economics.

REFERENCES

1. D. Patinkin, *Money, Interest and Prices*, Row Peterson, 1956.
2. J. R. Hicks, 'Mr Keynes and the Classics: a suggested interpretation', *Econometrica*, vol. 5, 1937, no. 2, pp. 147–59.
3. J. R. Hicks, *Value and Capital*, Clarendon Press, 1939.
4. B. Ohlin, 'Some notes on the Stockholm theory of savings and investment', *Economic Journal*, vol. 47, 1937, pp. 53–69, 221–40.
5. O. Lange, *Price Flexibility and Employment*, Principia, 1944.
6. F. Modigliani, 'Liquidity preference and the theory of interest and money', *Econometrica*, vol. 12, 1944, pp. 45–88.
7. J. M. Keynes, *The General Theory of Employment, Interest and Money*, Harcourt Brace, 1935, pp. v ff.
8. O. Lange, 'Say's law: a restatement and criticism', *Studies in Mathematical Economics and Econometrics*, edited by Lange, McIntyre and Yntema, University of Chicago Press, 1942, pp. 49–68.
9. R. M. Goodwin, 'The multiplier as matrix', *Economic Journal*, vol. 59, 1949, pp. 537–55.
10. H. Rose, 'Liquidity preference and loanable funds', *Review of Economic Studies*, vol. 24, February 1957, pp. 111–19.
11. H. Rose, 'The rate of interest and Walras' law', *Economica*, vol. 26, 1959, pp. 252–3.

12. D. Patinkin, 'Reply to R. W. Clower and H. Rose', *Economica*, vol. 26, 1959, pp. 253–5.
13. L. R. Klein, *The Keynesian Revolution*, Macmillan, 1952.
14. R. W. Clower, 'Keynes and the classics: a dynamical perspective'. *Quarterly Journal of Economics*, vol. 74, 1960, pp. 318–20.
15. B. Hansen, *A Study in the Theory of Inflation*, Allen & Unwin, 1951.
16. A. C. Enthoven, 'Monetary disequilibrium and the dynamics of inflation', *Economic Journal*, vol. 66, 1956, pp. 256–70.
17. F. H. Hahn, 'The Patinkin controversy', *Review of Economic Studies*, vol. 28, October 1960, p. 42, n.l.
18. P. A. Samuelson, *Foundations of Economic Analysis*, Harvard University Press, 1947.
19. D. W. Bushaw and R. W. Clower, *Introduction to Mathematical Economics*, Irwin, 1957.
20. V. L. Smith, *Investment and Production*, Harvard University Press, 1961.
21. G. Horwich, 'Money, prices and the theory of interest determination', *Economic Journal*, vol. 67, 1957, pp. 625–43.
22. G. C. Archibald and R. G. Lipsey, 'Monetary and value theory: a critique of Lange and Patinkin', *Review of Economic Studies*, vol. 26, October 1958, pp. 1–22, and 'Symposium on monetary theory', vol. 28, October 1960, pp. 50–56.
23. W. J. Baumol, 'Stocks, flows and monetary theory', *Quarterly Journal of Economics*, vol. 76, February 1962, pp. 46–56.
24. T. Negishi, 'General equilibrium models of market clearing processes in a monetary economy', *The Theory of Interest Rates*, Macmillan, 1965.
25. W. J. Baumol, *Economic Theory and Operations Analysis*, Prentice-Hall, 1961.
26. R. H. Strotz, 'The empirical implications of a utility tree', *Econometrica*, vol. 25, April 1957, pp. 269–80.
27 I. F. Pearce, 'A method of consumer demand analysis illustrated', *Economica*, vol. 28, November 1961, pp. 371–94.
28. J. M. Keynes, 'The general theory of employment', *Quarterly Journal of Economics*, vol. 51, February 1937, pp. 209–23.

9.5 Keynes and the Keynesians on Involuntary Unemployment*
[...]

NOTIONAL VERSUS EFFECTIVE EXCESS DEMANDS;
THE VALIDITY OF SAY'S PRINCIPLE AND THE
IRRELEVANCE OF WALRAS' LAW

This brings us back to Clower's contribution. The excess demand relations of the conventional general equilibrium model, Clower emphasizes, are based on the assumption that all traders can buy and sell whatever quantities they desire at the market prices at which trading actually takes place. In a *tâtonnement* exchange model with multiple markets, the individual trader considers only the vector of 'announced' prices in drawing up his budget plan. His demand curve for one of n commodities may be derived by holding $n-2$ relative prices constant and varying the numeraire price of the commodity in question, registering the desired purchases of this commodity for

* From A. Leijonhufvud, *On Keynesian Economics and the Economics of Keynes: A Study in Monetary Theory* (New York: Oxford University Press, 1968), ch. II. Copyright © 1968 by Oxford University Press, Inc. Reprinted by permission.

each alternative numeraire price. Aggregation of such individual schedules (uncompensated for real income changes) gives the conventional market excess demand function. As Clower points out, however, this procedure presupposes that the $n-2$ other markets will 'clear'. In considering his purchases or sales of a particular good for any announced vector of prices, the trader is supposed to face infinitely elastic supply and demand functions in all markets. His trading plans are drawn up so that the total value of his purchases will be *financed* by the total value of his sales *and* on the presumption that he will be able to *realize* any sales he desires at the announced price vector. *Excess demand schedules derived in this manner Clower terms 'notional' excess demand functions.*

The notional market excess demand functions thus represent the outcomes of a particular type of thought experiment, i.e., answers by individual transactors to hypothetical questionnaires which begin: 'Suppose that you will encounter no problems in buying or selling whatever quantities you wish at the following list of prices ...' etc.—answers which are then collated for each market. But *all* the notional transactions planned in this way can be carried out *only if* all markets clear at the price vector actually prevailing during trading. If actual demand falls short of notional supply in some markets, some suppliers in these markets find that they cannot finance their notional demands in other markets in the way originally planned. They must therefore curtail their demand in the latter markets. Thus:

... if realized current receipts are considered to impose any kind of constraint on current consumption plans, planned consumption as expressed in effective market offers to buy will necessarily be less than desired consumption as given by the demand functions of orthodox analysis.

Market excess demand functions which take into account constraints on the transactions quantities that people expect to be able to realize, we term '*effective*' *excess demand functions.*

Effective excess demands coincide with notional excess demands only when both are zero in all markets, i.e., only in full exchange equilibrium. Recontract models postulate continuous exchange equilibrium. Individual traders in such models need never consider action on any other set of prices than that which will clear all markets. Actual prices are always market-clearing prices. Such constructions posit *pure price adjustment*—real income is always at a full employment level.

Clower goes on to argue that 'Walras' Law, although valid as usual with reference to *notional* market excess demands, *is in general irrelevant to any but full employment situations*'. This, of course, is a most controversial assertion, mostly because no firmly established professional convention exists on a couple of relevant, terminological points. The lack of such conventions in itself reflects the fact that the substantive point made by Clower has not been recognized—and it is a point of great significance to the understanding of the economics of Keynes. Clower relies on a distinction between 'Say's Principle' and 'Walras' Law':

The familiar household budget constraint ... asserts ... that no transactor consciously *plans* to purchase units of any commodity without at the same time *planning* to finance the purchase either from profit receipts or from the sale of units of some other commodity.

Consequently, the individual budget has the property that the values of net demands and net supplies will sum to zero (as usual). This is *Say's Principle*. Since it is assumed to hold for each and every transactor, it holds for the system as a whole.

The budget of a 'pure' Walrasian price-taker is a *special case* of all budgets obeying Say's Principle. The quantities entering into this budget are 'planned' by an individual who has not considered the possibility that, at the 'given' prices, he may not succeed in selling all he wants to (in a deflationary disequilibrium) or in buying all he wants to (in an inflationary disequilibrium). The values of these 'notional' net demands and supplies sum to zero. If everybody is like that, we get *Walras' Law* (in the sense of Clower) for the system as a whole—a usage to which Walras could hardly have objected.

Suppose the 'facts of life' *do* intrude on the Walrasian price-taker—he fails to realize some of his notional sales. *Who is ever going to know what his notional demand quantities were?*

Assume that no one knows, so that notional demands do *not* 'provide the relevant market signals'. The information which traders acquire is based primarily on the actually realized exchanges. The forces tending to make an initial contraction 'cumulative'—i.e., the income-constrained process—can now be sketched. Transactors with unemployed resources (current revenues curtailed by the initial 'shock') will generally reduce their expenditures in other markets. *Effective demands* are thus reduced also in markets on which the initial disturbance may have had no impact. Unemployed resources emerge in these markets also and *the search instituted by unemployed workers and producers with excess capacity will yield information on 'effective' demands, not on 'notional' demands*. The 'multiplier' repercussions thus set in motion make the information acquired 'dated' even while it is being gathered.

Consider a multi-market system initially at equilibrium with an output vector, q, and a money price vector, p. Let there be a change in some parameter—e.g., investors' expectations—such that a new exchange-*cum*-production equilibrium can be defined by the vectors, q' and p', the latter being associated with lower aggregate demand in money terms. If information was perfect, traders would act, individually, so as to establish the new equilibrium instantly. The first reaction, however, will be characterized by some inflexibility of reservation prices and corresponding resource 'unemployment' and inventory accumulation. If realized current receipts 'impose any kind of constraint' on current expenditure plans, this will entail more than merely a 'frictional' slowing down of the system's motion towards the new equilibrium. The new information generated by the income-constrained process will not induce such a slow but direct movement towards the new position. Instead, the 'current income effects' operate to compound the confusion: Not only are transactors misled about potential aggregate money demand, but the contraction will ordinarily enhance the general uncertainty by generating changes in relative demands which are essentially unrelated to the required movement from (p,q) to (p',q'). The elasticity of demand with regard to current income will be of widely varying magnitude in different markets. The 'true' situation will be further obscured if price velocities for given excess supplies are highly unequal in different markets. There is no *deus ex machina* to straighten things out, no Walrasian auctioneer to ensure that prices tell the truth (and nothing but the truth) about how resources can and ought to be allocated. The cushion must be sought in a fixed 'outside' money stock or in a mixed inside-outside money supply held steady by the monetary authorities. A purely inside money system might 'implode' if the initial shock is heavy enough to set off a chain of defaults.

To illustrate, consider the standard aggregative model, and the typical process which brings that system into a Keynesian unemployment 'equilibrium'. The money supply is assumed to be an exogenously determined constant in the usual manner.

Effective excess demand table

	LABOR SERVICES	COMMODITIES	SECURITIES	MONEY	SUM
Initial equilibrium state	0	0	0	0	0
Stage 1	0	ES	ED	0	0
Stage 2	0	ES	0	ED	0
New income 'equilibrium'	ES	0	0	0	< 0

The initial state is one of full exchange-*cum*-production equilibrium. This is disturbed by an adverse shift in entrepreneurial expectations (a downward shift of the marginal efficiency of capital schedule). Entrepreneurs decide to order less investment goods and, correspondingly, to issue less securities. As yet, household income is unimpaired and their saving plans (demand for securities) unchanged. At Stage 1, therefore, we have effective excess supply of commodities coupled with an equal excess demand for secutities. Next, the interest rate falls, the securities market being 'ranked' as the fastest-adjusting in the system. Instead of having a constant-velocity money-demand function, however, we have Keynes' interest-elastic liquidity preference schedule. The funds channeled into security purchases by households are diverted into the hoards of bear speculators. At Stage 2, we consequently have excess supply of commodities—since the decline of market rate has stopped short of the new level of natural rate—and a corresponding effective excess demand for money. Inflexible reservation prices prevent the disequilibrium from being snuffed out simply by an appropriate change in the relative value of cash balances and commodities-labor services. The excess supply of commodities is removed instead by a contraction of output, which is amplified by the 'multiplier' repercussions previously described, and halted finally when the excess supply of commodities and excess demand for money simultaneously reach zero. At the money income level where effective attempts to hoard cease, however, we are left with excess supply of labor—the unemployed looking for jobs.

The usual ambiguity surrounds the use of the term 'unemployment equilibrium' with reference to the situation represented by the last line of the table. There are two ways in which the system may get out of this situation on its own: (a) The excess supply of labor implies some downward pressure on the wage rate. If wages were quite 'rigid', nothing would happen. When they are not, the question arises whether wage deflation will lead only to a *pari passu* decline of aggregate demand in money terms or whether the Pigou-effect or some other mechanism will come into operation to propel the system back towards full employment. This question we must postpone, as Keynes did, until a later chapter. (b) Even with 'rigid' money wages and no Central Bank or government action, an excess supply of money (spilling over ultimately into demand for commodities) should gradually develop in Keynes' case. Successive periods of persistently low short rates should cause the Keynesian bear speculators to revise their initial views of the future course of long rates. Such learning behavior would be reflected in a downward shift of the liquidity preference schedule and a corresponding decline of the (long-term) market rate. This however, is a long-run phenomenon and we will be concerned here with the short-run situation.

The last line of the table is written the way Clower would have it: '...the *constrained demand* functions...and the *notional supply* functions ...are the relevant providers of market signals.' And:

... in a state of involuntary unemployment, Walras' Law must be replaced by the more general condition...[that] *the sum of all* [effective] *market excess demands, valued at prevailing market prices, is at most equal to zero.*

But the last line of our table, it must be noted, contradicts the usual interpretation of the Keynesian unemployment 'equilibrium' as one in which the excess supply of labor has a counterpart in an excess demand for money of equal value. This is again a matter of terminology, namely whether the money that the unemployed are seeking to obtain in exchange for their services should be represented as an 'effective' excess demand for money. If we do so, obviously, we will be comforted to find that the last line 'sums to zero' as we are used to having it, thus enabling us to shrug off Clower's contention:

Contrary to the findings of traditional theory, excess demand may fail to appear anywhere in the economy under conditions of less than full employment.

From the standpoint of the information transmitted through the system, the unemployed indubitably do communicate to prospective employers the fact that they wish to earn some money. Yet I find the representation chosen in the table the more suitable because I prefer to associate the statement 'there is an excess demand for money', with a situation in which there is an ongoing tendency either for velocity to fall, or for the interest rate to rise or, more generally, both. None of this is true about Keynes' short-period unemployment 'equilibrium'. So I choose to describe this as a situation in which the *effective* excess demand for money is zero.

Whatever one's preference with regard to terminology, however, Clower's substantive point remains. It concerns the dynamic forces determining the disequilibrium motion of a money-using system and brings out the rationale for the strictures against the neglect of the means of payment function of money presented above.

Suppose we make a 'Walrasian questionnaire' investigation of the notional budgets (at the prices prevailing in Keynes' unemployment situation) of the unemployed. For simplicity (*only*), let us assume that the unemployed do *not* plan on building up their money balances (again) if they succeed in finding jobs. They plan just to restore their consumption and saving—in the form of accumulation of 'securities'—to accustomed levels. Checking the results of this experiment, therefore, we would find the *notional excess demand distribution*:

	LABOR SERVICES	COMMODITIES	SECURITIES	MONEY	SUM
Keynesian unemployment 'equilibrium'	ES	ED	ED	0	0

The experiment reveals, in Clower's words, that '*the other side of involuntary unemployment* [is] *involuntary under-consumption*'. But Walras' Law is 'obeyed': the excess supply of labor is equal in value to the sum of the unemployed workers' notional demand for consumption goods and for (indirect claims on) new investment goods. Assuming (with Keynes) that producers are always willing to pay labor its marginal product, that labor will accept jobs at a real wage equal to its marginal product, and that there are no unions or minimum-wage laws, etc., capable of preventing them from doing so, a 'Classical' economist would now conclude that the situation can and will be remedied by an adjustment of the real wage rate that will simultaneously wipe out these excess supply and demand magnitudes.

Why, then, is this Walrasian portrayal of the situation irrelevant to the movement of the Keynesian system? Clearly, because in that system *all exchanges involve money on one side of the transaction*. The workers looking for jobs ask for *money*, not for commodities. Their notional demand for commodities is *not communicated* to producers; not being able to perceive this potential demand for their products, producers will not be willing to absorb the excess supply of labor at a wage corresponding to the real wage that would 'solve' the Walrasian problem above. The fact that there exists a potential barter bargain of goods for labor services that would be mutually agreeable to producers *as a group* and labor *as a group* is irrelevant to the motion of the system. The individual steel-producer cannot pay a newly hired worker by handing over to him his physical product (nor will the worker try to feed his family on a ton-and-a-half of cold-rolled sheet a week). The lack of any 'mutual coincidence of wants' between pairs of individual employers and employees is what dictates the use of a means of payment in the first place.

Thus, *the dynamic properties of an economic system depend upon* what I will call *its 'transaction structure'*. That labor services are sold for money and that households obtain their consumption goods in exchange for money is one aspect of the transaction structure of Keynes' system. Another, equally important, lies in the postulate that savers and investors are 'not the same persons'—but we will come to that in later chapters.

In an economy of self-employed artisans our problem simply cannot appear. If it does appear in a posited system, say, of big farmers 'higgling and haggling' with prospective farm-hands over the room and board and other direct material benefits that are to constitute the real wage, it will be most smoothly solved in a thoroughly Walrasian manner.

The terminological thicket is a bother. Consider: *In the sense of Lange*, Walras' Law is the relation relevant to a money economy, whereas Say's Law applies only to barter systems and gives rise to 'false dichotomies' and like troubles if misapplied to a money-using system. *In the sense of Clower*, Walras' Law is irrelevant to the stability properties of a money economy, whereas Say's Principle expresses the transactor budget-constraints not just in a barter system, but in a money system as well.

All of this, it may be said, is fairly 'modern' stuff, still not digested and absorbed into the contemporary teaching of macroeconomics. It may help to make sense of Keynesian economics, but does it bear any relation to the 1936 efforts of that notoriously incompetent price theorist, John Maynard Keynes? This, obviously, must be our next question. In considering it, however, we must be realistic—we cannot expect or require the same analytical precision of Keynes that we find in the present-day discussion.

KEYNES ON THE SECOND CLASSICAL POSTULATE
AND SAY'S LAW; HIS CONCEPT OF
'INVOLUNTARY UNEMPLOYMENT'

The *General Theory* opens with Keynes' critique of 'The Postulates of the Classical Economics'. Initially, his attack focused on the second postulate of the Classical theory of employment, but by the end of Chapter 2 this attack is seen to have been but the preliminary opening of the breach through which an all-out assault on Say's Law is launched. The second Classical postulate Keynes put as follows:

The utility of the wage when a given volume of labour is employed is equal to the marginal disutility of that amount of employment.

The principal links in Keynes' argument are the following:

1. The Classical theory recognizes only 'voluntary' unemployment. It is extremely important to be clear on three things: (a) how very widely Keynes defined 'voluntary' unemployment; (b) that his own concern was entirely with the residual category of 'involuntary' unemployment and that it is with this unemployment that his theory of employment deals; (c) that his policy recommendations and remarks on the relative efficacy of fiscal and monetary policy measures refer specifically to the task of relieving 'involuntary' unemployment, so that his judgments on the usefulness of monetary policy, for example, apply to such situations and not in general.

With regard to (a), Keynes followed up his definition of the second postulate by noting that

Disutility must here be understood to cover *every kind of reason* which might lead a man, *or a body of men*, to withhold their labour rather than accept a wage which had to them a utility below a certain minimum (italics added)

The list of 'every kind of reason' supplied by Keynes is very long. But it embraces 'frictional' unemployment and seasonal unemployment in the broadest sense ('due to intermittent demand'). Most importantly here, the second postulate:

... is also compatible with 'voluntary' unemployment due to the refusal *or inability* of a unit of labour, *as a result of legislation or social practices or of combination for collective bargaining* or of slow response to change or of mere human obstinacy, to accept a reward corresponding to the value of the product attributable to its marginal productivity. (italics added)

This third category, we may designate as 'income-expenditure' unemployment. It is not, I think, unfair to do so—Keynes' followers have had persistent difficulties in assigning a clear meaning to his definition of 'involuntary' unemployment. In today's textbooks 'involuntary' generally means simply that the *individual* worker has no choice because unions or minimum-wage laws stand in his way. This to Keynes was an utterly 'Classical' idea:

Thus writers in the classical tradition . . . have been driven inevitably to the conclusion . . . that apparent unemployment . . . must be due at bottom to a refusal by the un-employed factors to accept a reward which corresponds to their marginal productivity. A classical economist may sympathize with labour in refusing to accept a cut in its money-wage . . . ; but scientific integrity forces him to declare that this refusal is, nevertheless, at the bottom of the trouble.

The imperatives of scientific integrity are still with us. Modern Keynesians tend to save the notion of 'involuntariness' by transferring the *blame* of the 'refusal to accept a reward corresponding to the marginal product' from the individual to unions, monopolies, or governments.

Keynes lumped all the above three categories of unemployment into 'voluntary' unemployment and paid no further attention to them *or to their causes.* The significance of his discussion of involuntary unemployment will be entirely missed unless one sees quite clearly that Keynes did not seek to assign 'blame' to anyone or *any group.* Neither individually nor collectively do the transactors of the system that he dealt with 'refuse to cooperate' in the way that a Classical economist would find 'proper'.

2. This is the main import of his definition:

Men are involuntarily unemployed if, in the event of a small rise in the price of wage-goods relatively to the money-wage, both the aggregate supply of labour willing to work for the current money-wage and the aggregate demand for it at that wage would be greater than the existing volume of employment.

This definition has been regarded as most tortuously contrived by most later interpreters. Two points should be made about it:

(a) It proposes a thought-experiment to *test* for the presence of involuntary unemployment. Note that *both* labor *and* producers are 'tested' for their willingness to cooperate in the way that the Classical theory of competitive markets would have them do. Producers are being tested for their willing-ness to employ labor up to the point where the product of the 'last' worker hired is no higher than his real wage—the first Classical postulate, which Keynes insisted on keeping—and, consequently, on their willingness to hire more workers if the real wage were to decline. The relevance of this, I take it, is that *were producers to act otherwise, their 'volition' would be to blame,* in which case employment would *not* be 'involuntary' in Keynes' sense. And workers, of course, are being tested for their willingness to take a real wage cut in order to become re-employed.

(b) The test involves a cut in real wages, but Keynes *insists* on one of the two possible versions, namely that of a rise in the price of wage goods (money wages constant) rather than that of a decline in money wages (price of wage goods constant). Yet, *from a partial equilibrium standpoint*, either labor-market experiment ought to work as well. But Keynes reiterates again and again that the test of the 'involuntary' nature of unemployment is that those unemployed 'though willing to work at the current wage' would *not* 'withdraw the offer of their labour in the event of even a small rise in the cost of living'.

On the other hand, he argued that there will be 'some resistance to a cut in money-wages, however small'. The juxtaposition of these two arguments seems to lead to the unavoidable conclusion that Keynes' theory was based on the assumption of 'money illusion' on the part of workers. Such an interpretation views his statements as referring to individual behavior in a single market. The appropriate perspective is that of the equilibrating tendencies of the entire system of interrelated markets. In disequilibrium, the system is 'confused' and transactors act on the basis of faulty information. In a sense, then, though hardly a useful sense, they may be said to act under an 'illusion' of one sort or another. But Keynes had no patience with this semantic point:

It is sometimes said that it would be illogical for labour to resist a reduction of money-wages but not to resist a reduction of real wages. For reasons given below, this might not be so illogical as it appears at first; and, as we shall see later, fortunately so. But, whether logical or illogical, experience shows that this is how labour in fact behaves.

3. Keynes had two separate objections to the second Classical postulate and the denial of the possibility of 'involuntary' unemployment that it implied. The first of these 'relates to the actual behaviour of labour' and 'is not theoretically fundamental'. It concerns the resistance to money wage cuts. Consider the kind of individual adjustment problem discussed in the previous section. The immediate reservation price of a worker will be set on the basis of his expectations of obtainable prices. What information relevant to these expectations will be most cheaply available to him? Two sets of data appear relevant: (a) *past (money) prices received* for the same services, and (b) *prices currently obtained by successful sellers* of such services.

All that Keynes needed to assert is that the worker who is threatened with a lay-off will not offer to take *any* cut necessary to retain his job. Nor, having been laid off, will he immediately resign himself to shining shoes or selling apples. One reason, of course, is that his views of what his services should be worth unavoidably are related to what he was paid only yesterday. His expectations are '*inelastic*' in the Hicksian sense and his decision to withhold his services from the market may therefore be described as *speculation* on the future course of (obtainable) wages. This is the way Keynes described the behavior of producers. The further analogy with the important role that speculation based on inelastic expectations (of the future course of long rates) plays in his analysis of securities markets lends a pleasing unity of conception to a theory which stresses this reason for 'some resistance' to money wage cuts. But, in dealing with the labor market (and labor services are, of course, 'perishable'), Keynes chose to emphasize the second set of data.

The second reason why the unemployed worker will not accept an arbitrarily large wage cut in order to regain employment immediately is that he sees many of his former mates still at their jobs at much the same money wage as before:

Since there is imperfect mobility of labour ... any individual or group of individuals, who consent to a reduction of money-wages relatively to others, will suffer a *relative* reduction in real wages, which is a sufficient justification for them to resist it.

This and other similar statements fail to make clear which of the following two hypotheses Keynes would stress: (a) the worker takes the wages of others purely as a piece of information on the remuneration that it is possible to obtain, or (b) his self-respect is involved—he simply will not accept that he suddenly is 'worth' less than those with whom he worked so recently. Here, however, a third interpretation, for which Keynes' text hardly gives much evidence, has gained some currency, namely that he meant to invoke a 'relative income hypothesis'. This is a static version of (b) above—current usage bases the 'relative income hypothesis' on the assumption that other people's earnings enter into the steady-state utility function of individuals. This interpretation seems implausible in view of the fact that Keynes' two chapters on the consumption function show no trace of such a 'keep up with the Joneses' hypothesis.

In any case, the fact that workers watch each others' wages imparts sluggishness to the behaviour of the general money wage level *despite* the assumed readiness of labor collectively to accept a required general wage cut. It is *because*:

...there is, as a rule, no means of securing a simultaneous and equal reduction of money-wages in all industries [that] it is in the interest of all workers to resist a reduction in their own particular case.

4. Keynes' 'theoretically fundamental' objection to the Classical theory of the labor market is that it *misrepresents the nature of the wage bargain* in presuming that it does not matter whether the analysis of the determination of wages is conducted in 'real' or money terms (and in opting for the former as more convenient). That Keynes regarded this point as pivotal in his attack on Classical economics is unmistakable, for he hammers away at it again and again, using the same language:

But there is a more fundamental objection. The second postulate flows from the idea that the real wages of labour depend on the wages bargains which labour makes with the entrepreneurs. It is admitted, of course, that the bargains are actually made in terms of money.... Nevertheless it is the money-wage thus arrived at which is held to determine the real wage. Thus the classical theory assumes that it is always open to labour to reduce its real wage by accepting a reduction in its money-wage.

The traditional theory maintains, in short, *that the wage bargains between the entrepreneurs and the workers determine the real wage*; so that, assuming free competition amongst employers and no restrictive combination amongst workers, the latter can, if they wish, bring their real wages into conformity with the marginal disutility of the amount of employment offered ...

But the ... more fundamental objection ... flows from our disputing the assumption that the general level of real wages is directly determined by the character of the wage bargain ... [This is] an illicit assumption. For there may be *no* method available to labour as a whole.... There may exist no expedient by which labour as a whole can reduce its *real* wage to a given figure by making revised *money* bargains with the entrepreneurs.

Thus, to repeat, the fact that there exists a potential barter bargain of goods for labor services that would be mutually agreeable to producers as a group and labor as a group is irrelevant to the motion of the system. In economies relying on a means of payment, the excess demand for wage goods corresponding to an excess supply of labor is but 'notional'—it is not communicated to employers as effective demand for output. The resulting miseries are 'involuntary' all around.

This, to my mind, is the only possible construction of Keynes' meaning. And it is, of course, recognized in the standard Keynesian argument that money wage cuts will, as Keynes had it, lead merely to a *pari passu* fall of aggregate demand in money terms as long as there do not emerge 'indirect effects due to a lower wages-bill in terms of money having certain reactions on the banking system and the state of credit'. That Keynes' position has *not* been fully assimilated, however, is most clearly demonstrated by the superficial, and at the same time quite contrived, interpretation of his assault on Say's Law that has become commonly accepted.

5. The attack on Say's Law follows directly upon the definition of involuntary unemployment. There are two prongs to the attack. Both arguments dispute the same 'Classical' notion: that excess supplies must have their counterpart somewhere (if only in the future) in *effective* excess demands of the same total value.

(a) The first argument again concerns the nature of the wage bargain. Keynes singled out a passage from J. S. Mill, the wording of which seems most flagrantly to assert that the offer of labor services constitutes effective demand for commodities:

What *constitutes the means of payment* for commodities is simply commodities.... Could we suddenly double the productive powers of the country.... Everybody would *bring* a double demand as well as supply; everybody *would be able to buy* twice as much, because everyone would have twice as much to offer in exchange. (italics added)

(b) The second argument became an almost incessant theme of later chapters:

As a corollary of the same doctrine, it has been supposed that any individual act of abstaining from consumption necessarily leads to, and amounts to the same thing as, causing the labour and commodities thus released from supplying consumption to be invested in the production of capital wealth.[1]

The 'same doctrine' is of course Say's Law, applied in the latter case to an intertemporal general equilibrium construction.

Say's Law is irrelevant to a money economy:

The conviction, which runs, for example, through almost all Professor Pigou's work, *that money makes no real difference except frictionally*, and that the theory of production and employment can be worked out (like Mill's) *as being based on 'real' exchanges* with money introduced perfunctorily in a later chapter, is the modern version of the classical tradition. (italics added)

And the relevance of the prevailing transaction is taken note of:

... these [Classical] conclusions may have been applied to the kind of economy in which we actually live by false analogy from some kind of non-exchange Robinson Crusoe economy, in which the income which individuals consume or retain as a result of their productive activity is, actually and exclusively, the output *in specie* of that activity.

According to the standard interpretation of these passages, Keynes accused the Classical economists of being addicted to Say's Law in the sense of Lange. It is assumed, in other words, that he sought to reaffirm Walras' Law, not to attack it. Say's Law in Lange's sense asserts that the sum of the values of the $n-1$ notional excess demands for the system's non-money goods is identically equal to zero, whereas Walras' Law is the same proposition applied to all n goods. Now, as previously pointed out, traditional general equilibrium models do not accord 'money' a special status—it is just one of n equally 'liquid' goods. The point of the distinction between the two 'Laws' has nothing specifically to do with the means of payment function of money. Walras' Law is logically correct simply because it reckons with all n goods.

[1] Compare, *General Theory*, e.g., pp. 104–5, where Keynes explicitly notes that 'present provision for future consumption' will be a source of aggregate demand, except 'in so far as our social and business organization separates financial provision for the future from physical provision for the future so that efforts to secure the former do not necessarily carry the latter with them ...' etc. The problem is explicitly regarded as one of the effective transmittal of the relevant information (p. 210): 'If saving consisted not merely in abstaining from present consumption but in placing simultaneously a specific order for future consumption, the effect might indeed be different.'

To assert that the sum of $n-1$ excess demands is identically zero violates the principles of the theory of exchange for a barter system, just as it does for a money-using system. Say's Law is just as invalid if some non-money good is excluded from the summation—it is false, for example, if we fail to reckon with Lerner's fabled peanuts. The standard interpretation, consequently, fails to explain why Keynes should insist that the crucial error of the Classical economists lay in their misrepresentation of the nature of the wage bargain and in their conviction 'that the theory of production and employment can be worked out as being based on "real" [i.e., barter] exchanges'. If there is money in the system, Say's Law is just as invalid, whether wage bargains are settled '*in specie*' or not.

From the perspective of the standard interpretation, moreover, Keynes' statement that, 'Nevertheless, [Say's Law] underlies the whole classical theory, which would collapse without it', is simply incomprehensible. However many statements suggestive of the 'invalid dichotomy', etc., may be found in pre-Keynesian writings, it is absurd to suggest that running over $n-1$ excess demands was an accepted convention 'underlying the whole classical theory'. And, even had this been true, of course, the discoverer of such a monumental blunder could never have argued that the theory 'would collapse without it'. Obviously, elimination of the error could only have strengthened received doctrine.

Keynes' charges against Classical theory were directed at three assumptions:

(1) that the real wage is equal to the marginal disutility of the existing employment;
(2) that there is no such thing as involuntary unemployment in the strict sense;
(3) that supply creates its own demand. . . .

One may, if one so wishes, piece together an interpretation of the *General Theory*'s second chapter by assuming that he invoked against Classical theory (a) the charge that Classical economists individually and generally were addicted to Say's Law in the sense of Lange, (b) the empirical hypothesis that workers seek to 'keep up with the Joneses', and (c) the empirical hypothesis that they also suffer from 'money illusion' (in the straightforward sense of being fooled by proportional changes in accounting prices). But one will then also have to assume that Keynes, basing his own position on this motley assortment of outlandish propositions, was brazen enough to argue that 'These three assumptions . . . all amount to the same thing in the sense that *they all stand and fall together*, any one of them logically involving the other two.'

One must conclude, I believe, that Keynes' theory, although obscurely expressed and doubtlessly not all that clear even in his own mind, was still in substance that to which Clower has recently given a precise statement.

SUMMARY

We have attempted to show that *'reconciling competition with unemployment' appears as a 'riddle' only when 'competition' is implicitly equated with 'perfect information'*. When a more realistic view is taken of the information problem which traders face, the emergence of unemployed resources is a predictable consequence of changes in demand. This unemployment further constrains effective demand: a 'cumulative' Keynesian process may be set in motion. Though the initial disturbance may have implied little change in the real wealth of the community had full employment equilibrium been continuously maintained, the 'illiquidity' of real resources in a situation of market disequilibria induces a contraction of money and real rates of aggregate expenditures. This contraction constitutes a new set of 'information inputs' causing adjustments by transactors which lead the system further away from equilibrium. This cybernetic chain of information feedbacks is the very essence of the income-constrained process. [...]

10. Macroeconomic Policy

Introductory Note

For the last twenty-five or so years, the governments of most industrialized countries have been committed to the use of the policy instruments available to them to pursue a variety of macroeconomic aims. These have included the preservation of a high and stable level of employment, price stability, a satisfactory rate of economic growth, and balance of payments equilibrium (though this last should more properly be regarded as a constraint which must in the end be satisfied, rather than as an end in itself). There have inevitably been conflicts between the directions which policy should take to achieve these ends, and much of the analysis of macroeconomic policy has been concerned with the nature of the conflicts and the appropriate means for resolving them. The greater part of this discussion has concentrated on the twin objectives of internal and external balance—full employment and balance of payments equilibrium—but analogous analyses can in general be constructed for conflicts between any other pair of objectives or, indeed, for a set of any number of objectives.

Meade [Reading 10.1] provides an exhaustive survey of the potential conflicts between policies for internal and external balance when only one policy instrument—financial policy, or 'demand management'—is available and when repercussions on a trading partner country are taken into consideration. Thus, for example, deflationary measures in country A will reduce employment and income in A; there will be a reduction in A's imports (B's exports) which will improve A's balance of payments and reduce B's levels of income and employment, and worsen B's balance of payments. If B takes no policy initiative, A faces no policy conflict: re-expansion of demand, for example by fiscal policy, will both raise A's employment and reduce its balance of payments surplus. By contrast, if A does nothing, B faces a policy dilemma: the reduction, via exports, of income and employment calls for reflation, the deterioration of the balance of payments for deflation. Meade examines all possible types of disequilibrium in this two-country situation and shows that, provided each country takes appropriate action when the direction of action is unambiguous (that is, when both external and internal objectives call for policy to be in the same direction), only a limited number of conflict situations arise. The number of conflict situations is, however, increased if one or other of the countries refuses to take appropriate action even when the direction is unambiguous.

When there are conflicts, it is evident that a second policy instrument is required. Both Swan [Reading 10.2] and Mundell [Reading 10.3] explore the appropriate combinations of two policies to attain the two objectives, Swan in the longer-run context of demand management coupled with alterations in the domestic/foreign price ratio, and Mundell in connection with the shorter-run mix of fiscal and monetary policies.

The core of Swan's argument is summarized in Fig. 10.1 and 10.2 (pp. 448 and 449). The vertical axis is an index of relative costs, reflecting the competitiveness of the economy. The horizontal axis measures real domestic expenditure on consumption and investment. At a given level of this expenditure, the more favourable is the cost ratio, the higher will be exports and the lower will be imports—thus the higher will be the levels of national income and employment, and the more favourable will be the balance of payments. Or, to put it in a more useful way, a given level of employment (internal balance) can be procured by *either* a highly favourable cost ratio and a relatively low level of domestic expenditure *or* by a less favourable cost' ratio offset by a higher level of expenditure: the locus of points of internal balance thus slopes downwards to the right. Similarly, a given balance of payments on current account can be obtained by a highly favourable cost ratio offset against a high domestic level of demand (increasing imports and decreasing exports) or by a less favourable cost ratio offset by a low domestic level of demand: the external balance locus thus slopes upwards to the right. Once the employment and balance of payments targets are set, the intersection of the appropriate curves gives the required cost ratio and level of domestic demand. Points other than this intersection reflect the four possible disequilibria—over-employment and external surplus, over-employment and external deficit, and so on. But since changes in either policy instrument—the cost ratio or the level of domestic expenditure—will affect *both* targets, each zone can be further divided into two segments. Thus in zone III of Fig. 10.2, for example, which indicates unemployment and external surplus, reflation of demand appears to be unambiguously called for. But there is also a need for improvement in the cost ratio. Thus to the right of the dotted line, improving the cost ratio to the level ruling at the equilibrium point will *more* than suffice to procure full employment, so that a measure of *deflation* is required. To put it another way, the required change in the cost ratio by itself would take the economy into zone IV.

Swan points out that the curves will tend to be flatter in the long run than in the short run, since the response of the economy to relative price changes is likely to be sluggish. This suggests that changes in the cost ratio—for example by alteration of the exchange rate or by means of changes in relative rates of wage and price inflation—should only be used to correct longer-run balance of payments disequilibria. In the short-run, fluctuations in the external balance should either be tolerated, if foreign exchange reserves are adequate, or corrected by means of quantitative import restrictions if the reserves are inadequate.

Mundell, by contrast, considers the situation when alterations in the exchange rate (and, by implication, other measures to change relative prices) are ruled out, and trade controls are considered inadvisable. It is shown that, provided it is the balance of payments on current *and capital* account (and not just on current account) which is the policy target, and provided that international capital flows are sensitive to interest-rate differentials between countries, fiscal and monetary policies can be employed as independent instruments to attain the twin targets of external and internal balance. Again (Fig. 10.3), external and internal balances can be respectively achieved by various combinations of fiscal and monetary policies (the former represented by the government's budget surplus, the latter by the level of the rate of interest). In this case, however, both lines slope downwards to the right: a given external deficit can be achieved either with a high budget surplus (fiscal deflation leading to low imports) and low interest rates (stimulating the domestic economy and raising imports, and also reducing capital inflows), or with a low budget surplus and high interest rates. On the domestic side, a given level of employment can be achieved with an expansionary fiscal policy offset by a restrictive monetary policy, or vice versa. The crucial point is that the external balance locus must be steeper than the internal balance locus. This is because of the responsiveness of capital inflows to changes in the interest rate. In the absence of such responsiveness, and taking exports as given, the sensitivity of the balance of payments to changes in fiscal and monetary policy will, assuming a constant propensity to import, exactly reflect the sensitivity of the domestic economy to these changes and the two loci would have the same slope. Since capital inflows *are* sensitive to changes in interest rates, the external balance will thus be relatively more sensitive to monetary policy than is the internal balance, and its locus of points of equilibrium will thus have a steeper slope.

It follows directly that fiscal policy should always be directed towards the achievement of internal balance, monetary policy towards external balance. This is most obviously true when a policy 'conflict' arises, that is, in the recession/deficit and excess demand/surplus cases. The use of monetary policy to correct the internal disequilibrium would require an offsetting fiscal change to restore external equilibrium which must of necessity take the internal account (which is relatively more sensitive to fiscal policy) even further into disequilibrium. This conclusion is no less true in the cases of recession/surplus and excess demand/deficit where there is no *qualitative* conflict between the two policies. In this case, inappropriate use of the two policies will in the first instance take the economy into one or other of the more troublesome zones, and the earlier analysis applies.[1]

---

[1] It is worth noting that the relative sensitivity of the balance of payments to monetary policy can be further increased if the authorities can alter the term structure of interest rates, since the capital inflow is influenced mainly by short-term rates and the domestic economy (via investment) by long-term rates. See Reading 4.3 above.

A general analysis of the balance of payments as a policy problem is offered by Johnson [Reading 10.4]. Johnson points out that the balance of payments (that is, the net inflow or outflow of receipts other than official reserves) can be regarded either as the difference between receipts from and payments to foreigners, or as the difference between total receipts and total payments by residents. Considering just the balance of trade:

$$B = X - M \tag{1}$$

or, since $Y = E + X - M$, where E is total domestic expenditure,

$$B = Y - E. \tag{2}$$

It is suggested that the 'traditional' approach to balance of payments problems—for example, the elasticities approach to the analysis of devaluation—takes (1) as its starting-point, while the advantage of (2) is that it focuses attention on the relationship between the balance of payments and the domestic economy. An important distinction is drawn between 'stock' and 'flow' deficits: a stock deficit—resulting for example from a decision by the community to switch from cash balances into stocks of commodities—is only a temporary problem, while a flow deficit—reflecting a decision to spend more than current income—will normally require corrective action, unless the domestic money supply is stabilized. In the latter case, cash balances of residents must fall, as money is transferred abroad, interest rates will rise and domestic expenditure will fall, so that the deficit will ultimately be self-correcting. Since foreign exchange reserves will generally be exhausted, however, before a sufficient reduction in the money supply takes place, the possibility of self-correction is largely academic.

It can be seen from the 'absorption' equation (2) that an improvement in the balance of payments requires either a reduction in expenditure relative to income, or a rise in income relative to expenditure. Since income and expenditure are interrelated, the required policies are not obvious. However, since a change in output normally induces a smaller change in expenditure, deflation (expenditure-reduction) will improve the external position. Policies to increase output in relation to expenditure are more complex: what is required is a switch of expenditure by both foreigners and residents from foreign output to domestic output—in more familiar terms, an increase in exports and in import-substitution. The required switch might, for example, be procured through the price mechanism by means of devaluation.

In a sense, equations (1) and (2) represent the demand and supply sides respectively of the determination of changes in the balance of payments. Consider the effects of a devaluation when the economy is at full employment. If export prices in home currency are kept constant, the foreign currency price falls and the demand for exports rises. Similarly, if foreign currency prices of imports are maintained, their home currency prices rise and the demand for imports falls. But the increased demand for exports and for import-substitutes can only be met, if output is already at the full-employment level, by a reduction in domestic expenditure. The success of devaluation thus requires (a) demand elasticities such that the increase in the volume of exports and decrease in the volume of imports are sufficient to more than offset the adverse movement in the terms of trade, and (b) sufficient reduction in domestic expenditure to permit the diversion of output to meet the increased demand for exports and import substitutes.[2]

The use of fiscal policy to stabilize the level of employment has so far implicitly been taken to be a perfectly straightforward matter: taxes should be cut or government expenditure raised in times of recession, taxes increased or expenditure cut in times of inflationary pressure. Baumol [Reading 10.5], however, shows that in the context of business cycles of the kind produced by the multiplier/accelerator interaction, apparently sensible stabilization policies—either attempting to counteract rises and falls in income (policy *a*) or attempting to equate actual and full-employment incomes (policy *b*)—will tend, depending on the lags with which the authorities react, either to increase the frequency of cycles or to increase their amplitude. Baumol's analysis is purely formal, but it is interesting to note that several analyses of fiscal and monetary policy in Britain have attributed a destabilizing role to government actions. For example, Dow writes:

As far as internal conditions are concerned, the budgetary and monetary policy failed to be stabilizing, and must on the contrary be regarded as having been positively destabilizing.[3]

Or again, Caves and associates conclude:

The level of unemployment, which normally triggers changes in policies for demand management, lags about a year behind changes in the growth rate of gross domestic product, the variable to be controlled. Destabilizing changes in fiscal and monetary policy have resulted from the failure to heed this relation, so that restrictive policies have taken hold only after the growth of aggregated demand has slackened.[4, 5]

10.1 Conflicts Between Internal and External Balance*

It will already be clear from the analysis of the preceding chapters that there may often be a conflict between financial policies for internal and for

---

[2] In practice, a host of other factors will of course influence the outcome of a devaluation: the extent to which domestic prices of exports in fact rise (though the consequential increase in the profitability of exporting may stimulate supply); the effect of the import price rise (which is itself expenditure-reducing) on the rate of wage/price inflation; the induced movements on capital account; the possibility of destabilizing expectations of future devaluation on stock-building and on capital flows; and so on.

[3] J. C. R. Dow, *The Management of the British Economy, 1945–60*, N.I.E.S.R. Economic and Social Studies XXII (Cambridge: Cambridge University Press, 1964), p. 384.

[4] Richard E. Caves and Associates, *Britain's Economic Prospects* (Brookings Institution, Washington; London: George Allen & Unwin, 1968), p. 489.

[5] These conclusions have, however, been challenged. For a review of the controversy, see G. D. N. Worswick, 'Fiscal Policy and Stabilization in Britain' in Sir Alec Cairncross (ed.), *Britain's Economic Prospects Reconsidered* (London: George Allen & Unwin, 1971).

* From J. E. Meade, *The Theory of International Economic Policy*, Vol. I; *The Balance of Payments* (published by Oxford University Press under the auspices of the Royal Institute of International Affairs, 1951), ch. X. Reprinted with permission.

external balance. On the other hand, there are often occasions on which the same financial policy is required for the preservation both of internal and of external balance. The example analysed at some length in Chapters V and VI provides a good illustration of both these possibilities.

There is a spontaneous deflation of domestic expenditure in A which (i) deflates national income in A, (ii) deflates national income in B, and (iii) causes the balance of payments to move favourably to A and unfavourably to B. A policy inflation of domestic expenditure is needed in A both in the interests of internal balance in order to put a stop to the domestic depression and also in the interests of external balance in order to put a stop to the reduction of the demand for imports in A and the movement of the balance of trade in A's favour. There is no conflict of policy so far as A is concerned. But if the authorities in A do not act in this way, the authorities in B are faced with a serious conflict of policy. A policy inflation of domestic expenditure is needed in B in the interests of her internal balance, as a means of offsetting the depression which has been 'exported' to B from A; but in the interests of external balance a policy deflation of domestic expenditure is required in B in order to restrict the demand for imports in B *parri passu* with the decline in the demand for B's exports in A. There is a sharp conflict of policy. The inflationary policy which will stabilize national income will put the balance of payments even more out of equilibrium, while the deflationary policy which will bring the balance of payments into equilibrium will only serve to intensify the depression of national income [...]

We may take next an example of a spontaneous change which will involve both countries in a conflict of choice between internal and external balance. In section 2 of Chapter VII we assumed that there is a shift of demand from A's products on to B's products within given levels of domestic expenditure in A and B. This will lead to (i) a deflation of national income in A, (ii) an inflation of national income in B, and (iii) an unfavourable movement in A's, and a favourable movement in B's, balance of payments. A policy inflation of domestic expenditure is needed in A in the interests of internal balance to offset the deflation in her national income; but in the interests of external balance a policy deflation of domestic expenditure is needed in A in order to restrain the demand for imports. In B, on the other hand, a policy deflation of domestic expenditure is required in the interest of internal balance and a policy inflation in the interests of external balance. If both countries adopt policies for internal balance, the balance-of-payments problem will be made the more acute. If both adopt policies for external balance, the internal deflation in A and/or inflation in B will become more serious.

We have discussed these possible conflicts on the assumption that there were only two possible criteria to be observed by the authorities of any one country in their choice between possible policies, namely, the effect on that country's national income and employment (internal balance) and the effect on that country's balance of payments (external balance). At our present level of abstraction this is correct, provided that the policy to be chosen by the authorities of any one country is to be judged solely from the point of view of that country's economic position; but if the effects of the policy upon the economy of the other country is to be taken into account, we must introduce a third criterion, namely, the effect of the policy to be adopted by the authorities of any one country upon the internal balance of the other country.

An illustration may serve to explain the point. There is a spontaneous rise in domestic expenditure in A which (i) inflates national income in A, (ii) inflates national income in B, and (iii) causes the balance of payments to move unfavourably to A and favourably to B. If the economy of A was in internal and external balance before the change, then a policy deflation of domestic expenditure will be required in A to offset the effects upon A's national income and balance of payments. But suppose that the economy of B was not in internal balance before the change,[1] but was suffering from heavy unemployment due to a deflated national income which the authorities in B were not finding it easy to offset by a policy inflation of domestic expenditure in B. The inflation of demand for B's exports proceeding from the spontaneous inflation of domestic demand in A might in these circumstances prove a great help in the restoration of internal balance in B.

We have, then, to ask of any policy of inflation or deflation of domestic expenditure in A the three questions: what will be its effect upon internal balance in A? What will be its effect upon internal balance in B? And what will be its effect upon external balance between A and B? There are now a large number of possible conflicts and agreements between these criteria.

These conflicts and agreements are set out schematically in Table 1. This table shows in its four rows (numbered on the right-hand side) the four possible situations which may arise by various combinations of the three criteria which have just been mentioned. Thus the first two situations (rows 1 and 2) refer to cases in which the national income of the surplus country is too low and needs to be inflated (column *a*). Of these the first situation (row 1) refers to the case in which the national income of the surplus country needs to be inflated (column *a*) and the national income of the deficit country is also too low and needs to be inflated (column *b*). And so on.

On the assumption made in the table that there is an existing disequilibrium in the balance of payments and in each national income, there is no single situation in the table in which the authorities in both countries have simultaneously an unequivocally clear duty from the standpoint of all three

---

[1] If A was in external balance, then B also must be in external balance, if we ignore the possibility that an accommodating payment (or receipt) to A (or B) may be an autonomous receipt (or payments) to B (or A). For B's adverse (or favourable) balance must in these circumstances be A's favourable (or adverse) balance.

criteria. There are two cases, namely, in rows 1 and 4, in which the authorities in one of the two countries have an unequivocally clear duty from all three points of view. ...

Row 1 describes a situation of general world depression. The national incomes of both countries need to be inflated. The authorities in the surplus country should in these circumstances engage in a policy of domestic inflation on all counts. Such a policy is required in order to stimulate the demand for the surplus country's products in the interests of internal balance in the surplus country; and in so far as it stimulates the demand in the

Table 1.

Conflicts of criteria for inflationary and deflationary financial policies

National income in the surplus country	National income in the deficit country	In the interests of		
		external balance	internal balance in the surplus country	internal balance in the deficit country
is too low (L) or too high (H)		there should be an inflation (S+) or deflation (S−) of domestic expenditure in the surplus country and an inflation (D+) or deflation (D−) of domestic expenditure in the deficit country.		
(a)	(b)	(c)	(d)	(e)
L	L	S+ D−	S+ D+	S+ D+	(1)
	H	S+ D−	S+ D+	S− D−	(2)
H	L	S+ D−	S− D−	S+ D+	(3)
	H	S+ D−	S− D−	S− D−	(4)

surplus country for the products of the deficit country it will help, both to restore equilibrium in the balance of payments and also to reflate the national income in the deficit country which is suffering from the world depression. The authorities in the deficit country, on the other hand, suffer from a serious conflict of policies. They desire to inflate domestic expenditure in order to increase demand in the interests of the domestic employment policy of the deficit country, which is also suffering from the general depression of demand.

But any such domestic reflation in the deficit country will also stimulate the demand in the deficit country for the products of the surplus country; and while this will be useful in helping to stimulate domestic economic activity within the surplus country, which is also depressed, it will unfortunately seriously increase the difficulties of the balance of payments.

The first conclusion about policy in such a situation is obvious. In a period of world depression it is the duty of the authorities in the surplus country to take the initiative in inflating domestic expenditure, since this will not only help their own problem of domestic depression but will also help to restore equilibrium to the balances of international payments and also to stimulate economic activity in the deficit country.

It is, of course, just possible that a given degree of such reflationary policy in the surplus country will serve to solve simultaneously all three problems, i.e. to raise both national incomes to the desired level and to restore equilibrium to the balance of payments. But this would, of course, be a pure coincidence. There are three other, and more probable, possibilities: (i) that, while the depressions of both incomes are serious, the balance of payments disequilibrium is slight, so that a given reflation of demand in the surplus country will restore equilibrium to the balance of payments before it has gone far enough to restore internal balance to either economy; (ii) that the internal disequilibrium in the deficit country is very slight, so that the reflation in the surplus country restores internal balance in the deficit country before it has restored external balance or internal balance in the surplus country; and (iii) that the internal disequilibrium in the surplus country is slight, so that internal balance in the surplus country is the first to be restored. Let us consider these three possibilities in turn.

(i) In the first case the situation in row 1 will continue merely with an interchange of countries. The inflation in the surplus country after a certain point will have caused such an increase in the demand in the surplus country for the products of the deficit country that the balance of payments will have become favourable to the previously deficit country at a time when reflation of demand is still required in both countries in the interests of internal balance. What is now required is that the authorities in the new surplus (previously deficit) country should take up the policy of reflation in order to reflate both national incomes and also in order to remove the disequilibrium in the balance of payments. In other words, if the balance-of-payments disequilibrium is not very great in a period of serious world depression of national incomes, the various countries should go ahead with policies of internal reflation as far as possible at a pace which will keep the balance of payments between them in equilibrium.

(ii) But sooner or later the reflation is likely to reach a point at which internal balance is restored in one country before it is restored in the other. We now suppose that, starting from row 1, the inflation in the surplus country proceeds to a point at which a small existing internal depression in the deficit country is removed without, however, removing the considerable depression in the surplus country or the disequilibrium in the balance of payments. If the inflation in the surplus country proceeds further, national income in the deficit country will be over-inflated and row 1 will give place to row 2, where inflation of national income in the surplus country and an improvement in the balance of payments of the deficit country are still required but national income in the deficit country now needs to be deflated. ...

(iii) Alternatively, it may be the internal depression in the surplus country which is the first maladjustment to disappear. In this case a continuation of a reflationary policy in the surplus country would cause the national income of the surplus country to become over-inflated, though national income was still depressed in the deficit country, and the balance of payments still in disequilibrium. We should have moved to the situation depicted in row 3, the treatment of which will be considered in due course.

So far, we have considered the situation of row 1—a world-wide depression with a disequilibrium in the balance of payments—on the assumption that the authorities in the surplus country can and will undertake the reflationary policy which is so clearly desirable on all grounds. It may be worth while giving some attention to the position in which the authorities in the deficit country would find themselves if the authorities in the surplus country failed to take such action. It is clear that there would be a straightforward conflict of policies between internal and external balance in the deficit country. If the authorities in the deficit country deflate in order to get rid of the balance-of-payments deficit, they make the internal depression of national income in the deficit country so much the worse; if they inflate in order to restore the home demand in the interests of employment policy, they intensify the deficit in the balance of payments. In this latter case they will, however, incidentally increase the demand for the products of the surplus country and thus help to restore internal economic activity in that country also; and if the failure of the authorities in the surplus country to inflate domestic expenditure to a sufficient degree and sufficiently quickly is due to some political or administrative inability to do so, it may be useful to all concerned that the authorities in the deficit country should adopt a policy of internal inflation in order to induce a restoration of demand for her own products as well as for those of the surplus country, in spite of the fact that this will actually intensify the existing disequilibrium in the balance of payments of the deficit country. But such an arrangement would, of course, depend upon the possibility of the authorities in the deficit country obtaining, if necessary by special arrangements, sufficient accommodating finance on sufficiently favourable terms to carry the cost of the abnormal balance-of-payments deficit during the period while the authorities in the surplus country are preparing themselves for the necessary action for the reflation of their own domestic expenditure. [...]

It is the row-3 type of disequilibrium which is the most intractable. Indeed this type of disequilibrium is the only one which cannot be handled solely by financial policy even if the authorities in both countries are willing and able to adopt the appropriate reflationary or disinflationary policies. In all the other cases (rows 1, 2, and 4) if the authorities in each country always inflate or deflate when an inflation or deflation is required both for the internal and the external balance of their own country, it will be seen from the preceding analysis that in all cases the disequilibrium will either be totally removed or else will be diminished until it is ultimately turned into a smaller disequilibrium of the row-3 type. Apart from row 3 a conflict policy can arise for the authorities in one country only if the authorities in the other country fail to adopt the policy which is appropriate to the situation.

But in a row-3 situation there is no combination of inflationary and deflationary financial policies which on our present assumptions of constant wage rates, constant rates of exchange, and constant barriers to international transactions, can deal with the disequilibrium. Row 3 depicts a situation in which there is an excessively high national income in the surplus country which requires deflation and an excessively low national income in the deficit country.

For the authorities in both countries there is now a conflict between financial policies for the internal and external balance of their own countries. If policies for internal balance are adopted in both countries, domestic expenditure will be deflated in the surplus country and inflated in the deficit country; but this will reduce imports into the surplus country still more and increase imports into the deficit country still more and the balance-of-payments problem will become even more acute. For such a situation to continue there would have to be a large flow of accommodating finance from the surplus to the deficit country; and this flow of accommodating finance would have to be permanent.

If the authorities in both countries adopt policies for external balance, domestic expenditure will be inflated in the surplus, and deflated in the deficit, country and this will help in increasing imports into the surplus country and reducing imports into the deficit country and thus removing the disequilibrium in the balance of payments. But this will be done at the expense of intensifying the existing excessive inflation of income in the surplus country and deflation of income in the deficit country.

In such intractable situations of conflict between policies of internal and external balance, what should the authorities concerned do? Should they adopt financial policies for external balance, allowing their national incomes to be excessively inflated or deflated and trusting that this will lead to a rise or fall in their whole wage and cost structures which will thereby restore internal balance as well? Or should they adopt financial policies for internal balance, inflating or deflating their domestic expenditures sufficiently to maintain the desired level of demand for their own products regardless of the immediate effect upon their balances of payments? And if so, should they then let the exchange rate between their currencies change as a means of regaining external balance without sacrificing internal balance? Or should they maintain their fixed exchange rates and adjust their balances of payments by direct controls (by exchange control, import restrictions, tariffs, export subsidies, and the like) over their international transactions so as to restore equilibrium to their balances of payments without disturbing their internal balance?[...]

10.2 Policies for Internal and External Balance*

I. INTRODUCTION

Since Keynes published *The General Theory* in 1936, it has been widely accepted that the two fundamental propositions of a full employment policy are (a) that incomes and employment depend on the level of spending; and (b) that there is no automatic mechanism to keep spending near its full employment level, without conscious action by economic and financial authorities. But the balance of payments equally depends on the level of spending. Must it be only a happy chance if the 'internal balance' and 'external balance' levels of spending coincide? Is there an automatic mechanism to ensure this, or what kind of conscious action by the authorities is required?[...]

II. HOW EMPLOYMENT AND THE BALANCE OF PAYMENTS ARE JOINTLY DETERMINED

Take productivity, the terms of trade, capital movements and other financial transfers as given, and assume no special import restrictions imposed on balance of payments grounds. Then Fig. 10.1 shows how employment and the balance of payments both depend on the level of spending *and* on the Australian relative cost situation. 'Real Expenditure' is total domestic investment and consumption (private and public) at constant prices, hereafter called E for short. The 'Cost Ratio', hereafter called R, is some sort of index measuring the competitive position of Australian industries—e.g., the ratio of an index of international prices (prices of imports and exports) to an index of local wages, with weights reflecting the sensitivity of supply and demand for different commodities to changes in relative costs.

A given level of employment can be sustained with E very low if R is high enough (i.e. if our costs are so favourable that we export a great deal and import very little), and *vice versa*. This is shown in the A-curves—A_1 for a given amount of unemployment, A_2 for 'full employment', A_3 for a given amount of 'over-employment'. On the other hand, a given balance of payments requires a combination of low E and low R, or high E and high R. This is shown in the B curves—B_1 for a surplus, B_2 for zero (equilibrium), B_3 for

* From T. W. Swan, 'Longer Run Problems of the Balance of Payments', in H. W. Arndt and W. M. Corden, *The Australian Economy* (Melbourne: F. W. Cheshire, 1963).

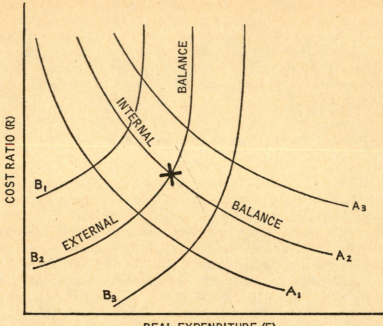

REAL EXPENDITURE (E)

FIG. 10.1

a deficit. The B-curves all turn up steeply near and beyond the A_2-curve of full employment, because as local resources are over-strained more and more of further increases in E must 'spill' overseas, till in the end an 'infinite' improvement in R is needed to offset any increase in E (i.e. an increasing deficit cannot be prevented by any cost adjustment whatever). There are, of course, as many A- and B-curves as we like to draw, for different levels of employment and the balance of payments.

Any combination of E and R along A_2 gives internal balance; any combination along B_2 gives external balance; only at their point of inter-section do we have both internal and external balance. The two curves of internal balance and external balance divide existence into four zones of economic unhappiness (Fig. 10.2).

However, between the two halves of each zone, as divided by the broken straight lines, the causes of disequilibrium differ. Only in Zones II and IV is the level of spending unequivocally too low or too high; only in Zones I and III are costs unequivocally too low or too high. Thus in each zone the necessary direction of adjustment of one of the two factors, E and R, is apparent, whereas the other may be either too high or too low, depending on our precise position in the zone. Conversely, overspending is consistent with both unemployment and over-employment, and with both at a balance of payments surplus and a deficit (but not with under-employment and a surplus

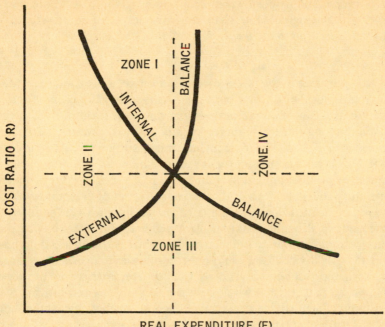

FIG. 10.2

Zone I: Over-full employment and balance of payments surplus.
Zone II: Under-full employment and balance of payments surplus.
Zone III: Under-full employment and balance of payments deficit.
Zone IV: Over-full employment and balance of payments deficit.

together); and so on. This is the source of many of the problems and errors of economic policy—if one factor is substantially out of line, the 'natural' indications for the other may be quite misleading. For policy, we need to know which *quadrant* we are in, whereas the mere facts of the employment situation and the balance of payments can tell us only which *zone* we are in.

Even these 'facts' fail to tell us anything directly, in the short-run, if for policy we want to distinguish between short- and long-run situations—e.g. if the terms of trade are temporarily better than their long-run average, we may appear to be in Zone I, although from a long-run viewpoint we are in Zone III. For the curves shift bodily with any change in the factors 'taken as given' above. Thus an improvement in the terms of trade or in capital inflow, etc., shifts all the B-curves, including the curve of external balance, to the right and downwards, permitting equilibrium with E higher and R lower. An improvement in productivity shifts all the A-curves to the right and upwards as well as all the B-curves to the right and downwards, permitting equilibrium with E higher and R probably lower (R higher if the productivity increase is concentrated in 'sheltered' home industries or if people insist on spending too high a proportion of their extra incomes on imports and exportables).

However, for many purposes it is convenient to think of the position of the curves as unchanged, while changes in the terms of trade, etc., shift the economic situation in the diagram in relation to the curves.

III. SHORT-RUN POLICIES

The importance of the policy distinction between the short- and the long-run arises from the fact that both the A-curves and the B-curves are much 'flatter' in the long-run than in the short-run, over most of their range (but even in the long-run the B-curves are still vertical or nearly vertical in the region where over-full employment has already strained local resources to the limit). This is because the longer is the time allowed for adjustments in the patterns of production and spending, the more sensitive are supplies and demands to different levels of R, whereas the effect of different levels of E is always immediate. Hence attempts to maintain short-run equilibrium by movements in R might involve violent and wasteful instability in the cost structure and distribution of incomes. Presumably the ideal would be (since we can hardly divide history into a series of discrete prospective long-runs) that R should respond very slowly to short-run changes in the economic situation, so that its level would reflect a sort of long-run moving average. This implies the use of international reserves as a buffer against the short-run fluctuations, and therefore the average size of these reserves will determine how long-run the adjustments of R can be.

This is the basic rationale of the use of quantitative import restrictions—as a short-run device to buy time for external balance, by economising on the average level of reserves needed to permit effective long-run relative cost adjustments to be made.

If restrictions are imposed only for sufficiently short and isolated periods and are sufficiently moderate in their impact, we may reasonably assume—

(a) that established trading habits will prevent any great element of 'profiteering' in licences and licensed goods, and that at the same time problems of the rationing of goods in short supply will not become acute.

(b) that recurrent periods of free importation or liberal allocation of new quotas will prevent ossification of the importing business and of trade connexions;

(c) that the prospect of early removal of restrictions will prevent any significant long-term investment in import-replacing industries; and

(d) that the margin of uncertainty, as to how serious a balance of payments deficit has to be before restrictions will be imposed, can be used to discourage speculative buying in anticipation of restrictions. [...]

With these assumptions, import restrictions do not differ in their effects from the running down of international reserves, except that we do not get the imports and that we still keep both the international reserves and their counterpart in domestic liquidity. There is, therefore, everything to be said for imposing import restrictions if otherwise we would be temporarily in Zone

III, with unemployment and a balance of payments deficit (provided that we make sure that the imposition of the restrictions does not itself carry us into a position of over-full employment). The resulting diversion of demand to domestic products and retention of domestic liquidity both help to sustain employment, without loss of international reserves, and without the upheaval of costs and incomes that would be otherwise needed to preserve short-run external balance.

But if we try to use import restrictions as a substitute for cuts in expenditure—in Zone IV, with over-employment and deficit—then the fact that we are keeping out goods and keeping in liquidity means that the problems of excess demand are made more acute than ever, local costs are driven up, and we move still further away from equilibrium: with little prospect of ending the restrictions unless we not only mend our ways and make the expenditure cuts that we hoped to dodge, but also take steps to undo the damage done to the relative cost situation in the meantime. [...]

At the same time, we must notice that an attempt to use exchange depreciation or tariff increases to protect reserves in Zone IV must have similar unfortunate results: for in this zone, so long as expenditure is kept too high external balance requires a more or less unlimited improvement in the relative cost situation, whereas internal balance requires, and over-full employment tends to produce, a movement in the opposite direction. And import restrictions do have the merit that they at least protect the reserves, while exchange depreciation and tariff increases, alongside rising money wages, might not do even that.

The moral is that there is no substitute, even in the short-run, for an effective limitation of expenditure to the level of the goods and services available from full employment output plus the maximum import surplus that we can afford after allowing for a temporary run-down of reserves. But if expenditure is effectively limited, then import restrictions are not merely a good substitute for, but a preferable alternative to, *temporary* cost adjustments which would otherwise be necessary. Indeed, import restrictions may often rightly be used in circumstances in which 'temporary' money wage cuts, depreciation, or tariff increases would be plain nonsense.

However, even in such circumstances, import restrictions should not be resorted to so readily and frequently that the assumptions on page 450 are seriously undermined. This is not an argument for trying to make what are essentially long-run adjustments do a short-run job, but rather an argument on the one hand for very careful consideration before quantitative restrictions are imposed and on the other hand for seizing every opportunity to build up reserves and to adjust relative costs in the long-run to a level which will make restrictions only rarely necessary. ...

In passing, we may note that the logic of quantitative restrictions as a device for temporarily short-circuiting the price mechanism, in circumstances in which it is ineffective, seems to rule out any case for the various proposals which have been made for the auctioning of licences, which would restore the price mechanism by the back door.

IV. LONG-RUN COST ADJUSTMENT

The argument of the preceding section implies that effective *short-run* control of Real expenditure (E) and effective *long-run* adjustments of the Cost Ratio (R) are both necessary to reconcile full employment with long-run external balance. The cost adjustments required are essentially adjustments of real wage rates (as we see, for instance, in the familiar propositions that exchange depreciation and money wage cuts are alternative routes to the same end, and that depreciation will not be effective if money wages rise proportionally with international prices in local currency, so as to preserve real wage rates unchanged). If long-run relative cost adjustments are not made, then import restrictions, imposed as a short-run device to eke out international reserves in specially 'bad' years (for the terms of trade), may have to become a permanent feature of the economy in 'good' years as well as 'bad'. Does this mean that the necessity for cost adjustments—for relating real wage rates to movements in productivity and the terms of trade—can be indefinitely postponed if only we can put up with quantitative restrictions of imports as a long-run institution?

The illusion of real wage rates might indeed be sustained in these circumstances with a certain amount of statistical success if with systematic price control and rationing the prices of permanently restricted imports were kept down to a cost-plus basis—but 'real wages' would have to be measured in terms of purchasing power over a basket of commodities consisting in part of empty import boxes, whereas actual wages would be spent on more expensive or less preferred home substitutes. The higher 'real wages' in this sense (as compared with their equilibrium level without import restrictions) the more empty boxes there would be, since export industries would be gradually squeezed out, till in the limit we could balance our international payments 'with nought on both sides and all of us flat on our backs'.

In practice, we must expect long-continued import restrictions (realistically assuming no price control and rationing) to lead inevitably to 'profiteering' in licences and imported goods to the extent of charging 'what the traffic will bear'. Thus if in the long-run real wages are not well regulated so as to make import restrictions unnecessary, they will be clipped to the necessary extent by the 'profiteering' of the importers and the dearness of available home substitutes—again, a process which reaches its limit with zero exports and imports.

Long run quantitative restrictions are in fact almost precisely the equivalent of a tariff, except that the licence-holder collects the duties instead of the Government. If the licences are interchangeable commodity-wise (as in Category B) the equivalent is a uniform *ad valorem* tariff; if they are specific (as in Category A), the equivalent is a tariff with differential *ad valorem* rates.

We should not complain if import restrictions encourage investment biased towards import-replacement. If the restrictions are really temporary, there is little danger of 'distortion'; if they are needed in the long-run, import-replacing investment is just what is called for and would anyway be encouraged by wage-cuts, depreciation, or tariff increases. But we may reasonably complain that both tariffs and quantitative restrictions (unlike wage-cuts and depreciation) encourage import-replacement without encouraging export-expansion; and perhaps we may complain also that quantitative restrictions, as usually administered, encourage in particular 'non-essential' import-replacement.

Certainly, tariffs are from almost every point of view preferable to long-run quantitative restrictions—if we must have one or the other. But we have been taught, on very respectable authority, that tariffs offer a way of sustaining real wages (at the expense of rural rents). Is there then still a hope of avoiding long-run relative cost adjustments in terms of real wages? It is true that a required adjustment of R may be made more 'economically', in terms of real wages, by raising only the relative price of imports (by means of a tariff) than by reducing domestic wages all round or by raising export and import prices all round, if the price of exportables is a significant element in real wages but their production is insensitive to changes in relative costs. (If exportables are not an element in the cost of living, a tariff which does not reduce real wages will neither encourage domestic industry nor reduce imports; if export production is sensitive to relative cost changes, a tariff may worsen the balance of payments even though it promotes import replacement.) This argument is strong in the short-run, but its force diminishes in the long-run, especially if we allow for the 'imperfections' which make investment in export industries depend to a considerable extent on average rather than marginal returns. In any case, the argument obviously cannot be carried too far, and once we have exploited its possibilities we are back with the necessity for real wage adjustments....

The 'official' mechanism for the control of wages is the Arbitration Court. It is by no means clear to what extent the judgments of the Court reflect a full understanding of the role of wages in relation to employment and the balance of payments, or to what extent its determinations have any important effect on the course of wages in the long-run. The only other obvious mechanism works in terms of the bargaining power of the trade unions, which depends largely on the state of the labour market. But whether this latter mechanism can be made to work in the direction of producing the necessary cost adjustments depends on how far the employment situation can be allowed to vary without departing too far from 'acceptable' standards of 'full employment'.

If there is no direct way of regulating real wages, other than through the state of the labour market, then official control of E must seek simultaneously to do two jobs—to keep the economy close to 'full employment', but sufficiently on one side or the other of it to keep real wages moving in proper harmony with the long-run trends of productivity and the terms of trade. The experience of recent years provides some reason to think that the acceptable range of 'full employment' is fairly wide, and that towards the lower limit of that range real wages can perhaps be restrained from increasing.

10.3 Fiscal and Monetary Policy for Internal and External Balance*

This paper deals with the problem of achieving internal stability and balance of payments equilibrium in a country which considers it inadvisable to alter the exchange rate or to impose trade controls. It is assumed that monetary and fiscal policy can be used as independent instruments to attain the two objectives if capital flows are responsive to interest rate differentials, but it is concluded that it is a matter of extreme importance how the policies are paired with the objectives. Specifically, it is argued that monetary policy ought to be aimed at external objectives and fiscal policy at internal objectives, and that failure to follow this prescription can make the disequilibrium situation worse than before the policy changes were introduced.

The practical implication of the theory, when stabilization measures are limited to monetary policy and fiscal policy, is that a surplus country experiencing inflationary pressure should ease monetary conditions and raise taxes (or reduce government spending), and that a deficit country suffering from unemployment should tighten interest rates and lower taxes (or increase government spending).

THE CONDITIONS OF EQUILIBRIUM

Internal balance requires that aggregate demand for domestic output be equal to aggregate supply of domestic output at full employment. If this condition is not fulfilled, there will be inflationary pressure or recessionary potential according to whether aggregate demand exceeds or falls short of, respectively, full employment output. It will be assumed here that, during transitory periods of disequilibrium, inventories are running down, or accumulating, in excess of desired changes, according to whether the disequilibrium reflects a state of inflationary or recessionary potential.

External balance implies that the balance of trade equals (net) capital exports at the fixed exchange parity. If the balance of trade exceeds capital exports, there will be a balance of payments surplus and a tendency for the exchange rate to appreciate, which the central bank restrains by accumulating stocks of foreign exchange. And likewise, if the balance of trade falls short of capital exports, there will be a balance of payments deficit and a tendency for the exchange rate to depreciate, which the central bank prevents by dispensing with stocks of foreign exchange.

*From R. A. Mundell, 'The Appropriate Use of Fiscal and Monetary Policy for Internal and External Stability', *I. M. F. Staff Papers*, 1962.

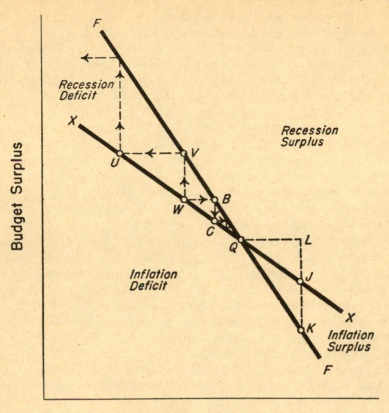

Rate of Interest

Fig. 10.3

In what follows it is assumed that all foreign policies and export demand are given, that the balance of trade worsens as the level of domestic expenditure increases, and that capital flows are responsive to interest rate differentials. Then domestic expenditure can be assumed to depend only on fiscal policy (the budget surplus) and monetary policy (the interest rate) at the full employment level of output. The complete system can thus be given a geometric interpretation in the two policy variables, the interest rate and the budget surplus (Fig. 10.3).

In the diagram the *FF* line, which will be referred to as the 'foreign-balance schedule', traces the locus of pairs of interest rates and budget surpluses (at the level of income compatible with full employment) along which the balance of payments is in equilibrium. This schedule has a negative slope because an increase in the interest rate, by reducing capital exports and lowering domestic expenditure and hence imports, improves the balance of payments; while a decrease in the budget surplus, by raising domestic expenditure and hence imports, worsens the balance of payments. Thus, from any point on the schedule an increase in the rate of interest would cause an external surplus, which would have to be compensated by a reduction in the budget surplus in order to restore equilibrium. Points above and to the right of the foreign-balance schedule refer to balance of payments surpluses, while points below and to the left of the schedule represent balance of payments deficits.

A similar construction can be applied to the conditions representing internal balance. The XX line, or 'internal-balance schedule', is the locus of pairs of interest rates and budget surpluses which permits continuing full employment equilibrium in the market for goods and services. Along this schedule, full employment output is equal to aggregate demand for output, or, what amounts to the same condition, home demand for domestic goods is equal to full employment output less exports. There is, therefore, only one level of home demand for domestic goods consistent with full employment and the given level of exports, and this implies that expenditure must be constant along XX. The internal-balance line must therefore have a negative slope, since increases in the interest rate are associated with decreases in the budget surplus, in order to maintain domestic expenditure constant.

Both the internal-balance and the foreign-balance schedules thus have negative slopes. But it is necessary also to compare the steepness of the slopes. Which of the schedules is steeper?

It can be demonstrated that FF must be steeper than XX if capital is even slightly mobile, and by an amount which depends both on the responsiveness of international capital flows to the rate of interest and on the marginal propensity to import. The absolute slope of the internal-balance schedule XX is the ratio between the responsiveness of domestic expenditure to the rate of interest and the responsiveness of domestic expenditure to the budget surplus. Now, if it is assumed for a moment that capital exports are constant, the balance of payments depends only on expenditure, since exports are assumed constant and imports depend only on expenditure. In other words, if capital exports are constant, the slope of FF also is the ratio between the responsiveness of domestic expenditure to the rate of interest and the responsiveness of such expenditure to the budget surplus. Therefore, apart from the effects of changes in capital exports, the two slopes are the same. It is then possible to see that the responsiveness of capital exports to the rate of interest makes the slope of FF greater in absolute value than the slope of XX.[1]

Consider, for example, what happens to an initial situation of over-all equilibrium at Q as this equilibrium is disturbed by an increase in the

[1] Both the absolute and relative values of the slopes depend on the particular fiscal policy in question. The discussion in the text applies to income tax reductions because that instrument tends to be neutral as between home and foreign spending. The conclusions would be strengthened or weakened, respectively, as the particular fiscal policy was biased toward or against home goods; the more the change in the budget surplus results from a change in spending on home goods, the greater is the difference between the slopes of XX and FF.

rate of interest equal to QL. Because of the higher rate of interest, there would be deflationary pressure and a balance of payments surplus at the point L. If the budget surplus is now lowered, the deflationary pressure can be eliminated at a point like J on the internal-balance schedule. But at J, expenditure is the same as it was at Q, and this means that imports, and hence the balance of *trade*, must be the same as at Q. The balance of *payments* is therefore in surplus at J because of capital imports attracted by the higher rate of interest; this makes necessary a further reduction in the budget surplus in order to bring the balance of payments again into equilibrium. It follows, then, that the point K on the foreign-balance schedule is below the point J on the internal-balance schedule, and that FF is steeper than XX. It can then also be concluded that the absolute difference in slopes is greater, the more mobile is capital (because this causes a larger external surplus at J) and the lower is the marginal propensity to import (because this necessitates a larger budget deficit to correct any given external surplus).

In Fig. 10.3, the two schedules separate four quadrants, distinguished from one another by the conditions of internal imbalance and external disequilibrium. Only at the point where the schedules intersect are the policy variables in equilibrium.

TWO SYSTEMS OF POLICY RESPONSE

Consider now two possible policy systems determining the behavior of fiscal policy and monetary policy when internal and external balance have not been simultaneously achieved. The government can adjust monetary policy to the requirements of internal stability, and fiscal policy to the needs of external balance, or it can use fiscal policy for purposes of internal stability and monetary policy for purposes of external balance.

It will be demonstrated first that the policy system in which the interest rate is used for internal stability, and fiscal policy is used for external equilibrium, is an unstable system. Consider, for example, a situation of full employment combined with a balance of payments deficit, represented by the point W. To correct the deficit by fiscal policy, the budget surplus must be raised from that indicated by W to that given by V. At V there will be equilibrium in the balance of payments, but the increased budget surplus will have caused recessionary pressure. If now the threatening unemployment is to be prevented by monetary policy, the rate of interest must be lowered from that indicated by V to that described by U. But at U there is again a balance of payments deficit, which in turn necessitates a further increase in the budget surplus. The process continues with the interest rate and the budget surplus moving ever further from equilibrium.[2]

---

[2] It need hardly be mentioned that the demonstration of instability in this instance (or of stability in the subsequent analysis) is not dependent upon the particular assumption that the government corrects imbalance first in one sector and then in the other, an assumption which is made only for expositional convenience. The conclusions follow, for example, even if the authorities simultaneously adjust fiscal and monetary policies.

To show formally that the system is unstable, it is sufficient to note that the payments deficit at *U*, after the first round of policy changes, exceeds the deficit at *W*. This is evident since it is known that the balance of *trade* at *U* and *W* is the same but, because of the lower rate of interest, the balance of *payments* at *U* is worse. It follows that this type of policy reaction is unstable.

On the other hand, the opposite type of policy is stable. Suppose that the authorities adjust the interest rate to correspond to the needs of external equilibrium and adjust fiscal policy to maintain internal stability. Then from the same disequilibrium point *W*, the rate of interest would be raised to *B*, thereby correcting the external deficit. But the tendency toward unemployment generated by the restrictive credit policy must now be corrected by a reduction in the budget surplus or increase in the budget deficit. At *C* there is again internal balance and a balance of payments deficit, as at *W*. But it is now possible to see that the deficit at *C* is *less* than the deficit at *W*. This follows, as before, because the balance of *trade* at *C* is identical with that at *W* but, since the rate of interest is higher at *C*, the balance of *payments* deficit must be less. The system is therefore stable.

The diagrammatic argument can be absorbed at once when it is realized that at *W*—or anywhere in the quadrant representing a deficit and recession—the interest rate is lower, and the budget surplus is higher, than is appropriate to the over-all equilibrium at *Q*. The use of fiscal policy for external balance, and monetary policy for internal balance, drives the interest rate and budget surplus further away from equilibrium, while the alternative system moves the instruments closer to equilibrium.

The same argument applies to an initial disequilibrium in the opposite quadrant, representing inflationary pressure and external surplus. To restore equilibrium, the interest rate must be reduced, and fiscal policy must be made more restrictive. Only if monetary policy is used for the external purpose, and fiscal policy for the internal purpose, will correction of the disequilibrium automatically ensue.

In the other two quadrants, monetary and fiscal policies will be moving in the same direction under either system of policy response, because both tighter monetary policy and an increased budget surplus correct inflationary pressure and external deficit, and both easier monetary policy and a reduced budget surplus tend to alleviate recession and external surplus. The distinction between the two policy systems appears less important in these phases of the international trade cycle; it nevertheless remains, since inaccurate information about the exact location of the point *Q* could propel the situation into one of the quadrants involving either recession and deficit or inflation and surplus.

CONCLUSIONS

It has been demonstrated that, in countries where employment and balance of payments policies are restricted to monetary and fiscal instruments, monetary policy should be reserved for attaining the desired level of the balance of payments, and fiscal policy for preserving internal stability under the conditions assumed here. The opposite system would lead to a progressively worsening unemployment and balance of payments situation.

The explanation can be related to what I have elsewhere called the Principle of Effective Market Classification: policies should be paired with the objectives on which they have the most influence. If this principle is not followed, there will develop a tendency either for a cyclical approach to equilibrium or for instability.

The use of fiscal policy for external purposes and monetary policy for internal stability violates the principle of effective market classification, because the ratio of the effect of the rate of interest on internal stability to its effect on the balance of payments is less than the ratio of the effect of fiscal policy on internal stability to its effect on the balance of payments. And for precisely this reason the opposite set of policy responses is consistent with the principle.

On a still more general level, we have the principle that Tinbergen has made famous: that to attain a given number of independent targets there must be at least an equal number of instruments. Tinbergen's Principle is concerned with the *existence* and location of a solution to the system. It does not assert that any given set of policy responses will in fact lead to that solution. To assert this, it is necessary to investigate the stability properties of a dynamic system. In this respect, the Principle of Effective Market Classification is a necessary companion to Tinbergen's Principle.

10.4 A General Theory of the Balance of Payments*

The theory of the balance of payments is concerned with the economic determinants of the balance of payments, and specifically with the analysis of policies for preserving balance-of-payments equilibrium. So defined, the theory of the balance of payments is essentially a post-war development. Prior to the Keynesian Revolution, problems of international disequilibrium were discussed within the classical conceptual framework of 'the mechanism of adjustment'—the way in which the balance of payments adjusts to equilibrium under alternative systems of international monetary relations— the actions of the monetary and other policy-making authorities being subsumed in the system under consideration. While the Keynesian revolution introduced the notion of chronic disequilibrium into the analysis of international adjustment, early Keynesian writing on the subject tended to remain within the classical framework of analysis in terms of international

---

* From H. G. Johnson, 'Towards a General Theory of the Balance of Payments', chapter VI of his *International Trade and Economic Growth: Studies in Pure Theory* (London: George Allen and Unwin; Cambridge, Mass.: Harvard University Press, 1958). Copyright © George Allen and Unwin, Ltd., 1958. Reprinted by permission of the publishers.

monetary systems—the gold standard, the inconvertible paper standard—and to be concerned with the role and adequacy in the adjustment process of automatic variations in income and employment through the foreign trade multiplier. Moreover, the applicability of the analysis to policy problems was severely restricted by its assumption of general under-employment, which implied an elastic supply of aggregate output, and allowed the domestic-currency wage or price level to be treated as *given*, independently of the balance of payments and variations in it.

The pre-war approach to international monetary theory reflected the way in which balance-of-payments problems tended to appear at the time, namely as problems of international monetary adjustment. Since the war, for reasons which need not be elaborated here, the balance of payments has come to be a major problem for economic policy in many countries. Correspondingly, a new (though still Keynesian) theoretical approach to balance-of-payments theory has been emerging, an approach which is better adapted to post-war conditions than the 'foreign trade multiplier theory' and 'elasticity analysis' of the pre-war period in two major respects: it poses the problems of balance-of-payments adjustment in a way which highlights their policy implications, and it allows for conditions of full employment and inflation.

The essence of this approach, which has been termed 'the absorption approach', is to view the balance of payments as a relation between the aggregate receipts and expenditures of the economy, rather than as a relation between the country's credits and debits on international account. This approach has been implicit to an important extent in the thinking of practical policy-makers concerned with balance-of-payments problems in post-war conditions.[...]

Let us first summarize the traditional approach to balance-of-payments theory. The balance of payments must necessarily balance, when all international transactions are taken into account; for imbalance or disequilibrium to be possible, it is necessary to distinguish between 'autonomous' international transactions—those which are the result of the free and voluntary choices of individual transactors, within whatever restrictions are imposed by economic variables or policy on their behaviour—and 'induced' or 'accommodating' international transactions—those which are undertaken by the foreign exchange authorities to reconcile the free choices of the individual transactors—and to define the 'balance of payments' to include only autonomous transactions. To put the point another way, balance-of-payments problems presuppose the presence of an official foreign exchange authority which is prepared to operate in the foreign exchange market by the use of official reserves so as to influence the exchange rate; and 'disequilibrium' is defined by changes in the official reserves, associated with imbalance between the foreign receipts and foreign payments of residents of the country, where 'residents' is defined to include all economic units domiciled in the country *except* the foreign exchange authority.

The 'balance of payments' appropriate to economic analysis may then be defined as

$$B = R_f - P_f \qquad (1)$$

where R_f represents aggregate receipts by residents from foreigners, and P_f represents aggregate payments by residents to foreigners. The difference between the two constitutes a surplus (if positive) or a deficit (if negative); a surplus is accompanied by sales of foreign currency to the exchange authority by residents or foreigners in exchange for domestic currency, and conversely a deficit is financed by sales of domestic currency by residents or foreigners to the authority in exchange for foreign currency. To remedy a deficit, some action must be taken to increase receipts from foreigners and reduce payments to foreigners, or increase receipts more than payments, or reduce payments more than receipts; and conversely with a surplus (though the rectification of a surplus is not generally regarded as a balance- of-payments problem').

The 'balance of payments' can, however, be defined in another way, by making use of the fact that all payments by residents to residents are simultaneously receipts by residents from residents; in symbols $R_r \equiv P_r$. Hence the balance of payments may be written

$$B = R_f + R_r - P_f - P_r = R - P. \qquad (2)$$

That is, the balance of payments is the difference between aggregate receipts by residents and aggregate payments by residents. A deficit implies an excess of payments over receipts, and its rectification requires that receipts be increased and payments decreased, or that receipts increase more than payments, or that receipts decrease less than payments; and conversely with a surplus. In what follows, however, surpluses will be ignored, and the argument will be concerned only with deficits.

The formulation of a balance-of-payments deficit in terms of an excess of aggregate payments by residents over aggregate receipts by residents constitutes the starting point for the generalization of the 'absorption approach' to balance-of-payments theory—what might be termed a 'payments approach'—which is the purpose of this chapter. It directs attention to two important aspects of a deficit—its monetary implications, and its relation with the aggregate activity of the economy—from which attention tends to be diverted by the traditional sectoral approach, and neglect of which can lead to fallacious analysis. These two aspects will be discussion in turn, beginning with the monetary implications of a deficit.

The excess of payments by residents over receipts by residents inherent in a balance-of-payments deficit necessarily implies one or other of two alternatives. The first is that cash balances of residents are running down, as domestic money is transferred to the foreign exchange authority. This can, obviously, only continue for a limited period, as eventually cash balances would approach the minimum that the community wished to hold in the process the disequilibrium would cure itself, through the mechanism of rising interest rates, tighter credit conditions, reduction of aggregate expenditure and possibly an increase in aggregate receipts. In this case, where the deficit is financed by dishoarding, it would be self-correcting in time; but the economic policy authorities may well be unable to allow the self-correcting process to run its course, since the international reserves of the country may be such a small fraction of the domestic money supply that they would be exhausted well before the running down of money balances had any significant corrective effect. The authorities might therefore have to take action of some kind to reinforce and accelerate the effects of diminishing money balances.

This last consideration provides the chief valid argument for larger international reserves. The case for larger international reserves is usually argued on the ground that larger reserves provide more time for the economic policy authorities to make adjustments to correct a balance-of-payments disequilibrium. But there is no presumption that adjustment spread over a longer period is to be preferred—the argument could indeed be inverted into the proposition that, the larger reserves, the more power the authorities have to resist desirable adjustments. The acceptable argument would seem to be that, the larger the international reserves in relation to the domestic money supply, the less the probability that the profit- or utility-maximizing decisions of individuals to move out of cash into commodities or securities will have to be frustrated by the monetary authorities for fear of a balance-of-payments crisis.

The second alternative is that the cash balances of residents are being replenished by open market purchases of securities by the monetary or foreign exchange authority, as would happen automatically if the monetary authority followed a policy of pegging interest rates or the exchange authority (as in the British case) automatically re-lent to residents any domestic currency it received from residents or foreigners in return for sales of foreign exchange. In this case, the money supply in domestic circulation is being maintained by credit creation, so that the excess of payments over receipts by residents could continue indefinitely without generating any corrective process—until dwindling reserves forced the economic policy authorities to change their policy in some respect.

To summarize the argument so far, a balance-of-payments deficit implies *either* dishoarding by residents, *or* credit creation by the monetary authorities —either an increase in V, or the maintenance of M. Further, since a deficit associated with increasing velocity of circulation will tend to be self-correcting (though the authorities may be unable to rely on this alone), a continuing balance-of-payments deficit of the type usually discussed in balance-of-payments theory ultimately requires credit creation to keep it going. This in turn implies that balance-of-payments deficits and difficulties are essentially monetary phenomena, traceable to either of two causes: too low a ratio of international reserves relative to the domestic money supply, so that the economic policy authorities cannot rely on the natural self-correcting process; or the pursuit of governmental policies which oblige the authorities to feed the deficit by credit creation. In both cases, the problem is associated fundamentally with the power of national banking systems to create money which has no internationally acceptable backing.

To conclude that balance of payments problems are essentially monetary is not, of course, to assert that they are attributable to monetary mismanagement—they may be, or they may be the result of 'real' forces in the face of which the monetary authorities play a passive role. The conclusion does mean, however, that the distinctions which have sometimes been drawn between monetary and real disequilibria, for example by concepts of 'structural disequilibrium', are not logically valid—though such concepts, carefully used, may be helpful in isolating the initiating causes of disequilibrium or the most appropriate type of remedial policy to follow.

Formulation of the balance of payments as the difference between aggregate payments and aggregate receipts thus illuminates the monetary aspects of balance-of-payments disequilibrium, and emphasizes its essentially monetary nature. More important and interesting is the light which this approach sheds on the policy problem of correcting a deficit, by relating the balance of payments to the overall operation of the economy rather than treating it as one sector of the economy to be analysed by itself.

An excess of aggregate payments by residents over aggregate receipts by residents is the net outcome of economic decisions taken by all the individual economic units composing the economy. These decisions may usefully be analysed in terms of an 'aggregate decision' taken by the community of residents as a group (excluding, as always, the foreign exchange authority), though it must be recognized that this technique ignores many of the complications that would have to be investigated in a more detailed analysis.

Two sorts of aggregate decision leading to a balance-of-payments deficit may be distinguished in principle, corresponding to the distinction drawn in monetary theory between 'stock' decisions and 'flow' decisions: a (stock) decision to alter the composition of the community's assets by substituting other assets for domestic money,[1] and a (flow) decision to spend currently in excess of current receipts. Since both real goods and securities are alternative assets to domestic money, and current expenditure may consist in the purchase of either goods or securities, the balance-of-payments deficit resulting from either type of aggregate decision may show itself on either current or capital account. That is, a current account deficit may reflect either a community decision to shift out of cash balances into stocks of goods, or a

---

[1] With the community defined to include the monetary authority, a substitution of securities for domestic money can only be effected by drawing securities from abroad in exchange for international reserves.

decision to use goods in excess of the community's current rate of production, while a capital account deficit may reflect either a decision to shift out of domestic money into securities or a decision to lend in excess of the current rate of saving.

The distinction between 'stock' and 'flow' balance-of-payments deficits is important for both theory and practical policy, though refined theoretical analysis has generally been concerned with 'flow' deficits, without making the distinction explicit. The importance of the distinction stems from the fact that a 'stock' deficit is inherently temporary and implies no real worsening of the country's economic position, whereas a 'flow' deficit is not inherently temporary and may imply a worsening of the country's economic position.

Since a stock decision entails a once-for-all change in the composition of a given aggregate of capital assets, a 'stock' deficit must necessarily be a temporary affair;[2] and in itself it implies no deterioration (but rather the reverse) in the country's economic position and prospects.[3] Nevertheless, if the country's international reserves are small, the economic policy authorities may be obliged to check such a deficit by a change in economic policy. The policy methods available are familiar, but it may be useful to review them briefly in relation to the framework of analysis developed here.

To discourage the substitution of stocks of goods for domestic currency, the economic policy authorities may either raise the cost of stock-holding by credit restriction or reduce its attractiveness by currency depreciation.[4] Under both policies, the magnitude of the effect is uncertain—depreciation, by stimulating de-stabilizing expectations, may even promote stock accumulation—while unavoidable repercussions on the flow equilibrium of the economy are set up. These considerations provide a strong argument for the use of the alternative method of direct controls on stock-holding, an indirect and partial form of which is quantitative import restriction.

To discourage the substitution of securities for domestic currency, the same broad alternatives are available: credit restriction, which amounts to the monetary authority substituting domestic currency for securities to offset

---

[2] A temporary deficit of this kind must be distinguished from a deficit which is 'temporary' in the sense that the causal factors behind it will reverse themselves, leading to a later compensating surplus: e.g. a deficit due to a bad harvest.

[3] The deficit involves the replacement of international reserves by stocks of exportable or importable goods and/or by holdings of internationally marketable securities, the change being motivated by private profit considerations. For this to constitute a deterioration from the national point of view, the alternatives facing private asset-holders must be assumed not to reflect true social alternative opportunities, or private asset-holders must be assumed to act less rationally than the economic policy authorities, or the national interest must be defined so as to exclude their welfare from counting. If any of these assumptions is valid, it indicates the need for a remedial policy, but not one conditional on the existence of a deficit or to be applied through the balance of payments. This point is argued more fully below, in connection with import restrictions.

[4] Stocks are built up by witholding goods from export or by increasing imports; depreciation makes both of these less attractive. A third policy might be increased taxation, either of stocks or of home-market sales of goods.

substitution of securities for domestic currency by the rest of the community; devaluation, which affects the relative attractiveness of securities only through expectations and may work either way; and exchange controls restricting the acquisition of securities from abroad. Considerations similar to those of the previous paragraph would seem to argue in favour of the use of controls on international capital movements as against the alternative methods available.

In both cases, evaluation of the policy alternatives suggests the use of control rather than price system methods. It should be recalled, though, that the problem is created by the assumed inadequacy of the country's international reserves. In the longer run, the choice for economic policy lies, not between the three alternatives discussed, but between the necessity of having to choose between them and the cost of investing in the accumulation of reserves large enough to finance potential 'stock' deficits. Also, nothing has been said about the practical difficulties of maintaining effective control over international transactions, especially capital movements.

In contrast to a 'stock' deficit, a 'flow' deficit is not inherently of limited duration. It will be so if the monetary authority is not prepared to create credit, but this is because its existence will then set up monetary repercussions which will eventually alter the collective decision responsible for it, not because the initial decision implied a temporary deficit. If the decision not to create credit is regarded as a specific act of policy equivalent to a decision to raise interest rates, it follows that the termination of a 'flow' deficit requires a deliberate change of economic policy. Further, a 'flow' deficit may imply a worsening of the country's capital position, providing an economic as well as a monetary incentive to terminate the disequilibrium.

In analysing the policy problems posed by 'flow' deficits, it is convenient to begin by abstracting altogether from international capital movements (other than reserve transactions between foreign exchange authorities) and considering the case of a current account deficit. In this case, if intermediate transactions are excluded, the balance of payments becomes the difference between the value of the country's output (its national income) and its total expenditure, i.e.

$$B = Y - E.$$

To facilitate analysis by avoiding certain complications associated with the possibility of changes in the domestic price level, income and expenditure are conceived of as being valued in units of domestic output. A deficit then consists in an excess of real expenditure over real income, and the problem of correcting a deficit is to bring real national income (output) and real national expenditure into equality.

This formulation suggests that policies for correcting current-account deficits can be classified broadly into two types: those which aim at (or rely on) increasing output, and those which aim at reducing expenditure. The distinction must, of course, relate to the initial impact of the policy, since income and expenditure are interdependent: expenditure depends on and varies with income, and income depends on and varies with expenditure (because part of expenditure is devoted to home-produced goods). Consequently any change in either income or expenditure will initiate multiplier changes in both. It can, however, readily be shown that, so long as an increase in income induces a smaller change in aggregate expenditure, the multiplier repercussions will not be large enough to offset the impact effect of a change, so that an impact increase in output or decrease in expenditure will always improve the balance on current account.[5]

The distinction between output-increasing and expenditure-reducing policies may usefully be put in another way. Since output is governed by the demand for it, a change in output can only be brought about by a change in the demand for it; a policy of increasing domestic output can only be effected by operating on expenditure (either foreign or domestic) on that output. Given the level of expenditure, this in turn involves effecting a switch of expenditure (by residents and foreigners) from foreign output to domestic output. The distinction between output-increasing and expenditure-decreasing policies, which rests on the *effects* of the policies, may therefore be replaced by a distinction between expenditure-switching policies and expenditure-reducing policies, which rests on the *method* by which the effects are achieved.

A policy of expenditure-reduction may be applied through a variety of means—monetary restriction, budgetary policy, or even a sufficiently comprehensive battery of direct controls. Since any such policy will tend to reduce income and employment, it will have an additional attraction if the country is suffering from inflationary pressure as well as a balance-of-payments deficit, but a corresponding disadvantage if the country is suffering from unemployment. Moreover, since the impact reduction in expenditure and the

---

[5] Differentiating the equation in the text, we obtain $dB = (1-e)dY + dE$, where e is the marginal propensity to spend out of income, dY is the total *increase* in output (including multiplier effects) and dE is the autonomous *decrease* in expenditure. If multiplier effects through foreign incomes are ignored,

$$dY = \frac{1}{1-e(1-m)} dA,$$

where dA is an autonomous change in demand for domestic output and m is the proportion of marginal expenditure leaking into imports. Splitting dA into two components, dO for output-increasing policies and $-hdE$ for expenditure-reducing policies (where h is the proportion of expenditure reduction falling on domestic output), gives the result

$$dB = \frac{1-e}{1-e+em} dO + \left(1 - \frac{(1-e)h}{1-e+em}\right) dE.$$

Hence either an output-increasing or an expenditure-reducing policy will improve the balance, so long as e is less than unity. (Alexander has argued that since e includes induced investment it may well exceed unity; this possibility is ignored in the argument of the text.) Expenditure reduction will in fact improve the balance so long as multiplier stability is present.

total reduction in income and output required to correct a given deficit are larger, the larger the proportion of the expenditure reduction falling on home-produced goods, and since different methods of expenditure-reduction may differ in this respect, the choice between alternative methods may depend on the inflationary-deflationary situation of the economy. Finally, since the accompanying reduction in income may lead to some reduction in the domestic price level, and/or a greater eagerness of domestic producers to compete with foreign producers both at home and abroad, expenditure-reducing policies may have incidental expenditure-switching effects.

Expenditure-switching policies may be divided into two types, according to whether the policy instrument employed is general or selective: devaluation (which may be taken to include the case of a deflation-induced reduction of the domestic price level under fixed exchange rates), and trade controls (including both tariffs and subsidies and quantitative restrictions). Devaluation aims at switching both domestic and foreign expenditure towards domestic output; controls are usually imposed on imports, and aim at (or have the effect of) switching domestic expenditure away from imports towards home goods, though sometimes they are used to stimulate exports and aim at switching foreigners' expenditure towards domestic output.

Both types of expenditure-switching policy may have direct impact-effects on residents' expenditure. Devaluation may result in increased expenditure from the initial income level, through the so-called 'terms-of-trade effect' of an adverse terms-of-trade movement in reducing real income and therefore the proportion of income saved. Trade controls will tend to have the same effect, *via* the reduction in real income resulting from constriction of freedom of choice.[6] In addition, trade controls must alter the real expenditure corresponding to the initial output level if they take the form of import duties or export subsidies uncompensated by other fiscal changes; this case should, however, be classed as a combined policy of expenditure-change (unfavourable in the case of the export subsidy) and expenditure-switch.

Whether general or selective in nature, an expenditure-switching policy seeks to correct a deficit by switching demand away from foreign towards

---

[6] These arguments conflict with the assumption, more frequently made in connection with trade controls than with devaluation, that the public will consume less because it cannot obtain the goods it prefers as readily as before. That assumption may well be valid in the case of a policy expected to be applied for a short period only, after which goods will become as available as before, or in the analysis of the short run during which the economy is adjusting to the change in policy; but it is invalid in the present context of flow disequilibrium, since it overlooks the effect of the policy change in reducing the future value of savings and hence the incentive to save. An example of this type of faulty reasoning is the assertion sometimes made that quantitative import restriction is particularly effective in under-developed countries because their economic structure allows little possibility of substitution for imported goods in either production or consumption.

One qualification to the argument of the text, which also applies to the final sentence of the paragraph, is that if the goods towards which domestic expenditure is switched are more heavily taxed than those from which expenditure is diverted (a type of complication which is ignored in the general argument of the text), real expenditure may fall rather than rise.

domestic goods; and it depends for success not only on switching demand in the right direction, but also on the capacity of the economy to make available the extra output required to satisfy the additional demand. Such policies therefore pose two problems for economic analysis: the conditions required for expenditure to be switched in the desired direction, and the source of the additional output required to meet the additional demand.

As to the first question, the possibilities of failure for both devaluation and controls have been investigated at length by international trade theorists, and require only summary treatment here. Export promotion will divert foreign expenditure away from the country's output if the foreign demand is inelastic, while import restriction will divert expenditure abroad if demand for imports is inelastic and the technique of restriction allows the foreigner the benefit of the increased value of imports to domestic consumers. Devaluation has the partial effect of diverting domestic expenditure abroad, *via* the increased cost of the initial volume of imports, and this adverse switch will not be offset by the favourable effect of substitution of domestic for foreign goods at home and abroad, if import demand elasticities average less than one half.

While the elasticity requirement for successful devaluation just cited is familiar, the approach developed in this paper throws additional light on what non-fulfilment of the requirement implies. From the equation $B = Y - E$, it is clear that, if direct effects on expenditure from the initial income level are neglected, devaluation can worsen the balance only if it reduces total world demand for the country's output. This implies that the country's output is in a sense a 'Giffen case' in world consumption; and that the market for at least one of the commodities it produces is in unstable equilibrium. Neither of these ways of stating the conditions for exchange instability makes the possibility of instability as plausible *a priori* as their equivalent, reached through sectoral analysis, in terms of elasticities of import demand.

The second, and more interesting, analytical problem relates to the source of the additional domestic output required to satisfy the demand for it created by the expenditure-switching policy. Here it is necessary to distinguish two cases, that in which the economy is under-employed and that in which it is fully employed, for both the relevant technique of analysis and the factors on which the outcome of the policy depend differ between the two.

If the economy has unemployed resources available, the additional output required to meet the additional demand can be provided by the re-absorption of these resources into employment: in this case the switch policy has the additional attraction of increasing employment and income. The increase in domestic output may tend to raise the domestic price level, through the operation of increasing marginal real costs of production, and conversely the foreign price level may tend to fall, thus partially counteracting the initial effects of the switch policy; but such repercussions can legitimately be analysed in terms of elasticity concepts, since under-employment implies that additional factors are available at the ruling price.

If the economy is already fully employed, however, the additional output required cannot be provided by increasing production; it can only be provided through a reduction in the previous level of real expenditure. This reduction may be brought about either by a deliberate expenditure-reducing policy introduced along with the switch policy, or by the inflationary consequences of the switch policy itself in the assumed full-employment conditions.

If the increased output is provided by a deliberate expenditure-reducing policy, the nature of this policy will obviously influence the effects of the expenditure-switching policy, since the composition of the output it releases may be more or less substitutable for foreign output in world demand. Thus, for example, an expenditure-reducing policy which reduces domestic demand for imports and exportable goods will be more favourable to expenditure-switching than one which reduces domestic demand for non-traded goods. The analysis of the effects of an expenditure-switching policy supported by an expenditure-reducing policy must therefore comprise the effects of the latter in determining the composition of the productive capacity available to meet the increased demand created by the former, as well as the elasticity relations which govern the effects of the interaction of increased demand with increased production capacity on the prices and volumes of goods traded.

If the expenditure-switching policy is not accompanied by an expenditure-reducing policy, its effect will be to create an inflationary excess of aggregate demand over supply, leading to price increases tending to counteract the policy's expenditure-switching effects. Inflation, however, may work towards curing the deficit, through various effects tending to reduce the level of real expenditure from the full employment level of output. These effects, which are familiar and have been analysed in detail by Alexander, include the effect of high marginal tax rates in increasing the proportion of real income absorbed by taxation as wages and prices rise, the possibility of a swing to profits increasing the proportion of income saved, and the effect of rising prices in reducing the real purchasing power of cash and government bonds held by the public, so reducing their wealth and propensity to consume. All of these effects, it may be noted, depend on particular asymmetries in the reactions of the sectors affected to the redistributive effects of inflation on real income or wealth, which may not in fact be present. The important point, however, is that these factors, on which the success of an expenditure-switching policy depends in this case, are monetary factors, and that the analysis required employs monetary concepts rather than elasticity concepts. As in the previous case, the elasticity factors are subordinate to the factors governing the reduction in aggregate real expenditure, in determining the consequences of the expenditure-switching policy for the balance of payments.

The argument of the previous paragraph—that in full employment conditions the success of expenditure-switching policies depends mainly on the effectiveness of the consequent inflation in reducing real expenditure—helps to explain both the prevalence of scepticism about, and hostility towards, exchange rate adjustment as a means of curing balance-of-payments disequilibria, and the fact that historical experience can be adduced in support of the proposition that devaluation is a doubtful remedy. The argument does not, however, support the conclusion frequently drawn from the analysis of devaluation in these circumstances, that import restrictions are to be preferred; this is a *non sequitur*, since import restrictions are equally an expenditure-switching policy. Rather, the proper conclusion is that expenditure-switching policies are inappropriate to full employment conditions, except when used in conjunction with an expenditure-reducing policy as a means of correcting the employment-reducing effects of the latter.

But what of the choice between devaluation and selective trade controls, to which reference has just been made? So far, it has not been necessary to distinguish between them, since from the point of view of the balance of payments both can be treated as expenditure-switching policies. It is from the point of view of economic welfare that they differ; and the arguments on their relative merits have nothing to do with the state of the balance of payments, except that if controls are preferable a deficit may offer an opportunity for introducing them with less risk of foreign retaliation than if trade were balanced.

The welfare arguments for controls on a country's international trade may be divided into two groups, those centring on controls as a means of influencing the internal distribution of real income, by discouraging imports consumed by the rich and encouraging those consumed by the poor, and those centring on controls as a means of increasing the country's gains from trade through exploiting its monopoly/monopsony power in foreign markets. The former are of doubtful validity, both because the ethics of disguising a real income policy as a trade policy are suspect, and because both the efficiency and the effectiveness of trade controls as instruments for governing real income distribution are dubious. The latter are valid, to the extent that the country has powers to exploit the foreigner and can use them without provoking sufficient retaliation to nullify the gains.

This is the familiar optimum tariff argument. Its application to balance-of-payments policy depends on the level of trade restrictions already in force, as compared with the optimum level of restrictions. If an expenditure-switching policy is required to correct a deficit, and the level of trade restrictions is below the optimum, restriction is preferable to devaluation until the optimum level is reached; in the opposite case, devaluation is preferable. But it is the relation of actual to optimum restrictions, and not the state of the trade balance, which determines whether restriction is desirable or not.

This concludes the analysis of alternative policies for correcting a 'flow' balance-of-payments deficit on current account. To complete the analysis of 'flow' disequilibria, it would be necessary to relax the assumption that international capital movements are confined to reserve movements between foreign exchange authorities, and to consider alternative policies for correcting a deficit on current and capital account combined. The central problem in this case is to determine the level of current account surplus or deficit, capital export or import, at which economic policy should aim. This raises two further problems too difficult to pursue here: the optimum rate of accumulation of capital for the community as a whole, and the degree to which it is desirable to discriminate in favour of investment at home and against investment abroad.

In conclusion, the argument of this chapter may be summarized as follows: formulation of the balance of payments as the difference between aggregate receipts and payments, rather than receipts and payments on international account only, has two major advantages. It brings out the essentially monetary nature of a deficit, which must be accompanied by dishoarding of domestic money or credit creation; and it relates the deficit to the operation of the economy as a whole. A deficit may reflect a 'stock' decision or a 'flow' decision by the community. The conditions which make a 'stock' deficit a policy problem indicate the use of direct control methods as against price system methods of correction. Policies for dealing with 'flow' deficits on current account may be divided into expenditure-reducing and expenditure-switching policies; in full employment conditions the latter must be supported by the former, or rely on inflation for their effect, which in either case cannot be analysed adequately in terms of elasticities. When capital account transactions are introduced into the analysis, the choice between policy alternatives requires reference to growth considerations not readily susceptible to economic analysis.

10.5 Pitfalls in Contracyclical Policy*

It is not generally recognized by economists that where governmental contracyclical policies are concerned common sense is a particularly dangerous tool. Policies—automatic or not—which appear to be properly designed may very well turn out to aggravate fluctuations. Miscalculations on delicate questions of timing or magnitudes can be crucial, and these matters may well be out of the range of competence of the good judgment and experience of most of the practical men who determine or advise on our monetary and fiscal policies.

This article describes tools which can be used to deal with at least some simple variants of these problems. Such tools can be particularly useful in

* From W. J. Baumol, 'Pitfalls in Contracyclical Policy: Some Tools and Results', *Review of Economics and Statistics*, 1961. Harvard University.

indicating the nature of the pitfalls in the area. In particular, I will describe two rather plausible types of contracyclical fiscal policy and show that they can lead to some rather surprizing results.

1. THE MODEL AND SOME CONTRACYCLICAL POLICIES

The discussion assumes that we are living in the world of the Samuelson accelerator-multiplier model. It will be recalled that the time path of national income, Y_t, in that model is described by the second-order linear difference equation:

$$Y_t = \text{consumption} + \text{acceleration investment} + \text{autonomous investment} + \text{net government outlay}$$

$$= kY_{t-1} + c(Y_{t-1} - Y_{t-2}) + A + G_t$$

where k is the marginal propensity to consume and c is the 'relation' of the acceleration principle. In other words, we have:

$$Y_t - (k+c)Y_{t-1} + cY_{t-2} - A - G_t = 0 \tag{1}$$

or, writing $b = -(k+c)$,

$$Y_t + bY_{t-1} + cY_{t-2} - A - G_t = 0. \tag{2}$$

In employing this model I am, as is so often done, ignoring important monetary phenomena, such as changes in interest rates and the real balance effect. However, I do not believe that this materially affects my conclusions.

Let us now suppose that the government determines to regulate its net outlays, G_t, in a way which reduces the severity of the cycle in income generated by (2). Let us consider several posibilities.

(a) A policy to offset income trends

Suppose the government decides to offset income trends by deficit spending ($G_t > 0$) when income has just been falling $[(Y_{t-1} - Y_{t-2}) < 0]$ and by collecting a budget surplus when income has been rising, and that the magnitude of this action is proportioned to the size of the change in income. This policy, which is designed to offset income trends, is described algebraically by:

$$G_{t,1} = -a(Y_{t-1} - Y_{t-2}) \tag{3.1}$$

where a is a positive constant.

Substituting from (3.1) into (2) and collecting terms we obtain:

$$Y_t + (b+a)Y_{t-1} + (c-a)Y_{t-2} - A = 0. \tag{2.1}$$

(b) A policy to adjust income levels

Suppose the government determines always to compensate for the difference between effective demand, Y, and some desired (near full employment) level, E. That is, it seeks to move effective demand toward the full employment level. If there is no lag in government response this yields:

$$G_{t,2} = w(E - Y_t) \tag{3.2}$$

where w is some positive constant. If there are one- and two-period delays in government reactions we have, respectively:

$$G_{t,3} = w(E - Y_{t-1}) \tag{3.3}$$

and

$$G_{t,4} = w(E - Y_{t-2}). \tag{3.4}$$

Substituting these expressions into (2), our basic income equation, we obtain respectively for the zero, one-period, and two-period lag cases:

$$Y_t + \left(\frac{b}{1+w}\right)Y_{t-1} + \left(\frac{c}{1+w}\right)Y_{t-2} - \frac{A+wE}{1+w} = 0 \tag{2.2}$$

$$Y_t + (b+w)Y_{t-1} + cY_{t-2} - A - wE = 0 \tag{2.3}$$

and

$$Y_t + bY_{t-1} + (c+w)Y_{t-2} - A - wE = 0. \tag{2.4}$$

It should be noted that equations (2.1)–(2.4) may be considered to approximate the much-discussed built-in stabilizers in our economy. For example, the fact that the government surplus tends automatically to rise (the deficit to fall) because tax payments as a proportion of income automatically go up when money incomes rise, and fall when money incomes decline, can be expressed by these relationships. Thus our analysis of (2.1)–(2.4) should shed some light on the contribution which these automatic stabilizers really make.

2. ANALYTIC TOOLS: ISO-STABILITY CURVES

Let us now develop some tools to help us analyze the effects of these policies on the stability of our model's behavior.

In Figure 10.4 the axes represent the coefficients, b and c, of the difference equation:

$$Y_t + bY_{t-1} + cY_{t-2} + r = 0.$$

Ignoring the nonhomogeneous term, r, every such equation can thus be represented by some point in the diagram and vice versa.

Triangle UVW is the locus of all points representing difference equations whose characteristic root of largest absolute value is of modulus unity.[1] Hence, these are the equations on the borderline between damping and explosion, i.e., stability and instability. The smaller triangles nested within UVW represent equations with stable solutions; the smaller the triangle, the smaller the absolute value of its dominant root and hence the less explosive

---

[1] In particular, UV represents complex root equations, WU represents equations with dominant unit root, and WV equations with dominant root $= -1$.

its time path. Similarly, the larger triangles outside UVW represent equations with unstable solutions; the larger the triangle, the larger the modulus of the dominant root. These triangles, then, constitute the family of second-order difference equation iso-stability curves. It is clear that any change in the coefficients of a difference equation which is represented by a move in the direction of the origin must represent an increase in stability. In particular,

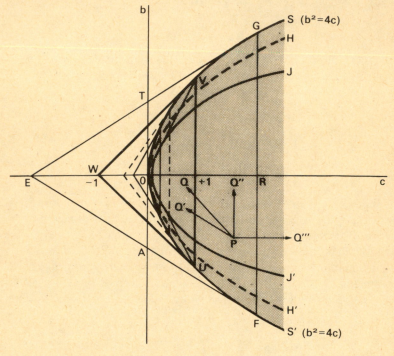

FIG. 10.4

stability must be increased by any leftward move inside the region bounded by the parabola SOS' (marked $b^2 = 4c$).

3. ISO-FREQUENCY CURVES: DIFFERENCE EQUATIONS

Parabola SOS' is the locus of all points which represent equations with multiple characteristic roots. All points inside this parabola involve complex roots and, hence, fluctuations. The family of iso-frequency curves, i.e., the loci of equations all of which yield a time path involving cycles of the same duration, must all lie within this shaded region. These iso-frequency curves are the parabolas such as HOH' and JOJ' which lie in this region. All of them are tangent to the b axis at the origin of the diagram, and they satisfy the equations $b^2 = 4k^2c$, where k is a number between zero and unity.[2]

[2] More specifically, if a cycle is of duration $2\pi/\theta$, we have $k = \cos\theta$.

In particular, the portion of the horizontal axis which lies to the right of the origin represents all equations whose cycles are four periods long. Points below the c axis represent cycles which are less frequent than this, up to the limiting case of lower arc OS' of the outermost parabola, $b^2 = 4c$. As we approach this arc the cycles become longer and longer, without limit, and their frequency approaches zero. Similarly, moving in the upward direction, we go toward arc OS and cycles whose length approaches two periods.[3]

In sum, any downward move within the shaded complex roots region reduces the frequency of cycles and is, in that sense, stabilizing.

4. EVALUATION OF STABILIZING POLICIES

The preceding diagrams now permit a simple and quick analysis of the stabilization effects of the policies which were described in the first section.

First let us look at the trend-offsetting policy (3.1). For this purpose we compare (2.1), the income difference equation in the presence of such a policy, with equation (2), in which G is now taken to be a constant. We note that in (2) the first coefficient, $b = -(k+c)$, is negative, and the second coefficient, c, is positive. Hence this equation is represented by a point in the south east quadrant of Figure 10.4. I assume also that (2) generates a cyclical time path so that it must be represented by a point, say P, within the lower half of the area bounded by the parabola $b^2 = 4c$.

Now, in the equation (2.1), coefficient b has been increased to $(b+a)$, and c has been decreased to $(c-a)$.[4] This means, in terms of Figure 10.4, that the point representing our difference equation has moved upward and to the left by the same amount, a. It has moved from P to, say, Q. The leftward move is, as we have seen, definitely stabilizing; any such move must increase the rate of damping of the cycle. But the upward move is very likely to involve an increase in frequency—that is, we are now likely to have more cycles in any given period of time than we would have in the absence of the trend-setting policy. Thus, such a measure may well turn out to be a mixed blessing.[5]

Let us see if our other policy alternative will do better. First comparing

[3] In the case of a difference equation it should be noted that a cycle less than two periods long is meaningless, since such an equation refers only to values of the variables at discrete points in time—one value per period—and since a cycle must have at least a high point and a low point, it must take on at least two such values, that is, it must occupy at least two time periods.

[4] This discussion ignores the effect of the various policy measures on the equilibrium income level via changes in the constant term of the equation. It is easy to add a constant amount of government expenditure to each of the policy equations to offset any effect on this constant term.

[5] It will be noted that nothing is being said about the effect of these policies on the amplitude of the cycle in the short run. That is because this amplitude in a linear model is so much a matter of initial conditions. It is, at any rate, possible to show that the policies cannot be depended upon to reduce cycle amplitude except through their effects on dampening of oscillations. In the long run, of course, a more damped time path will eventually have a smaller amplitude.

(2.2), our income equation in the case of a policy with zero lag in income adjustment, with the basic equation (2), we see that both b and c have been decreased in absolute value by the same proportion, $1/(1+w)$. That is, b will have been *increased* from its initial negative value whereas c will have fallen. The net result will thus be similar to that of the trend-offsetting policy, a north westward move in Figure 10.4—increased damping but more frequent cycles. Only in this case, the unfortunate increase in cycle frequency will *always* result, despite the zero lag in government response!

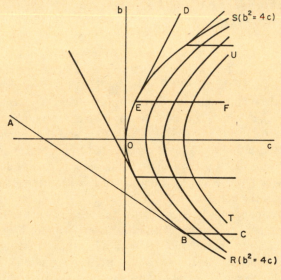

Fig. 10.5

In practice, of course, there are likely to be lags in government response to changes in economic data. As we shall now see, this is only likely to make things worse. Comparing (2.3) with (2) we see that a one-period lag in an income adjustment policy results in a rise in b to $(b+w)$ and no change in c. There is thus a move due north from P to Q'' in the point representing our equation in Figure 10.5—the policy now serves only to increase frequency of fluctuations without any compensating increase in cycle damping such as accompanies the two measures which we examined previously!

A two-period lag can perhaps be considered as making things worse still. For it leaves b unchanged and *increases* c to $(c+w)$. The net result is a move directly to the right in Figure 10.4 from P to Q'''. There is an increase in explosiveness of the cycle and no change in frequency!

5. CONCLUSION

The results of this discussion may reasonably be considered somewhat frightening. Plausible and reasonable contracyclical policies turn out to be capable of increasing the explosiveness and frequency of economic fluctuations. In fact, none of the possibilities examined proved to be entirely harmless in these respects, even in the highly simplified world of the multiplier-accelerator model. There would, therefore, seem to be little ground for confidence in such measures in the far more complex and unpredictable world of reality.

This, of course, is not meant to imply that good automatic stabilizers cannot be invented.[6] The relatively crude model and blunt tools of this article can be of little help in designing such policies, but it is certainly easy to argue, in principle, that effective stabilizers can be found. What the analysis does show clearly is that the design of an automatic stabilization policy is a dangerous game which requires careful calculation and testing. Certainly it is not a game for amateurs, not even those whose mathematical skill is considerable or those whose good common sense and workaday knowledge of monetary and fiscal institutions has in so many other ways been invaluable to the community.

[6] But common sense remains a dangerous ally. In the present model, for example, a good stabilization policy is one which has effects opposite from those of (3.4), i.e., it moves us directly leftward from a point like Q''' in the direction of P in Figure 10.4. But such a policy $[G_t = -w(E - Y_{t-2})]$ calls for a government deficit exactly two periods after every inflationary occurrence (and the reverse in the wake of periods of depression) no matter what the length of the cycle, and even if the inflationary pressure has not yet disappeared!

11. Econometric Models of the Economy

Introductory Note

In much of the macroeconomic theory with which previous chapters have dealt, a great deal depends on the numerical values which various parameters—the propensity to consume, the capital/output ratio, the interest-elasticity of investment, and so on—actually take. Estimates of these values can, given adequate appropriate data, be obtained by statistical analysis—notably, but not exclusively, the techniques of regression and correlation, and other methods of econometrics. In recent years, there has been an increasing number of attempts to use these techniques in the construction of complete macroeconomic models of the economy in which all the equations have estimated numerical values for the parameters. Such models serve two main purposes. They may be used for the analysis of the dynamic behaviour of the economy—to attempt to discover, for example, whether there is an inherent tendency towards cycles, or how powerful are the effects of changes in the money supply. Alternatively, they may be designed to forecast future changes in the economy as a guide to policy action by the authorities or as an aid to industrial investment planning, etc. In principle, there is no reason why models designed for these two purposes should differ in their structure, but in practice forecasting models are often constructed so as to allow for the incorporation of unquantifiable information—for example, surveys of the state of business confidence—which a purely analytic model cannot include. Nevertheless, the general principles of construction are common to both kinds of macroeconomic model.

Reading 11.1 describes the construction of a relatively small model of the U.K. economy designed for short-term forecasting purposes. The model is primarily demand-oriented: possible supply, or 'productive potential', is taken as given by the projection of past trend rates of growth of productive capacity. This reflects the short-run character of the model, which is a consequence of its use in planning counter-cyclical rather than long-run policy, and it means that the model casts no light on the factors governing the long-run rate of economic growth. Of the components of real national income, public current and capital expenditure and exports are treated as autonomous expenditure, and fixed investment (in the formal model described on pp. 493–4) is also determined outside the system. The endogenous types of expenditure are consumers' expenditure, investment in stocks (inventory accumulation), imports, and indirect taxes.

Of the functions underlying the behaviour of these expenditures, only the consumption function is substantially more complex than in a simple textbook macroeconomic model. There are six distinct stages in relating consumers' expenditure to national income in real terms:

(1) the distribution of income between sectors—income from employment to the personal sector, profits to the company sector, and so on;

(2) transfers from other sectors to the personal sector—transfer payments from the public sector and dividends from the company sector, for instance;

(3) payments of direct taxes;

(4) conversion of money into real income;

(5) allowance for monetary factors—especially changes in the availability of credit;

(6) the consumption function relating consumers' expenditure to real disposable income and credit.

Thus a number of areas of macroeconomics—notably the distribution of income and the analysis of price changes—are covered by the model not simply because of their intrinsic interest but also as necessary stages in accounting for the behaviour of consumption.

The remaining functional equations are straightforward: inventory investment is governed by a simple stock-adjustment model, modified to allow for unexpected changes in demand; imports are a function of total final expenditure with a special allowance being made for changes in inventories (which contain a large element of imported raw materials etc.); and indirect taxes are related to consumers' expenditure, on which they are almost exclusively levied.

The formal model is set out on pp. 493–4. Equations (1)–(3) determine the major components of personal income, while (4) and (5) are direct tax functions. Equation (6) is the consumption function, which excludes durable goods, (7) is a mark-up price equation for prices excluding indirect taxes—costs comprise unit labour costs (wages and salaries per unit of GDP) and import prices. Equations (9) and (10) are the stockbuilding 'flexible accelerator' and the import function. Equations (11)–(17) are identities. Some are national accounting identities, for example (15) and (17), while others incorporate behavioural hypotheses—(11) adds indirect taxes into the consumer price index, and (12) gives current transfers from the public sector a special weight in disposable income.

The remainder of Reading 11.1 describes very briefly both the use of such a model in producing forecasts and the exploration of its dynamic properties. In principle, the forecasting process is straightforward. Given forecast paths for the exogenous variables—public expenditure, exports, and so on—solution of the model will generate paths for the endogenous variables which will both obey the specified behavioural relationships and satisfy the national accounting and other identities. In practice, however, the model represents only a very simplified summary of how the highly complex real economy has behaved in the past and can be expected to behave in the future. Each behavioural relationship reflects only the most obvious influences on the dependent variable and, in forecasting, knowledge of likely future influences on the variable other than those specified in the equation will frequently need to be incorporated. Formally, this can be done by modifying any of the functional relationships by means of an adjustment term, or 'disturbance' at the discretion of the forecaster.[1] This has the important implication that, in assessing past forecasts made with the help of an econometric model, errors may reflect not only possible faults in the model, but also the judgements and guesses of its user.

The second use of macroeconometric models is in analysing the dynamic behaviour of the economy. This is most commonly done by means of the technique of simulation. The procedure is as follows. The model is first solved for given paths of the exogenous variables. One of these variables is then altered—government expenditure, or one of the parameters of the tax functions, for example, if the impact of fiscal policy is being explored—and the model solved again. The differences between the two solutions reflect the impact of the change in the exogenous variable. Attention is generally focused on the differences between the paths of GDP. In the first time period, the ratio of the change in GDP to the change in the exogenous variable—say government spending—gives the *impact multiplier*. If the change in government spending is maintained, the operation of the multiplier and accelerator will produce further changes in GDP over time. These changes may well be cyclical, and may be either damped or explosive. If they are damped, the change in GDP will ultimately settle down; the ratio of the ultimate change in GDP to the initial change in government spending is called the dynamic multiplier. Thus the N.I.E.S.R. model produces an impact multiplier for government spending on current account of $1 \cdot 13 (= 79 \times 1 \cdot 43/100)$; there is a very muted cycle, and the dynamic multiplier is $1 \cdot 10$. These low multipliers and the very damped cycle probably reflect the very high import and tax leakages in the British economy, and the absence from the model of a fixed investment function.

Fromm and Taubman [Reading 11.2] describe analogous experiments with a much larger model of the U.S. economy, the Brookings Quarterly Econometric Model. Not only is the model very much bigger—it contains some 150 behavioural equations—it is also more complete than the N.I.E.S.R. model in that it contains behavioural equations for fixed investment and a set of equations relating the monetary and real sectors (though the latter links are found to be relatively weak). After a brief description of the Brookings model and its current evolution, Fromm and Taubman list six kinds of simulation experiments which could be conducted. These are: random disturbances in the equations, disturbances with certain specified charac-

---

[1] Note the formal similarity with 'Type II' shocks in the simulation studies described by Adelman and Adelman—Reading 11.3 and p. 481 below.

teristics (see further Reading 11.3 below), changes in numerical parameters, changes in starting conditions, changes in either exogenous or endogenous variables, and changes in policy parameters. It is changes of this kind which are of direct interest in examining the effects of fiscal policy, and Table 1 on p. 503 gives the quarterly dynamic multipliers for unit increases in government expenditure on durable goods, on nondurable goods, and on employment, and unit decreases in income tax and income tax coupled with sufficient expansion of the money supply to leave interest rates unaffected. The results may be briefly summarized: changes in government expenditure have a more powerful effect on the economy than changes in taxation, as might be expected; there is some evidence of a very highly damped cycle (the expenditure changes tend to produce peaks in early-1961 and again in mid-1962); final multipliers, while larger than in the U.K., are not very large; and there is evidence of a significant damping effect of monetary feedbacks (compare the penultimate and final rows).

These simulation studies are primarily designed to throw light on the response of the economy to policy initiatives: they do not directly throw light on the central question of trade-cycle analysis—is the structure of the economy such as to produce an endogenous cycle? Adelman and Adelman [Reading 11.3] examine this question using the 1955 Klein–Goldberger model of the U.S. economy. First, the model was solved using stable trend growth paths of the autonomous variables (pp. 506–7). This produced, after an initial settling-down period, essentially trend growth in the endogenous variables. This essentially non-cyclical result is confirmed by the analysis of the response to a marked shock in government expenditure (pp. 508–9). Although this produced one cycle, the system again settled down to equilibrium. It thus seems that, if the Klein–Goldberger model is at all a satisfactory model of the economy, there is no inherent tendency towards continuing or explosive cycles of the sort assumed by, for example, Hicks (see Chapter 6 above). There remains, however, one important further possibility. How does the model respond to continuous random disturbance? Such shocks can be of two kinds—random variation in the exogenous variables (Type I) and random disturbances in the endogenous variables (Type II). The economic meanings of these two kinds of disturbance are clear: Type I shocks, for example, might reflect the impact of fluctuations in world trade on exports, while Type II shocks to consumption, for instance, will reflect the fact that consumption may be affected by a variety of factors not included in the consumption/income relationship of the model—changes in credit, wealth, expectations, and so on. It was found that the introduction of Type I shocks alone produced cycles of about the observed frequency, but with unrealistically small amplitude, but Type II shocks produced much more realistic cycles. Adelman and Adelman suggest that the more realistic case in which both types of shock are present would similarly produce cycles of about the 'right' frequency and amplitude, and conclude that the explanation of business cycles in terms of the superimposition of shocks on an essentially damped structural model is consistent with the evidence.

Goldberger [Reading 11.4] analyses the behaviour of a slightly altered version of the same Klein–Goldberger model in a different fashion. It will be recalled from Chapter 6 that the simple multiplier-accelerator model of the cycle consists of three linear equations—the national income identity, the investment accelerator, and the consumption function:

$$Y_t = C_t + I_t$$
$$C_t = (1-s)Y_t$$
$$I_t = v(Y_{t-1} - Y_{t-2}),$$

from which

$$Y_t - \frac{v}{s} Y_{t-1} + \frac{v}{s} Y_{t-2} = 0.$$

This second-order linear difference equation has dynamic properties which can be inferred from the values of its characteristic roots, which in turn depend on the numerical values of v and s. The same method of analysis can be applied to much larger systems of linear difference equations, though of course the solutions are considerably more complex. This is the analytic method employed by Goldberger. The Klein–Goldberger model is first linearized, since the method can only be applied to sets of linear equations— indeed, this restriction is a substantial disadvantage of the analytic method as compared with the simulation method of investigating the dynamic properties of models. Goldberger finds (pp. 517–8) a rather low dynamic government expenditure multiplier (2.34), and a highly-damped oscillatory component producing a cycle of about 7 years' frequency. Thus the Goldberger results broadly confirm those of the Adelmans: the evidence is consistent with a theory of the business cycle which imposes continuous random shocks on a structure which, undisturbed, would display only very damped cyclical characteristics.

This conclusion must, however, be extremely tentative. There are enormous problems in the construction of macroeconometric models, many of which have yet to be overcome. Data are often available only for the relatively recent past, and are frequently unreliable. There are formidable statistical problems in the estimation of the parameters of such models, and in particular in the estimation of the lag structures, which are of course crucial for the dynamic behaviour of a model. Last but not least, there is very little agreement about the correct specification of such models—how to treat monetary/real interactions, the determinants of inflation, the degree of disaggregation required, and so on. The role of econometric models in testing macroeconomic theory is clearly of the greatest importance; equally clearly, there is still a very great deal to be learned.

11.1 A Simple Econometric Model of the British Economy*

The analytic framework to be described deals in broad aggregates, generally in an economy-wide sense: exports, investment, consumption, and so on, relate to the economy as a whole and not to individual sectors or industries. Each of these aggregates represents a set of demands on economic resources; their sum represents, at a given time, the total demand on resources, which is supplied from domestic production and from imports of goods and services produced overseas. The level of domestic production is, of course, a major determinant of the level of employment. The capacity of the economy to produce goods and services will grow over time as technical and managerial progress increase the productivity of given factor resources; it will also be affected by the rates of change of factor inputs—the supply of labour and the stock of capital. Actual output in relation to the level which would keep resources fully employed is often referred to, in general, as the 'pressure of demand'.[1] In general terms, and without the intention of begging questions to be raised later, the pressure of demand may be taken to affect unemployment, the overseas trade balance, the rate of inflation and other key policy variables. Output—gross domestic product (GDP)—is thus the central point of the whole framework.

Following the main lines of development of macroeconomics since the appearance of Keynes's *General Theory*, the model is essentially demand-oriented.[2] Since the main interest is in demands on real resources, GDP and its components are measured at constant rather than at current prices. Quarterly figures, corrected for purely seasonal variation, are used throughout.

The expenditure account in the national accounting system is the starting point for the process of building a model of the economy. Taking 1969 as an example, Table 1 shows the expenditure aggregates at constant (1963) prices, their relative sizes and their average rates of growth over the period 1958–69. It will be seen that over half of total final expenditure is accounted for by consumers' expenditure, while the remainder is made up, in roughly equal parts, by public consumption, exports and fixed investment. Stockbuilding is, in comparison, a very small proportion of final expenditure, but year-to-year *changes* in stockbuilding have been an important source of variations in the rate of growth of the total.

* From M. J. C. Surrey, *The Analysis and Forecasting of the British Economy* (London: National Institute of Economic and Social Research, 1971), chs. 1 and 8.

[1] The pressure of demand can be measured in several ways. Unemployment itself can be used as a simple proxy; some writers have used a measure which combines the levels of unemployment and of vacancies. A more complex measure is the ratio of actual output to productive potential or capacity. The simplest measure of all is the ratio of output to its trend growth path, though this of course assumes that full-employment output grows with a steady trend.

[2] This is not to imply that the model is fully 'Keynesian'. In particular, there is at present no full monetary sector.

Of the total of final expenditure, less than three-quarters is met from domestic production as GDP. Part of the remainder represents net indirect taxes and subsidies,[3] and nearly a fifth is met from imports.

Table 1. *Expenditure on the gross domestic product in 1969*[a]

	Value	Proportion of total final expenditure	Average annual growth rate, 1958–69
	£m.	%	%
Consumers' expenditure	22,629	52·2	2·6
Public authorities' current expenditure	5,800	13·4	2·2
Gross fixed investment	6,602	15·2	5·3
Exports of goods and services	8,055	18·6	4·6
equals: Total final sales	43,086	99·4	3·3
plus: Stockbuilding	276	0·6	
equals: Total final expenditure	43,362	100·0	3·3
less: Imports of goods and services	7,784	18·0	4·6
Adjustment to factor cost	4,252	9·8	3·6
equals: Gross domestic product (at factor cost)	31,326	72·2	3·0

Source: Central Statistical Office, *National Income and Expenditure, 1969*, HMSO, 1970.
[a] At 1963 prices.

As it stands, Table 1 shows simply one accounting identity. It also illustrates, however, part of the causal structure of a simple model of the economy. Other things being equal, a rise in consumption, or in exports, investment and so on, will raise the level of GDP, and a rise in imports will correspondingly lower it. But a large number of other causal links exist. Consumers'

[3] This needs some elaboration. Expenditures are most conveniently measured (and in all probability are economically determined) at market prices, that is inclusive of any indirect taxation associated with the goods and services in question. When price indices are used to convert current price expenditures to base-year prices, these expenditures are thus implicitly being revalued inclusive of indirect taxes at base-year rates. But this indirect tax content does not, of course, represent a claim on resources; the factor cost adjustment is the sum of such contents, which must be subtracted from the total demands to give the total claim on real resources. When the portion of this claim which is met from overseas—imports—is deducted, the remainder represents the volume of total domestic output, usually referred to as GDP at base-year factor cost. In the present system of national accounts, base-year prices are those of 1963.

expenditure, for example, is principally determined by consumers' real incomes, so that a model must include the personal sector's income account, together with personal taxation. Again, since incomes are determined as money flows and not in real terms, an element of price forecasting is needed in order to derive consumers' real incomes and hence their consumption. And since the balance of payments is presented in current price terms, explanations of the behaviour of import and export prices are required.

Many of these aspects involve causal links in the reverse direction from those immediately apparent from Table 1. For example, although a rise in consumption will increase GDP, this will in turn raise employment incomes and hence consumption. Links of this kind make the system as a whole one of interdependent variables.

It was pointed out earlier that there are substantial areas where economic knowledge is inadequate or not relevant to the present framework. The elements of the national income affected must therefore be treated as exogenously determined. Public sector demands, for instance, are principally the result of government expenditure decisions rather than of well-understood economic forces. These demands thus cannot be explained within the model but must be fed in as data from outside. In practice, this distinction between exogenous and endogenous elements becomes blurred; in a very aggregated macroeconomic model of the economy almost every element represents an heroic simplification of infinitely complex reality and the behaviour of each endogenous element must be regarded as determined not exclusively by the major influences presented in the behavioural relationships, but also by other influences which are omitted. In forecasting, it may be possible to guess at the likely effect of some of these influences and to introduce them as further 'exogenous' elements.[4]

A working distinction is drawn between the behaviour of the domestic economy, centred round the level of domestic activity and cast predominantly in real terms, and the relationship between the domestic economy and the world economy, summarized in the balance of payments where money flows are most important. These two aspects are of course interdependent; in particular the level of exports, making up one large element in the balance of payments account, is also a determinant of the level of GDP, while the level of demand in the domestic economy is one of the principal determinants of the level of imports, another major element in the balance of payments.

Turning first to the domestic economy, the three main broad expenditure aggregates taken as being given exogenously (in the sense used above) are exports of goods and services, public authorities' current expenditure and public authorities' gross fixed investment. Other elements are taken as endogenous: for example, imports are related to total final sales and stock-building, stockbuilding to GDP, consumption to GDP (via an elaboration

[4] This aspect of forecasting is discussed in detail in chapters 3 and 9 below.

of the personal sector's income and expenditure accounts in which various other exogenous elements intrude) and indirect taxes to consumption. The system as a whole is thus one of simultaneous determination requiring a technique of simultaneous or iterative solution.

For the past, when the model is used for descriptive and analytic purposes, the recorded levels of the exogenous elements are taken as data. In forecasting however, future levels must be predicted. *Exports of goods and services* are forecast with reference principally to the expected level and composition of world trade. Both total world trade and the share in it of British exports are complex to forecast. World trade is assumed to depend primarily on the rates of growth of output in different countries, so that output forecasts are needed for each of the major industrial countries, and a view has to be taken about likely economic conditions in the developed sterling area and the underdeveloped countries. Britain's share of world trade has fallen steadily but at a rate which has varied with the rate of growth of world trade. More formally, relationships have been developed between British exports of manufactures and industrial countries' output and imports, and between British exports to underdeveloped countries and those countries' financial position. These relationships were all in terms of the value of exports, and a forecast of export prices was needed to convert the value forecast into the constant-price terms needed in the analysis of the domestic economy. Export prices are assumed to be affected by changes in home and import costs and by world trade.

Information on *public authorities' current expenditure* comes from estimates published by the government either in the annual White Paper on public expenditure or (since 1968) from the official forecasts of the economy published by the Treasury in the budget-time Financial Statement. *Public fixed investment* comprises investment in dwellings and other investment by both public corporations (broadly, the nationalized industries) and public authorities (both central and local government). Non-dwelling investment is also forecast by the government in the annual public expenditure White Paper. Public sector investment in dwellings can be forecast in broad terms in the light of ministers' announced forward plans, but information on contractors' orders and on dwellings currently under construction can also be used to provide a partially formal relationship between announced programmes of dwellings to be started and actual investment.

Private sector fixed investment is determined partly exogenously. Private investment in dwellings is assumed to be influenced by personal incomes and savings, by the supply of mortgage funds from building societies and local authorities, and by the availability of bank credit to builders. There is in addition some direct evidence from builders' reported intentions, but, as with public sector dwelling investment, the forecast is made in a largely informal way and is again essentially an exogenous element. The remainder of the private sector's fixed investment constitutes a more endogenous element in the framework for analysis and forecasting. A very simple lagged accelerator relationship between the level of business investment[5] and past changes in GDP provides a fairly good explanation of the behaviour of investment in the past. Investment by manufacturing industry alone can be explained with considerable precision when it is related to the (calculated) degree of capacity utilization in the industry, as well as to changes in output. The direct surveys of investment intentions carried out by the government are a further source of information, which may be used to modify, or even supplant, the prediction based on the formal relationships.

Investment in stocks — or stockbuilding — is treated as a wholly endogenous variable. The presumption is that stock-holders wish to maintain a given ratio of stocks to output (a ratio which appears to have declined gradually over the past fifteen years) but that the quarter-to-quarter levels of stockbuilding will be erratic, both because of lags in the adjustment of actual to desired stock levels and because of involuntary changes in stock levels associated with sharp changes in demand and output. The assumption of a relationship between the levels of stock and of output is reasonable: stocks are held principally as a buffer to smooth out short-term dislocations between supply and demand in different parts of the economy. Stocks of raw materials and intermediate goods are held in connection with immediate production, and stocks of finished goods in connection with consumption (by both producers and final consumers). At the most aggregate level, both of these rise in line with total domestic production.

Consumers' expenditure is related, though not in any simple way, to real personal disposable income and to changes in consumer borrowing.[6] Real personal disposable income depends on total personal income, on tax payments and on consumer prices. The main component of personal incomes is the wage and salary bill, forming about 60 per cent of the pre-tax total. The wage and salary bill is the product of average earnings and employment, each of which depends principally, though in different ways, on the pressure of demand.

The rate of change of average earnings depends both on changes in negotiated standard wage rates, and on other factors reflected as changes in wage-drift — that is the tendency for average earnings to rise faster than wage rates. Both negotiated wage rates and wage-drift are influenced by the demand for labour, though with differing emphasis.[7] Changes in wage rates are the outcome of formal negotiations between unions and employers, often at a national level and affecting workers irrespective of region, industry or type of labour. At local level, although earnings are affected by changes in basic or standard negotiated rates, they also reflect circumstances peculiar to

---

[5] That is, investment by the private sector other than in dwellings.

[6] Taken together, personal disposable income and changes in borrowing are sometimes called 'personal disposable funds'.

[7] Specifically, the pressure of demand appears to affect wage-drift both more strongly and more immediately than it affects negotiated wage rates.

the industry, locality, type of firm and so on. These local differences show up through changes in productivity, overtime and profitability. Overall these factors are a stronger influence on wage-drift the higher (and the more rapidly increasing) is the pressure of demand for labour. Wage rates are also influenced by the increase in retail prices—the cost of living. [...]

Employment is normally determined by a short-term relationship with output. Actual employment adjusts with a lag to 'desired' employment, which is dependent on the level of output in relation to a productivity trend and to normal hours of work. The trend of growth in productivity is estimated by regression analysis and, in forecasting, extrapolated from recent experience. In this short-term framework, no attempt is made to relate productivity to the rate of capital accumulation.[8]

Total personal income also includes income from self-employment, income from rent and dividends, and net receipts of interest. These are included together as 'other personal income' in the official national income quarterly accounts, though an annual breakdown is available. However, the absence of quarterly figures for these components of personal income has, so far, inhibited a systematic attempt at an empirical investigation of their determinants. Informally, incomes from self-employment seem to move in sympathy with the movement in wages and salaries, dividend payments to depend (after a lag) on company profits, and the rent and interest elements to grow in a trend-like way.

Current grants to persons from public authorities are determined primarily exogenously, by government decisions on, for example, benefit rates, but in principle the volume of such transfers also depends on the levels of unemployment and earnings, which are themselves functions of the pressure of demand. The remainder of personal income forces' pay and employers' contributions to National Insurance and private pension funds. Again, these are treated as exogenous elements.

The main deduction to be made from personal income is income tax, which depends on tax rates and the level of incomes. In the aggregate, a distinction is made only between the marginal tax rates on wages and salaries and on other personal income, the latter being significantly higher than the former, largely because this distinction between types of income corresponds roughly with the distinction between earned and unearned income which is reflected in the tax system. Deductions have also to be made for net transfers of cash abroad and for National Insurance and similar contributions by employees, both of which are assumed to be exogenously determined.[9] The resulting aggregate is personal disposable income at current prices.

[8] Partly, of course, because there is no consensus on how such a link could be specified theoretically, but also for the practical reason that, in the short term, such effects on the rate of growth of productivity seem likely to be small.

[9] National Insurance contributions will in fact be sensitive to changes in unemployment and earnings. As a first approximation, it is assumed that this sensitivity is small enough to be neglected.

Consumer prices are assumed to be set on a cost-plus basis, that is by the addition of a fixed profit margin to the average unit costs of production, which comprise labour costs and import costs. Unit labour costs depend on earnings and on productivity; one of the major problems in analysing the behaviour of prices is to decide whether entrepreneurs take actual productivity or the trend in productivity into account in setting prices. Prices are, of course, also affected by changes in indirect tax rates—purchase tax, excise duties, SET and so on. Personal disposable income, adjusted for increases in prices, is referred to as real personal disposable income.

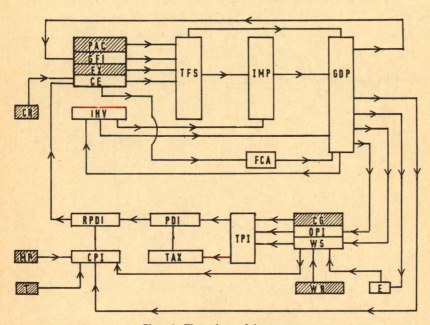

Chart 1. Flow chart of the economy

SYMBOLS: see p. 492. Shaded boxes contain exogenous variables (GFI is partly exogenous).
NOTE: The arrows indicate causal links and not simply quantitative flows.

Real personal disposable income is related to consumers' expenditure through the familiar consumption function. Incomes are disaggregated into income from current grants, disposable wages and salaries, and other disposable income, from each of which there are different marginal propensities to save. Current grants, accruing mainly to low-income families, lead to negligible savings; wages and salaries probably have a low, but not zero, savings propensity (empirically, about 8 per cent); while other personal income includes a much larger savings element (of the order of 20 to 25 per cent). Lags also differ: the consumption function is of a simple 'permanent income' type in which permanent income is a function of actual incomes for past periods with geometrically declining weights; the average lag is longer for other personal income than for wages and salaries or current grants. Special allowance has also to be made for the effect of changes in consumer credit. Such changes are very largely induced by changes in the regulations governing hire purchase transactions and by instructions or guidance given to the banks on personal overdrafts.

The *factor cost adjustment*, the indirect tax content of final expenditure at base-year tax rates, is in fact dependent almost wholly on consumers'

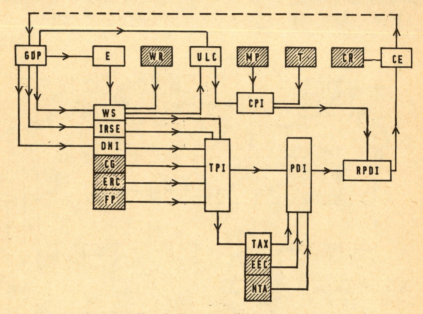

Chart 2. Flow chart of the personal sector

SYMBOLS: see p. 492. Shaded boxes contain exogenous variables.
NOTE: The arrows indicate causal links and not simply quantitative flows.

expenditure, since by comparison the indirect tax content of other kinds of final expenditure is negligible. Since constant (1963) tax rates are involved, a high degree of explanation is achieved by assuming a constant marginal ratio of factor cost adjustment to consumers' expenditure.

When these various forms of final expenditure—public authorities' current expenditure, fixed investment, exports, consumers' expenditure and stock-building—are added up, and the factor cost adjustment is deducted, the result is total final expenditure at factor cost. This is the total demand on resources which must be met either from domestic production or from imports. Since, in practice, it is assumed that the demand for imports is itself given by a simple relationship with total demand, it follows that it is now possible to deduce GDP or total domestic production as, essentially, a residual—that part of the final demand on resources which is not met from imports.

The relationship between total home demand and *imports of goods and*

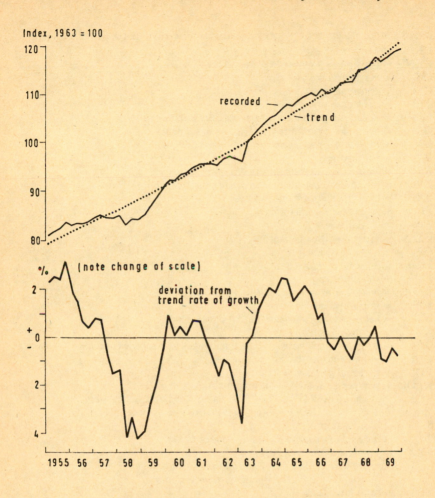

Chart 3. Output growth and output cycles

[a] Trend rate of growth of GDP = 2.87 per cent per annum compound.

services is a linear one, implying that the marginal propensity to import is constant. A distinction is drawn, however, between stockbuilding and the rest of final expenditure, since the import content of stocks is known to be much higher than the average import content of total final expenditure.

These main connections between the macroeconomic quantities are summarized in Charts 1 and 2. The first of these shows the main linkages for the economy as a whole, with the complex personal sector shown in an abbreviated form. The second shows the personal sector in more detail. Chart 3 shows the output cycles which the British economy has experienced since 1955.

SYMBOLS

(Italics indicate current prices; all other values are at constant prices.)

CE	= consumers' expenditure
CEND	= consumers' non-credit expenditure
CG	= *current grants to persons*
CPI	= consumer price index
CPI	= consumer price index
CPIFC	= consumer price index net of indirect tax content
CR	= *consumer credit* (hire purchase or bank debt)
DNI	= *income from dividends and net interest receipts*
E	= employment
EEC	= *employees' contributions to National Insurance*
ERC	= *employers' contributions to private superannuation schemes*
EX	= exports of goods and services
FCA	= adjustment to factor cost
FP	= *forces' pay*
GDP	= gross domestic product
GFI	= gross fixed investment
IMP	= imports of goods and services
INV	= stockbuilding
IRSE	= *income from rent and self-employment*
MP	= import prices
NI	= *net insurance contributions* (*ERC* less *EEC*)
NTA	= *net transfers abroad*
OPI	= *other personal income* (other than wages and salaries and current grants)
PAC	= public authorities' consumption
PDI	= personal disposable income
RPDI	= real personal disposable income
	made up of: RDW = real disposable wage and salary income
	RDO = other real disposable income
S	= level of stocks
T	= indirect tax component of consumer prices
TAX	= *personal income tax payments*
	made up of: *TAXWS = tax on wages and salaries*
	TAXO = tax on other incomes
TFS	= total final sales
TIM	= time
TPI	= *total personal income*
ULC	= *unit labour costs* (*WS*/GDP)
WR	= wage rates
WS	= *wage and salary bill*

The foregoing paragraphs have described the ways in which each of the aggregates making up the expenditure account of the national income is related to the rest and to other factors; this system of relationships as a whole was shown diagrammatically in the flow charts.[10] The system comprises a number of exogenous elements—exports, public expenditure, and so on—together with a simultaneously determined bloc in which, for example, consumers' expenditure as an element of demand influences GDP which, in

[10] See pp. 489, and 490.

turn, through the pressure of demand, affects incomes and prices and hence is a determinant of the level of consumers' expenditure.

If this system were wholly linear, it would comprise a number of simultaneous linear equations with, in general, a unique solution which could be found quite simply by solving the set in the familiar way. In fact, the system is non-linear in a number of important instances. This is ensured, for example, by the use of price indices, where the relation between value on the one hand and volume and price on the other is multiplicative, and by the inclusion of log-linear relationships. These non-linearities make the solution far more complex. Essentially, it is necessary to solve the system for given values of the exogenous variables by a process of successive approximation. A trial solution for GDP is taken, the values of the endogenous variables based on this trial value of GDP are calculated and the resulting GDP total compared with the initial trial value. On the basis of the discrepancy so revealed, a second trial value for GDP is taken and the process is repeated until consistency is achieved.

To perform the iterative procedure by hand can be extremely arduous, although until very recently there was no real alternative. But the accessibility of computer facilities makes it possible to solve the system in essentially the same fashion in a matter of seconds.

The somewhat blurred line between exogenously and endogenously determined elements has already been discussed. In the simplest form of the model there are eleven exogenous variables: exports, gross fixed investment and public authorities' consumption at constant prices; current grants to persons, forces' pay, net insurance contributions,[11] net transfers abroad and changes in hire purchase and bank debt at current prices; together with import prices, the indirect tax content of consumer prices, and time. These and the endogenous variables are interrelated either by behavioural relationships as described in earlier chapters, or by national income accounting or other identities, which can be shown schematically as follows:[12]

Behavioural equations

1. $IRSE$ $= f(GDP, IRSE_{-1})$
2. DNI $= f(GDP, DNI_{-1})$
3. WS $= f(GDP, WS_{-1}, \mathbf{TIM})$
4. $TAXWS = f(WS, \mathbf{TIM})$
5. $TAXO$ $= f(IRSE, DNI)$
6. CEND $= f(\mathbf{RDW}, \mathbf{RDO}, \text{CEND}_{-1})$
7. CPIFC $= f(WS, GDP, \mathbf{MP}, \text{CPIFC}_{-1})$
8. FCA $= f(\text{CE})$
9. S $= f(GDP, \text{TFS}, \text{FCA}, \text{S}_{-1})$
10. IMP $= f(\text{INV}, \text{TFS})$

[11] Employers' contributions to private pension schemes less employees' contributions to National Insurance, etc.

[12] With the standard notation (see p. 000), current-price values are in italics and exogenous variables are in bold type.

Identities

11. CPI $= \alpha\,\mathrm{CPIFC} + \beta T$
12. RDW $= (WS + FFP + NI + \gamma CG - TAXWS)/\mathrm{CPI}$
13. RDO $= (IRSE + DNI - NTA - TAXO)/\mathrm{CPI}$
14. CE $= \mathrm{CEND} + (\Delta CR)/\mathrm{CPI}$
15. TFS $= \mathrm{CE} + \mathbf{PAC} + \mathbf{GFI} + \mathbf{EX}$
16. INV $= S - S_{-1}$
17. GDP $= \mathrm{TFS} + \mathrm{INV} - \mathrm{IMP} - \mathrm{FCA}$

The formal model thus comprises ten behavioural equations and seven identities.

There is, however, an important complication. Each behavioural equation provides calculated values for the past which differ, quarter by quarter, from the actual values. These equation errors are presumed, statistically, to be distributed at random about a mean of zero. However, the reduction of enormously complex reality to a set of very simplified aggregate relationships necessarily means that discrepancies between actual and estimated values of a variable may not simply be random errors, produced for example by inaccurate recording of actual values, but may reflect the influences of other factors affecting the variable which have been left out of the specified relationship. This has important implications for the use of the model in forecasting. For it may be the case that such a factor, not included in the specified relationships, is expected to have a noticeable influence on the variable in the future. For example, it might be believed that the pursuit of a very stringent monetary policy (which did not operate in the past and whose effects thus cannot be objectively estimated by regression analysis) will cause stockbuilding to be lower in the future than would be expected from the behavioural relationship included in the model. In that case, the best forecast would be obtained by assuming that the future errors in the stockbuilding function will show random fluctuations not about a zero mean but about a negative mean. Since random fluctuations by their nature cannot be predicted, this implies making an exogenous adjustment to the relationship for the forecast period—in effect adjusting the intercept term and specifying different values for each quarter of the forecast.

The reasons for, and the shape of, such intercept adjustments will vary widely. The reasons for making an adjustment may range from the powerful and easily quantifiable assumption that exports delayed by a dock strike in the current quarter will be shipped out in the course of the next quarter with equal and opposite effects on stockbuilding, to a much vaguer belief about a relationship which has, say, underpredicted consumption over several recent quarters. In the latter case, where a gradual return to predicting correctly is assumed, the intercept adjustment required will return towards zero; if the assumption is that a constant underprediction will continue, the intercept adjustment will remain constant; if the underprediction is assumed to be growing, the rate of change being underpredicted, the intercept adjustment will grow over time.

In extreme cases, where a relationship has provided calculated values for the recent past which have diverged by a wide margin from the actual values, the relationship may have to be rejected altogether and an alternative explanatory hypothesis investigated. This has happened for example in the case of average earnings. In less extreme cases there may be room for a good deal of dispute as to why discrepancies have emerged and hence as to the intercept adjustment which should reasonably be made for the future. The paradigm case is that in which a new factor is thought to be influencing a relationship: there is, since the influence is a new one, no means of measuring its effect over the past. For example, wages and salaries have been rising more rapidly in the very recent past than would have been expected from established relationships with the pressure of demand. Possible new influences include the abnormal rise in consumer prices induced by the effect of devaluation on the prices of imported goods and the additional indirect taxation imposed as part of the devaluation strategy, reaction to the ending of incomes policy, and awareness by negotiators of inflation as a continuing aspect of the environment. Which hypothesis is believed will have an important influence on the intercept adjustment to be projected. The reaction to the devaluation-induced price rise will be a once-for-all effect, with earnings returning to a more normal rate of increase in time, though at a higher level than would otherwise have been expected. Adjustment to an inflationary environment, however, implies a continuing faster rate of increase, with the level of wages and salaries growing progressively higher than would otherwise have been expected. The adjustment to the ending of incomes policy might be more complex, with the level of earnings falling below the calculated value during the operation of the policy, rising above it in compensation after the ending of restraint and ultimately returning to the expected level. In the cases of other behavioural relationships it is easy to think of plausible ways in which current and future experience may differ from the average experience of the last ten or fifteen years over which the relationships were fitted.

To the eleven exogenous variables given above must therefore be added ten more—the intercept adjustment terms corresponding to the ten behavioural equations....

The error correlation matrix is shown in table 2. *A priori* expectations about the sizes of these correlations are rather obscure because of the simultaneity of the model. For example, overprediction of consumers' expenditure is likely to lead to consequential overprediction of GDP: to this extent a positive correlation of the errors in the two would be expected. Equally, the overprediction of GDP should lead to an overprediction of consumption thus reinforcing the expectation of a positive correlation. But in the case of imports, overprediction should lead to underprediction of GDP and hence to a negative correlation, while underprediction of GDP should lead to underprediction of imports, suggesting a positive correlation of errors.

Table 2. *Correlation matrix of simulation errors*

	IRSE	DNI	TAXO	WS	TAXWS	CE	CPI	FCA	INV	IMP	GDP
IRSE	1·00										
DNI	0·11	1·00									
TAXO	0·28	0·59	1·00								
WS	0·55	0·44	0·31	1·00							
TAXWS	−0·11	0·20	0·04	0·45	1·00						
CE	0·70	0·18	0·12	0·70	0·05	1·00					
CPI	−0·48	−0·28	−0·20	−0·39	0·09	−0·66	1·00				
FCA	0·38	−0·29	−0·27	0·23	−0·03	0·55	−0·37	1·00			
INV	0·03	0·12	0·11	0·08	0·29	0·07	−0·15	0·16	1·00		
IMP	0·51	0·10	0·12	0·57	0·06	0·64	−0·48	0·48	0·44	1·00	
GDP	0·40	0·50	0·38	0·52	0·22	0·57	−0·56	−0·08	0·43	0·50	1·00

Symbols: see p. 492.

In some cases, it is possible to say with some conviction in which direction the causal link between correlated errors operates. For example, the high correlation between errors in consumers' expenditure and the factor cost adjustment suggests that some of the errors in the latter are caused by errors in the former, for that link is strong and direct, whereas the link between the factor cost adjustment and consumers' expenditure through GDP and incomes is both weak and in the opposite direction. But, in general, the error correlation matrix provides little information about the important sources of error in the model.

SHOCKS, LAGS AND MULTIPLIERS

The essential properties of the model can be summarised by describing the impact on the economy which it implies, given an exogenous change in one variable or another. There are three aspects of the behaviour of the model following such a change. First, there are direct leakages: an increase of £100 million in consumers' expenditure, for example, will automatically raise imports by £21 million and the factor cost adjustment by £31 million even before multiplier effects, leaving a direct stimulus to output of only £48 million. Secondly, there are multiplier (and accelerator) effects which, thirdly, are lagged: the stimulus to output will, for example, raise employment and earnings, thus reinforcing the initial stimulus to consumption. A direct stimulus of £100 million to GDP gives rise to secondary expansion such that total GDP reaches £150 million by the third and fourth quarters, but then drops back very nearly asymptotically (there is in fact a highly damped cycle) to about £140 million. Thus the implied GDP multiplier is about 1·4; convergence is virtually complete after twelve quarters.

Table 3 summarises these properties of the model. The very muted cyclical variation shown in the last column reflects the operation of the accelerator implicit in the stockbuilding function. (It will be recalled that there is no fixed investment accelerator in the present form of the model; fixed invest-

Table 3. *Effects on GDP of exogenous stimuli*

£ *millions*

Leakages	Direct effect on GDP	The multiplier	Secondary effect on GDP
+100 in:		+100 GDP in quarter:	
Consumers' expenditure	+48	1	143
Public authorities'		2	145
consumption	+79	3	150
Gross fixed investment	+79	4	151
Exports	+79	8	145
Stockbuilding	+68	12	140
Imports	−100	16	137
Factor cost adjustment	−100	∞	139

Source: NIESR estimates.

ment is treated as wholly exogenous and thus invariant with respect to shocks of the kind under discussion. Clearly, an important next step in simulation studies will be to incorporate an accelerator element.)[...]

11.2 The Dynamic Behaviour of a Large Econometric Model*

INTRODUCTION

In the model, as in the economy (for any time period), certain variables [1] in the following diagram are largely determined by past values of other variables. Other sets of variables, [2] and [3], are for the most part simultaneously determined within the current period, while a final group [4], depends on the values of variables previously determined within the period. In all four instances, exogenous forces from outside the system (for example, long-term factors such as population and short-term influences such as government policy actions) may affect the solutions. This framework (which has become known as a block recursive structure) may be displayed as follows):

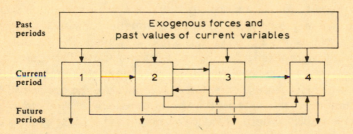

*From G. Fromm and P. Taubman, *Policy Simulations with an Econometric Model* (Washington, D.C.: The Brookings Institution, 1968), chs. 1 and 2. © 1968 by the Brookings Institution, Washington, D.C., U.S.A. Reprinted by permission.

Each block contains equations which relate so-called current endogenous dependent variables to other variables. For example, in the first block, business plant and equipment investment in the durable manufacturing sector is a function of lagged values of the industry's output originating and capital stocks, and long-term interest rates.

SECTORAL SPECIFICATIONS

Consumption

The consumption functions employed in the simulations of this volume are of a classical type, making expenditures (by category) dependent on income, relative prices, capital stock or lagged consumption, and a few additional variables. It seems likely, however, that outlays for durable goods are responsive to changes in credit terms and the availability of installment financing. This would have the effect of increasing the sensitivity of the model's 'real' sector to alterations in monetary policy and shifts in financial market conditions.

It is also desirable to develop improved measures of consumers' capital stocks of durable goods and to determine the impact of these holdings on consumption. Moreover, it may be desirable to examine whether a 'portfolio' approach with asset substitution and complementarities is relevant. That is, it might be helpful to postulate that consumers behave in such a way as to maximise utility, subject to income, financial assets, durables and housing assets, and inertial constraints. Also, the utility independence assumption could be relaxed to permit the consumption of each item to have an effect on the utility derived from consuming other items. This would lead to an 'optimal mix' formulation of the consumption function. Other questions in the consumption area which concern us are the independent impact of buying plans and expectations on expenditures and the degree to which the propensity to consume varies with different kinds (wages, salaries, transfers) and time paths of income.

Residential construction

In its present formulation, the equation for total new construction starts depends on the gap between household formation and removals plus vacancies, a relative price rental-construction cost index, the Treasury bill or bond rate of interest, and a distributed lag of past starts. The constant dollar value per start is a function of real income per household and the same rate of interest (which, for reasons of uniformity, should also be put in real terms). This dichotomy of the value per start being dependent on household income while the number of starts is independent of it, should be examined. One

* From G. Fromm and P. Taubman, *Policy Simulations with an Economical Model* (Washington, D.C.: The Brookings Institution, 1968), chs. 1 and 2. © 1968 by the Brookings Institution, Washington, D.C., U.S.A. Reprinted by permission.

should likewise investigate whether there is some relationship between credit conditions and housing *demand* or whether the influence of monetary factors impinges mainly on housing *supply* in the form of the willingness of builders to increase their inventories under construction.

It would also be appropriate to integrate the analysis of the housing and financial sectors since the two are functionally related. In particular, account should be taken of financial institutions' forward commitments of mortgage loans and the availability of funds from the Federal National Mortgage Association (FNMA). Furthermore, while U.S. Treasury interest rates serve as an indicator of the cost and availability of funds in the private housing market, they do so very imperfectly. Whenever possible, more direct measures should be used. This probably requires a substantial increase in detail in the housing-financial sectors. [...]

Inventories

In the initial work on this sector, the approach taken followed traditional lines by positing an inventory decision process based on a stock adjustment mechanism. Inventories were disaggregated by production sector (durable manufacturing, nondurable manufacturing, trade, and other), and some attention was given to industry capacity and government military orders. Other relevant factors were relative prices and short-term interest rates. While the performance of the final equations taken individually was satisfactory and comparable to the results obtained by other researchers, in the complete system they produced significant errors. Therefore, additional research was indicated and has already been initiated. [...]

Orders

The present model contains four orders functions for durable and nondurable manufacturing: two identities for the change in the level of unfilled orders (that is, new orders minus sales) and two new orders equations. In the latter, new orders are a function of current and lagged final sales, an own rate of change of price variable, and the first difference in government military outlays. [...]

Investment realizations

A significant result of the work on the Brookings model has been the demonstration (by Robert Eisner) that realization functions on investment intentions produce superior predictions of investment expenditures than the use of fixed automatic payout mechanisms on the intentions. Eisner's interpretation of his equations imputes a rate of return rationale for the included profits variable. [...]

Investment intentions

Dale Jorgenson's treatment of investment intentions is pioneering and powerful. However, it leaves room for further inquiry. As in the investment realizations functions, output originating might be considered the demand variable instead of sales. Also, the depreciation variable in the user cost of capital is in real replacement terms while, for tax purposes, a current, historical cost basis might be more relevant. Furthermore, no funds availability constraints are imposed, which implies that a firm, in any time period, can acquire unlimited capital at a marginal cost equal to the average user capital cost.

Then, too, the underlying production function is a homogeneous of degree one Cobb-Douglas, and technological change is exponential. Therefore, such change appears necessarily embodied, neutral, and time invariant. Also, it is implied that capital services per constant dollar of capital stock are fixed. These assumptions could be modified (discrete innovational shifts might be introduced) as could those relating to the lag structure of the investment decision, especially since the parameter estimates are highly sensitive to shifts in the lag distribution.

Moreover, the treatment of investment lags as being merely a technological phenomenon of the lag between placement of plant and equipment orders and their delivery is far too restrictive, given the uncertainty of future output, revenue, cost, and financing predictions. [...]

Foreign sector

The present formulation of the foreign sector is highly simplified and limited to U.S. import and export functions for a few classes of commodities. Constant dollar trade flows are related to real income, relative prices, production demands, and past levels of expenditures. [...]

Government revenues and expenditures

The government sector of the model offers one of the most extensive econometric descriptions of government fiscal activities ever prepared. For example, in the complete model, approximately twenty equations are employed to explain U.S. Treasury tax collections and to translate them into national income and product account statistics. [...]

Production functions and factor income payments

In what is equivalent to an implicit linear approximation of a production function, the model's employment and hours variables are dependent on the level and rate of increase of real output, beginning of period capital stocks, and their own lagged values. Judged by the usual statistical criteria these equations appear quite satisfactory; however, some restructuring of this framework may prove helpful. [...]

Wages and prices

The variables in the wage equations include the four-quarter change in the consumer price index, distributed lags of profits per unit of real output and the reciprocal of the unemployment rate, and past wage changes. [...]

In the area of prices, additional study is needed of the impact of purchased input costs on the market prices of goods and on trade, regulated, and
service sector margins (i.e. on the prices of value added). Also, for manufacturing, unfilled orders/output originating ratios may be better indicators of
demand conditions than corresponding inventory/output originating ratios.
Finally, in every period, wages and prices are closely connected; therefore, functions for these variables should be estimated as a simultaneous
subsystem. [...]

Agriculture

The condensed version of the agricultural sector is in many respects
similar in form and specification to the other production sectors: it includes
equations for investment, inventories, output originating, and employment.
The difference is that sales and production costs are treated explicitly and
rental income is divided into several components; more work is needed to
refine all the nonstandard equations (the standard equations are highly
satisfactory).

Labor force

The solutions presented below use a total aggregate labor force equation.
This function makes the absolute size of the labor force dependent on current
employment, the level and rate of change of unemployment in the previous
quarter, and a time trend. The unemployment variables have a positive sign,
presumably reflecting, on a net basis, the entrance of wives into the labor
force when their husbands lose their jobs and the discouragement of potential
or presently unemployed labor force participants. The positive sign on the
time trend can be interpreted as a net indicator of increased participation
of women in the labour force and a secular decline in the proportion of
teenagers seeking employment due to the longer average period of education
as well as a proxy for population growth. [...]

Monetary sector

The monetary subsector is one of the most interesting aspects of the model.
While previous model-building efforts have all but neglected monetary
influences, the complete Brookings model has an extensive set of equations
(numbering nearly 30) relating the financial and real sectors. Money and
near-money demands of households and businesses are treated separately as
are the various vlasses of financial institutions. However, the interactions
between the monetary and real sectors are weak, and are reflected only in the
form of interest rate terms in the housing, business investment, and factor
share distribution functions and income and investment terms in various
financial equations. A stronger linkage would probably be found if additional
variables were introduced. [...]

2. SYSTEM SIMULATIONS

Several different kinds of simulation studies might be conducted, with the response of the overall system observed in each case.

(1) Stochastic disturbances drawn from assured distributions (for example, multivariate normal distributions with mean zero and covariances equal to those of the equations in question) can be introduced into individual equations or blocks of equations.

(2) In addition to error variance characteristics which can be estimated from the data, these stochastic disturbances can be given assumed serial correlation or covariance properties.

(3) Selected parameters may be incremented.

(4) The initial conditions may be changed.

(5) Shocks can be imposed on certain endogenous or exogenous variables (for example, inventory change might be held to zero or the rate of population growth might be increased).

These tests are of a purely structural nature. Simulations of alterations in government policy parameters such as tax, transfer, expenditure, and monetary rates are of interest as well. Various structural and policy simulations can also be combined. In addition, parameters derived from applying different estimation techniques can be used.

Thus, a wide range of experiments is possible. In each instance the system's solution path (that is, the values of endogenous variables) over time would be computed. Obviously, for stochastic experiments (which by definition involve repeated trials) means, variances, and covariances should be calculated. As appropriate to the experiment, judgments can then be made about the system's stability, parameter sensitivity, and growth path characteristics. For policy experiments, interest centers on impact and dynamic multipliers, the net government cost of policy changes, Phillips curves, and induced rates of inflation. [...]

Dynamic multipliers

One method of analyzing the effect of the fiscal policies is to examine a set of dynamic multipliers.[1] Table 1 shows, by quarter, the increase in real gross national product over the original solution divided by the constant increase in real expenditures. For the tax cuts, the amount of the reduction is taken as the difference in tax rates multiplied by the personal income tax base before the change, divided by the implicit price deflator for personal consumption expenditures. The reduction varies from quarter to quarter, rising from $3·2 billion in 1906:3 to $3·8 billion in 1962:4, both in 1954 dollars.

[1] Dynamic multipliers are period-by-period response rates of endogenous variables to exogenous shifts in levels, flows, or parameters. That is, they measure the response along the transient path to final equilibrium positions. This is in contrast to static multipliers which give the equilibrium responses of the endogenous variables to exogenous changes.

Table 1. *Dynamic multipliers*

Increases in real gross national product per constant dollar of expenditure increase or tax reduction

	Multipliers									
	1960:3	1960:4	1961:1	1961:2	1961:3	1961:4	1962:1	1962:2	1962:3	1962:4
ΔG_{CD}^{54}	1·6	2·0	2·4	2·1	2·2	2·1	2·7	2·8	2·8	2·7
ΔG_{C}^{54}	1·4	2·0	2·3	2·4	2·5	2·4	2·8	2·9	2·9	2·9
ΔE_{G}	1·7	1·9	2·1	2·1	2·1	1·7	1·9	1·9	2·0	2·0
ΔG_{IC}^{54}	1·6	2·2	2·5	2·4	2·6	2·5	2·9	2·0	3·0	2·9
ΔY_{D}^{54}	0·8	1·0	1·2	1·1	1·2	1·2	1·2	1·2	1·2	1·2
$\Delta Y_{D}^{54} + MP$	0·8	1·0	1·2	1·3	1·4	1·5	1·7	1·8	1·8	1·8

The results show that, per dollar of expenditure increase or tax reduction, additional government employment is most effective and personal income tax cuts least effective in stimulating real *GNP* in the first quarter. By the second quarter, all the expenditure policies have nearly equivalent effects while the tax cut policies are even further behind. At the end of ten quarters, most of the lag influences have had their major impact and the multipliers should be nearly at their 'equilibrium' values. However, this is not strictly true of the income tax policies. Here, the reductions increase over time and, because of lagged adjustments in the system, the indicated multipliers are probably biased downwards. That is, the true tax cut multipliers are probably somewhat larger than those computed by dividing current period increases in real *GNP* by current period reductions in tax liabilities.

Moreover, because of various factors (including the impact of initial conditions), not too much emphasis should be given to the exact time path of increase of the various multipliers. A complex, dynamic, difference equation system is likely to have roots that produce fluctuating responses to any stepped changes in its forcing functions (exogenous inputs). Such a model is also likely to be influenced by specification choices and the techniques used to estimate parameters. Consequently, the dynamic multipliers fluctuate.

Notwithstanding these fluctuations, examination of the increases in real gross product per constant dollar of expenditure increase over the period indicates that the government durables, nondurables, and construction multipliers are approximately 2·8 to 3·0, while the employment expenditure multiplier is significantly lower, at about 2·0. This difference may be explained by the greater impact of the former expenditures on business investment. While the employment policy has a greater direct effect on the rate of unemployment, which is beneficial to consumption, this is not sufficient to override this investment advantage. The nonemployment policies would fare even better were it not for the greater leakages of their expenditures into corporate profits (and, therefore retained earnings and taxes).

Income tax multipliers would theoretically be expected to be less than expenditure multipliers. For simple, linear, income determination models, equal absolute amounts of ex post tax and expenditure increase, that is, a balanced government budget increment of zero, produce a multiplier of 1·0. For the same models, with an increase in tax *rates* yielding a balanced budget with the original ex ante tax base, the multiplier would be greater than 1·0 because of the growth in the tax base under the stimulus of higher government expenditures. Nevertheless, this type of growth is insufficient to explain the foregoing discrepancies between the 'pure' (without an accommodating monetary policy) income tax multiplier of 1·2 and those on expenditures of about 3·0.

Examination of the detailed simulation results indicates that many of these discrepancies were due to the complex, nonlinear nature of the model and, in particular, to the behavior of long-term interest rates. For the 'pure' income tax rise, equilibrium interest rates rose (thereby depressing investment), while for expenditures they were largely unchanged. This can be explained by the fact that direct impact of the tax reduction was larger than that of the expenditure increases on personal disposable income. The higher such income, the greater the desire of consumers to hold demand deposits and, with fixed bank reserves, the greater the pressure on interest rates. (Higher business income also tends to create such pressures; but higher business income, and cash flow, enables greater investment in plant and equipment, an offsetting influence to deposit demands.) In other words, for an income tax reduction to be fully effective, an accommodating monetary policy which allows for an expansion in bank reserves and the money supply must also be undertaken. Such a monetary policy might be defined as one which maintains interest rates as they would have been without the income tax reduction. This, in fact, is the simulation of an income tax cut with monetary policy that is reported in the foregoing tables. With it, the ten-quarter multiplier is 1·8, which gives about the expected difference between tax rate and expenditure policies. [...]

11.3 The Cyclical Behaviour of an Econometric Model: A Simulation Approach*

1. INTRODUCTION

One of the most vexing of the unsolved problems of dynamic economic analysis is that of constructing a model which will reproduce adequately the cyclical behavior of a modern industrial community. None of the schemes so far advanced have (yet) offered a satisfactory endogenous explanation of the persistent business fluctuations so characteristic of Western capitalism. It is true that there exist theories which lead to oscillatory movements, but,

*From Irma Adelman and F. A. Adelman, 'The Dynamic Properties of the Klein–Goldberger Model', *Econometrica*, 1959.

except under very special assumptions, these swings either die down, or else they are explosive in nature.[1] In the latter case, appeal is usually made to externally imposed constraints in order to limit the fluctuations of the system,[2] while, in the former case, exogenous shocks must be introduced from time to time to rejuvenate the cyclical movement.[3] Since recourse to either of these devices is rather artificial, it is of interest to seek a more satisfactory mechanism for the internal generation of a persistent cyclical process.

While it is desirable for an economic model (or any other model, for that matter) to be as simple as possible, it is almost certain that an adequate explanation of the business cycle cannot be found through approaches as idealized as those usually suggested. It may be of interest, therefore, to examine, from this point of view, the most complicated econometric description of the United States published in recent years—the 1955 forecasting scheme of Klein and Goldberger.[4] This structure, which consists of 25 difference equations in a corresponding number of endogenous variables, is nonlinear in character, and includes lags up to the fifth order. By its very nature it constitutes a description of a dynamic world, rather than a portrayal of comparative statics. Not only are the endogenous variables in each period functions of exogenous inputs, but also of lagged endogenous quantities and of stock variables. Thus, even if all the exogenous magnitudes were held constant, the economy represented by these equations would still vary with time.

But, while this model has been applied to yearly projections of economic activity in this country with some success, its dynamic properties have been analysed only under highly simplifying assumptions. In particular, it would be interesting to find out whether this construct really offers an endogenous explanation of a persistent cyclical process. We should like to learn whether the system is stable when subjected to single exogenous shocks, what oscillations (if any) accompany the return to the equilibrium path, and what is the response of the model to repeated external and internal shocks.

The purpose of this paper, then, is to investigate these issues in some detail. There are perhaps two major reasons which indicate why this work has not previously been done. First of all, the fact that Klein and Goldberger used observed quantities as inputs for their annual forecasts, rather than values generated by the model from earlier data, prevented them from studying, at the same time, the type of dynamic paths which would be traversed by the system in the absence of external interference. Secondly, the complexity of the model requires the use of modern high-speed com-

---

[1] P. A. Samuelson, 'The Interaction of the Accelerator and the Multiplier', *Review of Economic Statistics*, vol. XXI (1939), pp. 75–78.

[2] J. R. Hicks, *A Contribution to the Theory of the Trade Cycle* (Oxford, 1939).

[3] R. Frisch, 'Propagation Problems and Impulse Problems in Dynamic Economics', *Economic Essays in Honor of Gustav Cassel* (London, 1933), pp. 171–205.

[4] L. R. Klein and A. S. Goldberger, *An Econometric Model of the United States, 1929–1952* (Amsterdam, 1955).

puters for the long-run solution of the system in a reasonable length of time. [...]

2. THE DYNAMIC NATURE OF THE MODEL

Now, we are in a position to study some of the problems raised in the Introduction. First of all, what is the dynamic nature of the Klein–Goldberger model? That is, what sort of time path will these equations generate in the absence of additional external constraints or shocks? A priori, it is conceivable that the long-run extrapolation of this short-run predictive system will indicate that the economy so described is subject to a business cycle more or less analogous to that observed in modern industrialized societies. On the other hand, it is also possible that this model cannot offer even a qualitative picture of the economic growth process in the real world.

Our first machine data decided the issue unequivocally. After a brief 'settling-down' period, the system is quite monotonic and essentially linear. There is no hint whatever of any internally generated business cycle, and, indeed, even in the first few years, the shock of start-up is not sufficient to induce more than a single turning point in any variable. Of course, since most of the exogenous trends are fitted by straight lines, it is not surprising that the overall character of the solution is linear, rather than, say, quadratic, but the absence of oscillations is less obvious (a priori) and more significant.

The time paths of several of the more important quantities are depicted in Figure 11.1. The several curves in Figure 11.1 represent the projections of

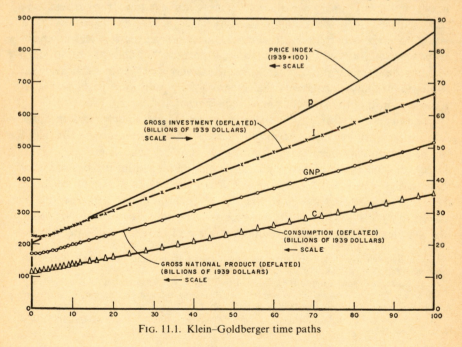

Fig. 11.1. Klein–Goldberger time paths

the price index and of the real values of GNP, consumer expenditures, and gross private investment, respectively. [...]

In an attempt to see whether the qualitative properties of the solution are at all sensitive to the starting conditions, we reduced the magnitudes of all but seven of the initial values of the real quantities by 10 per cent. The results of this calculation possessed the same general character as had been observed previously. As might have been anticipated, the new ordinates were invariably lower, and, except for corporate savings, the slopes of the curves tended to be the same or smaller. The linearity was even more marked with the reduced inputs; indeed, only two variables showed any turning points at all. These were corporate savings and corporate surplus, both of which were actually negative for several periods. Since, in view of these results, it was felt that small variations in our input would not lead to significant differences in the *nature* of our solution, a more detailed investigation of the influence of initial values upon the operation of the model was postponed to a future date.

The implications of these results are quite clear. Since the economic variables in the Klein–Goldberger model grow almost linearly with time, it is apparent that this scheme does not contain an intrinsic explanation of a persistent oscillatory process. That is, the complete lack of even a broad hint of cyclical behavior in the absence of shocks precludes the application of the Klein–Goldberger analysis to economies in which oscillations are presumed to develop spontaneously. The conclusions one may draw from this observation lie anywhere between the two extreme positions which follow. On the other hand, if one wishes to retain the hypothesis that periodic cumulative movements are self-generated in the course of the growth process in a realistic economy, one may contend that the Klein–Goldberger model is fundamentally inadequate, and hence that it is inapplicable to further business cycle theory. On the other hand, one may hold that, to the extent that the behavior of this sytem constitutes a valid qualitative approximation to that of a modern capitalist society, the observed solution of the Klein–Goldberger equations implies that one must look elsewhere for the origin of business fluctuations. Under the latter assumptions, cyclical analysis would be limited to an investigation of the reaction of the economic system to various perturbations. And, since the Klein–Goldberger model does present a more or less detailed description of the interactions among the various sectors of the economy, it could itself be utilized in the examination of the mechanism of response to shocks. Actually, as we shall see, exploitation of the latter alternative can prove extremely profitable.

3. STABILITY OF THE SYSTEM

It is apparent from the preceding discussion that, under ordinary conditions, the Klein-Goldberger model is non-oscillatory in nature. It remains to

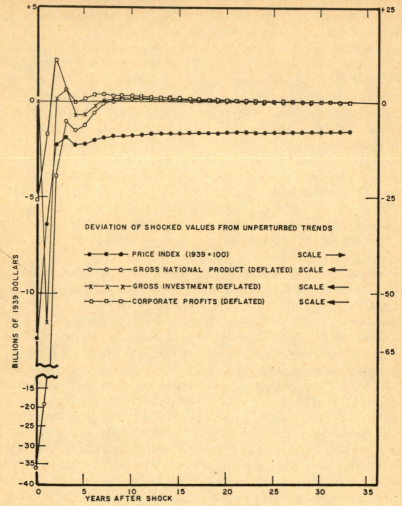

FIG. 11.2. Shocked time paths

be seen whether the economy described by this system is stable under large exogenous displacements.

In order to study this point, we solved the equations as in the preceding section, until the system was essentially on its long-run equilibrium path (about 8 years). Then, in the ninth period, we suddenly reduced the real magnitude of federal outlays from its extrapolated level of 37·5 to the much lower figure of 10; in the succeeding years government expenditures were returned to the values they would have had in the absence of external interference.

While it is obvious that such a discontinuity in an exogenous variable is basically equivalent to a change in initial conditions, it is equally obvious that the response of a dynamic system to large displacements may be quite different from its behavior under small perturbations.

Figure 11.2 presents some of the calculated results of this extremely severe shock to the economy. As is evident from these curves, the community was immediately thrown into a very deep depression by the sudden drop in federal outlays. The restoration of a normal governmental budget during the following year alleviated the situation only slightly, but, by the second year after the dip, the business world had more than recovered. The next period saw the return of national income, farm receipts, and total employment to their pre-shock trends. However, it was not until the fourth year after the disturbance that real private employee compensation achieved its unperturbed level, as the price index rose more rapidly than the wage rate. Meanwhile, possibly as a result of the fact that consumer expenditures lagged yet another period, there was a mild business recession in the fourth year, the effects of which were felt throughout the rest of the economy for the next two periods. The subsequent boom reached its peak (with respect to its unperturbed trend) about eight years later, and then tapered off extremely slowly over an additional 22 years or so. While calculations were not continued beyond this point, it appears that, after this 34 year cycle, the economy has essentially returned to its basic equilibrium path, except for the price and wage indices and for the cumulative corporate surplus (all of which remained lower).

While the details of the response of a Klein-Goldberger economy to a strong shock will depend on the nature of the perturbation, it would appear likely from this calculation that even a very strong shock will not permanently distort the long-run path of the economy. In other words, the Klein-Goldberger system is stable. Nevertheless, a sharp disturbance does suffice to create a business cycle of depth comparable to that which one would expect in an actual economy under a corresponding inpulse. And, while the duration of the cyclical movement is much longer than that normally observed in practice, it is probable that the later stages of such a cycle, if it really existed, would be observed by the intervention of new exogenous shocks.

4. INTRODUCTION OF RANDOM SHOCKS

So far, we have studied the dynamic properties of the Klein-Goldberger system by treating it as if it were composed of a set of exact functional relationships. That is to say, we have abstracted from the random elements which are inherent in the statistical specification of the equations. Furthermore, we have used smooth extrapolation procedures for predicting the magnitudes of the exogenous variables. We saw that under those assumptions the Klein-Goldberger equations are inadequate as an explanation of the cyclical behavior of our economy.

We cannot yet assess the validity of the Klein-Goldberger equations, however, as a representation of the United States economy over a long period of time because we must still analyse the time path of their system under the impact of random shocks.[5] After all, a model which differs from empirical fact by comparatively small and nonsystematic external factors may still be useful. It is therefore of great interest to see whether or not the introduction of relatively minor uncorrelated perturbations into the Klein-Goldberger structure will generate cyclical fluctuations analogous to those observed in practice.

With these considerations in mind, we exposed the Klein-Goldberger system to two distinct varieties of random impulses. First of all, random shocks were superimposed upon the extrapolated values of the exogenous quantities (shocks of type I). Secondly, random perturbations were introduced instead into each of the empirically fitted Klein-Goldberger equations (shocks of type II). In addition we made a set of calculations in which both kinds of disturbances were present.

5. SHOCKS OF TYPE I

Shocks of type I arise logically whenever exogenous quantities are projected in a smooth manner over long periods of time, for, while it is convenient to extrapolate these variables in a continuous fashion, even a cursory glance at the data over a period of a few years shows that these magnitudes tend to jump more or less erratically with respect to any smooth curve one might draw. It is, of course, obvious that a system that incorporates such statistical fluctuations may not be completely satisfactory for quantitative purposes. On the other hand, it may still prove fruitful to compare with economic experience the frequency of occurrence and the amplitudes of whatever cycles may arise.

We shall therefore modify our method of extrapolation of the exogenous variables in order to see what effects these random perturbations may have. For this purpose we define the value of an exogenous variable y_t at time t as its trend value $\bar{y}_t$ plus the shock term δy_t, and assume that δy_t has a Gaussian distribution with a mean of zero. In order that the shocks inflicted upon the system be of a more or less realistic magnitude at all times, we evaluate the standard deviation of δy_t over that portion of the data for which our least squares fit was made, and, for our subsequent calculations, we maintain the ratio of the standard deviation of δy_t to y_{t-1} at a value independent of time. It is interesting to note that these standard deviations are, in general, quite small; in fact, only three of them exceed 10 per cent of the trend value of the corresponding variable.

---

[5] The idea that economic fluctuations may be due to random shocks was first suggested in 1927 by E. Slutzky, 'The Summation of Random Causes as the Source of Cyclical Processes', translated into English in *Econometrica*, Vol. 5 (1937), pp. 105 ff. It was also suggested independently by R. Frisch, *op. cit.*

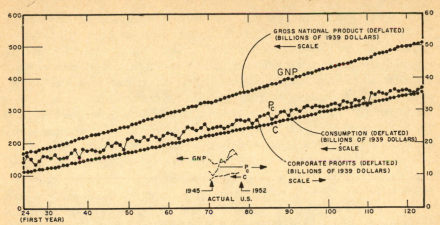

F<small>IG</small>. 11.3. Selected time paths under Type I impulses

Some of the results obtained with shocks of type I are summarized in Fig. 11.3. The solid lines in this graph portray the computed time paths of GNP, consumption, and corporate profits, while the dotted lines represent actual time paths of these variables for the postwar portion of the sample period. From this figure, it would seem that the introduction of forces of type I into the model generates 3 to 4 year swings in the variables of the system. However, the same graph also reveals that the average amplitude of the 'cycles' induced by random shock on exogenous quantities is unrealistically small. It would appear, then, that type I perturbations of reasonable magnitude superimposed upon the Klein-Goldberger model will not produce the sort of cyclical behavior observed in the actual economy. We shall therefore proceed to see whether shocks of type II will prove more promising.

6. SHOCKS OF TYPE II

To understand the origin of shocks of type II, one should recall that, in the process of fitting their empirical data, Klein and Goldberger endowed each of their behavioral equations with a random error term. At least three sources of irregularity could produce this term. In the first place, simplifying assumptions are inevitable whenever one wishes to construct a concrete model of a realistic economy. Some of these abstractions are made for convenience, others because the precise equations of motion of an economic system are not yet known. Variables which in practice exert a direct influence upon the solution may be suppressed from several of the equations, made exogenous, or omitted entirely; similarly, relationships which are an integral part of the description may be lost in the process of approximation. Moreover, in predictive models, inherently nonlinear relationships are often treated in a linear approximation for the sake of expediency. In view of these considerations, it is reasonable to expect that the inexactness of the functional form of the Klein-Goldberger equations as a representation of the economic behavior of our society contributes to the size of the random error term.

Secondly, even if the Klein-Goldberger relationships did have a functional form derived from indisputable theory, the fact that the coefficients are based upon empirical data would imply a random error term, as a result of the actual sampling fluctuations. These include, for example, the uncertainty of the degree to which the sample is representative of the universe, as well as the changes in accounting practices, coverage, and reporting techniques which generally occur in the collection of data over a long period of time.

A third potential contributor to the size of shocks of type II is of quite a different character. It arises from the possibility that some of the economic relationships which compose the Klein-Goldberger system may *never* be valid as exact equations. This situation will result if the aggregation of micro-economic quantities into macroeconomic variables is not a legitimate procedure. For example, if the value of total consumption depends upon the distribution of income as well as on its magnitude, a precise macroeconomic relationship between overall consumption and aggregate income will not exist. A similar effect, which will also be reflected in the size of the random error term, would occur if decision functions are probabilistic rather than single-valued.

It is therefore evident from the above discussion that the residuals of the several empirically fitted equations included in the Klein-Goldberger model can be attributed to a number of different types of irregularity. Since there would appear to be no *a priori* correlation among the many individual sources of fluctuation, the random error terms can be assumed for all practical purposes to be distributed in a Gaussian manner. We therefore postulate that each error term is distributed normally about a mean of zero, and we evaluate its standard deviation, just as in the case of shocks of type I, from the standard errors observed for the sample period.

In order to introduce perturbations of type II into the Klein-Goldberger model, we added a random error term to the right-hand side of each of the original non-definitional relationships. Then the same process of algebraic substitution which was used in the simplification of the unshocked system was applied to this new group of equations. These operations left us with a set of equations in which the several error terms appear as parameters, analogous to the exogenous and the lagged variables. Once the sizes and directions of these endogenous shocks are determined (by the selection of two-digit random numbers, as in the case of type I impulses), the system is solved as before. A similar procedure can be used to investigate the behavior of the Klein-Goldberger equations when both shocks of type I and shocks of type II are present simultaneously.

Some of the results of the computation with shocks of type II are plotted in Fig. 11.4. As in Fig. 11.3, the solid lines represent the calculated behavior of GNP, consumption, and corporate profits, respectively, while the dotted lines depict the time paths traversed by the same quantities during the postwar period in the United States. As before, we see that the shocked Klein-Goldberger system produces oscillatory movements with periods of 3 to 4 years. But, unlike the behavior of the model under the action of forces of type I, the swings generated here compare favorably in magnitude with those experienced by the United States economy after World War II. Thus, the superposition of impulses of type II upon the Klein-Goldberger equations leads to cycles whose gross properties are reasonably realistic.

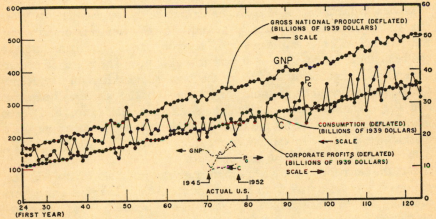

FIG. 11.4. Selected time paths under Type II impulses

Since the effects of shocks of type II are much larger than those of type I disturbances, the same statement can be made for a system in which both kinds of perturbations are present. And, in view of the fact that, on *a priori* grounds, either type of shock may be present in an actual economy, it would seem appropriate to carry out our more detailed analysis for the case in which both forces are present.

7. CONCLUSIONS

Our investigation into the dynamic nature of the econometric model of Klein and Goldberger suggests that their equations do not offer an immediate explanation of an internally generated cyclical process. For, in the absence of perturbations, the time paths of the economic variables are monotonic and essentially linear in character. Furthermore, the behavior of the model is remarkably stable, as evidenced by the fact that the solution resumes its unperturbed equilibrium growth trend even after a strong exogenous disturbance.

On the other hand, when random shocks of a realistic order of magnitude are superimposed upon the original form of the Klein-Goldberger equations, the cyclical fluctuations which result are remarkably similar to those described by the NBER as characterizing the United States economy. The average duration of a cycle, the mean length of the expansion and contraction phases, and the degree of clustering of individual peaks and troughs around reference dates all agree with the corresponding data for the United States economy. Furthermore, the lead-lag relationships of the endogenous variables included in the model and the indices of conformity of the specific series to the overall business cycle also resemble closely the analogous features of our society. All in all, it would appear that the shocked Klein-Goldberger model approximates the behavior of the United States economy rather well.

In view of these results, it is not unreasonable to suggest that the gross characteristics of the interactions among the real variables described in the Klein-Goldberger equations may represent good approximations to the behavioral relationships in a practical economy. There are, of course, a number of significant defects in the detailed workings of the Klein-Goldberger system. For example, the treatment of the monetary quantities and the interconnections between them and the real sector both need improvement. Nevertheless, the representation would seem to offer a good working basis for the investigation of cyclical fluctuations, especially if the deficiencies mentioned above are corrected.

But, the behavior of the Klein-Goldberger system under random perturbations is also suggestive from another point of view. Ever since the path-breaking article of Frisch on the propagation of business cycles, the possibility that the cyclical movements observed in a capitalistic society are actually due to random shocks has been seriously considered by business cycle theorists. The results we have found in this study tend to support this possibility. For, the agreement between the data obtained by imposing uncorrelated perturbations upon a model which is otherwise non-oscillatory in character is certainly consistent with the hypothesis that the economic fluctuations experienced in modern, highly developed societies are indeed due to random impulses.

Of course, these random impulses are not necessarily synonymous with an exogenous theory of the business cycle. For, as we saw in Section 6 above, it was primarily shocks of type II which led to agreement between the cyclical behavior of the model and that of the United States economy. And, the reader will recall, these shocks may reflect inexactness in the model, statistical inaccuracies in the fits, or inherent randomness in the decision functions of the economic units themselves. While none of these factors is, strictly speaking, endogenous to the particular Klein-Goldberger system investigated, this does not imply that the type of perturbations actually responsible for the observed cyclical behavior are exogenous to economic theory in general.

In conclusion, we should like to emphasize that, while we have shown that the shocked Klein-Goldberger model offers excellent agreement with economic fact, we have not proved either that the Klein-Goldberger model itself is a good representation of the basic interactions among the several sectors of our economy or that random shocks are the prime cause of business cycles. In view of the remarkable quantitative correspondence with reality, however, we are very tempted to suggest that the second of these hypotheses is true and that, in addition, the Klein-Goldberger system is, except for the deficiencies discussed, not very far wrong.

11.4 The Cyclical Behaviour of an Econometric Model: An Analytic Approach*

THE DYNAMIC PROPERTIES OF AN ECONOMETRIC MODEL

The type of analysis here employed is, in part, common in the recent literature on business cycles. A—usually simple—system of structural relationships is specified, and then reduced by algebraic manipulation, to a single 'final equation' in a single endogenous variable, current and lagged, together with dated exogenous variables. Corresponding to this 'final equation' is the 'characteristic equation' whose roots define the 'characteristic dynamic properties' of the system. The term 'characteristic dynamic properties' here refers to the inherent response characteristics of the structural system, i.e., to its stability or instability, periodicity and damping, if any. Values of the characteristic roots depend upon the values of the coefficients of the characteristic equation. These coefficients are the same as those of the endogenous variable in the final equation; these, in turn, are derived from, and hence depend upon, the values of the coefficients of the structural equations. In this manner, the structural coefficients are seen to be determinants of the dynamic properties of the system. The usual procedure is to consider certain numerical values—or certain ranges of values—for the structural coefficients and then to deduce the dynamic properties of the system.

As a classic case in point, we again cite Samuelson's multiplier-accelerator article. His structural system consists of a consumption function,

$$C_t = \alpha Y_{t-1}, \tag{1}$$

an investment relation,

$$I_t = \beta(C_t - C_{t-1}), \tag{2}$$

and the identity,

$$Y_t = g_t + C_t + I_t. \tag{3}$$

Here C is consumption, I induced investment, g governmental expenditure, and Y is national income. The endogenous variables are C, I, and Y; the

* From A. S. Goldberger, *Impact Multipliers and Dynamic Properties of the Klein-Goldberger Model* (Amsterdam: North Holland, 1959), ch. 6.

exogenous variable is g. The structural system (1)–(3) is reduced by algebraic manipulation to the single final equation

$$Y_t - \alpha[1+\beta]Y_{t-1} + \alpha\beta Y_{t-2} = g_t. \tag{4}$$

The corresponding characteristic equation is

$$x^2 - \alpha(1+\beta)x + \alpha\beta = 0, \tag{5}$$

whose two roots are:

$$x_1 = \frac{\alpha(1+\beta) + \sqrt{[\alpha(1+\beta)]^2 - 4\alpha\beta}}{2}$$

$$x_2 = \frac{\alpha(1+\beta) - \sqrt{[\alpha(1+\beta)]^2 - 4\alpha\beta}}{2}. \tag{6}$$

Depending on the values of these roots, the characteristic response of the system is damped monotonic, damped oscillatory, explosive monotonic, or explosive oscillatory. Since the values of the roots depend upon the values of the structural coefficients α and β, Samuelson is able to associate, in a simple fashion, any combination of values for α and β with a particular qualitative response pattern—damped or explosive, monotonic or oscillatory.

As our final dynamic model, we construct a reduced system for the endogenous-tax case.... The following set of reduced forms is suggested:

$$\dot{C} = 0.2380\dot{G} + 0.3219\dot{C}_{-1} + 0.0297(\dot{S}_C)_{-1} - 0.0278(\dot{P}_C)_{-1}$$
$$+ 0.2834\dot{D}_{-1} + 0.1027(\dot{W}_1)_{-1} - 0.0316\dot{K}_{-1} + 0.2827\dot{P}_{-1}$$
$$+ 0.1017(\dot{T}_E)_{-1} - 0.1502(\dot{T}_C)_{-1} - 0.1780(\dot{T}_N)_{-1}; \tag{7}$$

$$\dot{D} = 0.0516\dot{G} + 0.0134\dot{C}_{-1} + 0.0012(\dot{S}_C)_{-1} - 0.0012(\dot{P}_C)_{-1}$$
$$+ 0.0815\dot{D}_{-1} + 0.0043(\dot{W}_1)_{-1} + 0.0874\dot{K}_{-1} + 0.0815\dot{P}_{-1}$$
$$+ 0.0043(\dot{T}_E)_{-1} - 0.0759(\dot{T}_C)_{-1} - 0.0771(\dot{T}_N)_{-1}; \tag{8}$$

$$\dot{W}_1 = 0.2951\dot{G} + 0.0767\dot{C}_{-1} + 0.0071(\dot{S}_C)_{-1} - 0.0067(\dot{P}_C)_{-1}$$
$$+ 0.4939\dot{D}_{-1} + 0.2648(\dot{W}_1)_{-1} - 0.0247\dot{K}_{-1} + 0.4938\dot{P}_{-1}$$
$$+ 0.2646(\dot{T}_E)_{-1} - 0.0759(\dot{T}_C)_{-1} - 0.0771(\dot{T}_N)_{-1}; \tag{9}$$

$$\dot{P} = 0.7244\dot{G} + 0.1883\dot{C}_{-1} + 0.0077(\dot{S}_C)_{-1} - 0.0135(\dot{P}_C)_{-1}$$
$$+ 0.3443\dot{D}_{-1} - 0.1752(\dot{W}_1)_{-1} - 0.1492\dot{K}_{-1} + 0.3509\dot{P}_{-1}$$
$$- 0.1828(\dot{T}_E)_{-1} - 0.5184(\dot{T}_C)_{-1} - 0.5320(\dot{T}_N)_{-1}. \tag{10}$$

To close this system we may draw upon these structural equations:

$$\dot{I} = 0.7800(\dot{P} + \dot{D} - \dot{T}_C - \dot{T}_N)_{-1} - 0.0730\dot{K}_{-1}, \tag{11}$$

$$\dot{S}_C = 0.7200(\dot{P}_C - \dot{T}_C), \tag{12}$$

$$\dot{P}_C = 0.6800\dot{P}, \tag{13}$$

$$\dot{K} = \dot{I} - \dot{D} + K_{-1}, \tag{14}$$

$$\dot{T}_E = 0.1000(\dot{W}_1 + \dot{P} + \dot{D}), \tag{15}$$

$$\dot{T}_C = 0.5000\dot{P}_C, \tag{16}$$

$$\dot{T}_N = 0.3000(\dot{P} - \dot{T}_C - \dot{S}_C). \tag{17}$$

The eleven equations (7)–(17) contain eleven endogenous variables: $\dot{C}$, $\dot{D}$, $\dot{W}_1$, $\dot{P}$, $\dot{I}$, $\dot{S}_C$, $\dot{P}_C$, $\dot{K}$, $\dot{T}_E$, $\dot{T}_C$, and $\dot{T}_N$, and one exogenous variable, G—and therefore constitute a self-contained system. By substituting equations (11)–(17) into (7)–(10), a system of four equations in the four endogenous variables $\dot{C}$, $\dot{W}_1$, $\dot{P}$, and $\dot{D}$—and the exogenous $\dot{G}$—is obtained. In matrix form, this model is presented in (18):

$$
\begin{bmatrix}
1.0000 - 0.3219E - 0.0045E^2 & -0.1140E - 0.0016E^2 \\
-0.0767E - 0.0035E^2 & 1.0000 - 0.2942E - 0.0013E^2 \\
-0.1883E - 0.0212E^2 & 0.1956E - 0.0076E^2 \\
-0.0134E + 0.0124E^2 & -0.0048E + 0.0044E^2 \\
\\
-0.2312E - 0.0024E^2 & 0.0089E - 0.0028E^2 \\
-0.4450E - 0.0018E^2 & -0.2860E - 0.0022E^2 \\
1.0000 - 0.1470E - 0.0112E^2 & 1.1034E - 0.0134E^2 \\
-0.0556E + 0.0065E^2 & 1.0000 - 0.9216E + 0.0078E^2
\end{bmatrix}
$$

$$
\begin{bmatrix}
\dot{C}_t \\
(\dot{W}_1)_t \\
\dot{P}_t \\
\dot{D}_t
\end{bmatrix}
=
\begin{bmatrix}
0.2380 \\
0.2951 \\
0.7244 \\
0.0516
\end{bmatrix}
[\dot{G}_t]. \tag{18}
$$

To uncover the inherent response characteristics we put this model into the form:

$$
[1.0000 - 1.6837E + 0.9731E^2 - 0.2657E^3 + 0.0354E^4]
\begin{bmatrix}
\dot{C}_t \\
(\dot{W}_1)_t \\
\dot{P}_t \\
\dot{D}_t
\end{bmatrix}
$$

$$
= [\text{Adj } B]
\begin{bmatrix}
0.2380 \\
0.2951 \\
0.7244 \\
0.0516
\end{bmatrix}
[\dot{G}_t]. \tag{19}
$$

The corresponding characteristic equation is:

$$1.0000\lambda^4 - 1.6837\lambda^3 + 0.9731\lambda^2 - 0.2657\lambda + 0.0354 = 0. \tag{20}$$

The roots of this equation are:

$$\lambda_1 = 0.8468, \quad \lambda_3 = 0.1887 + 0.2353i,$$
$$\lambda_2 = 0.4595, \quad \lambda_4 = 0.1887 - 0.2353i. \tag{21}$$

Therefore the basic characteristic component of the time path of the endogenous variables has monotonic components corresponding to the two positive real roots λ_1 and λ_2 and an oscillatory component corresponding to the conjugate complex pair λ_3 and λ_4. The period of this oscillatory component is about 7 years and it is subject to a damping factor of $(0.3016)^t$. The absolute value of all roots is less than unity.

Again, the particular solution for the endogenous variables corresponding to a constant value of the exogenous variable may be derived. When government expenditures are specified to increase by 1.0, i.e., when

$$\dot{G}_t = \bar{G} = 1.0, \tag{22}$$

we have

$$\begin{bmatrix} \bar{C} \\ \bar{W}_1 \\ \bar{P} \\ \bar{D} \end{bmatrix} = \begin{bmatrix} 0.8792 \\ 1.1310 \\ 0.8317 \\ 0.1254 \end{bmatrix} \tag{23}$$

Again, these equilibrium values may be extended to investment and gross national product. We now find

$$\bar{I} = 0.4572, \quad \bar{Q} = 2.3364. \tag{24}$$

And once again, these results—which have been computed as the constant annual changes in endogenous variables compatible with a constant annual unit increase in government expenditures—may be interpreted as the change in the level of these variables that ultimately comes about in response to a sustained unit increase in the level of government expenditures. That is to say—under postwar tax rates—the equilibrium multiplier of government expenditures upon consumption is 0.88, upon private payrolls is 1.13, upon nonwage nonfarm income is 0.83, upon depreciation is 0.13, upon investment is 0.46, and upon gross national product is 2.34. [...]

THE DYNAMIC PROPERTIES OF THE K-G MODEL AS A WHOLE

In this chapter the dynamic properties of the K-G model have been investigated *via* several linearized and dichotomized versions. Some summary comments on the dynamic properties of the full are now in order. The previously cited study by the Adelmans is relevant for this purpose.[1]

In brief, the Adelmans take the entire non-linear K-G model (with taxes endogenous); insert, as initial conditions, the observed 1952 values of the

[1] [See Reading 11.3—Ed.]

variables; specify realistic trends for the exogenous variables; and with an electronic digital computer, trace out the resultant time path of all endogenous variables, year by year, for some one hundred years. The purpose is not to prepare realistic annual forecasts through the year 2052, but rather to see if the K-G model provides an endogenous explanation of business cycles. Also, several alternative specifications are made for government expenditures, and the responses to these are similarly traced out.

The basic calculation uses this set of specifications of the exogenous variables:

Government payrolls:

$$(W_2)_t = 1.82 + 0.578t$$

Government expenditures plus net foreign
   investment:

$$(G - F_I)_t = 19.892 + 0.567t$$

Entrepreneural employment:

$$(N_E)_t = 7.71 + 0.118t + \frac{2.12}{t - 15}$$

Government employment:

$$(N_G)_t = 2.01 + 0.321t$$

Population:

$$(N_P)_t = 97.39 + 2.589t$$

Labor force:

$$(N_L)_t = 44.53 + 0.964t$$

Hours worked index:

$$h_t = 1.062$$

Government farm subsidies:

$$(R_2)_t = 0.108 + \frac{0.0746}{t - 16}$$

Agricultural exports:

$$(F_R)_t = 171.86. \tag{25}$$

It will be noted that all of the influential exogenous variables are either held constant or given linear trends.

With these specifications and the initial position of the economy taken as 1952, the projection of the annual values of the endogenous variables proceeds iteratively. It is found that in keeping with the linear trends assumed for the key exogenous variables, the real variables move on to a linear expansion path which may be characterized as follows: Gross national product rises by 3·5 annually, consumption by 2·5, investment by 0·45, private payrolls by 1·7, nonwage nonfarm income by 0·35, and employment by 0·37. Since the initial position is somewhat above this moving equilibrium path, there is an initial adjustment period during which the variables switch onto this secular track. The length of this disequilibrium period differs from variable to variable; but by the sixth year all the real variables are moving linearly. The long-term trend in money wage rates and prices, however, is somewhat exponential in appearance.

Several conclusions follow from this set of results. The K-G model is, in the first instance, a stable one with respect to the real variables. A disturbance from equilibrium—such as that implicit in the initial conditions—is damped out. However, the monetary variables—prices and wage rates—tend to deviate more and more widely away from a linear moving equilibrium. This corresponds to the qualitative results obtained in our own study—a stable real sector and an essentially distinct monetary sector which at least verges on instability.

The changes in the endogenous variables are attributable to the changes in several exogenous variables operating jointly so that no pure multipliers may be referred from the results thus far cited. However, a supplementary calculation does permit the calculation of some government expenditure multipliers. In this supplementary calculation, the Adelmans introduce a temporary change in government expenditures in year 8. By that time, it will be recalled, the real variables have adjusted to their moving equilibrium path. Government expenditures are cut by 27·5 in year 8, and then immediately returned to their extrapolated path as specified in (25). The result of course is a severe jolt to the economy; the impact effect is to cut *GNP* to 36·0 below its trend value. The impact multiplier then is 36·0/27·5, or 1·3. This checks closely with our own estimates. The real variables return to their equilibrium trend is marked by some overshoot; again this corresponds to our findings. Again prices and wages move away from equilibrium.

From this correspondence in results, it may be inferred that the linearization and dichotomization employed in our own study for the sake of analytical and computational efficiency do not do violence to the character of the original K-G model. In particular, two key results of our own study hold up under this re-investigation. We will restate and briefly comment on these; this will conclude our analysis of this econometric model of the United States.

The first point relates to the real-money dichotomization. Although the initial formulation of the model by Klein and Goldberger allowed for numerous interdependencies between real variables and money variables, the estimated model shows few important plausible connections between them.

Clearly, at least two interpretations of this phenomenon are possible. It may be the case that the dichotomization of the K-G model simply reflects the situation in the real world. That is, the influence of monetary phenomena upon income, output, and employment is minimal. This is by no means a revolutionary idea in the history of economic thought. On the other hand, it may be held that the formulation of the K-G model did not allow for important links, which do exist, to manifest themselves. For example, interest rates and price fluctuations may be in reality important determinants of fixed investment and inventory accumulation, respectively, but the use of a too highly aggregated investment function has ruled them out of the K-G model.

This second position implies that the construction of an adequate structural model of the United States has as a prerequisite full-scale studies of the complex relationships within the monetary sector and of the sometimes subtle links which tie monetary and real variables. Alternatively, if one is impressed with the success of the K-G model in forecasting the real income and output variables, then adequate structural portrayal of monetary relationships may be forsaken, and priority given to a real-sector forecasting model. [...]

Returning to the key results, the second refers to the stability of the K-G model. As shown earlier, and as confirmed by the Adelmans' study, the model is damped. In the absence of repeated disturbances, deviations from equilibrium do not persist. In this sense the K-G model does not provide an endogenous explanation of a persistent cyclical process. Again, two interpretations are possible. It may be argued that the K-G model is inadequate in this respect. That is, in reality, periodic cumulative movements are self-generated; and that the formulation of the K-G model is deficient in that realistic lag patterns, ceilings, and floors are not specified. Alternatively, it may be argued that the K-G model mirrors reality; that is, the persistence of cyclical behavior is to be attributed to persistent exogenous stimuli.

To maintain this latter position, it is of course not necessary to assume that exogenous stimuli themselves behave cyclically. As Frisch has pointed out, 'A more or less regular fluctuation may be produced by a cause which operates irregularly. There need not be any synchronism between the initiating force or forces and the movement of the swinging system.'[2] Wicksell was apparently the first cycle analyst to note this: 'If you hit a wooden rocking-horse with a club, the movement of the horse will be very different to that of the club.'[3] More recently, Slutsky[4] and Goodwin[5] have illustrated the power of erratic shocks and lumped innovations to generate persistent cyclical fluctuations. The shape and duration of these cycles is in part determined by the endogenous mechanism of the system. Therefore, we may conclude that while the K-G model does not explain persistent economic fluctuations, it can serve as a component of such an explanation.

[2] R. Frisch, 'Propagation Problems and Impulse Problems in Dynamic Economics,' *Economic Essays in Honour of Gustav Cassel* (London: George Allen and Unwin, 1933), pp. 171–206.

[3] K. Wicksell, 'Krisernes Gata,' *Statsokonomisk Tidsskrift* (1907), pp. 255–286, quoted in Frisch, *op. cit.*, p. 198.

[4] E. Slutsky, 'The Summation of Random Causes as the Source of Cyclic Processes,' *Econometrica*, V (1937), 105–147.

[5] R. M. Goodwin, 'Innovations and the Irregularity of Business-Cycles,' *Review of Economics and Statistics*, XXVII (1946), 95–104.

Index